# The Higley
# Lesson Commentary

## 2010–2011

**Based on the
International Sunday
School Lessons**

**King James Version
78th Annual Volume**

**Editor**

Wesley C. Reagan

**Contributing Writers**

Gene Shelburne

John Comer

Doug deGraffenried

The Higley Lesson Commentary, in this 78th year of its life, renews its commitment to careful and reverent scholarship, clear and understandable language, practical and insightful application, and interesting and readable writing. We send it to you with a prayer that it will be a powerful resource for you.

# Foreword

What if you aspired to be an excellent teacher of the Scriptures and you enjoyed access to the following resources?

1) A balanced guide emphasizing key elements in each part of the Bible, with stress on the special holy days of the Christian faith such as Christmas, Easter, and Pentecost.

2) Tutors with years of training, experience, and a personal faith.

3) Libraries that the writers have access to with material gleaned to give you the best access that your schedule will allow.

4) Useful teaching helps such as exegesis, discussion questions, real life application, and evangelistic encouragement.

5) Words of uplift and inspiration that improve morale and provide motivation.

And, suppose that those resources were coordinated with the texts in your regular Sunday School Quarterly. And, suppose further, that you can enjoy that treasury of information for only pennies a week.

We are grateful to *The Higley Lesson Commentary* writers for their careful and poignant sharing of their hearts and faith in the pages that you now hold in your hand.

*Wesley C. Reagan, Editor*

*The Higley Lesson Commentary*
Soft Cover ISBN (13): 978-1-886763-38-8
Hard Cover ISBN (13): 978-1-886763-39-5
Lessons and/or Readings based on International Sundnay School Lessons. The International Bible Lessons for Christian Teaching, ©2007 by the Committee on the Uniform Series. Unless otherwise indicated, all Scripture references are taken from the King James Version of the Bible.

# PREFACE

The challenge to the adult Sunday School teacher is to find an understanding that the class can grasp. The class, then, can take that insight into their daily lives to live, to share, and to grow.

These lessons are layered in antiquity's dust. They involve translation nuances that require the teacher to seek with diligence for a means to relate the insights to class members. The teacher's guide is provided to keep us mindful of God and His love for His creation. His creation survives all time and all people in all languages and all places with a grace that exceeds our understanding. This guide is like a compass and while God is the true North, the teacher must remain faithful to the course that keeps all lessons centered on God's promise.

The Scriptures burst into reality, much like a spring blossom, when we look for the result that love and grace have nourished. The seed of the Word becomes the beauty of the mature bloom. Prayer is the connection. The smiles of understanding are the response to our challenge.

Sam Kinsey

*Editor's Note – Sam Kinsey has taught an adult church school class for the last 20 years. His career includes owning and operating an auto parts store and teaching automotive skills to troubled youths.*

# FALL QUARTER
## *The Inescapable God*

Unit I: God Reveals (Lessons 1-4)
Unit II: God Sustains (lessons 5-9)
Unit III: God Protects (Lessons 10-13)

# WINTER QUARTER
## *Assuring Hope*

Unit I: Comfort for God's People (Lessons 1-5)
Unit II: A Future for God's People (Lessons 6-9)
Unit III: Jesus, the Promised Servant-Leader (Lessons 10-13)

# SPRING QUARTER
## *We Worship God*

Unit I: A Guide for Worship Leaders (Lessons 1-4)
Unit II: Ancient Words of Praise (Lessons 5-9)
Unit III: John's Vision of Worship (Lessons 10-13)

# SUMMER QUARTER
## God Instructs the People of God

Unit I: God's People Learn from Prosperity (Lessons 1-5)
Unit II: Listening for God in Changing Times (Lessons 6-10)
Unit III: A Case Study in Community (Lessons 11-13)

# Lesson Cycle, 2010-2013
## Arrangement of Quarters according to the
## Church School Year, September 2010 through August 2013

| *Fall 2010* | *Winter 2010-2011* | *Spring 2011* | *Summer 2011* |
|---|---|---|---|
| GOD | HOPE | WORSHIP | COMMUNITY |
| **The Inescapable God** | **Assuring Hope** | **We Worship God** | **God Instructs the People of God** |
| Exodus | Isaiah | Matthew | |
| Psalms 8, 19, 46, | Matthew | Mark | Joshua |
| 47, 63, 66, 90, 91, | Mark | 1, 2 Timothy | Judges |
| 139 | | Philippians 2 | Ruth |
| | | Jude | |
| | | Revelation | |

| *Fall 2011* | *Winter 2011-2012* | *Spring 2012* | *Summer 2012* |
|---|---|---|---|
| TRADITION | FAITH | CREATION | JUSTICE |
| **Tradition and Wisdom** | **God Establishes a Faithful People** | **God's Creative Word** | **God Calls for Justice** |
| Proverbs | Genesis | John | Exodus |
| Ecclesiastes | Exodus | | Leviticus |
| Song of Solomon | Luke | | Deuteronomy |
| Matthew | Galatians | | 1, 2 Samuel |
| | | | 1, 2 Kings |
| | | | 2 Chronicles |
| | | | Psalm 146 |
| | | | Isaiah |
| | | | Jeremiah |
| | | | Ezekiel |

| *Fall 2012* | *Winter 2012-2013* | *Spring 2013* | *Summer 2013* |
|---|---|---|---|
| FAITH | GOD: JESUS CHRIST | HOPE | WORSHIP |
| **A Living Faith** | **Jesus Is Lord** | **Beyond the Present Time** | **God's People Worship** |
| Psalm 23, 46 | Matthew | | Isaiah |
| Matthew | John | Daniel | Ezra |
| Mark | Ephesians | Luke | Nehemiah |
| Luke | Philippians | Acts | |
| 1 Corinthians | Colossians | 1, 2 Peter | |
| 13:1-13 | 1 John | 1, 2 Thessalonians | |
| Hebrews | | | |
| Acts | | | |

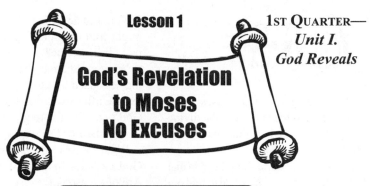

# God's Revelation to Moses
# No Excuses

## Exodus 3:1-6, 13-15

Now Moses kept the flock of Jethro his father in law, the priest of Midian: and he led the flock to the backside of the desert, and came to the mountain of God, even to Horeb.

2 And the angel of the LORD appeared unto him in a flame of fire out of the midst of a bush: and he looked, and, behold, the bush burned with fire, and the bush was not consumed.

3 And Moses said, I will now turn aside, and see this great sight, why the bush is not burnt.

4 And when the LORD saw that he turned aside to see, God called unto him out of the midst of the bush, and said, Moses, Moses. And he said, Here am I.

5 And he said, Draw not nigh hither: put off thy shoes from off thy feet, for the place whereon thou standest is holy ground.

6 Moreover he said, I am the God of thy father, the God of Abraham, the God of Isaac, and the God of Jacob. And Moses hid his face; for he was afraid to look upon God.

13 And Moses said unto God, Behold, when I come unto the children of Israel, and shall say unto them, The God of your fathers hath sent me unto you; and they shall say to me, What is his name? what shall I say unto them?

14 And God said unto Moses, I AM THAT I AM: and he said, Thus shalt thou say unto the children of Israel, I AM hath sent me unto you.

15 And God said moreover unto Moses, Thus shalt thou say unto the children of Israel, The LORD God of your fathers, the God of Abraham, the God of Isaac, and the God of Jacob, hath sent me unto you: this is my name for ever, and this is my memorial unto all generations.

**Memory Verse**
Exodus 3:6

**Background Scripture**
Exodus 3

**Devotional Reading**
Luke 20:34-40

1

What was going on in Moses' mind as he shielded his face from the divine glory that flamed in that marvelous bush?

After forty years herding sheep in that barren desert, was he shocked to find out that God still remembered him?

Years after his scrape with the law in Egypt, was he still afraid that Pharaoh might find him and haul him back to pay for his crime?

Whatever he may have been thinking, it caused him to begin generating excuse after excuse not to say Yes to God's call for him to go back to Egypt to lead the Lord's people to freedom.

What causes you and me to offer God excuses instead of obedience? Are our reasons for disobedience any more valid than the ones Moses came up with?

ഇൻൽ

## For a Lively Start

An attorney in my city surprised all of us who knew him when he accepted the call to become a senior pastor of the largest church in the area. This good man shuttered his law practice, cleaned out his posh office, and shifted gears in his life.

Now, instead of arguing high visibility cases before prestigious judges, this for-mer lawyer spent much of his time comforting widows and preparing homilies for the handful of worshipers who came back to church Sunday evenings.

Then, as suddenly as the call came, that door closed. The elders of the church asked for his resignation. Over night, he was an attorney again, but one without a practice. Like Moses at the bush, he had to listen closely to hear God's voice in this second call. Is it sometimes hard for you to hear God's call?

| Teaching Outline | Daily Bible Readings |
|---|---|
| I. The Bush That Burned—3:1-3 | Mon. A God of the Living<br>*Luke 20:34-40* |
| A. In the Desert of Midian, 1 | Tue. God Has Spoken<br>*Numbers 23:18-26* |
| B. On the Mountain of God, 2-3 | Wed. Waiting for God to Speak<br>*Psalm 62:5-12* |
| II. The Voice That Called—3:4-6 | Thu God Speaks Through the Son<br>*John 3:31-36* |
| A. God's Voice, 4 | Fri. God Knows Our Suffering<br>*Exodus 3:7-12* |
| B. Moses' Fear, 5-6 | Sat. God Will Relieve Our Misery<br>*Exodus 3:16-22* |
| III. The Man Who Answered—3:13-15 | Sun. God Speaks and Reveals<br>*Exodus 3:1-6, 13-15* |
| A. Moses' Question, 13 | |
| B. God's Reply. 14-15 | |

# Verse by Verse

Exodus 3:1-6, 13-15

## I. The Bush That Burned—3:1-3
### A. In the Desert of Midian, 1

**1 Now Moses kept the flock of Jethro his father in law, the priest of Midian: and he led the flock to the backside of the desert, and came to the mountain of God, even to Horeb.**

Forty years before this day, Moses fled to Midian. He was on the lam after that unfortunate day when his efforts to defend a fellow-Hebrew from an Egyptian taskmaster turned deadly.

Deep in the desert, Moses had fallen in with a Midianite priest named Jethro (later in the story called Reuel). Moses had married one of the priest's daughters, Zipporah, and she had borne him two sons.

As this episode begins, Moses seems to be contentedly and competently herding his father-in-law's sheep, way south in the barren country near Mt. Horeb (also known to us as Mt. Sinai).

### B. On the Mountain of God, 2-3

**2 And the angel of the LORD appeared unto him in a flame of fire out of the midst of a bush: and he looked, and, behold, the bush burned with fire, and the bush was not consumed.**

**3 And Moses said, I will now turn aside, and see this great sight, why the bush is not burnt.**

Throughout the Bible, God often makes His presence known to His people through fire. When His Presence filled the Tabernacle, a pillar of fire settled above it. Any Israelite in the camp could look out and see that God was with them.

Tongues of fire leapt up above the heads of the apostles when God's Spirit filled them on the day of Pentecost described in Acts 2. The fire was visual proof to the assembled Jews that God was present.

Likewise, the fire in the bush was Moses' first clue that he was about to have a life-changing encounter with the Almighty.

What really caught Moses' attention was not just the flames. Fire alone was not all that unusual a sight. What aroused his curiosity was the fact that the bush burned but was not consumed. It just kept on burning without suffering any apparent damage. Moses quickly knew that this was a phenomenon worth observing more closely. He called it "a great sight."

## II. The Voice That Called—3:4-6

### A. God's Voice, 4

**4 And when the LORD saw that he turned aside to see, God called unto him out of the midst of the bush, and said, Moses, Moses. And he said, Here am I.**

Once God had Moses' full attention, He spoke to him. Sometimes the hardest thing for God to do is to get our attention. We are so easily distracted and mesmerized by the trivial things of this world.

God's communication with His future leader is quite personal. God addresses him by name. Years later the Bible will assure us that the Good Shepherd knows His sheep by name. The God we serve is not an impersonal Force. He knows each of us and has plans for each of us individually.

A small church in Maui invites various stateside preachers to come be their visiting pastor for a month. One man who accepted this invitation spent the month before his visit to the island studying the photos of the families in the church and memorizing their names. Imagine how impressed those Christians were when their visiting pastor—a stranger to most of them—greeted them that first Lord's day by name. That is how God greeted Moses that fateful day on His holy mountain.

### B. Moses' Fear, 5-6

**5 And he said, Draw not nigh hither: put off thy shoes from off thy feet, for the place whereon thou standest is holy ground.**

**6 Moreover he said, I am the God of thy father, the God of Abraham, the God of Isaac, and the God of Jacob. And Moses hid his face; for he was afraid to look upon God.**

Does it seem strange to you that you cannot get into your local McDonald's without your shoes on, but Moses could not step on the holy ground before the bush without taking his shoes off?

Moses' first act of obedience—his first way to show his awe before the Almighty—was to take off his sandals. Without protest, he immediately did what God told him to do.

By identifying Himself as the God of Abraham, Isaac, and Jacob—the God of the Jews' great fathers—the Lord instantly put into play the centuries-old covenant He had made with those patriarchs of old. This is not just any God in that bush. This is Abraham's God. All the promises God had made to the father of the Jewish people were suddenly back on the table when God told Moses who He was.

Moses reaction was a wise one. It was the same reaction all godly men have when the Almighty draws near. He hid his face. He covered his eyes. "Woe is me!" Isaiah would moan years later, "for mine eyes have seen the King, the Lord of hosts!"

## III. The Man Who Answered —3:13-15

### A. Moses' Question, 13

**13 And Moses said unto God, Behold, when I come unto the children of Israel, and shall say unto them, The God of your fathers hath sent me unto you; and they shall say to me, What is his name? what shall I say unto them?**

People in Egypt worshiped dozens of

gods and goddesses. If Moses came to them saying, "God has sent me to set us free," their logical response would be, "Which god? Identify him for us."

Six decades ago if anybody in America referred to God, nobody who heard the word would have asked, "Which god?" Not so today. With the arrival of New Age cults and the burgeoning of eastern religions, the word "god" may apply to more possible deities than the Egyptians had heard of. Like Moses, we now find ourselves needing to be able to name God to our neighbors before they can have any idea which god we are preaching to them.

**B. God's Reply, 14-15**

**14 And God said unto Moses, I AM THAT I AM: and he said, Thus shalt thou say unto the children of Israel, I AM hath sent me unto you.**

**15 And God said moreover unto Moses, Thus shalt thou say unto the children of Israel, The LORD God of your fathers, the God of Abraham, the God of Isaac, and the God of Jacob, hath sent me unto you: this is my name for ever, and this is my memorial unto all generations.**

In this holy name God asserts, among other things, His timelessness. He is not the God who used to be. He is the God who one day will show up to bless His people. He is the God who presently exists. In all times and in all places He exists. I AM sets Him above all the restrictions that limit our human existence.

This majestic name also reveals our Lord God as the only deity who deserves honor and praise. Before Him alone should we bow down. The Egyptians might be confused about which god controlled their fate and prospered their land. Some prostrated themselves before the god of the great river Nile. Others had greater reverence for the god who controlled the sun. The list of possible deities was virtually endless. Yet, I AM WHO I AM was Yahweh's way for telling His people that He shared His might and power with no other deity. He alone merited their fear and their undiluted faith.

We do well to hear the Lord's final description of His name as the one He intends for His people to use forever. His people in all ages will know Him as the great I AM. This means that today, in the present confusion of gods vying for allegiance in the American heart, the great God I AM is unwilling to play the diversity game. He will not be just one possible god among many. As Jesus teaches us, "Him only shalt thou serve."

ഇറെ

## Evangelistic Emphasis

God never gives up on us, even when we have made huge mistakes.

Some of the great heroes of our faith are, what the world would consider, losers! How about "father Abraham?" He was seventy-five before he ever left home; talk about arrested development. We see him at one moment lying to the king of Egypt to save his skin, no matter that the lie placed Sarah in moral peril. Yet, Abraham becomes the father of a great nation.

David had a bad experience with Bathsheba in the bath. They both got into a lather and Uriah's bubble ended up being busted. David, after this experience, was known as "man after God's own heart." These two losers become mom and dad to the wisest of Israel's kings, Solomon.

Moses stands at that burning bush a loser. He was a fugitive from Egyptian law. He could only find work in his father-in-law's employ. Yet Moses was standing at that burning bush receiving a commission that would change the course of Hebrew history.

God does not have winners and losers, He has children. His children are all precious in His sight and worthy of a second chance, and a third, or even a fourth. That is the good news, that those the world calls loser, in Jesus Christ can becomes saint.

Have you experienced God's gracious second chance?

## ৪৩

## Memory Selection

**"God called unto him out of the midst of the bush, and said, Moses, Moses. And he said, Here am I."**

*Exodus 3: 4*

Moses was 80 when we witnessed the burning bush.

He was well past a mid life crisis. He was comfortable heading into the sunset years of his life. Contented tending the flocks of his father-in-law Jethro, Moses had little to hope for from life. The burning bush experience with God handed Moses a challenge that would change his life and the course of Hebrew history. We learn from the story that this burning bush was on fire, yet the fire did not consume the burning bush.

Perhaps you have wondered why that detail is placed in the story. If the fire consumes the burning bush, we can forget about it. The bush is no longer there. Now if the bush represents your calling, or a challenge to change your life, and it is consumed you can easily forget about the pressure to change the bush represents. But what if the bush is always there? What if God wanted to leave the bush intact, so that Moses would see it later as he was leading the people of Israel through the journey? The bush becomes a reminder of the call that God placed on Moses, a call that lasts for a lifetime.

Burning bushes in your life are very personal. But the bush is always there. God leaves reminders in our lives of our need to trust him with each decision, and our need to rely on him for our daily living.

What is the burning bush challenge for your life?

## Weekday Problems

Laramie worked for a national retail store. She had worked for that company since she graduated from college. Although rare in these times, this was the only employer Laramie had ever known. She was very good at her job. She was friendly to the customers and a pleasure to work with. Laramie was shocked when the regional manager stopped by the store one Friday and asked to speak to her.

Laramie was brought into an office and the regional manager proceeds to tell her about the downsizing that was going on nationally. He told her that she would not have a position at the beginning of the next month. He slid a pile of papers across the desk and asked her to sign the top sheet, which was her official notification of termination.

Laramie had given everything to this company. She had sacrificed Saturday football games. She had postponed meaningful relationships in her life. She had even worked on Sunday mornings, because it was good for the company. She had been faithful and loyal to that company and now she was cast aside in the name of "corporate restructuring." She was angry and very hurt at the way she was treated by the corporate structure.

Have you ever felt like you were cast aside, or forgotten in some important times of life?

Discuss how Moses must have felt before the burning bush, especially in terms of being "cast aside."

# Skydiving

A blonde is watching the news with her husband when the newscaster says, "Six Brazilian men died in a skydiving accident today." The blonde starts crying and sobs to her husband, "That's horrible."

Confused, he says, "Yes, dear, it is sad, but they were skydiving, and they knew there was risk involved."

After a few minutes, the blonde, still sobbing, asks, "How many is a Brazilian?"

# This Lesson in Your Life

Nothing amazes us until the Lord God takes hold of us. We know what we have done and left undone and are often amused and amazed that God would have anything to do with us. We clean up pretty well to go to church. We act properly in public, but many of us know the darkness lurking in our souls. Then there are the faults that everyone can see, but we are blind to them. In many ways, we are not perfect and need a savior.

While we long for a closer walk with the Lord, we have our excuses and reasons for not having that experience. We will spend hours at a hobby and only minutes with the Lord. We can travel thousands of miles to see an old friend, but will not drive down the street to attend a worship service. We think, and often hope, that, because of our duplicitous natures, God cannot really use us for anything important.

Moses would have been a good guest for Oprah. Early in life, he was full of hope and promise. He was a celebrity only surpassed by Pharaoh. He was the golden boy and heir apparent to the throne of Egypt. In an expression of his anger over the beating of a Hebrew slave, Moses lost control and killed an Egyptian. Everyone saw him do it, and because he was who he was, he could have gotten away with it. Moses, in today's culture, could have received a pass. His mother, who floated him down the river in a basket, abandoned him. He was raised in a foster home. He was forced to learn Egyptian culture, which flew in the face of his Hebrew heritage. Moses could have pled victimization led to his misbehavior.

Not wanting to see what would happen next. Moses fled Egypt. The prince is now a fugitive.

Moses ran to the most desolate place he could imagine, Mount Horeb. There he found Jethro and his beautiful daughter. Moses settled down as a married shepherd of the people of Midian. His dreams of power, glory, and leadership had faded as dull as the boulders surrounding Horeb.

Part of this lesson must be a discussion of how "living life" often saps the energy out of our dreams. Have you noticed how one thing leading to another always keeps us from living out the dream or vision that God has given us for our lives? We can never seem to get around to doing what we know in our heart God desires for us. We become too busy or create too many excuses to follow the dream that God has placed on our heart.

Moses forgot his dream. He also forgot the hurting Hebrew cousins back in Egypt. Often the dream that God gives us is for the betterment of others and leading them to Christ.

People who forget the dreams God has placed in their lives, confront "burning bushes" daily. God will not let go of us and his call in our lives cannot be revoked because of what we have done or failed to do.

God is calling you by name, can you say, "Here I am?"

**1. As the third chapter of Exodus unfolds, what details are learned about the life of Moses?**

Moses was tending the sheep of his father-in-law, Jethro, at the west end of the wilderness.

**2. What is the profession of the father-in-law of Moses?**

Jethro, who was Moses' father-in-law, was a priest of Midian. It is likely that Midian refers to a people rather than to a pagan God.

**3. As Moses tended the flocks near the west end of the wilderness, he came to the mountain of God. What happened there?**

Moses saw a strange sight on the mountain of God. The angel of the Lord appeared to Moses out of a burning bush. The bush burned with flames but it was not consumed.

**4. What happened after Moses saw the strange sight of the bush that burned but it was not consumed?**

Moses did what most of us would do; his curiosity got the best of him. Moses decided to get a better look at this strange sight.

**5. The Lord spoke to Moses from the burning bush with immediate instructions for Moses. What were the instructions?**

Moses was to come no closer to the burning bush. He was also instructed to take off his shoes because he was standing on holy ground.

**6. God made himself known to Moses in a very special way. What was that way?**

God identified himself as the God of Abraham, Isaac, and Jacob. This was the way God reminded people of the covenant relationship.

**7. What did God tell Moses about the condition of the Hebrews back in Egypt?**

God told Moses that he had observed the affliction of his people back in Egypt. He had heard their cries for deliverance. He also knew their pain.

**8. What actions had God decided to take in regards to his people?**

God was going to set the people free from the captivity of the Egyptians and give them a land flowing with milk and honey.

**9. What peoples were living in the land that was flowing with milk and honey?**

The Canaanites, Hittites, Amorites, Perizzites, the Hivites, and the Jebusites occupied that land.

**10. Moses was commanded to go back to Egypt and place God's demands for the Hebrews freedom before Pharaoh. How did Moses respond to this call?**

Moses was not excited with the challenge to deliverer the Hebrew people from Egypt. Moses gave God several excuses as to why Moses was a bad choice as a leader.

Have you seen the bumper sticker that reads, **"God doesn't call the qualified, he qualifies the called."** That is power. God makes it possible for you to serve Him. He provides the means, the method, the motivation, the material, the mission, the message, and the Messiah. He gives it all to you, not for your personal enjoyment and pleasure, but for you to carry out His will in our world. We have gotten it all backwards in the church. We fill out gift inventories to find out where our spiritual gifts are. Moreover, we cannot imagine serving God in an area in which we are not gifted. If God has called you, He will equip you. That is the point. God is not limited by your spiritual gifts, or lack of spiritual gifts. God sends the Holy Spirit to make provision for you.

For every objection, Moses could raise about doing this great thing in going to Pharaoh, God supplied not only an answer, but also a proof that God would take care of Moses.

God will provide. When you learn that you can trust God for everything, you can become bold in your living. You can trust God for forgiveness of sins, for power for daily living, for a way through the storm, and for a way out. When you stop trying or pretending to be God, you are freed from the anger and frustration that so many feel, because they are playing God. A role will not bring peace of mind. When you let go, you let God bring change to your life.

When we hear the call of God, we are like the old Snaggle Puss cartoon, "Exodus, stage left." We want to run as far, as fast as we can.

The point is God equips us when he calls us. He does not select us, and then send us to crash and burn. Although we may not have the natural desires, convictions or qualifications to do God's work in the world, although we may not seem suited for God's service, God addresses us, invites us, challenges us, and empowers us to do his mission in the world.

The call of God is not about us. It is all about God. We never should lose sight of this. It is never about us. God calls us to serve Him and to do His will. However, He seeks us out because we are uniquely gifted to do His purpose. Moses was an authentic leader because he had some personal weaknesses. He was not articulate. He was not overly confident. He was not even sure of the validity of the calling of God. He accomplished the purpose for which God sent him, not because of personal greatness. He found himself in places where he had to put his complete trust in God. Yet, because he was willing to trust God to equip him and guide this endeavor, Moses became a great hero of the Hebrew people.

Our mission, like that of Moses, is to liberate people from bondage. The call comes to us every day as God declares us to be one in a billion, and to engage in a sacred and life-saving mission that can only be done the way we can do it.

God equips us when he calls us!

# Lesson 2

# God's Covenant with Israel
# Who's the Boss?

## Exodus 20:1-11

And God spake all these words, saying,

2 I am the LORD thy God, which have brought thee out of the land of Egypt, out of the house of bondage.

3 Thou shalt have no other gods before me.

4 Thou shalt not make unto thee any graven image, or any likeness of any thing that is in heaven above, or that is in the earth beneath, or that is in the water under the earth:

5 Thou shalt not bow down thyself to them, nor serve them: for I the LORD thy God am a jealous God, visiting the iniquity of the fathers upon the children unto the third and fourth generation of them that hate me;

6 And shewing mercy unto thousands of them that love me, and keep my commandments.

7 Thou shalt not take the name of the LORD thy God in vain; for the LORD will not hold him guiltless that taketh his name in vain.

8 Remember the sabbath day, to keep it holy.

9 Six days shalt thou labour, and do all thy work:

10 But the seventh day is the sabbath of the LORD thy God: in it thou shalt not do any work, thou, nor thy son, nor thy daughter, thy manservant, nor thy maidservant, nor thy cattle, nor thy stranger that is within thy gates:

11 For in six days the LORD made heaven and earth, the sea, and all that in them is, and rested the seventh day: wherefore the LORD blessed the sabbath day, and hallowed it.

**Memory Verse**
Exodus 20:2-3

**Background Scripture**
Exodus 20

**Devotional Reading**
John 1:14-18

11

Some of us by nature are rule-keepers. We always drive under the speed limit. We stop at stop signs. We get to work on time. We do not even tear tags off mattresses.

Others see rules as a challenge. In almost every situation they push the envelope of proper behavior, stretching the limits just as far as they can without losing their job, going to jail, or getting divorced.

When God gave these famous ten rules for living, He promised His people that keeping them would greatly enhance their happiness. It follows that the built-in penalty for breaking any of these rules will be self-inflicted misery and woe.

Why should we keep these rules? The Lord himself explains: "That it may be well with you."

## For a Lively Start

The first four commandments of the famous Ten shape our relationship with God. We obey the six that follow because of our reverence for Him, but these later rules define a right relationship with the people around us.

Jesus recognized this division of the Decalogue when He compressed the Ten Commandments into two: 1. Love God totally, 2. Love your neighbor as yourself. These two commandments summarize the Law of Moses, Jesus said.

Breaking any one of the final six commandments inflicts obvious damage on our relationship with somebody. Stealing a man's wheels or lying to a spouse will spark instant trouble. Can we see as clearly that violating any of the first four commandments does just as much damage to our relationship with God?

| Teaching Outline | Daily Bible Readings |
|---|---|
| I. No Other Gods—20: 1-3 | Mon. Your Law Is My Delight<br>*Psalm 119:73-77* |
| II. No Idols—20:4-6 | Tue. The Tablet of Your Heart<br>*Proverbs 7:1-5* |
| A. What Kind of Images, 4 | Wed. The Law with Grace and Truth<br>*John 1:14-18* |
| B. What Kind of God, 5-6 | Thu Righteousness That Comes From Faith<br>*Romans 10:5-13* |
| III. Rightly Using God's Name—20:7 | Fri. Justified Through Faith<br>*Galatians 2:15-21* |
| IV. Keeping the Sabbath—20:8-11 | Sat. God's Claims on Our Relationships<br>*Exodus 20:12-21* |
| A. Man's Rest, 8-10 | Sun. God's Claims on Us<br>*Exodus 20:1-11* |
| B. God's Rest, 11 | |

# Verse by Verse

## Exodus 20:1-11

**I. No Other Gods—20:1-3**

**1 And God spake all these words, saying,**

**2 I am the LORD thy God, which have brought thee out of the land of Egypt, out of the house of bondage.**

**3 Thou shalt have no other gods before me.**

As they left Egypt, the Israelites not only were leaving behind the oppression and misery of slavery. God also intended for them to make a clean break from all the pagan gods and goddesses they had learned to worship and fear during their centuries in Egypt.

The prohibition of actual idols will follow in Commandment No. 2. This first command leaves room in Israelite hearts only for Yahweh. God cites His mighty act of breaking the bonds of slavery and bringing them safely out of Pharaoh's cruel control as proof that He outranks all the deities they bowed down to in Egypt. Now the Hebrew nation was to worship and serve Him alone.

This rule has special significance to us in modern America where the God of Abraham, Isaac, and Jacob now must compete with the God of Mohammed or the spirits of Hinduism or even with Satanism's evil lord. The true God expects His people to be single-minded in their devotion to Him. We cannot allow our desire to be tolerant and irenic to beguile us into granting equal status between our God and elements found in other religious traditions such as Wicca, Zoroastrianism, or Buddhism. "No other god" is Yahweh's unmistakable requirement for His people.

**II. No Idols—20:4-6**

**A. What Kind of Images, 4**

**4 Thou shalt not make unto thee any graven image, or any likeness of any thing that is in heaven above, or that is in the earth beneath, or that is in the water under the earth:**

Not only in Egypt, where these people had been, but also in the Canaanite territory where they were headed, the locals bowed down to idols that depicted everything from planets and stars to fish and reptiles. Canaan's Baal gods paid tribute to the virility of prime breeding bulls. Those who deified the animals, credited their calves, fashioned of stone, precious metals, and clay, with power to control the fertility not only of their fields, but also of human and animal wombs.

Events, such as the classic golden calf scene in Exodus 32, show how greatly such worship displeased God. As the true Giver of life, God objected not only to the sordid worship practices (fertility god worship usually encouraged wanton sexual activity and drunken debauchery), but also to the unthinkable insult of playing a secondary role to gods who were not gods.

The detailed completeness of the list of prohibited idol forms should make it clear to God's people just how total He intends this ban to be.

**B. What Kind of God, 5-6**

**5 Thou shalt not bow down thyself to them, nor serve them: for I the LORD thy God am a jealous God, visiting the iniquity of the fathers upon the children unto the third and fourth generation of them that hate me;**

**6 And shewing mercy unto thousands of them that love me, and keep my commandments.**

God's prohibition in this second commandment has a double thrust. He forbids His people to participate in physical worship before an idol or to fear and obey the pagan deities in everyday life.

Why does God enforce such a rule? To explain how serious He is about this restriction, God compares Himself with a jealous husband who simply will not tolerate the dalliances of a cheating wife. Those of us who have read the prophet Hosea's sermons know that he expands this imagery of God the offended husband and Israel the profligate wife. Curiously, Hosea extracts two opposite messages from the Wanton Wife image, just as God uses it here to underline two sides of His character. Like a wronged husband, God insists that his spouse be faithful, even punishing Israel's unfaithfulness for generations to come. Yet, like many an aggrieved husband, the Lord also repeatedly chooses to forgive His misbehaving mate. Israel "goes a-whoring after other gods", to use a phrase of the late prophets. God just keeps forgiving her and taking her back. He is indeed a God of mercy, especially to those who are careful to obey His commandments.

**III. Rightly Using God's Name— 20:7**

**7 Thou shalt not take the name of the LORD thy God in vain; for the LORD will not hold him guiltless that taketh his name in vain.**

Even those of us who grew up in Christian homes with godly parents somehow learned to cuss before we reached our teen years. Ugly, profane language may be a universal plague and an un-muted evidence of Original Sin. Go to any nursing home and visit the sweet, gentle, God-fearing grandmas whose minds and inhibitions have left them, and you had better cover your ears. Incredibly, some women who for years had been the epitomes of properness will now be swearing like sailors, shouting the Lord's name in profane, angry tirades.

Profanity is one of the hardest habits for any human to break. Once we learn to say the words, they just seem to slip out whenever anger or stress slips up on us. Is this the sin in focus in Commandment No. 3? Possibly. If so, we do well to avoid any profanity that includes references to God or His Son.

Nevertheless, the purpose of this commandment may be to curb a much more serious offense. What if a witness in a trial solemnly intones, "I swear to tell the truth, the whole truth, nothing but the truth—so help me God," while all along this witness intends to climb into the stand and lie shamelessly? Is this not a more wicked way of taking the name of the Lord in vain?

What about a bride or a groom, who stands before God in the sanctuary of a church, and there before the community of faith promises to live with

14

their new spouse "for better, for worse, for richer, for poorer, until death do us part," while all along in their heart they really mean, "or until it is not fun anymore"? Cussing is not a laudable habit, but is it not a far more serious sin to make holy promises we really do not intend to keep? This may be the worst possible way to take the name of the Lord in vain. AIn vain," of course, means emptily, or without meaning it. All Christians are aware, surely, that Jesus simplified this commandment by warning us to keep our speech simple—just Yes or No—without elaborate oaths sworn "by God" or by holy things.

**IV. Keeping the Sabbath—20:8-11**

**A. Man's Rest, 8-10**

**8 Remember the sabbath day, to keep it holy.**

**9 Six days shalt thou labour, and do all thy work:**

**10 But the seventh day is the sabbath of the Lord thy God: in it thou shalt not do any work, thou, nor thy son, nor thy daughter, thy manservant, nor thy maidservant, nor thy cattle, nor thy stranger that is within thy gates:**

For the nation of Israel, the Sabbath command was not a requirement to dress up in their finest and go to worship. A few times a year, a Jewish festival might fall on a Sabbath. Most of the time, however, the only requirement during the Sabbath was to do nothing. It was a God-ordained and God-enforced day off.

Later elaboration in Exodus and Leviticus show us how extensive God intended this prohibition to be. Food for the Sabbath was to be prepared Friday so that the women in the home also got a day to rest. They required farmers, doctors, and anybody with nonstop duties to tend only to true emergencies. The rest could wait until the Sabbath was past. They would include travel later in the growing list of forbidden Sabbath activities. Moses likely would have frowned on Sabbath soccer leagues or weekend trips to the lake. While many Christians wisely try to incorporate into their schedules God's provisions for significant rest, it would be hard to find any modern believer who is as strict about such matters as were these early Israelites. They stoned to death one poor fellow who dared to pick up firewood sticks on the Sabbath (Num. 15:32-33).

Note that the day of rest was not Sunday. Some of us call Sunday the Sabbath and apply some of the Old Testament restrictions to our Sunday activities, but here in Exodus and all through the Bible the prescribed day of rest is clearly Saturday, the seventh day. How we use the term Sabbath today likely does not matter a lot, but when we are reading our Bibles, we will often miss the point unless we define the term as they did back then.

**B. God's Rest, 11**

**11 For in six days the Lord made heaven and earth, the sea, and all that in them is, and rested the seventh day: wherefore the Lord blessed the sabbath day, and hallowed it.**

If anyone doubts that the Sabbath is the seventh day, they should read this verse. It clears up the issue beyond any doubt. Harking back to the creation story, God explains Commandment No. 4 by basing our rest on His. In creation God rested on the seventh day. Now, many centuries later, He asks His people to imitate Him and do the same.

**15**

## Evangelistic Emphasis

Evangelism and the Ten Commandments do not seem to belong together. Most evangelists use the Ten Commandments as the reason people need to experience an evangelist appeal. The sermon has a predictable pattern. We have broken the Ten Commandments no matter how good we are. We are guilty of the violation of the law, and deserve punishment. The punishment we deserve is death. Jesus came to pay the price of our violation of the law and by accepting Him as our Lord and Savior, we are forgiven by God and given eternal life.

We find ourselves in discussions about the relationship between law and grace. They are held in juxtaposition. Law and grace have nothing to do with each other, right?

The Ten Commandments are part of the salvation story. They are good news! The Good news is that God has no secret rules we must keep. He keeps his word and tells us what is acceptable and unacceptable. These commandments are words of grace. When we live them out, we avoid those behaviors that separate us from God and from humanity. The commandments keep us out of trouble.

Just one example should suffice. When you keep holy the Sabbath, and take that time of rest, your body, soul, and mind are refreshed. You are more open to the movement of the Spirit. When you keep that commandment, you make time and space for God.

That is just one example of the words of grace known as the Ten Commandments.

෧෯ඖ

## Memory Selection

"I am the LORD thy God, which have brought thee out of the land of Egypt, out of the house of bondage. Thou shalt have no other gods before me." *Exodus 20: 2-3*

Idolatry is such a quaint term. Seminary students know about it as do preachers, but you do not find the word used much in conversation. Rarely will a group of Christians come together to pray and one shares a prayer concern that goes, "I'm struggling with idolatry in my life." Just because we do not use the word does not mean idolatry is not part of our sin problem.

The modern idolatry is spatial in nature. Relationships breaking up often have the theme of one party claiming, "I need my space." The fastest growing industry in America is the self-storage industry, with over three billion square feet of storage space in America. Why do we need all this storage space? Because we are purchasing more stuff and we need room for our old stuff. It even happens in church life, when we ask members to serve in the church and they reply, "I don't have any space on my calendar for another activity." The modern imagery for idolatry is space.

If that is the case, then God is saying to us, "don't let anything take up My space in your life." Idolatry is anything in your life that displaces God's space. Idolatry happens as we replace or displace God from our lives.

What is filling your life? Throughout history, faithful people have filled their lives with all sorts of activities that are good, but they have filled up the space belonging to God, and that is called idolatry.

16

## Weekday Problems

We find legalists in all faith communities. No denomination has cornered the market on these folks. They were around in the time of Jesus, they tormented Paul, and, in our time, they have discovered the mass marketing appeal of the Internet. They are the rules people. For the legalist, life is black and white, good or evil. There is no middle ground. There is no room for God's grace or forgiveness. You keep the rules, because breaking them brings out the wrath of God.

The funny thing about legalists is that they are list makers. They track behavior and can tell you quickly which of the Ten Commandments have been violated. They will not modify their understanding of the law for anyone, except. . .

Have you ever noticed that legalist do not see their behavior as sinful? They just do not get it, when the words of Jesus are read about those "blind guides" otherwise known as the Pharisees. The legalistic Jews mentioned in the book of Galatians do not bother them. The sins of others bother them, but rarely do they hold themselves to the same standards by which they judge the rest of us.

The truth is that most of us are legalists. We have our own personal lists of intolerable behavior and unforgivable sins. Many of our lists have nothing to do with the Bible and everything to do with how we were raised.

Talk about your communities' list of "every day" sins. Notice how the lists will differ.

# Unanswered Prayer?

The preacher's 5-year-old daughter noticed that her father always paused and bowed his head for a moment before starting his sermon. One day, she asked him why he did that.

"Well, Honey," he began, quite proud that his daughter was so observant of his messages. "I'm asking the Lord to help me preach a good sermon."

Innocently, she asked, "How come He doesn't do it?"

# This Lesson in Your Life

In the time before Jesus, the Jews added to the law. They had laws that explained the law; they expanded the Ten Commandments to over 600 rules and regulations. When people came to Jesus and asked questions about the law, many had a serious quandary about these laws. The Ten Commandments admonished people to keep the Sabbath holy. The Rabbis determined that work was one of the things that would not be allowed on the Sabbath. Over the years, questions about work were asked. What was work? By the time of Jesus, work was defined as the energy expended to carry the ink to make a jot or a tittle. It was enough ink to dot an "i." No wonder the people saw the law as a burden. Rather than being words of grace and offering hope, the Ten Commandments and the commentary on the law, enslaved the Hebrew people.

Part of the consternation that Jesus felt from the Jewish leadership, related to his simplification of the Jewish legal system. Jesus summarized the law in two commandments: to love God and then love each other. That was how Jesus boiled down the Ten Commandments.

Even our culture is about making things simple. As you think about the Commandments, perhaps it might be helpful if you would think about the Ten Commandments in the manner of Jesus. The Ten Commandments call us to love God. The first section through the keeping of the Sabbath all have something to do about honoring God with the choices and decisions one makes. Keeping the Sabbath is important because that day allows us to honor God and to make sure that nothing else is in God's holy space.

Honoring our father and mother begins the next section of the Ten Commandments. My mother used a phrase about "putting our feet under her table." By eating at my mother's table there was an unwritten rule that a person eating the food had agreed to live by the moral and ethical rules of my mother. Many a time, I have received the lecture that began, "Young man, if you put your feet under my table, you will... or will not..." We knew our mother had certain expectations of behavior. We honored our mother by keeping her rules.

The second section of the Ten Commandments is where we agree to love God and live according to his rules. In this second section, the negations of not killing, no adultery, no coveting, and keeping our word, all have to do with behaviors of people who have God as our Father. To behave differently would dishonor the name we carry as Christians.

Every time we celebrate the Lords' Supper, we are "putting our feet under the Lords' table" while we are reminded of His love for us. We are also reminded of that second section of the Ten Commandments to live in a way that keeps the community of faith in harmony. We are challenged to live before others a "life that becomes the gospel."

**1. What is the first commandment and what is unique about it?**

The first commandment is actually an affirmation. "I am God who brought you out of the land of Egypt."

**2. What is the second commandment? What is the meaning of that commandment?**

The second commandment deals with making images, shapes, or forms of God. There is a danger of making a representation of God, because it is easy to worship that representation.

**3. The third commandment is about taking the name of God in vain. What is the meaning of that commandment?**

The word "vain" means to "make light." Taking the name of God in vain is about using the name of God for felonious purposes. Declaring God is on "your side" of an issue is most likely taking his name in vain.

**4. The fourth commandment is about honoring the Sabbath. What is the significance of the Sabbath?**

The Sabbath was the day of rest. After creation was complete, God rested on the seventh day. We rest to allow God to recreate our spirit.

**5. There is a question about the numbering of the ten commandments. Can you think of a way to renumber this first section?**

There is a discussion of whether, "Thou shalt have no other Gods before me" is a separate commandment or an explanation of the first commandment.

**6. What stands out about the commandment to honor our Father and Mother?**

This commandment is the only one with a promise attached to it. The promise is that there would be long life in the land.

**7. The next commandment deals with killing. Does this commandment forbid all killing?**

The Hebrew word is not the word "to kill." The word here is the Hebrew verb to murder.

**8. If we keep the commandment that forbids stealing, what do you think that includes?**

There might be some interesting discussions on this subject. For instance, if you are checking your personal email at work, is that stealing from the company?

**9. What does it mean to be a false witness?**

Again, this is a good point to have discussion. Is this commandment just limited to falsehood in a legal proceeding or is something else going on?

**10. Another word for coveting is lusting. What are we to avoid lusting after?**

We are not to covet the possessions of our neighbors and we are also not to covet their primary relationships.

Your sweet little angel bolts from the car while you are untangling yourself from the child seat. Before you are even aware, he is running toward the street just as fast as his chubby little three-year-old legs will take him. Do you reason with him at this moment? Do you tell him that you love him and do not want harm to come to him? Do you wonder if restrictive rules will damage his budding self-esteem?

No. You shout at the top of your lungs. "NO. Stop. Come back here."

Ah, but that is not letting the child find boundaries for himself. Yes, but it is keeping him from harm.

We have to understand the commandments in the light of the redemptive word that God is the one who brought the Hebrews out of Egypt. The commandments must be heard in terms of redemption. They were given for God's community. They do not belong to everyone. They were not meant for everyone. They were given to the redeemed.

To make sure, our very living was a reflection of God's desires for us. The commandments are authoritative. They are right. That is a strange concept today. Right and wrong. Why must *we* blur the lines? Human beings created the "gray areas."

There is an old story of the golfer Chi Chi Rodriguez. He was driving down the street with his friend. He was driving a lot faster than he should have been. A light changed from yellow to red ahead of him, and he zoomed right through it. Didn't even slow down.

His friend almost had the "big one." He looked over at Chi Chi and sputtered, "Chi Chi, what in world are you doing? You went right through a red light. Don't you stop for red lights?

"My brother taught me to drive," Chi Chi replied, "and he doesn't stop for red lights. So I don't stop for red lights." Sure enough, a little farther down the road the pro golfer approached another intersection and blasted right through the red light.

His friend was a nervous wreck by then. "C'mon man!" he said. "You're gonna get us killed. What in the world are you thinking?"

Chi Chi repeated, "My brother taught me to drive, and he doesn't stop for red lights. So I don't stop for red lights."

Driving a little farther, they came to an intersection with a green light. This time, Chi Chi put on his brakes and stopped, nervously looking both ways.

"Why are you stopping, now?" his friend asked. "This is a green light."

"I know," Chi Chi said, "My brother might be coming."

We are all accomplished at changing green lights into red lights, and red lights into green lights, aren't we? Maybe we would rather have all the lights yellow, so we could look around quickly and keep on going the way we want to go. In other words, what we think and whatever we feel is fine. Always fine! Yet, we need a moral authority such as these relational commandments. They govern our relationship with God and our relationship, as people of faith, with each other. These commandments are eternal. Jesus made that clear.

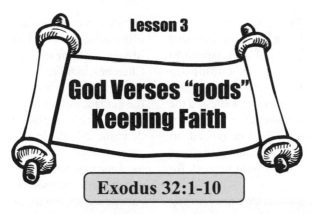

# Lesson 3

# God Verses "gods" Keeping Faith

## Exodus 32:1-10

And when the people saw that Moses delayed to come down out of the mount, the people gathered themselves together unto Aaron, and said unto him, Up, make us gods, which shall go before us; for as for this Moses, the man that brought us up out of the land of Egypt, we wot not what is become of him.

2 And Aaron said unto them, Break off the golden earrings, which are in the ears of your wives, of your sons, and of your daughters, and bring them unto me.

3 And all the people brake off the golden earrings which were in their ears, and brought them unto Aaron.

4 And he received them at their hand, and fashioned it with a graving tool, after he had made it a molten calf: and they said, These be thy gods, O Israel, which brought thee up out of the land of Egypt.

5 And when Aaron saw it, he built an altar before it; and Aaron made proclamation, and said, To morrow is a feast to the LORD.

6 And they rose up early on the morrow, and offered burnt offerings, and brought peace offerings; and the people sat down to eat and to drink, and rose up to play.

7 And the LORD said unto Moses, Go, get thee down; for thy people, which thou broughtest out of the land of Egypt, have corrupted themselves:

8 They have turned aside quickly out of the way which I commanded them: they have made them a molten calf, and have worshipped it, and have sacrificed thereunto, and said, These be thy gods, O Israel, which have brought thee up out of the land of Egypt.

9 And the LORD said unto Moses, I have seen this people, and, behold, it is a stiffnecked people:

10 Now therefore let me alone, that my wrath may wax hot against them, and that I may consume them: and I will make of thee a great nation.

**Memory Verse**
Exodus 32:8

**Background Scripture**
Exodus 32

**Devotional Reading**
John 5:39-47

 All of us have seen what can happen to a champion athletic team that loses its legendary coach. Perhaps we have witnessed the decline of a solid church when their longtime pastor died or retired, or the downturn of a booming business whose strong CEO went to work for a competitor.

Strong organizations need strong leaders. When the hand at the helm vanishes, previously successful groups often wind up like Israel did when Moses disappeared on Mt. Sinai. Churches, families, schools, or nations easily lose their way when they lose the guidance of a trusted leader.

Could this explain the growing domestic disorder in an age of single-parent homes? In a time when too many local and national leaders alike disgrace and discredit themselves, far too many Americans imitate the orgy of leaderless Israel around that golden calf.

 ## For a Lively Start

ഇരുൽ

How would this story have changed if Aaron had rebuffed the people's request for new gods? What if he had told them, "No way!" when they came up with this idea? Quite likely one man's faith could have won the day and held back the entire nation from the debacle that followed. Yet, Aaron played the patsy. He went right along with their misguided scheme.

All of us should be steadfast in our faith, but this kind of strength is crucial for those vested with the leadership of God's people. If the Church has entrusted us by putting us in charge of some part of her work, part of our duty may include resisting popular demands to pursue agendas that clearly will violate the Lord's instructions to His people. In this event Aaron shows us how *not* to do it.

| Teaching Outline | Daily Bible Readings |
|---|---|
| I. The Missing Moses—32: 1 | Mon. Warnings Against Idolatry *1 Corinthians 10:1-11* |
| II. Aaron's Role—32:2-4 | Tue. Flee from Idol Worship *1 Corinthians 10:14-21* |
| A. His Idea, 2-3 | Wed. Idols–The Work of Human Hands *Psalm 135:13-18* |
| B. His Creation, 4 | Thu Keep Yourselves from Idols *1 John 5:13-21* |
| III. Worshiping the Calf—32:5-6 | Fri. Confronting Idolatry *Exodus 32:15-24* |
| IV. God's Response—32:7-10 | Sat. The Consequence of Idolatry *Exodus 32:30-35* |
| A. God's Report to Moses, 7-8 | Sun. The Infidelity of Idolatry *Exodus 32:1-10* |
| B. God's Anger, 9-10 | |

# *Verse by Verse*

**Exodus 32:1-10**

**I. The Missing Moses—32:1**

**1 And when the people saw that Moses delayed to come down out of the mount, the people gathered themselves together unto Aaron, and said unto him, Up, make us gods, which shall go before us; for as for this Moses, the man that brought us up out of the land of Egypt, we wot not what is become of him.**

The text tells us "Moses delayed to come down" from the holy mountain. Earlier, in Exod. 24:18, we find out that he spent forty days atop Sinai the first time he went up to get the holy stone tablets.

Awed by Moses' ability to unleash the catastrophic plagues in Egypt and later by his display of power when he parted the Red Sea for their incredible escape, the people had followed Moses from oasis to oasis down the western slopes of the Sinai Peninsula. Now they encamped in the shadow of the rumbling mountain, hunkered down in unfamiliar territory many miles from anything they had ever called home. Then Moses vanished.

Minus their legendary leader, the Hebrews lost what little sense of purpose or direction they had. With hearts and eyes still focused backwards on Egypt, they begged Moses' substitute to fashion for them some physical gods they could touch and see. They thought these gods would be a welcome change from the unseeable deity who thundered at them from the clouds atop the mountain.

"We wot not," is Elizabethan English meaning simply, "We know not." Clearly, the absence of Moses was the key factor that triggered their panicky loss of faith and their yearning to return where they had come from. He had left them stranded in a harsh, strange land. Without him they felt that all hope was gone.

**II. Aaron's Role—32:2-4**

**A. His Idea, 2-3**

**2 And Aaron said unto them, Break off the golden earrings, which are in the ears of your wives, of your sons, and of your daughters, and bring them unto me.**

**3 And all the people brake off the golden earrings which were in their ears, and brought them unto Aaron.**

It seems a bit surprising that Aaron, the man God chose to become Israel's first high priest, would so quickly join his people in idolatry. This turn of events may remind us that Aaron and his people are only a few days of travel removed from a land where idolatry was the norm. At the time of this calf-creating event in Exod. 32, the ink on the Ten Commandments is hardly dry. To those of us who have treasured these commandments for several thousand years, Aaron's lack of hesitance to break the first two commandments is hard to comprehend.

Aaron's command for the people to "break off" their earrings seems strange to our modern ears. All the later English versions change this terminology to "take off" the earrings, using the verb we usually associate with such jewelry. With earrings from several million ears—both female and male, according to the text here, Aaron should have had sufficient gold to fashion an impressive "graven image."

**B. His Creation, 4**

**4 And he received them at their hand, and fashioned it with a graving tool, after he had made it a molten calf: and they said, These be thy gods, O Israel, which brought thee up out of the land of Egypt.**

Aaron's worst sin was not the creation of the calf itself. Far more serious, were his blasphemous words that credited this short-lived, handmade god with the power to free the Hebrews from Egyptian slavery. To this mute, motionless creature of gold Aaron attributed the power behind the spectacular plagues that had terrorized all Egypt. According to Aaron, this powerless idol had opened the waters of the Red Sea and then drowned Egypt's mighty army beneath its waves.

The Israelite nation, so immature in their faith at this point, could not see the foolishness of Aaron's theology.

**III. Worshiping the Calf—32:5-6**

**5 And when Aaron saw it, he built an altar before it; and Aaron made proclamation, and said, To morrow is a feast to the LORD.**

**6 And they rose up early on the morrow, and offered burnt offerings, and brought peace offerings;**

**and the people sat down to eat and to drink, and rose up to play.**

From the description offered here, the altar Aaron built and the various kinds of offerings he taught the people to present sound very much like the later worship forms specified for the true Hebrew worship in Leviticus.

This similarity is less surprising when we discover in v. 5 that Aaron and his idolatrous people fully believed that they were using this visible deity as a stimulus for their worship of Yahweh. They saw no more conflict between their idol-worship and their devotion to the true God than we did when we idolize our families, our homes, our professions, or our 401-K's and still show up to sing hymns and pray to the unseen God of heaven on the Lord's day.

The calf-worship became "play" that was not nearly as innocent as that word infers. Worship of fertility gods such as the calf usually involved all manner of sexual activity. In other times and places most of the temples to the various fertility deities housed orders of shrine prostitutes who were there to engage in sexual acts with those who came to worship. This "play" before the golden calf was in fact a drunken orgy. Many of those who were misbehaving were so absorbed in their lustful activities that they totally ignored Moses' angry demands that they cease their sinning. The swords of the Levites struck them dead while they indulged in sex.

**IV. God's Response—32:7-10**

**A. God's Report to Moses, 7-8**

**7 And the LORD said unto Moses, Go, get thee down; for thy people, which thou broughtest out of the land of Egypt, have corrupted themselves:**

**8 They have turned aside quickly out of the way which I commanded them: they have made them a molten calf, and have worshipped it, and have sacrificed thereunto, and said, These be thy gods, O Israel, which have brought thee up out of the land of Egypt.**

High up on the mountain, lost in the clouds and darkness, Moses heard from God as He reported on the faith fiasco taking place down in the valley. God notes how briefly His people had been obedient to the laws He had given them. Still, it may be significant that at this point He did not claim them as His people. Instead, he spoke to Moses about "*your* people." "The people *you* brought up from Egypt" have run amok, God informed Moses.

The term "molten calf" means one made from melted metal. Note that God is offended not only by their making of the idol and their prostration before it. He also objects to the lying words Aaron used to describe the idol. God knew who really set Israel free from the Egyptians. He expected His people to know and remember it too. His mighty acts in Egypt were to be the foundation of their national faith for centuries to come. On every Passover, they were to rehearse those great events of Redemption and renew their loyalty to the One who set them free, just as we Christians replay the events of the Cross and renew our covenant with the One who saved us.

**B. God's Anger, 9-10**

**9 And the LORD said unto Moses, I have seen this people, and, behold, it is a stiffnecked people:**

**10 Now therefore let me alone, that my wrath may wax hot against them,**

**and that I may consume them: and I will make of thee a great nation.**

In the scene that begins with these verses we see compelling pictures both of God and of Moses.

C. S. Lewis in his grand Narnia tales often addressed our modern tendency to domesticate God. When Lewis' young characters would attempt to get too familiar with the great Christ-figure lion, Aslan, some mature character in the novel would wisely remind the youngsters, "He is not a tame Lion."

Embedded in biblical events like the golden calf story is a warning we moderns need to hear: "He is not a tame God." When the Hebrew people disobey Him so flagrantly and so thoughtlessly attribute His power to man-made images, we see God get furious with them. We see His wrath "wax hot," the King James Version says in archaic English which means that His anger burned with a scary intensity. When God sees the orgy before the golden calf, He gets mad enough to wipe out the nation He just freed from Pharaoh. He is angry. Red-hot, dangerously angry.

This is not a view of God we enjoy seeing, but it is a theological reality we need to see. This passage can help us see and deal with God's wrath toward sin.

In this chapter, we get our first look at an endearing side of Moses. Instead of encouraging God's anger and endorsing His intention to wipe out Israel and start over, Moses stands beside his people and pleads with the Almighty to show mercy. What a marvelous example Moses gives here for any frustrated pastor or church leader.

25

## Evangelistic Emphasis

In all my growing up years, I was not lost one time! My mother had a hard time locating me at times, but I knew where I was at all times. There were times that I did not understand why she was so upset when she could not locate me immediately, because I always knew my spatial relationship to her. I never left town or the country. Yet, she would be upset when I came in late from the place where I was. I knew I was going to be late, but I did not tell her. She would fuss, when I was not by her side in the department store. What little boy wants to be beside his mother when she is looking at towels, when the little boy can look at all the model airplanes? Parents needlessly worry about children, who are not lost. The children know where they are. Parents worry when their children are lost.

We do not hear the word *Lost* very often in church. With GPS devices installed in our cars, we always know right where we are. How can people be lost when they are well aware of their location? I have had some amusing back door comments after preaching a sermon to the lost.

The story from Exodus 32, is the story of the people of God who are spiritually lost at the base of the very mountain of God. That should give us pause. If people can be lost that close to God, I wonder about the people who never knock at the door of a church. Maybe we should dismiss Sunday school class today and go tell the lost about Jesus.

## Memory Selection

&)CR

**"They have turned aside quickly out of the way which I commanded them:"** *Exodus 32:8*

Last Sunday, what were the major points of your pastor's sermon? What music was sung in the worship service? Was anyone baptized last week? What scripture lesson was read in church? Do you remember the Sunday school lesson from last week? I can tell you it was about the Ten Commandments, because in the world of Sunday school literature, I wrote it last night. How long is your memory?

I want to help the Hebrews out for a moment and defend them by saying they had a very short memory. They had been wandering in the wilderness for so long they had forgotten their bondage in Egypt. They waited on Moses so long that they had forgotten his face. They had been outside, living in tents they simply forgot that God was not in idols. He was not in idols before the Ten Commandments and he has not been in idols since. The Hebrews were simply forgetful and that is why they were in trouble. What we share with the Hebrews is that we have short memories too.

God said, "They turned aside quickly." They forgot fast.

*Remember* is an important word in our Bible. We remember the lessons of the past because they encourage us toward faithful living today. When we keep remembering the lessons, they drop deep into our souls where they cannot be forgotten. That is why we repeat sermons and Sunday school lessons, so you will not forget!

# Weekday Problems

Holly tried to stay up on the latest of technology. She was a youth counselor of her church. She thought that by keeping up on technology, she would be more effective in touching the youth of the church. For the most part, Holly was right about using technology to keep up with the youth. She signed up for one of those social networking sites called "Facebook." Once on that program, she quickly connected with many of the youth. Holly had forgotten just one small problem; even the things she did not want the youth to read on "her" page were visible to them. Holly was also a single young person and there was much attention from single men on her Facebook page.

Holly would post pictures of her activities with the youth. Holly also posted a picture of her social life. For the most part, Holly lived a very conservative life, faithful to her Lord and to the church.

One Saturday morning, Holly woke up late, went to her computer, and posted a message to her Facebook that read, "Took full advantage of happy hour and now suffering the consequences." The youth who saw the post immediately began sending the youth counselor advice on getting over a hangover quickly. Other youth asked her where she went to happy hour and did they make good drinks there.

When she saw the faces of the youth, and of the parents, Holly knew she had made a very large mistake, doing something that, at the time, seemed so small.

So, how do small innocent acts get us into trouble? You might compare that to something innocent like making a representation of God out of gold.

## Discovery

TEACHER: Maria, go to the map and find North America.

MARIA: Here it is.

TEACHER: Correct. Now class, who was it that discovered America?

CLASS: Maria.

# This Lesson in Your Life

Harry Emerson Fosdick said, "Atheism is not our greatest danger, but a shadowy sense of God's reality."

Our North American problem is not atheism. How many pure atheists do you know? It is the height of arrogance to say, "I know that God does not exist." Atheism is intellectually dishonest. We are, at the core of our being, religious people. We have a heart that longs for God. However, in our culture the biggest danger is the "shadowy sense of God's reality."

Rather than having the God of Sinai, or the Lord of Calvary, some people have chosen the god of popular culture. God is a grandfather figure who would never hold his children accountable. He wants all to be happy, just the way they are without any repentance or life changing experience. This is a god of the immediate and does not demand patience or perseverance. This god of popular culture also pampers us when we express our needs. Rather than calling for sacrifice, this god is interested in our prosperity.

Aaron needed to fashion a god quickly. The children of Israel were in open rebellion against Moses, who has been gone for 40 days and nights. People did not want to be patient. They would never think about repentance; they wanted instant access to and gratification from their new god. Aaron did the best he could at theological crowd control.

In the midst of their anxiety, the Hebrews demanded that a god be fashioned for them. A teachable moment in your class might be to discuss how people handle anxiety. When God is quiet in the midst of a time of turmoil, or when life does not seem to be working out, how do we respond in those moments? Do we look for quick fixes to the pain and the problems? Do we seek the face of God? Are we willing to wait on the Lord? The Hebrews worried about their future and their leader. They panicked and demanded that the religious leader produce some expression of god that would help them with their immediate anxiety.

The other interesting discussion for your class might be on the whole role of leadership. Moses is an example of a person totally committed to following the will and purpose of God. Yet, none of us would really want Moses to be our pastor. While he was in touch with God, his devotional time was keeping him from the people. Although God wanted him on that mountain, Moses was absent from the people. Jesus talked about the problems created when His people are "like sheep without a shepherd." Spiritual leadership has to make tough choices, balancing the presence of God with the needs of the people.

Aaron was also a weak leader. Rather than seeking and following the will of God, Aaron was too interested in the perceived needs of the people. Wanting to keep the flock happy, Aaron did not protect the sheep from the evils of idolatry. Discuss the qualities of leadership, especially in a crisis, and you will find rich experience learning from this story of the Golden Calf.

## GETTING
## THE FACTS STRAIGHT

**1. What factor led to the people of Israel going to Aaron and demanding that he fashion the golden calf?**

The people of Israel saw that Moses delayed from coming down from the mountain. They did not know if Moses was even alive or would come back.

**2. What did they think had happened to Moses on Mount Sinai after forty days and nights on the mountain?**

The people of Israel did not know what happened to Moses. From the phrase, "this Moses," they were certainly not confident that he would ever return to lead them.

**3. The children of Israel went to Aaron with a demand that would be a solution to the absence of Moses. What was that proposal?**

The children of Israel, knowing Moses had led them, wanted a false god to take over leadership of the people. They demanded that Aaron fashion a god for them.

**4. What was the source of the gold for the golden calf?**

The gold came from the earrings of the wives, sons, and daughters of the men making the demand on Aaron to fashion a god.

**5. What did Aaron do with the gold he had collected from the people?**

Aaron fashioned the gold with a graving tool and made a molten calf for the people of Israel.

**6. What affirmation did the people make with regard to this newly formed molten calf?**

The people were told, "these are the gods that brought you up out of the land of Egypt."

**7. Aaron requested that the people do something the next morning. What did the people of Israel do?**

The people rose up early and brought offerings to the altar. They sat down to eat and drink, and then they rose up to play.

**8. The Hebrews are at the foot of Sinai having a party in front of the golden calf. What happens next?**

The Lord looked down and told Moses that the people have quickly turned aside and made a molten calf and are committing adultery.

**9. What did God plan to do with the children of Israel?**

God told Moses that His anger would burn against the children of Israel. God would let his anger destroy the children of Israel but would spare Moses.

**10. What did Moses do in response to the idolatry of the people and the anger of the Lord?**

Moses begged that God would be merciful and spare the children of Israel from his wrath.

An American tourist, on a safari in the Sahara Desert, takes a wrong turn and becomes hopelessly lost. After a long morning in the hot sun, he spots a man riding toward him on a donkey.

"Please help me," cries the tourist. "I'm dying of thirst!"

"I'm sorry," says the stranger. "All I have are neckties."

"Neckties?" cries the tourist. "I need WATER."

"I like you," says the peddler, "and here's what I'm going to do. I normally get $15 each for these ties. But seeing as you're suffering, I'll let you have two of them for 25 bucks."

Whereupon the tourist turns away in disgust and walks off. Three hours later, he sees an oasis. By now, he is on his knees, and as he crawls toward it, he looks up to see a man in a tuxedo standing under a palm tree.

"Please," he asks, "do you have any water?"

"Oh, sure! PLENTY of water."

"Great, great. Where do I go?"

"This way, sir. The restaurant is right inside. Unfortunately, I can't let you in without a tie."

The party in the shadow of Mount Sinai proves that we human types do not get it. What the children of Israel needed was an experience of the living God. God had been leading His children to this point, where they would receive His law. Rather than wait for these words from the Lord, the Hebrews demanded that Aaron do something and create a representation of God to lead them the rest of the way.

Like the man who declined the tie, they did not understand that the law was what they would need to live faithfully in the Promised Land. They would need the law later on. At Sinai, God was making preparation for the rest of the journey. The Hebrews could not see the big picture. They could not see beyond today, and because of their shortsighted vision, they short-circuited the blessings of God. The Hebrews had yielded to the tyranny of the immediate circumstances.

What do you need in your life right now? What are you constantly talking to God about giving you, or changing for you? Those are rewarding prayers if we do not take some short cut trying to lend God a hand by hastening the process.

The other insight from this lesson is that it is not about you. The Hebrews made self-centered decisions and suffered the consequences of forgetting that it is about God. It is about God's will for our life. It is about being obedient to the leadership of the Holy Spirit. It is about being patient so God can work His plan rather than working around our efforts at constructing life.

It is not about what we need now, but what God wants us to have and experience tomorrow. It is as simple and as strange as buying the tie from that man in the desert.

# Lesson 4

## God Promises an Awesome Thing Steadfast Love

### Exodus 34:1, 4-10

And the LORD said unto Moses, Hew thee two tables of stone like unto the first: and I will write upon these tables the words that were in the first tables, which thou brakest.

4 And he hewed two tables of stone like unto the first; and Moses rose up early in the morning, and went up unto mount Sinai, as the LORD had commanded him, and took in his hand the two tables of stone.

5 And the LORD descended in the cloud, and stood with him there, and proclaimed the name of the LORD.

6 And the LORD passed by before him, and proclaimed, The LORD, The LORD God, merciful and gracious, longsuffering, and abundant in goodness and truth,

7 Keeping mercy for thousands, forgiving iniquity and transgression and sin, and that will by no means clear the guilty; visiting the iniquity of the fathers upon the children, and upon the children's children, unto the third and to the fourth generation.

8 And Moses made haste, and bowed his head toward the earth, and worshipped.

9 And he said, If now I have found grace in thy sight, O Lord, let my Lord, I pray thee, go among us; for it is a stiffnecked people; and pardon our iniquity and our sin, and take us for thine inheritance.

10 And he said, Behold, I make a covenant: before all thy people I will do marvels, such as have not been done in all the earth, nor in any nation: and all the people among which thou art shall see the work of the LORD: for it is a terrible thing that I will do with thee.

---

**Memory Verse**
Exodus 34:6

**Background Scripture**
Exodus 34:1-10

**Devotional Reading**
Acts 3:19-26

---

Through the centuries, believers have emphasized one side of God's nature while ignoring or reducing the other.

Some evangelists have seemed to enjoy proclaiming hellfire and damnation. They have thundered sermons of judgment, depicting their listeners as "sinners in the hands of an angry God."

Other evangelists proffered grace as God's only response to sin. Their sermons have offered only the blood to cleanse but seldom the fire to punish or to refine.

On the mountain, God reveals to Moses both sides of His eternal nature—His holy justice and His compassionate mercy. Martin Luther called it the "sermon on the name of the Lord" because it features both attributes of God.

ℰℐℭℛ

## For a Lively Start

Would it make us more controlled, careful people if we knew that we would always have to fix whatever we break?

In righteous indignation, Moses hurled down the original stone tablets. In his disgust, because his people were violating half the commandments on the tablets, the angry leader of Israel shattered them into pieces.

Do you suppose he realized that God would later require him to replace them? Maybe the old man would have expressed his anger is a different way if he had known he, not only would have to hew new tablets, but then God would require him to return with those stones back up the mountain.

What if our anger breaks hearts instead of stone?

| Teaching Outline | Daily Bible Readings |
|---|---|
| I. Fixing What's Broken—34:1 | Mon. God's Mercy *Psalm 57:1-5* |
| II. New Tables of Stone—34:4 | Tue. God's Faithfulness *Lamentations 3:22-26* |
| III. Proclaiming the Lord's Name— 34:5-7 | Wed. God's Forgiveness *Psalm 103:1-5* |
| IV. Bowing Before Him—34:8 | Thu God's Justice *Psalm 103:6-10* |
| V. Moses' Prayer—34:9 | Fri. God's Compassion *Psalm 103:11-16* |
| VI. God's Covenant—34:10 | Sat. God's Steadfast Love *Psalm 103:17-22* |
| | Sun. God's Inheritance *Exodus 34:1, 4-10* |

# Verse by Verse

Exodus 34:1, 4-10

## I. Fixing What's Broken—34:1

**1 And the LORD said unto Moses, Hew thee two tables of stone like unto the first: and I will write upon these tables the words that were in the first tables, which thou brakest.**

We have few clues as to how large the stone tablets might have been. Artists through the ages have envisioned them large and small. All we know from the Scriptures is that they were small enough for an 80-year-old man to carry them up and down the rugged slopes of Mt. Sinai. They also had to be small enough to fit inside the Ark of the Covenant, whose dimensions are not in doubt (Exod. 37:1).

The fact that God would engrave the laws on the face of the stone—on both sets—is one way of telling us that these laws are not of human origin. They came directly from the Lord. So they deserve our utmost respect.

Is there a hint of blame in the final three words of this verse, where God quietly reminds Moses that he broke the first set? Or is God simply distinguishing one set from the other?

During the centuries that follow, these stone tablets will be treated as the holiest treasures of Israel, housed in the Most Holy Place, concealed from human sight. The fact that Moses survived his treatment of the first set of stone tablets may tell us something of his stature in God's estimation.

## II. New Tables of Stone—34:4

**4 And he hewed two tables of stone like unto the first; and Moses rose up early in the morning, and went up unto mount Sinai, as the LORD had commanded him, and took in his hand the two tables of stone.**

The last time Moses climbed the mountain, his lengthy stay led to the golden calf debacle. Evidently, that shameful episode turned out to be a learning experience for God's people. Now Moses spent another forty days on the mountain, but this time the people behaved while he was absent from the camp.

Does this experience teach us that nothing can erase God's eternal word? Years later a surly king would burn Jeremiah's scroll that contained God's judgments against the evil potentate. God just repeated His indictments of the monarch and Jeremiah wrote them down a second time, this time with some damning embellishments against the scroll-burner. "Heaven and earth shall pass away," our Lord assures us, Abut my words shall not pass away."

## III. Proclaiming the Lord's name—34:5-7

**5 And the LORD descended in the cloud, and stood with him there, and proclaimed the name of the LORD.**

**6 And the LORD passed by before him, and proclaimed, The LORD, The LORD God, merciful and gracious, longsuffering, and abundant in goodness and truth,**

**7 Keeping mercy for thousands, forgiving iniquity and transgression and sin, and that will by no means clear the guilty; visiting the iniquity of the fathers upon the children, and upon the children's children, unto the third and to the fourth generation.**

During the exodus era, God often uses clouds to show His Presence. Israel's route through the desert was marked at night by fire and in the daytime by a cloud. When the Tabernacle stood in its place, God would signal His Presence by the same signs.

Recall that at the time when the Tabernacle was first dedicated, the Scriptures tell us, "Then a cloud covered the tent of the congregation, and the glory of the LORD filled the tabernacle. And Moses was not able to enter to the tent of the congregation, because the cloud abode thereon, and the glory of the LORD filled the tabernacle" (Exod. 40:34-35).

It should not surprise us, then, that the Lord drew near to Moses atop the mountain "in a cloud." What does stretch our imagination is the following statement that God "stood with" Moses. To convey God's actions, the writers of Scripture often speak of Him doing human things such as looking at us, listening to us, turning his face toward us or away, walking, talking,

smiling, or doing something with His hand. The writers do not mean to infer by these expressions that the Lord is a huge human—some Jolly Green Giant. They are simply using the only metaphorical language that adequately expresses heavenly ideas to human minds. However, the picture of God "standing with" Moses atop Sinai, reaches a level seldom touched by the other anthropomorphic metaphors. It is akin to God's "walking and talking" with Adam in the Garden.

Proclaiming "the name of the Lord" is the same as telling about His nature. In the New Testament when we are told to "do everything in the name of the Lord," the command is not prescribing words we should speak before every action. Instead it is telling us to be Christ like in all we do—to imitate His nature.

The description of God in vv. 6-7 was so precious to His people that they repeated it generation after generation (Num. 14:18; 2 Chron. 30:9; Neh. 9:17; Jonah 4:2). Mature believers value both God's mercy and His justice. One tends to be meaningless without the other. A God who forgives His children when they sin but still expects them to behave is not unlike a mother who has learned the value of tough love.

### IV. Bowing Before Him—34:8

**8 And Moses made haste, and bowed his head toward the earth, and worshipped.**

Both the Presence of the Lord and His proclamation accelerated Moses' reaction to what was going on before him. He bowed low (not always an

34

easy task for an octogenarian). "Worshipped" also describes his body position. They imply some combination of bowing, stooping, or kneeling. Our Catholic and Episcopalian friends could help Protestants understand and practice the Bible's often-repeated indication that posture and piety go together. When our bodies kneel or bow, our souls follow. Likewise, when our souls are prostrated before the Almighty, our bodies should feel the need to follow suit.

### V. Moses' Prayer—34:9

**9 And he said, If now I have found grace in thy sight, O Lord, let my Lord, I pray thee, go among us; for it is a stiffnecked people; and pardon our iniquity and our sin, and take us for thine inheritance.**

Moses' prayerful response to the Lord's description of His dual nature asks God to embrace the Hebrews with both His grace and His justice. Humbly Moses confesses that the Israelites he is trying to lead are some hardheaded, sinful people. In spite of this reality, Moses begs the Lord to aid the Hebrews and claim them as His nation.

The TEV puts Moses' prayer into everyday language that clearly conveys what he wants from God. "Lord, if You really are pleased with me," Moses prays, "I ask You to go with us. These people are stubborn, but forgive our evil and our sin, and accept us as Your own people."

### VI. God's Covenant—34:10

**10 And he said, Behold, I make a covenant: before all thy people I will do marvels, such as have not been done in all the earth, nor in any nation: and all the people among which thou art shall see the work of the LORD: for it is a terrible thing that I will do with thee.**

As so often happens, the Lord answers by telling Moses that He will do far more than Moses has asked. Israel will be His covenant people. What He would do for them in the years just ahead would far surpass all the great works He had done to deliver them from Egypt. God said He would be sure that the surrounding nations witnessed His mighty works so that they would know He was backing up Israel.

God's promise that He would do a "terrible thing" through and for Israel does not mean exactly what we often mean today when we say something is terrible. The word has gradually changed since the days of King James. Some newer versions have picked up the over-used modern term "awesome" to replace "terrible." God's great works for and through Israel would indeed inspire awe in the hearts of their neighbor nations. Other modern versions capture the root of the original word when they describe God's works as "fearful." They will prompt fear in the pagan observers. This is precisely the response we find in Jericho when Rahab tells the spies what her neighbors think about Israel and their God. They are scared stiff.

ೲ

## Evangelistic Emphasis

An aphorism says, "You don't get a second chance to make a first impression." Our witness for Jesus is so important that we must carefully guard our first impression, both as individuals and as congregations.

I want to suggest that while that adage is good human relationship advice, it is not adequate theology. A theme of the life of Moses is the theme of a second chance. He was floated down the Nile in that basket and given a second chance at having a life. After murdering the Egyptian, Moses fled into the wilderness. Years later when Moses was just a memory to both Hebrews and Egyptians, God called to him from the burning bush. Moses would have a second chance to be a leader, this time he would be leading God's people.

Now Moses was invited back to Sinai with a new set of blank tablets. God was going to write the law for the people again. Moses and the children of Israel were all receiving yet another second chance from the Lord. That is the nature of God's grace. God offers to us another chance or a new beginning when we have so richly deserved and earned something much worse.

We must rethink this notion of evangelism. Evangelism happens when you make a phone call to a person you have not seen in a while and you say, "I have missed you." Evangelism begins when you practice love and forgiveness in your daily walk with colleagues at work and children at home. Evangelism means letting someone "off the hook" in Jesus name.

ॐ

## Memory Selection

**"And the LORD passed by before him, and proclaimed, The LORD, The LORD God, merciful and gracious, longsuffering, and abundant in goodness and truth,"** *Exodus 34:6*

I was the oldest child in our family. Growing up as the oldest child had certain advantages when it came to siblings. I was also the undisputed wrestling champion of all my siblings. Wrestling usually happened in the middle of the living room floor as a way of determining who took possession of some trivial item. We wrestled until someone in the wrestling match yelled uncle. The way one won the contest was to get the other one to yell "Uncle." "Uncle" was usually yelled by the one who had his head in a headlock.

Crying Uncle is the childhood equivalent of "begging for mercy." We do not beg for anything in our culture, especially mercy. Honestly, mercy is not something powerful people need. We might distribute some, but need it? Never! Not us.

Our pride blocks our ability to ask God for mercy. Maybe we have some childhood hang up about "crying Uncle!" Maybe our belief is that God understands our sins and we are "off the hook."

Our need is to be open to God's mercy. We do that by going to the Lord as we confess our sins. Not that we try to remind God, for he saw them, we need to remind ourselves that we have sinned. In repentance, we turn back to God, and as we do that, His mercy is poured out on us.

Jesus told us, "Blessed are the merciful for they shall receive mercy."

## Weekday Problems

Who do you believe Jesus is?

Your eternal salvation rests on whom you believe Jesus is. More importantly, your "weekday problems" will be solved or will remain based on whom you believe Jesus is. If you believe that He is a religious teacher of the tradition of great religious teachers, you will look to Him for advice or wisdom when you face your "weekday problems." You might read the pages of Scripture looking for a saying of His that deals with your immediate situation.

If you believe that Jesus was a good man, you will face your problems with that kind of motif. You might even try to live by the golden rule, because Jesus lived by the golden rule and was good to all. I would hope you remember that the Jewish authorities had this good man crucified. Besides, trying to determine how a good person would handle a situation does not solve all of your problems.

You might think that Jesus was crazy. Some people believe that He was distracted with some populist desire. I cannot imagine how you could face any problem with a concept of Jesus that held He was crazy.

This lesson is about second chances, which Jesus offers. This lesson is also about Moses having a clear understanding of the character of God before the children of Israel continued their journey.

Understanding God, as Jesus reveals Him will help you face your "weekday problems."

# The Beginning and the End

Adam blamed Eve.

Eve blamed the snake.

And the snake didn't have a leg to stand on.

One inquisitive Young Lifer wanted to know, "When I get to heaven, what should I say when God sneezes?"

# This Lesson in Your Life

The second giving of the law, gives us one more insight into the character and holiness of God. Our culture does not like this strong image of a holy God who demands holiness of us. We prefer a softer concept of God.

Secularism banished God back to the heavens. Spirituality has found God among us. Contemporary spirituality defines God as an equal opportunity employer. God is the universal source of energy. Modernism believes that He is waiting to be tapped by all of us. What we believe is not important; the challenge is to understand ourselves in light of the higher power within us. If we need forgiveness, we must simply grant it to ourselves. We have broken the commands of no personal God, since there is no God to offend. There is no God whose forgiveness we must seek. The craze is self-salvation by self-knowledge. If you are going to save yourself, then you cannot have a God who makes rules.

Nietzsche, facing the implication of disbelieving in a transcendent God wrote:

"How shall we, murderers of all murderers, comfort ourselves? Who will wipe the blood off of us? What water is there for us to clean ourselves? What festivals of atonement, what sacred games shall we have to invent? Is not the greatness of this deed too great for us?"

To put this in modern context, we could say, "We have redefined God, we have stolen his transcendence, His personhood, and now there is no one left to tell us we are forgiven."

On the other hand, people who do not have a balanced view of God, and who must save themselves, must sacrifice to make God happy. All major religions have sacrificed, they reason, so we need a sacrifice that will make us acceptable to God.

There are some "sacrifices" that God will not accept. One is the gift of sincerity. Some think God should receive them because they mean well. Another is the gift of service, some remember all the good they have done, and think God owes them acceptance for their basic decency. A third is the gift of their own spiritual quest. In addition, many bring the gift of guilt. They flagellate themselves, believing that if they feel sorry enough, they will pay for their own sins and God will accept them.

Martin Luther wrote, "What makes you think that God is more pleased with your good deeds than he is with his blessed Son."

The Hebrews dancing before the Golden Calf did not get it. They did not understand that God has rules and the rules are there to protect us from ourselves. Moses in his anger at the people did not get it either. While God has rules about certain behaviors, He is also slow to anger and abounding in steadfast love.

The empty spirituality of today's world is an easy path. Believe, feel, and do as you wish and God will be happy. The faith of our fathers expressed in these stories of Moses gives a much different picture. God is loving, yet demanding. He is jealous and also merciful.

This is not an easy journey we walk as we seek to understand the biblical image of God, but it is a journey that leads to Jesus, the Way, the Truth, and the Life.

**1. Exodus 34 is the story of the second set of tables upon which the law was written. What happen to the first set?**
As Moses and Joshua were coming down from the mountain, they heard the noise associated with the Golden Calf. In his anger, Moses threw the stones down and broke them.

**2. God gave Moses specific instructions regarding the second tablets. What were those instructions?**
Moses was to cut two tablets of stone like the first and then God would write the law on the stones as before.

**3. What is interesting about the instructions that were given to Moses about those second tablets?**
God himself would write the law as He had done on the first set of tablets.

**4. How was Moses to receive the law from the Lord?**
Moses was to get up the next morning, go to the top of the mountain, and present himself before the Lord.

**5. What other orders did God give to Moses as he prepared to go up to Mount Sinai again?**
No one was to go with Moses on the mountain. There was to be a complete quarantine of the mountain, not even animals were allowed on the mountain.

**6. What happened when Moses arrived on the top of Mount Sinai?**
God descended from heaven in a cloud that rested on the top of the mountain, and the Lord stood with Moses.

**7. How did God describe Himself to Moses?**
God was merciful and gracious; slow to anger, abounding in steadfast love and faithfulness, keeping steadfast love for thousands.

**8. What warning was given as God described Himself to Moses on Mount Sinai?**
God would not clear the guilty and he would visit the iniquities of the fathers on their children's children.

**9. How did Moses respond to the self-revelation of God on Mount Sinai?**
Moses quickly bowed his head to the earth and worshiped the Lord.

**10. What request did Moses make of God?**
Moses requested that God forgive the children of Israel and continue to lead them toward the Promised Land.

An empty frame.

For years, it was hanging in the lobby of the courthouse in Pulaski County, Kentucky. It was a blank and a void, and it looked rather ridiculous — but this picture of nothing was not nailed to the wall as a joke. Instead, it was put up as a testimony to something that had been taken away.

The frame used to contain the Ten Commandments, but in 2001 a U.S. district judge ordered that the display be removed, a decision that was upheld by a federal appeals court in 2003. It was determined that courthouse postings of the Ten Commandments violate the First Amendment of the Constitution, an amendment that forbids Congress from making any law "respecting an establishment of religion."

Down came the commandments, by order of the court.

But the frame remained.

A number of Kentuckians rose up to fight this ruling, and took their arguments all the way to the Supreme Court. In 2004, Darrell BeShears, the judge-executive of Pulaski County, traveled to Washington with 200 others to witness the proceedings. More than anything else, BeShears wanted to refill that frame, and return the Ten Commandments to public prominence.

As you might imagine, there has been no lack of intensity around this issue. "It's about our heritage. It's about our history," said Christian-radio owner David Carr to the *Lexington Herald-Leader* (March 3, 2005). "It's about the future of our children."

However, others say no, as Americans we have to maintain separation of church and state.

Therefore, the arguments go on, and no doubt will continue to go on for many years to come. Nevertheless, as we ponder this issue, it is clear that "Pulaski's empty frame" does raise for each of us the question of where the Ten Commandments belong in our own lives. We need to ask ourselves: Am I displaying them clearly in my own daily words and deeds? Am I keeping them prominently posted in my personal life?

Or am I an empty frame?

As people of faith, we must fill our frames with not only the Ten Commandments, but with the Great Commandment Jesus gave us, as well as all the virtues of a Spirit-filled life.

It is true that the commandments contain a list of rather daunting "thou-shalt-nots," but these 10 rulings are not meant to drag us down into a state of negativity. In fact, they are intended to give us a very positive framework for the living of our lives. The first four commandments provide us with guidance for our relationship with God, and the last six explain what it means to have a healthy relationship with each other.

෪෬

# God's Majesty and Human Dignity Caring for Creation

## Psalm 8

To the chief Musician upon Git'-tith, A Psalm of David.

O LORD our Lord, how excellent is thy name in all the earth! who hast set thy glory above the heavens.

2 Out of the mouth of babes and sucklings hast thou ordained strength because of thine enemies, that thou mightest still the enemy and the avenger.

3 When I consider thy heavens, the work of thy fingers, the moon and the stars, which thou hast ordained;

4 What is man, that thou art mindful of him? and the son of man, that thou visitest him?

5 For thou hast made him a little lower than the angels, and hast crowned him with glory and honour.

6 Thou madest him to have dominion over the works of thy hands; thou hast put all things under his feet:

7 All sheep and oxen, yea, and the beasts of the field;

8 The fowl of the air, and the fish of the sea, and whatsoever passeth through the paths of the seas.

9 O LORD our Lord, how excellent is thy name in all the earth!

**Memory Verse**
Psalm 8:6

**Background Scripture**
Psalm 8

**Devotional Reading**
Genesis 1:26-31

41

Standing beside the thundering cascade of Niagara Falls, I was overwhelmed by the immensity of its non-stop power and my own puniness.

The first time I gazed upward at the top of a towering redwood tree I felt dwarfed by that mighty creation of God.

Perched on the precipice of Grand Canyon, flying what seemed a few arm-lengths from the snowy peak of Mt. McKinley, or watching the relentless waves battering the Carolinas' barrier islands, I have been awed by Creation's beauty and might. Beside such marvels, man seems so minuscule.

The psalmist felt these same sensations when he peered into the night skies and pondered the precision and scope of the stars. The apostle Paul was right when he said that humans in all ages and places have been able to discern the greatness and glory of the Creator just by looking at what He made (Rom. 1:20).

## For a Lively Start

An unbeliever who contemplates the power and beauty and complexity pent up in Nature will ask the same question the ancient psalmist did. "What is man?" all humans wonder when they compare themselves with the grandeur of God's other creations.

Yet, the unbeliever comes out at a different spot than the psalmist did.

ಎಂಬ

The psalmist recognizes that God has put all of Nature under humanity's control, and he marvels that this is so. The unbeliever, bereft of God and dwarfed by Nature, sees only our insignificance, so he despairs.

Abandoning the Judeo-Christian view of creation, the unbeliever allows Nature to outrank man. Then whales and wolves matter more than we do.

| Teaching Outline | Daily Bible Readings |
|---|---|
| I. Praising His Excellent Name—8:1a | Mon. A Faithful Creator<br>*1 Peter 4:12-19* |
| II. Beholding His Greatness—8:1b-3 | Tue. The Creator of the Earth<br>*Isaiah 45:9-13* |
| A. His Glory in the Heavens, 1b | |
| B. His Praise from Toddlers, 2 | Wed. God Rules Over All<br>*1 Chronicles 29:10-16* |
| C. His Handiwork in the Skies, 3 | Thu Remember Your Creator<br>*Ecclesiastes 12:1-8* |
| III. Marveling at Man's Place—8:4-8 | |
| A. His Insignificance, 4 | Fri. All God's Works Give Thanks<br>*Psalm 145:8-13* |
| B. His Crown of Glory, 5 | |
| C. His Dominion Over Everything, 6-8 | Sat. God's Image in Humanity<br>*Genesis 1:26-31* |
| IV. Praising His Excellent Name—8:9 | Sun. God's Majesty in All the Earth<br>*Psalm 8* |

# *Verse by Verse*

## Psalm 8

### I. Praising His Excellent Name—8:1a

**1 To the chief Musician upon Git'-tith, A Psalm of David.**

**O LORD our Lord, how excellent is thy name in all the earth!**

The performance directives that preface many psalms at times are perplexing, for they often contain terms that baffle the translators. In this psalm, however, most agree that the performance leader is being instructed to accompany the psalm with a flute-like instrument from the Philistine town of Gath.

Most of us will recall David's early encounter with the giant, Goliath from the town of Gath. He was a formidable enemy, but the men of Gath later protected David. As the weeping king fled his murderous son, "bsalom, 2 Sam. 15:18 tells us that Asix hundred Gittites who had accompanied him from Gath" led his armed retreat. This flute from Gath was said to produce a joyful sound.

In this verse, even as in Exod. 34:5 in the previous lesson, the "name" of the Lord stands for His total nature—for all that He is. So to praise the excellence of His name is to praise Him.

### II. Beholding His Greatness—8:1b-3

#### A. His Glory in the Heavens, 1b

**... who hast set thy glory above the heavens.**

Higher than the sky is the majesty of our God. His greatness tops anything we can witness or imagine. We moderns with our Hubble telescope have scanned distant galaxies millions of miles beyond anything David could behold, but the glory of the Creator continues to outstrip anything we can behold. Many of us have seen on the Internet some beautiful Hubble photos of distance planets. For those of us who believe in the Creator, these majestic scenes bear mute testimony to His glory. He made all things well.

#### B. His Praise from Toddlers, 2

**2 Out of the mouth of babes and sucklings hast thou ordained strength because of thine enemies, that thou mightest still the enemy and the avenger.**

Almost all Bible versions use the Hebrew translation "strength" to describe what comes out of the mouth of the little ones. Yet the Greek translation (the Septuagint) used by Jesus and His apostles tells us the babies were voicing "praise." Jesus cited this reading of the psalm when He silenced His critics

43

on Palm Sunday (Matt. 21:16).

While the Greek reading of "praise" fits the message of the complete psalm, the choice of "strength" according to the Hebrew text gives us a message God often repeats to His people. How typical it is of our God to use what is weak (infants here) to quell the power of His enemies. He loves to use what is foolish to destroy the wise, or what is humble to shame the proud (1 Cor. 1:27-29). In this psalm, David accepts, as a little child accepts, that our God is so great that He can use infants to wipe out avengers. He can use a baby's cry to put a menacing army to flight.

**C. His Handiwork in the Skies, 3**

**3 When I consider thy heavens, the work of thy fingers, the moon and the stars, which thou hast ordained;**

In all ages, human beings have observed the planets with awe. Very specially, the immensity of the nighttime skies has fascinated and humbled people. Ancient cultures such as the Aztecs and Incas tracked the stars so precisely that their temples aligned perfectly with the seasonal shifts high above. Egyptian pyramids still amaze us as we discover how their angles coordinate with the position of the sun and moon on high. At Stonehenge the exacting spacing of the Druids' masonry shows us how carefully they had studied the heavens.

Even those cultures that were not blessed with God's written revelation still caught glimpses of His greatness when they pondered the stars. Without Bibles to describe Him, these ancient people figured out from the heavens that some great Power designed the solar system and kept it spinning right on time.

**III. Marveling at Man's Place— 8:4-8**

**A. His Insignificance, 4**

**4 What is man, that thou art mindful of him? and the son of man, that thou visitest him?**

In typical Hebrew poetry form, David repeats his thought in this line. He asks the same question twice, using different words. "Son of man" is Hebrew vernacular for "man," so asking "What is man?" is really no different from asking, "What is the son of man?"

Again, in the last half of each phrase, David repeats his thoughts: To be "mindful" of man means the same thing as to "visit" him. "Visit" is used here in the Elizabethan English sense of "caring for." The TEV reflects this by translating, "What is man, that you think of him; mere man, that you care for him?"

It is baffling, isn't it, that in a world existing in a limitless cosmos, God chooses to pay special attention to a being as tiny and finite as man. In contrast to the stars and the endless space beyond them, a human is less than a flyspeck. How remarkable it is, then, that God invests so much love and care on us.

**B. His Crown of Glory, 5**

**5 For thou hast made him a little lower than the angels, and hast crowned him with glory and honour.**

Not only does God take care of us humans, David marvels, but also He exalts us. He bestows dignity on us above any other creature or any other work of His hands. Right now the angels outrank us, but not by much, David notes. By creating man in His image, God has made us nobler than any other earth-bound being. The animals exist for our good. All of them. We humans eat them, train them, work them, and hunt them at our pleasure, because none of them reflects God's image like we do. We alone wear the God-given crown of glory and honor.

**C. His Dominion Over Everything, 6-8**

**6 Thou madest him to have dominion over the works of thy hands; thou hast put all things under his feet:**

**7 All sheep and oxen, yea, and the beasts of the field;**

**8 The fowl of the air, and the fish of the sea, and whatsoever passeth through the paths of the seas.**

At this point in his psalm, David echoes the mandate of God from the creation account in Gen. 1:26, "Let us make man in our image, after our likeness: and let them have dominion over the fish of the sea, and over the fowl of the air, and over the cattle, and over all the earth, and over every creeping thing that creepeth upon the earth." Into this familiar verse David meshes the Lord's later pronouncement to Noah and his clan, "The fear of you and the dread of you shall be upon every beast of the earth, and upon every fowl of the air, upon all that moveth upon the earth, and upon all the fishes of the sea; into your hand are they delivered. Every moving thing that liveth shall be meat for you; even

as the green herb have I given you all things" (Gen. 9:2-3).

God put man over everything He made. Much of the political conflict in our world today arises when unbelievers turn this order on its head, subjecting humans to Nature and valuing animal rights above those of mankind. It is clear from Genesis that God intended for humans to be good stewards of the world He created for them. From the earliest days—even before the Fall—Adam was expected to tend the Garden. He had duties as both a botanist and a zoologist. Still, God gave man dominion over all created things with the right to use animals, plants, energy, and minerals for his benefit. Those who would reverse this order do not project a biblical worldview, and they grow in numbers today.

**IV. Praising His Excellent Name— 8:9**

**9 O Lord our Lord, how excellent is thy name in all the earth!**

In David's song, he points to this dominant position of humans to express his amazement that the Creator would honor us so highly. What is there about us, David asks, that the One who made everything would put us in charge of it? The fact that He did put us in charge shows how highly He esteems us. Then this, in turn, causes us to honor Him even more. So again, we laud His holy name.

## Evangelistic Emphasis

What are you?

That question is more than just a boy or girl question. It goes to the very core of your relationship with others, with the creation, and with your Creator.

Our educational system now teaches children that human beings are a distant cousin to some animal that slithered out of the primordial ooze. We are related by D.N.A. and archeological evidence to some kind of monkey that decided to get out of the tree and walk up-right. Science holds its collective breath that with each new dig the proverbial "missing link" will be discovered and we can definitively say we evolved. If we are just the result of random acts of evolution, then we are nothing very special. We are mostly water, with about two dollars and fifty cents worth of chemicals poured in for good measure. If we were nothing special, then treating others as though they were relatives of pond scum would be perfectly appropriate.

But...

If we are the unique creation of God, created in His image, and He breathed into our nostrils the breath of life, then we are something special. If we are made by God, that would mean that other people are made by God and should be treated as being special to God. If we are created by God, then it makes sense that He would want to redeem his creation and live in relationship with us.

So, what are you?

## Memory Selection

℘)(℃

"**Thou madest him to have dominion over the works of thy hands; thou hast put all things under his feet:**" *Psalm 8:6*

There is order to the creation.

In writing to the Romans, Paul said that because we have the creation that points to God, everyone is without excuses in terms of knowing God. According to Paul, the problem is that we creatures start worshipping the creation rather than the Creator.

You do not have to listen long before someone will mention "global warming." The problem with that political football is that it creates a system that does exactly what Paul described. The movement has at its heart the notion that we human beings are somehow responsible for changing the earth's climate. That is the height of human arrogance. Our actions cannot change the climate! They have not in the past and they will not in the future! Global warming is a modern idolatry that calls the benighted to worship the creation rather than the Creator.

As Christians, we are to care for the creation that God has given us. We are to renew and replenish our earth. We are called to live in proper relationship with our creation. I believe that most Christians have that as their unspoken covenant with creation.

While we conduct good environmental practices, honoring what God has given us, we need to be careful not to go too far and start worshipping "mother earth." I believe God warned about having "no other God's before me," that includes our planet.

# Weekday Problems

Lisa and Sam met while attending church youth meetings. Sam moved with his family to a small rural community only a year before being promoted into the youth department of the church. Lisa was a lifelong member of the church. After college, they began their careers, Lisa as an administrative assistant at a small community college, and Sam as a coach and teacher. They married, bought a small house, and became even more active in their church. There was one thing that Lisa and Sam wanted more than anything, and that was a baby. Years went by, and finally Lisa discovered that she was infertile. It was like a death. They grieved for the baby that was not meant to be.

Then Sam read an article about little girl babies in China who had been given to orphanages by their birth parents. Sam and Lisa prayed, asking God if this was the answer to their prayers. After almost two years of red tape and constant correspondence, they flew to China and met little Sue. She was only three months old and they fell in love immediately.

When they got home, there were many adjustments. Sue's body clock was set for "China Time"—daylight in the U.S. meant darkness in China. But Sam and Lisa's love for their new daughter did not need adjusting. They wanted to keep her Chinese heritage by giving her a name in her native tongue. That name means "flower" in English. Lisa had often been bitter that God had not made her body "perfect" in order to have a child. Now, she and Sam realize that their adopted daughter Sue represented God and His perfect creation.

# Wisdom and Wit

Typical of Will Rogers' down-home humor were these bits of wisdom hiding behind a chuckle:

1. Never slap a fellow who's chewing tobacco.

2. Never kick a cow chip on a hot day.

3. There are two theories about arguing with a woman. Neither one works.

4. Never miss a good chance to shut up.

5. Always drink upstream from the herd.

6. If you find yourself in a hole, stop digging.

# This Lesson in Your Life

When we think of deer, we think of Bambi - that cute cartoon critter with big eyes, long eyelashes and an adorable human expression.

Walt Disney's talented artists certainly knew what they were doing. They devised an irresistibly infantile look for Bambi, and then sealed the deal by dubbing in a charming childish voice. You can be sure that a controversy is going to be created whenever someone recommends the systematic killing of deer.

What people hear - deep down inside - is that Bambi must die or that bad things happen to cute animals.

This controversy arises every year, when springtime deer populations explode. Recently in Milford, Michigan, public hearings were held over plans to kill deer in three parks in the region.

In one of the parks, the deer herd is five times too large, resulting in many malnourished deer. Because of overgrazing, at least 19 plant species have disappeared, and 23 more are threatened. The local authority's plan is to bring in a sharpshooter to kill some of the 528 deer.

Of course, people are upset. Animal rights groups have protested, saying that if the herd is too large, deer will naturally reproduce less. Some also suggest sterilization, a feeding ban, or a relocation of the animals. Will the problem be solved peacefully and permanently?

Not a chance.

Emotions are going to run high whenever someone implies that Bambi must die. While a service of worship is neither the time nor the place to recommend a particular policy for controlling animal overpopulation, this issue does raise for us the question of how humans are to relate to nature. We need to take a clear-eyed look at what it means to have dominion over animals, be good stewards of creation and live responsibly in the midst of a world that is wild and free.

Psalm 8 is an excellent place to begin. This hymn of praise is not only a proclamation of the supreme authority of God, but also an affirmation of the exalted status of human beings. "O Lord, our Sovereign, how majestic is your name in all the earth!" it begins, extolling God for his magnificent work as the Creator of heaven and earth. "When I look at your heavens, the work of your fingers, the moon and the stars that you have established; what are human beings that you are mindful of them, mortals that you care for them?"

This psalm reminds us that the Creator of an infinite universe has chosen to be "mindful" of us and to care for us - an amazing attitude for an almighty Lord to have. When the psalm writer says to God, "You have given [people] dominion over the works of your hands; you have put all things under their feet", he is clearly not envisioning any abuse of creation by the people of the world. Instead, he expects us to be mindful of other creatures and to care for them - "all sheep and oxen, and also the beasts of the field, the birds of the air, and the fish of the sea, whatever passes along the paths of the seas."

**GETTING THE FACTS STRAIGHT**

**1. What about the Lord is above everything on the earth?**

The majestic name of God is over everything on the earth.

**2. Where is this glory and this majesty spoken and what is the contrast between the witness for God and the enemies of God?**

The glory of the Lord is spoken out of the mouth of babes and infants and the enemy and avengers are silent.

**3. What assumptions might be made from the reading of the first three verses?**

The first three verses might lead us to believe that the majesty and glory of God are understood by simple acts of faith.

**4. What are the works of the fingers of God?**

The heavens, the moon, and the stars are all the result of the work of God's fingers.

**5. As the Psalm continues, what rhetorical question is asked?**

The Psalmist asks the rhetorical question, "what are human beings that you are mindful of them?"

**6. What might we learn from the phrase, "what are human beings that you are mindful of them?"**

We might learn that human beings have a special place in God's creation and that He cares for us in special ways.

**7. How are humans described with reference to heavenly beings?**

Various translations will read that human beings are a little lower than the angels are or a little lower than God.

**8. What is the relationship that human beings share with the created order?**

We are to have dominion over all the works of God's hands.

**9. What are the works of God's hands?**

The works of God's hands include all sheep and oxen, the beasts of the field and the birds of the air, as well as the fish of the sea.

**10. What does having dominion over all these parts of creation mean?**

It means that we have a responsibility to care for creation as well as the blessing of enjoying creation.

For the next weeks, we will be studying the Psalms together. The collection of Psalms is called the Psalter. The Psalter was and is the Jewish hymnal. Many of the songs we sing in church remind us of these Psalms. Therefore, in this section, you might be reading words of a hymn that reminds you of the Psalm you have just studied.

The importance of music in our faith development cannot be ignored. Most of us learned our first bit of theology singing, "Jesus loves me this I know for the Bible tells me so." Many of the passages from Paul entered the collective consciousness because they became the great hymns of doxologies of our faith. The songs we sing land deep in our souls and stay with us for a lifetime.

Our Hebrew ancestors sang and so do we, here is one example:

O Lord, our Lord, how splendid is your name,
In all the whole wide earth how great your fame.
Above the heavens, your majesty you show.
Because of opposition from the foe,
From babes and children's lips, praise you ordained,
The foe and the avenger, you restrained.

When in the heavens your fingers' work I trace,
The moon and stars which you have set in place.
What is a man, so mindful you're of him?
Why do you care so for the son of man?
Only below the angels he's been placed,
But with a crown of glory, he's been graced.

Over your hands' works given rule to wield -
All flocks and herds and beasts out in the field,
All placed beneath his feet by your decree -
Birds of the air, beasts, fish that swim the sea.
O Lord, our Lord, how splendid is your name,
In all the whole wide earth how great your fame.

This song is a translation and interpretation of the great hymn of Praise. It captures in modern language the eloquence of the Psalm.

Perhaps as part of your class time, you would make the assignment to take the eighth Psalm and work it into a hymn or a modern praise song.

ଧଞ

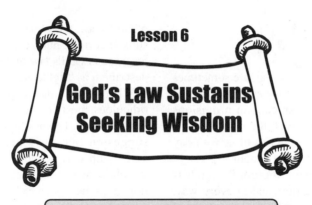

# Lesson 6

## God's Law Sustains Seeking Wisdom

### Psalm 19:7-14

The law of the LORD is perfect, converting the soul: the testimony of the LORD is sure, making wise the simple.

8 The statutes of the LORD are right, rejoicing the heart: the commandment of the LORD is pure, enlightening the eyes.

9 The fear of the LORD is clean, enduring for ever: the judgments of the LORD are true and righteous altogether.

10 More to be desired are they than gold, yea, than much fine gold: sweeter also than honey and the honeycomb.

11 Moreover by them is thy servant warned: and in keeping of them there is great reward.

12 Who can understand his errors? cleanse thou me from secret faults.

13 Keep back thy servant also from presumptuous sins; let them not have dominion over me: then shall I be upright, and I shall be innocent from the great transgression.

14 Let the words of my mouth, and the meditation of my heart, be acceptable in thy sight, O LORD, my strength, and my redeemer.

Oct. 10

**Memory Verse**
Psalm 19:7-8

**Background Scripture**
Psalm 19

**Devotional Reading:**
1 Chronicles 22:7-13

# focus

Laws made by man are sometimes not fair. Recent laws enacted by the U. S. Congress contain provisions designed to enrich the family of one lawmaker. To the rest of us who pay taxes, this is clearly unfair.

Nevertheless, the Lord's Torah is good all the time and in every way. David almost exhausted his stock of positive adjectives in his descriptions of God's law. It is perfect, he said, and sure. It is right, pure, clean, and true. So good is God's law that David can describe it as "righteous altogether."

When we feel that a speed limit is ridiculous, most of us tend to ignore it. Centuries ago, Thomas Aquinas wisely suggested that laws people don't agree with may actually cause them to behave worse, not better. Prohibition might be a good example of such a law. But God's laws are clearly just and right. Our only sensible response to them is to obey.

## For a Lively Start

Some people see rules as oppressive restrictions on their fun, so they skirt the rules and dodge the requirements at work, at school, on the highway, or on the ball field. Rules cause them to rebel.

Those who are wise enough to keep God's rules, however, will find that by doing so they have received a reward.

For God's rules always bless those who obey them.

In this psalm, King David lists some of the rewards inherent in obeying God's laws. If we keep them, God's laws can revive our souls, make wise the simple, gladden our hearts, and enlighten our eyes. David says the pleasure of obeying God's laws is akin to receiving gold or tasting honey.

| Teaching Outline | Daily Bible Readings |
|---|---|
| I. Qualities and Effects of God's Law—19:7-9 | Mon. The Testimony of Creation<br>*Psalm 19:1-6* |
| A. Perfect and Sure, 7 | Tue. An Everlasting Covenant<br>*Psalm 105:1-11* |
| B. Right and Pure, 8 | Wed. The Law as Revelation<br>*Deuteronomy 29:25-29* |
| C. Clean and True, 9 | Thu The Law as Obedient Love<br>*Deuteronomy 30:1-10* |
| II. Blessings in God's Laws—19:10-11 | Fri. The Law as Witness<br>*Deuteronomy 31:19-26* |
| A. Like Gold or Honey, 10 | Sat. The Law as Covenant<br>*Jeremiah 31:31-37* |
| B. Offering Warnings and Rewards, 11 | Sun. The Testimony of the Law<br>*Psalm 19:7-14* |
| III. Protection from Sins—19:12-13 | |
| IV. A Prayer for This Prayer—19:14 | |

# Verse by Verse

Psalm 19:7-14

## I. Qualities and Effects of God's Law—19:7-9

### A. Perfect and Sure, 7

**7 The law of the Lord is perfect, converting the soul: the testimony of the Lord is sure, making wise the simple.**

"Perfect" can mean flawlessly and without error. It can also mean completely, as in a perfect circle. Perfect can also describe something that fits just right. A husband may tell his wife, "That necklace is just perfect with that outfit." Which meaning do you think David intended here? Almost every Bible version uses the word "perfect" here, but it is up to us to define the term.

Evidence of the perfection of God's law, the KJV tells us, is that it "converts" the soul. Our traditional use of the word "convert" in Christian evangelism may throw us a curve here. The meaning of David's original word can be seen by comparing this verse in several later Bible versions. The NIV echoes the RSV and the NLT in telling us here that God's law "revives" the soul. The NASB says it "restores" the soul. The basic idea comes clear in the TEV, which says "it gives new strength" to our souls.

How many terms can you think of that are synonyms for "law"? David must have thoroughly searched his thesaurus to come up with so many

ways to say "law." In this verse, he uses "testimony" (not meaning the anecdotes we tell when we testify). In the verses to come he will use statutes, commandments, fear, and judgments, among others.

The statement here, that God's law will "make wise the simple" is so well translated that virtually every Bible we can find repeats it. TEV simplifies "the simple" by telling us that God's law "gives wisdom to those who lack it." Most of us know right from wrong, don't we? If there is ever any doubt, however, God's law usually contains the instruction we need.

### B. Right and Pure, 8

**8 The statutes of the Lord are right, rejoicing the heart: the commandment of the Lord is pure, enlightening the eyes.**

When we make rules, we often have to use them for a spell before we can know for sure if the new regulation will fix our problems or cause new ones. Rules for taxes, schools, medications, or safety often turn out to be flawed. This is not the case of God's laws in our lives. We can count on them. Therefore, our various Bible versions in this verse tell us that they are trustworthy. They are sure. They are right.

53

Consequently, God's rules fill us with joy. If we obey them, they make us happy. If we contemplate them, our reaction is positive, because we can see that God's commands are right on target. IRS regulations often fill us with frustration. The new green rules may make us angry. Yet, God's laws are so clearly sensible and effective that they stir joy in our hearts.

In v 8, the original adjective translated "pure" gives the Bible translators a hard time. Using the concluding phrase about "light for the eyes" as a clue to the word's meaning in this place, the NIV says God's laws are "radiant," and the NRSV describes them as "clear." The purity involved here obviously has something to do with helping us to see. Instead of providing light or enlightenment for the eyes, the NLT applies this metaphor and tells us that the Lord's laws will "give insight for living." Surely, this captures David's intent.

## C. Clean and True, 9

**9 The fear of the Lord is clean, enduring for ever: the judgments of the Lord are true and righteous altogether.**

"Fear" at first seems a strange word to use right here in David's chain of synonyms for "laws." If we balance this phrase, ("the fear of the Lord is clean") with the total series of descriptions that precede and follow it, we doubt that David used it to refer to our being afraid of God in the usual sense of the word. Even the TEV translation of "reverence for the Lord" does not seem to fit with the phrases before and after this one.

The respected Old Testament commentator C. F. Keil explains that the expression here "is not the fear of God as an act performed, but as a precept, it is what God's revelation demands, effects, and maintains; so that it is the revealed way in which God is to be feared." The word David used here probably refers to the Jewish religion as a whole—the way of life God willed for His people.

That way of life is "clean," David tells us. It rises above both the physical and moral filth that degraded so much of the pagan society around God's nation. Even today it can be seen that those countries that order their society in keeping with Judeo-Christian ethics and standards enjoy a level of sanitation and a general quality of life unseen in most pagan lands.

David concludes his litany of praise for God's laws by asserting that they are "true and righteous altogether." Several versions reflect the fact that the word here for "righteous" often will be translated "just" or "fair." Can anything more complimentary be said about any ordinance? If the rule turns out to be fair to all concerned, then it is clearly a good rule worthy to be accepted and obeyed. Such are all God's laws.

## II. Blessings in God's Laws— 19:10-11

### A. Like Gold or Honey, 10

**10 More to be desired are they than gold, yea, than much fine gold: sweeter also than honey and the honeycomb.**

David's poetic flair shines here. Would you like to have a lot of gold? That is how much we will want God's laws if we understand them. Would you relish a tasty helping of honey? That is how sweet the laws of the Lord will be if we learn them and live by them. If fact, David dares to assert that the divine Torah is more desirable than wealth and sweeter than honey.

All who order their lives according to the laws of the Lord will join David in affirming that the pleasure of righteous living far surpasses anything enjoyed by those who choose to break those laws.

## B. Offering Warnings and Rewards, 11

**11 Moreover by them is thy servant warned: and in keeping of them there is great reward.**

So much heartache and suffering befall people who mess up simply because they do not know any better. They are like the newlyweds who lost their new car this month. It was repossessed, towed away from their home, on the same day when the fellow who holds their home mortgage showed up to warn them that foreclosure looms. These good people simply lack the training and the financial experience to make and follow a simple budget. Early in their marriage, they have broken most of the rules for handling money. Now they are paying the price.

God's laws provide us the simple instructions that can keep us from ruining our lives. His rules about sex, alcohol, courtship, money, work, sanitation, and a host of other everyday activities can keep us out of all manner of trouble. The person who pays attention to God's rules will enjoy a better, happier life.

## III. Protection from Sins—19:12-13

**12 Who can understand his errors? cleanse thou me from secret faults.**

**13 Keep back thy servant also from presumptuous sins; let them not have dominion over me: then shall I be upright, and I shall be innocent from the great transgression.**

Even men and women with good hearts and pure motives will have blind spots that keep them from seeing their own offenses. Those who pride themselves on being thrifty may stray into stinginess. Those who seek to be disciplined may not realize how controlling they have become. All of us need to be constantly praying that God will purge us of those failings that we are unaware of.

Worse, however, are "presumptuous sins"—those transgressions that we know to be wrong but persist in anyway. A mother who shrieks at her children knows she should not, but still she may allow herself often to inflict this angry abuse. A man who knows his overspending on minor vices will deprive his family of basic needs still does not curtail his indulgence. These sins are willful sins, sins we commit with open eyes and hard hearts. They easily develop into hurtful habits that dominate our lives and ruin our relationships.

David wisely guides us into fervent prayers that God may keep us free of both kinds of sin.

## IV. A Prayer for This Prayer—19:14

**14 Let the words of my mouth, and the meditation of my heart, be acceptable in thy sight, O Lord, my strength, and my redeemer.**

Can you think of a finer prayer to commit to memory and to offer often to the Lord?

There is a wonderful Chasidic story about the child of a rabbi who used to wander in the woods. At first, his father let him wander, but over time, he became concerned. The woods were dangerous. The father did not know what lurked there. He decided to discuss the matter with his child.

One day he took him aside and said, "You know, I have noticed that each day you walk into the woods. I wonder why do you go there?"

The boy said to his father, "I go there to find God."

"That is a very good thing," the father replied gently. "I am glad you are searching for God. But, my child, don't you know that God is the same everywhere?"

"Yes," the boy answered, "but I'm not."

The story reminds us that nature and the power of nature allows us to change our perspective and to see things about God we might not always see. Walking out doors on a fall afternoon, and watching the beauty of the leaves changing colors brings beauty to our souls and causes us to ponder that power that created all the beauty.

The creation is always pointing the creature to the creator. The good news is that creation is always reminding us that God is looking for us, and through His love and grace, He is always seeking to be a part of our lives.

## Memory Selection

ഇരു

**"The law of the LORD is perfect, converting the soul: the testimony of the LORD is sure, making wise the simple. The statutes of the LORD are right, rejoicing the heart: the commandment of the LORD is pure, enlightening the eyes."** *Psalm 19: 7-8*

There is an important sequence of words in these verses. The Psalmist speaks of the law, the testimony, the statues, and the commandments of the Lord. All of these things are good and perfect. The result of experiencing these expressions of God's love is that the eyes are enlightened.

Do you have enlightened eyes? Do you see God's hand moving in your life or in the lives around you? Can you see the umbrella?

The fields were parched and brown from lack of rain, and the crops lay wilting from thirst. People were anxious and irritable as they searched the sky for any sign of relief. Days turned into arid weeks. No rain came. The ministers of the local churches called for an hour of prayer on the town square the following Saturday. They requested that everyone bring an object of faith for inspiration.

At high noon on the appointed Saturday, the townspeople turned out en masse, filling the square with anxious faces and hopeful hearts. The ministers were touched to see the variety of objects clutched in prayerful hands - holy books, crosses, rosaries.

When the hour ended, as if on magical command, a soft rain began to fall. Cheers swept the crowd as they held their treasured objects high in gratitude and praise. From the middle of the crowd, one faith symbol seemed to overshadow all the others. A small 9-year-old child had brought an umbrella.

## Weekday Problems

Gene was an attorney in town. He had barely passed law school and he had to take the bar exam a couple of times to receive his law license. He was not much of an attorney and had been placed on probation a couple of times for bad practices related to clients' money. He had his law license suspended over one incident.

However, he was reinstated to the practice of law. He was still not much of an attorney. He found himself as a public defender. About the only people proud of Gene were his parents. Gene's only claim to public defender fame was getting a child molester off with probation.

Gene was hired to defend a man who shot a police officer. The officer had succumbed to his wounds leaving a widow and three small children. It was an easy case for the District Attorney, and since Gene was not much of a lawyer, it would be even easier. Everyone in the country was anticipating the trial, and the almost guaranteed guilty verdict.

On the morning the trial was to begin, the local newspaper discovered that Gene had not kept his law license current and at the time was not licensed to practice law. The judge was forced to declare an immediate mistrial and justice was delayed.

In your class discuss how not following the law can hurt innocent people and how justice is often delayed for both the perpetrator and victim.

# Rev. Ole and Pastor Sven

Reverend Ole was the pastor of the local Norwegian Lutheran Church, and Pastor Sven was the minister of the Swedish Covenant Church across the road.

One day the two pastors were seen pounding into the ground a sign that warned: "DA END ISS NEAR! TURN YERSELF AROUND NOW BEFORE IT'S TOO LATE!"

As a car sped past them, the driver leaned out his window and yelled, "Leave us alone, you religious nuts!" Around the curve they soon heard screeching tires and a big splash.

Rev. Ole turns to Pastor Sven and asked, "Do ya tink maybe da sign should yust say, 'Bridge Out'?"

# This Lesson in Your Life

Recently, a scientist, who is also a leader in his congregation, prepared a devotional for his local church board based upon a reading from Genesis 1. His comments were prompted by an essay in *The Washington Post* by Henry Brinton, a Presbyterian pastor and a regular contributor to *Homiletics*, on the debate within his congregation between proponents of Intelligent Design and Evolution.

The scientist began by describing himself as a scientist and a Christian. He went on to explain the difference between a scientific theory and a hypothesis: The first is proven by a rigorous testing of hypotheses; the second is not provable by a set of repeated tests and thus remains a hypothesis. Theory is not the same as hypothesis

Then he stated his own conviction regarding creation. "God did it. The Genesis stories of creation, while different in detail, agree that God did it. This theme runs throughout the Bible. That God did it does not suggest *how* God created us, and I find it somewhere between amusing/annoying/irritating/maddening that people might have the temerity to insist that God did it in a way that is pleasing to them. I feel that God has given us the intelligence to explore the world around us and to do our best to understand it."

This approach, combining the pursuit of truth through scientific discovery while humbly acknowledging that there are some things known only to God, allows for an embrace of science and faith. It allows one to pursue the data that science reveals, including data about the origins of life, while praising God as the magnificent author of all that is.

This, in fact, was the approach of many of the great scientists of history, including Galileo, Kepler and Einstein. The pursuit of truth is what animated them. If one believes that God is the author of all truth, then the pursuit of scientific truth is not to be feared but rather pursued with joy and delight in the discoveries that will render the manifold splendor of God's truth. Truth is truth, therefore, scientific truth need not be held in opposition to revealed, or religious, truth; they are different aspects of the truth that leads us to knowledge of God.

Generations of believers have embraced the prayer of Psalm 19 in just this way.

"The heavens are telling the glory of God; and the firmament proclaims his handiwork. Day to day pours forth speech, and night to night declares knowledge ."

The Psalmist gazes at the beauty of creation and utters praise to God, the sovereign author of it all. This praise offering comes from a truth born of faith. This is not science asserting, it is faith affirming. Science talks the talk; faith walks the walk. Science can do no more; faith can do no less.

GETTING
THE FACTS STRAIGHT

**1. What do the heavens and the firmament tell about God?**

The heavens tell the glory of God and the firmament declares the handiwork of God.

**2. What do day and night share about God?**

The day pours forth speech and the night declares knowledge about God.

**3. What does the Psalmist say about this speech of day and night?**

The day and the night do not use words and there is no speech involved in the message they are proclaiming.

**4. With no words or speech involved how far does this type of communication travel?**

The message about God, carried by day and night, travels throughout the world even to the ends of the earth.

**5. How is the daily journey of the sun described?**

The sun is described as a bridegroom leaving his chamber and like a young man running for joy.

**6. What level of desire should there be for the law of the Lord?**

The law is to be desired more than gold or more than the honey that drips from the honeycomb.

**7. Other than desire what is the other benefit of the law of the Lord?**

By keeping the law of the Lord, the servant of the Lord is warned and in keeping the law there is great benefit.

**8. From which kind of sins does the Psalmist desire to be protected?**

The Psalmist prays that he would be protected from presumptuous sins.

**9. What are the rewards of avoiding presumptuous sins?**

The Psalmist would be blameless and innocent of great transgressions.

**10. What are the most familiar words from this Psalm?**

"Let the words of my mouth and the mediations of my heart be acceptable to you, O Lord, my rock and my redeemer."

Isaac Watts wrote this hymn based on Psalm 19:

> The heav'ns declare Thy glory, Lord,
> In every star Thy wisdom shines
> But when our eyes behold Thy Word,
>
> We read Thy Name in fairer lines.
> The rolling sun, the changing light,
> And nights and days, Thy power confess
> But the blest volume Thou hast writ
> Reveals Thy justice and Thy grace.
>
> Sun, moon, and stars convey
> Thy praise Round the whole earth, and never stand:
> So when Thy truth begun its race,
> It touched and glanced on every land.
>
> Nor shall Thy spreading Gospel rest
> Till through the world Thy truth has run,
> Till Christ has all the nations blest
> That see the light or feel the sun.
>
> Great Sun of Righteousness, arise,
> Bless the dark world with heav'nly light;
> Thy Gospel makes the simple wise,
> Thy laws are pure, Thy judgments right.
>
> Thy noblest wonders here we view
> In souls renewed and sins forgiv'n;
> Lord, cleanse my sins, my soul renew,
> And make Thy Word my guide to Heaven.

Is this hymn in your songbook? Your class might ask the musicians to plan to play this as part of the worship service on this Sunday. Maybe you would familiarize yourself on the story behind the writing of this particular hymn by Isaac Watts.

Have your class investigate Isaac Watts and his contribution to the hymn traditions of the church. Lowell Mason wrote the modern musical score for this hymn and you might look up his biography to see how he contributed to the growth of church music.

## Lesson 7

# God Provides Refuge
# Seeking Refuge

**Psalm 46:1-7**

To the chief Musician for the sons of Ko'-rah, A Song upon Al'-a-moth.

God is our refuge and strength, a very present help in trouble.

2 Therefore will not we fear, though the earth be removed, and though the mountains be carried into the midst of the sea;

3 Though the waters thereof roar and be troubled, though the mountains shake with the swelling thereof. Selah.

4 There is a river, the streams whereof shall make glad the city of God, the holy place of the tabernacles of the most High.

5 God is in the midst of her; she shall not be moved: God shall help her, and that right early.

6 The heathen raged, the kingdoms were moved: he uttered his voice, the earth melted.

7 The Lord of hosts is with us; the God of Jacob is our refuge. Selah.

Oct. 17

**Memory Verse**
Psalm 46:1

**Background Scripture**
Psalm 46:1-7

**Devotional Reading**
Hebrews 6:13-20

61

# fOCuS

Those who have lived through times of national distress such as Pearl Harbor or 9/11 will surely recall how deeply shaken most Americans were by these unthinkable events. Sobered and silenced by those unexpected disasters, frightened citizens across the land turned to God. People gathered in their communities to pour out their combined prayers to the One Who alone could aid them.

## For a Lively Start

For centuries, Christians have affirmed their hope in the face of terrifying troubles by singing Martin Luther's grand hymn, "A Mighty Fortress Is Our God."

In the face of a flood of what Luther aptly described as mortal ills, "we will not fear for God is near."

Luther used the language and metaphors of battle to describe the struggles we encounter against every form of evil Satan throws at us. The psalmist pictures the same life crises as upheavals of the Earth so violent that the mountains and the seas get rearranged.

In either case the people of God stand firm and unmoved because the Lord of hosts—our present help—is with us.

World-shaking disasters do not always break forth on a national scale. Any family whose retirement funds and future hopes were swallowed in the Madoff scandal likely felt more threatened by these personal losses than by the larger national crises. Likewise, anyone whose oncologist has just told them they have an aggressive cancer will feel like their whole world is coming apart on them.

The 46th Psalm addresses this kind of life-shattering catastrophe and points us to the God Who alone can help us in such times of dire need.

ഓരൂ

| Teaching Outline | Daily Bible Readings |
|---|---|
| I. Our Refuge and Strength—46:1-3 | Mon. Our Strong, Yet Gentle God<br>*Isaiah 40:6-11* |
|   A. Always Present, 1 | Tue. Our Faithful God<br>*Deuteronomy 7:7-11* |
|   B. Banishing Our Fear, 2-3 | Wed. Our Comforting God<br>*2 Corinthians 1:3-7* |
| II. A Glad, Holy Place—46:4-5 | Thu Our Rescuing God<br>*2 Corinthians 1:8-11* |
|   A. A Well-Watered, Holy Place, 4 | Fri. God Before and After Us<br>*Isaiah 52:7-12* |
|   B. God's Present Help, 5 | Sat. God's Provision for the Needy<br>*Psalm 68:4-10* |
| III. Vanquished Enemies—46:6-7 | Sun. God's Help in Times of Trouble<br>*Psalm 46:1-7* |
|   A. Their Voice, and His, 6 | |
|   B. Our Sure Safety, 7 | |

# Verse by Verse

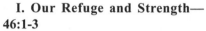

**Psalm 46:1-7**

## I. Our Refuge and Strength—46:1-3

### A. Always Present, 1

**1 To the chief Musician for the sons of Ko'-rah, A Song upon Al'-a-moth.**

**God is our refuge and strength, a very present help in trouble.**

Several of the psalms are connected to the sons (descendants) of two great Hebrew musicians, Asaph and Korah. Psalms 50 and 73-83 are linked to Asaph. Psalms 42-29 and 84-88 are tied to Korah. Translators are not agreed on whether the psalms were written by or for the Asaphites and the Korahites, but these two names show up often in the Psalter.

Musicians from both families show up in the account of one of King Jehoshaphat's battles. 2 Chronicles 20 tells us that the army of Judah was embattled by several united and fierce enemies who were endangering Jerusalem. A man from Asaph's family, Jahaziel, received a message from God promising an unexpected victory the next day. Jehoshaphat surprised his foes by attacking them with a battalion led by a choir of singers from Korah's clan. With God's help, the men of Judah won.

Whether Psalm 46 is for or from (of) Korah's family is unclear. Translators also are not positive about the next phrase that refers to "Alamoth." The NLT tells us this means the psalm was "to be sung by soprano voices." The NASU agrees.

Few lines in the psalms have been more cherished by God's people than the first line of this psalm, possibly because most of us know how much we need God's strength and protection when we are in trouble.

Troubles come to believers and unbelievers alike. Living by God's laws can keep us out of some of life's worst messes. Sin always brings suffering and death. Even the righteous who trust in the Lord share the common maladies that afflict all human beings. Believers are not exempt from catching the flu or breaking bones when they slip on icy sidewalks. We will have to wait for heaven to be free from pain, tears, and grief. It is a blessing to know that the help and strength of God are there for us when our troubles pile up the highest.

### B. Banishing Our Fear, 2-3

**2 Therefore will not we fear, though the earth be removed, and though the mountains be carried into the midst of the sea;**

**3 Though the waters thereof roar and be troubled, though the mountains shake with the swelling thereof. Selah.**

Not because we are so strong, wise, or tough, but because God is present to help us, we will not be afraid when life turns tough.

To let us know that he does not have just minor problems in mind, the psalmist, at this point, conjures up some extreme metaphors. The troubles in focus here are so great that we might feel like they are remodeling the terrain of the world. Things are really shaking when mountains start sliding into the ocean, undermined by swelling, roaring waves. This is a scene out of the wildest typhoon or hurricane we can imagine.

Some students of the psalms suggest that the psalmist's vivid language in these lines depicts a reversal of creation. Originally, the Creator caused the mountains and dry land to emerge from the chaotic depths of the sea. Now in this moment of physical upheaval, it appears that the raging sea may drag the rocky crags back into the ocean.

Are there times when everything about our world seems to be coming apart, when troubles mount up so fiercely that everything we count on seems to be vanishing? This is the kind of trouble the psalmist has in mind when he assures us that our God is a present help in the hard times of life. At such moments, when all seems lost, we can turn to Him and find refuge—a safe place—secure while the storms of life threaten to undo us.

The word "Selah" at the end of this verse has puzzled Bible commentators for centuries and has been the occasion of many pages of speculation. Most do agree that it is some sort of musical instruction for the director or the choir. Some see it as an interlude for instruments. The term used to translate it in the Greek version of the Old Testament (the Septuagint) causes some to see it as marking a time to rest, a time for silence. It could be both—a time for the voices to hush while the harps or trumpets carry on.

## II. A Glad, Holy Place—46:4-5
### A. A Well-Watered, Holy Place, 4
**4 There is a river, the streams whereof shall make glad the city of God, the holy place of the tabernacles of the most High.**

In contrast to the disintegrating landscape ravaged by storm and endangered by troubles we now step into the holy city of God, a peaceful, fertile, happy place watered by an abundant river whose tributaries supply all its needs.

The apostle John in his final picture of the New Jerusalem echoes some of the imagery in this psalm. The Temple of the Most High and the river dominate the scene. The overarching sense of well-being shared by all in God's city stems in part from the bounty of His provisions for all who dwell there. They are "made glad" by the ever-flowing streams.

This picture here is not a scene in heaven. John is showing us heaven, but the psalmist is calling us to see that God's rich provision for His children—even in troubled times—gives us reason to be satisfied and grateful. In God's presence and safekeeping we should never grumble or complain. In His city, we are made glad.

### B. God's Present Help, 5

**5 God is in the midst of her; she shall not be moved: God shall help her, and that right early.**

Any of us who are familiar with Revelation 21-22 will see again that John borrowed this line to picture God's presence as the center of everything in the New Jerusalem. However, the psalmist is not heaven gazing. He is celebrating the fact that even when enemies most seriously threaten earthly Jerusalem, she is safe because the Lord is there "in the midst of her."

Not only will He help Jerusalem, but also He will come to their aid soon ("right early"), the psalmist assures them.

When troubles beset us, one of the hardest things we do is to wait for the Lord's solutions. Sometimes God's timetable seems slower than ours, so waiting for His aid tests our patience. Often the real problem may be that He does send us help "right soon," but we fail to recognize it because it is not precisely the solution we hand in mind.

**III. Vanquished Enemies—46:6-7**
**A. Their Voice, and His, 6**
**6 The heathen raged, the king-doms were moved: he uttered his voice, the earth melted.**

Angry pagans surrounded Jerusalem screaming threats and curses at God's people in the holy city. In King Hezekiah's day, the representative for the enemy king scared the men of Judah encamped inside the city walls. Then God spoke and the enemy army vanished. Pagan yells seemed scary. Divine answers melted the challengers.

We can expect the same kind of victory when God speaks to the powers of Satan that threaten us.

**B. Our Sure Safety, 7**
**7 The Lord of hosts is with us; the God of Jacob is our refuge. Selah.**

God's army is on our side. We are like Elisha when the Syrian troops camped around his village that night, but the horses and chariots of fire in God's holy divisions filled the mountains surrounding the enemy.

When we know for sure that the winning power and sure shelter belong to us, we can relax and praise God for His care. If "Selah" really means to be silent, we can rest our souls, secure in the Lord's protection.

ℬℭ

## Evangelistic Emphasis

Troubles, unbidden, chiefly beset us with demands that are beyond our coping abilities, let alone our resources. Where can we turn for relief? The psalmist tells us that God is our refuge and strength, a tested help in times of trouble.

When we have troubles, we seek a secure refuge. For example, the ability to overcome a serious illness needs to come as quickly as possible. In the case of cancer, we need a cure for it in the present time. In a similar manner, we should not postpone a joyful expectation of a permanent relationship with God. Furthermore, we must not delay in overcoming any form of fear.

We give peace to our coping abilities to minimize inconvenient difficulties when we place them within the presence of God.

In the *For a Lively Start* narrative, we introduced Martin Luther's hymn, Ein' Feste Burg, (as translated by Thomas Carlyle, "A safe stronghold our God is still.") Some forty-eight years ago, in our thirtieth annual volume (1963), our exegete described Luther's "A bulwark never failing" as follows:

The first three verses of this Psalm are enough to lift the spirits of any stricken soul.

Just to read or repeat them aloud gives comfort and strength. If the almighty, eternal God is with us, what need we fear? Even though the strongest, sturdiest mountains around us—morally, socially, spiritually—all seem to be swept away; even though the waters of trouble come pouring in on us in an overwhelming flood—still we can know that we are secure in God's care.

## Memory Selection

೫೦೧೪

"God is our refuge and strength, a very present help in trouble." *(Ps. 46:1)*

All people have trouble at one time or another. Their hope for rescue is from God.

He is our refuge, or place of safety. He is a place of security, like a bomb shelter, or army tank, or a house with a solid foundation. He is like a cave or military unit.

His refuge is a very present help. It comes now, when it is needed. It provides rescue in a time of emergency. Rescue that comes after the emergency is over is not much rescue at all.

If a person has a serious illness, or a life-threatening car accident, or is caught up in a natural disaster, he needs the help now.

Not only is it important that God rescue us from troubles of all kinds. It is also vital that His refuge comes in a timely way. He saves us when the need is most urgent. Therefore, we can appeal to God when our need is great. We know to whom to appeal, what to expect, and when the rescue can be expected. Each of these is vital.

It is God from whence refuge comes. Our strength to overcome our problems is from a Divine source, and help comes when it is needed - now. The fact is that we all have troubles. The strength to overcome is now.

# Weekday Problems

There are three classic answers to the rhetorical question, "Why are these bad things happening?"

The first classic answer is found in 1Peter. We learned somewhere that when bad things are happening to Christians there must be some kind of lesson involved. After all Simon Peter wrote, " That the trial of your faith, being much more precious than of gold that perisheth, though it be tried with fire, might be found unto praise and honour and glory at the appearing of Jesus Christ" (1Peter 1:7). The implication of this verse is that our faith will be put to the test. The result of the testing is that all impurities will be "burned away."

The second image comes from our Lord. Jesus told His disciples to take up their crosses and follow Him. He was clear about self-denial and self-sacrifice. You have heard many persons refer to some hardship in their lives as "the cross they must bear." Yet, from the words of Jesus, it is evident that the cross is something that is willingly taken up. It is not something thrust on an unwilling victim.

The third image is that of the violation of God's covenant. When we break faith with God, the consequences of our actions often come to bear on our souls. If you walk too close to the edge of a cliff, you might slip. If you slip you do not break the law of gravity, you prove that it is true. It might happen that a person who smokes heavily will develop lung cancer. It might happen that a sedentary person, who eats high fat food, develops heart disease.

So with these three things in mind ask yourself the following question:

* Are my trials a result of God's testing, a sin, or is it my cross to bear?

---

## Puns for Educated Minds

1. The roundest knight at King Arthur's round table was Sir Cumference. He acquired his size from too much pi.

2. I thought I saw an eye doctor on an Alaskan island, but it turned out to be an optical Aleutian.

3. She was only a whiskey maker, but he loved her still.

4. A rubber band pistol was confiscated from algebra class, because it was a weapon of math disruption.

5. No matter how much you push the envelope, it'll still be stationery.

6. A dog gave birth to puppies near the road and was cited for littering.

# This Lesson in Your Life

Today, we study the seeking of refuge within the sustaining power of God. This beautiful Psalm 46 is one of the Psalms of personal trust. There is another one, Psalm 23. It is hard to consider one without the other. Yet, it is easy to conjoin them when we reflect on the security of trust and safety. We can think of them as prayers of consolation (peace, joy, serenity, kindness, beauty) and prayers to overcome desolation (threats, trauma, alienation, hostility, catastrophe).

As a preface to our lesson for Psalm 46, let us pay a short visit to David's Psalm 23 probably the best-loved verse in the Old Testament, if not in the whole Bible. It has brought comfort and assurance to millions of people in times of stress. Its worth as a security of trust cannot be weighed in gold. Where I meet the day, there is a refreshing credo on the first two beautiful scenes of green pastures and still waters using a 23-word version of Psalm 23:

The Lord's  My Shepherd I'll not want;  He makes me down to lie
In pastures green; He leadeth me  The quiet waters by.

The metaphor of the Lord as the Shepherd of His people occurs frequently in the Scriptures. This Psalm portrays the Shepherd's preservation and provisions. With the shepherd's help, we know that we shall safely reach our heavenly home, to dwell in the house of the Lord forever. There we find consolation.

Regarding Psalm 46, Asaph wrote the psalm sometime between the late eleventh century B.C., to the sixth century, B.C. The place of origin is unknown. This psalm was not found within the Psalter at Qumran (The Dead Sea Scrolls). History aside, there is no rush to condense Psalm 46 with 46 words. In 1529, Martin Luther came close in the first stanza of his Ein' Feste Burg, (A Mighty Fortress Is Our God) with his 48-word glissade. Psalm 46 affirms that because God is our refuge, we will not fear. We do not have to live a life of anxiety and insecurity. We can live with confidence and hope. We know that God will take care of our every need. We are sure that whatever we ask of Him, He will gladly give. When our security is threatened, we feel confused and fearful. Yet, we are protected from all harm and rest with the confidence that God will take care of us in this life and in the next. In a somewhat archaic manner of speaking, God will help us at the "turning of the morning" (daybreak). There we can avoid desolation.

Yet, people of faith are not always rescued in the face of physical calamity. How are we to square the saving message of this psalm with the death or destruction of those who are faithful? There has been unrest in Africa nearly every day of my life. Must we conclude that there are geographic locations for an absentee God? It is immature governance and pride that diminishes providential help. Faith allows us to place our trust in a well-proved help in trouble, the One who is our personal refuge.

## GETTING
## THE FACTS STRAIGHT

**1. How is God described in Psalm 46:1 and what is the significance of this?**
He is our refuge and our strength. He is our place of safety and the power by which we are protected.

**2. How will we respond to this protection?**
We will not be afraid even though the earth is removed and the mountains are carried into the midst of the sea.

**3. What might happen in the world?**
The waters may roar and the mountains may shake with swelling.

**4. What is the reaction of the people to this demonstration of the power of God?**
The city of God will be made glad.

**5. Where is God?**
He is in the midst of the city and He shall not be moved. He will easily help the city in her time of need.

**6. What happened when the earth revolted against God?**
The heathen raged, the kingdoms were moved, He uttered His voice, and the earth melted.

**7. Whom can we depend on to be our Lord and our refuge?**
We can depend on God for our safety and protection.

**8. We should seek the refuge of God and how should we respond to it?**
Safety is in the arms of God. We should trust it and respond with confidence.

**9. What is the Lord of hosts?**
It is the power of God in the midst of Jacob. It is the power of the multitude that can overcome the powers of evil.

**10. How do adults feel about where they can turn in difficult times?**
They feel an insecurity that makes it important to experience a trust in God.

There was a Broadway musical (Wiz) that sings the refrain, "Don't Nobody Bring Me No Bad News." Those words, in need of a grammarian, revolt against any news that would produce stress, trauma, fear, or anxiety. Although that trope borders on urban cant, it is delightfully optimistic— it overlooks the fact that in every life there are personal pains. Not long ago, we used to refer to current events as news. It did not take long for cultural illiteracy to overtaken the countryside with an amnesia of eternal verities transforming the word "news" as an equivoque for "bad news."

As life's events keep charging on, we need help in overcoming its never-ending troubles. Surely, we need to do more than dreaming to deal with the assault of bad news. Just for starters, we may need to pray with greater fervor or work harder in order to find a way to make things better. That, of course, involves the rejection of bad news.

Adults feel confusion and fear when their security is threatened. They do not want any bad news because of the uncertainty. They do not want to be troubled by problems, sickness, or bad fortune. Many times the uncertainty does not represent an actual misfortune. It may be the fear of what is to come or the anxiety of an unknown future .While an injury or a sickness may be a fact, it may be one's imagination or an exaggeration of a situation that is real.

Yet, there are times of gratitude and joy—times to live in peace, good health, and prosperity. These are not days of bad news, but days of brightness and happiness. As such, they bring days of blessings with goodness. The phrase, "Don't Nobody Bring Me No Bad News," is not applicable to them.

In either case, bad or good, we do not want to receive bad news with their dreaded dark clouds. We want blue skies and sunshine. In the final analysis, relief triumphs over pain and eternal joy over sorrow.

On the lighter side, the singer with third grade grammar was Mabel King and Charles Smalls wrote the lyrics, ghosted by Nietzsche for added emptiness. If this is all that Broadway has to offer, we might want to "refrain" from such negative works. As populist concoctions, the temporal mediators "broke their legs" some while ago and became another "no show."

# God Is in Charge
# Good Leaders

## Psalm 47

To the chief Musician, A Psalm for the sons of Ko'-rah.

O clap your hands, all ye people; shout unto God with the voice of triumph.

2 For the Lord most high is terrible; he is a great King over all the earth.

3 He shall subdue the people under us, and the nations under our feet.

4 He shall choose our inheritance for us, the excellency of Jacob whom he loved. Selah.

5 God is gone up with a shout, the Lord with the sound of a trumpet.

6 Sing praises to God, sing praises: sing praises unto our King, sing praises.

7 For God is the King of all the earth: sing ye praises with understanding.

8 God reigneth over the heathen: God sitteth upon the throne of his holiness.

9 The princes of the people are gathered together, even the people of the God of Abraham: for the shields of the earth belong unto God: he is greatly exalted.

**Oct. 24**

**Memory Verse**
Psalm 47:6-7

**Background Scripture**
Psalm 47

**Devotional Reading**
Jeremiah 10:6-10

Younger Americans may not realize how much the world they inherited was shaped by World War II (an ancient event in the eyes of today's adolescents).

Before WW II, most Americans preferred that the country remain isolated from international economic and political involvements. Before the war, the majority of Americans were parochial. Many had never been outside their own county or state. The war scattered men all over the globe. They came home freshly aware of the world. They now understood that God really was "the king of all the earth."

At the same time, in what appears contradictory, WW II stirred up a level of patriotism likely unequaled in any other era of American history. Proud of their victorious defense of the free world, most Americans praised God because "He subdued peoples under us, and nations under our feet" (Ps. 47:3, NRSV). The writer of this psalm recognizes the legitimacy of both parochial and patriotic traditions.

## For a Lively Start

Although God chose the Jews to be the bloodline for His Son, at no time in history has God been less than the God of all nations in all places.

In Genesis 12, God stated His intent to save the whole world through Abraham's family. He loved all of us—Jews and non-Jews—and embraced all of us in His plan to save the world through Christ.

Just as the psalmist welcomes everybody to worship the Lord ("Clap your hands, all ye people"), Jesus sends us to teach and baptize "all nations" (Matt. 28:18). People from every tribe, nation, tongue, and land will surround God's eternal throne. God's plans for His people defy all prejudice and racism.

| Teaching Outline | Daily Bible Readings |
|---|---|
| I. Universal Call to Worship—47:1 | Mon. There Is None Like God<br>*Jeremiah 10:6-10* |
| II. The Most High God—47:2-4 | Tue. The Lord Is King<br>*Psalm 97* |
| A. King Over All the Earth, 2 | Wed. The Lord Rules over All<br>*2 Chronicles 20:5-12* |
| B. Victor for His People, 3-4 | Thu The Lord Delivers<br>*Psalm 3* |
| III. Call to Loud Worship—47:5-6 | Fri. The Lord Keeps Safe<br>*Deuteronomy 33:26-29* |
| IV. Our Global God—47:7-8 | Sat. The Lord Loves Justice<br>*Psalm 99* |
| V. God Exalted by All—47:9 | Sun. The Lord Is Worthy of Praise<br>*Psalm 47* |

# Verse by Verse

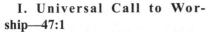

### Psalm 47

**I. Universal Call to Worship—47:1**

**1 To the chief Musician, A Psalm for the sons of Ko'-rah.**

**O clap your hands, all ye people; shout unto God with the voice of triumph.**

Several of the psalms are marked as "for" or "from" the sons of Korah. See the comments on 46:1 in the Verse-by-Verse section of the previous lesson.

There is an exuberant tenor of worship throughout this psalm. Solemnity and dignity have their place in some worship assemblies, but they are not the order for this outpouring of praise.

Some Christian fellowships have fretted among themselves about the propriety of handclapping in worship. In this setting, everybody is expected to "put their hands together," as some modern worship leaders put it.

Bible commentators differ among themselves about who is included in "all ye people." Some link this psalm (and the other involving Korah's descendants) to the military victory of King Jehoshaphat over his Gentile neighbors, so they hear this as a call to all Jews to recognize God's hand in conquering their foes. Later in the psalm, several lines clearly seem to reflect this limitation of "all ye people" to "all you Jewish people."

Other commentators, however, choose to link this phrase to the later praise of God as "the king of all the earth," so they see "all people" here in v. 1 as a call to all humanity regardless of race or tribe.

**II. The Most High God—47:2-4**
**A. King Over All the Earth, 2**

**2 For the Lord most high is terrible; he is a great King over all the earth.**

Most of the newer Bible versions capitalize all three words in "Lord Most High," thereby clearly showing in English that all three terms are God's name. Several of the versions translate Yahweh Elyon as "the Lord, the Most High" (NRSV, TEV, among others). The paraphrase of the Living Bible explains "Most High" as meaning "the God above all gods."

Martin Luther styled this psalm as a tribute to the Lord because of His Ascension.

In English, the word terrible conveys negative tones not intended by the Hebrew wording. To those who love Him, the Lord is in no way repulsive. The term here is entirely positive, pointing to the absolute power, glory, and control of God as awe-inspiring.

He outranks all spiritual beings.

Our God also enjoys dominion over all human rulers—"over all the earth." At times when He led His people to decisive victories over alliances of pagan rulers, God's people sang these words to acknowledge the real reason they had won.

## B. Victor for His People, 3-4

**3 He shall subdue the people under us, and the nations under our feet.**

**4 He shall choose our inheritance for us, the excellency of Jacob whom he loved. Selah.**

"Us" in these two verses clearly referred to the Jews in the original context of this psalm, and "the nations" denoted the Gentile nations who at times rose up against them.

The use of "our inheritance" and "Jacob whom he loved" in the parallel members of this verse are likely intended to remind us of the promises made first to Abraham in Gen. 12 and in later chapters to Isaac and Jacob that the land of Canaan would belong to their descendants. The TEV captures this intent in v. 4; "He chose for us the land where we live, the proud possession of his people, whom he loves."

In later centuries, "Jacob" signified the entire Jewish nation and not just the patriarch in the last half of Genesis.

We think "Selah" was a musical notation, possibly signaling the choir director either to pause for silence or for an instrumental interlude.

## III. Call to Loud Worship — 47:5-6

**5 God is gone up with a shout, the Lord with the sound of a trumpet.**

**6 Sing praises to God, sing praises: sing praises unto our King, sing praises.**

Instead of "gone up," the NIV reads that God "has ascended." Christians will, of course, hear in this a different connotation than would an ancient Jew who knew nothing about Christ's Ascension. The TEV clarifies "gone up" by telling us that "God goes up to his throne." Whether the throne in focus is the royal throne in Solomon's palace in Jerusalem or God's eternal throne in heaven is not specified.

Shouting and trumpet fanfares further enhance the exuberance of the worship begun with hands clapping. Nothing about this worship is restrained.

Those who make light of modern praise songs, calling them 7-11 songs because they repeat 7 words 11 times, would do well to consider how many times this inspired psalm repeats "sing praises."

## IV. Our Global God—47:7-8

**7 For God is the King of all the earth: sing ye praises with understanding.**

**8 God reigneth over the heathen: God sitteth upon the throne of his holiness.**

The psalmist returns here to his emphasis that God rules over all the earth. No race or nation lies outside His dominion. He is not America's God alone. He was not a Hebrew deity exclusively. "All the earth" is His domain, including "the heathen," the psalmist reminds us here.

Despite his repeated calls for loud and vigorous worship, this psalm's author evidently had some concern about quality of worship. "Sing ye praises with understanding" turns into "sing praises with a psalm" in the RSV or "with a song" in the TEV. However, the NASB specifies "a skillful psalm," a thought likely mirrored in the Living Bible's call for us to "sing thoughtful praises." Shakespeare caught this drift in his famous warning that "words without thoughts never go to heaven."

## V. God Exalted by All—47:9

**9 The princes of the people are gathered together, even the people of the God of Abraham: for the shields of the earth belong unto God: he is greatly exalted.**

In its original use, "the people of the God of Abraham" surely meant the Hebrew nation. In later centuries, all who are familiar with the apostle Paul's teaching about spiritual Israel will see all believers as linked to God through Abraham.

Instead of "shields," the NIV reads "kings." Other modern versions either repeat "shields" or use words that describe the weapons and might of armies. God controls all armies; one more proof that He is indeed the Most High as the One exalted above all kingdoms, rulers, and powers anywhere.

ഌഝ

## Evangelistic Emphasis

Have you ever been stuck behind a truck pulling a "wide-load" mobile home? They are infuriating on the interstate because they slow traffic. They are dangerous in towns because they do not turn corners well. They are also a symbol for our culture in the last part of this century. Nothing is permanent. Even homes, once called the American dream, have become mobile.

With a mobile society and a disposable culture, the idea of loyalty has almost become foreign to our thinking. The idea of a "company store" is as remote to us as having a barber administer medical treatment and care. Since people move with such ease and frequency, they no longer feel the need to maintain personal, community, or product loyalty. Gone are the days of denominational loyalty, or of belonging to the same church through several generations of a family.

God is old-fashioned. He believes in loyalty. He is loyal to us to the end. "Behold, I am with you always" is the promise of our Lord.

God as king is old fashioned, He is loyal to his word, and His actions are consistent in bringing blessing to His people. Isn't that in stark contrast to the elected leadership in our nation?

God is loyal to us and He asks that we respond by giving Him our loyalty.

## Memory Selection

ৰ৹ঞ

"Sing praises to God, sing praises: sing praises unto our King, sing praises. For God is the King of all the earth: sing ye praises with understanding."

*Psalm 47:6-7*

Eudora Welty is one of our greatest living writers; she describes her experience in a southern Methodist Sunday School.

"In the primary department of Sunday school, we little girls rose up in taffeta dresses and hot white gloves, with a nickel for collection embedded inside our palms, and while elastic bands from our Madge Evans hats sawed us under the chin, we sang songs led and exhorted by Miss Hattie. This little lady was a wonder of animation, also dressed up, and she stood next to the piano making wild chopping motions with both arms together, a chair leg off one of our Sunday school chairs in her hand to beat time with, and no matter how loudly we sang, we could always hear her even louder: 'Bring them in! Bring them in! Bring them in from the fields of sin! Bring the little ones to Jesus!'

"Those favorite Methodist hymns all sounded happy and pleased with the world, even though the words ran quite the other way. ' Throw out the lifeline! Throw out the lifeline! Someone is sinking today!' went to a cheering tune. 'I was sinking deep in sin, Far from the peaceful shore, Very deeply stained within, Sinking to rise no more' made you want to dance, and the chorus — 'Love lifted me! Love lifted me! When nothing else would help, Love lifted me!' — would send you leaping. And of course so many of the Protestant hymns reached down to us from the same place; they were old English rounds and dance tunes, and Charles Wesley and the rest had - no wonder - taken them over"

76

## Weekday Problems

Betsy sat in the pastor's office in tears. For two years, her marriage had been on the rocks. Her husband Paul was not attentive to her. He didn't like the fact they lived in a home owned by Betsy's father. Paul really didn't like the fact that their children appeared to be closer to their maternal grandfather than they were to him.

Paul had told Betsy on many occasions that everything would be better if they would only move from that community. Paul worked 30 miles away in another town. He told his wife that a move would help him at work, and help their family situation. When Betsy hesitated, Paul demanded that she choose him or her father.

"Pastor, I am not comfortable moving," Betsy said. "Paul has changed jobs five times in seven years. He doesn't seem to have any loyalty to any job or anything else for that matter. I know I promised to love and cherish him. The preacher even read about Ruth in our ceremony. I just can't make myself believe that moving will make things better between us. What should I do?" she asked.

Is the loyalty of a husband and wife for each other absolute? When might this loyalty not be absolute?

Could Betsy's fears of moving be based on her perception that Paul has never been loyal to a company or employer?

How do loyalties often become problems in our lives?

How does loyalty play into our understanding as God as the King of all nations?

# Pulling the Plug

During a visit to the mental asylum, I asked the Director, "How do you determine whether or not a patient should be institutionalized?"

"Well," the Director replied, "we fill up a bathtub. Then we offer the patient a teaspoon, a teacup, and a bucket and ask him or her to empty the bathtub."

"Oh, I get it," I said. "A normal person would use the bucket because it's bigger than the spoon or the teacup."

"No," the Director responded. "A normal person would pull the plug. Do you want a bed near a window?"

# This Lesson in Your Life

What images come to mind with the phrase "heavenly worship?" Where do you fit in those images?

When we compare Western liturgy (Roman Catholic and mainline Protestant) to Eastern Orthodox liturgy, one element stands out: the East emphasizes the unity of heaven and earth in the praise of God. If we look hard enough, we can find references to that unity in our worship, but its simplified nature makes that connection easy to overlook. We just do not expect to see an angel at our side in prayer at Mass.

This notion of uniting heaven and earth in worship is not new. Indeed, a close reading of Psalm 47 reveals such an assumption. The psalm was a call to Temple worship in song, shouts, and trumpet blasts (47:1, 5) mixed with the image of God seated on His throne in His heavenly court (47:6-8). In the midst of praise and celestial imagery, the psalm proclaimed a short creed for the Israelite: YHWH was the Lord of all nations and He favored His people over any other with His covenant (47:4). The psalm has military overtones: the nations were to be subjects of Israel (47:3) and the commoner among God's people were equal to the princes of the nations (47:9). In total, this song made a common belief among ancient people: their holy ground and holy ritual paralleled heaven and its worship. For the Israelites, the Temple in Jerusalem was a copy of the heavenly court; their worship joined the praise of the angels.

There is one more notion that can be teased out of this psalm: the sense of God's time. God rising up and seated on this throne echoes the belief in the Day of the Lord, Judgment Day. Many Jews and Christians hold that the Final Judgment will take place in Jerusalem. The Lord will come and sit in judgment over the peoples of the earth. Psalm 47 may not directly refer to the end of days, but the imagery of divine judgment-glory and sense of the eternal moment evoke such a belief.

With this background in mind, we can easily see why Christians have interpreted 47:5 (God mounting his throne) as the Ascension of Christ into heaven. The Ascension was seen as the heavenly coronation.

When we pray either at church or outside, whether with others or alone, we should take a moment and consider our place before the Lord. We praise Him with the angels. They are at our side. The Lord sits in glory and judgment over us. The present moment is the eternal moment. Now is the end of days.

That reflection on prayer might seem overpowering, but it serves a purpose. When we pray, we are on God's time, on God's turf, depending on God's favor. Yet, this is not a burden but a joy, for he loves us.

Praise God in heaven!

**1. What physical actions does the Psalmist call God's people to engage in to give praise to God?**
People are to clap their hands and use their voices to shout for joy to the Lord.

**2. What role, in relationship to the world, does the Psalmist say the Lord has?**
The Lord is a great king over all the earth.

**3. As the king of the earth, how do many translations describe the Lord?**
The Lord is described as terrible, a great king over all the earth. Terrible is leading to the idea of fearing the Lord.

**4. What did the Lord allow the Israelites to do?**
The Lord subdued the peoples and allowed the Israelites to put the nations under their feet.

**5. "God has gone up with a shout." What do you think that means?**
This is certainly an affirmation that the Lord, as king, has ascending to His throne.

**6. With the Lord on His throne, what is the response of the people?**
The people are to praise the Lord.

**7. What is God's relationship with the nations?**
God reigns over the nations and sits on His holy throne.

**8. What happens when God gathers the nations?**
The princes of the people are gathered as the people of God of Abraham.

**9. What do you think this verse means?**
It means that God is the ruler of all the earth, and that we are under His control.

**10. What do you think it means to praise the Lord?**
This is a class discussion opportunity.

This is a hymn from Charles Wesley based on the 47th Psalm. Mr. Wesley wrote the words to this hymn in 1743, so it stands as one of his earliest hymns. Over his lifetime, Wesley would write thousands of hymns; many of them remain in use in churches today. The great evangelist and musician Ira Stankey penned the tune to this hymn.

Clap your hands, ye people all,
Praise the God on Whom ye call;
Lift your voice, and shout His praise,
Triumph in His sovereign grace!

Sons of earth, the triumph join,
Praise Him with the host divine;
Emulate the heavenly powers,
Their victorious Lord is ours.

Glorious is the Lord most High,
Terrible in majesty; He
His sovereign sway maintains,
King o'er all the earth He reigns.

Shout the God enthroned above,
Trumpet forth His conquering love;
Praises to our Jesus sing,
Praises to our glorious King!

Jesus is gone up on high,
Takes His seat above the sky:
Shout the angel-choirs aloud,
Echoing to the trump of God.

Power is all to Jesus given,
Power o'er hell, and earth, and Heav'n!
Power He now to us imparts;
Praise Him with believing hearts.

Wonderful in saving power,
Him let all our hearts adore;
Earth and Heav'n repeat the cry,
"Glory be to God most High!"

# God's Presence Comforts and Assures Filling Our Emptiness

## Psalm 63

A Psalm of David, when he was in the wilderness of Judah.

O God, thou art my God; early will I seek thee: my soul thirsteth for thee, my flesh longeth for thee in a dry and thirsty land, where no water is;

2 To see thy power and thy glory, so as I have seen thee in the sanctuary.

3 Because thy lovingkindness is better than life, my lips shall praise thee.

4 Thus will I bless thee while I live: I will lift up my hands in thy name.

5 My soul shall be satisfied as with marrow and fatness; and my mouth shall praise thee with joyful lips:

6 When I remember thee upon my bed, and meditate on thee in the night watches.

7 Because thou hast been my help, therefore in the shadow of thy wings will I rejoice.

8 My soul followeth hard after thee: thy right hand upholdeth me.

9 But those that seek my soul, to destroy it, shall go into the lower parts of the earth.

10 They shall fall by the sword: they shall be a portion for foxes.

11 But the king shall rejoice in God; every one that sweareth by him shall glory: but the mouth of them that speak lies shall be stopped.

**Oct. 31**

> **Memory Verse**
> Psalm 63:1
>
> **Background Scripture**
> Psalm 63
>
> **Devotional Reading**
> Psalm 3:1-6

## focus

A top Christian publisher wrote down his random thoughts on a tough subject he hoped one of his best-selling authors would tackle. The result was a rambling two-page document the publisher entitled "Scattershooting."

This might be a good title for the 63rd Psalm. David put pen on scroll and brain dumped. He engaged in scatter shooting. All through the psalm, David's dependence on God and his yearning for the Lord's closeness are obvious, but his perspective on life and on God shift verse by verse in a disconnected way.

Have you ever been so stressed and weary that you could not keep your thoughts straight? David's writing here sounds a bit like that. He is crying out to God, praising Him, longing for Him, recalling His goodness, but his outcries keep changing direction and focus. He leaps from metaphor to metaphor without warning, sounding very much like a fellow running for his life, which he was.

## For a Lively Start

ဆာ

Out in the Arizona desert, every year somebody is lost or stranded. Without shade or water in that oven-like heat they don't last long. Dehydration soon saps their strength and unthinkable thirst ravages them in their final hours.

As David wrote the opening lines of Psalm 63, he was hiding in the Judean desert. Unlike the tourists who die in Arizona, David was prepared for the desert dangers. Still, he knew firsthand its burning thirst, and he chose this apt metaphor to describe his intense longing for the Lord. So he prayed,

my soul thirsts for you;

my flesh faints for you,

as in a dry and weary land where there is no water (NRSV).

| Teaching Outline | Daily Bible Readings |
|---|---|
| I. Thirsting for God—63:1-2 | Mon. Hiding from God's Presence<br>*Genesis 3:1-8* |
| II. Praising with Lips and Hands—63:3-4 | Tue. Fleeing from God's Presence<br>*Jonah 1:1-10* |
| III. Praising in the Night—63:5-6 | Wed. Trembling at God's Presence<br>*Psalm 114* |
| IV. Shaded by His Wings—63:7-8 | Thu Coming into God's Presence<br>*Psalm 100* |
| V. Protected from Enemies—63:9-11 | Fri. Refreshing at God's Presence<br>*Acts 3:17-26* |
| A. Headed to the Grave, 9-10 | Sat. Praising in God's Presence<br>*2 Samuel 22:2-7* |
| B. Lying Stopped, 11 | Sun. Dwelling in God's Presence<br>*Psalm 63* |

# Verse by Verse

## Psalm 63

**I. Thirsting for God—63:1-2**

**1 A Psalm of David, when he was in the wilderness of Judah.**

**O God, thou art my God; early will I seek thee: my soul thirsteth for thee, my flesh longeth for thee in a dry and thirsty land, where no water is;**

**2 To see thy power and thy glory, so as I have seen thee in the sanctuary.**

Those who know the details of David's life may be tempted to place this psalm at the time when murderous Saul pursued him "in the wilderness of Judah." Further reading in the psalm erases this assumption because David, in that period of his life, could not and would not refer to himself as king as he does in the final verse. The only other time that fits, would be the time when David made his way through the Judean wilderness while he fled from Absalom (2 Sam. 19).

Few of us have ever known thirst like that of a person stranded in a burning desert—"in a dry and thirsty land, where no water is." Surely, this metaphor leapt into David's mind as he confronted the barren Judean desert, which was almost as dangerous as the foes that were chasing him.

To us, David's request in these verses seems backwards. We go to the sanctuary and wish that there we could see the Lord's grandeur as vividly as we behold Him when we roam mountains or forests or deserts in our leisure. David journeys through the outdoors, thirsting to see the Lord's power and glory with the same immediacy he normally would see in the sanctuary.

**II. Praising with Lips and Hands—63:3-4**

**3 Because thy loving kindness is better than life, my lips shall praise thee.**

**4 Thus will I bless thee while I live: I will lift up my hands in thy name.**

At a moment when David's own flesh and blood had betrayed him and risen up against him, David saw in contrast the constancy of God's love. Friends and family let him down, but God was always there for him.

In place of the somewhat dated but stately word lovingkindness, the newer versions describe God's love as "steadfast" (RSV), "unfailing" (NASB), or "constant" (TEV). David knew he could count on God and so can we. Because God's love never failed him, David resolved to praise Him all of his life, opening his lips and lifting his hands.

**83**

Many in Protestant fellowships tend nowadays to overlook the link between bodily posture and effective worship. Our ancestors through the centuries recognized this link. Not many generations ago, it was unthinkable that any man in even the humblest meetinghouse would attempt to pray without kneeling. Now most of our mainstream churches do not lift a hand in praise.

If our worship settings discourage physical expressions of humility or rejoicing before the Lord, at least in our private devotions we should seek to recapture the prayer postures often mentioned in the psalms. It is amazing how much better we can see God when we are on our knees.

### III. Praising in the Night—63:5-6

**5 My soul shall be satisfied as with marrow and fatness; and my mouth shall praise thee with joyful lips:**

**6 When I remember thee upon my bed, and meditate on thee in the night watches.**

David shows a command of metaphors—twice in two verses—that would make pundits jealous. David first recalls how good it feels to be stuffed after a hearty meal. He predicts the same sort of pleasure and contentment for his soul that God ministers to all as he envisions the joyful praise his lips will offer to the God who blesses him so richly.

Then, suddenly, it is nighttime and David is on his bed. The metaphor changes again without warning. David diverts his schedule to where he feels moved to offer praise and petitions to his God.

Late at night, "in the night watches"

when soldiers guarded, David lay on his bed and contemplated the goodness and glory of the Lord. Any believer afflicted with insomnia would agree that David's approach is surely more satisfying and effective than counting sheep.

### IV. Shaded by His Wings—63:7-8

**7 Because thou hast been my help, therefore in the shadow of thy wings will I rejoice.**

**8 My soul followeth hard after thee: thy right hand upholdeth me.**

Present faith is usually the result of experience. As we recall the times when God's faithfulness and love have steadied us through life's valleys, we can walk with confidence that He will be there with us no matter how rough our path becomes. David had felt God's protection in many a tough time. He was certain—and here a new and brilliant metaphor appears—he was sure that the shadow of God's wing would shelter him from harm. Will those who read this psalm today recognize the imagery here of a mother hen or a mama eagle gathering her chicks under her wings to hide them from the predator prowling nearby? Thus, the Lord shields us from evil.

Instead of "my soul followeth hard after thee," virtually all the modern Bible versions say something here about "clinging" to the Lord. David is telling God that even in the difficult circumstances facing him he will not turn loose of Him. In return, David is assured that the Lord's hand will faithfully and powerfully hold on to him. As one devotional writer has graphically said, "If you feel separated from God, know assuredly that He was not the one who turned loose."

## V. Protected from Enemies—63:9-11

### A. Headed to the Grave, 9-10

**9 But those that seek my soul, to destroy it, shall go into the lower parts of the earth.**

**10 They shall fall by the sword: they shall be a portion for foxes.**

Having focused totally on God up to this point in the psalm, David now allows himself to look for a moment at his evil enemies. They are out to kill him. The success of their revolution depends on David's being dead.

Because the Lord is a just and loving God, David is sure that his enemies will be the ones who die. That is what it means to "go into the lower parts of the earth." David's army will surely defeat them; the swords of his men will deal death to them. Wild animals then will feed on their bodies. Instead of "foxes" as here in the KJV, most versions read "jackals"—a fiercer, hungrier, uglier animal far more likely to feast on remains. What a humiliating end for those who have raised their hand against the king. David relishes the image of their total downfall.

### B. Lying Stopped, 11

**11 But the king shall rejoice in God; every one that sweareth by him shall glory: but the mouth of them that speak lies shall be stopped.**

Referring to himself in third person (David is "the king"), David credits God's love and power for his victory over his foes. All those on God's side (those who "swear by him") will have reason to celebrate—to "glory." However, their enemies won't be part of that celebration. David's foes were false fellows who deceived him and his supporters to mount the present rebellion. David describes them as "them that speak lies." When David's defenders and the jackals get through, prevaricators won't tell any more lies.

ഏരള

## Evangelistic Emphasis

A man bought a new hunting dog. Eager to see how he would perform, he took him out to track a bear. No sooner had they gotten into the woods than the dog picked up the trail. Suddenly he stopped, sniffed the ground, and headed in a new direction. He had caught the scent of a deer that had crossed the bear's path. A few moments later, he halted again, this time smelling a rabbit that had crossed the path of the deer. On and on it went until finally the breathless hunter caught up with his dog, only to find him barking triumphantly down the hole of a field mouse.

That is the way you and I become lost. We go chasing after passions that will never satisfy us. We indulge appetites that will never feed our hearts. Even in the church, we become passionate about things that will not cause our church to grow into Christ likeness.

Our waywardness is why Christ came to earth. He came to give us an example of holy living. He showed us the way, the truth, and the life, giving us a pattern for being faithful to God in our daily walk.

The good news is that all of us have sinned. We have given in to those passions that have us looking down the hole of a field mouse. Christ gives us the second chance to stand tall and be the people we were created to be.

For what does your soul thirst?

## Memory Selection

ৰাৎ

"O God, thou art my God; early will I seek thee: my soul thirsteth for thee, my flesh longeth for thee in a dry and thirsty land, where no water is;"

*Psalm 63:1*

Methodists talk about John Wesley's rising habits. According to Methodist legend, John Wesley began his day at four in the morning. By five in the morning, he was preaching in his chapel to an average of 2000 people. Early rising is considered a virtue in our work-a-holic honoring world.

Now some scientists have determined that early risers have some kind of mutated gene. I am wondering if the gene mutates after the boys are girls graduate from college and get jobs of their own. Prior to that time, it seems that young folks have some gene that allows them to sleep all of the time.

The Psalmist said that he rose early in the morning to seek God. That is a sign of a passion for God would you not agree?

In your life, getting up just a few minutes earlier to center, your day might allow you to discover God's blessings during the day. There is something about getting to work early that seems to make your day more productive. It might have to do with the phone not ringing. Therefore, might we assume that joining our Lord in prayer early in the morning might cause your day, and life, to flow more smoothly?

So tomorrow, do not hit that snooze button, get up 15 minutes earlier. Go to a quiet place and have a conversation with the Lord. You will find the Lord ready to meet you any time of day.

## Weekday Problems

A boy scout came into a troop meeting with a black eye. "How did you get that black eye?" the troop leader asked.

"I was trying to help an old lady across the street," the scout answered.

"But she didn't want to go!"

David was made the leader of Israel at a tender young age. His only experience was leading and tending sheep. Looking at all the things that matter to you and me, David was a poor choice for a leadership role. Yet, we are reading and studying scripture inspired by God and authored by that young king of Israel.

In your faith community, how are your leaders selected? Who is leading your Sunday school class? Too often in the church, we find the willing and turn them loose with whatever they are willing to do. Of course, we have standards to determine who might be willing. They have to be members of the church forever. They must contribute generously. They cannot disturb the way "it has always been done." If they meet our guidelines, they might be worthy of asking if they are willing. How many people are we excluding because we do not see them as God does?

Ask the question in your faith community about how leaders are selected. Do the leaders in your faith community seem to hunger and thirst for God? Does it appear that they are rising early to spend time with God?

## Back to School

TEACHER: Donald, what is the chemical formula for water?
DONALD: H I J K L M N O.
TEACHER: Where did you come up with that?
DONALD: Yesterday you told us it was H to O.

TEACHER: Winnie, name one important thing we have today that we didn't have ten years ago.
WINNIE: Me!

# Ths Lesson in Your Life

I came across a sad story this week. This is a story about a honeymoon disaster. The newlyweds arrived at the hotel in the wee hours with high hopes. They had reserved a large room with romantic amenities. That is not what they found.

Seems the room was skimpy. The tiny room had no view. No flowers. A cramped bathroom and worst of all--no bed. Just a foldout sofa with a lumpy mattress was the only thing to sleep on. You know the kind that has the bar in the middle of your back and your back hurts all day the next day, kind of sofa. The springs even had the nerve to sag. It was not what they had hoped for; consequently, neither was the night.

The next morning the sore-necked groom stormed down to the manager's desk and ventilated his anger. After listening patiently for a few moments, the clerk asked, "Did you open the door in your room?"

The groom admitted he had not. He returned to the suite and opened the door he had thought was the closet.

There, complete with fruit baskets and chocolates, was a spacious bedroom.

Can't you just see them standing in the doorway of the room, they had overlooked? Oh, it would have been so nice but they missed it. How sad. Cramped, cranky and uncomfortable while comfort was a door away. They missed it because they thought the door was a closet.

*Why didn't you try?* I was asking as I read the piece. Get curious. Check it out. Give it a shot. Take a look. Why did you just assume the door led nowhere?

Perhaps our spiritual life would be like that big honeymoon room if we were more passionate about our relationship with the Lord. Like that groom on the honeymoon, too many North American Christians are happy just going to church and maybe staying for your Sunday school lesson. They do not move much past an occasional fellowship dinner as something they consider extra in their faith experience. They are dissatisfied because they have not experienced the power that comes from practicing the presence of God.

This lesson is about passion, a hunger, and a thirst for God. Some of the members of your class are passionate about the "things of the church" but they have failed to translate that passion into seeking God. You have an opportunity to challenge members to a deeper walk as you challenge them to be as passionate about the things of God as they are about their "pet areas" of church life.

For what does your soul hunger and thirst, are you passionate about the things of God, or have you stopped in the anteroom of faith?

**GETTING THE FACTS STRAIGHT**

**1. If David's soul thirsts for God and his soul faints for God what might that mean?**

It likely means that David was seeking God with his whole being; there was nothing he was holding back from seeking God.

**2. Thirsting and fainting for God is compared with what real life situation David likely faced?**

Thirsting and fainting for God is like being in a dry and weary land without water to sustain him.

**3. David in his spiritual seeking discovers God. How is that described?**

David looked upon God in the sanctuary and beheld the glory and the power of the Lord.

**4. How did David describe the steadfast love of the Lord?**

The steadfast love of the Lord is better than life itself.

**5. Because God's steadfast love is better than life. How did David respond?**

David said he would bless the Lord for as long as he lived and he would lift his hands and call upon God's name.

**6. God's presence with David, satisfied David. How was that described?**

David said that his soul feasted as with marrow and fat and his mouth again gave praise to God.

**7. Was there a time in David's day in which he did not think of God?**

He said that even on his bed he meditated on the things of God, and in the watches of the night he continued to consider God.

**8. What had David discovered about the Lord?**

The Lord had been David's help and had hidden him in the shadow of God's wing.

**9. What other protections had God offered David and how did David respond?**

The Lord hid David in the shadow of His wing and he had been clinging to God and felt the protection of God's right hand.

**10. What will happen to the enemies of David?**

Those enemies will go down to the depths of the earth and they shall be given over to the power of the sword and be prey for jackals.

John Wesley translated this hymn from Spanish. The author of the hymn is unknown. Most church musicians are aware of the prodigious hymn authorship of Charles Wesley, but his brother, John also authored hymns that have been used in the church for generations.

> O God, my God, my all Thou art!
> Ere shines the dawn of rising day,
> Thy sovereign light within my heart,
> Thy all enlivening power display.
>
> For Thee my thirsty soul doth pant,
> While in this desert land I live;
> And hungry as I am, and faint,
> Thy love alone can comfort give.
>
> In a dry land, behold I place
> My whole desire on Thee, O Lord;
> And more I joy to gain Thy grace,
> Than all earth's treasures can afford.
>
> More dear than life itself, Thy love
> My heart and tongue shall still employ
> And to declare Thy praise will prove
> My peace, my glory, and my joy.
>
> In blessing Thee with grateful songs
> My happy life shall glide away;
> The praise that to Thy Name belongs
> Hourly with lifted hands I'll pay.
>
> Abundant sweetness, while I sing
> Thy love, my ravished heart o'erflows;
> Secure in Thee, my God and King,
> Of glory that no period knows.

One exercise your church musicians might aid your class in, is to take these words and put them with familiar music. That is a good way to teach new hymns to a class and to a congregation. Is singing a part of your class time?

If you are interested in further research on hymns based on scripture there are several websites that can you help you find more information about the hymns or the songs you sing in church every Sunday. Also many denominational hymnals have scripture indexes located in the back of the hymnal. It adds depth to the worship experience if you understand most of the scriptural allusions that the hymn writers used.

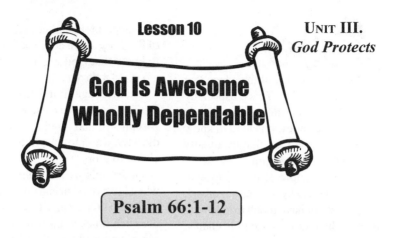

# God Is Awesome Wholly Dependable

## Psalm 66:1-12

To the chief Musician, A Song or Psalm.

Make a joyful noise unto God, all ye lands:

2 Sing forth the honour of his name: make his praise glorious.

3 Say unto God, How terrible art thou in thy works! through the greatness of thy power shall thine enemies submit themselves unto thee.

4 All the earth shall worship thee, and shall sing unto thee; they shall sing to thy name. Selah.

5 Come and see the works of God: he is terrible in his doing toward the children of men.

6 He turned the sea into dry land: they went through the flood on foot: there did we rejoice in him.

7 He ruleth by his power for ever; his eyes behold the nations: let not the rebellious exalt themselves. Selah.

8 O bless our God, ye people, and make the voice of his praise to be heard:

9 Which holdeth our soul in life, and suffereth not our feet to be moved.

10 For thou, O God, hast proved us: thou hast tried us, as silver is tried.

11 Thou broughtest us into the net; thou laidst affliction upon our loins.

12 Thou hast caused men to ride over our heads; we went through fire and through water: but thou broughtest us out into a wealthy place.

**Memory Verse**
Psalm 66:5

**Background Scripture**
Psalm 66

**Devotional Reading**
Psalm 40:1-5

Nov. 7

All of us have heard the adage that "hindsight is 20/20." This is especially true of our most difficult times. While we are in the valley, it is hard to know that we are on a road that eventually leads to the mountaintop.

A good example of this is Joseph. Sold into slavery by his angry brothers, Joseph did not have much to celebrate as he trudged toward Egypt in chains.

At that point, he did not know the rest of the story as we do, so he had no way to know that God was leading him on a path to a throne.

Chained again and thrown into a prison because of a loose woman's lies, Joseph still had no clue that his latest disaster was moving him one notch closer to glory.

James tells us to "count it all joy" when life turns sour and times are tough. As Psalm 66 declares, God will usually use such times to bless us in ways we can't imagine during the trial.

## For a Lively Start

For the Hebrew nation, those early events in the Exodus when God delivered His people from Egyptian slavery were the defining moments in their faith. During subsequent generations, the Jews rehearsed the Passover night, the parting of the Red Sea, and the wilderness events to explain their belief in a God who delivers.

For the same reason, we Christians continue to reenact the historical roots of our faith: the Cross, the Resurrection, and the Ascension. We expect the same saving power to rescue us from Satan's power.

Likewise, families who can recall occasions when God sustained them in dark days have reasons to hope when the going gets tough again.

| Teaching Outline | Daily Bible Readings |
|---|---|
| I. Worship Call No. 1—66:1-4 | Mon. Deliver Us This Day! |
|   A. A Joyful Noise from All Lands, 1-2 | *Judges 10:10-16* |
|   B. All the Earth Sings of God's Works, 3-4 | Tue. Direct Your Heart to the Lord *1 Samuel 7:3-13* |
| II. Worship Call No. 2—66:5-7 | Wed. The Lord Will Save Me *1 Samuel 17:31-37* |
|   A. Remembering the Red Sea, 5-6 | Thu God Gives a New Song *Psalm 40:1-5* |
|   B. His Might Still Rules, 7 | Fri. God Hears My Prayer *Psalm 66:13-20* |
| III. Worship Call No. 3—66:8-12 | Sat. God Rules over the Nations *Psalm 22:19-28* |
|   A. God Protects Us, 8-9 | Sun. God Rules Forever *Psalm 66:1-12* |
|   B. God Tests Us, 10-12 | |

# *Verse by Verse*

Psalm 66:1-12

## I. Worship Call No. 1—66:1-4

### A. A Joyful Noise from All Lands, 1-2

To the chief Musician, A Song or Psalm.

Make a joyful noise unto God, all ye lands:

2 Sing forth the honour of his name: make his praise glorious.

Using the word noise to describe the music of worship has always seemed a bit ludicrous. Some congregations are more musically gifted than others are, but noise seems like a harsh word to use to describe anybody's sincere outpouring of praise. The majority of our later Bible versions instead use the word shout, as in the NLT: "Shout joyful praises to God."

All of the psalms in our Bible are part of the Hebrew hymn book, of course, but they often look beyond their own heritage to call for all people everywhere to bow down to the Lord and praise Him. So this worship call is addressed to "all ye lands."

Verse 2 makes the simple argument that since God is glorious, our praise to Him should also be glorious.

### B. All the Earth Sings of God's Works, 3-4

3 Say unto God, How terrible art thou in thy works! through the greatness of thy power shall thine enemies submit themselves unto thee.

4 All the earth shall worship thee, and shall sing unto thee; they shall sing to thy name. Selah.

"Awesome" or "amazing" are words that better capture what "terrible" meant in the day of King James. This is a positive adjective—a compliment and not an accusation. Curiously, in the Greek version of the Old Testament (the Septuagint) that Jesus and the apostles always used, the phrase that begins, "How terrible. . ." in Verse 3 is the very same phrase sung centuries later by the heavenly harpists in Rev. 15:3, "Great and marvelous are Thy works."

In Phil. 2, the apostle Paul predicts that in the End when our Lord returns, every knee will bow to Him and every tongue will confess His name. That grand scene is prefigured here in Ps. 66 where "all the earth"—including the enemies of the Lord—sing His praise. Some will sing because they recognize His unequalled greatness and goodness, but others who have chosen to oppose the Almighty will

93

still find themselves prostrate in praise when they witness His power.

## II. Worship Call No. 2—66:5-7

### A. Remembering the Red Sea, 5-6

**5 Come and see the works of God: he is terrible in his doing toward the children of men.**

**6 He turned the sea into dry land: they went through the flood on foot: there did we rejoice in him.**

"Terrible" occurs here again and should be read as "awesome." "The children of men" is a Hebrew poetic expression that simply means "humans." Almost all the newer Bible versions are similar in their readings for v. 5: "Come and see what God has done, how awesome his works in man's behalf!" (NIV).

What has the great God in Heaven done for His human creatures on Earth? Instantly, the Jews recall the day when the Almighty rolled back the waters of the Red Sea, clearing a dry path for His people to escape their armed pursuers. The un-named writer of this psalm correctly recalls that the new nation of Israel paused after their close escape in order to praise the Lord after He had saved them (Exod. 15). They were led in their music and dancing by none other than Moses' sister, Miriam, thereafter known as a prophetess among her people.

### B. His Might Still Rules, 7

**7 He ruleth by his power for ever; his eyes behold the nations: let not the rebellious exalt themselves. Selah.**

The psalmist points out that God, not only used to be powerful enough to do great and glorious deeds, but also that He is still glorious in power; there never will be a time when He does not control the entire world by that great power. As the Scriptures remind us, "The Lord is the same yesterday, today, and forever" (Heb. 13:8).

No rebels should dare to rise up against God or His people, the psalmist warns, because God watches all nations. No one can get away with defying Him.

## III. Worship Call No. 3—66:8-12

### A. God Protects Us, 8-9

**8 O bless our God, ye people, and make the voice of his praise to be heard:**

**9 Which holdeth our soul in life, and suffereth not our feet to be moved.**

Probably the "people" being addressed originally in v. 8 were of the Hebrew nation. Although it is true that the Lord protects and cares for all of His own today, the praise in this section first arose because God had led His people through some dangerous moments in their history.

Some Bible commentators have ventured guesses about the precise events referred to in v. 9. No one doubts that the people of Israel probably felt such feelings of gratefulness and adoration for their God when he saved them from the Assyrian armies in King Hezekiah's time. However, many scholars see clues elsewhere in this psalm that it was written before the times of Captivity.

Whatever experience gave rise to these words of praise, they express sentiments that all mature believers have shared at some time. All of us can join this psalmist in praising God because "he has preserved our lives and kept our feet from slipping" (NIV).

**B. God Tests Us, 10-12**

**10 For thou, O God, hast proved us: thou hast tried us, as silver is tried.**

**11 Thou broughtest us into the net; thou laidst affliction upon our loins.**

**12 Thou hast caused men to ride over our heads; we went through fire and through water: but thou broughtest us out into a wealthy place.**

The word proved is an old English usage, which really means "tested." The metaphor of refining precious metals reminds us of the apostle Peter's words: "In this you greatly rejoice, though now for a little while you may have had to suffer grief in all kinds of trials. These have come so that your faith—of greater worth than gold, which perishes even though refined by fire—may be proved genuine and may result in praise, glory and honor when Jesus Christ is revealed" (1 Peter 1:6-8, NIV). Both Peter and the psalmist could see the value of suffering as it tests the quality of our faith in the Lord.

The psalmist quickly shifts his testing metaphors in the next verses, referring to several tough experiences God's people might have been through at the hands of their enemies. "The net" might refer to a bird hunter's net; some versions use this reading, calling it a "trap." Others think it more likely describes a prison or the cell within a prison, so they translate in that vein.

All these "tests" are attributed by the psalmist to the hand of God. In whatever hard time he has in mind, the Lord evidently allowed the enemies of the Hebrews to afflict them severely. However, the psalmist is not complaining, nor is he calling on us to accuse God. Instead, he rehearses all these hard times in order to praise God for bringing them safely through the difficulties and into a time of great blessings. "But in the end, you brought us into wealth and great abundance" (TLB).

80C3

**Evangelistic Emphasis**

Do you remember a time when your elementary school class had something called, "show and tell"? I am not sure of the educational purpose of this exercise, but it seems those of us of a certain age, all participated in this time. Show and tell offered a chance to bring strange things from your home and share them with your classmates.

In the Christian realm, our invitation is "come and see." In the Old Testament, the word was to come and see the mighty works of God. Those mighty works included the exodus. The time when God made the bottom of the Red Sea dry land for his people to walk over, was considered the moment of salvation for the children of Israel. The people of God were reminded that their ancestors walked on the dry land in the middle of a sea. Later, this dry land would become sea again when the Egyptians tried to cross over.

Our faith is bolstered by moments when we "see" the hand of God working in our lives or in the lives of those around us. Sometimes faith needs to see.

The invitation of the Disciples of Christ was to "come and see" the Lord. The church continues to offer that invitation to the world, "come and see" the risen Christ. The invitation is opened to all people, no matter their status in life. Jesus invites good people to come and see, and He invites those of us who are sinners to "come and see."

ഇൗരു

**Memory Selection**

"Come and see the works of God: he is terrible in his doing toward the children of men." *Psalm 66: 5*

Andre Gide, the twentieth century French novelist, playwright, essayist, diarist, wrote in 1919 a short meditation on Christianity and the dangers of "the free interpretation of the Scriptures" entitled "The Pastoral Symphony," which was later adapted into a three-act play and motion picture. It revolves around the relational dynamic between a beautiful young woman named Gertrude, blind from birth, and a devout Swiss minister, who rescues her from a hovel and guides her from darkness into light. Yet the light is blinding, more blinding than her blindness. When surgery suddenly enables her to see, two things awaken her soul with crushing pain. One is that "my eyes opened on a world more beautiful than I had ever dreamt it could be . . . the daylight so bright, the air so brilliant, the sky so vast." The other thing that struck her powerfully, and that precipitated her death, was the way people's faces were "so full of care, pain, and emptiness." She almost wishes that her eyes had never been opened by the miracle.

People see pain all around. Whether individuals, groups, or nations, the pain in our world is evident on the evening news or surfing the Internet. We see so much pain that we become blinded to it.

I wonder if we also see the hand of God so often that we have become unable to discern the miracles that surround and sustain us. As a preparation for leading the lesson this Sunday, make a list of the times you were aware that God was active this week. We invite the world to "come and see." Are you willing to share what you SAW?

## Weekday Problems

Members of the worship committee at First Church were tackling the age-old mystery of communion, which some call the Lord's Supper. The tradition of First Church had held for many years that communion was served on the first Sunday of every month. In both their traditional and contemporary services, First Church had communion every first Sunday. Every first Sunday as communion was being served the members of the worship committee noticed a drop in attendance. It was not a big drop, but the people who kept numbers noted that worship dropped every first Sunday.

Since they were a committee and they were meeting, the worship committee tried to do what all committees try to do; first, they wanted to know "who was to blame for the drop in worship on the first Sunday." Second, they wanted to know "what the responsible party was going to do about the drop in worship." The discussion went on for quite a few moments as each member of the worship committee expressed his not well thought out emotional responses to the problem.

It was decided that since the committee could not reach consensus, they needed to form a study committee to further investigate the matter.

One member noted that just as communion seemed to have nothing to do with real life issues, the worship committee could not seem to come to terms with real life problems.

How is communion an opportunity to "come and see" what God has done?

## Back to School

In the small town of Mt. Vernon, Texas, when a bar owner began construction of a better building, the local Baptist Church did everything they could to stop the project. They passed out petitions. They held prayer meetings.

Work progressed despite the Baptists' objections. Then, in the week before its grand opening, lightning struck the new building and burned it to the ground.

The church folks were a bit smug until the bar owner filed suit against the church, claiming they were ultimately responsible for the fate of his building. In their legal reply, the church vehemently denied any responsibility for the loss.

At the first public hearing the judge commented wryly, "I don't know yet how I will decide this case, but from all the paperwork so far it appears that we have here a bar owner who believes in the power of prayer, and an entire congregation of Baptists who do not."

# This Lesson in Your Life

Psalm 66 is a good example of how much of the Old Testament does theology, by interpreting present reality through the lens of God's past actions on behalf of Israel. You see it throughout the OT; the Ten Commandments begin with a recitation of God's deeds. The whole book of Deuteronomy is a witness to God's work and a call to respond in obedience; "for you were slaves in Egypt" is Deuteronomy's oft-spoken refrain. The Psalmist is quick to remind his audience that God was active on behalf of the children of Israel.

In this psalm, you have dual testimony; you have testimony about God's great deeds in the past alongside God's great deeds in the present. Especially key to the memory of God's past doings is the memory of the exodus event, shown here in verses six and seven. The Old Testament is best understood as the story of faith leading up to the exodus and the story of faith and apostasy leading to the exile into Babylon.

In Isaiah, the exilic prophet anticipates restoration as a new exodus from Egypt, declaring boldly to the exiles: "Do not remember the former things, or consider the things of old. I am about to do a new thing; now it springs forth, do you not perceive it?" (This will be used in one of your lessons in the second quarter; you might read ahead to the lesson about Isaiah 43). This same theme and way of understanding the present through the past is at work in Psalm 66 as well, tying the testimony of God's past deeds (exodus) to the individual testimony of God's present deeds, seen as a kind of new exodus in the life of the testifier or in the life of Israel who the testifier speaks on behalf of.

The worship found in Psalm 66 is not worship for the sake of worship, but is worship because of the confidence found in God's deeds on behalf of God's people. It is not worship so that we might get something in return, but worship because of what God has already done for us. Further, it is worship intended to do more than just give thanks, but to invite others to share in the celebration: "Come and hear, all you who fear God, and I will tell you what he has done for me" (verse 16). It is worship as testimony about God, about who God is and what God has done for God's people. In addition, in response to this kind of God, the psalm suggests, we should freely and joyfully offer praise, thanksgiving, and blessing.

Therefore, we have always been a story-telling people. We tell stories about what happened to us in the past, especially when our children or grandchildren are the captive audience. Most of our stories are designed to instruct and sometimes to inspire a change in behavior for people. Psalm 66 invites us into the story of God's people, the story of God's working on their behalf to instruct and inspire us.

Have you invited someone to "come and see" the works of God?

**GETTING THE FACTS STRAIGHT**

**1. What invitation is issued to all the earth?**

The earth is invited to make a joyful noise to God, sing the glory of His name, and give Him glorious praise.

**2. What is the earth to "say to God?"**

The earth is to say to God, "how terrible are thy deeds, so great is thy power that thy enemies cringe before thee."

**3. What is the three-fold expression of praise to God about his mighty deeds?**

All the earth worship God, sing praises to God, and sing praises to the name of the Lord.

**4. After praise, what is the earth invited to do?**

The earth is invited to "come and see what God has done, he is terrible in his deeds among men."

**5. What specific event in the history of Israel is remembered?**

God turned the sea into dry land, man passed through the river on foot.

**6. What events are referred two in verse seven?**

There are two historical allusions possible in this verse, the first is the Exodus via the Red Sea, the second is the crossing of the Jordan River, as the Hebrews entered the Promised Land.

**7. What is God's relationship to the nations of the world?**

God keeps watch over all the nations of the earth, so "let not the rebellious exalt themselves."

**8. What part of the human body is mentioned and why is it significant?**

God keeps our feet from slipping. This is important because it signifies that God walks with us and guards our steps.

**9. What sacrifices will the Psalmist make in worship to the Lord?**

The Psalmist will bring burnt offerings and pay the vows he made when he was in trouble.

**10. The Psalm ends with two images of hope, what are they?**

God has not rejected the prayer of the Psalmist and the steadfast love of God would not be removed from him.

*Come All Ye People and Bless Our God* is based on Psalm 66:

Come, all ye people, bless our God,
And tell His glorious praise abroad,
Who holds our souls in life,
Who never lets our feet be moved

And, though our faith He oft has proved,
Upholds us in the strife.
We come with offerings to His house,
And here we pay the solemn vows,

We uttered in distress;
To Him our all we dedicate,
To Him we wholly consecrate
The lives His mercies bless.

Come, hear, all ye that fear the Lord,
While I with grateful heart record
What God has done for me;
I cried to Him in deep distress,
And now His wondrous grace I bless,
For He has set me free.

The Lord, who turns away the plea
Of those who love iniquity,
Has answered my request;
He has not turned away my prayer,
His grace and love He makes me share;
His Name be ever blest.

*Let All the World in Every Corner Sing*, is also based on Psalm 66:

Let all the world in every corner sing, my God and King!
The heavens are not too high, His praise may thither fly,
The earth is not too low, His praises there may grow.
Let all the world in every corner sing, my God and King!

Let all the world in every corner sing, my God and King!
The church with psalms must shout, no door can keep them out;
But, above all, the heart must bear the longest part.
Let all the world in every corner sing, my God and King!

**100**

# God Is Forever Life Is Short

## Psalm 90:1-12

A Prayer of Moses the man of God.

Lord, thou hast been our dwelling place in all generations.

2 Before the mountains were brought forth, or ever thou hadst formed the earth and the world, even from everlasting to everlasting, thou art God.

3 Thou turnest man to destruction; and sayest, Return, ye children of men.

4 For a thousand years in thy sight are but as yesterday when it is past, and as a watch in the night.

5 Thou carriest them away as with a flood; they are as a sleep: in the morning they are like grass which groweth up.

6 In the morning it flourisheth, a nd groweth up; in the evening it is cut down, and withereth.

7 For we are consumed by thine anger, and by thy wrath are we troubled.

8 Thou hast set our iniquities before thee, our secret sins in the light of thy countenance.

9 For all our days are passed away in thy wrath: we spend our years as a tale that is told.

10 The days of our years are threescore years and ten; and if by reason of strength they be fourscore years, yet is their strength labour and sorrow; for it is soon cut off, and we fly away.

11 Who knoweth the power of thine anger? even according to thy fear, so is thy wrath.

12 So teach us to number our days, that we may apply our hearts unto wisdom.

**Memory Verse**
Psalm 90:2

**Background Scripture**
Psalm 90

**Devotional Reading**
1 Timothy 1:12-17

Nov. 14

How old do you suppose Moses was when he wrote his only psalm?

He cites 70 years as the average length of life at that time. A healthy person might make it to 80, he mused. Does this imply that Moses was younger than 80 when he wrote these words? Not necessarily.

Moses finally lived to be 120, well past the actuarial table he quoted. During his first 40 years, he herded sheep in the desert of Midian. The final 40 years of his life, he spent shepherding God's people in the Exodus. Somehow, psalm writing seems more likely to be the activity of a pastor rather than a shepherd, doesn't it. Nevertheless, we should not overlook the fact that Moses, the psalmist, began his work among sheep.

Only God knows how many times the words of this psalm have been read at a funeral to acknowledge both the brevity of life and the eternal nature of God.

Moses' metaphors for the shortness of life are graphic. Life, he says, is like going to sleep one night—no longer than that. We humans are here one minute and gone the next, as if we were swept away by a raging flood.

We are like weeds that sprout in the morning and wither by night; like plants that survive one short season, then die, dry, and blow away, never to be thought of again.

However, the God who made us is eternal. Time means nothing to Him. We come and go quickly, but He always has been and always will be—forever.

| Teaching Outline | Daily Bible Readings |
|---|---|
| I. Our Everlasting God—90:1-2 | Mon. The King of the Ages |
| II. Our Short Lives—90:3-6 | *1 Timothy 1:12-17* |
|   A. Destined to Dust, 3 | Tue. Stand Up and Bless the Lord |
|   B. God's Timelessness, 4 | *Nehemiah 9:1-5* |
|   C. Metaphors of Brevity, 5-6 | Wed. God's Eternal Purpose |
| III. God's Wrath and Our Sins— | *Ephesians 3:7-13* |
|   90:7-11 | Thu God's Eternal Power |
|   A. God's Anger, 7 | *Romans 1:18-24* |
|   B. Our Sins, 8 | Fri. An Eternal Weight of Glory |
|   C. Short Stories, 9-10 | *2 Corinthians 4:13-18* |
|   D. Powerful Wrath, 11 | Sat. All Our Days |
| IV. Numbering Our Days—90:12 | *Psalm 90:13-17* |
| | Sun. From Everlasting to Everlasting |
| | *Psalm 90:1-12* |

# *Verse by Verse*

## Psalm 90:1-12

### I. Our Everlasting God—90:1-2
**1 A Prayer of Moses the man of God.**

**Lord, thou hast been our dwelling place in all generations.**

**2 Before the mountains were brought forth, or ever thou hadst formed the earth and the world, even from everlasting to everlasting, thou art God.**

Unlike many of the notations at the beginning of the various psalms, the authenticity of this line about Moses is virtually unchallenged by scholars.

Referring to God as "our dwelling place" means that we run to Him for security when dangers threaten us. See Ps. 71:1, 3, for example, where the psalmist says, "In you, O Lord, I have taken refuge; let me never be put to shame. . . . Be my rock of refuge, to which I can always go" (NIV). Similarly, in the next weekly chapter, Ps. 91:9-10, "If you make the Most High your dwelling—even the Lord, who is my refuge—then no harm will befall you, no disaster will come near your tent" (NIV). Taking refuge in the caves on the rugged sandstone cliffs was a well-known strategy in the Judean desert. It may be the basis for this metaphor.

All the way back to Creation—even before the time that the earth took form at God's command—God was God. He always has been and He always will be. This is one of the grandest descriptions of God anywhere in the Scriptures.

### II. Our Short Lives—90:3-6
#### A. Destined to Dust, 3
**3 Thou turnest man to destruction; and sayest, Return, ye children of men.**

Almost every Bible version except the KJV reads that the Lord turns us back to "dust." He sends us back to where we came from.

Compared to our eternal Maker, without beginning or end, we humans are temporary creatures; we were never meant to last.

#### B. God's Timelessness, 4
**4 For a thousand years in thy sight are but as yesterday when it is past, and as a watch in the night.**

Those of us who enjoy Bible prophecy should be warned that this verse is not intended as a key to unlock the apocalyptic imagery in Bible books like Zechariah or Revelation. This is not a mathematical or historical formula. It is a metaphor, a poetic figure, intended to be read as such.

That this is true should be appar- .

ent on the surface, for the "thousand years" of God are equated here to two human time spans—first to a single day (yesterday), and then to "a watch in the night" (which was usually three hours). If this is a mathematical key, then 1,000 simply cannot equal both lengths of time.

The metaphor is a beautiful way of saying that our God is timeless. Calendars and clocks mean nothing to One who is eternal. In this psalm, Moses contrasts God's timelessness with the brevity of our allotted time.

### C. Metaphors of Brevity, 5-6

**5 Thou carriest them away as with a flood; they are as a sleep: in the morning they are like grass which groweth up.**

**6 In the morning it flourisheth, and groweth up; in the evening it is cut down, and withereth.**

There are at least three metaphors here to accentuate the idea that our lives are short. First, we vanish as if swept away by raging floodwaters. Here one minute, gone the next. Second, our life is as brief as a nap (or one version says, as a dream). Third, and more elaborate here, we are like plants that spring up in the morning and are chopped down by evening time, never to be missed or remembered.

The TEV helps to clarify these verses: "You carry us away like a flood; we last no longer than a dream. We are like weeds that sprout in the morning, that grow and burst into bloom, then dry up and die in the evening."

Compared to God who always is, none of us creatures stays around long.

### III. God's Wrath and Our Sins— 90:7-11

#### A. God's Anger, 7

**7 For we are consumed by thine anger, and by thy wrath are we troubled.**

Moses attributes the maladies or threats that cut short our lives to God's displeasure with us. If we trace all sickness and death to the Fall, his reasoning here likely is valid.

Instead of saying we are "troubled" by God's wrath, most of the later versions read that we are either "overwhelmed" or "terrified" by His wrath.

#### B. Our Sins, 8

**8 Thou hast set our iniquities before thee, our secret sins in the light of thy countenance.**

The Lord has more than adequate reason to afflict us due to His anger, for our wrongdoings are totally known to Him. Even the sins we thought we had concealed from all who know us—"our secret sins"Care exposed by the brightness of His face. He knows everything we have ever thought or done—and loves us still. Doesn't this make us grateful for His blood and His grace?

#### C. Short Stories, 9-10

**9 For all our days are passed away in thy wrath: we spend our years as a tale that is told.**

**10 The days of our years are threescore years and ten; and if by reason of strength they be fourscore years, yet is their strength labour and sorrow; for it is soon cut off, and we fly away.**

Every minute that we live takes place under the watchful eye of God, exposed to His holiness and disapproval of sin. Our lives are not as lengthy as a Tolstoy novel. Instead, they are like an O. Henry short story—"a tale that is told." Moses did not add Shakespeare's embellishment: "a tale told by an idiot," but the bard of Avon was not wrong.

A "score" is an old English word for twenty years. The math here is not very tough. People's lives in the era of Moses were not very different in length from our own. Even those among us who hang around the longest feel that their lives have been much briefer than they can believe.

Was Moses a sad sack? Was he a pessimist, needlessly morose? Perhaps. He certainly was convinced that life is ugly, hard, and sad. The "strength" of our years, to use the KJV language, means the main thing about them—their dominant qualities. Moses says these primary features about our lives are strenuously hard work filled with deep grief. Does that accurately describe your life?

Regardless of the quality of our years, they end sooner than we are ready for them to. We are "soon cut off," like a weed or a pruned tree limb.

Like a bird, we fly away and vanish forever from this life.

### D. Powerful Wrath, 11

**11 Who knoweth the power of thine anger? even according to thy fear, so is thy wrath.**

Again, Moses asserts that the shortness of our lives and the quickness of our deaths are somehow the result of God's wrath. The strange ending of this verse may become clearer to us in the NLT: "Your wrath is as awesome as the fear you deserve."

### IV. Numbering Our Days—90:12

**12 So teach us to number our days, that we may apply our hearts unto wisdom.**

In preparing our hearts receptive to wisdom, Moses reaffirms that we must understand that our forthcoming death results from God's wrath at our sinful, rebellious nature. Wisdom dawns when we realize that God's loathing of our sins overwhelms our weak attempt to measure our days in awe and wonder of His creation, let alone our attempt to master a life within it. All of us would do well to pray, as often as we can, this exceedingly fine psalm—Moses' Psalm 90.

ഇ൬ൈ

## Evangelistic Emphasis

How are your numbers?

Not your income numbers, but the numbers that determine the length of your days. Those numbers are your weight, your blood pressure, your blood sugar, and your cholesterol. According to medical science, if those numbers are in certain parameters, you should just about live forever. We are always trying to make those numbers better. We pop pills, exercise, and eat right all in an attempt to get those number to the right level. However, everyone reading these words and the one writing them, all share a common future. We will all die. You are not going to be the first one to escape that exit from this life.

Psalm 90 gives us the word from the Lord on this subject. "The years of life are threescore and ten, or even by reason of strength fourscore." According to the Bible, the lifespan of a person is 70 to 80 years. Now many people are outliving that lifespan, with taking care of keep those life numbers in the proper boundaries.

The word of the Psalmist is not about the specific length of our life, but just a warning that we will not live forever on this earth. That challenges us to make the most of every day, to see each new day as a blessing from God. It also serves as a warning that one day we will run out of days to "get things right with the Lord."

Are you sharing the good news with the way you are spending your days?

### ☙ ❧

## Memory Selection

**"Before the mountains were brought forth, or ever thou hadst formed the earth and the world, even from everlasting to everlasting, thou art God."** *Psalm 90:2*

This verse reminds us that God was before creation, but this eternal God had a unique way of revealing His love to us.

Finding God is like playing a game of hide-and-seek. Playing hide-and-seek with a 3-year-old is hilarious. Ever done it? The 3-year-old hides behind the sofa and we are to find her. Pretending, we search the other side of the room, saying loudly so she can hear, "I wonder where she could be." She darts out, face beaming, "Here I am! Here I am!"

God steps out and shouts, "Here I am! Here I am!" We look and do we see God? No! What do we see? A person! A human! A baby! Jesus!

It is ridiculous! A contradiction to the obvious: God and humans are not the same. We are not God. Nevertheless, that is the gospel proclamation: God reveals Himself in a person who was born in a stable in Bethlehem, grew up in the town of Nazareth, worked as an itinerant minister for three years, helping people and telling people of God's will, crucified for what he said, and resurrected from death to live both in God's glory and in the hearts of his followers.

This everlasting God had to limit himself to the form of a man so that He could speak to us in a way that we would understand. The power that created the heavens and the earth and raised Jesus from the dead is available to us today through the presence and power of God's Holy Spirit.

That means that the everlasting God is still creating His world, in and through us.

**106**

## Weekday Problems

Debbie and Mike had been married for 25 years. They had two children who had grown into adulthood and were starting families of their own. Mike and Debbie had many of the advantages that came since both were college graduates. However, for 20 years of their marriage Mike and Debbie had struggled with Mike's physical problems.

At the age of 26, Mike was diagnosed with Parkinson's disease. The disease had left him unable to drive his own car. He could no longer speak clearly. As the disease progressed into other stages, the doctors became unable to treat his condition. Mike lost control of most of the muscle functions that allowed him to enjoy life. Soon it became evident that Mike would need care beyond Debbie's ability to give.

Debbie, who had a deep faith in the Lord, was changing as Mike's disease progressed. She became angry and bitter about the unfairness of his suffering and the problems his illness had brought to her and her family. Debbie disassociated herself from all other people who loved and cared about her. She could scarcely hide her anger at God and stopped coming to church services. She still claimed that she had faith, but still she had big questions about why all of this had happened and why God had not heard her prayers for Mike's healing.

Because our lifespan is limited, how do we talk about faith and hope to those who have endured suffering like Mike and Debbie?

What is the word of hope found in Psalm 90 in this situation?

# The Bottom Line

Dan was a single guy living at home with his father and working in the family business. He found out that he was going to inherit a fortune when his sickly father died so he decided he would need a wife with whom to share his fortune.

One evening at an investment meeting he spotted the most gorgeous woman he had ever seen. Her natural beauty took his breath away. "I may look like just an ordinary guy," he said to her, "but in just a few years, my father will die, and I'll inherit $65 million."

Impressed, the woman obtained his business card and, a week later, she became his stepmother.

Women are so much better at financial planning than men.

# This Lesson in Your Life

There are some good discussion points in the 90th Psalm.

One topic for you to build a lesson around is the idea of God as the creator of the universe. As we look deeper into our universe, we marvel at the size and complexity of our cosmos. Actually, we are looking back into history even as we look up. Imagine that the light from the nearest star has taken decades to arrive at our night sky. Creation shouts that God is the creator and we are the creature.

Genesis affirms that God created our cosmos, yet the first book does not tell us how God created the universe. In many cases, science and our faith do not have to be in conflict about creation. However, at the point we are viewed as the sum total of some random acts of genetic mutation, it is time to state clearly the biblical affirmation that we are created in the image of God. We are special in God's creation.

Another topic for discussion would be on the eternal nature of God. God has always been, and he will always be. John says, "In the beginning was the Word and the word was with God and the word was God." John settles the matter that Jesus and God co-existed from the beginning. Jesus has always been with God. The creation He came to redeem was what He created.

God, who has always been, deserves our praise. God is eternal and we are dust. Our best efforts might yield 80 years. We cannot understand, but we can still praise the idea of an eternal God. Our lives are guided by One who has the perspective of eternity and it not bound in time.

For us creatures to praise the Creator is to acknowledge our contingency, a contingency that is more than the psychological state of dependence. Rather, this contingency is a built-in status to which we refer when we speak of God's transcendence. God's transcendence is not a matter of DISTANCE between heaven and earth but is one of "being" DIFFERENT. In praising the transcendent God, we agree that H. Richard Niebuhr got it right in saying, "We are in the grip of power that neither asks our consent before it neither brings us into existence nor asks our agreement to continue us in being beyond our physical death." To praise the Creator is to acknowledge joyously, not grudgingly, that we did not make ourselves, but are contingent on the One who cannot and must not be reduced to the guarantor of our cultures and causes, however noble their aims and achievements. To praise the transcendent Creator is to acknowledge that it is not the divine Reality that is contingent on us, but we on it.

In other words, authentic praise of God acknowledges what is true about God; it responds to qualities that are "there" and not simply "there for me." God is to be praised because God is God, because of what God is and does, quite apart from what God is and does for me.

Praise God!

**1. What is the significance of God being described as a dwelling place from all generations?**

With Moses as the author of this Psalm, it was written before the Hebrews had a homeland. They were still nomads.

**2. How long has God been the everlasting God?**

Before the mountains were brought forth, before the earth or the world was formed, God was the everlasting God.

**3. How long does a thousand years last from God's perspective?**

A thousand years is as a day or a part of a day from the perspective of eternity.

**4. What two images are used to describe the transitory nature of man's lifespan?**

A human lifespan is as a dream, or like the grass that is renewed in the morning and withers in the afternoon.

**5. What is the result of God observing our sinfulness and our iniquities?**

We are consumed by the wrath of God and we are overwhelmed by the anger of God.

**6. According to the Psalmist what is the expected lifetime of a person?**

The normal lifespan is threescore and ten, and sometime a person might live fourscore years.

**7. How long is a "score?"**

A score is generally considered to be 20 years.

**8. How is human life on earth described?**

Our lifespan is toil and trouble. Our years are done and we fly away.

**9. As a result of the wrath and anger of God and the short span of human life, what should we do?**

We should number our days, which is the heart of wisdom.

**10. What does it mean to number our days?**

It means that we should see each day as important and not take any one of them for granted.

*O God Our Help in Ages Past* is a hymn that appears in almost every hymnal in America. Isaac Watts wrote the hymn. It reflects the theology of Psalm 90, and is based solely on that Psalm. Watts penned the hymn in 1719.

Our God, our help in ages past,
Our hope for years to come,
Our shelter from the stormy blast,
And our eternal home.

Under the shadow of Thy throne
Thy saints have dwelt secure;
Sufficient is Thine arm alone,
And our defense is sure.

Before the hills in order stood,
Or earth received her frame,
From everlasting Thou art God,
To endless years the same.
Thy Word commands our flesh to dust,

"Return, ye sons of men:"
All nations rose from earth at first,
And turn to earth again.
A thousand ages in Thy sight

Are like an evening gone;
Short as the watch that ends the night
Before the rising sun.
The busy tribes of flesh and blood,

With all their lives and cares,
Are carried downwards by the flood,
And lost in following years.

Time, like an ever rolling stream,
Bears all its sons away;
They fly, forgotten, as a dream
Dies at the opening day.

Like flowery fields the nations stand
Pleased with the morning light;
The flowers beneath the mower's hand
Lie withering ere 'tis night.

Our God, our help in ages past, Our hope for years to come, Be Thou our guard while troubles last, And our eternal home.

## God Delivers and Protects Where Is My Security Blanket?

### Psalm 91:1-6, 9-16

He that dwelleth in the secret place of the most High shall abide under the shadow of the Almighty.

2 I will say of the Lord, He is my refuge and my fortress: my God; in him will I trust.

3 Surely he shall deliver thee from the snare of the fowler, and from the noisome pestilence.

4 He shall cover thee with his feathers, and under his wings shalt thou trust: his truth shall be thy shield and buckler.

5 Thou shalt not be afraid for the terror by night; nor for the arrow that flieth by day;

6 Nor for the pestilence that walketh in darkness; nor for the destruction that wasteth at noonday.

9 Because thou hast made the Lord, which is my refuge, even the most High, thy habitation;

10 There shall no evil befall thee, neither shall any plague come nigh thy dwelling.

11 For he shall give his angels charge over thee, to keep thee in all thy ways.

12 They shall bear thee up in their hands, lest thou dash thy foot against a stone.

13 Thou shalt tread upon the lion and adder: the young lion and the dragon shalt thou trample under feet.

14 Because he hath set his love upon me, therefore will I deliver him: I will set him on high, because he hath known my name.

15 He shall call upon me, and I will answer him: I will be with him in trouble; I will deliver him, and honour him.

16 With long life will I satisfy him, and shew him my salvation.

---

**Memory Verse**
Psalm 91:14

**Background Scripture**
Psalm 91

**Devotional Reading**
Isaiah 52:7-12

Nov. 21

Isn't it strange that one of the best-known verses in Psalms is familiar to us Christians because it was quoted by Satan?

That's right. When Satan came to tempt Jesus in the desert, he dared Jesus to dive off the Temple heights just to see if God would really keep His promise in Ps. 91:11-12, "For he shall give his angels charge over thee. ... They shall bear thee up in their hands, lest thou dash thy foot against a stone."

Satan was right, of course, in suggesting that such a performance would have been quite a show. However, Jesus was also correct when He rebuffed Satan with another scripture, "You shall not tempt the Lord thy God" (Luke 4:10-11).

Those who use this psalm to teach God's people a "health and wealth" gospel that promises them exemption from all disasters and diseases run dangerously close to Satan's use of it.

## For a Lively Start

One of the finest modern praise songs is Michael Joncas' "On Eagle's Wings." In his lyrics, Joncas develops the key metaphors of the 91st Psalm, adding in the refrain his own strong imagery of the Lord holding us in the palm of His hand.

In the psalm, the wings cover God's people, hiding them from harm. In Joncas' song, the musician uses Isaiah's metaphor where he pictures us being borne aloft on wings like eagles' (40:31). The rest of Joncas' classic hymn tracks closely with Psalm 91, using its word pictures to assure God's people that His strength and protection belong to all who trust in Him.

| Teaching Outline | Daily Bible Readings |
|---|---|
| I. Personal Confession—91:1-2 | Mon. Call upon the Lord<br>*Psalm 18:1-6* |
| II. Assurances to Others—91:3-6, 9-13 | Tue. A Refuge for the Poor<br>*Psalm 14* |
| A. No Reason to Fear, 3-6 | Wed. A Refuge for the Needy<br>*Isaiah 25:1-5* |
| B. No Evil to Dread, 9-10 | Thu A Refuge for the Children<br>*Proverbs 14:22-27* |
| C. Angels to Attend, 11-12 | Fri. A Refuge for the Future<br>*Jeremiah 16:14-21* |
| D. Dangers Neutralized, 13 | Sat. God Is My Fortress<br>*Psalm 59:1-10* |
| III. God's Promises—91:14-16 | Sun. Those Who Love the Lord<br>*Psalm 91:1-6, 9-16* |
| A. Deliverance, 14 | |
| B. Answered Prayer, 15 | |
| C. Long Life, 16 | |

# Verse by Verse

**Psalm 91:1-6, 9-16**

## I. Personal Confession—91:1-2

**1 He that dwelleth in the secret place of the most High shall abide under the shadow of the Almighty.**

**2 I will say of the Lord, He is my refuge and my fortress: my God; in him will I trust.**

Along the streets of many neighborhoods in America today, one can see an assortment of security company signs warning would-be intruders that somebody is watching that property. The signs also tell us that property owners in this area do not feel entirely safe. So burglar alarms, surveillance cameras, dead bolt locks, and a host of other security technologies are being employed to ward off criminals. The companies that sell these gadgets and services really are marketing peace of mind.

God promises a sense of security and safety to all who trust in him. The writer begins this psalm by stating his intention to trust in the Lord as his place of safety. The metaphors he uses are a bit odd to us today. Almost all modern Bible versions replace "the secret place" with "shelter." The term here refers to one's personal place of retreat—a place where one is hidden from the dangers that prowl the outside world.

Being "under the shadow" of the Lord may be an echo of Ps. 17:8—"Hide me in the shadow of your wings" (NIV). On the other hand, it could be a reference to Isaiah's familiar line about "a shadow of a rock in a weary land" (32:2). Only those who have known the fierce heat of the desert sun can appreciate how welcome and life saving such a shadow may be.

## II. Assurances to Others—91:3-6, 9-13

### A. No Reason to Fear, 3-6

**3 Surely he shall deliver thee from the snare of the fowler, and from the noisome pestilence.**

**4 He shall cover thee with his feathers, and under his wings shalt thou trust: his truth shall be thy shield and buckler.**

**5 Thou shalt not be afraid for the terror by night; nor for the arrow that flieth by day;**

**6 Nor for the pestilence that walketh in darkness; nor for the destruction that wasteth at noonday.**

To give us assurance of the full extent of God's shield against danger,

**113**

the psalmist lists multiple sources of potential fear and the ways the Lord will shelter us from those dangers.

"The snare of the fowler" is a trap used to catch birds. God keeps us safe from the traps set for us by the wicked. "Noisome" (in v. 3) is a seldom used word that has changed its meaning since the KJV was translated. The promise here is that the Lord will keep us safe from "fatal plagues" (LB) or "deadly diseases" (TEV). To a generation whose fear of serious disease tops their list of anxieties, this promise should be particularly precious to us.

The psalmist uses the familiar image of God sheltering us as a bird shields her young with her wings. Then he shifts to a military metaphor. God's "truth" referred to here is His "faithfulness" (NASB and others). The fact that we can count on Him to love and protect us becomes our sure armor, the psalmist says.

Different dangers threaten us at different times of the clock. Evil tends to lurk in the night, but ancient warfare tended to be a daytime danger. Whether the threat to us is disease at midnight or mayhem in the morning, the psalmist assures us that God is still our most dependable source of security and peace of mind.

**B. No Evil to Dread, 9-10**

**9 Because thou hast made the Lord, which is my refuge, even the most High, thy habitation;**

**10 There shall no evil befall thee, neither shall any plague come nigh thy dwelling.**

A sense of safety and well-being belong to those who have "made the Lord their habitation," to use the KJV terminology. This means to make God our dwelling place—to abide where He abides, to live near to Him, where He lives.

**C. Angels to Attend, 11-12**

**11 For he shall give his angels charge over thee, to keep thee in all thy ways.**

**12 They shall bear thee up in their hands, lest thou dash thy foot against a stone.**

Most of us will recognize these verses are the familiar lines Satan quoted when he tried to tempt Jesus atop the Temple.

In the psalmist's mouth instead of the devil's, however, these lines become a precious promise that God will have His angels watching over those who trust in Him for aid and care. We can expect angelic assistance when we are threatened.

**D. Dangers Neutralized, 13**

**13 Thou shalt tread upon the lion and adder: the young lion and the dragon shalt thou trample under feet.**

The "adder" here is a kind of poisonous snake, identified by some modern translations as a cobra (NKJV). No other Bible versions use the word "dragon" in this verse. All of them reflect that the Hebrew word here is another term that means "serpent."

What we have in this verse is the familiar Hebrew poetic device of saying something and then repeating it in a parallel statement that means the same although the words have been slightly changed.

**III. God's Promises—91:14-16**

**A. Deliverance, 14**

**14 Because he hath set his love**

**upon me, therefore will I deliver him: I will set him on high, because he hath known my name.**

The psalm began with the writer confessing his own dependence in God. In v. 3 he shifted focus, giving assurances to all who trust in the Lord. Now in the final three verses the speaker in this psalm is the Lord Himself.

Anyone who loves the Lord and who acknowledges Him as Savior and Protector ("hath known my name") will enjoy God's deliverance and protection. To be "set on high" calls forth the image of warriors scaling a desert peak to enjoy the relative safety of the high ground in a battle. God promises here to put us in a safe place if we trust in Him.

**B. Answered Prayer, 15**

**15 He shall call upon me, and I will answer him: I will be with him in trouble; I will deliver him, and honour him.**

Our prayers in troubled moments are not wasted words, God promises us. If we trust in Him, we can expect Him to respond to our prayers and to be present with us when we need Him most.

The last part of this verse is astounding. In the usual order of things, God is the One who receives honor from us. However, if we trust in Him to protect us when life really gets tough, He promises here to honor us. What a promise!

**C. Long Life, 16**

**16 With long life will I satisfy him, and shew him my salvation.**

This is probably not a blanket promise that everybody who trusts in the Lord will live to advanced years. Obviously this is not always so. In the context of this psalm's assurances, it is more likely that this verse tells us that those who reach out to the Lord for help and protection may survive the threats. Thus, their lives will be extended.

The "salvation" promised here may, as in most other Bible verses, refer to either eternal saving or to immediate rescue in this life. Possibly, it is intended here to encompass both meanings of the word. God promises to save His children both here and in the hereafter.

છ૭ભ

## Evangelistic Emphasis

A little Spanish boy in Vigo who became a devout Christian was asked by an Englishman what had been the influence under which he acted.

"It was all because of the odd sparrow," the boy replied.

"I do not understand," said the Englishman in surprise. "What odd sparrow?"

"Well, Senor, it is this way," the boy said, "A gentleman gave me a Testament, and I read in one gospel that two sparrows were sold for a farthing. Again, in Luke, I saw, 'Are not five sparrows sold for two farthings?' And I said to myself that Nuestro Senor (our Lord) Jesus Christ knew well our custom of selling birds. As you know, sir, we trap birds, and get one chico for two but for two chicos we throw in an extra sparrow. That extra sparrow is only a makeweight, and of no account at all.

"Now, I think to myself that I am so insignificant, so poor, and so small that no one would think of counting me. I'm like the fifth sparrow. And yet, oh, marvelous, Nuestro Senor says, 'Not one of them is forgotten before God.'

"I have never heard anything like it, sir. No one but He could ever have thought of not forgetting me."

What a great image that we are not forgotten by our God, that He protects us under the shadow of His wing. That is good news!

## Memory Selection

ℰ)ℭℛ

"**Because he hath set his love upon me, therefore will I deliver him: I will set him on high, because he hath known my name.**" *Psalm 91: 14*

God protects those whom He loves.

The late pastor Tom Rietveld tells the following story of West Side Baptist Church in Beatrice, Nebraska:

Normally all of the good choir members of the West Side Baptist Church in Beatrice, Nebraska, came to church on Wednesday night to practice, and most of them even came early. That meant they showed up well before the 7:30 starting time.

But one night, March 1, 1950, one by one, two by two, they all had excuses for being late. Marilyn, the church pianist overslept on her after-dinner nap, so she and her mother were late. One girl, a high-school sophomore, was having trouble with her homework. That delayed her, so she was late. One couple could not get their car started. They, and those they were to pick up, were subsequently late.

In fact, all 18-choir members, including the pastor and his wife, were late. Every single person had a good excuse.

Then, on that Wednesday evening, at 7:30, the time the choir rehearsal was supposed to begin, not one soul was in the choir loft. This had never happened before. But here's the rest of the story.

That night, the only night in the history of the church that the choir was not starting to practice at 7:30, was the night that there was a gas leak in the basement of the West Side Baptist Church. At precisely the time at which the choir would have been singing, the church furnace ignited the gas leak and the whole church blew up.

And... The furnace room was right below the choir loft!

# Weekday Problems

John was approaching his 50th birthday.

He had been married a couple of times. He had children from both marriages and had maintained a close relationship with his ex-wife and his children by that marriage. But turning 50 was starting to eat at John. The first sign was his change in wardrobes. He traded his conservative business clothes for some clothes that would look better on a kid attending a college class. He did trade in his very pragmatic form of transportation for a two-seat sports car that had all of the gadgets on it. In stereotypical fashion, John's personal life also changed. He stopped coming home right after work and started frequenting the local watering hole, which was also a place where many single women gathered. John's work ethic changed. Perhaps related to his nocturnal activities, or just out of laziness, he came in later in the morning and would leave for long lunches.

John's church attendance was fading too. His wife would insist that he go to church because of the kids and that argument was beginning to be ignored. John declined from an every Sunday person to an every now and then church attendee.

When confronted by his behaviors by his pastor, John's response was predictable. He told his pastor that he was not getting any younger and he wanted to live fully, before he died.

How does the Psalmist warning about the "destruction that wastes at noon day" affect your understanding of John's plight?

---

# Gobbler Gags

Which side of the turkey has the most feathers?
The outside.

Why can't you take a turkey to church?
Because they use such fowl language.

If April showers bring May flowers, what do May flowers bring?
Pilgrims!

What do you get when you cross a turkey with an octopus?
Enough drumsticks for a great Thanksgiving.

If the Pilgrims were alive today, what would they be most famous for?
Their age.

What kind of music did the Pilgrims like?
Plymouth Rock.

# This Lesson in Your Life

The most amazing thing about this Psalm is that there is one constant theme. . . Safety. God calls us into the secret place, under His Wings, covered with His feathers. He is a refuge, fortress, truth, a deliverer. We can trust Him, He assures us. He is called the MOST High, meaning there is no other higher than He is. It follows, then, that as a deliverer, protector, shelter, we can have the assurance that when problems arise, He is there.

Darkness falls. The kids go to bed just like any other evening, ready for school in the morning. Then in the middle of the night, you are awakened by a call from another room. It is one of the girls. You rush in to find that your daughter has a high fever, something you did not even suspect earlier in the day. She had been so active. Supper was uneventful. Now, she is quite ill. What happened? Pestilence.

For some reason, unknown to you, you cannot sleep more than a few minutes at night. Each time you go to bed, you pray that THIS time sleep will be continuous, that you will not be tired yet again. However, again, you are awake after having only a couple hours of sleep. What is this about? These days someone would say that you are plagued by sleeplessness. They could be right. Pestilence.

In this verse, "Nor for the pestilence that walketh in darkness"; we can once again have the assurance that we do not have to take this. The enemy chooses his fights carefully. He strikes at a time when you are at your lowest point. Late at night, the body is trying to regenerate through sleep. If a person is deprived of sleep, the body cannot regenerate. If a person is susceptible to illness, the time for it to strike is late at night. However, God says that we can live in His shadow, under His Wings. The first four verses have already given you the surety that you have His protection. In verse five, we learned that He tells us not to be afraid. If He commands it, then it is certainly possible that we do not have to keep fear. It can be thrown off. It is a choice. I love that. We can CHOOSE not to be afraid of the pestilence in the dark. That stalker cannot harm us!

Time is running out and you have to get to work. You are already late. By the time you do get there, the boss is in a mood and will not listen. This job is all the income you have. It is vitally important that it not be shaky. Regardless of what you do, the day is all wrong. Your friends cannot understand you. The boss is on you about everything. Nothing works right. The machines break down when you touch them. Alarms sound in your head that something is very unbalanced but you cannot put your finger on it. Then the boss put his finger on you. You are FIRED! Destruction that wastes.

Our Father says that we are not to be concerned with this. "nor for the destruction that wasteth at noonday." Because of the promises that God has made, we can go into that secret place, in the shelter of His shadow, under His Wings. Prayer is such a wonderful place, that secret place. Ask and it shall be given to you. Seek and you shall find. Knock and the door shall be opened to you (Matthew 7:7).

**GETTING THE FACTS STRAIGHT**

**1. How can one affirm that the Lord is "my refuge and my fortress in whom I trust?"**

A person who is dwelling in the shelter of the Most High and abiding in the shadow of the Almighty can make that affirmation.

**2. What kind of deliverance will God give to those who trust in Him?**

He will deliver from the snare of the fowler and from deadly pestilence.

**3. What other images are used of God's protection?**

God will cover us with his pinions and will give us shelter under his wings. His faithfulness is a shield and a buckler.

**4. God protects his people during the day. What specific times are mentioned in this affirmation of our protection?**

We need not fear the terror of the night, the arrow that flies in the day, the pestilence that stalks in the darkness. The specific time mentioned is noonday.

**5. What are we not to fear at noonday and what is your understanding of it?**

We are not to fear the destruction that wastes at noonday. The destruction that wastes at noonday is boredom.

**6. What might the Psalmist see that he is not to fear?**

The Psalmist might see people falling at his side, but this destruction will not befall the Psalmist. The Psalmist will see the recompense of the wicked.

**7. Because the Psalmist has made the Lord his refuge and Most High his habitation, what benefit will come to the Psalmist?**

Because the Lord is protection, the Psalmist will have no evil befall him and no scourge will come to his tent.

**8. Who will God give charge over our care?**

The Lord has given his angels charge over us and will guard us in all of our ways.

**9. What kind of protection to the angels gives?**

The angels will "bear you up lest you dash your foot against a stone.

**10. What kind of animals will we be able to overcome?**

We will tread on the lion and the adder and the young lion and the serpent you will trample under foot.

*The Day is Past and Over* is a hymn from the sixth century AD. It was translated into English by John Neale in 1853. This hymn is based on the words and images of the 91st Psalm. In Neale's preface to Hymns of the Eastern Church, where this translation was first published, he wrote:

"This little hymn, which, I believe, is not used in the public service of the Church, is a great favorite in the Greek Isles. Its peculiar style and evident antiquity may well lead to the belief that it is the work of St. Anatolus. It is, to the scattered hamlets of Chos and Mitylene, what Bishop Ken's evening hymn is to the village of our land, and its melody is singularly plaintive and soothing."

The day is past and over;
All thanks, O Lord, to Thee!
We pray Thee that offenseless
The hours of dark may be.
O Jesus, keep us in Thy sight,
And guard us through the coming night.

Lord, that in death I sleep not,
And lest my foe should say,
"I have prevailed against him,"
Lighten mine eyes,
I pray: O Jesus, keep me in Thy sight,
And guard me through the coming night.

The joys of day are over;
We lift our hearts to Thee,
And call on Thee that sinless
The hours of dark may be.
O Jesus, make their darkness light,
And guard us through the coming night.

The toils of day are over;
We raise our hymn to Thee,
And ask that free from peril
The hours of dark may be.
O Jesus, keep us in Thy sight,
And guard us through the coming night.

Be Thou our souls' Preserver,
O God, for Thou dost know
How many are the perils
Through which we have to go.
Lord Jesus Christ, O hear our call
And guard and save us from them all.

# Lesson 13

# God Is All-knowing Comforting Awareness

## Psalm 139:1-6, 13-16, 23-24

To the chief Musician, A Psalm of David.

O Lord, thou hast searched me, and known me.

2 Thou knowest my downsitting and mine uprising, thou understandest my thought afar off.

3 Thou compassest my path and my lying down, and art acquainted with all my ways.

4 For there is not a word in my tongue, but, lo, O Lord, thou knowest it altogether.

5 Thou hast beset me behind and before, and laid thine hand upon me.

6 Such knowledge is too wonderful for me; it is high, I cannot attain unto it.

13 For thou hast possessed my reins: thou hast covered me in my mother's womb.

14 I will praise thee; for I am fearfully and wonderfully made: marvellous are thy works; and that my soul knoweth right well.

15 My substance was not hid from thee, when I was made in secret, and curiously wrought in the lowest parts of the earth.

16 Thine eyes did see my substance, yet being unperfect; and in thy book all my members were written, which in continuance were fashioned, when as yet there was none of them.

23 Search me, O God, and know my heart: try me, and know my thoughts:

24 And see if there be any wicked way in me, and lead me in the way everlasting.

---

**Memory Verse**
Psalm 139:4

**Background Scripture**
Psalm 139

**Devotional Reading**
1 John 3:18-24

---

Nov. 28

121

In a time when race riots raged and American cities burned, the voice of a black university chaplain, Dr. Howard Thurman, sounded a courageous but calming note not just to his own people but also to all Christians who struggled after generations of prejudice.

Dr. Thurman said in one of his books that if the entire Bible was destroyed and he was allowed to preserve only one part of it, he would save Psalm 139.

He began his powerful little book, *The Luminous Darkness*, reflecting on a possible double meaning in David's words in Ps. 139:12, "Even the darkness is not dark to thee, . . . for darkness is as light with thee" (RSV). After that cleverly fashioned beginning, he spoke in reconciling, thought-provoking words to Christians on both sides of the racial gulf in those difficult days.

## For a Lively Start ℘ℭ

The woman at the well in John 4 described Jesus to her neighbors as a man who told her everything she had ever done. He did not, of course, but after their conversation at the well that day, she was convinced that He could.

Psalm 139 confronts us with a God who knows everything about us, including everything we have ever thought or done. That is not always a comforting view of God; we also learn to see Him as a God who cares about us despite what we have done. This is precisely the Bible's definition of God's love. "While we were yet sinners, Christ died for us" (Rom. 5:8).

| Teaching Outline | Daily Bible Readings |
|---|---|
| I. God Knows All About Me—139:1-6 <br>   A. Everything I Do, 1-3 <br>   B. Everything I Say, 4 <br>   C. Everywhere I Go, 5-6 <br> II. God Made Me Marvelously—139:13-16 <br>   A. My Body, 13-16a <br>   B. My Days, 16:b <br> III. Search Me and Know Me—139:23-24 | Mon. God Sees and Knows All <br>   *Matthew 6:1-8* <br> Tue. God Keeps Watch over All <br>   *Proverbs 15:1-7* <br> Wed. God Knows Our Ways <br>   *Job 23:8-13* <br> Thu The Expanse of God's Presence <br>   *Psalm 139:7-12* <br> Fri. The Expanse of God's Understanding <br>   *Psalm 147:1-6* <br> Sat. The Expanse of God's Knowledge <br>   *Psalm 139:17-21* <br> Sun. The Intimacy of God's Knowledge <br>   *Psalm 139:1-6, 13-16, 23-24* |

# *Verse by Verse*

Psalm 139:1-6, 13-16, 23-24

I. God Knows All About Me—139:1-6

A. Everything I Do, 1-3

1 To the chief Musician, A Psalm of David.

O Lord, thou hast searched me, and known me.

2 Thou knowest my downsitting and mine uprising, thou understandest my thought afar off.

3 Thou compassest my path and my lying down, and art acquainted with all my ways.

This grand psalm celebrates God's omniscience and His omnipresence. The fact that He knows everything about us and that He tracks us in all places and in all times give us abundant reason to praise Him with awe.

The Hebrew word used here for "search" means to drill down deeply. God has fathomed the depth of our being and knows all there is to know about us. The word came to mean an exacting, precise search.

No change in our position or posture will diminish God's awareness of us.

The poet includes enough varied stances—sitting, standing, lying down, or traveling—to convey the idea of God's complete surveillance of our lives.

"Compassest" is an Elizabethan era word partially reflected in our modern word "encompass." Translators for the various modern Bible versions try to capture the "God has us surrounded" concept by telling us that God knows all about us whether we are coming or going. God keeps up with us at every point on the round trips in our lives.

When we have been married to the same person for several decades, we get so well acquainted with our spouse's habits that we can predict what they will do or how they will react. God knows us even better than that.

B. Everything I Say, 4

4 For there is not a word in my tongue, but, lo, O Lord, thou knowest it altogether.

"Even before a word is on my tongue, lo, O Lord, thou knowest it altogether," the RSV clarifies here. God knows what we are about to say.

C. Everywhere I Go, 5-6

5 Thou hast beset me behind and before, and laid thine hand upon me.

6 Such knowledge is too wonderful for me; it is high, I cannot attain unto it.

"Beset" conveys something of a negative tone, almost implying that God is afflicting us. This is the opposite of the message intended. V. 5 is the psalmist's praise to God because the Lord covers our back and secures the road ahead of us.

Dr. Peterson does a good job of capturing this concept in The Message: "I look behind me and you're there, then up ahead and you're there, too—your reassuring presence, coming and going. This is too much, too wonderful—I can't take it all in!" The truth celebrated in this psalm—the fact that the Lord knows so much about us and cares so much for us—is amazing.

## II. God Made Me Marvelously—139:13-16

### A. My Body, 13-16a

**13 For thou hast possessed my reins: thou hast covered me in my mother's womb.**

**14 I will praise thee; for I am fearfully and wonderfully made: marvellous are thy works; and that my soul knoweth right well.**

**15 My substance was not hid from thee, when I was made in secret, and curiously wrought in the lowest parts of the earth.**

**16 Thine eyes did see my substance, yet being unperfect;**

Both believers and unbelievers are amazed at the intricacy of our physical bodies. The more we learn about our genetics and about the micro-workings in our anatomy, the more we are in awe that such finely engineered systems could ever have been fashioned. Many years before we discovered DNA or tracked proteins with atomic microscopes, the psalmist had seen enough of his physique to write these lines that still adequately express our feelings on such matters.

In King James days "reins" (in v. 13) referred to internal organs that were then linked by medical theories to human emotions. To say that God "possessed" our emotions does not say much to our modern minds. Nor do we catch the meaning of the next part of the verse that says God "covered" the

psalmist in his mother's womb.

Instead of "possessed," almost all the modern versions say that God "created," and for "reins," the NIV says "my inmost being." Several of the later versions (NKJV,NRSV, and NASB) read "my inward parts." NLT says God made "the delicate inner parts of my body." These terms are understandable to us today.

Further, instead of our being "covered" in the womb, several modern versions say that we were "knit together" (NLT, NIV) or "woven" (NASB) inside our mothers. TEV simplifies the metaphor by saying God "put me together" in my mother. The concept becomes clear in any of the later readings that the Creator was at work fashioning us during our mother's' pregnancies. That is how well He knows us and how important was His hand in how we are granted the gift of life.

The psalmist extols the Lord for His genius and care in constructing the psalmist's unborn body. We indeed are "fearfully and wonderfully made." If all we knew about the natural universe were our own bodies, this alone would be enough to make us bow in amazement before the One who made us.

The gist of v. 15 is that nobody else besides the Lord could see what was going on while he was gestating inside his mother "in secret." Some scholars suggest that the metaphor behind "curiously wrought" is that of sewing or knitting, suggesting that God's creation of the baby in the womb was akin to the needle work on a fine tapestry.

Our modern minds are puzzled by the reference here to "the lowest parts of the earth." In more Victorian eras when it was considered unseemly to refer to any part of inception or pregnancy in mixed company, some Bible commentators explain this phrase as a delicate way to define the womb. That is possible. In some way that we cannot explain, it refers to the absolute secrecy of the baby's gestation, seen and known only by God.

"Yet being unperfect" in v. 16 does not mean the baby was flawed. "Perfect" here means complete; we would then say that a baby was brought to a "full-term." God knew us completely before it was time for us to make our appearance in this world.

**B. My Days, 16:b**

**16b and in thy book all my members were written, which in continuance were fashioned, when as yet there was none of them.**

The difficult phrasing here is clarified by all our modern Bible versions. They unanimously agree that David meant for us to hear something akin to the RSV: "In thy book were written, every one of them, the days that were formed for me, when as yet there was none of them."

Few scholars would contest the meaning of the words in this verse. Yet, the truth contained in these words has stirred much discussion throughout the centuries. That God, in His omniscience knows everything about our lives long before we are born nobody, but atheists, doubts. All Christians, with healthy beliefs, agree that God has known everything about human history since before He created the world.

Discussions center on whether God forces these things to happen and just how much input humans have in the outcome of single events. Because God is sovereign in all things, does this mean that He controls the outcome of all human experiences?

Reasoning that God has already assigned each of us a certain number of days, some soldiers in battle have abandoned all caution. It could be argued that this kind of determinism has needlessly cost some good people their lives. In almost every Bible study, it is likely that we will have participants with strong feelings on both sides of this issue.

**III. Search Me and Know Me— 139:23-24**

**23 Search me, O God, and know my heart: try me, and know my thoughts:**

**24 And see if there be any wicked way in me, and lead me in the way everlasting.**

"Lead me in the way everlasting." This is the ancient way of God to the Israelites through Moses. We can find a glimpse of the ancient way in Jer. 6-16. It comes without a GPS device: "Stand at the crossroads and look; ask for the ancient paths." That way of the ancients is still our safest toll-free route. There we find the unchangeable Lord who, in later generations, as the Son of God, leads us with His "I am the way, the truth, the life." What better directions could any of us receive from the One who knows everything about us?

Inspired by this Psalm, we offer this fitting prayer as we end the lessons of this quarter: Lord, Lead us in the Ways of thy light and thy love, and help us to follow.

## Evangelistic Emphasis

The late Lewis Smedes, professor at Fuller Seminary joined Bill Moyers and others on a PBS television series that centered on the book of Genesis.

In the discussion of the story of Jacob wrestling with an angel, Smedes broke in to tell his own story: "You don't have to be in the ghetto to feel abandoned," he said in response to a pastor who spent most of his life ministering in ghetto situations. "You can feel abandoned in Bel Air. There I was a few years ago, undergoing a pretty tough experience of depression. That's a feeling of abandonment. I went to an island in Puget Sound alone for three weeks — no newspapers, no books, no telephone, no TV, no radio. Nothing.

"About a week and a half later, I had an experience as real as being with you here. I was feeling the deepest sense of abandonment when I heard my mother say, 'I can't help you.' I heard good friends say, 'I can't help you.' I felt utterly lost. Then at some miraculous moment, I felt a powerful sense: 'No, you are not lost. I am here, underneath you. I am holding you up.'

"I arose, and I thought for the first time in my life, 'I know the meaning of joy.' It felt so marvelous. I said to myself, 'Now I know what the Psalmist means, Even when you make your bed in hell, I will be there, and I will hold you up.'"

The good news of Jesus is that we are never abandoned; God watches over us and cares for us.

ℰℴℭℛ

## Memory Selection

**"For there is not a word in my tongue, but, lo, O LORD, thou knowest it altogether."** *Psalm 139: 4*

God knows us. A small-town prosecuting attorney called his first witness to the stand in a trial — a grandmotherly, elderly woman. He approached her and asked, "Mrs. Jones, do you know me?"

She responded, "Why, yes, I do know you, Mr. Williams. I've known you since you were a young boy. And frankly, you've been a big disappointment to me. You lie, you cheat on your wife, you manipulate people and talk about them behind their backs. You think you're a rising big shot when you haven't the brains to realize you never will amount to anything more than a two-bit paper pusher. Yes, I know you."

The lawyer was stunned. Not knowing what else to do he pointed across the room and asked, "Mrs. Williams, do you know the defense attorney

She again replied, "Why, yes I do. I've known Mr. Bradley since he was a youngster, too. I used to baby-sit him for his parents. And he, too, has been a real disappointment to me. He's lazy, bigoted, he has a drinking problem. The man can't build a normal relationship with anyone and his law practice is one of the shoddiest in the entire state. Yes, I know him."

At this point, the judge rapped the courtroom to silence and called both counselors to the bench. In a very quiet voice, he said with menace, "If either of you asks her if she knows me, you'll be jailed for contempt!"

God knows what she would have said; He knows your words too!

# Weekday Problems

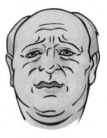

Robert McBain was thinking that he would have been better suited to be a wrestling referee than the pastor of First Church would. It seemed, recently that Robert found himself in the middle of all kinds of messy situations. Most of the people coming to him with problems wanted Robert to choose sides; of course, he was to choose THEIR side.

The latest upset was over the matter of whether the choir should buy blue robes with white piping or white robes with blue piping. The issue had clearly divided the choir right down the middle and the sopranos were no longer speaking to the tenors. The battle had begun to enter the "regular church members" as both sides tried to rally support for their choir robe position. The choir director was at odds with the organist.

A committee had been formed to try to settle the matter and they had asked the Rev. McBain to weigh in on the matter before the choir. Of course, they did not want pastoral guidance; they wanted Robert to pick a color. When Robert refused to become engaged in their choral color dilemma, many of the choir members were mad! They doubted the "backbone" of their preacher.

How many "dumb" things have caused problems in your faith community?

Do you suppose that if God knows the words before they are on our lips, He also knows our selfishness? Does He see us when we are a church misbehaving?

---

# Teaching the Teacher

TEACHER: Glenn, how do you spell "crocodile"?
GLENN: K-R-O-K-O-D-I-A-L
TEACHER: No, that's wrong
GLENN: Maybe, but you asked me how I spell it.

TEACHER: Glen, why do you always get so dirty?
GLEN: Well, I guess I'm a lot closer to the ground than you are.

TEACHER: Millie, give me a sentence starting with I.
MILLIE: I is . . .
TEACHER: No, Millie. You must always say, "I am."
MILLIE: All right . . . "I am the ninth letter of the alphabet."

# This Lesson in Your Life

One of the most familiar and beautiful of the Hebrew Psalms, Psalm 139 stresses two main theological points: God's omniscient omnipresence and God's role as creator, not only of the created universe, but also as the divine parent of every human being. In order to illustrate God's omnipresence, the psalm begins by employing a merismus in both verses two and three. God knows the Psalmist's "sitting down and rising up," as well as the Psalmist's "departure and return" (translated in English, "my path and my lying down"). In other words, there is nothing that the Psalmist does in the normal course of a day of which God is unaware.

Beyond a mere knowledge of one's comings and goings, God also knows the content of the human mind and heart. God knows words before they are spoken, and as the next merismus indicates, God surrounds the human being "behind and before" and God's power (literally "hand") governs all things in human life. In verses 7-10 are the familiar expansions on this theme - "If I ascend to heaven, you are there; if I make my bed in Sheol, you are there." There are no barriers to God's power. There are no borders around God's presence. God is constantly in control of the universe and continually surrounds the human experience, a concept that flies in the face of other ancient belief systems in which many gods were confined each to their own small areas of influence and power. There are no such constraints on Israel's God.

Throughout this psalm, the Psalmist acknowledges that God's power and wisdom are superior to that of human beings. God's wisdom is inexplicable, and God's work in creating the human being is a sign of God's divine power. The Hebrew describes these acts of creation as "fearful" and "wonderful," but the nouns made off the verbal bases of these adjectives are used to mean "miracle." Clearly, our very physiology is one of the miraculous acts by which one can see the presence of the living God in nature. It is less clear what the Psalmist is describing when it is said that we were "woven together in secret, in the depths of the earth." The verb for weaving is the one used to describe striped or variegated cloths such as those used in the making of the tabernacle (Exodus 38). It is unclear why the depths of the earth are described here. Elsewhere, this is another way of describing Sheol (Job 40:13; Isaiah 45:19). It is puzzling why the site of creation should be located in Sheol unless this is a reference to our being made out of clay as in Genesis 2. If this is the case, however, it is an interesting combination of female images for God and male ones. God in Genesis 2 is generally described as male - but a weaver, as God is described here, was virtually always a woman in the ancient Near East.

Another unusual notion presented by this psalm is the idea of a scroll in which God records all the events of a human being's life even before they occur. Elsewhere we are told that God has a book with the names of the righteous written in it (Malachi 3:16), but only here in Psalm 139 and in Psalm 40:7 are we led to believe that God keeps more extended data in such records than just names. The concept behind this image is clear, however. We are fully known to God, and our very actions are known in advance.

## GETTING THE FACTS STRAIGHT

**1. What does the Lord know about us?**

The Lord knows when we sit down and when we rise up. He knows the thoughts of our hearts.

**2. The second verse parallels the first verse in affirming that God knows us. What does verse two indicate about God's knowledge of us?**

God searches our path and our lying down and is acquainted with all of our ways.

**3. What does God know about what we say?**

Before we utter a word, or the word is formed in our minds, God knows that word.

**4. What theological conclusion might be drawn from the fact that God knows our words before we speak them?**

The theological concept is omniscience. God knows everything before it happens.

**5. How can God know everything before it happens?**

The simple answer is that God is not bound by time, that God transcends time.

**6. How protected are human beings?**

God is watching and caring for us from before us and behind us.

**7. What does the Psalmist say about the knowledge that God has concerning us?**

This knowledge is too wonderful for the Psalmist to grasp, and so high that the Psalmist cannot attain it.

**8. When did God form the Psalmist?**

The Psalmist was "knit together in his mother's womb." This affirms that God knows us before we are born.

**9. What does the Psalmist affirm about how human beings are made?**

People are fearfully and wonderfully made because the works of God, of which we are the apex, are wonderful.

**10. According to the Psalmist where does God keep records of all that is?**

God writes everything down in a book. Discuss the book mentioned in Psalm 139 and the Book of Life found in the Revelation.

Allusions to Psalm 139 appear in several of our hymns.
Isaac Watts wrote, In All My Vast Concerns with Thee in 1719:

In all my vast concerns with Thee,
In vain my soul would try
To shun Thy presence, Lord, or flee
The notice of Thine eye.

Thy all-surrounding sight surveys
My rising and my rest,
My public walks, my private ways,
And secrets of my breast.

My thoughts lie open to the Lord
Before they're formed within;
And ere my lips pronounce the word
He knows the sense I mean.

O wondrous knowledge, deep and high!
Where can a creature hide?
Within
Thy circling arms I lie,
Beset on every side.

So let Thy grace surround me still,
And like a bulwark prove,
To guard my soul from every ill,
Secured by sovereign love.

Lord, where shall guilty souls retire,
Forgotten and unknown?
In hell they meet Thy dreadful fire, In
Heav'n Thy glorious throne.

Should I suppress my vital breath
To 'scape the wrath divine,
Thy voice would break the bars of death,
And make the grave resign.

If winged with beams of morning light
I fly beyond the west,
Thy hand, which must support my flight,
Would soon betray my rest.

If o'er my sins I think to draw
The curtains of the night,
Those flaming eyes that guard Thy law
Would turn the shades to light.

## Lesson 1

**2ST QUARTER—**
*Unit I.*
*Comfort for*
*God's People*

**Dec. 5**

# The Highway for God Receiving Comfort and Strength

### Isaiah 40:1-5, 25-26, 29-31

Comfort ye, comfort ye my people, saith your God.

2 Speak ye comfortably to Jerusalem, and cry unto her, that her warfare is accomplished, that her iniquity is pardoned: for she hath received of the LORD's hand double for all her sins.

3 The voice of him that crieth in the wilderness, Prepare ye the way of the LORD, make straight in the desert a highway for our God.

4 Every valley shall be exalted, and every mountain and hill shall be made low: and the crooked shall be made straight, and the rough places plain:

5 And the glory of the LORD shall be revealed, and all flesh shall see it together: for the mouth of the LORD hath spoken it.

25 To whom then will ye liken me, or shall I be equal? saith the Holy One.

26 Lift up your eyes on high, and behold who hath created these things, that bringeth out their host by number: he calleth them all by names by the greatness of his might, for that he is strong in power; not one faileth.

29 He giveth power to the faint; *weary* and to them that have no might he increaseth strength.

30 Even the youths shall faint and be weary, and the young men shall utterly fall:

31 But they that wait upon the LORD shall renew their strength; they shall mount up with wings as eagles; they shall run, and not be weary; and they shall walk, and not faint.

**Memory Verse**
Isaiah 40:29

**Background Scripture**
Isaiah 40

**Devotional Reading**
Ephesians 2:11-22

131

Like so many of Isaiah's fine lines, these words in the early part of Chapter 40 have been made familiar and precious to serious Bible readers because of the way they are used in the New Testament. Most of us recognize vss. 3-5 as Isaiah's prophecy of the ministry of John the Baptist. We Christians treasure those words because John prepared hearts for the coming of our Lord Jesus.

When we view these verses in the broader setting of this entire chapter, we can see that this heartwarming piece of news—the good news that God is getting ready to send His Son to save us from our sins—comes to Israel at a time when life for them has been bleak and harsh. Now God wants to comfort their souls. Just as He heard the groaning of His people as they slaved in Egypt, now He hears their anguish while captives in Assyria. He also hears us when we are struggling in the wildernesses of life.

**For a Lively Start**

Almost any list of favorite Old Testament verses will include the last half of Isaiah 40. The unequaled description of God and the promises of His strength to bolster us when we are weary combine to lift up our hearts in a way that few Scriptures can.

Isaiah's recurring challenge, "To whom then will ye liken God?" effectively reminds us that the Lord we serve stands higher, taller, wiser, and stronger than any being that might challenge Him.

Unequaled in strength, this mighty God reaches out to us and restores us when we are weary. Instead of collapsing under our burdens, we receive His divine uplift to soar on eagles' wings.

| Teaching Outline | Daily Bible Readings |
|---|---|
| I. God's Comfort for His People—40:1-5 | Mon. God's Glory Revealed *Deuteronomy 5:22-27* |
| A. Comfort After Failure, 1-2 | Tue. God's Glory Declared *1 Chronicles 16:28-34* |
| B. Getting Ready for God's Help, 3-4 | Wed. God's Glory Praised *2 Chronicles 5:11-14* |
| C. God's Glory Revealed, 5 | Thu God's Glory Beseeched *Psalm 79:5-10* |
| II. God's Greatness—40:25-26 | Fri. God's Glory Above the Nations *Isaiah 40:12-17* |
| A. Greater Than Any, 25 | |
| B. Keeper of the Stars, 26 | Sat. God's Glory Above the Earth *Isaiah 40:18-24* |
| III. God's Strength—40:39-31 | |
| A. Our Weariness, 29-30 | Sun. God's Coming Glory *Isaiah 40:1-5, 25-26, 29-31* |
| B. His Power, 31 | |

# *Verse by Verse*

Isaiah 40:1-5, 25-26, 29-31

**I. God's Comfort for His People—40:1-5**

**A. Comfort After Failure, 1-2**

**1 Comfort ye, comfort ye my people, saith your God.**

**2 Speak ye comfortably to Jerusalem, and cry unto her, that her warfare is accomplished, that her iniquity is pardoned: for she hath received of the LORD's hand double for all her sins.**

Pain and heartache come in all sizes, shapes, and colors. Our health may fail, our job may be downsized, our best friend may betray us, or our dearest loved one may die. The sun only shines part of the time anywhere. That sometimes clouds will gather or storms will blast us is inevitable. God knows our anguish. He understands our pain. It is His will to comfort us, His people.

Some of our worst times are the result of our own misdeeds or failures. During at least the first half of Isaiah's life, the kings of Judah were faithless, foolish men who turned their backs on God and led their people into idolatry and immorality. God punished them— they "received of the Lord's hand double for their sins"—by sending Assyria's cruel armies to ravage the Holy Land.

However, the days of punishment were over. Now it was God's will to send comfort to the people He had chastened. The time of war was past.

**B. Getting Ready for God's Help, 3-4**

**3 The voice of him that crieth in the wilderness, Prepare ye the way of the LORD, make straight in the desert a highway for our God.**

**4 Every valley shall be exalted, and every mountain and hill shall be made low: and the crooked shall be made straight, and the rough places plain:**

Before Assryia's armies could invade a land like Judah, their engineers and road crews had to widen highways, bridge valleys, and cut through mountains that blocked the way of the machines and men of war.

In this extended period of warfare, Isaiah's readers would have been familiar with this metaphor. So were the people years later who heard the same imagery used by John the Baptist to describe how God would prepare the hearts of men and women for the coming of God's Kingdom. Likewise, God's Spirit must prepare the way for God to come into our hearts.

## C. God's Glory Revealed, 5

**5 And the glory of the LORD shall be revealed, and all flesh shall see it together: for the mouth of the LORD hath spoken it.**

God's rescue of His people from Captivity would reveal His majesty, His power, and His greatness to them because He had foretold that He would bring them home. Not only would the Israelites be awed by this display of His saving power, but also "all flesh"—a common Bible expression for "everybody everywhere"—would witness His goodness to His people.

In the same way, when God puts us back together today after major disasters have come upon us, our restoration can be a strong witness to all around us that our Lord is gracious indeed.

## II. God's Greatness—40:25-26

### A. Greater Than Any, 25

**25 To whom then will ye liken me, or shall I be equal? saith the Holy One.**

The question here echoes vs. 18 of this chapter. The first time it was the prophet who asked it. Now God Himself asserts His uniqueness. In a world and time when numerous gods and goddesses vied for the allegiance and trust of His people, it was a pertinent question.

Increasingly in our modern world, now that America is no longer seen either at home or abroad as a Christian nation, we need to remind even our own children that the God we serve really does excel above any competitor espoused by any other religion or by any deity-denier.

One of Isaiah's favorite names for God is "the Holy One." Holy implies not only absolute purity but also it asserts God's otherness. He is not like us or like any of His creatures. Isaiah later will record God's claim, "As the heavens are higher than the earth, so are my ways higher than your ways and my thoughts than your thoughts" (55:9, NIV).

### B. Keeper of the Stars, 26

**26 Lift up your eyes on high, and behold who hath created these things, that bringeth out their host by number: he calleth them all by names by the greatness of his might, for that he is strong in power; not one faileth.**

The reference here is to the stars on high. "Bringing out the host by number" is a poetic way of describing how the stars appear each night, seeming to pop out in the sky one by one as the last rays of the sun fade and the growing darkness makes the stars visible, the brightest ones first, but then with surprising suddenness the entire sky full of them.

Do you and your children know the names of the various planets and the constellations of stars? How fortunate is the person whose parents or grandparents taught them to recognize at least the major features of the night sky. Few things in creation demonstrate more clearly the greatness and power of our Creator. Not in our lifetime (nor in recorded history) has one of the major planets vanished from the sky. Isaiah tells us not only that God's power put them there, but also His might keeps them there. Moreover, that strength is what protects and blesses us, His people.

## III. God's Strength—40:29-31

### A. Our Weariness, 29-30

**29 He giveth power to the faint; and to them that have no might he increaseth strength.**

**30 Even the youths shall faint and be weary, and the young men shall utterly fall:**

When Israel was in bondage, they knew how powerless they were to resist or escape their captors. They were "faint." They "had no might," to use the descriptions Isaiah has chosen here. To people in that shape the gift of divine deliverance would be particularly appreciated. If they had been strong enough to free themselves, then in their mind God would have been unnecessary.

His saving power seems to be most meaningful today to those whom the Lord has rescued from circumstances they simply could not fix by themselves. The alcoholic who has struggled through repeated failures before finally finding sobriety pays homage to more than just "a Higher Power" when she thanks God for granting her victory over her bottle. The man who has endured endless midnights of grief prays especially fervent prayers of thanksgiving when God's light finally shines again in his dark world. This text pictures God's goodness coming to those who need it most.

In addition, all of us do need it terribly at times. As the prophet says, even strong, virile young bodies run out of energy. Even those with the vigor of youth get tired to the point of exhaustion. All of us at times run out of steam. Then we need the spiritual stamina God provides.

### B. His Power, 31

**31 But they that wait upon the LORD shall renew their strength; they shall mount up with wings as eagles; they shall run, and not be weary; and they shall walk, and not faint.**

Some of the finest praise songs heard among Christians today find their inspiration in this verse. To "wait upon the Lord" means to "hope in" Him (NIV) or to "trust in" Him (TEV). He comes through for those who expect Him to.

ℰ☙ℂℛ

## Evangelistic Emphasis

A good way to understand Isaiah's message is to go to your local pharmacy. Whole sections in large national pharmacy chains are labeled, "pain killers." Count the number and variety of these medicines. If you have a pain, one of those "pain killers" will be custom tailored to your ailment. While we have all of these remedies for pain, we are still living with so much of it.

The words to Isaiah, "Comfort ye, Comfort ye my people." (Is 40:1) are words of comfort and hope for our day. Notice that the Lord did not say, "Comfortable are my people." The avoidance of pain and the seeking of pleasure have become obsessions in our day. Even the church has bought into the Faustian deal. Some times deep within our psyche we feel as though suffering is the direct result of sin, and thus deserved. Yet, in our own lives, when dark days come we wonder at the source and reason for our pain. Scripture assumes that suffering and pain are a part of living, and cannot be completely avoided even through righteousness.

The words of comfort from our Lord speak volumes to us. God does not offer His people a way out, but a way through the pain. His words calm our spirits when the dark days come. Our Lord's words of comfort help us deal with our pain and suffering without losing hope. These words of comfort do not answer the "why" of suffering, but explain "how" we will endure.

For a hurting planet, with suffering people, the words, "Comfort ye, Comfort ye my people." are a gracious invitation to meet the Christ of consolation.

## ✠ Memory Selection

**ഈറ**

**"He giveth power to the faint; and to them that have no might he increaseth strength."** *Isaiah 40:29*

I enjoy going to the mall at this time of year. I admit I am a crowd watcher and watching them shop for Christmas brings me great joy. I am fascinated by the multi-tasking moms I see. They are dragging a minimum of three children around from store to store, they know exactly what they are going to shop for, and they dare anyone to get in their way.

I am fascinated by their source of strength. I want to know if they have a personal relationship with Christ, and if they are shopping in the spirit. What gives them the patience and the strength to do this feat?

Christmas shopping is an example of how celebrations can wear us down. Christmas is the middle of the holiday season. You have been going and doing since October and it will not stop until January. What gives you the ability to do all of this?

The point is that the Lord, through the presence of the Holy Spirit gives us the power for daily living. God will not disappointment us and will be there for us. So when you are about to "fall out" when you think that you cannot go on with whatever it is, do you call upon the name of the Lord for strength?

That is the point Jesus was making when He told us to "pray for our daily bread," the bread is a symbol of God sustaining his people.

## Weekday Problems

Helen was in church every Sunday, reluctantly. She was the youngest daughter of her widowed mother who was making certain that she "grow up in church." Helen led a duplicitous life. Most Sunday's she had to fight the effects of the Saturday night before in order to "endure" the lesson, then the sermon. Helen's acting job was fooling everyone in the church.

Therefore, everyone was in shock when Helen announced that she was expecting a child in five months. As far as anyone knew, she did not even have a steady boyfriend. True to their Christian faith, the women in the church tried to surround Helen with love and compassion. Her pregnancy and delivery were uneventful. However, there were complications with the baby. The doctor told Helen's mother that the baby had a heart defect because of Helen's abuse of cocaine.

Helen's mother, who did not handle the pregnancy well, was not about to take this latest revelation of her daughter's dark activities "in stride." The doctor had to tell both Helen and her mother that there was little or no hope for this child's survival. After only a few precious days of life, Helen's baby died.

A month later, Helen was again in church. This time not dutifully, but with a big question hanging over her heart. Helen was looking for hope and for comfort in her life.

God said, "Cry unto her (Jerusalem) that her iniquity is pardoned." (Is 40:2) How would this passage apply to Helen?

How do the concepts of sin, judgment, comfort, and forgiveness express themselves in this situation?

---

# Balloon Anatomy

One wise grandfather never lets a weekend go by without a phone call to his grandson in a distant state. Grandpa was chuckling when he showed up at church right after a recent call.

"Papa Lee," the precocious two-year-old had just asked him, "did you know that balloons have belly buttons?"

# This Lesson in Your Life

This lesson could take many forms as you explore the various paths through this Scripture passage.

The first path leads to a discussion of the nature and consequences of sin. The children of Israel found themselves in captivity because of their rebellion against God. They were sternly warned by prophets to "return unto the Lord." Yet, knowing the dire consequences of their actions, they continued to ignore the Lord and His messengers. The parallels to our day are frightening. There are many sins we must confess. Our sins are both corporate and individual. There are other sins that we refuse to acknowledge and will reap the results thereof.

The second path arises out of the first. This lesson has words to speak on the matter of suffering. In this text, suffering is a direct result of the sin of the people. However, in life that is not always the case. You might discuss ways in which sin and suffering are and are not related. Be prepared, traveling this path, to deal with guilt and anxiety in the many ways they will be manifest among class members dealing with suffering in their lives. People "rush to judgment" when tragedy occurs. They find some satisfaction and some comfort in being able to clearly place the blame for a tragedy. Often, these people are left pointing their fingers of judgment in their own direction. They feel guilty. These persons need to hear the rest of the story. They need the good news that Jesus offers forgiveness.

The third path is comfort and consolation. Recognizing the Hebrews culpability, God still was willing to forgive and forget. He was the source of the good news that Jerusalem's debt had been paid. One cannot have a healthy discussion of sin and suffering unless he is balanced with the Biblical concept of forgiveness and comfort. God always offers a way out of the problem of sin and suffering. That "way out" is through prayer, repentance, and forgiveness. In your class, there is at least one person who is blaming him or herself for the pain in their life. While he may have clearly heard the relationship between suffering and sin, has he as clearly heard the words of comfort from God?

The fourth path deals with our responsibility in all of this. As we will see later on in Isaiah, there is a steep price paid to be a messenger for God. Yet, as a teacher of His people, you have a calling to proclaim and teach faithfully the message of God's love. It is easy to condemn sin on all levels, but what about offering faithful solutions for those living with the terrible consequences of sin in their lives. Is it equally easy to offer God's word of assurance and reconciliation? We are the vessels that God uses to proclaim His gracious love.

Another direction this lesson might travel would be a discussion of the frailty of life. Isaiah 40 gives us that pattern for what is permanent. Our lives will be fleeting and temporary. God's Word, His message is eternal. This is our hope that we trust in a Lord who is never changing, yet never caught off guard by the cultural changes we endure every day.

## GETTING THE FACTS STRAIGHT

**1. What message of comfort is to be proclaimed to Jerusalem?**

The message to Jerusalem is that "her term has been served" and "her penalty is paid." (Isaiah 40:2) These images well could apply to a prison sentence. In God's grace, the remaining sentence is forgiven. The people of Israel are being released.

**2. In terms of severity, the sentence carried out against Jerusalem was described in what terms?**

Jerusalem had received a "double" portion for her sin and folly. (Isaiah 40:2) This is a Hebrew idiom stressing the severity of the punishment.

**3. The source of pain and suffering often remains a mystery, according to Isaiah 40:2, who is the source of the woe falling upon Jerusalem?**

Jerusalem's sentence and penalty came from "the Lord's hand."

**4. According to Luke 3: 4-6, John the Baptist utters words from the prophet Isaiah, which verses does John quote?**

John the Baptist is quoting from Isaiah 40: 3-4. His ministry was to prepare the people for the coming Christ.

**5. "Preparing the way of the Lord" involves what actions?**

The way of the Lord is prepared by making straight the highway, lifting up the valley, bringing down the mountain, and level the uneven and rough ground. (Isaiah 40: 3-4)

**6. How is the faith of the people of God described?**

Their faith (constancy) is like the grass and flowers of the field. Both of these things wither and die. (Isaiah 40: 6-8)

**7. What is the only enduring truth in our world?**

"But the word of our God will stand forever." (Isaiah 40:8)

**8. Zion and Jerusalem are to preach. What is the essence of their message?**

They are both to proclaim to the world and to the people of Israel, "Here is your God!" (Isaiah 40: 9)

**9. How is the Lord described as coming to Judah?**

He is described as a mighty ruler. His reward is with him. His recompense is before Him. (Isaiah 40:9)

**10. Verse 11 offers a contrast to verse 10, what is that contrast?**

In verse ten, God is described as a mighty conqueror. In verse eleven, God is pictured as a shepherd tending His sheep.

Isaiah's prophecy described the dream of men like Henry Joy: straight, smooth, level highways from coast to coast.

By the 1939 World's Fair in New York, the dream was much closer to being a reality. The most popular exhibit at the fair was General Motors' Futurama -- a diorama of the futuristic world of 1960 replete with tiny streamlined model cars whizzing along super-highways only dreamed of in 1939. The opening of the first American superhighway was less than a year away. "America's Dream Road," was our first superhighway. It was the Pennsylvania Turnpike, 160 miles of four-lane divided highway, connecting Pittsburgh and Harrisburg, that gave us our first national taste of the straight, smooth, level highways prophesied in the Futurama exhibit. The first travelers along the turnpike were rhapsodic in their praises.

However, the Futurama dream also unintentionally foreshadowed the night-mares to come: When one of the tiny streamlined cars would occasionally be stuck in its groove, the others would crash into it, creating a massive, miniaturized glimpse of future gridlock.

As we all know, when highway traffic slows, tempers rise. Aggressive driv-ing, road rage, ordinary Jekyll-citizens change into sociopathic, ranting, deadly Hydes—we have all seen it or felt it. What can we do?

Whatever we do, we know that adding capacity will not solve the traffic prob-lem, nor will it solve the time problems we have in our own lives. Adding more capacity, more time, will not treat the basic issues of how to unclutter our lives and prepare for the coming of the Lord.

In fact, there are a few possibilities to explain the congestion and frustration in our lives as we enter this Advent season. We might consider that as we start packing to meet God, we may be on the wrong highway. God may not be found on the roads of consumerism and materialism. If we find that our lives are gridlocked, it is because we are on the same road as everyone else. Time to get off that road and onto another.

Even if we are on God's road, it may need some smoothing out. It is very easy for seasonal and distracting potholes to create a bumpy ride on the way to meet God.

On the other hand, it might not be the road at all. It may be the travelers on the road. We do not need better roads; we need to be better travelers. Perhaps we need to get rid of some baggage. There may be something more significant than long lines and toy shortages at the heart of our Christmas preparation woes. Something more significant than a lack of money is at the heart of our financial woes. Something more significant than a lack of time is at the heart of our feeling hurried all the time. Something more significant than a lack of entertainment is at the heart of our boredom.

In these and many other ways, we tend to seek solutions through our American genius for efficiency—the straight, smooth, level highway philosophy applied to life in general. We seek the better highway, the better job, the bigger store, the right pill. We often succeed, at least for a while.

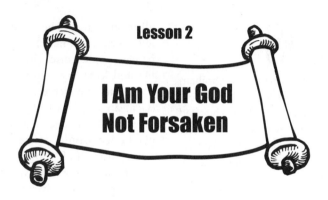

## Lesson 2

# I Am Your God
# Not Forsaken

## Isaiah 41:8-10, 17-20

But thou, Israel, art my servant, Jacob whom I have chosen, the seed of Abraham my friend.

9 Thou whom I have taken from the ends of the earth, and called thee from the chief men thereof, and said unto thee, Thou art my servant; I have chosen thee, and not cast thee away.

10 Fear thou not; for I am with thee: be not dismayed; for I am thy God: I will strengthen thee; yea, I will help thee; yea, I will uphold thee with the right hand of my righteousness.

17 When the poor and needy seek water, and there is none, and their tongue faileth for thirst, I the LORD will hear them, I the God of Israel will not forsake them.

18 I will open rivers in high places, and fountains in the midst of the valleys: I will make the wilderness a pool of water, and the dry land springs of water.

19 I will plant in the wilderness the cedar, the shittah tree, and the myrtle, and the oil tree; I will set in the desert the fir tree, and the pine, and the box tree together:

20 That they may see, and know, and consider, and understand together, that the hand of the LORD hath done this, and the Holy One of Israel hath created it.

**Memory Verse**
Isaiah 41:10

**Background Scripture**
Isaiah 41:1-42:9

**Devotional Reading**
1 John 4:13-19

God's reference in vs. 1 to Abraham as "my friend" impressed the New Testament writer James. When he cited Abraham's example of active faith, he tacked on the observation, "And he was called the Friend of God" (2:23). Can you think of anybody else in the Bible who was so highly honored?

God's close relationship with Abraham resulted in eternal blessings for

### For a Lively Start

ഇൗ

Present-day Israel is an agricultural marvel, given the arid nature of that landscape. Nothing that resembles the description of luxuriant terrain described here by Isaiah exists there now, nor has this area ever been that green.

Some see in vss. 17-20 a poetic message to Israel during their most hopeless days of Captivity—God's promise of how much better things were going

all of humanity. The Lord explicitly tells us that "all nations on earth will be blessed, because Abraham obeyed me and kept my requirements, my commands, my decrees and my laws" (Gen. 26:4-5, NIV). What a remarkable thing that one man's faith and obedience would create an eternal ripple effect of blessings.

Long after Abraham was dead, the same explanation is given for God's later goodness to Israel: "He remembered his holy promise given to his servant Abraham" (Ps. 105:42). Who may be blessed because of your faith in the Lord?

to be for them because of His grace. In his famous commentary, C. F. Keil saw in these verses "a description of the miraculous change which would take place in the now comfortless and helpless condition of the exiles." Almost all Bible scholars recognize the over-the-top language here—the flowing water and the burgeoning greenery—as symbolic language promising huge blessings from the Lord.

| Teaching Outline | Daily Bible Readings |
|---|---|
| I. God's Chosen Ones—41:8-10 | Mon. A God of Love<br>*1 John 4:13-19* |
| A. Descendants of Abraham, 8 | Tue. A God of Grace and Mercy<br>*2 Chronicles 30:6-9* |
| B. Chosen Ones from Afar, 9 | Wed. A God Ready to Forgive<br>*Nehemiah 9:16-21* |
| C. Still God's People, 10 | Thu A God of Hope<br>*Psalm 71:1-6* |
| II. Rich Blessings to Come—41:17-20 | Fri. The Lord, First and Last<br>*Isaiah 41:1-7* |
| A. Rivers for the Thirsty, 17-18 | Sat. Do Not Fear<br>*Isaiah 41:11-16* |
| B. Shade in the Desert, 19 | Sun. The Lord's Promise to Protect<br>*Isaiah 41:8-10, 17-20* |
| C. Proof of God's Goodness, 20 | |

# *Verse by Verse*

## Isaiah 41:8-10, 17-20

### I. God's Chosen Ones—41:8-10
### A. Descendants of Abraham, 8

**8 But thou, Israel, art my servant, Jacob whom I have chosen, the seed of Abraham my friend.**

To our modern American ears, the word *servant* suggests the humiliation of a servile relationship. To us the term is demeaning. Yet, that is the opposite of the sense intended here. When God calls the nation of Israel his "servant," He is complimenting them with a title of special honor. If a king were to refer to his most trusted advisor and highest official as "my servant Jacob," nobody would consider it a put-down. Nor is one intended here.

Instead, the next phrase that describes Jacob as one God has "chosen" conveys the positive nature of this entire line. It is an honor to win an election—to be "chosen." On the sandlot baseball field, players who are "chosen" first always feel especially valued. To be chosen for an honor at work or at school exalts us in the eyes of our associates. So it is for Israel—God's chosen.

"Jacob" in this line means not the shyster in the Genesis tales but, instead, all of his descendants, the Jewish people. The name is used here as an appositive to "Israel," showing

that the two words mean exactly the same thing. This use of "Jacob" is quite common in the writings of the prophets.

A second appositive describes Israel as the descendants ("the seed") of Abraham. What an extraordinary distinction that old patriarch enjoyed to be designated here and elsewhere in Scripture as God's friend. No wonder the apostle Paul was pleased to call him our father in the faith.

### B. Chosen Ones from Afar, 9

**9 Thou whom I have taken from the ends of the earth, and called thee from the chief men thereof, and said unto thee, Thou art my servant; I have chosen thee, and not cast thee away.**

Without fail, all the newer Bible versions correct the KJV reading "the chief men thereof." The NKJV, instead, translates here "the farthest regions." All agree that the Hebrew word here means something like that. God is describing the ancient origin of the Jewish nation. Genesis 11 preserves the record that God first called Abraham's family from Ur of Chaldea— from the farthest east reaches of the Fertile Crescent—a long way off. To a man on foot or riding a camel in those ancient days, Ur must have seemed a world away.

Here in vs. 9 is that word "servant" again, and again God is bestowing honor and privilege on the nation when He tells them, "I have chosen you to be my servant." He stresses that since He Himself made that choice, He is not likely to unselect them and reject them. They might feel like He had done that when He allowed them to become captives, but He assures them here that they are still His people, His chosen ones.

### C. Still God's People, 10

**10 Fear thou not; for I am with thee: be not dismayed; for I am thy God: I will strengthen thee; yea, I will help thee; yea, I will uphold thee with the right hand of my righteousness.**

Christ's most frequent greeting to His men was, "Fear not!" In that case, they were at least temporarily frightened of Him. Here in Isaiah, the fear is generated not by the Lord's Presence but by the circumstances His people were enduring. The Lord is assuring His people—even as He would assure us—that they do not need to be undone and alarmed by the hardships they face, because He will be with them to strengthen, help, and uphold them.

Where the KJV inserts the connecting word *yea* between God's promises, the Hebrew connector does more that link the phrases. It has the effect of piling them up one on the other to emphasize the fact that the Lord is doing all of these things for His people at the same time.

### II. Rich Blessings to Come—41:17-20
### A. Rivers for the Thirsty, 17-18

**17 When the poor and needy seek water, and there is none, and their tongue faileth for thirst, I the LORD will hear them, I the God of Israel will not forsake them.**

**18 I will open rivers in high places, and fountains in the midst of the valleys: I will make the wilderness a pool of water, and the dry land springs of water.**

The original Bible readers lived in an arid land, so the often-used imagery of freely flowing water spoke cogently to them as a symbol of the Lord's blessings. In the first Psalm, a righteous man is described as like "a tree planted by the rivers of water." Christ borrowed this metaphor in John 7 to describe a person filled with the Spirit: "Out of his heart shall flow rivers of living water." On more than one occasion, Jesus offered "the water of life" to all who thirsted for it. In Paradise to come, one dominant feature is "the river of life."

Isaiah uses this water imagery to its fullest in these verses. Thirst represents virtually all of humanity's deepest desires, especially those that are accentuated by deprivation. God has a soft spot in His heart for the thirsty, Isaiah tells us. He listens when they cry out to Him. It was true for Israel in Captivity. It is true for any of us today. The more acute our sense of longing and need, the more likely it may be that God is paying attention to our cries.

### B. Shade in the Desert, 19

**19 I will plant in the wilderness the cedar, the shittah tree, and the myrtle, and the oil tree; I will set in the desert the fir tree, and the pine, and the box tree together:**

144

We could make a mistake by trying to identify each variety of trees mentioned here. We may lose sight of the intended image of verdant shade now made available by God in a land known for its blistering desert sun.

Nevertheless, a couple of the trees denoted in the KJV raise inevitable questions because they mean nothing to the average reader. *Shittah* is a close transliteration of the Hebrew word right here (which means the translators at the time had no idea what it meant, so they reproduced the Hebrew they could not interpret). Most modern verses tell us the intended tree here is the acacia. The "oil tree" in the KJV is an understandable naming of the olive tree, from which we get olive oil.

The type of trees involved here really does not matter. Isaiah is not giving us an agronomy lesson. He is opening a catalog of tree types in order to paint the lush greenery and delicious shade God will provide to his desert-scorched people.

No one reading this catalog would expect evergreen trees to start sprouting in the desert wastelands of Judah. They were not going to fuss at God and accuse Him of going back on His promise if thick forests did not begin to cover the foothills west of Jerusalem. They realized that Isaiah was not promising actual trees. Instead, the prophet was using the symbol of shady trees to embody God's comfort and protection for the people He still loved.

That divine comfort and protection still shelter those who trust in the Lord.

**C. Proof of God's Goodness, 20**

**20 That they may see, and know, and consider, and understand together, that the hand of the Lord hath done this, and the Holy One of Israel hath created it.**

Not all the blessings and protections Isaiah describes here are designed just to make the Jewish people safe and comfortable. They were sent primarily to show them that God still loves and cares for them.

ൠരൂ

145

## Evangelistic Emphasis

In the [Bob Dylan] song, "When the Deal Goes Down," we see the prophet as a vulnerable traveler, lost like Dante in the deep forest of night:

*In the still of the night, in the world's ancient light*

*Where wisdom grows up in strife*

*My bewildering brain, toils in vain*

*Through the darkness on the pathways of life ...*

*We live and we die, we know not why ...*

God speaks this to the bewildered pilgrim: *I'll be with you when the deal goes down.*

What is "the deal" going down? It is mortality and death. Cancer, heart disease, plane crashes, terrorism and the threat of nuclear holocaust. Preachers and prophets do not speak of death as "the deal," but old bluesmen do. In the plain and repetitive tones of the blues, Dylan has rediscovered a mode of speaking that enables him to communicate not with irony but rather with the authority of the prophet spreading his message of God's undying love for all times and for all people.

When "the deal" goes down in your life, where do you find your foundation and your strength? Jesus holds our future in His hands and we are in very compassionate powerful hands.

&oଔ

## Memory Selection

"Fear thou not; for I am with thee: be not dismayed; for I am thy God: I will strengthen thee; yea, I will help thee; yea, I will uphold thee with the right hand of my righteousness." *Isaiah 41: 10*

"The Boy and the Crèche" is the true story of what happened one Christmas Eve in front of the Holy Trinity Episcopalian Church in New York City. The story is told by the Reverend Clarke Kimberly Oler, who was pastor at the time.

Oler says that a street urchin, barely 6 years old, showed up at the Nativity scene on Christmas Eve. He had been around before but had always run off when approached. The streets at this time of night were deserted. The little boy peered at the life-sized figures and stared at the manger. Then, suddenly, he climbed inside and curled up in the straw. Oler writes, "I felt as though I had been granted a momentary look into a lonely child's heart.... All I could do was breathe a prayer that somehow he had been comforted by Mary's unchanging expression of love."

The promise of love, of life eternal, of the divine fulfillment of all our longings and desires, is offered anew to us this season. Just as our Nativity scenes and crèches are set out each year, so are the promises, that the baby Jesus embodies, reaffirmed every Christmas. With that little boy, we should all take turns climbing into that cradle and allow the power of the promise to wash over us, encouraging us, and filling us with promise for the coming year.

146

## *Weekday Problems*

Tony was at the end of his rope. His shift had been notified that the plant was "downsizing" and all workers on the third shift would be laid off. He could either wait for an opening on another shift, or accept transfer across the country. Moving was out of the question because Tony was taking care of his mother, who recently suffered a stroke.

If the job was not enough, Pam was giving Tony fits at home. She had wanted a baby for years. The time never seemed to be right and now seemed as if it was running out. She and Tony tried and failed to have children. This depressed Pam and she took her depression and anger out on Tony.

Hal Martin was a life-long friend of Tony. They played a few holes of golf together once a month. One afternoon Hal stopped by. He caught Pam and Tony in one of their tiffs. Sensing the anger in the room, Hal invited himself in for a glass of tea. He sat for a moment in silence.

Tony said, "Boy, I'll bet we look silly, don't we?"

Hal continued to sit. As the minutes unfolded into a couple of hours, Hal listened patiently to both Tony and Pam. He offered no advice. He took no sides. Hal made it clear that he heard and understood each one of them.

How can one offer encouragement without using words?

What words from Isaiah offer encouragement for you?

---

# A Christmas Story

In the bustle of Christmas shopping a lady lost her handbag. It was found by a honest little boy. He checked her I.D. info, called her, and returned it to her.

After a quick inventory of her purse, the woman commented, "Hmmmmmm . . . That's funny. When I lost my bag, there was a $20 bill in it. Now there are twenty $1 bills."

"That's right lady," the boy quickly replied. "The last time I found a lady's purse, she didn't have any change for a reward."

# This Lesson in Your Life

Isaiah speaks the truth about Israel. Isaiah is probably talking about the nation of Israel when he speaks of God's servant. He is reminding them that they are the Lord's chosen people, with a mission of sharing God's teachings with the world and establishing justice on the earth. "I have given you as a covenant to the people," says God through the prophet, "a light to the nations, to open the eyes that are blind" (vv. 6-7).

Did Isaiah get this right? Yes, he did. In fact, Israel did prove to be a light to the nations, opening the eyes of people around the world to the teachings and justice of the one true God. Without Israel, we never would have been introduced to the God of Abraham and Sarah, Isaac and Rebekah, Jacob and Rachel.

We never would have gotten to know God's Son Jesus, either.

Isaiah speaks the truth about Jesus. Here is where Isaiah's prophecy gets interesting. It may have first revealed a truth about Israel, but it later unveiled the true nature of Jesus the Messiah. When Jesus was baptized by John, the Spirit of God descended like a dove and a voice from heaven said, "This is my Son, the Beloved, with whom I am well pleased" (Matthew 3:17). These words could have come straight out of Isaiah 42, in which God says, "Here is my servant ... my chosen, in whom my soul delights" (v. 1).

Clearly, what Isaiah got right is Jesus. He is the servant of the Lord with God's "spirit upon him" (v. 1), the one who "will faithfully bring forth *mishpat* — justice" (v. 3). Jesus will be "a covenant to the people, a light to the nations" (v. 6), a savior who will "bring out the prisoners from the dungeon" (v. 7). Isaiah sensed what God was up to, and he spoke the truth about Jesus, the Messiah of God.

This reveals a key fact about good prophets, one that we need always to keep in mind. They are not supposed to be fortune-tellers who predict precisely what will happen in the months and years to come. Instead, they are supposed to be truth-tellers who speak clearly about what is happening *right now!*

A good prophet paints a clear picture of the state of the world, with all its pain, brokenness, sin, and selfishness. A good prophet speaks the truth in love, and points people to where God is at work in the middle of all our human failings,

*A good prophet is a truth-teller, not a fortune-teller.*

Take Paul Ehrlich, a respected professor at Stanford University. In 1968, he wrote a book called *The Population Bomb*, which stated that people would have many babies in the future. He saw the population growth around him, and he spoke clearly about it. That is truth telling. That is good prophecy.

However, Ehrlich went on to say that "hundreds of millions of people will starve to death," and he predicted that India would run out of food in 1971. That is fortune telling. That is bad prophecy.

Isaiah is a good prophet because he paints a clear picture of the state of the world. He speaks the truth in love, and points people to where God is at work.

**GETTING THE FACTS STRAIGHT**

**1. Isaiah 41 begins with an invitation. What is that invitation?**

The coastlands are to listen to God in silence; the people are to draw close in silence and God and the people will draw close for judgment.

**2. What image is Isaiah 41 portraying?**

The image that Isaiah 41 is portraying is that of a judicial proceeding with God and his people as opponents.

**3. What is the first question that God asks in the court?**

God inquires about who has raised up kings from the east and defeated armies. He has also called generations from the beginning.

**4. Who are the witnesses to the mighty acts of God?**

The coastlands have seen and the ends of the earth tremble, they have drawn near and are witnesses to the hand of God.

**5. What historical event is probably referred to in the first section of Isaiah 41?**

The background to this scene is the victories of Cyrus, King of Persia.

**6. What two images are used to describe the people of Israel?**

They are the people of Abraham, a friend of God and they are chosen of God.

**7. What word of hope is given to the people of Israel?**

They are not to be dismayed for God will strengthen them, help them, and uphold them with His victorious right hand.

**8. What is the significance of the right hand?**

The right hand and arm of God are always symbolic of the might or the power of God. Jesus is seated at the right hand of God, the mighty side of God.

**9. What will happen to the enemies of Israel?**

They shall be put to shame and confounded. They will be as nothing and shall perish.

**10. How will God restore the men of Israel?**

He will make them a threshing sledge; new, sharp and having teeth. They will have the power to crush the mountains.

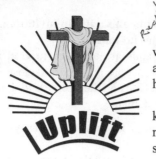

This Uplift section continues the thoughts about what the prophet Isaiah got right. He was right about Israel and Jesus. There is a third thing Isaiah had right.

Isaiah speaks the truth about us. Even better, this kind of prophecy steers us in the direction that we need to go. Isaiah does not just get right that God's servant is coming — he creates a template that we can use for our own actions and attitudes. Bringing forth justice and being a light to the nations are not just the responsibility of Jesus the Messiah — they are also part of the job description of anyone who follows Jesus.

The prophet is speaking about us, right along with Jesus. What Isaiah affirms *is the need for servants of God to bring forth* mishpat *justice in every time and place.*

True story: A homeless man named Ben walked into a Virginia church one afternoon, asking to see the pastor. He was suffering from kidney stones, and had a prescription for a painkiller — but no money to pay for it. Ben asked if the pastor had funds to fill the prescription for him.

Now Rev. Mike, let us call him, had a ton of stuff to do that afternoon, and Ben's predicament was way down on his list. But Rev. Mike just happened to be studying Isaiah 42, and had just read an important line about the character of the servant of God— "a bruised reed he will not break, and a dimly burning wick he will not quench; he will faithfully bring forth justice" (42:3).

Homeless Ben was a bruised reed, a dimly burning wick. Rev. Mike knew that health care is a constant struggle for the uninsured poor of our country, and sensed that he really needed to do something. If he was going to be God's servant, and "faithfully bring forth justice," he needed to help fill that prescription.

The next morning, the two of them went to the pharmacy, looking like a rather strange couple — Ben, all covered with tattoos, and Rev. Mike in a dress shirt with a cheap tie. They picked up the painkillers, and then on the car ride back to church Ben told his story: He had grown up on a dairy farm in Ohio, with an abusive father who ended up shooting Ben's mother and then killing himself. Ben had served in the military and worked as a truck driver, and now he was meeting with a mental health counselor to get himself into a group home.

When they said goodbye, Rev. Mike wished Ben well and invited him to worship. He was glad that he had been God's servant that morning, doing what he could to bring forth a little bit of *mishpat* justice, and offer a ray of light to a man who was dwelling in deep darkness.

What Isaiah knew is that servants of God exist; in the nation of Israel, in Jesus Christ, and in each of us. May we live our days in ways that make this prophecy come true.

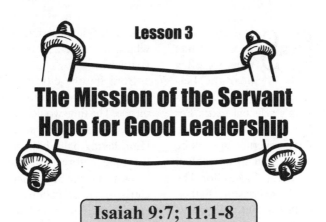

# Lesson 3

# The Mission of the Servant
# Hope for Good Leadership

## Isaiah 9:7; 11:1-8

Of the increase of his government and peace there shall be no end, upon the throne of David, and upon his kingdom, to order it, and to establish it with judgment and with justice from henceforth even for ever. The zeal of the Lord of hosts will perform this.

11:1 And there shall come forth a rod out of the stem of Jesse, and a Branch shall grow out of his roots:

2 And the spirit of the Lord shall rest upon him, the spirit of wisdom and understanding, the spirit of counsel and might, the spirit of knowledge and of the fear of the Lord;

3 And shall make him of quick understanding in the fear of the Lord: and he shall not judge after the sight of his eyes, neither reprove after the hearing of his ears:

4 But with righteousness shall he judge the poor, and reprove with equity for the meek of the earth: and he shall smite the earth with the rod of his mouth, and with the breath of his lips shall he slay the wicked.

5 And righteousness shall be the girdle of his loins, and faithfulness the girdle of his reins.

6 The wolf also shall dwell with the lamb, and the leopard shall lie down with the kid; and the calf and the young lion and the fatling together; and a little child shall lead them.

7 And the cow and the bear shall feed; their young ones shall lie down together: and the lion shall eat straw like the ox.

8 And the sucking child shall play on the hole of the asp, and the weaned child shall put his hand on the cockatrice's den.

---

**Memory Verse**
Isaiah 11:5

**Background Scripture**
Isaiah 9:1-7; 11:1-9;
Matthew 1:18-25

**Devotional Reading**
John 4:19-26

Especially at Christmas time, we often hear the Isaiah's cherished prediction that prefaces this lesson's selected text: "For unto us a child is born, unto us a son is given: and the government shall be upon his shoulder: and his name shall be called Wonderful, Counsellor, The mighty God, The everlasting Father, The Prince of Peace" (9:6). We know, of course, that the only "child" who fits this incredible description is the baby whose birth the angels announced at Bethlehem.

Born in "the city of David," this baby would grow up to sit on David's throne. The time would come when the citizens of Jerusalem would welcome Him, laying palm branches to carpet the road before Him and shouting, "Hosanna to the Son of David!" Today, Christians of all nations acknowledge Him as their King and herald Him as the Prince of Peace.

## For a Lively Start

ଽଠଔ

Isaiah's imagery in 11:1-9 depicts a world none of us has ever known. In the real world, wolves and lambs don't mix. Leopards and goats cannot coexist. Infants do not play with cobras. No jungle or zoo on this earth houses straw-eating lions. What is the prophet trying to tell us with otherworldly language like this?

Some Christians read these verses as a description of Heaven—a peaceful Paradise where danger simply does not exist and fear is unknown.

Other believers, however, think Isaiah is giving us a highly poetic description of the peace and safety that should mark all of our relationships in the present Kingdom of God under the reign of His Son, the Prince of Peace.

| Teaching Outline | Daily Bible Readings |
|---|---|
| I. The Endless Reign of David's Son—9:7 | Mon. The God of Peace *Romans 15:25-33* |
| II. A Shoot Out of Jesse's Royal Roots—11:1-5 | Tue. The Gospel of Peace *Ephesians 6:13-17* |
| A. God's Spirit Upon Him, 1-3a | Wed. Peace with God *Romans 5:1-5* |
| B. Justice for the Helpless, 3b-4a | Thu Peace Given to You *John 14:25-31* |
| C. Wrath for the Wicked, 4b | Fri. A Child Is Born *Isaiah 9:1-6* |
| D. Robed in Righteousness, 5 | Sat. His Mission—Our Mission *Matthew 28:16-20* |
| III. A Kingdom Free from Fear—11:6-8 | Sun. The Prince of Peace *Isaiah 9:7; 11:1-8* |

# *Verse by Verse*

**Isaiah 9:7; 11:1-8**

## I. The Endless Reign of David's Son—9:7

**9:7 Of the increase of his government and peace there shall be no end, upon the throne of David, and upon his kingdom, to order it, and to establish it with judgment and with justice from henceforth even for ever. The zeal of the LORD of hosts will perform this.**

Many years before Isaiah's time, God promised David he would always have a son on the throne. "I will raise up your offspring to succeed you . . . , and I will establish his kingdom. . . . I will establish the throne of his kingdom forever. I will be his father, and he will be my son." Then the Lord emphasized the eternal nature of the reign of David's son. "Your house and your kingdom will endure forever before me; your throne will be established forever" (2 Sam. 7:12-16, NIV). Now Isaiah echoes the divine promise that the reign of David's son and the peace during His rule will have "no end." This righteous reign will continue "from henceforth even forever," the prophet assures us.

Some commentators point out that the promise of a peaceful Kingdom that has "no end" is couched in a He-brew word that could apply either to time or to space. Instead of describing a Kingdom that is eternal, this promise may offer one that just keeps on expanding—an apt description of the reign of Christ on earth.

The very idea of a human government that just keeps on increasing sounds more hellish than heavenly to some Christians, but the King on this throne reigns with absolute justice and righteousness, guaranteeing peace and security to His subjects. None of us has ever known a government like this, so it is hard to imagine what a blessing its ever-increasing growth could be.

## II. A Shoot Out of Jesse's Royal Roots—11:1-5

### A. God's Spirit Upon Him, 1-3a

**1 And there shall come forth a rod out of the stem of Jesse, and a Branch shall grow out of his roots:**

**2 And the spirit of the LORD shall rest upon him, the spirit of wisdom and understanding, the spirit of counsel and might, the spirit of knowledge and of the fear of the LORD;**

**3 And shall make him of quick understanding in the fear of the LORD:**

All the later Bible versions use the word *shoot* in place of the old English

**153**

*rod*, and most of them replace the KJV *stem* with *stump*, as in the stump of a tree.

The parallelism of Hebrew poetry helps us here. The meaning of the first half of vs. 1 is identical to that of the last half. Isaiah's horticultural metaphor compares the dynasty of King David to a tree that has been cut down. The stump of most trees does not die when cut off during the peak of the growing season. Before long new shoots begin to emerge from the edges of the stump as the life in the tree roots asserts itself; new branches try to grow where once the tree stood proud and tall. Even so, Isaiah tells us, the family of David will not be dead and gone just because they appear to have been cut off.

The Spirit of the Lord will impart special gifts to this new Ruler in David's line. His wisdom, understanding, insight, and knowledge will be legendary, as will the resulting power of his Kingdom. "Quick understanding" in vs. 3 is translated "delight" in many newer versions such as the NKJV. This great new King will take pleasure in all who respect or "fear" the Lord.

**B. Justice for the Helpless, 3b-4a**

**3b and he shall not judge after the sight of his eyes, neither reprove after the hearing of his ears:**

**4a But with righteousness shall he judge the poor, and reprove with equity for the meek of the earth:**

When Jesus commands, "Judge not by appearances, but judge with righteous judgment" (John 7:24), He has in mind exactly what Isaiah does in vs. 3. This new King on David's throne will be a fair man who does not jump to conclusions, but instead assesses true motives and pays attention to the heart.

The next part of Isaiah's compliment—the fact that this King's judgments will not be made "after the hearing of his ears"—means that He will not base His rulings on "hearsay" (TEV and NLT). To find out what actually happened, He will seek genuine evidence instead of relying on palace gossip.

In many places today, it is hard for a poor, powerless person to get justice from a judge or a bureaucrat, but David's son will extend fair treatment to peasants and widows—to those without political influence. Again, the parallelism of Hebrew poetry helps us in the two phrases in vs. 4a. "The poor" in the first part of the line are the same as "the meek" in the last part. They will receive from the Davidic King "righteous judgment" and "equity."

Those of us, who bow down to Christ, the Son of David, find a grand description of our Lord in these verses. In His earthly ministry, Jesus demonstrated special gentleness and patience with publicans, sinners, widows, and children. His ministry provided special esteem and care for "the last, the least, the lost, the little, and even the dead"— those who could not reward Him or repay Him in any way. He fit perfectly in Isaiah's description. We should not expect that His priorities have shifted as He rules from Heaven.

**C. Wrath for the Wicked, 4b**

**4b and he shall smite the earth with the rod of his mouth, and with the breath of his lips shall he slay the wicked.**

Unlike the kings and magistrates of the earth, who tend to favor the rich and unprincipled with their justice-warping bribes, Isaiah tells us that this son of David will deal out harsh treatment to the worthless and wicked. His innocent subjects will rejoice in the uncommon fairness of this kind of governing.

Isaiah compares the words of this just Ruler to the rod of discipline wielded by an executioner. The parallel members of vs. 4b again repeat the same concept in the first and last parts. In both segments, those who deserve punishment will receive it because of what this righteous Ruler speaks.

Is this not the ideal for any official who governs us? We need them not only to be just and kind to the powerless, but also we need them to be unerringly severe toward all who pervert the system and break the rules. Judges, cops, or legislators on the take make life hard for all who are trying to abide by the law. The pattern of hurt and corruption established by some notoriously wicked government officials provide a dark relief against which, the fairness and righteousness of David's son shine with winsome brightness. Isaiah pictures for us a most attractive King.

**D. Robed in Righteousness, 5**

**5 And righteousness shall be the girdle of his loins, and faithfulness the girdle of his reins.**

This son of David will be clothed in goodness and fairness, Isaiah is telling us. "Girdle" is old English for "belt." It had special meaning in biblical days when men wore bathrobe-type garments that needed to be cinched up with a broad belt. The meaning of this verse with its archaic terms becomes clear in the reading of the NIV: "Righteousness will be his belt and faithfulness the sash around his waist."

**III. A Kingdom Free from Fear— 11:6-8**

**6 The wolf also shall dwell with the lamb, and the leopard shall lie down with the kid; and the calf and the young lion and the fatling together; and a little child shall lead them.**

**7 And the cow and the bear shall feed; their young ones shall lie down together: and the lion shall eat straw like the ox.**

**8 And the sucking child shall play on the hole of the asp, and the weaned child shall put his hand on the cockatrice's den.**

These obviously are not scenes in our world. These animals do not hang out together and small children do not safely supervise them. We do not let our babies and toddlers play with poisonous snakes—with "asps" (vipers) or "cockatrices" (cobras). Isaiah pictures, with these extreme images, a time and place where danger and fear no longer exist. His next verse sums up God's intentions in this imagery: "They shall not hurt nor destroy in all my holy mountain." Whether this very safe realm is Heaven to come or Christ's present reign on Earth depends on what Christian teacher happens to be explaining it to us.

შოცჳ

155

## Evangelistic Emphasis

Across the street from a famous New Orleans restaurant is an even more famous tree. The tree is an oak tree that is more than one hundred and fifty years old. Neither the age nor the stature of the oak is unique to that species. What makes this tree special is the other tree. This oak has a palm tree growing in the oak tree. Some bird or animal deposited the important part of a coconut in the bough of the oak. A full-grown palm tree now resides some fifteen feet off the ground in the middle of that oak.

Seeds can grow any place they have protection and nourishment. That message is important for us. God can plant seeds and have them grow any place he chooses. He can even cause "shoots to come from a stump." (Is. 11:1) The surprise of the gospel of Christ is that the seeds of grace and peace grow in the strangest places.

Jesus planted his seeds of forgiveness and mercy in the lives of sinners, tax collectors, and other assorted malcontents. Those seeds grew into tall oaks of faith. Jesus can also plant his seed of mercy in your life, and in the life of the biggest sinner you know. If he can make a stump spring forth, he can certainly forgive our sinful world. This is the good news, that God has planted the seeds of his kingdom all around. Have you seen any of his seed growing recently? Have you planted any?

## Memory Selection

### ઠ૭ભ

"And righteousness shall be the girdle of his loins, and faithfulness the girdle of his reins".

*Isaiah 11: 5*

There is a story told that, one day during the course of the American Revolution, an officer on horseback wearing civilian clothes rode past a group of soldiers repairing a small redoubt. He asked their commander, who was busy shouting instructions, why he was not assisting his exhausted men. "Sir," the officer retorted indignantly, "I am a corporal!"

The stranger apologized, dismounted, assisted the soldiers himself, and, some time later, turned to the corporal. "Corporal," he declared, "next time you have a job like this and not enough men to do it, go to your commander-in-chief, and I will come and help you again."

The stranger? George Washington, of course.

The messianic king pictured by Isaiah is a man who is humble. With an attitude of righteousness and faithfulness, his attitude toward those0 around him is one of help and consolation. Righteousness is living in right relationship with God and with our fellow human being. Faithfulness is being the kind of person that not only keeps the word of God but also keeps his own word and does as he promises.

Jesus said that He came not to be served but to serve others and to give His life as a ransom for many. Jesus was a man of righteousness and faithfulness, and showed us how to live within that lifestyle.

# Weekday Problems

Jack Jackson was a youth director with an uncanny ability to get himself in all kinds of trouble. It wasn't that he intentionally sought it out. Trouble seemed to find him. His last little jaunt had once again landed him in hot water. He had purchased mugs with the name and picture of New Harmony Church on them. The mugs were sold by the youth group as the "perfect Christmas gift" idea. While Jack dutifully logged each mug sale, he neglected one of the finer points of business. He neglected to pay the vendor who made the mugs.

After a nasty phone call to Rev. Mitchell, the vendor received his check and Reverend Mitchell and Jack had a meeting.

Reverend Mitchell had "covered" many mistakes that Jack had made. The youth seemed to love him. The parents of the youth were a little unsure of him. Jack Jackson had managed to alienate almost all of the leadership of the church. On Christmas Eve, when the Finance Chairman found out about Jack's latest ploy, he told the Pastor that Bro. Jackson should be terminated. An impromptu census of the leadership felt the same way.

Brother Mitchell had heard these comments before. This time, he felt that Jack must be confronted with the long (and growing longer) list of the things he had done wrong.

When the meeting ended, Jack Jackson was as white as a sheet.

How could Jack's ministry at New Harmony been "saved?"

In what ways do we avoid problems and conflicts?

Is the avoidance of conflict the way to bring about the song of the angels, "Peace on earth, goodwill toward men?"

## Mary, Did You Know?

He was created of a mother whom He created.

He was cared for by hands that He formed.

He cried in the manger in wordless infancy, He the Word, without whom all human eloquence is mute.

—*St. Augustine of Hippo, 4th century*

# This Lesson in Your Life

Christmas is a time for and about children. Children get the most wrapped up in the holiday and have the fewest "headaches." They do not have to deal with crowds in the mall and parts that were not in the box. They simply anticipate, then open presents with gusto and vigor on Christmas morning. The whole "reason for the season" was another baby. This baby was foretold by prophets long ago, and fulfilled in the person of Jesus Christ. The ministry of this most special child is the miracle of the season.

Isaiah saw that the Christ would create a world in which "the wolf shall live with the lamb, the leopard shall lie down with the kid, the calf and the lion and the fatling together." (Is 11:6) The "natural evil and animosity" of creation will be removed by the kingdom of God. Not only is the natural order effected, humanity also benefits from the coming of this child.

People will be judged and treated fairly. This is a word of hope for all of us. A good discussion starter might be to ask your class how many of them are worried about one or more of the Christmas gifts they have purchased. We are often judged this time of year by the expense of the presents we purchase and give to friends and family. Others are judged by the number of cards they do or do not receive.

We long for someone who "knows the real us." Isaiah promised such a one as that. Christ judges us only in terms of his righteousness. The bad news is that in terms of his righteousness, we all fall miserably short. The good news is that when we ask for forgiveness and mercy it is given freely and generously. He knows us completely and loves us unconditionally.

The old familiar Christmas story should remind us of that. Jesus' birth was not announced in palatial halls or the Roman colonnades. His birth was announced to shepherds who where were on the night shift. The real first line shepherds worked the day shift. These fellows had nothing to do at night but drink wine and watch the sheep sleep. Being a shepherd often rendered the person ceremonially unclean. It was just assumed these fellows were also liars and thieves. Because of that assumption, they were not allowed into the temple area. Thus, they were not allowed to participate in the acts of worship that would lead to the forgiveness of their sins. If they worked, they could not be a part of the temple.

To these who were trapped by their circumstances, the birth of Jesus was announced. That is what the story of Christmas is all about. A God who judges us and treats us not by some impossible standards of divinity, but in love and understanding. These shepherds were the first to hear about the wonderful child born in Bethlehem. On that first Christmas, they were the ones that needed the message the most.

Does that message bring you comfort and hope on this day? Christmas is about children, for children—children like you and me.

**GETTING
THE FACTS STRAIGHT**

**1. What is the significance of the mention of Jesse?**
Jesse was the father of David, the greatest king of Israel. The Messiah comes from the lineage of David.

**2. What are the results of the "Spirit resting" on the Messiah?**
The Spirit will give the Messiah wisdom and understanding, counsel and might, the spirit of knowledge and the fear of the Lord.

**3. Fear of the Lord is mentioned here and again as describing the shepherds. What does fear mean in these contexts?**
Fear, in these two contexts, carries with it the notion of the awe of the divine. The shepherds felt that awe and the "regular" kind of fear, too.

**4. How shall the Lord judge his people?**
He will not use his eyes or his ears. His judgment is not based on external actions, but on internal righteousness.

**5. As a result of the leadership of this child, what will the lion do that is out of character?**
The meat-eating lion will eat grass.

**6. What was the sign for the shepherds looking for the savior?**
The shepherds would readily understand the image of a manger. They were very much used to seeing mangers.

**7. What was the good news that was announced to the shepherds?**
The savior had been born, and through him, God was bringing peace on earth.

**8. Isaiah mentions two categories of people that would also qualify as describing the shepherds of Luke 2. What are these two kinds of people?**
The poor and the meek of the earth.

**9. What is the meaning of Isaiah 11: 6?**
Natural and moral enemies will relate to each other in new ways. These ways will be indicative of the Messiah's righteousness and pattern for creation.

**10. What two items of clothing are mentioned in this passage?**
The girdle of righteousness and the girdle of faithfulness. In modern vernacular, one is a T-shirt and the other running shorts.

Jesus not only is the Lion of the tribe of Judah; he is the Lamb of God that takes away the sins of the world. Not only is Jesus both the Lion and the Lamb, he makes both to lie down together. The light of the world was snuffed out on the cross, but returned brighter than ever.

We have all heard litanies of oxymorons—those unique combinations of terms that both make sense and nonsense. Jumbo shrimp, long shorts, fresh frozen, pretty ugly, holy war, inactive Christian. However, have you ever considered that we have just celebrated one of the biggest oxymoron ever considered: "Silent Night."

Is anyone out there a Christmas Eve shopper? There are some people who either because they want to take advantage of all the last-minute price markdowns they can or because they love the madhouse atmosphere of a shopping mall on December 24, intentionally do all their shopping the day before Christmas.

Of course, some of us will admit that it is just plain old procrastination that forces us to fight our way through hoards of other desperate shoppers on Christmas Eve. Cash registers ringing, bags and boxes crunching and crashing, harried shoppers bustling and bumping, parking lots filled with screeches and honks—these are the real sounds of our "Silent Night."

Even if we avoid the mall madness, what is the decibel level like at our own homes? The sounds of kids home for the holidays—fighting over the TV, fighting over the stereo, fighting over the scissors, paper, and tape. The sound of the holiday chef in the kitchen, trying to get as much done as possible for the massive meals the next day—dishes clatter, pans rattle, cupboards slam. The sound of the official toy-assembler, muffled perhaps by the walls of the basement, garage, or attic workspace he or she is crammed into—bangs, groans, curses, kicks—these are the other honest, real sounds of our "Silent Night."

Even if we go to church on Christmas Eve, we seldom get more than a suggestion of "Silent Night." There are the sounds of greeting friends, the sounds of giggling nervous children dressed like wise men and shepherds, the sounds of the choir, the preacher, the pageant. Then maybe if we are lucky, there is the sound of singing "Silent Night," which may in fact be followed by a few moments of silence. But how quickly the silence is over. Then we rush out again to fill the rest of that not-so-silent night with as much hustle and bustle as we possibly can before crashing exhausted into bed.

It is appropriate that our Silent Night should be filled with sound and turmoil. Everything about Christmas is an oxymoron.

The Lord, the creator of heaven and earth, came to earth and was born as a human baby. His birth happened in a manger attended by the animals. Perhaps we need to get back to God's oxymoron about Christmas rather than the mess we have created.

## Lesson 4

# I Will Be with You
# Whom Shall I Follow?

### Isaiah 43:1-7, 11-12

But now thus saith the LORD that created thee, O Jacob, and he that formed thee, O Israel, Fear not: for I have redeemed thee, I have called thee by thy name; thou art mine.

2 When thou passest through the waters, I will be with thee; and through the rivers, they shall not overflow thee: when thou walkest through the fire, thou shalt not be burned; neither shall the flame kindle upon thee.

3 For I am the LORD thy God, the Holy One of Israel, thy Saviour: I gave Egypt for thy ransom, Ethiopia and Seba for thee.

4 Since thou wast precious in my sight, thou hast been honourable, and I have loved thee: therefore will I give men for thee, and people for thy life.

5 Fear not: for I am with thee: I will bring thy seed from the east, and gather thee from the west;

6 I will say to the north, Give up; and to the south, Keep not back: bring my sons from far, and my daughters from the ends of the earth;

7 Even every one that is called by my name: for I have created him for my glory, I have formed him; yea, I have made him.

11 I, even I, am the LORD; and beside me there is no saviour.

12 I have declared, and have saved, and I have shewed, when there was no strange god among you: therefore ye are my witnesses, saith the LORD, that I am God.

---

**Memory Verse**
Isaiah 43:2

**Background Scripture**
Isaiah 43

**Devotional Reading**
Isaiah 63:7-14

---

ian's armed assaults during Isaiah's own lifetime, we may not be able to determine with certainty.

God's comforting command, "Fear not," rings out not once but twice in these early verses of Isaiah 43. Clearly, some distress was stirring anxiety or panic in the hearts of His people. Whether it was the cruelty of captivity in Babylon, as some Bible scholars surmise, or some earlier time of national disaster such as the Assyr-

Still, this message from the Lord addresses His children in every time and place. At times, all of us are shaken by threats that could undo us. IRS calls. Cancer tests come back positive. Business goes bad. Crimes take place too near. In these and a dozen other unnerving situations, we need to hear our Creator bidding us to trust in Him and "fear not."

## For a Lively Start

When the apostles Peter and John were brought before the Jewish court, do you suppose Peter had recently pondered the text we call Isaiah 43:11? I wonder if this were so because of the similar truth in both places.

God tells His people through his prophet, "I am the LORD; and beside me there is no saviour." Peter told his accusers in the Sanhedrin, "Neither is

there salvation in any other: for there is none other name under heaven given among men, whereby we must be saved" (Acts 4:12).

God never has been big on diversity. "You shall have no other gods before me," was the first of His commandments. Likewise, Jesus intends to be our only Savior.

| Teaching Outline | Daily Bible Readings |
|---|---|
| I. Fear Not. I Have Redeemed You.—43:1-4 | Mon. Remember God's Mercy *Isaiah 63:7-14* |
| A. Past Blessings, 1 | Tue. Chosen by God *Isaiah 43:8-10* |
| B. Future Care, 2 | Wed. God Forgets Our Sin *Isaiah 43:22-28* |
| C. Ransomed by God, 3-4 | Thu Obey and Find Mercy *Jeremiah 42:7-17* |
| II. Fear Not. I Am with You.—43:5-7 | Fri. The Lord Is with You *Haggai 1:7-15* |
| A. A Scattered People, 5-6 | Sat. God with Us *Matthew 1:18-25* |
| B. God's Creation, 7 | Sun. No Other Savior *Isaiah 43:1-7, 11-12* |
| III. No Other Savior—43:11-12 | |

# *Verse by Verse*

## Isaiah 43:1-7, 11-12

### I. Fear Not. I Have Redeemed You.—43:1-4

**A. Past Blessings, 1**

**1 But now thus saith the LORD that created thee, O Jacob, and he that formed thee, O Israel, Fear not: for I have redeemed thee, I have called thee by thy name; thou art mine.**

Twice in this short section of Isaiah's prophecy, the Lord reminds His people that He made them. Surely, it is no accident that the same words are repeated like a drumbeat both in vs. 1 and in vs. 7. Called. Created. Formed.

None of us doubts for a minute that God has made us. The mere mention of the word *created* transports most Bible readers instantly to the Genesis story and the beginning pronouncement that "in the beginning God created." The language of Isaiah automatically diverts most of us to the dawn of time. We can hardly keep from hearing in Isaiah's words a description of the God who created us in that context of the beginning of creation.

Notice, however, that Isaiah's message is addressed to, "thee, O Jacob"— and then in typical Hebrew parallelism to, "thee, O Israel." In focus here, is the creation or forming the establishment of the nation of the Jews. God made them, named them, and claimed them. They are His.

In the same way, God has created His Church. He raised us, cleansed us, named us, and claimed us in Jesus. We are His.

**B. Future Care, 2**

**2 When thou passest through the waters, I will be with thee; and through the rivers, they shall not overflow thee: when thou walkest through the fire, thou shalt not be burned; neither shall the flame kindle upon thee.**

The focus of vs. 1 was on what God had done in the past to establish and claim His people. Now, He promises to take care of them through all danger and hardship in the days to come.

Could any Jew read the description of the dangers, though, without sensing allusions to the Red Sea and the Jordan River, as the Lord led His people out of Egypt and into Canaan? The same God is still their God and He tells them He is still willing and able to care for them as He did in the past.

Few of us can read the words about walking through the fire without immediately recalling Daniel's friends in the fiery furnace. When they came out of the intense flames, they did not even smell like smoke. They experienced exactly the kind of care that God promised to His children here in Isaiah's book.

Isaiah's words were not intended to tempt us to try daredevil stunts. He was not counseling his Jewish neighbors to use less than reasonable care when confronting natural disasters or occupational hazards. Nor should we interpret these words as a divine invitation for us to abandon due caution.

## C. Ransomed by God, 3-4

**3 For I am the LORD thy God, the Holy One of Israel, thy Saviour: I gave Egypt for thy ransom, Ethiopia and Seba for thee.**

**4 Since thou wast precious in my sight, thou hast been honourable, and I have loved thee: therefore will I give men for thee, and people for thy life.**

Nobody knows for sure what God is referring to in these verses, when He reminds the Jews that He "ransomed" them by paying the price for three nations mentioned here.

Had Ethiopia and Seba not been included in the ransom, the most obvious sense of these verses would be that God ravaged the land of Egypt to free His people from the cruel slavery in Moses' time. Scripture often tells us God "redeemed" Israel from that time of bondage. The countries south of Egypt, Ethiopia and Seba (the Sabeans), are never mentioned in the early Exodus accounts. God may be referring here to another part of Jewish exile history.

Several Bible commentators note that the Assyrian king Sennacherib, who threatened Jerusalem during the

reigns of Hezekiah and his predecessors, spared the holy city in order to divert his troops to attack Egypt, Ethiopia, and points south of them. Therefore, it could legitimately be said that God gave up those nations in order to spare His own.

In either case, Egypt and its southern neighbors were conquered in place of Israel because God willed it to be so. Today, do others sometimes suffer tragedies in order to divert those troubles from God's children?

## II. Fear Not. I Am with You.—43:5-7

### A. A Scattered People, 5-6

**5 Fear not: for I am with thee: I will bring thy seed from the east, and gather thee from the west;**

**6 I will say to the north, Give up; and to the south, Keep not back: bring my sons from far, and my daughters from the ends of the earth;**

This is the second "Fear not" in five short verses. The first one was "Fear not" because of what I the Lord have done for you. Now, God says to Israel, "Fear not" because of what I am doing for you. Both past and present experiences with the Lord give His children adequate reasons to have courage and confidence.

God promises to gather scattered Israelites from all over the globe. "Thy seed" means "your descendants." His promise echoes His promise in the early verses of Deuteronomy 30: "Wherever the LORD your God disperses you among the nations, and when you and your children return to the LORD your God and obey him with all your heart and with all your soul according to everything I command you today, then the LORD your God will restore your fortunes and have compassion on you and gather you again from all the nations where he scattered you. Even if you have been banished to the most distant land under the heavens, from there the LORD your God will gather you and bring you back. He will bring you to the land that belonged to your fathers" (NIV).

Many Christians think this promise is at work today, as Jews worldwide return to the land of Israel. Others are convinced that the promise was fulfilled when God moved the Persian king, Cyrus, to release the Jewish captives to return to their homeland and rebuild the Temple in Jerusalem.

**B. God's Creation, 7**

**7 Even every one that is called by my name: for I have created him for my glory, I have formed him; yea, I have made him.**

To be called by the Lord's name means to be recognized as His child. Sons wear the name of their father. God promises to bring back to the Promised Land all those who are His.

Then follows Isaiah's echo of 43:1, where God asserts that He created, formed, and made Israel. This is His basic explanation for the blessings and security He is promising to them.

**III. No Other Savior—43:11-12**

**11 I, even I, am the LORD; and beside me there is no saviour.**

**12 I have declared, and have saved, and I have shewed, when there was no strange god among you: therefore ye are my witnesses, saith the LORD, that I am God.**

"Savior" is a synonym for rescuer, healer, or deliverer. Although it is used in the Bible to denote the Lord's work in saving our souls eternally, far more often "savior" refers to physical healing or rescue. The name of Joshua, Israel's great leader during the years of the conquest, means savior. He was their national champion, their deliverer, in those perilous times. Jesus was so named, the angel explained, because He came to "save his people from their sins." However, the same word for saving was used more often in the Gospels to refer to the physical healings our Lord performed.

God's finest blessings belong to His people when they are devoted to Him alone, when they trust in His arm alone, when they acknowledge Him as their only Savior.

80Q8

165

## Evangelistic Emphasis

Do you understand the events in your life? I mean understand why they are happening to you at this moment? Do you find yourself reaching out to God in ways you never dreamed possible? If the events in your life seem inexplicable, I need to warn you about something.

C.S. Lewis once said that he felt sorry for atheists. He felt sorry for people who tried to live their lives without God because in his words, *"God is so resourceful, so unscrupulous in keeping his own."*

The Lord is unscrupulous when it comes to loving us and caring for us. Think about that. He is the shepherd who notices that when one lamb is lost, He will leave the 99 in the fold. He will leave them and search for the one lost lamb until that lamb is found. We would be guarding with all of our power the 99 remaining, but not the Lord! The Lord loves that one lost sheep so much, He will take the chance of leaving the herd to find the one lost lamb.

The Lord tells about a father who waits for his youngest son to come back from the foreign land and, when he son returns, the father has a party. The same father leaves the pouting older brother in the field.

Isaiah proclaims God as a savior. He is our only savior and He is unscrupulous when it comes to showing love for us.

## Memory Selection

### ✱☞

"When thou passest through the waters, I will be with thee; and through the rivers, they shall not overflow thee: when thou walkest through the fire, thou shalt not be burned; neither shall the flame kindle upon thee."          *Isaiah 43: 6*

Speaking of passing through the waters, here is a story:

While sport fishing off the Florida coast, a tourist capsized his boat. He could swim, but his fear of alligators kept him clinging to the overturned craft.

Spotting an old beachcomber on the shore, the tourist shouted, "Are there any gators around here?"

"Naw," the man hollered back. "They ain't been around for years!"

Feeling safe, the tourist started swimming leisurely toward the shore. About halfway there, he asked, "How'd you get rid of the gators?"

"We didn't do nothin'," the beachcomber said. "The sharks got 'em."

The truth of this text might send some of the modern television preachers screaming into the night. In this text from Isaiah, we are not promised uninterrupted prosperity or happiness. We are promised that we will arrive in heaven but some of us might have some bruises when we arrive.

Jesus calmed the storm for the disciples struggling in the boat, but the text says nothing about the disciples having dry feet. Isaiah gives us a true word about how life really is, and that is a word of hope. Rather than promise us a good life with no problems, the Lord promises that He will be with us and sustain us through the fire.

Don't you relate to the Isaiah text when you are having a bad day?

**166**

## Weekday Problems

Tricia was reaching for another Kleenex as she told her long saga to Pastor Carl. Tricia and her husband had grown up in the church. It was in Sunday school when they met, during their days in Junior High. They had their first kiss at church camp, and awhile later, announced their engagement at the student ministry on their college campus. Their children were being raised to go to church and to love singing as they served others. If you were keeping score of people who should be blessed by God, Tricia and her husband should have been near the top of the list.

Yet things were not going well for Tricia. Her husband, Mike, who was a salesman, was not making any money in the economic downturn, while their bills kept piling up. With their home mortgage facing foreclosure, they were unable to give an offering to the church. Life was spinning out of control and Tricia was reduced to tears.

She was trying to keep a positive outlook but she was wondering aloud in front of Pastor Carl if God could be trusted. She wondered why God was allowing all of these bad things to happen in her life. She wanted to know where God was.

Pastor Carl decided to share Isaiah 43:2 with Tricia and asked her how she felt this verse applied to her situation. How would you respond, if you were Tricia to the news that God does not get us out of every situation unscathed?

## Chuckle

As a young man, McKerry was an exceptional golfer. At the age of 26, however, he decided to become a preacher. He was assigned ttoa church that had a strict rule that their Pastor must not engage in sports, including golf. This was difficult for McKerry, but he agreed.

One Sunday morning, Pastor McKerry woke up and, decided he just had to play golf. So . . . he told the Associate Pastor that he was feeling sick and convinced him to give the sermon for him that day. As soon as the Associate Pastor left the room, Pastor McKerry headed out of town to a golf course about forty miles away.

Setting up on the first tee, he was alone. After all, it was Sunday morning and everyone else was in church! At about this time, Saint Peter leaned over to the Lord while looking down from the heavens and exclaimed, "You're not going to let him get away with this, are you?"

The Lord said, "No, I guess not." Just then, Pastor McKerry hit the ball and it shot straight towards the pin, dropping just short of it, rolled up and fell into the hole. It WAS A 420 YARD HOLE IN ONE! St. Peter was astonished. He looked at the Lord and asked, "Why did you let him do that? The Lord smiled and replied, "Who's he going to tell?"

# This Lesson in Your Life

Some years ago, on a hot summer day in South Florida, a little boy decided to go to the old swimming hole behind his house. In a hurry to dive into the cool water, he ran out the back door, leaving behind shoes, socks, and shirt as he went. He flew into the water, not realizing that as he swam toward the middle of the lake, an alligator was swimming toward the shore. The boy's father, working in the yard, saw the two get closer and closer together. In utter fear, he ran toward the water, yelling to his son as loudly as he could.

Hearing his dad's voice, the little boy became alarmed and made a U-turn to swim to his father. It was too late. Just as he reached his father, the alligator reached him. From the dock, the father grabbed his little boy by the arms just as the alligator snatched his legs. That began an incredible tug-of-war between the two. The alligator was much stronger than the father was, but the father was much too passionate to let go.

A farmer happened to drive by, heard screams, raced from his truck with his gun, took aim, and shot the alligator. Remarkably, after weeks in the hospital, the little boy survived. His legs were extremely scarred by the vicious attack. Even on his arms were the deep scratches where his father's fingernails dug into his flesh in an effort to hang on to the son he loved.

A newspaper reporter who interviewed the boy after the trauma asked if he would show him his scars. The boy lifted his pant legs. Then, with obvious pride, he said to the reporter, "But look at my arms. I have great scars on my arms, too. I have them because my dad wouldn't let go."

Isaiah pictures a time when the Hebrews are in captivity. All they know of normal living has been taken away from them. Because of their sinfulness, they have been carried into captivity. They are in troubled waters in a foreign land far from the Temple and all that reminded them of God's love and grace. They felt estranged and lonely in the environment of their captors' homeland.

They had a sense that they had been abandoned and that God was no longer on their side. However, as the book of Isaiah unfolds, we learn that this captivity was in the plan of God for His people. We will learn that God never left them and would never leave them and that even as they wondered about His love and care, He was raising up one named Cyrus who would allow the Hebrews to return to Palestine.

In your life, do you feel that you are being tested by fire or that you have to cross through the deep waters? It is part of our faith journey that times come that test the depth and the character of our faith. We certainly feel as though we are in "over our heads." Some times, we even come out of these spiritual times with cuts and scrapes on our soul.

What we discover is that those marks are really the places where Jesus was holding on to us and not letting us go.

## GETTING
## THE FACTS STRAIGHT

**1. Israel and Jacob are mentioned in the first verse of the 43ʳᵈ chapter. What is the significance of this reference?**

This verse makes it clear that God created and formed both the southern and the northern kingdoms of Israel. Both nations were God's people.

**2. What attitude are the people of God to have about their current circumstance?**

The people are not to be afraid of what is happening to them, because God has redeemed them.

**3. How are the redeemed of Israel described?**

The ones who have been redeemed have been called by name and God says they belong to Him.

**4. What is the promise to those who have been redeemed?**

When they pass through the waters and through the rivers, the waters will not overwhelm the redeemed.

**5. What other promise is made to the redeemed?**

Not only are they protected from the waters, they are also protected from the fire and the flame. They will not be burned or consumed.

**6. How does God describe Himself to the redeemed?**

God is the "Lord your God, the Holy One of Israel, your savior."

**7. What tender language does God use in describing His relationship with His people?**

God says, "you are precious in my eyes, and honored, and I love you."

**8. The encouragement to "fear not" because God is with the people, to whom else does the promise extend?**

God will gather "your offspring from the east and from the west God will gather the very people of Israel." So they should not fear.

**9. The Hebrews were in captivity. From where will God call them back home?**

All four points of a compass are mentioned that God will call His people from the north, south, east, and west.

**10. In the closing verses of the text for the lesson, what is the affirmation that God makes about himself?**

God is unique. There are no others before Him and only He is the savior of Israel. There is no other.

God will carry us through rough waters, but not with the glitzy Vegas-style amenities of a luxury cruise ship. Thalassophobia. *Thalassa* means "sea," and *phobos* means "fear," so Thalassophobia is "fear of the sea."

This is a legitimate phobia, when you think about it. The ocean can be a place of danger and even death. Take to the water, and you have to deal with waves, wind, tides, currents, rocky shorelines, and ever-changing weather conditions. You know what lies at the bottom of the ocean and twitches, don't you?

A nervous wreck.

When you venture out onto the ocean, you want to be surrounded by as large a ship as possible. Fortunately, Royal Caribbean cruise line has now launched an authentic sea monster. Called *Oasis of the Seas*, it is the largest, tallest, widest, heaviest, and costliest passenger ship ever built.

How big is it? According to *The Atlantic* magazine (June 2009), it dwarfs a Nimitz-class aircraft carrier, stands taller than a 20-story building and carries 8,000 people.

It is not a boat. It is a floating city.

*Oasis of the Seas* features 21 swimming pools, including a water park, a beach pool, and two wave pools. On-board actors and actresses offer Broadway-style productions in a playhouse that seats almost 1,400, while water ballerinas present shows in an outdoor Aqua Theater. In the middle of the ship is a green space called Central Park, which is half the size of a football field and full of tropical plants and 20-foot trees.

Walking in the park, passengers can easily forget that they are at sea.

To power this enormous vessel, six massive generators produce enough electricity to light up 105,000 homes. Snaking through the ship are 3,300 miles of electrical cables, enough to stretch across the United States. In addition, 158,000 gallons of paint were needed to cover the ship — sufficient to paint the George Washington Bridge three times.

Now if your thalassophobia kicks in while you are cruising on *Oasis of the Seas*, you can go inside and enjoy a restaurant, bar, theater, or casino. The interior space is "a celebration of excess," writes Rory Nugent; the ship is packed with "glitzy amenities and attractions of the sort usually associated with Las Vegas." Vacationers who want to take a ride on the wild side can even visit a wash-off-tattoo parlor and get themselves inked.

"When you pass through the waters, I will be with you," promises God in the book of Isaiah, "and through the rivers, they shall not overwhelm you" (43:2). This is a stirring and beautiful passage, but just what exactly is God saying here?

ഇരുള

170

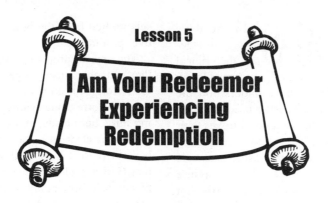

## Lesson 5

# I Am Your Redeemer
# Experiencing
# Redemption

## Isaiah 44:21-26

Remember these, O Jacob and Israel; for thou art my servant: I have formed thee; thou art my servant: O Israel, thou shalt not be forgotten of me.

22 I have blotted out, as a thick cloud, thy transgressions, and, as a cloud, thy sins: return unto me; for I have redeemed thee.

23 Sing, O ye heavens; for the LORD hath done it: shout, ye lower parts of the earth: break forth into singing, ye mountains, O forest, and every tree therein: for the LORD hath redeemed Jacob, and glorified himself in Israel.

24 Thus saith the LORD, thy redeemer, and he that formed thee from the womb, I am the LORD that maketh all things; that stretcheth forth the heavens alone; that spreadeth abroad the earth by myself;

25 That frustrateth the tokens of the liars, and maketh diviners mad; that turneth wise men backward, and maketh their knowledge foolish;

26 That confirmeth the word of his servant, and performeth the counsel of his messengers; that saith to Jerusalem, Thou shalt be inhabited; and to the cities of Judah, Ye shall be built, and I will raise up the decayed places thereof:

**Memory Verse**
Isaiah 44:22

**Background Scripture**
Isaiah 44

**Devotional Reading**
Psalm 106:40-48

171

In the days long before Jesus, the original readers of Isaiah 44 would not have understood the metaphors the apostles used to assure Christians that the Lord forgives their sins. We are blessed, for example, by the imagery of being washed and made clean. The apostle John can assure us that, "the blood of Jesus His Son continually cleanses us of every sin" (1 John 1:7, WET), and that assurance

sets us free from the burden of guilt over past failures.

The ancient prophet could not use that metaphor. Instead, he compared God's forgiveness of Israel's sins with the way storm clouds vanish or morning mists burn away, quickly leaving the sky as clear as if they had never been there. Isaiah assured his people that God had chosen to remove any hint of their former guilt, so they could draw near to the Lord without fearing any residual wrath or punishment for their past misbehavior. That same assurance is ours in Christ.

෨෭ෘ

## For a Lively Start

In the harder moments of our lives, what would any one of us give for a fresh start? When we have made terrible mistakes and burned bridges we now regret, what would it mean to us to have our reputations restored and our options opened once more?

Isaiah's poetic language wonderfully describes the joy his people should feel because God was redeeming them and giving them another chance. Jubilant music should ring in the highest heavens and in the lowest parts of the earth as all creation praises the Creator for His goodness in allowing Israel a new opportunity to do it right this time.

All of us need that kind of grace, don't we? Thank God, it is ours in Jesus.

| Teaching Outline | Daily Bible Readings |
|---|---|
| I.  God Made Us—44:21 | Mon. My Redeemer Lives! <br> *Job 19:23-27* |
| II.  God Blots Out Our Sins—44:22 | Tue.  Know That I Am with You <br> *Genesis 28:10-17* |
| III. A Reason to Sing—44:23 | Wed. Do Not Fear <br> *Isaiah 44:1-5* |
| IV. Proofs of God's Greatness—44:24-26 | Thu  God's Steadfast Love <br> *Psalm 106:40-48* |
| A. He Made Everything, 24 | Fri.  Redeemed to Be Heirs <br> *Galatians 4:1-7* |
| B. He Humbles Pretenders, 25 | Sat.  Assured of the Future <br> *Isaiah 44:6-8* |
| C. He Confirms Prophecies, 26 | Sun. Rejoice in Redemption <br> *Isaiah 44:21-26* |

# *Verse by Verse*

## Isaiah 44:21-26

### I. God Made Us—44:21

**21 Remember these, O Jacob and Israel; for thou art my servant: I have formed thee; thou art my servant: O Israel, thou shalt not be forgotten of me.**

In effect, God was making a deal with the Jewish nation in this verse. Although God's offer to His people is dead serious, its language has lightness in its tone. "If you'll remember, I'll remember," is the gist of the Lord's offer.

"Jacob and Israel" are names used interchangeably by the psalmists and the prophets to refer to the nation of the Jews. The reason God gives for them to pay attention to His instructions and promises is that they would not exist if He had not "formed" them. Because of God's redeeming power and love, they became a nation when He freed them from slavery and led them out of Egypt.

God assures Israel that He will not forget them. They belong to Him as do all of us who believe in Jesus. "You are not your own," the apostle Paul reminds us. "You were bought with a price" (1 Cor. 6:20-21, RSV). Instead of demeaning us, being owned by God gives us the assurance that He will always remember us and seek what is best for us.

### II. God Blots Out Our Sins—44:22

**22 I have blotted out, as a thick cloud, thy transgressions, and, as a cloud, thy sins: return unto me; for I have redeemed thee.**

Those who live in the semi-arid areas of the American Southwest may find this metaphor of a "blotted out" cloud more meaningful than those in areas where clouds last for weeks or even months at a time. In dryer climates like the Holy Land or west Texas, storm clouds may gather quickly and then vanish suddenly. One moment the sky may be dark, only to be clear and bright an hour later. Isaiah uses the idea of vanishing clouds to illustrate how God had "swept away" (RSV, TEV) or "wiped out" (NASB) the sins that had caused Him to punish Israel in an earlier time. After sending them away into captivity to pay for their wickedness, He will now draw them back to His side.

Telling Israel that God has "redeemed" them alludes to the imagery of slavery, wherein a slave often paid for his own freedom or, perhaps, some-

173

one paid the price to ransom him. God tells Israel He will set them free from bondage, just as He sets us free from the enslavement of our sins.

### III. A Reason to Sing—44:23

**23 Sing, O ye heavens; for the LORD hath done it: shout, ye lower parts of the earth: break forth into singing, ye mountains, O forest, and every tree therein: for the LORD hath redeemed Jacob, and glorified himself in Israel.**

In the reference here to "heavens," some see into the angelic realm where the seraphim give praise to the Almighty. It seems more likely, however, that Isaiah was expanding metaphors to identify natural elements as a source of praise to the Lord. If this is true, then the "heavens" would mean the upper altitudes of the Earth's atmosphere, and the prophet would be enlisting the highest and the lowest parts of the created world to join in praising the Creator.

Calling on the trees and animals and oceans and other parts of God's creation to praise Him, is a common refrain of the prophets and psalmists. A good example of this is Psalm 96:11-12: "Let the heavens rejoice, let the earth be glad; let the sea resound, and all that is in it; let the fields be jubilant, and everything in them. Then all the trees of the forest will sing for joy" (NIV).

The reason Isaiah uses for this cosmic outpouring of praise, is that the Lord has "redeemed Israel." He has reached out to His people and reaffirmed to them that they indeed are His.

Does the happiness of this scene resemble our own celebrations of the Lord's goodness and grace? Does the music of our worship resound with the joy and exuberance of this scene? If our hymns are faint and our praise sounds anemic, what does this say about our hearts? What does it say about our gratitude to God for His surpassing grace?

### IV. Proofs of God's Greatness—44:24-26

#### A. He Made Everything, 24

**24 Thus saith the LORD, thy redeemer, and he that formed thee from the womb, I am the LORD that maketh all things; that stretcheth forth the heavens alone; that spreadeth abroad the earth by myself;**

As evidence of His ability to redeem and bless His people in any way He sees fit, the Lord shows His impressive credentials as an unequaled Creator. He puts us together within our mother's womb. Nothing exists that He has not made, from planets to atoms. He had no need for help when He decided to unfurl the heavens with all their majesty and complexity. Solar systems were a snap for Him; planets and galaxies were a breeze. Alone, the Creator "spread out" the earth with all its grandeur and immensity.

This wonderful God, for Whom creation was a simple task that required no exertion or assistance, now offers His aid to His people. Restoring Israel was an easy assignment for Him. Restoring us, when we fall, would present no challenge to Him.

#### B. He Humbles Pretenders, 25

**25 That frustrateth the tokens**

of the liars, and maketh diviners mad; that turneth wise men backward, and maketh their knowledge foolish;

Another proof of God's capability, Isaiah tells us, lies in His ability to embarrass those who make claims to special knowledge or insight. The TEV simplifies this verse for us: "I make fools of fortunetellers and frustrate the predictions of astrologers. The words of the wise I refute and show that their wisdom is foolishness." The variations in translations show that our Bible translators struggle a bit here to know exactly what occult skills were claimed by the group the KJV calls "the liars," but that translation reflects the universal truth that shamans and witch doctors of every sort have always relied on trickery and deception to intimidate and befuddle their clients. One sign of God's greatness is how easily He exposes them as charlatans.

"Diviners" could include fortunetellers, astrologers, palm readers—all sorts of mentalists—who claim to be able to predict the future or to know facts hidden from most mortals. God makes them look like fools ("mad" in the sense of mindless) and thereby exhibits His own greatness.

The apostle Paul echoes the last part of vs. 25 in 1 Corinthians 1. He begins by quoting Isaiah 29:13 and then expands on this whole idea: "I will destroy the wisdom of the wise, and the discernment of the discerning I will thwart.' Where is the one who is wise? Where is the scribe? Where is the debater of this age? Has not God made foolish the wisdom of the world? . . . For God's foolishness is wiser than human wisdom" (vss. 19-20, 25, NRSV).

**C. He Confirms Prophecies, 26**

**26 That confirmeth the word of his servant, and performeth the counsel of his messengers; that saith to Jerusalem, Thou shalt be inhabited; and to the cities of Judah, Ye shall be built, and I will raise up the decayed places thereof:**

God further confirms His greatness by making sure that His prophets actually predict what happens. In particular, when Isaiah's prophecies that Jerusalem and Judah will again be home for the Jewish people come true, all of Israel will recall the prophet's words and praise God. Even more impressive will be the fact that, 200 years before it happened, Isaiah could foretell by name which Persian king (Cyrus) would liberate the Jews. How could they doubt that he was inspired by an all-seeing God? If we believe God's word, the same fulfilled prophecy should convince us, too, of His awesome power to bless us.

෨෮ඏ

175

## Evangelistic Emphasis

Here is a good definition: "Insanity is doing the same thing over and over again and expecting different results."

What is your favorite holiday in the year? Many of us would say, "Thanksgiving" because we concentrate more on our family, friends, and faith then we do at other times of the year.

Your children might say "Christmas" because of the presents they receive from relatives and Santa. They might also like "Halloween" because of the candy. Others pick the Fourth of July, an anniversary, or a birthday.

Personally, New Years Day is one of my favorite times. It is undeniable proof that on that on this day—everything changes. It is the first day of a brand new year. We are forced to change. It is the best time of the year to commit to being a better person. Let us stop the insanity and grow. Let us put on a new attitude, behavior, and let us keep it going throughout this month and the rest of this year.

It only takes twenty-one days to create a new habit and change a life. As 2011 begins, this passage from Isaiah will challenge us to have hope—not in false idols but in our God. Have you made a good beginning to this New Year that God has given you?

What changes would God have you make this year?

## Memory Selection

ℰᎧᏯ

**"I have blotted out, as a thick cloud, thy transgressions, and, as a cloud, thy sins: return unto me; for I have redeemed thee."** *Isaiah 44:22*

One cold day at the police court, they brought a trembling old man before Fiorello La Guardia, charged with stealing a loaf of bread. His family, he said, was starving.

"I've got to punish you," declared La Guardia. "The law makes no exception. I can do nothing but sentence you to a fine of $10 dollars." La Guardia reached into his pocket as he added, "Well, here's the $10 dollars to pay your fine. And now I remit the fine." He tossed a $10 dollar bill into his hat.

"Furthermore," he declared, "I'm going to fine everybody in this courtroom 50 cents for living in a town where a man has to steal bread in order to eat. Mr. Bailiff, collect the fines and give them to this defendant!"

The hat was passed, and a shocked old man left the courtroom with a stake of $47.50.

The promise of Isaiah is that our sins have been forgiven. Not only has God forgiven our sins, He has forgotten them. That is a wonderful promise of scripture. If God has removed our sins from his memory, who are we that we keep reminding Him of those things He has forgotten.

Like the surprised man leaving Mayor La Guardia's courtroom, we should rejoice in what Jesus has done for us in removing our sins.

So, which sins are you needlessly hanging on to and why?

## Weekday Problems

Billy was baffled at the behavior of his bride. They began married life happily enough. Recently Sheila was exhibiting some uncharacteristically poor decision making traits. She was shopping all the time. Running up the credit card bills faster than Billy could keep them paid. She was spending several evenings a week out with the "girls." She was not taking care of her children, those tasks falling to Billy.

He was a patient and loving man. He found himself at the end of his rope in his pastor's office one day. He confessed that he was angry with her because of how she was behaving. He had confronted her. He had pleaded with her. He had taken the credit cards away from her and she got more. He faced a decision whether his children were better off living in an environment that was hostile, or whether they would be better off raised

 by him alone. He told his pastor he was ready to decide that very moment. His hesitation was in not knowing what decision would be best for his children.

His pastor listened and then talked to Billy about the necessity of forgiving Sheila and seeking to have a renewal of their relationship. Billy was very frustrated because he seemed to be forgiving her for the same things over again.

If you were Billy's pastor what advice would you give?

How does forgiveness help keep a marriage together?

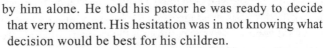

# More Puns for Educated Minds

1. A grenade thrown into a kitchen in France would result in Linoleum Blownapart.

2. Two silk worms had a race. They ended up in a tie.

3. A hole has been found in the nudist camp wall. The police are looking into it.

4. Atheism is a non-prophet organization.

5. Two hats were hanging on a hat rack in the hallway. One hat said to the other: "You stay here; I'll go on a head."

6. I wondered why the baseball kept getting bigger. Then it hit me.

# This Lesson in Your Life

God proclaimed through Isaiah that He has announced from of old, and what was spoken has happened. God's spoken word is powerful. His power is much more than the false idols described as being fashioned by man. God speaks, He communicates. Idols cannot communicate.

In a former day, God spoke through his prophets. You can read about the antics of the prophets in the Old Testament. They were quite a group of individuals. Some were fiery preachers while others were reluctant evangelists. They lived for God and spoke for God in a culture that had little care for God. Their message was not warmly received and some lost their lives for preaching the judgment of God. All the prophets pointed to a day when Messiah would come and would speak for God.

Jesus came and spoke for God. His message was not well received by His own people. He was God and lived out God's love in a culture that cared little for God. He showed God to be a God of love and grace. Jesus was beaten and crucified for His message of God's love for all.

God continues to speak through the ministry of the Holy Spirit. God gives us counsel and help with our daily living. The Spirit reminds us that we are to live Godly lives in the midst of a culture that cares little for God. Do you sense a pattern here? As God continues to speak through the Spirit, we have assurance that this revelation will not contradict the words of Jesus.

If God continues to speak, how are we doing as listeners?

We rename our sins and dress them up, but we are still sinners in need of a Savior. God has been reaching down to us and offering us a message of hope. The message has not changed, but some of the language has. Revelatory theology says that God is still speaking to His people. God desires a faith response from His people.

The Hebrews were in captivity because they had not listened to the word that God had proclaimed. He gave the law and they had not listened. Their failure to listen had landed them in the hands of a foreign power. As God prepared them for a return to Palestine, He gave Isaiah the image of the artisans who fashioned idols out of wood and iron. These idols, fashioned by man, did not have the power to speak. They could give no law. They could give no guidance. They could speak no words of forgiveness. They could do nothing for the people of Israel.

The words of Isaiah 44 are words of God's forgiveness, of His willingness to put the sins of the Hebrews away and allow the possibility of a new relationship.

We are called to communicate, within our world, the power of God's forgiveness and the offer of His grace through our Lord Jesus Christ. God's word in Jesus is still powerful and redemptive.

**GETTING
THE FACTS STRAIGHT**

**1. Who is the servant of the Lord?**
Jacob is called the servant of the Lord and Israel the one whom God has chosen.

**2. Do you think that the reference to Jacob and Israel is to a nation or to a person?**
Many scholars believe that this is one of the servant passages of Isaiah and refers to an individual. Many of the same scholars identify the servant of Isaiah as Jesus.

**3. How long has God had a relationship with His servant?**
God has known His servant since "you were formed in the womb."

**4. God makes a promise to His servant. What is that promise?**
God will pour out water on the thirsty land and streams on the dry ground.

**5. God makes a promise to His people Israel. What is the promise made to the people?**
God will pour out His spirit upon their descendants and His blessings upon their offspring.

**6. The promise of restoration of the people is given using what image?**
The people of God will "spring up like grass amid waters and like willows by flowing streams."

**7. How was the uniqueness of God described?**
God is described as "the first and the last and besides me there is no god."

**8. What word of hope was given to the Israelites as they faced the days ahead?**
The Israelites were told "fear not, nor be afraid because what the Lord has said of old has happened."

**9. What three kinds of idol makers are described by Isaiah?**
Isaiah describes idol makers who make idols from nothing, from iron, and from wood.

**10. What is the folly of idols made by human hands?**
Idols made by human hands are not god and have no power although they were trusted by many.

Computer technicians who talk to the public about computer problems should get extra credits of grace in Heaven with God.

One technician was on the phone fifteen minutes with a woman working on a "not so complex computer problem." The woman on the other end of the phone claimed that she was quite familiar with the workings of a computer.

Tech support: "Now click, OK."

Customer: "Click, OK?"

"Yes, that is correct, click OK"

"Click, OK?

"Yes ma'am that is correct, click OK."

*Long pause*

Customer: "I clicked cancel."

Tech support: "You were supposed to click OK."

Customer: "I thought you said click CANCEL."

Tech support: "No ma'am I said click OK. Now we have to start all over again."

So they go through the same routine and get all the way to the last step in the process. This took another fifteen minutes to accomplish.

Tech Support: "Are you ready to click OK?"

Customer: "Yes."

Tech Support: "Great, click OK."

*Long pause.*

Customer; "I clicked CANCEL."

And the tech support man said, "And people wonder why my mouse pad has a bright red target on it with the words, BANG HEAD HERE.

You know that God must share similar frustration with our inability to follow His clearly spoken words of direction. In the Garden of Eden, it was just God and that sweet couple. His instructions could not have been clearer. "Don't eat of the fruit of that tree." We all know what Adam and Eve did. Human obedience to divine communication has not been great. We repeat the mistakes of the past. We ignore God at the same place.

Communication is an art. Jesus was God's masterpiece of communication. God showed the world His true nature in the life and ministry of His Son. He clearly communicated His love toward us. Looking at the world, one has the impression that we have not done a good job of listening to God.

God has communicated clearly in His Son Jesus. We have a record of that communication in the Bible. God still speaks through His Spirit.

God is the beginning and the end. His creative word fills all the blanks. Are we listening to all the ways that God is speaking to us?

෨ඦ

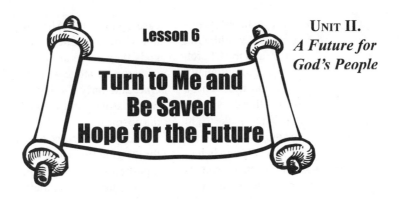

**Lesson 6**

# Turn to Me and Be Saved
## Hope for the Future

**Isaiah 45:18-24a**

For thus saith the LORD that created the heavens; God himself that formed the earth and made it; he hath established it, he created it not in vain, he formed it to be inhabited: I am the LORD; and there is none else.

19 I have not spoken in secret, in a dark place of the earth: I said not unto the seed of Jacob, Seek ye me in vain: I the LORD speak righteousness, I declare things that are right.

20 Assemble yourselves and come; draw near together, ye that are escaped of the nations: they have no knowledge that set up the wood of their graven image, and pray unto a god that cannot save.

21 Tell ye, and bring them near; yea, let them take counsel together: who hath declared this from ancient time? who hath told it from that time? have not I the LORD? and there is no God else beside me; a just God and a Saviour; there is none beside me.

22 Look unto me, and be ye saved, all the ends of the earth: for I am God, and there is none else.

23 I have sworn by myself, the word is gone out of my mouth in righteousness, and shall not return, That unto me every knee shall bow, every tongue shall swear.

24 Surely, shall one say, in the LORD have I righteousness and strength:

Jan. 9

---

**Memory Verse**
Isaiah 45:22

**Background Scripture**
Isaiah 45

**Devotional Reading**
Exodus 15:11-18

---

181

In our skeptical world, God and the Church are continually on trial. Those without faith dismiss those who believe in a Creator. They make light of all who dare to suggest that Intelligence brought our universe into being.

In Isaiah 45, the prophet reverses this picture and puts the unbelievers on trial. In vss. 20-21, he dares the doubters and pagans to present their case against the Almighty. They do not stand a chance, of course. The gods they serve are mindless chunks of wood or stone—no match for the One and only God who made that wood, stone, and everything else in the cosmos.

Today's skeptics are little match for the One true God. Long after their arguments have crumbled and they are returned to dust, their Creator will continue to run the world He brought into being. Then it will be clear that those of us who serve Him were on the right side.

ഇൗരു

## For a Lively Start

Although these words are addressed originally to the Jews who would be captives in Babylon and Persia, what God intended was for Isaiah's stirring message to be heard and treasured by people in "all ends of the earth" (v. 22). The God of Heaven never was, and never will be, just the God of the Jews. His eternal agenda has been the salvation of all people in all nations.

"Go into all the world and preach the gospel to every creature," Jesus instructs His Church (Mark 16:15). The universal nature of God's appeal makes His Kingdom an expansive undertaking. We deceive ourselves if we reduce His love and grace to one group of believers sequestered in a limited locale. God's focus is worldwide.

| Teaching Outline | Daily Bible Readings |
|---|---|
| I. The Greatness of Our God—45:18-19 | Mon. The People God Redeemed *Exodus 15:11-18* |
| A. Creator of the Earth, 18 | Tue. Two Different Opinions *1 Kings 18:17-29* |
| B. Speaker of Truth, 19 | Wed. Answer Me, O Lord *1 Kings 18:30-38* |
| II. A Summons to Court—45:20-21 | Thu The Prayer of Faith *James 5:13-18* |
| A. The Gods of the Nations, 20 | Fri. Building God a House *2 Chronicles 36:15-23* |
| B. The Only True God, 21 | Sat. The Lord Creates Weal and Woe *Isaiah 45:1-8* |
| III. The God of All—45:22-24a | Sun. A Righteous God and Savior *Isaiah 45:18-24a* |
| A. Salvation for All, 22 | |
| B. Honored by All, 23-24a | |

# Verse by Verse

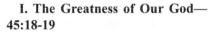

Isaiah 45:18-24a

## I. The Greatness of Our God—45:18-19

### A. Creator of the Earth, 18

**18 For thus saith the Lord that created the heavens; God himself that formed the earth and made it; he hath established it, he created it not in vain, he formed it to be inhabited: I am the Lord; and there is none else.**

In this verse, Isaiah starts to report a proclamation by the Lord, but the quotation is interrupted by the prophet's rather lengthy description of the God Who is about to speak. By either punctuation or formatting, newer versions make it a bit clearer to us that the first nine words in the verse introduce God's statement in the last eight words. "Thus saith the Lord . . .I am the Lord."

Even the descriptive phrases are interrupted with passing thoughts. The result is a rather complex, possibly confusing verse. NRSV's use of parentheses helps to clarify it: "For thus says the Lord, who created the heavens (he is God!), who formed the earth and made it (he established it; he did not create it a chaos, he formed it to be inhabited!): I am the Lord, and there is no other."

Isaiah tells of the power of God to create the heavens and the earth to establish His right to address Israel in the following verses. The word that Isaiah used to describe how the Lord created the world gives all translators some trouble. KJV tells us the creation was "not in vain." NKJV echoes this, but RSV tells us the creation of earth was "not in chaos"—quite different in meaning. Even more varied is the NASB's reading, "not a waste place," a word choice mimicked by the TEV, which tells us God did not make the world "a desolate waste." Obviously, the best translators are not quite sure what the meaning of this Hebrew word is. Even though the choice of wording in this phrase is uncertain, most of the translating committees managed to preserve the link between vs. 18 and vs. 19, where the same word is used in both verses. Vs. 19 says God did not intend for His people to see Him "in vain," "in chaos," "in a waste place," or in whatever sort of place the same word describes the newly created world in vs. 18. It does not seem likely that this repetition of the same unusual word was accidental. Isaiah did this to connect Israel's search for the activities of God as Creator.

### B. Speaker of Truth, 19

**19 I have not spoken in secret, in a dark place of the earth: I said not**

**unto the seed of Jacob, Seek ye me in vain: I the LORD speak righteousness, I declare things that are right.**

Some scholars think the Lord's words here may be a deliberate comparison of Himself to pagan gods, such as the Delphi, whose oracle came from the depths of a dark cave. God, on the other hand, speaks openly and directly to His people.

Others suggest that God's claim here in vss. 18-19 is the same as His declaration in Deuteronomy 30:11: "This commandment which I command thee this day, it is not hidden from thee, neither is it far off." If this is so, then the NLT conveys the Lord's basic message: "I publicly proclaim bold promises. I do not whisper obscurities in some dark corner. I would not have told the people of Israel to seek me if I could not be found. I, the Lord, speak only what is true and declare only what is right."

## II. A Summons to Court—4 5:20-21

### A. The Gods of the Nations, 20

**20 Assemble yourselves and come; draw near together, ye that are escaped of the nations: they have no knowledge that set up the wood of their graven image, and pray unto a god that cannot save.**

What God is saying here about those who set up and worship gods of wood is plain, but just who the Lord is addressing with His satirical call to stand trial we cannot be sure. "Ye that are escaped of the nations" means that they are refugees, survivors, fugitives, or castoffs, but their precise identity is not clear. Is God

confronting Gentiles who once lived among idolaters but now are living among people who know the Lord? That is a possibility. Others think He may be talking to former Jewish captives who now are back in the Holy Land after a hard sojourn in a land of Captivity. That reading makes sense. Whether the object of vs. 20 was held prisoner by "the nations" or was a former member of them we do not know. In either case, the basic truth remains the same. The idols the refugees observed were senseless, powerless, and ridiculous compared to the Almighty.

### B. The Only True God, 21

**21 Tell ye, and bring them near; yea, let them take counsel together: who hath declared this from ancient time? who hath told it from that time? have not I the LORD? and there is no God else beside me; a just God and a Saviour; there is none beside me.**

Those assembled in "court" by the Lord have been brought there to hear the indisputable ruling that God is the only true God. He assures the "witnesses" that He is a "just" or "righteous" God, one who rescues His people when they are in distress. No other deity is like Him. In fact, no other deity exists.

### III. The God of All—45:22-24a

### A. Salvation for All, 22

**22 Look unto me, and be ye saved, all the ends of the earth: for I am God, and there is none else.**

The target of this verse may suggest the proper answer to the question of who just was invited to court. "All

184

ends of the earth" would include all the non-Jews. Here is the God of Israel inviting all non-Israelis to come and experience His salvation.

In this invitation, we hear an early announcement of the Lord's intention to include every man and woman on Earth in the salvation that is coming through Jesus. "Go teach all nations," Jesus told His men. With no restrictions, He commanded them to baptize people of every race and every place. In these verses, Isaiah tips us off to the universal nature of God's plans to bless all of us in Jesus.

**B. Honored by All, 23-24a**

**23 I have sworn by myself, the word is gone out of my mouth in righteousness, and shall not return, That unto me every knee shall bow, every tongue shall swear.**

**24 Surely, shall one say, in the LORD have I righteousness and strength:**

Before Jesus warned us not to, men swore by God. Nevertheless, as the writer of Hebrews wryly observes, God could not find anyone greater than Himself on whom He could make an oath. With this rather extreme language ("I have sworn by myself"), the Lord assures all who hear Him that the words He speaks here—the prediction He makes—will come true without doubt. He is predicting that the time will come when not just the Hebrew nation, but also every human being will bow down before Him and swear allegiance to Him as their God.

Christians can hear echoes of this verse in the writings of the apostle Paul. Most clearly, we hear this verse borrowed by Paul in Philippians 2:10-11. Paul tells us that God has exalted Jesus, "so that at the name of Jesus every knee should bend, in heaven and on earth and under the earth, and every tongue should confess that Jesus Christ is Lord, to the glory of God the Father" (NRSV).

In Romans 14:10-11, as he warns his readers to avoid judging one another, Paul gives us this verse from Isaiah 45: "We shall all stand before the judgment seat of Christ For it is written, As I live, saith the Lord, every knee shall bow to me, and every tongue shall confess to God."

We fulfill Isaiah's prediction today when we look to the one true God for our salvation and strength.

ℰℭ

185

## Evangelistic Emphasis

This lesson has an important message about the exclusive source of salvation. The prophet says in NIV, "Turn to me, and be saved . . . for I am God, and there is none else."

We meet our many needs in life in multiple ways. We might seek one source of medical care, another for food, another for relaxation, and still another to improve physical fitness. There are many sources of bread and entertainment; yet, there is one place we may find salvation. We can turn to other sources for other needs, but the only source of salvation is God.

This does not mean that there is a limited offer of salvation. It simply specifies the place where we can seek and find it. The righteous and the unrighteous may find it, but only in God. The saint and the sinner may find it, but only in God. It is not limited to those who are pious, religious, or morally pure. For it is freely available to all, but it is from a single source.

The good news here is that salvation is freely available to you. The fact is that it is only available from God. If you wish to give the greatest of gifts to a friend, loved one, or even a critic or enemy, you have an unlimited supply, and may give freely. If your friend wishes to seek salvation from a source, other than from God, he will know the depths of disappointment.

The book of Isaiah gives a magnificent picture of God freely giving salvation to His children. Yet it also warns that God's salvation is exclusively from God and not from any other source.

## Memory Selection

ℰᏯᏒ

"Turn to me and be saved, all the ends of the earth: for I am God, and there is none other." *Isaiah 45:22*

This verse teaches us that people do not earn salvation but that it is a gift from God.

Even though we do not earn it, we must receive it. God does not force the gift of an eternal relationship with Him on any man. It is freely given, but we must also freely receive it. No one is a Christian because someone forces him to be one. Those who are Christians have chosen to be so. They have chosen to turn the other cheek, go the second mile, and love their enemies. In short, they have determined to be as much like Jesus as they can. They are volunteers on a Christian journey. No one is an unwilling recruit. This is not a restricted invitation

Does that mean that nothing is expected of a Christian? Not at all. Christians expect to love, serve, and give, as did their Master. Christians grow toward that kind of a person as Christ. This effort and growth is not an attempt to earn anything. It is an attempt to honor and show gratitude to the One who died for him.

Not only does God offer His gifts, but we must also receive them thankfully. We must always remember that God freely offers, but it is up to us to turn to the Lord for salvation.

## Weekday Problems

In the world, there is a struggle for Christian faith. There are many contradictions and uncontrollable confusion. Rivals speak with different voices. First one and then another disagree on doctrine and practice. Churches do not live together in peace and goodwill, but engage in backbiting and jealousies.

I remember one story about a church engaged in a power struggle. There was hatefulness and ugliness. At last, the church split into two groups and built churches across the road from each other. Instead of preaching good news to the sinner, they spoke bitterness to those who should be brothers.

This passage teaches that we find hope for the Christian church in its being truthful, merciful, and forgiving. We do not find hope for the Christian future in winning battles, prevailing in debate, or castigating of one's brother.

Rather we find Christian hope in turning the other cheek, going the second mile, and forgiving one's enemies. It is participating in a society in which the lion lies down with the lamb and every competitor lives together in peace. In this way, we can realize Bible policy by way of letting there be peace on earth and good will among men.

Our task, as teachers is not to kindle enmities, seek victory in religious argumentation, or prove oneself superior to others. It is rather to seek peace and offer forgiveness. When we do so, we will be like the Galilean who came to serve—to give His life as a ransom for others.

---

# It's Elemental, Dear Watson

Recent hurricanes and climate changes have led to the discovery of the heaviest chemical element yet known to science.

The new element, Governmentium (Gv), has one neutron, 25 assistant neutrons, 88 deputy neutrons, and 198 assistant deputy neutrons, giving it an atomic mass of 312.

These 312 particles are held together by forces called morons, which are surrounded by vast quantities of lepton-like particles called peons. Governmentium can be detected, because it impedes every reaction it comes into contact with. A minute amount of Governmentium can cause a reaction (that would normally take less than a second) to be delayed from four days to fourteen years.

Governmentium has a normal half-life of two to six years; it does not decay, but instead undergoes a reorganization in which some of the assistant neutrons and deputy neutrons exchange places.

# This Lesson in Your Life

"And the world was without form, and void, and darkness was upon the face of the deep." Ge 1:2

From a world that was waste and void, God created order and beauty. The Bible repeatedly speaks of the order that God put into a world that was formerly chaotic. Since that time, the world has consistently sought the order that God put into it in the beginning.

We have sought order in the form of peace, order in the creation of beauty, order of the stimulus of the intellect, and order in the development of health. We have sought order in the just distribution of food and shelter.

In our own lives, we have sought the harmony of eliminating incongruity and conflict. We seek instead to find beauty, peace, and health. This results in consistency, predictability, and hope. It does not leave us floundering in confusion and chaos. In one sense, we are trying to restore in heaven what was forfeited in Eden.

On a more personal scale, we search for the order that we yearn to live in a predictable and consistent manner. We are not comfortable when we live in doubt and insecurity. That does not mean, of course, that there is a blueprint of our lives. In all lives, there are times of uncertainty. We do not know when sickness and death will come. Yet we do know that we are in the hands of a loving God who will keep us secure both in this world and in the world to come. This relationship with God guarantees our peace and happiness with Him.

While there is an ultimate disorder, heaven is the ultimate harmony. Hell is the ultimate chaos and heaven the ultimate peace and harmony. This makes it easy to understand that what was lost in Eden is restored in heaven. When Cain killed Abel, it was a time of disorder.

When God restored a time when there were no fears, He returned order.

ଚ୨ଙ୍କ

**GETTING THE FACTS STRAIGHT**

**1. What does Isaiah say about the exclusive sovereignty of God?**

He has formed the earth and formed it to be inhabited. There is none other than He.

**2. What does God say about the manner in which He has spoken to Israel?**

That He has not spoken in secret and darkness but has declared righteousness openly.

**3. What is the result of praying to the wood of a graven image?**

It is praying to a God who cannot save.

**4. For those who have rejected God, what alternative is there?**

There is none.

**5. Where should we look for salvation?**

To God for there is none else.

**6. Can we depend on God's promise?**

He has sworn by Himself and His word shall not return.

**7. How will God's word be acknowledged?**

"Every knee shall bow, every tongue shall swear." (Is. 45:23)

**8. What will be the reaction of all who are incensed against God?**

They will be ashamed.

**9. While the wicked shall be ashamed, what shall be the reaction of the righteous?**

They will glory in their salvation.

**10. What should Bible teachers teach their students about God?**

That He is exclusive and all-powerful.

In Mark 8:31-38, Jesus was trying to prepare the disciples for the fact that he was going to have to go through a hard time and they did not want to hear it. We are like that. Even if we are having a hard time now we want to believe that things are going to get better. We want to believe that good times are the norm and bad experiences are the exception. We may have had a difficult time all of our lives, but we may still believe that we are about to break through to a time of happiness and success.

We do not like to be told, "Things are tough, and they are going to get tougher." Nevertheless, this is sometimes true. This is what Jesus told his disciples. Peter surely did not like it. Jesus, more surely, knew it was going to happen whether Peter liked it or not.

The Lord further warned that it was going to happen, not only in His life, but in the lives of the disciples as well. Our purpose in this lesson is to help our class members deal with the bad news that inevitably comes into our lives.

Our inclination is to want to reject our troubles, as Peter wanted to reject the painful message that Jesus was giving him. However, to do so is to be unrealistic in a way that leaves us unprepared to deal with the pain that will certainly come. We cannot respond to pain with the cliché, "All God's chillun's got troubles." Not all people have the same problems. Some clearly have more than others and some have larger problems than others do. We cannot discount the seriousness of another's pain by saying, "Everybody's got problems. Live with it."

However, it is important to realize that everyone has problems. Realizing this helps us to avoid the feeling of being discriminated against when bad news arrives. If we feel that our problems are a part of what befalls humanity, we do not feel alone in our distress. We can then deal with the anguish in a simpler and a more healthy way. Our struggles will be easier with a sense of community, rather than a feeling of isolation. This will help us avoid the feeling that we are treated unfairly.

# Lesson 7

## Reassurance for God's People Putting the Past Aside

## Isaiah 48:14-19, 21-22

All ye, assemble yourselves, and hear; which among them hath declared these things? The LORD hath loved him: he will do his pleasure on Babylon, and his arm shall be on the Chaldeans.

15 I, even I, have spoken; yea, I have called him: I have brought him, and he shall make his way prosperous.

16 Come ye near unto me, hear ye this; I have not spoken in secret from the beginning; from the time that it was, there am I: and now the Lord GOD, and his Spirit, hath sent me.

17 Thus saith the LORD, thy Redeemer, the Holy One of Israel; I am the LORD thy God which teacheth thee to profit, which leadeth thee by the way that thou shouldest go.

18 O that thou hadst hearkened to my commandments! then had thy peace been as a river, and thy righteousness as the waves of the sea:

19 Thy seed also had been as the sand, and the offspring of thy bowels like the gravel thereof; his name should not have been cut off nor destroyed from before me.

21 And they thirsted not when he led them through the deserts: he caused the waters to flow out of the rock for them: he clave the rock also, and the waters gushed out.

22 There is no peace, saith the LORD, unto the wicked.

Jan. 16

---

**Memory Verse**
Isaiah 48:20

**Background Scripture**
Isaiah 48

**Devotional Reading**
1 Kings 8:33-40

---

# focus

Do you know some people who seem to be born with a special talent for doing the wrong thing? They talk when they should be listening. They lose their temper when they need to stay cool. They spend when they should be saving, play when they should be laboring, and tell lies when the truth would serve them better. Some people have the gift of foul-

## For a Lively Start

ⰔⰒⰓ

When Christians gather to worship, they dwell on the saving acts of God at the Cross-and the Resurrection. When the Jews bowed before the Lord, their hope and trust were rooted in the saving acts of God during the time of the Exodus. God's mighty deeds in the past (as in 48:21) give His people

ing up. For such people, "there is no peace."

If we listen to the Lord, however, He promises to help us avoid such life-ruining foolishness. "I'll show you what works best," He promises in 48:17. "I will show you the way that you should go."

However, God will not force us to take the right road. He never makes us choose the wise and moral path. He shows us what is right and then lets us decide which way to go. Blessed is the person who walks in the counsel of the Lord.

ⰔⰒⰓ

reason to expect His rich blessings in the future.

Can you, with your family, or your congregation, recall times in your past when God came through for you? Rehearsing these moments of grace with your children, and with their children, should help you and your loved ones trust in His goodness in days to come.

| Teaching Outline | Daily Bible Readings |
|---|---|
| I. A Wise God Versus Dumb Idols—48:14a | Mon. God Hears Confession *1 Kings 8:33-40* |
| II. God's Man, Cyrus—48:14b-15 | Tue. God's Chosen Instrument *Acts 9:3-6, 10-18* |
| III. God's Message to His People—48:16-19 | Wed. God Will Deliver *Jeremiah 15:19-21* |
| A. A Call to Listen, 16 | Thu God Spoke Long Ago *Isaiah 48:1-5* |
| B. Identifying the Lord, 17 | Fri. God Discloses New Things *Isaiah 48:6-8* |
| C. The Fruits of Obeying Him, 18-19 | Sat. God, the First and the Last *Isaiah 48:9-13* |
| IV. Past Proof of God's Goodness—48:21 | Sun. God Leads the Way *Isaiah 48:14-19, 21-22* |
| V. God's Warning to the Wicked—48:22 | |

# Verse by Verse

## Isaiah 48:14-19, 21-22

### I. A Wise God Versus Dumb Idols—48:14a

**14a All ye, assemble yourselves, and hear; which among them hath declared these things?**

This verse picks up in the middle of Isaiah's attack against the worthless idols some Israelites have chosen to worship—pieces of rock or wood fashioned to resemble insignificant replica. Whereas the Lord God instructs His people with wisdom and foretells their future with accuracy, Isaiah points out, that none of those senseless idols ever imparted a similar message.

That comparison alone should have been enough to convince God's people to replace fabricated gods. We should realize how little our own idols (sex, money, fun, vocational success) have to offer, and how undependable they are compared to the eternal God. He alone can save us.

### II. God's Man, Cyrus—48:14b-15

**14b The LORD hath loved him: he will do his pleasure on Babylon, and his arm shall be on the Chaldeans.**

**15 I, even I, have spoken; yea, I have called him: I have brought him, and he shall make his way prosperous.**

As in the first half of vs. 14, the meaning of this last half depends on the preceding verses. "Him" refers to the Persian king Cyrus. God empowered this king to defeat the mighty Babylonian empire, who thought they were invincible. Isaiah accurately predicted that Cyrus would "do his pleasure in Babylon." Whose pleasure? We may ask. In the phrase that follows, whose "arm" is going to be "on the Chaldeans"?

"His" in these phrases can refer either to God or to His man Cyrus. The verse makes good sense with either antecedent, so many of the standard Bible translations choose to preserve this ambiguity, allowing us to read it either way. On the other hand, the NKJV uses: let it be God's pleasure and God's arm; it shows us this choice by capitalizing "His" in both instances. The TEV re-words the verse to reflect this same option.

Vs. 15 casts some question on this decision, though, for all the third-person pronouns in this verse clearly seem to identify Cyrus. God called *him*. God will bring *him* to the throne to accomplish God's purposes against Babylon. *He* (Cyrus) will succeed— *his* way will prosper, the Lord predicts. Since all these pronouns refer to Cyrus, it seems likely that previous ones in vs. 14b also would.

The verbiage may be a bit confusing, but we can learn from it that success awaits anyone whom God chooses to bless.

### III. God's Message to His People—48:16-19

### A. A Call to Listen, 16

**16 Come ye near unto me, hear ye this; I have not spoken in secret from the beginning; from the time that it was, there am I: and now the Lord GOD, and his Spirit, hath sent me.**

Several of the newer Bible versions format the text to show a break after vs. 15. Having dismissed the idols and having predicted Cyrus' success, the Lord now addresses a message to His people of Israel. It is difficult to tell just who in vs. 16 is issuing the invitation to draw near and hear God's words.

One obvious choice is Isaiah. As God's inspired messenger, he may be the one summoning an audience for the Lord.

An interesting possibility, however, is that Christ might be speaking here.

The NASB projects this option by choosing a unique way to capitalize "Me" in this verse:

Come near to Me, listen to this:

From the first I have not spoken in secret,

From the time it took place, I was there.

And now the Lord GOD has sent Me, and His Spirit.

If this is a valid translation, then some Bible scholars point out that we have the Trinity present in this verse,

with Jesus inviting, God speaking the message that follows, and the Spirit inspiring the message.

The meaning of this verse depends on the "caller" for us to come near. If the spokesman is Isaiah, then he is reminding his readers that he has always been where they needed him during all the difficult days of his ministry. If the Inviter is either God or Jesus, then the message that follows is being prefaced with a reminder to Israel of the openness of divine communication with them from their beginning.

### B. Identifying the Lord, 17

**17 Thus saith the LORD, thy Redeemer, the Holy One of Israel; I am the LORD thy God which teacheth thee to profit, which leadeth thee by the way that thou shouldest go.**

God's description of Himself as One who teaches Israel "to profit" has nothing to do with monetary gain or commercial profit as we usually use the word today. God is reminding Israel that He shows them what is best for them, what will give them success if life. The next description is a good equivalent: God leads us in the way we should go. Contrast this with, "the way of the ungodly" in Psalm 1.

### C. The Fruits of Obeying Him, 18-19

**18 O that thou hadst hearkened to my commandments! then had thy peace been as a river, and thy righteousness as the waves of the sea:**

**19 Thy seed also had been as the sand, and the offspring of thy bowels like the gravel thereof; his name should not have been cut off nor destroyed from before me.**

"Peace" in vs. 18 translates the

familiar Hebrew *shalom*. "Righteousness" in some versions reads either "success" or "prosperity." The metaphor of a flowing river or rolling waves is a way of telling Israel how rich and pleasant life could have been for them if they had paid attention to the Lord.

Comparing "the offspring of thy bowels" to "gravel" is ancient English that misses most of us today. The NKJV simplifies and modernizes this verse: "Your descendants also would have been like the sand, And the offspring of your body like the grains of sand." If only Israel had listened to God, their population would have multiplied.

### IV. Past Proof of God's Goodness—48:21

**21 And they thirsted not when he led them through the deserts: he caused the waters to flow out of the rock for them: he clave the rock also, and the waters gushed out.**

God reminds His people of Exodus events that all of them would have known. At Rephidim, early in Israel's journey from Egypt to Mt. Sinai, the Hebrews and their cattle were waterless. They faced deadly dehydration in the desert. God watered the people and their flocks by causing water to flow from a huge rock that Moses struck with his miracle-working staff (Exod. 17). Years later the apostle Paul wrote, "That rock was Christ."

The Lord always has provided adequately for His people when they trust Him, and He always will.

### V. God's Warning to the Wicked—48:22

**22 There is no peace, saith the LORD, unto the wicked.**

When Israel decided to ignore God's commandments and began to indulge in the debauchery of pagan idolatry, they chose a lifestyle that would cause them more trouble than they could imagine. So it for us today. Peace belongs to the righteous. Wickedness always brings us woe.

છଓଓ

## Evangelistic Emphasis

The Lord is the rescuer of His people. Isaiah said they thirsted not when he led them through the desert. He caused the waters to flow out of the rock for them. He clave the rock and the waters gushed out.

In our lives, we find ourselves in situations that are beyond our control. We thirst and can find no access to water. We struggle and can find no way of escape. We seek to meet health needs, economic needs, and relationship crises and can find no way out of our problems.

Forgiveness of our sins and eternal hope through Christ is the only way of escape. These gifts from God will rescue us from every danger and difficulty.

How do we receive these gifts? Others who are already believers share the good news.

We, in turn, share it with those who have need of it. That gives us a great responsibility as well as a great opportunity. Those who have needs and struggles can learn from us the good news about the Lord who loved them so much he died for them. A simple conversation about the love of Christ can be the means of blessings that will endure forever.

Guilt can be forgiven, hope can be born, and fresh starts can be offered. It is a magnificent message that we can gladly share with others. We call it evangelism, the spreading of good news.

### ಬಿೞಚೞ

## Memory Selection

**Go ye forth of Babylon, flee ye from the Chaldeans, with a voice of singing declare ye, tell this, utter it even to the end of the earth; say ye, The Lord hath redeemed his servant Jacob.**

*Isaiah 48:20*

The nation of Israel gladly fled from the Babylonians. Babylon was a fierce and powerful enemy. Their cruelty could wreak havoc in Israel. Escaping from them created a time of singing and rejoicing. The people of Israel responded from this rescue with joy and praise. They sang, "The Lord has redeemed His servant."

In our present day lives, we face enemies that can be vicious. Escape from them is a time for singing and rejoicing. Perhaps that is one of the reasons that the worship of joyful singing is so dominant in the Christian Church.

The admonition of the Memory Selection is that the people of God should seek refuge in the power of God. This refuge should give joy with singing.

# Weekday Problems

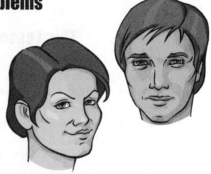

Many problems that we have in life are not major events, but are annoying smaller vexations. In one case, Tom and Mary are struggling with financial difficulties when car problems stretch the budget with an additional $800 expense. Just last month they had to put a new water heater in their house so their expenses were already at breaking point.

These problems are not large compared to the serious sickness of a family member, the loss of a job, or an injury from an accident. Yet they produce strains and create anxieties.

Most of us have serious problems at one time or another in life. Yet it may not be the disasters, but rather the annoyances, that cause us the most grief.

Life is not problem-free. It is problem solving with faith. We can deal with the smaller problems—the major ones can be trusted to God. Right now, we are thinking about relatively petty problems that seem to drive us crazy sometimes. It may be the mosquitoes and not the lions that devour us.

It is heartening to know that God will be with us in the minutia of life as well as the catastrophes of life. We will not let petty vexations worry us more than the disasters that befall us. We can be sure that we have God's help with their financial problems as well as their serious illnesses.

## Little Did They Know

We got married for better or for worse.
He couldn't do any better.
I couldn't do any worse.

An old man's wife asked him, "Whatcha doin'?"
He said, "Nothin'."
She barked back, "You did that yesterday."
He explained, "I didn't get finished."

# This Lesson in Your Life

There are some practical guidelines for Christian living in this passage. One is that adults need help to move beyond the mistakes they have made in life. No one is without mistakes. Many of our mistakes are beyond our ability to correct. For this reason, we need the help of God to recover.

Christianity is not a self-help religion. It is a reliance on God. We want to be better than that which we create by ourselves. That requires divine assistance. God forgives our mistakes and, with His help, we are able to make a fresh start. Then a person has a new birth. He no longer suffers from guilt and shame. Instead, he has a new beginning. With a clean slate, hope replaces fear—instead of looking forward to death, one looks forward to an eternal relationship with God.

These benefits are not the result of our achievement. Rather they are the gifts of God. He gives them without restraint and we receive them, not with arrogance, but with gratitude.

Adults need to be open to the counsel that will improve their lives. Some are so opinionated that they are not able to consider the alternative views that others hold. When this happens, a person may repeat his mistakes. It is an openness of spirit that stimulates growth. The ability to grow in a positive direction is a mark of maturity.

Another lesson in this text is that actions have consequences. Some people continue in long-time paths neither learning nor growing. They repeat their mistakes with damaging consequences. The illusion that decisions and actions have no consequences is a false one.

This text also affirms that we can overcome the erring acts and words of the past. We are not doomed to permanent punishment by the deeds of the past. Past sins are serious and we need to treat them with great care. Yet they are also forgivable–allowing us to rise above them.

Christians understand that human repentance is possible because of God's forgiveness. Although sinfulness has consequences, there is a way of escape within God's forgiveness.

**1. What did the Lord do to supply Israel's need for water?**
He caused the waters to flow out of the rock and clave the rock so that the waters gushed out.

**2. Do we ever find ourselves beyond our control?**
Yes. We thirst and find no access to water. We struggle and find no way of escape.

**3. What is the only way of escape from these disasters?**
It is the forgiveness of our sins and the possession of eternal hope through Christ.

**4. How are we to receive these gifts?**
Others who have already received the good news share it with us. In turn, we share it with those who have need of it.

**5 What does it mean to say that actions have consequences?**
It means that there is significance to what we do. When we take an action, there is a result to that action. When we neglect doing well, it leaves the poor without relief, the hungry without food.

**6. What is "The way you should go?"**
It is the way the way of Gods righteousness.

**7. How can we tell the difference between New Year's resolutions and God's salvation?**
A New Year's resolution is a resolve to improve one's own life with discipline and personal effort. God's salvation is yielding oneself to the actions of God so He will heal and improve you.

**8. How is God's salvation to be disseminated?**
By the efforts to teach the gospel to those who hunger for it.

**9. Compare God's help with examples proposed in self-books.**
Compile lists of the remarkable things God has done for man and contrasting lists of the results of man controlling his own life.

**10. How can we, as teachers, help those who struggle to serve God?**
We can set examples, teach Bible truths, and encourage people to live godly lives.

**Uplift**

Mike, at an early age, suffered from polio. He spent his life in an iron lung. Can you imagine growing through boyhood confined to a huge breathing device? Although he was unable to run and play, he was still able to laugh. As he passed into early adulthood, he was unable to participate in routine boyhood experiences. He could not participate in normal athletic and social experiences.

Mike's paralysis was in his arms and hands—and he had to have help in breathing. Yet, he maintained a quickness of intellect and a steady smile.

Mike was the son of devout parents. They not only were genuine in their faith, but their loyalty to their son was unwavering. They never tired of providing him with cheerful care. They bought him stacks of books that he devoured with consuming absorption. They purchased a specially equipped van for Mike's transportation. In addition, they provided him the education that permitted his growth and perception.

His mind was bright as were those of his father and mother. Not only did his parents free him to grow, but also he allowed them to develop their abilities and careers. The family was remarkably normal in spite of difficulties that would intimidate many.

Mike wrote extensively of his experience fighting a handicap. He was determined not to allow his physical limitations shape his life. Instead, he wanted to determine his future.

Remarkable Mike could not use his hands to write, so he learned to write with his feet. Later he learned to type. Knowing his history, a publishing company agreed to publish Mike's writing. This opened another avenue of expression for Mike. Again, instead of lying in the iron lung in self-pity, he challenged life's problems. Once again, his challenge was successful.

Because of courage and love from both the son and the parents, there were three successful lives in this family. The father was a capable and compassionate minister to a large church. The mother was not only a good homemaker but also a professional teacher who was a role model to many young people. Mike, himself, had art, literary, and journalistic ability.

Neither the son nor the parents intruded on each other's independence, and growth. They loved each other and admired the accomplishments of other family members.

෧෮

# Lesson 8

# The Servant's Mission in the World
# Pay It Forward

## Isaiah 49:1-6

Listen, O isles, unto me; and hearken, ye people, from far; The LORD hath called me from the womb; from the bowels of my mother hath he made mention of my name.

2 And he hath made my mouth like a sharp sword; in the shadow of his hand hath he hid me, and made me a polished shaft; in his quiver hath he hid me;

3 And said unto me, Thou art my servant, O Israel, in whom I will be glorified.

4 Then I said, I have laboured in vain, I have spent my strength for nought, and in vain: yet surely my judgment is with the LORD, and my work with my God.

5 And now, saith the LORD that formed me from the womb to be his servant, to bring Jacob again to him, Though Israel be not gathered, yet shall I be glorious in the eyes of the LORD, and my God shall be my strength.

6 And he said, It is a light thing that thou shouldest be my servant to raise up the tribes of Jacob, and to restore the preserved of Israel: I will also give thee for a light to the Gentiles, that thou mayest be my salvation unto the end of the earth.

**Jan. 23**

**Memory Verse**
Isaiah 49:6

**Background Scripture**
Isaiah 49:1-6

**Devotional Reading**
Hebrews 10:19-25

# *fOCuS*

Most Christians are familiar with the way Christ uses the metaphor of light. In the Sermon on the Mount, for example, He says to His followers, "You are the light of the world." Moreover, he charges us, "Let your light so shine before men that they may see your good works and glorify the Father."

Most of us recall the apostle Paul's description of his converts as stars that shine brightly in a dark and mixed-up world (Phil. 2:14).

Perhaps both Christ and Paul were recalling the Lord's charge to Israel, "I will give you as a light to the nations, that my salvation may reach to the end of the earth" (Isa. 49:6, NRSV). Christ's Great Commission charges all of us who know and love Him to be shining the light of the Gospel into distant lands worldwide. After all, none of us would know Jesus if someone had not shared the light in other times and places.

## *For a Lively Start*

"We have all the mission work we can handle right here in our own back yard," the minister of one mega-church replied to a missionary pleading for assistance. No doubt, the minister told the truth, not just for his congregation but also for all of us involved in spreading the Gospel. In our communities, we will never run out of people who need to hear the word or evangelistic projects that need support.

But preaching just at home does not fulfill our Lord's command to "go into all the world." It does not recognize God's concern in Isaiah 49:1 for people "in distant lands"—people who are "far away." If we neglect missions abroad, we rob ourselves, and our churches, of some of the excitement that can inspire our Gospel preaching here at home.

| Teaching Outline | Daily Bible Readings |
|---|---|
| I. God's Message to People Afar—49:1-3 | Mon. The Lord Has Chosen You *Isaiah 49:7-11* |
| A. People in Distant Lands, 1a | Tue. Faithful or Unfaithful Servants *Matthew 24:45-51* |
| B. A Pre-natal Call, 1b | Wed. The Greatest as Servant *Matthew 23:2-12* |
| C. Armed to Preach, 2-3 | Thu Made a Slave to All *1 Corinthians 9:19-23* |
| II. The Frustrated Preacher—49:4 | Fri. A Testimony to the Gentiles *Matthew 10:16-24* |
| III. Salvation for Jews and Gentiles—49:5-6 | Sat. Hope for the Gentiles *Matthew 12:15-21* |
| A. Restoring Israel, 5 | Sun. A Light to the Nations *Isaiah 49:1-6* |
| B. Saving Gentiles, 6 | |

# *Verse by Verse*

## Isaiah 49:1-6

**I. God's Message to People Afar—49:1-3**

**A. People in Distant Lands, 1a**

**1a Listen, O isles, unto me; and hearken, ye people, from far;**

In these verses, we wish that identifying the speaker were as easy as determining to whom he speaks. The word "Isles" means "coastlands" in many Bible versions. As the appositive that follows clearly tells us, the message here is intended for people who live far away in distant lands. The worldwide scope of God's grace, so often spelled out in God's word, is once more made clear in this address.

**B. A Pre-natal Call, 1b**

**1b The LORD hath called me from the womb; from the bowels of my mother hath he made mention of my name.**

To identify the speaker here, we must look not only at this line but also at the verses that immediately follow. Some see the speaker as the entire nation of Israel, called by God to convey His salvation to all who inhabit the globe. The description he gives of himself in vs. 5 seems to distinguish him from the Jewish nation and, at the same time, to set him apart as an individual.

The two individuals usually suggested as our spokesperson in these verses are the Messiah and the prophet Isaiah. Bible scholars give good reasons for our choice of either Christ or Isaiah; yet other solid reasons are offered for rejecting the choice of the first one and then the other. The issue here is complex indeed, and the evidence for one choice or the other is not airtight. When all is said and done, the reader of these verses has to decide which speaker to listen to, while knowing all along that the choice was partly a guess.

We will assume, for the next few paragraphs, that Isaiah is the speaker.

**C. Armed to Preach, 2-3**

**2 And he hath made my mouth like a sharp sword; in the shadow of his hand hath he hid me, and made me a polished shaft; in his quiver hath he hid me;**

**3 And said unto me, Thou art my servant, O Israel, in whom I will be glorified.**

Vs. 2 contains an extended metaphor in which God's servant (perhaps Isaiah) was prepared by the Lord for his assignment, just as a warrior would carefully make ready his weapons. The sharp sword in the mouth revives in Christian minds of our Lord's self-description in Revelation 2:12. This is a classic description of a well-prepared prophet with an incisive message. His tongue is sharp, his message cutting. The polished shaft is an arrow, as the following reference to the quiver indicates. God's message will fly accurately to its intended target.

In vs. 3, we see the beginning of the message God wants Isaiah to deliver. It is a message in keeping with what He has been saying to Israel, His servant, from the beginning of Isaiah 42 and throughout the following chapters. In His redemption of Israel from Captivity, and in His later blessing of them through the Messiah, God certainly will be glorified among all nations. They will see His power and goodness.

## II. The Frustrated Preacher—49:4

**4 Then I said, I have laboured in vain, I have spent my strength for nought, and in vain: yet surely my judgment is with the LORD, and my work with my God.**

If God's servant here really is Isaiah, it is easy to see why the prophet would lament that all his work has been fruitless. Isaiah's call to ministry came during the reign of faithless kings on Judah's throne. The prophet himself tells of times when King Ahaz was virtually deaf to all God's encouragement and instruction. Thus was the time in Isaiah 7-8, when through Isaiah, God offered the king a sign that He would save him from the attacking Assyrian armies. However, Ahaz turned out to be a faithless soul who rejected all of God's assurances. During the lengthy tenure of two faithless kings, Isaiah

preached, but the morals and faith of God's people continued to decline. Surely, in those dark days before Hezekiah, the aging prophet must have thought all his efforts were wasted. Yet, he reminded himself that the final assessment was up to the Lord. God was in charge of his ministry.

Are there not times when all pastors need to remind themselves of this and follow Isaiah's example? God does not call us to be successful in ministry. He calls us to be faithful.

## III. Salvation for Jews and Gentiles—49:5-6

### A. Restoring Israel, 5

**5 And now, saith the LORD that formed me from the womb to be his servant, to bring Jacob again to him, Though Israel be not gathered, yet shall I be glorious in the eyes of the LORD, and my God shall be my strength.**

If our speaker is the prophet Isaiah, we have little difficulty understanding his statement here about the Lord's preparing him to be His servant even while he was in his mother's womb. The idea of God's choosing and preparing a worker before birth is common in the Scriptures. God told Jeremiah, "Before I formed you in the womb I knew you, and before you were born I consecrated you; I appointed you a prophet to the nations" (Jer. 1:5, RSV). "God in his grace chose me even before I was born, and called me to serve him," the apostle Paul tells us (Gal. 1:15, TEV). The older versions tell us Paul was called while he was in the womb.

It is easy to see why pro-life advocates value the message of verses like these, but abortion is not Isaiah's subject. He mentions his divine call before birth to emphasize both the greatness of the God who called him, and the crucial nature of the message God entrusted to him for the nation of Israel.

Does God still select key people, and put them into place, to carry out His plans, and to communicate His message in critical times and places? What promising young person in your present fellowship might be someone God is grooming to play a special role in a high-visibility situation years from now? Does thinking about this change the way we relate to that youngster?

In almost all of the later Bible versions, Isaiah tells us in this verse that God chose him for the task of bringing Israel ("Jacob") back to Him. This could mean "back" from the paganism and faithlessness during the reigns of kings like Jotham and Ahaz. It could also mean back from Assyrian captivity. In either case, Isaiah tells us that he feels honored to have been given this task, and he knows that the strength to accomplish it will have to come from the Lord.

**B. Saving Gentiles, 6**
**6 And he said, It is a light thing**
**that thou shouldest be my servant to raise up the tribes of Jacob, and to restore the preserved of Israel: I will also give thee for a light to the Gentiles, that thou mayest be my salvation unto the end of the earth.**

The statement that God started to make at the beginning of vs. 5, He now speaks in vs. 6. He tells Isaiah that saving Israel will be a small part of the job that God has in store for the prophet. God's real target for his ministry is the salvation of all peoples everywhere. Isaiah's message will be, "a light for the Gentiles."

Vss. 5 and 6 take on a different flavor, of course, if we think the servant here is the Messiah instead of the prophet. The NKJV translators assume this, so they capitalized the pronouns in vs. 6 to make it read as a statement to Jesus:

It is too small a thing that You should be My Servant

To raise up the tribes of Jacob,

And to restore the preserved ones of Israel;

I will also give You as a light to the Gentiles,

That You should be My salvation to the ends of the earth.

ဆာ

## Evangelistic Emphasis

William Carey, the great missionary to India, spent nearly 30 years on the mission field before he witnessed his first conversion. That was more than a century ago. One wonders, whether Carey would have stayed 30 years if he lived today. We are so accustomed to instant results in all our endeavors. The idea that some of the work we will do will not bear fruit is foreign to our sense of pride and to our work ethic.

The Servant of Isaiah admitted that his work has been fruitless. Yet, in the midst of that claim, the servant still trusted the Lord who called him. "I have labored in vain, I have spent my strength for nothing and vanity; yet surely my right is with the Lord, and my recompense with my God." (Isaiah 49:4)

As we share the gospel of Jesus Christ, our minds should hold the truth that God called us not to be successful, but to be faithful. There is a world of difference between the two. The parable of the sower (Mk 4:3-8) is our Lord's call to be faithful despite paltry results. When you read the parable, one discovers that the sower had only 25% of his seed bear fruit. Three quarters of the sowers work was in vain. Yet, because of his faithfulness in sowing, the seed that did sprout, brought forth abundant fruit.

Not all of your efforts for Christ will succeed. The call of today's Scripture is not to worry about failures, but to trust God to bring success in His time, in His way. Living like that is called being faithful.

## Memory Selection

ಣಲೇಬ

"I will also give thee for a light to the Gentiles, that thou mayest be my salvation unto the end of the earth." *Isaiah 49:6*

Once we moved into our new home, my son Andrew, who was only nine at the time, commandeered the night light we had put in the hallway. I never asked him why he put the light in his room. Even today, I am amused by all the things that give off "light" in my house. My alarm clock, my iPhone, and even my shaver charging in the bathroom, all give off comforting light. We crave light to drive the darkness away.

Darkness comes in many forms. While we know it best as sin, darkness can also be fear of the unknown, moving, or the loss of a loved one. Darkness comes as that anxiety in the middle of the night that we cannot name. Darkness also happens in moments when we are feeling tempted to do something that does not glorify God.

Many good church people walk in that dark valley at some time or another. We are called, like Christ to bring light into their lives. Whether you are aware of it, you are the light that is shining in some darkened life. Your words of encouragement, your acts of love, even your own faith serve as a light shining in an other person's darkness. Often you may never be aware that you are helping a person, but you are. Rejoice that God is using you for such a vital task.

Are you lighting the way for others to come to Christ?

# Weekday Problems

Mr. Coy never went to church. He worked as a bridge tender for 30 years. For 30 years, ministers from every denomination had visited Mr. Coy in his bridge-house. For 30 years, he told them he worked on Sunday. The reason he worked on Sunday, was so he could have off on the weekday afternoons.

Mr. Coy was also a Little League umpire. In the fall and spring, he was also a basketball referee. He loved "his children" as he referred to them. He told preachers that too. As long as he could officiate, and be with his children, he would always work the weekends. That meant as long as he was an umpire, he would not come to church. Many a preacher used Mr. Coy as a sermon illustration on the evils of working on Sunday.

These same preachers never did really know Mr. Coy. On the baseball field as well as the basketball court, Mr. Coy was sharing the love of God in Jesus Christ. He could do more for the work of the kingdom during a basketball time out than most preachers did all week. Mr. Coy never did give up his weekend work. He umpired well into his late sixties. When he finally died, the church was filled with children, sitting with their fathers, who had all been touched by Mr. Coy's ministry.

How are people faithful to God's calling outside the regular activities of the church?

Do you think a person can be faithful and not be in church every Sunday?

Considering all the things that Christ called us to do, how much is not seen or understood by the world?

---

# More Puns for Educated Minds

1. A sign on the lawn at a drug rehab center said: "Keep Off the Grass."
2. The short fortune-teller who escaped from prison was a small medium at large.
3. The corporal who survived mustard gas and pepper spray is now a seasoned veteran.
4. A backward poet writes inverse.
5. In a democracy it's your vote that counts. In feudalism it's your count that votes.
6. When the cannibals ate their missionary, they got a taste of religion.

# This Lesson in Your Life

Ray Kroc was a man with a purpose. His purpose in life was to serve the best hamburger that he could. He did not allow his individually owned franchises to vary his formula at all. He demanded performance and perfection from those who sold his hamburgers. You have eaten one of Ray Kroc's hamburgers if you have ever eaten at McDonald's. Some people live for interesting things. Ray Kroc lived for hamburgers; they gave his life purpose and meaning. Before we look down on that, we need to ask, "what gives meaning to my life?"

The Servant of God had been called by God from his mother's womb. He knew what his purpose in life was. Therefore, he could handle the disappointments that came because of his calling and ministry. With his eyes on the goal, the hard times were just bumps in the road to accomplishment.

Discouragement is the result of not having a clearly defined purpose in life. When we set our goals, and decide we are going to meet them, hard times become learning experiences. Setbacks can then be viewed in terms of the big picture of our goal. Not everything Ray Kroc did turned out right. He personally like the "hula burger" that was two pieces of cheese and a ring of pineapple. I will bet you have never eaten one of those at a McDonald's. The reason is, that burger was a miserable failure. For Kroc, who loved them, it was a learning experience.

The Servant said, "I have spent my strength for nothing and vanity." (Is. 49:4) He was uttering words of frustration. Even persons with clearly defined purposes in life, get frustrated. The problem that arises in the church is that we do not appropriately express that frustration. The Servant did it in terms of a prayer of faith in God. Even though things were not working out, God was still the source and the object of the purpose. That could not be taken away or diluted. When one of your brilliant ideas for the church does not work out, it is appropriate to be frustrated. We can honestly express that frustration to the Lord. Moreover, we should keep that frustration to ourselves. As God is the source and object of our purpose, he will understand our feelings and help us deal with them constructively.

Little, or even major, setbacks should not deter us from our purpose in serving Him. Our purpose is to live faithfully, because God has called us to a high task. "It is too light a thing that you should be my servant to raise up the tribes of Jacob and to restore the preserved of Israel; I will give you as a light to the nations." (Is 49:6). Our task is to take the gospel of Jesus Christ to the world. From that purpose, we must not be deterred. Now, everything we do is a small task, compared to the call to evangelize the world. We are given as a light to the nations as we begin our sharing of the gospel with our closest neighbors. From that task, small setbacks should not deter us.

Carrying out our purpose is important because of the people who are living in darkness. We are their light. A soul may be uncertain, waiting on your faithfulness.

**1. Who is commanded to listen to the message of the Servant?**

The coastlands and people who live far off are the audience to whom the message is addressed.

**2. At what point was this Servant called into his ministry by the Lord?**

From the time the Servant was in the womb of his mother, God had placed His call on the Servant.

**3. What else was unique about the Servant's name?**

The name of the Servant was given to His mother, prior to the birth of the child.

**4. What does this selection and naming prior to birth of the Servant remind you of?**

It is a prediction of the calling of Jesus and His being named prior to His birth.

**5. In reading verses two and three, how are you reminded of the ministry of Jesus Christ?**

Discuss this with your class.

**6. What is the feeling of the Servant toward His ministry?**

Verse four indicates the frustration the servant felt with his ministry, but that his ultimate vindication come by the hand of God.

**7. What were the original limitations placed on the ministry of the Servant?**

His ministry was primarily to "raise up the tribes of Jacob and to restore the preserved of Israel."

**8. How was the ministry of the Servant expanded?**

Beyond his original mission (question seven), he was called to bring the salvation of the Lord to the ends of the earth.

**9. How are you reminded of the ministry of Jesus and the church?**

While ministering to some Gentiles, Jesus' ministry was primarily to His own people. The church expanded on that ministry taking the gospel to the ends of the earth.

**10. How will the salvation of the Lord reach to the ends of the earth?**

It will come as God's people shine as lights. Those in darkness will see this light. These persons will be drawn to this light.

Whether you are just hanging in or hanging out, it is no way to go through life.

We have all seen it. That poster of a clinging kitten, hind feet dangling in the air, only its front paws, claws dug in frantically, keeping the kitty somewhere above the ground. Underneath the picture of this panicked kitten is the admonition, "Hang In There!"

We are told that this is the kind of visual message we need at 7:00 a.m. Friday morning to encourage us to make it through the day and stick it out to the weekend. Yet, there are two strange facets of this picture of a hanging cat.

First, why does this picture evoke a grin, a chuckle, from us when we look at it? Surely, we are not all abusive cat-haters, pleased at the distresses of all frantic felines. No, we smile for the same reason we laugh at slapstick comedy. Our laughter is a burst of relief that, at least this time, we are not the one falling. We sympathize. We even empathize. However, we also give a sigh of thanks for our own safety.

The second mystery of this poster is that we seem to assume that some rescue awaits that kitten... if only it can just "hang in there" long enough. In all the versions of this portrait I have seen, the viewer cannot see beyond a few inches below the kitten's toes. We cannot tell if she is afraid to let go and drop three inches to a grassy lawn–or if she is dangling above the open jaws of a snarling pit bull or the traffic of a four-lane highway. We assume there will be a happy ending or a safe landing. Otherwise, the encouragement to "hang in there" would not make any sense.

Most of us encounter little crises in our lives that can be weathered by just "hanging in there." A frustrating week of work is followed by a weekend. A nagging car trip with the kids will end. Head colds do eventually loosen their grip and go away. Even tedious meetings finally adjourn. Sometimes "hanging in there" is all that is required.

But there are other situations in our lives that call us to do much, much more than simply court disasters. When your ship is sinking, you cannot just "hang in there." You have to get moving, break out the life rafts, and start rowing for all you are worth.

God has sent His servant in the world to tell us more than "hang in there." The Servant will show us how to live faithfully in the power of God. Through the power of God's Holy Spirit residing in us, we are able to face the challenges of daily living. Like the Hebrews in exile, who were renewed with memories of Jerusalem and the hope of return, we are renewed knowing that Christ is with us and that one day we will all be gathered with Him in heaven.

# Lesson 9

## Healed by His Bruises Suffering for Others

### Isaiah 53:4-6, 10-12

Surely he hath borne our griefs, and carried our sorrows: yet we did esteem him stricken, smitten of God, and afflicted.

5 But he was wounded for our transgressions, he was bruised for our iniquities: the chastisement of our peace was upon him; and with his stripes we are healed.

6 All we like sheep have gone astray; we have turned every one to his own way; and the LORD hath laid on him the iniquity of us all.

10 Yet it pleased the LORD to bruise him; he hath put him to grief: when thou shalt make his soul an offering for sin, he shall see his seed, he shall prolong his days, and the pleasure of the LORD shall prosper in his hand.

11 He shall see of the travail of his soul, and shall be satisfied: by his knowledge shall my righteous servant justify many; for he shall bear their iniquities.

12 Therefore will I divide him a portion with the great, and he shall divide the spoil with the strong; because he hath poured out his soul unto death: and he was numbered with the transgressors; and he bare the sin of many, and made intercession for the transgressors.

Jan. 30

**Memory Verse**
Isaiah 53:5

**Background Scripture**
Isaiah 53

**Devotional Reading**
2 Corinthians 5:16-21

The last half of Acts 8 contains the story of an Ethiopian man who had just visited Jerusalem. He was riding along in his chariot reading what we call Isaiah 53, when the Christian preacher Philip thumbed a ride with him.

As the Ethiopian puzzled over the verses about a man who suffered in silence, like a sheep being shorn with-

out protest, he asked Philip, "Who is this about? Is Isaiah describing himself or somebody else?" The Bible tells us that Philip began at that verse to preach to his questioner about Jesus. The entire 53rd chapter of Isaiah is about our Lord's trial and death and the atonement He provided on Calvary for our sins.

Before that chariot ride was over, its owner asked the preacher to baptize him. Isaiah's gospel message had reached his heart and saved his soul.

## For a Lively Start

ഇ൭൫

"All we like sheep have gone astray," Isaiah wrote, thereby acknowledging one of the core truths of the Christian faith. Even the best of us is a sinner. To use the often-repeated word of Isaiah 53, all of us are "transgressors." "There is none righteous; no, not one," Paul asserted as the basis for his famous exposition of God's grace in the book

of Romans. "If any person says he has no sin," John agreed, "he is a liar and no truth abides in him."

Since all of us are stained with the guilt of our transgressions, Isaiah's picture of One who comes to suffer willingly in our place speaks convincingly to all who trust in Jesus. That the ancient prophet could describe Christ's suffering in detail seven centuries in advance, adds to our amazement at this text.

| Teaching Outline | Daily Bible Readings |
|---|---|
| I. His Suffering for Our Sins—53:4-6<br>A. Our Fault, 4<br>B. His Suffering, 5<br>C. Our Sins, 6<br>II. His Suffering Pleases God—53:10a<br>III. His Suffering Rewarded—53:10b-12<br>  A. Lasting Blessings, 10b<br>  B. Satisfying Results, 11<br>  C. Allotted Spoils, 12 | Mon. Reconciled Through Christ<br>    *2 Corinthians 5:16-21*<br>Tue. A Sacrifice for All Time<br>    *Hebrews 10:10-18*<br>Wed. Offering and Sacrifice<br>    *Ephesians 4:25-5:2*<br>Thu Grace and Righteousness<br>    *Romans 5:12-17*<br>Fri. Despised and Rejected<br>    *Isaiah 52:13-53:3*<br>Sat. Oppressed and Afflicted<br>    *Isaiah 53:7-9*<br>Sun. Wounded and Crushed<br>    *Isaiah 53:4-6, 10-12* |

# Verse by Verse

Isaiah 53:4-6, 10-12

## I. His Suffering for Our Sins—53:4-6

### A. Our Fault, 4

**4 Surely he hath borne our griefs, and carried our sorrows: yet we did esteem him stricken, smitten of God, and afflicted.**

"Who is the prophet talking about here?" the Ethiopian eunuch asked his hitchhiker as they considered these verses. "Is he talking about himself or about someone else?" It was a perceptive question, one that has been asked repeatedly during the centuries since then.

Some of Isaiah's later readers have chosen to identify the suffering Servant in these passages as a contemporary of Isaiah. A few have even dared to name specific people in Isaiah's time as likely candidates.

That day in the chariot, the evangelist Philip did not hesitate to tell the Ethiopian questioner that Isaiah was writing about Jesus, the Messiah. In the centuries since, most Christians have read Isaiah 53 in that light. While many have acknowledged the possibility that the prophet was also describing someone in his own day, Christians traditionally have chosen to look beyond that servant to the One sent by God to suffer for the transgressions of humankind. This reading is so widely accepted that reputable translations, such as the NKJV and the NASB, have elected to capitalize "He" and "Him" in all the verses describing the Sufferer.

"Griefs" and "sorrows," in the KJV, look beyond our usual use of those words to describe the aftermath of death. The TEV catches the broader viewpoint: "He endured the suffering that should have been ours, the pain that we should have borne. All the while, we thought that his suffering was punishment sent by God."

### B. His Suffering, 5

**5 But he was wounded for our transgressions, he was bruised for our iniquities: the chastisement of our peace was upon him; and with his stripes we are healed.**

All of us, who trust in the Cross for our salvation, see the suffering of our Savior in these familiar phrases. We can also benefit, though, in seeing how men and women who imitate the unselfish sacrifice of our Lord have blessed others by suffering on their behalf. The apostle Paul said, for example, "I bear in my body the marks of Jesus" (Gal. 6:17). He urged his converts not to be discouraged because of his sufferings for them (Eph. 3:13). He said that all of us should strive to belong to "the fellowship of sharing in his sufferings, becoming like him in his death" (Phil. 3:10, NIV). Our world is a much better place because people like Mother Teresa have chosen to suffer for the good of those who are unable to repay such acts of sacrifice and kindness.

Still, the main reference of these phrases is the actual suffering of our Lord. In addition, the truth is unavoidable that all the pain He endured was caused by our iniquities. "The chastisement of our peace," reads more clearly in versions that characterize it as, "the punishment that makes us whole." Do not miss the contrast that the "stripes"— the wounds—that so brutally injured Jesus actually healed us.

## C. Our Sins, 6

**6 All we like sheep have gone astray; we have turned every one to his own way; and the LORD hath laid on him the iniquity of us all.**

Most Bible readers today have had little, if any, contact with sheep. We may miss the aptness of Isaiah's metaphor to describe the waywardness of humanity. Sheep tend to wander aimlessly into all sorts of dangers. Jesus' famous parable of the 99 sheep that remained gathered focused on one egregious lamb. Just as shepherds through the centuries have invested far more energy to locate and rescue the roamers in their flocks, so Jesus focused the bulk of His energy and concern to seek and save those who are lost.

The truth clearly stated in this verse, however, is the fact that all of us are lost. All of us have "gone astray." Ignoring the Lord's instructions, we have chosen selfish, hurtful paths. We have insisted on doing it our way. The price for our waywardness was the awful suffering of our Savior. The thief beside Him was right. Jesus had done nothing to deserve such agony. Still, on Calvary, God had Him pay the price for our sinfulness. "By this," Paul tells us, "we know just how much God loves us—while we were yet

sinners Christ died for us" (Rom. 5:8).

The whole idea of the substitutionary atonement—one person suffering because of another's wrongdoing—is a hard concept for some people to embrace. C. S. Lewis struggled with this in his early years as a Christian. The other New Testament metaphors that explain the cross—being washed clean, being ransomed from slavery, being raised from death to new life—spoke to his heart and mind. Yet, he said he blocked up on the idea of an innocent man being punished for a guilty one. In fact, Lewis' conversion from atheism was delayed as he wrestled with this common biblical explanation of Christ's atonement. Nowhere is this concept taught more plainly than here in Isaiah 53.

## II. His Suffering Pleases God— 53:10a

**10a Yet it pleased the LORD to bruise him; he hath put him to grief:**

It may be hard for some of us to wrap our human logic around God's thinking in the atonement, but this text could not be clearer in telling us that God was delighted to save us by this method. Lewis resolved some his quarrels with substitutionary atonement (the innocent suffering in place of the guilty) by recognizing that the One who suffered in this instance was God Himself. Instead of sending someone else to be flogged, mocked, shamed, and slaughtered, He went Himself to the Cross. "God was in Christ reconciling the world to himself," the Scriptures explain (2 Cor. 5:19).

Again, in this verse "grief" does not imply that Jesus had any later regrets about the crucifixion. "Grief" in King James days was a broader word that implied all types of pain and hurt. It was God's eternal plan that He would suffer the agony of death so that His sinful creatures might have life.

## III. His Suffering Rewarded—53:10b-12

### A. Lasting Blessings, 10b

**10b when thou shalt make his soul an offering for sin, he shall see his seed, he shall prolong his days, and the pleasure of the LORD shall prosper in his hand.**

The language in this verse is one of the main reasons some choose to apply Isaiah 53 to a sufferer other than Jesus, for obviously (despite Dan Brown's claims in his best-selling novels) Jesus had no sons or daughters—no descendants ("his seed") that He would later see in old age.

The Messiah would rise from the grave to see multitudes of people in the centuries to come rising from the grave of baptism to share in His new life. In this way, they were His spiritual descendants. Moreover, He was raised from death to live forever, to enjoy not just a few days but eternity in which to rejoice in the results of His suffering.

### B. Satisfying Results, 11

**11 He shall see of the travail of his soul, and shall be satisfied: by his knowledge shall my righteous servant justify many; for he shall bear their iniquities.**

"Travail" compares the agony Jesus suffered to childbirth pains. The suffering here was not physical but "of his soul." Sometimes we overlook this part of what He endured for us. However, Isaiah says Jesus would look back and be pleased with the way it all turned out. His death makes it possible for all who trust in Him to be justified (to be made right with God), because He has taken care of our sins.

### C. Allotted Spoils, 12

**12 Therefore will I divide him a portion with the great, and he shall divide the spoil with the strong; because he hath poured out his soul unto death: and he was numbered with the transgressors; and he bare the sin of many, and made intercession for the transgressors.**

The metaphor early in this verse is that of a king or soldier returning from war with victory booty to share with his officers. The TEV makes this clear: "I will give him the honors of a victorious soldier, because he exposed himself to death." In Ephesians 4, Paul uses this figure, comparing the ascending Christ to a conquering king lavishing gifts when he returns home victorious from war.

Not only did Jesus suffer for us, but also and more importantly, He suffered as one of us. He "was numbered with the transgressors." Not only was he executed as a criminal among criminals, but also he died as a sinner among sinners. "He was made like us in every way" (Heb. 2:17). It had to be that way. "Because God's children are human beings—made of flesh and blood—the Son also became flesh and blood. For only as a human being could he die, and only by dying could he break the power of the devil, who had the power of death" (Heb. 2:14-15, NLT).

Like the high priest in Old Testament days, entering the Holy of Holies on Yom Kippur to intercede for his nation, Jesus has now entered Heaven, there to present His blood for our sins and to intercede for us before the Throne on high.

## Evangelistic Emphasis

This is a weekend for winners and losers. Traditionally this will be Super Bowl Sunday. People all over the land will gather in front of the television for an evening of football. Emerging out of the game will be one winner and one loser. We will be able to remember and list the winner, but years from now we will forget the loser. This "All-American" concept of winners and losers has blurred our view of the servant ministry.

The servant of Isaiah is traditionally known as the "Suffering Servant" primarily because of the text for this day. By today's standards, this man was a loser. He did not come out on top. He was "smitten, afflicted and wounded." Those are traits that would automatically classify him as weak. It was through his weakness that others found life and redemption.

Who could relate to a God who knew no pain? Could you relate to a God who had never been touched by human tragedy? Could you relate to a God who was "superhuman?" In the "Suffering Servant" image that Jesus adopted for his ministry, we find a God who understands us. Our plans for success and ladder climbing often do not work out. We find ourselves "smitten, wounded and afflicted." It is in those moments we can reach out to one who knows us and who has experienced our pain first hand.

The Good News is found in the fact that our God knows. He knows what pain is like. In that process, He can bring healing.

ଈଠଔ

## Memory Selection

"But he was wounded for our transgressions, he was bruised for our iniquities: the chastisement of our peace was upon him; and with his stripes we are healed." *Isaiah 53: 5*

My wife's favorite indoor sport is moving furniture. She decides to move it on major holidays. New Year's Day and Labor Day are two of her favorites. I always know that when she is looking in a room with her hands on her hips, something is about to be moved. Around our house, you can be certain that furniture will be rearranged at least every six months. The interesting thing is that she often moves it by herself. I have actually seen triple dressers relocated after arriving home from work!

We have recently found that moving furniture together is more fun. She tells me where she wants a piece of furniture to be located, and together we move it. I figure the weight of the furniture is at least halved. In a perfect world, people would come and move the furniture for us, that way all the weight would be gone.

Sin is heavy. Some of you, walking around with it in your lives, know what that statement is all about. Jesus Christ takes the weight of sin off our shoulders. Aren't you glad that weight is gone?

He literally took the weight of our sins on His shoulders; He was bruised for our iniquities. The "weight" of our sin was placed on Him. By his suffering on the Cross we are healed.

# Weekday Problems

Sam Johnson did not like anyone. Top on his dislike list was himself. Sam was the second son of Jack and Janice Johnson. He was not kidding when he told everyone that mom and dad liked his older brother best.

Jack, Jr. had everything going for him. He was the first-born son. He grew up and became a successful engineer. He held many patents related to petroleum products he had developed over the years. Jack married the prettiest woman in town and they had three perfect children.

Sam's relationship with Jack, Jr. went way beyond sibling rivalry. Sam could not do anything as good as Jack, Jr. could according to his father. He was compared to his older brother by his parents, by preachers, by teachers, and even by football coaches. In trying to deal with that perceived rejection of himself, Sam rejected everything that Jack Johnson stood for.

He faced the end of his brother's life now, knowing that the worthy one would die and he would live. Jack, Jr. had been diagnosed with terminal cancer. He would have only weeks to live.

Mustering courage and grit, Sam visited Jack in the hospital. His brother was cordial, even friendly. Sam tried but he could not feel any kind of love and warmth for his brother. His anger was now compounded by his guilt. In the hallway, Sam heard his father tell his mother, "I don't understand why this happened to Jack. Sam is the one who has lived the hard life. Jack has always been so good."

How do we "reject" persons without being aware of it?

---

# Down-Home Truths

In his cow-puncher drawl Will Rogers had an off-handed way of muttering truths that would sneak up on you. Like these:

1. The quickest way to double your money is to fold it and put it back in your pocket.

2. Good judgment comes from experience, and a lot of that comes from bad judgment.

3. If you're ridin' ahead of the herd, take a look back every now and then to make sure it's still there.

4. Lettin' the cat outta the bag is a whole lot easier'n puttin' it back in.

# Ths Lesson in Your Life

Rejection is a topic of which we are all aware. At one time in our lives, we have been rejected. That rejection runs the gamut from a love to a job proposal. It is as universal as life itself. Some times reasons are valid, other times they are as capricious as the zip code in which you might live.

Humans started this whole problem. Way back in the Garden of Eden our ancestral parents, Adam and Eve, decided to reject the love of God. They did not see obedience as something a loving God should impose on humanity. They found a way of rebelling against the rules that God placed on inhabitants of the Garden. From then on, Scripture reads like one rejection slip after another. It seems though, that it is humanity turning its back on God.

Perhaps that is what the prophet meant when he said, "All we like sheep have gone astray, we have turned everyone to his own way." Is 53:6. When our way was chosen over God's way, rejection took place. The creature rejected the loving protection and guidance of the Creator. We see that played out so often in homes with teenagers. They reject the loving counsel and guidance of parents who love them so.

In rejecting our God, we placed ourselves at risk. We had to turn to one another for guidance and direction. Unfortunately, humanity's resume in those two areas is woefully lacking. We wandered though life, looking for a replacement for God. Continuing by our actions and inaction to reject His love we replace Him with god's of our own making. Something had to be done, or humanity would have been destroyed.

God sent His only Son into the world, to try to bring us back into the fold. Guess what? You got it; we rejected that plea from God. When God made His loving message perfectly clear in the person of Jesus, we found ways of crucifying that love.

Even today, we find modern ways of rejecting His love. I wonder, does the amount of time you spend with a Bible exceed the amount of time you spend at a computer terminal? How about the time you spend at the lake, does it compare favorably with the time you spend on a pew? How about the time you give as a booster for your favorite sporting team, does that compare with the time you spend in Christian service?

I can hear some of you protesting that in our world, one has to make choices. Those choices must be based on priorities that bring us the greatest amount of fulfillment. Our children, careers, and leisure must be priorities. What are we doing? Well, we are simply finding new, more creative ways of rejecting God's love.

God's love, in Jesus has promised us abundant living and the fulfillment of the purpose for which we were created, to glorify God.

**GETTING THE FACTS STRAIGHT**

**1. What is the reception that the prophet's message about the Suffering servant receives?**

The people do not believe a word he is saying. They cannot comprehend the ministry of the Suffering Servant.

**2. How will this Servant grow up among the people?**

He will not call attention to himself. No one will pay particular attention to him. There are no physical features that make him stand out.

**3. How do the other people around this Servant relate to him?**

They reject him and cause his life to be miserable. He is a man acquainted with sorrows.

**4. Of whom does this description remind you?**

The prophet is describing the public ministry of Jesus Christ, who was rejected by the very people he came to redeem.

**5. How have you experienced rejection because of your religious beliefs?**

Have your class discuss this issue.

**6. What kind of animal is used as an image to describe man's relationship with God?**

We are described as sheep who are determined to go our own way.

**7. What kind of animal is used as an image to describe the ministry of the Suffering Servant?**

He was described as a lamb. This lamb made no sound of complaint as it faced it's "shearers."

**8. Who is responsible for the suffering of this Servant?**

While humanities' sin has brought this about, the Lord has laid upon the Servant the iniquity of us all.

**9. What is the recurring theme of Isaiah that is found again in this passage?**

The RSV translates verse eleven, "Out of his anguish he shall see light." The light image is a recurring one in Isaiah.

**10. How does Isaiah 53 predict the earthly ministry of Jesus Christ?**

This is another question your class might discuss.

Born to missionary parents in India in 1914, Paul Brand went on to become a world-renowned orthopedic surgeon who devoted his life to the research and treatment of leprosy. Yet, this brilliant and distinguished doctor sought neither prestige nor wealth.

*How My Faith Survived the Church*, Philip Yancey recalls the first time he met Brand in Carville, Louisiana, at the National Hansen's Disease Hospital and Research Center. Yancey writes:

"I knew of Brand's stature in the world medical community in advance of my visit: the offers to head up major medical centers in England and the United States, the distinguished lectureships all over the world, the hand-surgery procedures named in his honor, the prestigious Albert Lasker Award, his appointment as Commander of the Order of the British Empire by Queen Elizabeth II, his selection as the only Westerner to serve on the Mahatma Gandhi Foundation. Yet I awaited our interview in a cubbyhole of an office hardly suggestive of such renown. Stacks of medical journals, photographic slides, and unanswered correspondence covered every square inch of an ugly government green metal desk. An antique window air conditioner throbbed at the decibel level of an unmuffled motorcycle.

"Most speakers and writers I knew were hitting the circuit, packaging and repackaging the same thoughts in different books and giving the same speeches to different crowds. Meanwhile Paul Brand, who had more intellectual and spiritual depth than anyone I had ever met, gave many of his speeches to a handful of leprosy patients in the hospital's Protestant chapel. At the Brands' insistence, I attended the Wednesday evening prayer service during my week at Carville. If I recall correctly, there were five of us in the choir and eight in the audience. Margaret Brand had drafted me into the choir, pleading, 'We haven't had a male voice in ever so long. Paul is giving the sermon, so he is not available. You simply must sing with us.' She brushed aside my mild protests. 'Don't be silly. Half the people who attend are deaf because of a reaction to a drug we use in treating leprosy. But a guest chorister would be such a treat — they'll enjoy just watching you.' To that motley crew, Brand proceeded to deliver an address worthy of Westminster Abbey. Obviously, he had spent hours meditating and praying over that one sermon. It mattered not that we were a tiny cluster of half-deaf nobodies in a sleepy bayou chapel. He spoke as an act of worship, as one who truly believed that God shows up when two or three are gathered together in God's name."

Paul Brand reflected the glory of Jesus, one who came to us as a sufferer not as a king. The suffering servant is not a popular image in our culture, but gives us an incarnate image for a way of changing lives.

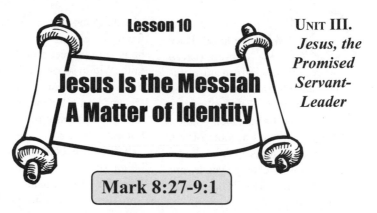

## Lesson 10

### Jesus Is the Messiah A Matter of Identity

### Mark 8:27-9:1

And Jesus went out, and his disciples, into the towns of Caesarea Philippi: and by the way he asked his disciples, saying unto them, Whom do men say that I am?

28 And they answered, John the Baptist: but some say, Elias; and others, One of the prophets.

29 And he saith unto them, But whom say ye that I am? And Peter answereth and saith unto him, Thou art the Christ.

30 And he charged them that they should tell no man of him.

31 And he began to teach them, that the Son of man must suffer many things, and be rejected of the elders, and of the chief priests, and scribes, and be killed, and after three days rise again.

32 And he spake that saying openly. And Peter took him, and began to rebuke him.

33 But when he had turned about and looked on his disciples, he rebuked Peter, saying, Get thee behind me, Satan: for thou savourest not the things that be of God, but the things that be of men.

34 And when he had called the people unto him with his disciples also,

he said unto them, Whosoever will come after me, let him deny himself, and take up his cross, and follow me.

35 For whosoever will save his life shall lose it; but whosoever shall lose his life for my sake and the gospel's, the same shall save it.

36 For what shall it profit a man, if he shall gain the whole world, and lose his own soul?

37 Or what shall a man give in exchange for his soul?

38 Whosoever therefore shall be ashamed of me and of my words in this adulterous and sinful generation; of him also shall the Son of man be ashamed, when he cometh in the glory of his Father with the holy angels.

9:1 And he said unto them, Verily I say unto you, That there be some of them that stand here, which shall not taste of death, till they have seen the kingdom of God come with power.

**Feb. 6**

---

**Memory Verse**
Mark 8:29
**Background Scripture**
Mark 8:27-9:1
**Devotional Reading**
Luke 3:7-18

---

**focus** In Mark 8, the apostle Peter demonstrates how a mere human being can grasp crucial truths and affirm their correctness. "You are the Christ," Peter volunteers when Jesus asks His men their opinion of Him. In Matthew's account of this same experience, Jesus applauds Peter. "That truth was revealed to you by my Father in Heaven," He tells the apostle (Matt. 16:17).

However, in these few verses the apostle Peter also shows us just how wrong a believer can be—even when he is very correct on other matters of faith. Within seconds of his confession of Jesus, Peter heard Jesus calling him "Satan" and rebuking him for opposing the most basic purposes of Jesus' ministry.

It should encourage us to see that being so wrong did not disqualify Peter for later valuable service to the Lord. Jesus set him straight, but He did not reject him because of his mistake. Such is the Lord's grace to all of us who love Him.

## For a Lively Start

Even when Jesus walked among them, people in Galilee held all sorts of opinions about who Jesus might really be. Some guessed that He might be John the Baptist (possibly resurrected). Based on Malachi's prophecy, quite a few posited that He might be Elijah back on Earth. Numbers of other great prophets from the past were among those who wondered who Jesus might be.

Things have not changed much, have they? Like those Galileans, our neighbors reflect a wide assortment of ideas about the identity of Jesus. Our Jewish and Muslim neighbors may grant that He was a great moral teacher. Others think He was a deluded fellow who should have been locked up. Some doubt He even existed. Our task is to help others know Him as God who became man.

| Teaching Outline | Daily Bible Readings |
|---|---|
| I. What Do Others Say About Me?—Mark 8: 27-28 | Mon. The Messiah Promised *Jeremiah 33:14-18* |
| II. What Do You Say?—Mark 8:29-30 | Tue. The Messiah Expected *Luke 3:7-18* |
| III. Predictions of the Cross—Mark 8:31-33 | Wed. The Messiah Sought *Matthew 2:1-6* |
| A. Christ's Prediction, 31, 32a | Thu The Messiah, Are You the One? *Luke 22:66-70* |
| B. Peter's Objections, 32b | |
| C. Christ's Rebuke, 33 | Fri. The Messiah Disclosed *John 4:16-26* |
| IV. Living by Dying—Mark 8:34-35 | |
| V. The Worth of Our Soul—Mark 8:36-37 | Sat. The Messiah Found *John 1:35-42* |
| VI. Ashamed of Jesus—Mark 8:38 | Sun. You Are the Messiah! *Mark 8:27-9:1* |
| VII. The Coming Kingdom—Mark 9:1 | |

# *Verse by Verse*

Mark 8:27-9:1

## I. What Do Others Say About Me?—Mark 8: 27-28

**27 And Jesus went out, and his disciples, into the towns of Caesarea Philippi: and by the way he asked his disciples, saying unto them, Whom do men say that I am?**

**28 And they answered, John the Baptist: but some say, Elias; and others, One of the prophets.**

Just as churches today often take their people on mountain retreats to help them focus on Kingdom matters, the Lord took His chosen men to the mountain country north of Galilee. There He could lead them into a deeper understanding of Who He is, what He hoped to accomplish, and how He would go about it.

The Twelve had just returned from a short ministry session across Galilee. This retreat to Caesarea Philippi gave Jesus a chance to encourage them and to find out what they had heard from the people they visited. The people seemed to be convinced that Jesus was someone extraordinary. Just look at the names they put on the table: John the Baptist, Elijah, or one of the prophets they revered.

Just two verses before the Old Testament ends, God promises to send Elijah back to bless His people. The people clearly were aware of that prophecy, so the miracles and excitement surrounding Christ's ministry triggered their hopes that the great prophet had arrived.

## II. What Do You Say?—Mark 8:29-30

**29 And he saith unto them, But whom say ye that I am? And Peter answereth and saith unto him, Thou art the Christ.**

**30 And he charged them that they should tell no man of him.**

Peter's confession confirms to Jesus that His men know more about Him than do the populace. With the help of Heaven, they know that this Man they have chosen to follow is indeed the Messiah, just as they had hoped.

"Do not tell anyone," Jesus instructs them. Why? Quite likely, for the same reason He earlier told the healed leper to keep quiet (Mark1:43). Probably, for the same reason He instructed His men to tell no one what they had seen when He raised Jairus' daughter from death (Mark 5:43). Excitement about the promised Messiah created a volatile situation, since many of the people shared the Zealots' belief that the coming King would rally the Jews to mount a revolution against the occupying Roman powers. Anything Jesus and His men did to fan those militant dreams could unleash an uprising. Therefore, Jesus and his men had to use great care in order that the false hopes of the people do not ignite a war.

## III. Predictions of the Cross—

## Mark 8:31-33

### A. Christ's Prediction, 31, 32a

**31 And he began to teach them, that the Son of man must suffer many things, and be rejected of the elders, and of the chief priests, and scribes, and be killed, and after three days rise again.**

**32 And he spake that saying openly.**

Today, when we read the events in Jesus' ministry, all of us know that He is headed inevitably to Calvary. When those events were unfolding, however, His men could not imagine such a thing. Nothing could have been farther from their expectations. At this point in His ministry, the Lord began telling His men "openly"—clearly and without placing anything in parables—that He would be tried, crucified, and then would rise on the third day.

We know what He was talking about, but they did not have a clue. At this point, the apostles knew nothing about the Cross or the unselfish love that caused Jesus to pursue such an end.

### B. Peter's Objections, 32b

**32b And Peter took him, and began to rebuke him.**

The KJV reading that Peter "took him" means that the stalwart apostle "took him aside." Peter had the finesse not to challenge Jesus within the hearing of the other disciples, but he also loved Jesus too much to accept even for one moment that His Lord would face a roman trial and die as a criminal. Even from the mouth of the Messiah he adored, Peter could not listen to such an outlandish prediction. Obviously, at this point he was not able to imagine what events lay ahead for his Leader.

### C. Christ's Rebuke, 33

**33 But when he had turned about and looked on his disciples, he rebuked Peter, saying, Get thee behind me, Satan: for thou savourest not the things that be of God, but the things that be of men.**

Jesus made sure the other Eleven heard his reply to Peter. It was time for all of them to learn the true nature and purpose of His ministry, especially if they harbored the same, false Messianic expectations that fired up the crowds. It was time for His men to know about the Cross—time for them to learn that self-denial and sacrifice were His way.

Those were hard lessons for His men. They are still hard truths for many in the modern Church. From the day we are born, our culture aims us toward success. From youth, we learn to do our best to get ahead. Then Jesus turns all of this on its head. This self-interested approach to life is the way men think, He warns. The things of God lie down a different path. Peter's aversion to the Cross put him squarely in opposition to God, so much so that Jesus called him "Satan."

What a put-down for a fellow who had just been complimented as the recipient of the greatest truth ever revealed from Heaven!

### IV. Living by Dying—Mark 8:34-35

**34 And when he had called the people unto him with his disciples also, he said unto them, Whosoever will come after me, let him deny himself, and take up his cross, and follow me.**

**35 For whosoever will save his life shall lose it; but whosoever shall lose his life for my sake and the gospel's,**

**the same shall save it.**

Now Jesus expands His audience to include "the people" as well as His chosen Twelve. He does not reveal the coming Cross to the crowds, but He does teach them about the spirit that explains the Cross.

We should remember that when Jesus talks here about denying oneself and taking up a cross, nobody in that crowd had an inkling that Jesus would soon be crucified. They simply did not hear these words the way we do.

Do we understand any better than they did what Jesus meant about saving our lives by losing them? The self-preservation and self-advancement instincts that caused Peter to object so strongly to the idea of the Cross, often cause believers today to vie for honor and power in Christian circles. Saving life by losing it is a hard concept to sell in any circle—even to those of us who wear Jesus' name.

**V. The Worth of Our Soul—Mark 8:36-37**

**36 For what shall it profit a man, if he shall gain the whole world, and lose his own soul?**

**37 Or what shall a man give in exchange for his soul?**

The attitude that makes Peter protest his Master's dying is the same misguided spirit that causes people to give up everything in order to reach goals and acquire possessions that turn out in the end to be without value.

Some newer Bible versions read "life" instead of "soul." Other modern versions stick with "soul," but the NLT footnote explains that the word for "soul" means our "self." The price being paid for seeking the wrong goals for the wrong reasons is not eternal salvation. Instead, Jesus is warning here that a person can lose his personal integrity or can waste all the time, talent, and energy that make up his life. The selfish approach Peter sought would cost a person everything that matters in life.

**VI. Ashamed of Jesus—Mark 8:38**

**38 Whosoever therefore shall be ashamed of me and of my words in this adulterous and sinful generation; of him also shall the Son of man be ashamed, when he cometh in the glory of his Father with the holy angels.**

Tie this verse back to the idea that provoked Jesus' rebuke to Peter. As Christians, our only message is Christ crucified (1 Cor. 1:23). If we choose the sophistication of this world in place of the sacrificial humility modeled by our Lord, this may be the equivalent of being "ashamed" of Jesus and His way.

Peter did learn the lesson Jesus taught him on this day described in Mark 8. In the end, Peter would go to his own physical cross because of his devotion to the crucified One. He was not ashamed of his Lord.

**VII. The Coming Kingdom—Mark 9:1**

**9:1 And he said unto them, Verily I say unto you, That there be some of them that stand here, which shall not taste of death, till they have seen the kingdom of God come with power.**

Christ predicts that God's Kingdom would come in its power while some in the crowd that day were still alive. Some scholars link this verse to Jesus' words about the fall of Jerusalem in Mark 13:30.

## Evangelistic Emphasis

A recent cartoon shows a man worshipfully kneeling at an altar. Instead of the expected symbol, perched on top of this altar is a huge replica of a #1 lottery ball. The man is soulfully closing a just-uttered prayer with the words, "For thine is the kingdom, the power ball, and the glory forever. Amen."

Our culture's growing addiction to gambling is one clear indication of this new and alarming commitment to "success-by-chance." All across America small towns and big cities left with big holes in their local economies are embracing gambling casinos and lottery games as their tickets to salvation.

State-run lottery games are used to fund public education. We would rather buy a lottery ticket than approve local school budgets. We like to take any short cut that keeps us from responsibility. We are good at preaching to others but are very slow at taking up our cross and following Jesus. Self-denial is painful.

The good news is that in a world gone crazy, Jesus is still the answer. The confession, "you are the Christ the son of the living God" still brings redemption. Our challenge is to confront the popular paths to salvation with THE WAY. Jesus redefines success as being willing to make a sacrifice. When we give up our human efforts at salvation and trust His sacrifice, we all can know salvation. That is the essence of sacrifice; and we are to pattern our lives after Jesus who made one great sacrifice for us.

ଔଔଔ

## Memory Selection

"And he saith unto them, But whom say ye that I am? And Peter answereth and saith unto him, Thou art the Christ." *Mark 8: 29*

Most of us feel an affinity for Simon Peter. He was a big buffoon who let his mouth write checks that his spiritual life could not cash. He gives us hope that you and I, as flawed individuals, can have the hope of being faithful disciples of Christ.

With Peter seen as a buffoon by many, he still was right a couple of times. The second time was when Peter asked Jesus if he could get out of the boat and walk to the Lord on the water. Before he sank, Peter did take a few steps on the water. Simon Peter knows what it feels like to walk on water, if for a few steps.

This is the first time that Simon Peter was right. Jesus was asking who the people were saying He was. The disciples had given Jesus all of the ideas of popular opinions. When Jesus asked who the disciples thought He was, it was Simon Peter who made this confession.

"You are the Christ!" Peter understood that Jesus was the Messiah. It is obvious from further conversation that Peter had a very limited concept of what Messiah meant, but he was right. He was willing to say in front of others what was on his mind. Of course, we learn that Peter did not have much of a problem speaking his mind, but this time he was right!

Who do you say that Jesus is?

## Weekday Problems

Scott was the most spiritual person at First Church and he was quick to tell everyone so. Each Sunday in worship, his feet were tapping, arms waving, and he was singing at the top of his lungs. His Bible was always with him. It was worn out from all the page turning he did. Scott loved anything spiritual. He loved talk about spiritual life and especially spiritual warfare. He was always at Bible studies and prayer groups. Scott also loved to talk to others about his spiritual life and how their lives did not add up quite like his standards would have them.

Scott would be contacted almost every time the Habitat for Humanity coordinator needed help with a house. Scott would always be busy praying or going to some spiritual training event. He would not teach Sunday school because he liked to go to another church on Sunday to "get more food." Scott would not DO anything in the church.

He was quick to answer that he was saved by grace through faith. He could never answer the question about "taking up his cross and following Jesus." He said he would have to pray about it.

Have you known people who were so heavenly minded they were no earthly good?

How should our belief in Jesus transform us into "servants?"

Discuss the relationship between faith and works?

# Love Marks

One little boy was often embarrassed because he had so many freckles.

"I love your freckles," his grandmother told him as she knelt beside him. "When I was a little girl I always wanted freckles," she said, while tracing her finger across the child's cheek. "Freckles are beautiful."

The boy looked up, "Really?"

"Of course," said the grandmother. "Why, just name me one thing that's prettier than freckles."

The little boy thought for a moment, peered intensely into his grandma's face, and softly whispered, "Wrinkles."

# This Lesson in Your Life

What Jesus said about denying self and taking up the cross flies in the face of some popular theology.

The first wrong attitude toward healing is peculiar to the West in recent times– the belief that suffering has no rightful place in the world and certainly no place in the redeemed order of things. Such complacency is surely one cause of the spiritual poverty of the Western church. Jesus did not have that view, neither did the writer to the Hebrews– nor C.S. Lewis, nor John Donne. Suffering has its place and value in this life, no matter how much we yearn for its absence. 1 Peter tells us that suffering is the opportunity for God to "burn off" all that is false in us, leaving us as the pure metal we should be in Jesus Christ. Suffering has been seen in theological history, as a time that God has called both individuals and societies to repentance.

Instead of fully understanding and redeeming suffering, we pray for its removal while harnessing it to become more Christ like. We have ignored it and impoverished ourselves in an attempt to make practical steps toward its amelioration.

The second idea is that preacher's cliché—instant gratification. We all know about this, and yet we continually diminish our capacity for perseverance by accepting it. This is especially true when we have minor afflictions, and might be excusable if we actually did anything worthwhile with our lives.

Where is the concept of self-denial? Where is the notion of following Christ in the way of suffering? We have lost both denial and suffering in our instant gratification. God wants you healthy, wealthy, and wise according to American theology.

We have endured economic set backs and trials over recent years. Many have personally experienced lay-offs, foreclosures, the loss of wealth, and the anxiety that comes with a major economic downturn. While the media would like to tell us that things are on the mend, perhaps you are not finding that to be the case. You have experienced true suffering. What have you done with that suffering? What have you discovered about instant gratification in the past years? Haven't you found more pleasure in delaying purchases and in saving money for that proverbial "rainy day?"

Jesus suffered humiliation and death at the hands of the Pharisees and the temple authorities. Yet, our modern expression of the Christian faith has lost the notion of that suffering. You can actually watch this happen in some congregations. We go immediately from Palm Sunday to Easter with no stopping at Good Friday to consider the cross.

What opportunities does suffering bring you to grow in the faith of Jesus Christ?

How do you talk to others about suffering and faith?

**1. What information did Jesus seek from his disciples as they traveled through Caesarea Philippi?**
Jesus asked his disciples, "Who do the people say that I am?"

**2. What was the popular opinion about Jesus according to the disciples?**
Some thought Jesus was John the Baptist. Others thought He was Elijah. Still others thought he was one of the prophets.

**3. What specific question did Jesus pose to His disciples after hearing about public opinion?**
He asked them, "Who do YOU say that I am?"

**4. Who answered for the group and what was the essence of his answer?**
Peter was the spokesman for the group. He answered, "You are the Christ."

**5. What did Jesus tell the disciples they should do with the information about His identity?**
Jesus sternly ordered the disciples that they were not to tell anyone about Him.

**6. What did Jesus begin to teach the disciples about how the Christ was to be treated?**
He taught them that He must undergo much suffering by the chief priests. He would be killed, and on the third day, he would rise again.

**7. How did Peter respond to this new insight to the role of the Christ?**
Peter took Jesus aside and attempted to correct His theology about the nature of the Christ.

**8. How did Jesus respond to Peter's theological correction?**
Jesus rebuked Peter saying, "Get behind me Satan, for you are setting your mind not on divine things but on human things."

**9. What were the conditions that Jesus gave the crowd for discipleship?**
The disciple must deny himself, take up his cross, and follow Jesus.

**10. What happens to those who are ashamed of Jesus and His words?**
"Those who are ashamed of me ... of them the son of Man will be ashamed when he comes in the glory of His Father.

When Peter confessed that Jesus was the Messiah, he finally took a leap of faith, a genuine risk. He quit being an "armchair disciple," and for just a moment became an airborne "extreme disciple"—risking everything for the thrill of claiming Jesus as Messiah totally and completely. When Jesus followed Peter's big risk by revealing the God-sized risk He Himself would undertake, Peter lost his nerve.

Peter had come to recognize Jesus as Messiah because of the "glory days" and good times of Jesus' Galilean ministry. Peter could not believe that his newly confessed Messiah was "big enough" to embrace the ignominy, and defeat, the suffering, and ridicule, the torture, and death that Jesus predicted were to come. Peter thought he had to protect Jesus from this future, shielding Him from exposing the divine reputation to such a high-level risk. Despite his confession of faith, Peter's concept of the Messiah, his understanding of God's power and purpose, was not "big enough."

God took the biggest risk in all of history when He created mankind and gave the freedom to choose or reject a relationship with God. This divine risk was so huge that eventually it necessitated another God-ordained gamble—a crucified Christ. Jesus incarnated God's risk-taking love for humanity by offering us a new way back to the wholeness God intended for creation.

Peter's worries were ridiculous. With God's help, Jesus was big enough to shoulder the cross, big enough to bear the suffering of the world, big enough to endure the scorn and rejection, big enough to accept the judgment of death. Jesus the Christ, Jesus the Messiah, was big enough to endure all this, to take this ultimate risk because He knew first-hand a God who was big enough—big enough to break through the hate with love, big enough to relieve the suffering forever, big enough to roll away the rock at the tomb's entrance, big enough to break the bonds of death itself and big enough to bring about the glory of the Resurrection.

Jesus' first formal lesson on discipleship taught that there was no risk we can take that is so great it could ever separate us from God's redemption and God's love. Our greatest risk, Jesus cautioned, comes when we try to "play it safe" and avoid any risk-taking ventures—"those who want to save their life will lose it, and those who lose their life for my sake, and for the sake of the gospel, will save it."

Jesus wants us to be "extreme Christians." The body of Christ must become the "extreme church." We have a big-enough God, a big-enough Savior, to handle whatever risks may emerge from our extreme behavior. We have a God who risked loving us beyond all else.

୫০୯ଷ

**230**

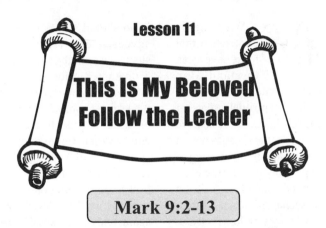

## Lesson 11

# This Is My Beloved / Follow the Leader

## Mark 9:2-13

And after six days Jesus taketh with him Peter, and James, and John, and leadeth them up into an high mountain apart by themselves: and he was transfigured before them.

3 And his raiment became shining, exceeding white as snow; so as no fuller on earth can white them.

4 And there appeared unto them Elias with Moses: and they were talking with Jesus.

5 And Peter answered and said to Jesus, Master, it is good for us to be here: and let us make three tabernacles; one for thee, and one for Moses, and one for Elias.

6 For he wist not what to say; for they were sore afraid.

7 And there was a cloud that overshadowed them: and a voice came out of the cloud, saying, This is my beloved Son: hear him.

8 And suddenly, when they had looked round about, they saw no man any more, save Jesus only with themselves.

9 And as they came down from the mountain, he charged them that they should tell no man what things they had seen, till the Son of man were risen from the dead.

10 And they kept that saying with themselves, questioning one with another what the rising from the dead should mean.

11 And they asked him, saying, Why say the scribes that Elias must first come?

12 And he answered and told them, Elias verily cometh first, and restoreth all things; and how it is written of the Son of man, that he must suffer many things, and be set at nought.

13 But I say unto you, That Elias is indeed come, and they have done unto him whatsoever they listed, as it is written of him.

**Memory Verse**
Mark 9:7

**Background Scripture**
Mark 9:2-13

**Devotional Reading**
Malachi 4:1-5

**focus** What a heady experience that must have been to stand atop that Galilean mountain shoulder to shoulder with the spiritual greats of all time, Moses, Elijah, and Jesus! We can understand why the apostles would want to prolong that summit meeting as long as they possibly could. However, Heaven changed that idea. A cloud obscured the scene, and when it lifted, the RSV says, "they saw Jesus only."

So should we. We must not allow advocates of diversity demoting Jesus to just another prophet alongside Mohammed, Moses, or Buddha. He is not just another philosopher whose views must compete with Marx, Kant, or Sarte. Nor is He the founder of a cult who must give equal time to an assortment of kooks and gurus. We can be nice about it, but we must be firm in our conviction that Jesus only can save us. Only Jesus died and rose again. Only Jesus was God in the flesh. The Transfiguration should teach us to see Jesus only.

## For a Lively Start ℬℭ

Episode by episode, Mark in his Gospel presents Jesus to us as the Son of God. In his opening scene, God affirms the just-baptized Jesus by saying, "This is my Son." In subsequent events, Mark lets us watch Him commanding demons, raising the dead, calming storms, walking on the water, feeding multitudes, and healing dreaded diseases—doing things that cause His incredulous followers to exclaim, "What manner of man is this?"

Now, at the high point in our Lord's ministry, Mark lets us listen while God once more verifies Jesus' true credentials. "This is my beloved Son," the voice booms from Heaven. What better evidence could we possibly find?

| Teaching Outline | Daily Bible Readings |
|---|---|
| I. Atop the Mountain—Mark 9:2-8 | Mon. Moses, Elijah, and the Coming Day *Malachi 4:1-6* |
|   A. Jesus' Changed Appearance, 2-3 | Tue. Moses on the Mountain *Exodus 19:1-6* |
|   B. Their Honored Guests, 4 | Wed. Elijah on the Mountain *1 Kings 19:11-18* |
|   C. Peter's Suggestion, 5-6 | |
|   D. Heaven's Answer, 7-8 | Thu A Mountain of Revelation *Ezekiel 40:1-4* |
| II. On the Way Down— Mark 9:9-13 | Fri. Come Up to the Mountain *Isaiah 2:1-4* |
|   A. Jesus' Command, 9 | Sat. Ponder God's Love *Psalm 48:9-14* |
|   B. Resurrection Questions, 10 | |
|   C. Elijah Concerns, 11-13 | Sun. Listen to My Son! *Mark 9:2-13* |

# Verse by Verse

## Mark 9:2-13

### I. Atop the Mountain—Mark 9:2-8

**A. Jesus' Changed Appearance, 2-3**

**2 And after six days Jesus taketh with him Peter, and James, and John, and leadeth them up into an high mountain apart by themselves: and he was transfigured before them.**

**3 And his raiment became shining, exceeding white as snow; so as no fuller on earth can white them.**

The Gospels tell us that on three occasions Jesus took Peter, James, and John with Him to share in special moments denied to the other apostles. On one occasion, He took them to Jairus' home, where they watched the Lord raise the man's dead daughter. On another occasion, He took them deep with Him into Gethsemane where He agonized in prayer before the mob dragged Him away to die. Then here—"apart by themselves," Mark emphasizes—Jesus treated these special friends to a morning on the mountain with Moses and Elijah. Several decades later Peter would recall this extraordinary day, "We were eyewitnesses of his majesty. For he received honor and glory from God the Father when the voice came to him from the Majestic Glory, saying, 'This is my Son, whom I love; with him I am well pleased.' We ourselves heard this voice that came from heaven when we were with him on the sacred mountain" (2 Pet. 1:16-18, NIV).

"Transfiguration" is the word that identifies this Gospel event to all English-speaking Christians—a word imparted by the KJV language. "Figure" refers to shape or appearance. "Trans" is a prefix that implies change. On the mountain, the apostles watched as Jesus' appearance was changed so that His clothing shone with a luminous whiteness described as whiter than any scrubbing tool ("fuller"—KJV) could produce.

**B. Their Honored Guests, 4**

**4 And there appeared unto them Elias with Moses: and they were talking with Jesus.**

Evidently, the three apostles were not included in this one-of-a-kind conversation. Moses and Elijah showed up to talk with Jesus. Luke tells us that the main topic of their discussion was Christ's coming death (9:31). If you were about to die, would it help to visit with two heroes who had already been dead for several hundred years?

How could we possibly come up

233

with two more prestigious spiritual representatives than Moses and Elijah? No wonder Peter wanted to keep them around for a while.

### C. Peter's Suggestion, 5-6

**5 And Peter answered and said to Jesus, Master, it is good for us to be here: and let us make three tabernacles; one for thee, and one for Moses, and one for Elias.**

**6 For he wist not what to say; for they were sore afraid.**

The word "tabernacles" in the older texts has confused many Bible readers, conjuring up images of massive construction projects to build three impressive chapels or cathedrals atop the mountain. Peter had nothing like that in mind. "Tabernacles" is the same word we encounter in the Feast of Tabernacles. In our modern versions, it is rendered Feast of Booths or Huts. The structures Peter wants to erect are the same kind of temporary shelters the Jews built and lived in during the Yom Kippur festival, shelters not unlike pup tents or fair booths, easily erected and quickly dismantled. These modest structures would have briefly shielded Jesus and their honored guests from sun or rain.

"He wist not" in vs. 6 is archaic English that means "he did not know." Peter is like some of us who get a serious case of fright. He spoke because he did not know what to say—not a very good reason to start talking.

Notice that the apostles' reaction to this supernatural event was not to say, "Oh, great!" Instead, fear gripped them. One version says they were "terrified" (NRSV), which is the only sensible response by any human who comes into such close contact with the divine.

### D. Heaven's Answer, 7-8

**7 And there was a cloud that overshadowed them: and a voice came out of the cloud, saying, This is my beloved Son: hear him.**

**8 And suddenly, when they had looked round about, they saw no man any more, save Jesus only with themselves.**

The same Voice that verified Christ's Sonship at His baptism speaks again here on the Mount of Transfiguration. The message is also the same. "This is my Son—my Beloved—the One I love." This heavenly endorsement must have been a great source of encouragement to Jesus when He was launching His ministry. Now that the prospect of an awful death appears before Him, the Father's reaffirmation of His love for His Son surely must impart strength and comfort at this critical moment.

When that momentary cloud lifts, the apostles can see that, just as suddenly as their heavenly visitors had appeared, the visitors vanished. The apostles are now alone with their Master, and He looks normal again.

### II. On the Way Down—Mark 9:9-13

### A. Jesus' Command, 9

**9 And as they came down from the mountain, he charged them that they should tell no man what things they had seen, till the Son of man were risen from the dead.**

All of us who have been blessed by marvelous mountaintop experiences at spiritual retreats know that the bliss and excitement of those times are temporary. We always have to come back down the mountain and resume normal life. So do the apostles. Difficult tasks and hard days await them down below.

Telling the masses about the Transfiguration at that moment could have triggered the pandemonium of revolution at a time when Jesus did not need that distraction. After the Resurrection, there would be time enough for telling.

### B. Resurrection Questions, 10

**10 And they kept that saying with themselves, questioning one with another what the rising from the dead should mean.**

We read these verses and have no doubt what Jesus means when He speaks here about rising from the dead. We celebrate Easter; and we know the Good News of the Resurrection. However, the apostles are hearing these words before the Cross—before the empty tomb. Jesus' instruction to tell no one about the events atop the mountain until after He rises leaves Peter and his friends scratching their heads.

### C. Elijah Concerns, 11-13

**11 And they asked him, saying, Why say the scribes that Elias must first come?**

**12 And he answered and told them, Elias verily cometh first, and restoreth all things; and how it is written of the Son of man, that he must suffer many things, and be set at nought.**

**13 But I say unto you, That Elias is indeed come, and they have done unto him whatsoever they listed, as it is written of him.**

In the final verses of the Old Testament, Malachi foretold the return of Elijah before the appearing of the Messiah. Jesus had already told His people plainly that this prophecy was fulfilled by John the Baptist (Matt. 11:11-14), but these three apostles evidently were not paying attention. Having just seen Elijah on the mountain, they start trying to connect what they have seen to what Malachi predicted. Jesus corrects them, reaffirming that John the Baptist was the Elijah they were looking for. Then Jesus tries to get His apostles to see that the same Scriptures that foretell Elijah's return also foretell that the Messiah will suffer much mistreatment. Nevertheless, the fledgling apostles at this moment are still less able to hear the truth about the Cross than the truth about Elijah's coming. How often our preconceptions keep us from seeing the plainest truths in God's word.

## Evangelistic Emphasis

There is an old rabbinic story about the man who left his village, weary of his life, longing for a place where he could escape all the struggles of this earth. He set out in search of a magical city—the heavenly city of his dreams, where all things would be perfect.

He walked all day and by dusk found himself in a forest where he decided to spend the night. Eating a crust of bread he had brought, he said his prayers, and before going to sleep, placed his shoes in the center of the path, pointing them in the direction he would continue the next morning.

Unbeknownst to him, however, someone appeared in the night and turned his shoes around, pointing them back in the direction from which he had come.

The next morning, in all the innocence of folly, he got up, gave thanks to the God of the universe, and started on his way again in the direction his shoes pointed. For a second time, he walked all day and toward evening finally saw the magical city in the distance. As he got closer, it looked curiously familiar. But he pressed on, found a street much like his own, knocked on a familiar door, greeted the family he found there and lived happily ever after in the magical city of his dreams.

What God does in the night is turn our shoes around and point us toward home. The Transfiguration is about calling us to point our shoes in another direction.

## Memory Selection

ഇൗരു

"And there was a cloud that overshadowed them: and a voice came out of the cloud, saying, "This is my beloved Son: hear him." *Mark 9:7*

Airplane pilots enjoy flying under visual flight rules. Visual flight rules mean that pilots do not have to be qualified to use the navigational instruments in a plane's cockpit in order to be able to fly. They can see the horizon in VFR conditions and can keep the plane oriented and headed in the proper direction. VFR days are days of good weather.

IFR means the pilot must be qualified to use the various instruments in the plane's cockpit that are for flying in conditions in which the pilot cannot see the horizon in order to keep the plane properly oriented. Many a pilot has lost his life when weather conditions changed from VFR to IFR (Instrument Flight Rules). These pilots trusted their instincts and their skills as a pilot and failed to heed the direction that was coming from "inside the cockpit."

There are times when the clouds of trouble and pain surround us and we cannot find our way. These are moments that we often trust our instincts and our skills to get us out of these situations. Often our abilities are inadequate for navigating through life without the ability to see the horizon. Out of that cloud, the voice called to the disciples. We need to learn a lesson here, that at times when we "can't see the horizon," Jesus is there with us and we can arrive safely at our destination if we will keep our hearts tuned to His voice.

# Weekday Problems

Becky was back in the pastor's office again. Her complaint was the same that it had been for the last dozen times she had been in the office of the pastors. Her complaint was that the choir was just not what it used to be. She had been the volunteer director of the choir for 30 years. In the past dozen or so years, the church had grown to the point that the choir director was now a paid position. When the position became a part time paid position, Becky had made it clear that she was not interested in the paid position, but that she would continue to sing in the choir.

Now years later, and a couple of pastors later, Becky was lamenting the fact that the choir seemed to have lost the commitment they once had to the church. She noted that participation in rehearsals was down significantly. The choir was having all sorts of trouble recruiting new members to the choir. Becky was particularly upset that the younger people in the church did not seem to be interested in church music. She told the pastor that she made these requests and issues known every Wednesday night at choir practice, and she talked about these issues with members of the church.

Becky was wondering what the benefit of having a paid choir director was, since it seemed the choir was so much better back when she was the choir director.

She told the pastor she did not want him to take any action, she was simply describing the problem to him.

How are we often stuck in the past? Do you think Peter wanting to build booths reflects a desire to hold on to the way it was?

## Barbie Dolls

A father buying a present for his daughter asked the toy store clerk, "How much are those Barbies in the window?"

"That depends," she replied. "We have Barbie Goes to the Gym for $19.95, Barbie Goes to the Ball for $19.95, Barbie Goes Shopping for $19.95, Barbie Goes to the Beach for $19.95, Barbie Goes Nightclubbing for $19.95, and Divorced Barbie for $265.00"

"Wow!" the father exclaimed, "Why is the Divorced Barbie so expensive when all the others cost only $19.95?"

"That's obvious" the sales lady says. "Divorced Barbie comes with

Ken's house, Ken's car, Ken's boat, Ken's furniture . . ."

# This Lesson in Your Life

Thomas Merton once said that at the root of all war is fear - not so much the fear we have of one another but the fear we have of everything. How right he is. Fear makes all of God's creatures do strange things. Once adrenalin hits the bloodstream, who can predict what ways of fight or flight follow? For example, unlike other bears, grizzlies merit extreme caution from hikers because they have a highly unstable adrenal gland and are "high" on this fight-flight drug most of the time. Imagine having your insides—your nerves, stomach, and heart—jangling, reeling, and pounding all the time as if you had just seen the latest Alien movie. Poor bears! Poor anyone who gets in their way!

The disciples experienced that mouth-drying, heart-thumping, knee-buckling kind of fear on the mountaintop at the Transfiguration. After rejoicing at the presence of Elijah and Moses, they were suddenly reduced to blubbery, quaking jelly by the power and splendor of the voice from above. They could not comprehend the magnificence of the divine presence, or the implications of what the voice was saying. The entire experience was a mystery way beyond their previous life events. No wonder they reacted by curling into defensive little fear-balls at Jesus' feet.

The glory of the transfiguration event shines as brilliantly and as incomprehensibly today as it did for those disciples nearly 2000 years ago. If we still cannot understand this vision, we can at least learn how Jesus would have us behave to events that challenge our comprehension and threaten to paralyze us with fear. While Jesus did not explain the meaning behind the Transfiguration mystery, He did give us a map for coming back down from the mountaintop experiences in our lives.

Jesus' counsel to the disciples, as He helped them to their feet, might be paraphrased as, "Get up, come down, keep quiet (until the time is right), then yell!" These four steps, for getting off the mountain, work just as effectively in our lives today. When God does something dramatic, or something "mysterious" happens in our lives, we too can get scared. Depending on genetic predispositions toward adrenalin overload, we react with "fight-fear" or "flight-fear," lashing out in panic or retreating in misery.

After the sudden death of a loved one, we ask–how can lives and God still be good? After the recessive economy strikes home, where suddenly we have no job, no career, and no self-identity, we ask–how can we find a new path for life? Even positive experiences confuse and confound. God calls us, challenging us to serve in ways that threaten the stability and comfort for which we have worked so hard. How can we respond?

Some times, we need to stand in silence, letting that cloud surround us, and then hear the promise of God. "This is my son, listen to him."

## GETTING
## THE FACTS STRAIGHT

**1. The story of the Transfiguration begins "and after six days," six days after what event?**

Six days after Jesus had made a prediction about His coming death, he took Peter, James, and John up on the mountain and was transfigured in front of them.

**2. Who did Jesus take up on the mountain with Him and what was the significance of that selection?**

Jesus took Peter, James, and John with Him on the mountain. These three disciples become Jesus' inner circle of disciples.

**3. Jesus was transfigured in front of them. How was the transfiguration described?**

Jesus' changed and His garments became glistening, intensely white, and whiter than anyone could have bleached them.

**4. Who appeared with Jesus on the mountain?**

Elijah and Moses appeared with Jesus in His transfigured state.

**5. What was the significance of Elijah and Moses appearing with Jesus?**

Moses represented the Old Testament law and Elijah represented the prophets of the Israel.

**6. What were Elijah and Moses doing, and from other gospel writers what do you know about what they were saying to Jesus?**

Moses and Elijah were talking to Jesus. They were talking to Him about His death.

**7. What happened next in the story?**

Peter was frightened, or just needed to talk and said, "Let's build three booths, one for each of you."

**8. What do you think the significance of the booths was?**

The booths probably symbolize Peter's desire to capture the moment or to be able to stay on that mountain indefinitely.

**9. Why did Peter say what he did?**

He spoke because he was exceedingly afraid according to the text.

**10. What happened after Peter spoke?**

After Peter spoke, a cloud covered the mountain and there was a voice heard from the cloud. The voice said, "this is my beloved Son, listen to Him."

The Transfiguration confounds even preachers. We ministers sometimes avoid it because it is hard to explain in a sermon. It is not easy to explain in written Sunday school materials. There are times that we need to believe rather than have all the things explained to us. We look for a logical explanation of the Transfiguration and look for some meaning we might learn from it that will help us with our daily living. We do not mean to, but tend to ignore passages that are not practical. We get nervous at times when the Bible appears to speak of Jesus in mysterious terms. This is one of those times.

John M. Buchanan, Senior Minister of Fourth Presbyterian Church in Chicago, tells of receiving, a couple of years ago, "an interesting and important note" from the sixth and seventh grade church school class. It read as follows:

Dear Dr. Buchanan:

We have some questions about Christmas.

Did the star stand still? Were the shepherds and wise men real? How was Jesus born if his parents didn't have sexual intercourse?

Please meet us next Sunday and tell us the answers to our questions. Merry Christmas, The Sixth and Seventh Grade Church School Class

Dr. Buchanan writes: "Well, my first response was that back in the dark ages when I was in sixth grade, the phrase 'sexual intercourse' had not yet been uttered aloud in my hearing. In fact, one didn't encounter that particular phrase until ninth grade health class, if I remember correctly, and for certain, it was not a phrase one would use in a note to one's minister.

"My second response is that no one ever tells you, nor do seminaries and divinity schools provide training in one of the unwritten lines in a clergy job description, namely, serving as a court of final appeal for questions no one else wants to answer. Parents can always say, 'Why don't you ask your Sunday school teacher about that?' The teachers apparently say, 'Let's ask the minister.' . . . I met the class the following week at a doughnut shop and learned, once again, a fundamental lesson of theological discourse, and that is that 'I don't know' is a legitimate and respectable answer to some questions. And I also discovered a wonderful thing about sixth-graders, and that is they are quite capable of handling the fact that there are some things we do not, and probably will not, understand; and that there just may be more important questions about those things, such as 'What do they mean? What are they saying to us?' The sixth-graders understood that when we talk about the virgin birth, we are not as concerned about Mary of Nazareth's sexual behavior as we are about the nature and identity of her Son."

ജര

240

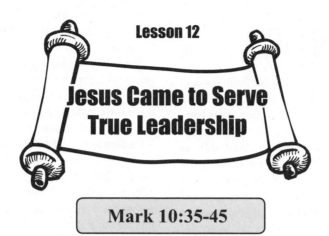

# Lesson 12

## Jesus Came to Serve
## True Leadership

### Mark 10:35-45

And James and John, the sons of Zebedee, come unto him, saying, Master, we would that thou shouldest do for us whatsoever we shall desire.

36 And he said unto them, What would ye that I should do for you?

37 They said unto him, Grant unto us that we may sit, one on thy right hand, and the other on thy left hand, in thy glory.

38 But Jesus said unto them, Ye know not what ye ask: can ye drink of the cup that I drink of? and be baptized with the baptism that I am baptized with?

39 And they said unto him, We can. And Jesus said unto them, Ye shall indeed drink of the cup that I drink of; and with the baptism that I am baptized withal shall ye be baptized:

40 But to sit on my right hand and on my left hand is not mine to give; but it shall be given to them for whom it is prepared.

41 And when the ten heard it, they began to be much displeased with James and John.

42 But Jesus called them to him, and saith unto them, Ye know that they which are accounted to rule over the Gentiles exercise lordship over them; and their great ones exercise authority upon them.

43 But so shall it not be among you: but whosoever will be great among you, shall be your minister:

44 And whosoever of you will be the chiefest, shall be servant of all.

45 For even the Son of man came not to be ministered unto, but to minister, and to give his life a ransom for many.

---

**Memory Verse**
Mark 10:45

**Background Scripture**
Mark 10:35-45

**Devotional Reading**
John 13:3-16

Feb. 20

## fo(us

Much of the unpleasantness and strife both in congregations and in broader fellowship circles stems from the efforts of some to finagle positions of authority and honor. Mark tells us that when the ten other apostles heard what the sons of Zebedee were up to, "they began to be much displeased with James and John." Most of us are just as unhappy when we hear that someone in our ranks is playing the ecclesiastical version of King of the Mountain.

Peaceful churches are led by humble saints with servant hearts—by people who aspire to be shepherds instead of bosses. Repeatedly Jesus tried to teach His apostles that true greatness in His Kingdom belonged to those who were willing to be least in the sight of men, but they kept clambering for positions of honor and power. It seems to be just as hard for Him to teach many of us this lesson today.

## For a Lively Start

Being Christ-like is a grand goal for any believer. It would be fine if we could pray as He did (although His all-night sessions do seem extreme). Should we not aspire to live without sinning, even as He did (none of us will make it, of course, but it is still a great goal)? Surely, our hearts should be as soft as His was, full of compassion

ഇവര

for those who are hungry, sorrowful, or tired.

Striving to be Christ-like seems to be a worthy effort until we recall that being like our Lord involves a cross. Imitating Jesus sounds noble until we realize that it could entail "drinking the cup" of suffering and enduring the "baptism" of torture and shame. Then, how enthusiastic are we to be like Him?

| Teaching Outline | Daily Bible Readings |
|---|---|
| I. The Request of James and John—10:35-37 | Mon. Serving Like a Slave<br>*Luke 15:25-32* |
| II. Jesus' Reply—10:38-40 | Tue. Choosing the Better Part<br>*Luke 10:38-42* |
| A. "You Know Not", 38-39 | Wed. As One Who Serves<br>*Luke 22:24-30* |
| B. "Not Mine to Give", 40 | Thu Come, Follow Me<br>*Mark 10:17-22* |
| III. Ten Unhappy Apostles—10:41 | Fri. Serving and Following<br>*John 12:20-26* |
| IV. Instructing the Twelve—10:42-45 | Sat. An Example Set<br>*John 13:3-16* |
| A. This World's Values, 42 | Sun. Greatness Through Service<br>*Mark 10:35-45* |
| B. Kingdom Values, 43-44 | |
| C. Christ's Example, 45 | |

# Verse by Verse

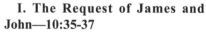

Mark 10:35-45

## I. The Request of James and John—10:35-37

**35 And James and John, the sons of Zebedee, come unto him, saying, Master, we would that thou shouldest do for us whatsoever we shall desire.**

**36 And he said unto them, What would ye that I should do for you?**

**37 They said unto him, Grant unto us that we may sit, one on thy right hand, and the other on thy left hand, in thy glory.**

The kind of blank-check request James and John pose to Jesus would raise red flags for any boss, wouldn't it? "Please agree to do whatever I ask you to," opens up a Pandora's box of possibilities—not all of them good ones.

Jesus plays along with the sons of Zebedee. Instead of agreeing to give them whatever they might request, the Lord asks them to be more specific before He says Yes. One reason He hesitates to grant their wishes is that He knows how ruinous their selfish goals would be. If He agrees to give them positions of status and authority, they could be ruined eternally. Could this be the reason our prayers sometimes seem to go unanswered? Could it be that the Lord is protecting us from ourselves?

In Jewish thought, the right hand of the king was the place of greatest prominence, and the left hand was the next-best honor. James and John obviously have bought into the popular concept of the Messiah as an earthly king who would reign over the Jews with all the pomp and power of David or Solomon. Sensing that things are about to come to a head in Christ's ministry, these two apostles try to take advantage of the other ten. They want to own the top political positions. In effect, they are asking Jesus, "Please make us Secretary of State and Secretary of War."

## II. Jesus' Reply—10:38-40

### A. "You Know Not ", 38-39

**38 But Jesus said unto them, Ye know not what ye ask: can ye drink of the cup that I drink of? and be baptized with the baptism that I am baptized with?**

**39 And they said unto him, We can. And Jesus said unto them, Ye shall indeed drink of the cup that I drink of; and with the baptism that I am baptized withal shall ye be baptized:**

James and John have no idea what they have just asked for. Top positions in Jesus' Kingdom would not be a

243

ticket to power and honor. Instead, they would expose a person to abuse and suffering beyond their imagination.

"Can you drink the cup I drink?" is Jesus' way of asking if they can endure a trial like the one He will be subjected to. Can they face nails and thorns, as He will? Can they stand and let men lie about them and jeer at them, as He must? Are they very eager to go to Calvary with Him?

Jesus changes the metaphor when He asks, "Can you share my baptism?" Yet, the question is still the same. Of course, James and John are not like us. They have not read the Gospel story as we have. They know nothing about the trial and the crucifixion. Jesus has been predicting it, but their growing hopes of sharing Messianic power keep them from hearing a word Jesus says about suffering and death. They are equally deaf when Jesus responds to their ignorant request with metaphors about suffering.

"We can," is their quick but deluded response when Jesus asks, "Can you?" If tears are not in our Lord's eyes, surely they are in His heart as He answers His own question. "Yes, these men He loves so dearly will indeed drink the cup with Him and endure the baptism of suffering He faces." No doubt, He knows how much mistreatment and persecution they will go through one day as His faithful emissaries. He knows the answer to His question, but they do not even comprehend the question.

### B. "Not Mine to Give ", 40

**40 But to sit on my right hand and on my left hand is not mine to give; but it shall be given to them for whom it is prepared.**

If James and John are in the dark during most of this conversation, so are we when Jesus makes this statement. Sitting at His right and left hands clearly indicates positions of power, but what do we know about such positions in the Kingdom of our Lord. He goes on to explain the inverted values of the heavenly Kingdom, telling us how the highest positions involve the most humiliation and drudgery. With great difficulty, we can grasp this, but who are "those for whom it is prepared"? Would top honors in Heaven not be recognized until the Lord saw who suffered the most and who offered the most degrading service to his fellows? When Jesus tells us this, we have to line up alongside James and John and scratch our heads too.

### III. Ten Unhappy Apostles— 10:41

**41 And when the ten heard it, they began to be much displeased with James and John.**

Matthew tells us in his Gospel that the request of James and John for honored spots is actually presented to Jesus by their mother (Matt. 20:20). The very idea that James and John have someone recommending them could have disappointed the other disciples, not to mention the fact that this woman is unfairly trying to obtain the powers that all of the others want.

If the Twelve—those men closest to our Savior—became upset with each other, why should it surprise us that Christ's followers today sometimes become upset with each other?

### IV. Instructing the Twelve— 10:42-45

**A. This World's Values, 42**

**42 But Jesus called them to him, and saith unto them, Ye know that they which are accounted to rule over the Gentiles exercise lordship over them; and their great ones exercise authority upon them.**

When Jesus knows His disciples are contending for who will run the coming Kingdom, He gathers them for the exercise of authority. His illustration is the way all the kingdoms of the world (those who rule over the Gentiles) define and parcel out power. In that worldly political realm, the most powerful dominates the others. The most powerful king subdues his own people and anyone who tries to oppose him. Greatness in that realm is determined by who has the biggest army, or who has the most resources. It is a power game, an exercise of control.

**B. Kingdom Values, 43-44**

**43 But so shall it not be among you: but whosoever will be great among you, shall be your minister:**

**44 And whosoever of you will be the chiefest, shall be servant of all.**

Christ's lesson here drives a nail into the coffin of the dreams these misguided men had about power and status in an earthly dictatorship. My Kingdom will not run like any kingdom you have ever seen, Jesus tries to tell His disciples. His Kingdom's values will be superior compared to anything they have ever known or imagined. The biggest will be the smallest. The top will be the bottom. The "chiefest" (KJV) will be the lowest servant among them. Surely, the minds of these immature apostles are whirling as they try to make sense of such an upside down realm.

**C. Christ's Example, 45**

**45 For even the Son of man came not to be ministered unto, but to minister, and to give his life a ransom for many.**

You and I look back at this encounter, and the one thing that causes it to make sense to us is our Lord's example. The word "minister" in the KJV can be confusing. We often use the term to refer to some sort of government position. Nothing could be farther from Jesus' meaning here. He is talking about "serving" as the lowest of slaves. "Ransom" is also a concept foreign to our time. The "ransom" that Jesus refers to is the price paid for that freedom when someone purchases the freedom of a slave or a prisoner. Jesus gave His life to buy us back from the slavery of sin and death. That He came to give and not to receive is His lesson here. We, too, should be givers and not takers if we hope to be like Him.

℘℘℘

## Evangelistic Emphasis

America is a nation with a "number one" mentality. We want the best, the brightest, and the biggest. We make assumptions based on this mode of thinking.

A tourist was visiting New York City with his seven-year-old daughter when a man approached to ask for change. The little girl asked what the man wanted.

"He wanted money," her father explained.

The little girl asked why.

"The man is hungry," he said.

At that, his daughter's eyes widened. "They eat money in Manhattan?"

We have some strange view about money, things, and servant-hood in the church.

The most faithful Christian is often not the wealthiest. The neediest person is often not the poorest. James and John found out that Jesus measures people on a completely different scale. The greatest in the kingdom will be servant of all.

If you want to be first with Jesus, you must become the servant of all. He lived this out in a manner that His disciples could see and they still did not really "get it." In our world, can you think of ways in which you might be a servant and thus reflect the love of Christ?

ഇരുൽ

## Memory Selection

"For even the Son of Man did not come to be served, but to serve, and to give His life a ransom for many." *Mark 10: 45*

Mark it down. Anytime you see a happy family, it did not happen by accident. Somebody sacrificed. That person sacrificed convenience, comfort, time, power, and the right to make unilateral decisions. There is no success without sacrifice.

We live in the era of the pampered athlete, executive, politician, educator, student, parishioner, preacher, and nation. What has happened to sacrifice? Sacrifice is the sacrament of love. Jesus made the ultimate sacrifice on our behalf. In Philippians, Paul wrote, "Let the same mind be in you that was in Christ Jesus, who, though he was in the form of God, did not regard equality with God as something to be exploited, but emptied himself, taking the form of a slave, being born in human likeness. And being found in human form, he humbled himself and became obedient to the point of death—even death on a cross." This passage from Philippians affirms the word from Mark that Jesus humbled Himself and became a servant, and that sacrifice He made meant His death on the cross. Jesus put all of creation above Himself in dying on the cross.

Putting someone's needs before our own is the essence of being like Christ. Perhaps our culture would hear the message of sacrifice clearer than the message of prosperity, if God's people practiced sacrificial living. Some in the church seem to have them confused.

# Weekday Problems

Carl Rife tells of being chosen to be the drum major of a new marching band his senior year in high school. "Most of us had absolutely no experience of marching in parades. I still remember leading the band down West Market Street in York, Pennsylvania. My basic job was to march in front of the band and every so often blow my whistle in a certain cadence to strike up the band. As we were marching down West Market Street for a short time, I heard someone from the crowd who had gathered to watch the parade holler to me, 'Mister, you lost your band.' I sneaked a look back and sure enough, there was the Central High School marching band about three-quarters of a block behind."

How do we in the church sometimes lose our bands? Whether it is the Sunday school class we lead or the choir, do we get so caught up in leading we leave them behind? Can you recall a time when being helped by a servant leader renewed your faith? How can we be leaders for Christ and still have the servant attitude that Jesus has called us to have?

Effective Christian leadership means that we put the needs of those we serve above our own needs. As you reflect on the groups of which you are a part, how is servant leadership lived out in these various groups?

How did Jesus give an example of servant leadership as He led the disciples during his public ministry?

---

# Grave Humor

In a London, England cemetery:

Ann Mann
Here lies Ann Mann,
Who lived an old maid
But died an old Mann.
Dec. 8, 1767

In a Ruidoso, New Mexico, cemetery:

Here lies
Johnny Yeast
Pardon me
For not rising.

# This Lesson in Your Life

In the past couple of years, the church has become concerned about saving itself. Part of this crisis of faith stems from the economic conditions of our country. Congregations have laid off staff members, rolled back programming, and even cut the salary of their pastor all to keep the doors opened. Some congregations have even been forced to close because they could not remain financially viable. In the middle of this crisis, some churches have re-examined their mission statement and their expression of the gospel of Christ.

The church is not in this world to serve and save itself. Many congregations have a goal to survive; they desire to keep safe by forming inward looking circles. Missionary discipleship denies that there is any need for the church to "just keep going" if it is not "going" anywhere. Can you state the reason your church exists? Do you know what the mission of your Sunday school class is?

The church has become much too fixated on how to save itself rather than saving the world. The community of faith, the circle of believing disciples, must face the world with its message. The difference between an inward-circle faith and an outward-circle faith is the difference between "Churchianity" and "Christianity." It is time for us to dismount that dead "churchianity" horse in favor for the leadership of the Holy Spirit. That means anything that we have "never done before" ought to be the very things we are doing. Why is it that we keep trying the same things and expecting different results? The answer is that we want to save ourselves and our churches rather than saving the lost by presenting them with the gospel of Jesus Christ.

The number of people parking themselves on a psychiatrist's couch each week, for years on end, testifies to the fact that we all feel ourselves to be fascinating subjects of attention. There are whole churches that share this self-fixation. What would happen if both individually and as a congregation we shook ourselves out of this self-absorption and began to look for the key to our psychological and spiritual health outside ourselves. Jesus counseled that those who seek to save their lives would lose them. Let us look outside the familiar circle of our own problems, our own concerns, and find healing, wholeness, and health in giving ourselves in service to others.

We will save the world and the church as we open our familiar circles outward and start looking at our world differently. Looking to the needs of others will allow those persons to see Christ in us, and that is the purpose of being a Christian.

Jesus came not to be served, but to serve others and give His life as a ransom for many. How do we live that out in our Christian discipleship? How are you "walking the walk" of servant leadership and discipleship? This is the question that the world of the 21$^{st}$ century is waiting for us to answer, and answer it in ways that transforms lives.

## GETTING
## THE FACTS STRAIGHT

**1. As Jesus was walking along the road to Jerusalem, there were two responses to him among those in the crowd. What were they?**
They were amazed and they were afraid at the same time.

**2. What did Jesus do as this group traveled toward Jerusalem?**
Jesus took the disciples aside and told them again what would happen to Him in Jerusalem.

**3. What did Jesus tell the disciples would happen to him in Jerusalem?**
He would be condemned to death and be handed over to the Gentiles. They would mock Him, spit on Him, flog Him, and kill Him. After three days, He would rise again.

**4. After Jesus spoke words about his crucifixion, two disciples came with a question. Who were they?**
James and John the sons of Zebedee came to Jesus with a request.

**5. What was the request that James and John made of Jesus?**
The sons of Zebedee wanted to sit one on the right hand and the other on the left when Jesus came into His kingdom.

**6. In response to their request, Jesus asked a question of them. What was that question?**
"Are you able to drink the cup that I drink, or to be baptized with the baptism with which I am baptized."

**7. What did Jesus tell James and John about their request?**
He told them that He was not able to grant their request.

**8. When the other disciples heard about the request of James and John, what was their response?**
The ten, when they heard it, were angry with James and John.

**9. Jesus talked about the Gentiles and their social structure. What was that structure?**
The Gentiles lord it over them, and their great ones are tyrants over them.

**10. What did Jesus tell the disciples about greatness?**
Whoever wants to be great must be servant of all, and whoever wishes to be first must be slave of all.

Uplift

You have been in a lift line for 45 minutes, waiting to catch a chair that will take you to a black diamond death run down Peak 9.

Or, you are standing in line for a ride at Disney World.

Or, you are one of scores of people with baggage in a line that snakes toward two ticket agents at the airport.

Then, a VIP, or a rich person who has paid more money or something, or someone who knows someone else, gets to go to the front of the line, bypassing all the others who have been waiting with reasonable patience for their turn.

Perhaps there is no line at all, but you still are not allowed to pass because of — the rules. Remember Ben Stiller's scene in Meet the Parents? He is at the airport waiting to board a plane. The agent announces that boarding is beginning for all first-class, frequent flyers, and premier executive flyers. Except there are no first-class, frequent flyers, or premier execs to board. Stiller's character assumes he is free to board for coach. But the agent will not let him. So they both stand in silence until the appropriate amount of time has passed — and then he can board.

Another example. You are in traffic after work, headed home. They call it the "rush hour." What a joke.

But there is hope. On many of the nation's toll roads, rather than stopping at a toll-booth to toss some change in a hopper, you can now purchase a transponder, sometimes called an EZ-Pass, and zip through in the left lanes without even slowing down to the acceptable speed limit.

Instead of cash, tickets, and paper receipts, it is a microchip tag placed on your windshield containing pertinent data that eases your way. Your data is quickly read by a tollbooth electronic antenna as your car passes on through. It automatically deducts your appropriate toll tax. This computerized collection system then sends a monthly statement to your home with tallies of times and places for your records. EZ-Pass is like a debit card for your car, only quicker.

No more stop, go, stop, go, stop, go, stop, and go to the tollgate, the narrow gate.

Jesus says," I am the narrow gate." There is no quick way in. There is no shortcut. Through me, or not at all (John 10:7; Matthew 7:13).

If he were not the Christ himself already, He would be the perfect patron saint of tollgates.

Everybody wants the easy way to the front of the line, a quick way to glory and fast track to success, including James and John, the brothers Zebedee, who want front-row seats numbering two and three.

How about you, do you want an EZ pass to faithfulness?

## Lesson 13

# Coming of the Son of Man The Return!

### Mark 13:14-27

But when ye shall see the abomination of desolation, spoken of by Daniel the prophet, standing where it ought not, (let him that readeth understand,) then let them that be in Judaea flee to the mountains:

15 And let him that is on the housetop not go down into the house, neither enter therein, to take any thing out of his house:

16 And let him that is in the field not turn back again for to take up his garment.

17 But woe to them that are with child, and to them that give suck in those days!

18 And pray ye that your flight be not in the winter.

19 For in those days shall be affliction, such as was not from the beginning of the creation which God created unto this time, neither shall be.

20 And except that the Lord had shortened those days, no flesh should be saved: but for the elect's sake, whom he hath chosen, he hath shortened the days.

21 And then if any man shall say to you, Lo, here is Christ; or, lo, he is there; believe him not:

22 For false Christs and false prophets shall rise, and shall shew signs and wonders, to seduce, if it were possible, even the elect.

23 But take ye heed: behold, I have foretold you all things.

24 But in those days, after that tribulation, the sun shall be darkened, and the moon shall not give her light,

25 And the stars of heaven shall fall, and the powers that are in heaven shall be shaken.

26 And then shall they see the Son of man coming in the clouds with great power and glory.

27 And then shall he send his angels, and shall gather together his elect from the four winds, from the uttermost part of the earth to the uttermost part of heaven.

**Memory Verse**
Mark 13:26

**Background Scripture**
Mark 13

**Devotional Reading**
Isaiah 2:5-12

Feb. 27

251

 Some consider Mark 13 to be the most difficult chapter in the Gospels. It may be hard for two main reasons: because we are not familiar with the prophets that Jesus quotes or alludes to, and because of preconceptions that some bring to this text.

Old Testament prophets often used apocalyptic imagery to predict God's historical judgment on certain cities or nations. These symbols always sounded like "the End is near," but the prophetic message was about the end of some kingdom or place, not the End of the world. Jesus uses this imagery just as the prophets did—to predict Jerusalem's destruction in A.D. 70. Early Christians heard this warning, but many today hear Jesus talking instead about the End of time.

Those who have studied this material primarily in Matthew 24, are more likely to hear all of it as End-time predictions, because Matthew omits the clarifying information in Mark 13:1-4 and Mark 13:30.

## For a Lively Start

When the apostles asked Jesus when the Temple in Jerusalem would be torn down, He began his answer by warning them not to let anyone deceive them concerning the matters He was about to reveal.

All who believe Jesus expect Him to return. All who love Him will also "love His appearing" (2 Tim. 4:8). Those who truly adore Him will join the saints in praying, "Come quickly, Lord Jesus." We will do our best to be ready.

This ardent desire for Jesus' speedy return, however, can cause the acceptance of dubious End-time theories. Through the centuries, many charlatans have miss-used End-time predictions to frighten and beguile God's people. We need to hear Jesus' warning to be careful when pondering these matters.

| Teaching Outline | Daily Bible Readings |
|---|---|
| I. The Abomination of Desolation—13:14-20 | Mon. Terror for the Proud and Lofty *Isaiah 2:5-12* |
| A. Safety in the Mountains, 14-16 | Tue. Peril in Distressing Times *2 Timothy 3:1-9* |
| B. Dangerous Circumstances, 17-18 | Wed. The Day of Judgment *2 Peter 3:3-10* |
| C. Unequaled Affliction, 19-20 | Thu What You Ought to Be *2 Peter 3:11-18* |
| II. False Christs and Prophets—13:21-23 | Fri. Beware! *Mark 13:1-13* |
| III. Apocalyptic Images—13:24-27 | Sat. Be Watchful! *Mark 13:28-37* |
| A. Solar System Spectacles, 24-25 | Sun. Coming of the Son of Man *Mark 13:14-27* |
| B. Coming in the Clouds, 26-27 | |

# *Verse by Verse*

## Mark 13:14-27

**I. The Abomination of Desolation—13:14-20**

**A. Safety in the Mountains, 14-16**

**14 But when ye shall see the abomination of desolation, spoken of by Daniel the prophet, standing where it ought not, (let him that readeth understand,) then let them that be in Judaea flee to the mountains:**

**15 And let him that is on the housetop not go down into the house, neither enter therein, to take any thing out of his house:**

**16 And let him that is in the field not turn back again for to take up his garment.**

Jesus tells us plainly that He is alluding here to Daniel's famous "abomination of desolation" (Dan. 11:31, 12:11). Most Bible scholars agree that Daniel used this ominous term to predict the coming of Antiochus Ephiphanes, the Greek general who marched into Jerusalem with his army and defiled the Jewish Temple with the blood of a sow. Jesus does not expect Antiochus to be resurrected. Instead, Christ uses the prophecy that is quite familiar to all Jews in His time to warn that another foreign general will be marching into Jerusalem to target the Temple one more time. In A.D. 70, when the Ro-

man general Titus invaded Jerusalem with his army, the historian Eusebius tells us many Christians remembered Jesus' warning words, and fled to the heights of Pella to escape the carnage in the holy city.

Looking at Mark 13, we can see that Jesus was answering His followers' question about when the Temple would be destroyed. Reading the later history, we can see that the early Christians understood our Lord to be warning about the coming of the Romans, who destroyed the Temple.

Notice that the warnings in these verses are specifically given to people in Judea. They are to head to the hills without delaying for any reason. Going back into town or into their homes to retrieve provisions or other possessions would let them fall into Roman hands.

Most of us know that these verses have been incorporated into various millennial or End-time systems, but their original application clearly pertained to the invasion of the foreign army during the lifetime of those Jesus addressed (see Mark 13:30).

**B. Dangerous Circumstances, 17-18**

**17 But woe to them that are with child, and to them that give suck in those days!**

**18 And pray ye that your flight be not in the winter.**

The Judean Christians who escaped to Pella managed to slip out of town as the Roman invaders were pouring into the city on the other side. For a pregnant woman ("them that are with child") or a mother with a breast-feeding infant ("them that give suck"), it would be hard to move fast enough or furtively enough to get away.

In addition, all those trying to run for their lives would be in much greater danger—the chance of their escaping would be greatly reduced—if Titus attacked during harsh winter weather. Those who did make it to the safety of the mountains without coats, food, and other supplies would be in much worse distress if it were freezing cold.

**C. Unequaled Affliction, 19-20**

**19 For in those days shall be affliction, such as was not from the beginning of the creation which God created unto this time, neither shall be.**

**20 And except that the Lord had shortened those days, no flesh should be saved: but for the elect's sake, whom he hath chosen, he hath shortened the days.**

Jesus rightly foretold that the days of the Roman invasion of Jerusalem would be a terrible time for the people. Titus' siege on the holy city would reduce the populace to near-starvation before his assault that left so many maimed or dead. Although we cannot always depend on his statistics, the Jewish historian Josephus tells us about 1,100 people died during Titus' invasion. He says the casualty count would have far surpassed this if the Romans had prolonged their assault on the city. A longer campaign would have made it tough for those who were hiding unsheltered and without food in the Judean hills.

Over 40 years before Titus' attack on Jerusalem, Jesus was able to predict that it would come, and He knew that God would cause the ordeal to be shortened to protect Christians ("for the elect's sake, whom he hath chosen").

Obviously, those who incorporate these verses into their theories of End time tribulations will align various aspects of their own predictions with those of Jesus in this chapter.

**II. False Christs and Prophets— 13:21-23**

**21 And then if any man shall say to you, Lo, here is Christ; or, lo, he is there; believe him not:**

**22 For false Christs and false prophets shall rise, and shall shew signs and wonders, to seduce, if it were possible, even the elect.**

**23 But take ye heed: behold, I have foretold you all things.**

Historians tells us that in the decade of A.D. 60-70 a series of false Messiahs stirred up the population of Judea and led short-lived revolutions against the occupying Roman forces. The final siege of Titus on the holy city came at least in part because of Rome's frustration with these repeated uprisings. Our Lord accurately foretold this unrest over three decades before it happened, and He warned His own followers that these false Christs would mislead even some of the Christians on the scene. If they listened to what Jesus told them in these verses, they might escape both the slaughter during the main Roman attack, as well as the earlier dangers of being involved in unsuccessful revolutions led by leaders who were deceivers. Our Lord's predictions would protect His own.

### III. Apocalyptic Images— 13:24-27

#### A. Solar System Spectacles, 24-25

**24 But in those days, after that tribulation, the sun shall be darkened, and the moon shall not give her light,**

**25 And the stars of heaven shall fall, and the powers that are in heaven shall be shaken.**

If the sun and moon stop giving light and the stars fall from the sky, this universe is done for, isn't it? The End has come. Yet, it is easy to see why some think Jesus is predicting the End of time in these verses.

Repeatedly in the Old Testament, we hear the prophets using these exact images to foretell heavenly judgment that was about to fall on some city or kingdom. They speak of the solar system disintegrating, but clearly they are predicting the historical end of some specific place—not the End of time. See these same apocalyptic images in Isaiah 13:10; 34:4; Ezekiel 32:7; and Joel 2:10; 3:15. Jesus is quoting some of these passages almost word for word. In every case, the Old Testament passage predicts the end of a city or nation, so it should not surprise us that Jesus uses the images the same way—to predict a city's end.

#### B. Coming in the Clouds, 26-27

**26 And then shall they see the Son of man coming in the clouds with great power and glory.**

**27 And then shall he send his angels, and shall gather together his elect from the four winds, from the uttermost part of the earth to the uttermost part of heaven.**

Since Jesus is predicted to return some day in the clouds (Acts 1:11; 1 Thess. 4:17; Rev. 1:7), it is hard for us to read these verses without seeing that prediction. Surely, we do no violence to Mark's text if we do see Christ's End-time return in these words. Our Lord's primary meaning here, however, applies to God's judgment that would befall Jerusalem in A.D. 70. Again, Jesus is echoing the apocalyptic language of the prophet Daniel. He referred to the Lord coming in the clouds—not at the End of the world—but to inflict some divine judgment on a wicked people (Dan. 7:13). Vs. 27 is almost a verbatim quotation of Zechariah 2:6. Our Lord is mindful of this Old Testament imagery. To understand Him, our heart and mind must also be receptive to this imagery.

80CR

## Evangelistic Emphasis

Have you heard that the world is coming to an end on December 21, 2012? That happens to be the date of the winter solstice and the day the Mayan calendar ends. Some geniuses in the media and the Internet world have decided to cash in on the Mayan calendar ending. There is a website, www.december212012.com, you can visit and find out anything you wanted to know about this date. It has everything from the bizarre to scriptural interpretation that leads to the conclusion that December 21, 2012 is that date. Now if that is true, how will you be living between now and then? You have less than two years to go if this date is even close.

The truth is that since the resurrection of Jesus there have been forty major predictions of the second coming of Christ and the end of the world. Not only are "0" dates very popular, but also years that end in "33" are popular selections. Jesus has not come back yet, but He will.

The promise of scripture is that Jesus will return to conclude history. For the Christian, this is a word of hope that our struggle will be over and our work for Jesus will be done. For those that do not know Jesus as Lord and Savior, the second coming of Christ is an anxiety producing time.

So, how do you see the coming of Christ and the end of the world? How can we communicate, with those who do not know Jesus, the immediacy of being ready for His coming again?

ℰℭ

## Memory Selection

**"And then shall they see the Son of man coming in the clouds with great power and glory."** *Mark 13:26*

Thankfully, some purveyors of doomsday succeed more in lightening our hearts than chilling our souls. Consider the "Omega Letter" which advertises itself as being "a book on Bible prophecy that automatically updates itself every single month!" Those who are lucky enough to be subscribers are promised "front row seats to those very events that will culminate in the soon return of our Lord and Savior Jesus Christ!" Richard John Neuhaus, who discovered this publication, notes "that there is a special reduced rate for three year subscriptions." Neuhaus suggests none of us get too concerned until the publisher "will only take your money one month at a time."

The first time Jesus came to us, He did so as the baby of Bethlehem. He came in humility. He came to show us God's love and grace. He came to make a sacrifice on our behalf on Calvary's cross.

When Christ comes again, He comes as the "king of Kings and Lord of Lords." He will come to judge the living and the dead. He comes to separate the righteous and the sinner. He will judge those who have not received Him and at the "judgment seat of Christ, judge those of us who have.

When Christ comes again, "every knee shall bow and every tongue confess that Jesus is Lord to the glory of God the father."

## Weekday Problems

Pastor Greg was sitting in his office one Friday working very hard on a sermon. It has been one of those crazy weeks, where there was a wedding, a funeral, and a volunteer who did not show up to teach a Bible study and Pastor Greg found himself at the end of the week with little to say on Sunday morning.

Not wanting to be disturbed, the Pastor closed his door to work on the sermon. There was a knock and before he could get up, the door opened. A very tall man wearing overalls barged in the office. The man said, "I have only one question, do you preach the second coming of Jesus?" Pastor Greg assured the stranger that he did. The stranger walked over and sat down at the pastor's desk and said, "I have been sent here from God and I have a special word for your congregation about the coming of Jesus Christ." Greg tried to be nice and said, "What do you have to share."

The man refused to tell Pastor Greg the contents of his "secret" knowledge about the coming of Jesus, but assured him that the congregation would be blessed by hearing this "secret" message on Sunday morning. The stranger then demanded that Pastor Greg allow him to preach on Sunday in order to share this "secret" information with the congregation.

Pastor Greg reached the end of his patience and told the stranger that he really did not want to hear any "secret" knowledge about the second coming of Jesus Christ.

Why do you suppose there are so many people talking about the second coming of Jesus? How should we approach this subject?

---

# Best Headlines from a Recent Year

Police Begin Campaign to Run Down Jaywalkers

Iraqi Head Seeks Arms

Teacher Strikes Idle Kids

Juvenile Court to Try Shooting Defendant

Red Tape Holds Up New Bridges

New Study of Obesity Looks for Larger Test Group

---

# This Lesson in Your Life

For many baby boomers, one of the earliest memories of elementary school was going through a periodic safety drill known as "duck and cover."

During the early part of the Cold War, when Americans feared a missile attack from the Soviet Union, it was common for teachers to instruct students on what to do in the event of a nuclear war. If the air raid sirens ever went off, the teachers advised the students, they were to duck down immediately under their desks, pull their knees up to their chins, and cover their heads with their hands.

Today, of course, this advice seems absurd. If nuclear war ever were to burst forth upon the earth, a school desk would provide scant protection. That is why America's schools stopped conducting duck-and-cover drills decades ago. They were pointless and only served to increase everyone's anxiety level.

Jesus' advice to his disciples is just the opposite of duck and cover. Rather than advising them to hunker down in hard times and hope for the best, he instructs them to "Stand up and raise your heads." It sounds counter intuitive. Who would even think of raising their heads when the fury of Judgment Day is raging all around?

A Christian, that is who. A Christian who believes God's promises and knows them to be true. This life has things to be feared, no doubt about that. If we did not fear the worst-case scenarios — illness, poverty, pain, suffering, and all the rest — we would be considered foolish. Yet, Jesus is sharing good news here. He is telling us that all our fears are ultimately a waste of time, when compared with the great plans God has for this world.

When you hear of the signs of the end of time, or when your life seems to be falling apart, here is some good advice from Jesus:

First, Jesus said that there would be very bad days and very bad times like the end of the world. Jesus did not tell his disciples to get in the boat so they would drown. He told them to come with Him to the other side. Jesus never promised those disciples would arrive at the other side without having wet feet. Sometimes, storms toss water into the boat.

Second, Jesus told us to face today and tomorrow with faith, not fear. Since Jesus is with us every step of the journey, we are never alone. Because we have a traveling companion, there is nothing we need fear.

Third, Jesus told us to watch and pray during our lives. How can we have anxiety when we have given our lives to Jesus and when we stay in constant communication with Him through prayer? Prayer invites us to keep our eyes focused on the face of Jesus as opposed to looking at the storms associated with the end of times, storms that cause worry. Worry will not happen, when we pray.

**GETTING**
**THE FACTS STRAIGHT**

**1. What is the meaning of the "desolating sacrilege" set up where it ought not to be?**
The meaning of the phrase is not clearly understood, although it means some intrusion of Gentile practice into the temple area.

**2. The "desolating sacrilege" is the sign that those who live in Judea should take action, what action?**
The desolating sacrilege is the sign that those in Judea should flee to the mountains.

**3. How fast should the people flee from Judea?**
They are to flee so fast that they do not go down from the housetops, nor do they enter their house to get anything.

**4. What do you suppose the image is of the person who does not go down from his rooftop?**
Jesus was giving us the image of a person seeing the sign, jumping off the roof of his house, and running for his life.

**5. What particular group did Jesus feel for?**
Jesus feels sorry for those women who are with child or who are nursing a small child when they see the sign of this coming.

**6. What historical event is often associated with the "desolating sacrilege?"**
The "desolating sacrilege" is often seen as the invasion of Jerusalem by the Roman army who eventually destroyed the Temple in 70 A.D.

**7. How does Jesus describe the tribulation that is coming in these days?**
The tribulation to come "as has not been seen from the beginning of creation until now and never will be."

**8. On behalf of the elect, what happens to the tribulation that is coming?**
Unless the tribulation was shortened, no one would have survived it, but because of the elect, the tribulation is shortened.

**9. Who will appear during this time of tribulation?**
During the time of tribulation, many will arise and claim they are the Christ, and false prophets will arise and do signs and wonders.

**10. What is the goal of these false prophets and these false Messiahs?**
By doing many signs and wonders they hope to lead the elect astray.

Many of us have a clock radio on our bedside table. Each evening, upon retiring, we are faced with a choice. We can set the radio for either "music" or "alarm."

Of the two, music is by far the most pleasant. Set the switch to music, and the dulcet tones of our favorite radio station will ease us into wakefulness — a process that can take some time.

On the other hand, a process may not happen at all. Many of us have learned that the music setting is just a bit unreliable. The morning concert may be so relaxing, it just works its way into our dreams, and we oversleep. The station that came in crystal clear the evening before may have somehow drifted during the daytime. Morning may bring only white noise that would not rouse an insomniac.

No, some of us have learned that if we really want to get up at a certain time, there is no substitute for the "alarm" setting.

Don't you hate it when that blame thing goes off? It is loud and raucous. It makes us jump. It sets us flailing around with our arms until we hit the snooze button, which converts the alarm to a few minutes of lovely music — after which, if we haven't mistakenly turned the thing off altogether, the alarm will go blasting once again.

Still, were we forced to make a choice; many of us would pick the alarm over the music. Much as we dislike it, there are times when the consequences of staying asleep are just too dire.

The Bible's apocalyptic passages are like the alarm on a clock radio. No one likes them; their message is disturbing. That is why they are in the Bible. Their function is to disturb, to shake up, and to blast us into wakefulness.

As we approached the year 2000, can you remember the "gloom and doomers" that predicted all sorts of maladies coming our way? They were like those alarms blaring us into wakefulness, and yet, nothing happened that was so dire.

We again face the same kind of "alarmists" as the world approaches 2012. There will be "gloom and doomers" sounding the alarms of all the dire things that are coming our way. The alarms will annoy most and frighten some. However, it is better being prepared for something that does not happen than being caught off-guard.

How does one prepare for the end of the world? Like the title of this section, we lift UP our heads so that we can see our redemption drawing close. We work, pray, and remain faithful witnesses for Jesus Christ until that day, whenever that day arrives.

When we see that Son of man coming in glory and power, that will be a good day for His people.

 හිඳ

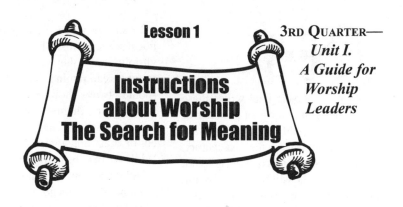

**Lesson 1**

3RD QUARTER—
*Unit I.*
*A Guide for*
*Worship*
*Leaders*

Mar. 6

## Instructions about Worship
## The Search for Meaning

**1 Timothy 2:1-6; 3:14-16**

I exhort therefore, that, first of all, supplications, prayers, intercessions, and giving of thanks, be made for all men;

2 For kings, and for all that are in authority; that we may lead a quiet and peaceable life in all godliness and honesty.

3 For this is good and acceptable in the sight of God our Saviour;

4 Who will have all men to be saved, and to come unto the knowledge of the truth.

5 For there is one God, and one mediator between God and men, the man Christ Jesus;

6 Who gave himself a ransom for all, to be testified in due time.

These things write I unto thee, hoping to come unto thee shortly:

15 But if I tarry long, that thou mayest know how thou oughtest to behave thyself in the house of God, which is the church of the living God, the pillar and ground of the truth.

16 And without controversy great is the mystery of godliness: God was manifest in the flesh, justified in the Spirit, seen of angels, preached unto the Gentiles, believed on in the world, received up into glory.

**Memory Verse**
1 Timothy 2:5

**Background Scripture**
1 Timothy 2:1-6; 3:14-16

**Devotional Reading**
Hebrews 8:6-12

When the apostle Paul writes these words, he is in chains—a prisoner of the man who would kill more Christians than any other ruler in the first century, the Roman emperor Nero. Paul does not know whether he will be released or put to death by this increasingly mad ruler, but he still bids Timothy and his friends in Ephesus to pray for kings and others in authority over them.

In an age when the American political scene seems to be growing more vitriolic and uglier year by year, this scripture can remind us that Christians should always show respect for those who govern them—even those that seem most incompetent, most misguided, or most antagonistic to our faith. While we may be politically powerless to influence policies that seem unwise or immoral, we can go "over the heads" of bad leaders by praying for them. Our prayers may do more to improve bad government than our insults and angry criticism ever can.

## For a Lively Start

We cannot know exactly how the first-century Christians utilized the words in 3:16, but we treasure it as one of the earliest recorded creeds in our faith. In short, easy-to-remember phrases it states the core of what we believe:

God was manifested in the flesh,

justified in the Spirit,
seen of angels,
preached unto the Gentiles,
believed on in the world,
received up into glory.

Like the great creeds we recite today, surely it enabled them to reaffirm their faith and enter into worship.

| Teaching Outline | Daily Bible Readings |
|---|---|
| I. Praying for Rulers—2:1-6 | Mon. The Ministry of the Mediator *Hebrews 8:6-12* |
| A. For All in Authority, 1-2a | Tue. Worship and Thanksgiving *Psalm 95:1-7* |
| B. Promoting Peace, 2b | Wed. Prayer and Supplication *Ephesians 6:18-24* |
| C. What God Wants, 3-4 | Thu The Spirit's Intercession *Romans 8:22-27* |
| D. Our Testimony, 5-6 | Fri. Instructions on Prayer *Luke 11:1-13* |
| II. The Church of the Living God—3:14-15 | Sat. The Goal of Instruction *1 Timothy 1:1-7* |
| III. The Mystery of Godliness—3:16 | Sun. The Great Mystery *1 Timothy 2:1-6; 3:14-16* |

# Verse by Verse

**1 Timothy 2:1-6; 3:14-16**

## I. Praying for Rulers—2:1-6

### A. For All in Authority, 1-2a

**1 I exhort therefore, that, first of all, supplications, prayers, intercessions, and giving of thanks, be made for all men;**

**2a For kings, and for all that are in authority;**

We are hard pressed to explain exactly what Paul means by the string of prayer words he uses in vs. 1, but the gist of his exhortation is clear. He wants Christians to be busy praying for rulers and other governing officials. Most of us will quickly recognize the difference in giving thanks for the king versus interceding for God on that person's behalf. "Supplications" is replaced in other Bible versions with "petitions," "requests," or "entreaties." "Prayer" is a more general term that would seem to include all of the others. If somebody prays for us, they might thank God for us, plead to the Lord on our behalf, or offer to God any number of specific requests.

Praying for our President, our Congressmen, or our local leaders certainly implies a more benevolent spirit than we often hear today in political conversations. If Jesus taught us to pray for our enemies and to bless those who wrong us, this instruction should cover political leaders who seriously displease us, shouldn't it? We Christians ought to be setting an example of love, patience, kindness, and gentleness in our attitudes toward all elected officials. In our democracy, thankfully, we do not have to agree with all of our leaders, but to obey this passage we do have be respectful toward them.

### B. Promoting Peace, 2b

**2b . . . that we may lead a quiet and peaceable life in all godliness and honesty.**

The purpose behind our prayers for those in public office involves our own good as well as theirs. The specifics of such prayers will vary depending on the immediate concerns of society, but the general goal is to have laws and policies in place that will encourage peace and righteousness in our day-to-day lives.

### C. What God Wants, 3-4

**3 For this is good and acceptable in the sight of God our Saviour;**

**4 Who will have all men to be saved, and to come unto the knowledge of the truth.**

Paul's writing teacher would have used up some red ink on vs. 3, because Paul failed to make clear just what "this" refers to. Is Paul telling us here that praying for rulers is good and acceptable to the Lord? Perhaps, he means to say that living quiet and peaceable lives in all godliness and honesty is something God heartily approves. Either idea makes sense. Either idea seems appropriate to the surrounding text.

"God our Savior" is an expression Paul uses often in the Pastoral Letters—twice in 1 Timothy and three times in Titus. The same name for God appears often in Psalms, so Paul's use of the term may reflect a deepening of his personal devotional life, possibly because of his recent prison time.

Vs. 4 may not be a basis for universalism's thesis that every single human being will be saved. God's desire is that "all men" be saved and learn the truth about Jesus, but the core truth of the gospel is that God never forces His desires on people. If we choose to sin and ignore the truth, He lets us walk on the path to our own destruction. Peter expresses the same idea when he tells his readers that God does not want anybody to perish (2 Pet. 3:9), but he is quite clear in asserting that the wicked will be lost.

The "truth" that God wants all men to know must be the same truth Paul identifies in Ephesians 4:21, wherein he reminds his converts that they had learned "the truth that is in Jesus" (NIV).

**D. Our Testimony, 5-6**

**5 For there is one God, and one mediator between God and men, the man Christ Jesus;**

**6 Who gave himself a ransom for all, to be testified in due time.**

Some suggest that the ideas in vss. 5-6 are the "truth" alluded to in the previous verse, but none of the major translations reflects this concept. Instead, all of them introduce vs. 5 with the word "for," which is used here in the sense of "because." Paul is telling us in this extended passage that God wants all men to know that Jesus serves as our mediator to reconcile us to our Maker. To do that, Jesus paid the price to ransom us from the slavery of sin.

The writer of Hebrews stresses that Jesus is the mediator of the new covenant between God and humanity (8:6; 9:15; 12:24). The work of Jesus to reconcile us to the Father is also often mentioned in the New Testament (Eph. 2:16; Col. 1:20). Perhaps the clearest text about the reconciling work of Jesus can be found in 2 Corinthians 5:18-20:

All this is from God, who reconciled us to himself through Christ and gave us the ministry of reconciliation: that God was reconciling the world to himself in Christ, not counting men's sins against them. Moreover, he has committed to us the message of reconciliation. We are therefore Christ's ambassadors, as though God were making his appeal through us. We implore you on Christ's behalf: Be reconciled to God (NIV).

**II. The Church of the Living God—3:14-15**

**14 These things write I unto thee, hoping to come unto thee shortly:**

**15 But if I tarry long, that thou mayest know how thou oughtest to behave thyself in the house of God, which is the church of the living God, the pillar and ground of the truth.**

In the opening verses of 1 Timothy, we learn that Paul sent Timothy to minister to the churches in Ephesus and that area of Asia. Paul continued on his journey to the northwest to visit the Macedonian churches (which would include Philippi, Thessalonica, and Berea).

Just what might detain Paul on the trip, he does not tell us and we have no way to know. It is apparent from these lines that he is not working on a strict timetable. Ministry demands in these important Macedonian churches might delay his return, so he gives Timothy a rather lengthy set of instructions for dealing with the problems he faces in the Ephesian fellowship.

The reference about how to "behave thyself in the house of God" does not mean how Timothy should act in the physical edifice where they worshiped. Paul uses "house" to refer to the family of God. Most of the modern Bible translations speak here about "the household" of God. Paul in this letter is describing how members of the family of God are expected to act.

Paul's closing metaphor in vs. 15 compares the church to the massive stone that served as the foundation for a building. The people who serve God in Christ are that foundation, the buttress, or support of the truth of the Christian gospel.

**III. The Mystery of Godliness—3:16**

**16 And without controversy great is the mystery of godliness: God was manifest in the flesh, justified in the Spirit, seen of angels, preached unto the Gentiles, believed on in the world, received up into glory.**

"The mystery of godliness" means the truth God revealed to humanity about how He intends to save the world—the truth found in the early creed that summarizes the main points of God's plan.

1) "God was manifested in the flesh" reminds us of the incarnation of God in Christ.

2) "Justified in the Spirit" refers to Jesus, not us. The Spirit fell on Him at His baptism, verifying His Sonship.

3) "Seen by angels" affirms that Heaven was fully involved in Jesus' earthly ministry, with angels present from His birth to His resurrection and ascension.

4) "Preached unto the Gentiles" states a truth fulfilled in Jesus' own days when He left Jewish lands to address Gentiles. It also describes the rapid spread of the gospel to Gentile lands during Paul's own ministry.

5) "Believed on in the world" is a contrasting truth to the one that follows,

6) "Received up into Glory," a clear reference both to the Ascension and to Christ's present high priestly role in Heaven.

80C3

## Evangelistic Emphasis

The relationship between the Apostle Paul and Timothy just has "Evangelistic Emphasis" written all over it. In Acts 16, we read about these two being acquainted. It was early in Paul's second missionary trip that he met this young disciple who had an excellent reputation among other believers in the area.

From this point, Timothy traveled with Paul and became his trusted and reliable helper. He was with Paul through thick and thin, and when there was a difficult job to be done, Timothy often got the assignment.

This is what we find happening as we read 1st Timothy. There were problems in the church in Ephesus. The very heart of the Christian evangelistic message was being threatened. Timothy's responsibility was to right the wrong. He was to command certain teachers to hold to the basic doctrine of Jesus Christ.

Apparently, that church's worship gatherings must have reflected some of the improper teaching they had received. The life of the church, with its assemblies and other activities, should reflect the authenticity of the evangelism that first brought the message of Christ.

The Church at worship reflects its core values. So it is that Timothy was to remind the Ephesians of their foundational Christian faith, and give instructions for worship. This reminder is appropriate for today's Church also.

### Memory Selection

ഇറ

"For there is one God, and one mediator between God and men, the man Christ Jesus." *1 Timothy 2:5*

Timothy needed to get the Ephesian church back to basics. It is a basic truth in the New Testament that the gospel is for "all the world," including "every creature" (See the Great Commission, Mark 16:15-16).

The prayers of the Ephesian church needed to "be made for all men" (2:1). They were reminded that God "will have all men to be saved, and to come unto the knowledge of the truth" (2:4).

This leads us right into our memory verse. There is not one God for Jews and another for Gentiles. There is not one for Greeks, while the Ethiopians have their own. There is one God, and only one mediator between God and mankind.

In cities throughout the Roman Empire there were temples to many gods. Acts 19:23-41 tells about Ephesus' main temple, dedicated to the goddess Diana (also known as Artemis). Take time to read about Paul's experience there.

The first two of the Ten Commandments (Exodus 20) tells us what we need to know about multiple gods and their images, and Jesus lets us know that He is our only mediation between God and mankind. He said that no one comes to the Father except through Him (John 14:6).

In present-day America, plurality is on the increase. Men such as Paul and Timothy will help guide us as we do so. They encourage us to pray for all mankind, including unbelievers who do not yet honor the "King eternal, immortal, invisible" (1:17).

## Weekday Problems

We Christians have different ways of "doing church." Some churches are more formal and liturgical – very "high church." Others range all the way to the opposite extreme. Wherever we "do church," and whatever activities and worship style that church may have, we want to make sure the basics are in place.

Many years ago, there was a newspaper report about Billy Graham being shown a lavish new church building. It had been praised for its architecture and the great addition it would make to the city. After he had seen it and had been told about all its high points, someone asked what he thought about it. His answer was to the effect that he saw a place in that church for everything except Jesus.

The church in Ephesus may have been heading toward a similar situation. Their teaching had been largely off-base (chapter 1) and that is why Paul wanted Timothy to bring them back to Christian fundamentals.

Can you see a problem here that you and I might share with these people? How can we keep church "real" and keep Jesus alive in our hearts? Can we keep the great truths of Christianity viable in our twenty-first century lives?

How would you evaluate a church? I once heard someone say he liked a particular church because it had a great band. I'll admit that I might be discouraged with a church that had a really bad band, but shouldn't we care even more about the core beliefs of that church? The Church is the house of the living God. It rests on the pillar and ground of truth (3:15). Remembering this may help us make wise decisions and avoid some weekday (and lifetime) problems.

## Marriage—As Men See It

A successful man is one who makes more money than his wife can spend.

A successful woman is one who can find such a man.

To be happy with a man you must understand him a lot and love him a little. To be happy with a woman you must love her a lot and not try to understand her at all.

A woman marries a man expecting he will change, but he doesn't.

A man marries a woman expecting that she won't change and she does.

A woman worries about the future until she gets a husband, while a man never worries about the future until he gets a wife.

There are two times a man doesn't understand a woman—before marriage and after marriage.

Only two things are necessary to keep your wife happy. One is to let her think she is having her way, and the other is to let her have it.

# This Lesson in Your Life

It is interesting that as Paul began his "to-do list" for helping the Ephesian church, he started by calling attention to the church's prayers.

One point he emphasized was that prayers should "be made for all men." We, along with the Ephesians, need to remember that the Church has a worldwide mission, and shares God's concern for every person everywhere. Let us remember John 3:16. God loved the world, not just one little corner of it. "Whosoever believeth" reaches all around the globe.

It cannot be ignored that kings and all who are in authority were to be included in their prayers. At that time Emperor Nero was a one-man terrorist organization, threatening the whole Roman Empire. Do you suppose they hesitated to include him in their Sunday prayer list?

Let us do some thinking about respecting those who are in positions of authority. Several news media spokespersons have recently observed that American society is becoming more crude and rude. They suggest that civility and respectful behavior are in a sharp decline, and especially noticeable in our conduct toward elected officials. (Not to mention the conduct of some elected officials toward their constituents!)

In the state where I live, citizens are allowed to wear registered weapons in public. As the U.S. President visited our city, one man wore his pistol and assault rifle as he stood in the crowd gathered outside the building where the president was speaking. It was his way of expressing his feeling toward the president with a not too-subtle armed threat. It was legal, but it was wrong. The worst part of the story is that this behavior was encouraged by the man's pastor, who says he prays for the president's death. The media also reports an out-of-our-state pastor who shares the same views about the president's wellbeing. We can hope and pray that such ugly and disrespectful behavior will not spread.

Scripture takes a very positive approach toward "the higher powers" (Romans 13 1-7). It says they are ordained of God, and the person in authority is the minister of God to do good. (This places quite a responsibility on all our government officials.)

First Peter 2:13-17 says that we should be law-abiding citizens, and "Honor all men. Love the brotherhood. Fear God. Honor the king."

It may be that those who report that Americans are becoming more disrespectful are correct in their assessment. This does not mean that you and I must adopt boorish ways either toward office-holders or with each other.

Let us do what Paul told the Ephesian church to do. Our national leaders, as well as state and local officials, should be prayed for in our churches. We need to be praying for each other, too.

**GETTING THE FACTS STRAIGHT**

**1. What are the four categories of praying that 2:1 mentions?**

There should be supplications, prayers, intercessions, and giving of thanks made for all men.

**2. In prayers for kings and other authorities, what should be the object?**

These people should allow us to lead quiet, peaceable lives in godliness and honesty.

**3. How will God feel about such prayers?**

This will be good and acceptable in his sight. It reminds us that all our prayers (as our lives) should be in the spirit of "Thy will be done."

**4. Verse 4 suggests another favorable result that might come from such prayers. What is it?**

God wants everyone to be saved and know the truth. The prayers include everyone, including officials.

**5. There is one God and Christ Jesus is the only mediator between God and men. What else is said about the mediator?**

He gave Himself as a ransom for all.

**6. Paul hoped to come to Ephesus soon. In case he was delayed, what action did he take?**

He wrote this letter so they would have the instruction they needed about church.

**7. What kind of behavior was he concerned that they learn?**

He wanted them to know how to behave themselves in the house of God. Lesser standards than those set by God are not acceptable.

**8. Paul describes the house of God in what terms?**

The house of God is the church of the living God, the pillar and the ground of the truth.

**9. Paul said that the mystery of godliness is very great. What six things did he say about it?**

God was manifest in the flesh, justified in the Spirit, seen of angels, preached to the Gentiles, believed on in the world, and received up into glory.

**10. Three of the above points were on earth. The other three were more heavenly. Name the three that were on earth.**

The three earthly ones: Manifest in the flesh, preached to the Gentiles, and believed on in the world.

269

The church where I preach always seems to find a special comfort when in Bible studies we connect our present Christian convictions with significant biblical events of the distant past. So much in life is shallow, fads come and quickly go, generations pass and are largely forgotten. We all need something to hold onto that has endured the ages. We need stability and continuity.

When we read the Ten Commandments, we are amazed to think that we share in what happened on that mountaintop so long ago, and that we read what was written by the finger of God. As we say or sing the Lord's Prayer we are in the company of the apostles and the earliest of Christ's followers. This is both exciting and comforting at the same time.

Our present lesson gives us words that may well have been spoken in unison in churches when the apostles were still alive. As we read 3:16, we can visualize some house church in Ephesus, or Rome, or Jerusalem as they spoke these words in Greek, Latin, or Aramaic:

God was manifest in the flesh,
justified in the Spirit,
seen of angels,
preached unto the Gentiles,
believed on in the world,
received up into glory.

These words probably form one of the earliest Christian creedal efforts to summarize basic beliefs about Christ. It gives us a sense of belonging, of permanence, as we share in something so ancient.

The traditional creeds of the Church do much the same thing. They represent the thinking of Christian minds at the time when they were written. As we read or say them we are following in the footsteps and sharing the faith with long-gone saints.

The Apostle's Creed (not written by them, but apostolic in what it says), in a modern English version begins: "I believe in God, the Father almighty, creator of heaven and earth. I believe in Jesus Christ, God's only Son, our Lord, who was conceived by the Holy Spirit . . . ." The Nicene Creed begins much the same way.

In his commentary, William Barclay states that Philippians 2:11 is the first creed the Christian church ever had: "Jesus Christ is Lord." He further states that we would do well to go back to it. There is both simplicity and depth in it.

The point of discussing creeds here, either biblical or those that came later, is simply to say that part of their value lies in their ability to make us feel good about who and what we are, and that in faith we are keeping good company.

## Lesson 2

# Qualifications of Worship Leaders Choosing a Good Leader

## 1 Timothy 3:1-13

This is a true saying, If a man desire the office of a bishop, he desireth a good work.

2 A bishop then must be blameless, the husband of one wife, vigilant, sober, of good behaviour, given to hospitality, apt to teach;

3 Not given to wine, no striker, not greedy of filthy lucre; but patient, not a brawler, not covetous;

4 One that ruleth well his own house, having his children in subjection with all gravity;

5 (For if a man know not how to rule his own house, how shall he take care of the church of God?)

6 Not a novice, lest being lifted up with pride he fall into the condemnation of the devil.

7 Moreover he must have a good report of them which are without; lest he fall into reproach and the snare of the devil.

8 Likewise must the deacons be grave, not doubletongued, not given to much wine, not greedy of filthy lucre;

9 Holding the mystery of the faith in a pure conscience.

10 And let these also first be proved; then let them use the office of a deacon, being found blameless.

11 Even so must their wives be grave, not slanderers, sober, faithful in all things.

12 Let the deacons be the husbands of one wife, ruling their children and their own houses well.

13 For they that have used the office of a deacon well purchase to themselves a good degree, and great boldness in the faith which is in Christ Jesus.

**Memory Verse**
1 Timothy 3:9

**Background Scripture**
1 Timothy 3:1-13

**Devotional Reading**
1 Peter 5:1-5

As Timothy selected lay leaders for the congregations in Ephesus, Paul's list of attributes to look for and traits to avoid protected him from choosing people who might be detrimental to the young churches.

Long before Paul wrote this list in 1 Timothy 3 and the similar one in Titus 1, the apostles in Jerusalem set standards for deacons—standards just as lofty as Paul's but stated in terms that are more general. Those first deacons were to be men "known to be full of the Holy Spirit and wisdom" (Acts 6:3, TEV). Paul's fuller description in the later texts stated what the simpler criteria required.

In our denominations today, we may vary the titles we use for church offices and each group has its own definition of the duties to be performed by various leaders, but all of us agree with Paul that our church leaders must be exemplary people, above reproach both in and out of the church fellowship.

&)Q&

## For a Lively Start

Some denominations try to refer to their church officers by the terms used in Scriptures such as 1 Timothy 3. They try to define the duties of various church leaders to comply with those duties occurring in the days of the apostles.

Yet, other churches choose to use leadership titles and job descriptions that are traditional to their heritage. To avoid confusion, Bible readers in this latter group need to know that when Paul speaks of a deacon or a bishop, the office he has in mind may be quite different from that of their leaders bearing the same title today. Consider, for example, that the duties of bishops in Protestant groups today may not resemble those of a Catholic bishop, and neither of them may fill the role Paul refers to in 1 Timothy 3. We do not have to adopt Paul's vocabulary, but to understand what he writes; we must discern how he uses the titles involved.

| Teaching Outline | Daily Bible Readings |
|---|---|
| I. Traits of a Bishop—1 Timothy 3:1-7<br>A. Personal Demeanor, 1-3<br>B. His Home, 4-5<br>C. Avoiding Satan's Snare, 6-7<br>II. Attributes of a Deacon—1 Timothy 3:8-13<br>A. Personal Demeanor, 8<br>B. Personal Faith, 9<br>C. Tested and Approved, 10<br>D. Their Wives, 11<br>E. Their Homes, 12<br>F. Their Reward, 13 | Mon. Tending the Flock of God<br>*1 Peter 5:1-5*<br>Tue. Leading God's People Astray<br>*Isaiah 9:13-17*<br>Wed. Leaders as God's Stewards<br>*Titus 1:5-9*<br>Thu Imitate Your Leaders' Faith<br>*Hebrews 13:1-7*<br>Fri. Obey Your Leaders<br>*Hebrews 13:17-25*<br>Sat. Good Stewards of God's Grace<br>*1 Peter 4:7-11*<br>Sun. Qualifications of Leaders<br>*1 Timothy 3:1-13* |

# *Verse by Verse*

## 1 Timothy 3:1-13

**I. Traits of a Bishop—1 Timothy 3:1-7**

**A. Personal Demeanor, 1-3**

**1 This is a true saying, If a man desire the office of a bishop, he desireth a good work.**

**2 A bishop then must be blameless, the husband of one wife, vigilant, sober, of good behaviour, given to hospitality, apt to teach;**

**3 Not given to wine, no striker, not greedy of filthy lucre; but patient, not a brawler, not covetous;**

In the New Testament days, the hierarchy of church leaders as we know it had not yet been developed. Today in many fellowships "bishop" denotes a church leader who exercises authority and oversight over multiple congregations and/or pastors. However, in Paul's time the word "bishop" (overseer) was used to refer to a lay leader who guided a single congregation. In the New Testament, the term is used interchangeably with "pastor" and "elder." See, for example, Acts 20:28 where Paul says to the *elders* in Ephesus, "Keep watch over yourselves and all the flock of which the Holy Spirit has made you overseers (*bishops*). Be shepherds (*pastors*) of the church of God" (NIV). Although we may not use these words exactly as Paul did, his high requirements for those who lead the church still apply.

Such a leader must be "blameless"— above reproach. "Husband of one wife" in the original Greek is literally a "one-woman man." In addition, "sober" or "temperate" are modern synonyms of the KJV term "vigilant." "Given to hospitality" is an archaic way of saying "hospitable." "Apt to teach" means that a bishop must be ready and capable of imparting knowledge and discipline.

Obviously, a respected church leader should be filled with goodness. He should not be a drunkard. "Striker" is old English for "a violent man." Church leaders should be gentle peacemakers. "Filthy lucre" is King James language for "dirty money." A church leader should never accept such a position because he is greedy for gain. Neither should a bishop be one who is prone to enter fights (a "brawler"), nor be someone who is desirous of others' property ("covetous").

**B. His Home, 4-5**

**4 One that ruleth well his own house, having his children in subjection with all gravity;**

**5 (For if a man know not how to**

273

rule his own house, how shall he take care of the church of God?)

Paul tells Timothy that one good way to tell if a man is suited to serve as a bishop in the church is to see how he handles his family. Many of the same skills it takes to guide and mold children are the abilities one must have to lead and teach God's people.

This verse is a clear indication that in the first-century Church all the bishops were male. Obviously, the moral rectitude and social aptitudes Paul prescribes for these men should be required of any female considered for church leadership today.

### C. Avoiding Satan's Snare, 6-7

**6 Not a novice, lest being lifted up with pride he fall into the condemnation of the devil.**

**7 Moreover he must have a good report of them which are without; lest he fall into reproach and the snare of the devil.**

Paul describes two ways that Satan may use to destroy a church leader. If the leader is a "novice"—if he is new in the faith, he may entertain a flattering opinion of himself if he is elevated too quickly to a position of trust and authority. In a similar way, if the prospective leader's reputation has been sullied, Satan may use this previous failure as a trap to ruin him.

To state these two verses positively, we should select church leaders who are mature, proven Christians who have unblemished reputations. Both requirements are protections for the man who might be chosen.

## II. Attributes of a Deacon—1 Timothy 3:8-13

### A. Personal Demeanor, 8

**8 Likewise must the deacons be grave, not doubletongued, not given to much wine, not greedy of filthy lucre;**

"Deacon" is a transliteration of the Greek word that means "servant." The title refers to those who served their fellow-Christians in the Church. The TEV calls them "church helpers."

Many of the qualifications for deacons echo those set forth earlier for the church's overseers. Those we have explained earlier.

"Grave" translates a word that can point in two directions. It can mean "reverent" (NIV) or "serious" (RSV), thus describing the bearing of the deacon himself. Alternatively, it may describe how other people see him, possibly as a man with "good character" (TEV) or a person "worthy of respect" (NIV).

We understand "doubletongued" to mean dishonest. Sometimes we say that a fellow speaks with a forked tongue, meaning the same thing. Paul is requiring here that a deacon be a man of integrity, a person who can be trusted.

### B. Personal Faith, 9

**9 Holding the mystery of the faith in a pure conscience.**

The personal faith of a deacon must embrace the core truths of Christianity without any hidden doubts or unspoken reservations.

### C. Tested and Approved, 10

**10 And let these also first be proved; then let them use the office of a deacon, being found blameless.**

Being "proved" means being "tested." Before a deacon is selected, he needs to show the church that he is capable and willing to perform the required services.

To "use the office" does not imply underhanded, manipulative miss-use as the term often signifies today. Paul is simply saying that if a man passes the test, he should "serve" as a deacon since the testing period has shown him to be fit.

## D. Their Wives, 11

**11 Even so must their wives be grave, not slanderers, sober, faithful in all things.**

The Greek word translated "wives" is the usual word for "women." Bible scholars cannot agree as to whether this verse refers to deacons' wives or to female deacons ("deaconesses"—NIV footnote or "women deacons"—NLT footnote). The qualifications here echo some of those earlier applied to the male deacons. If deacons' wives are described in this verse, we certainly can recognize that no church leader can ever be any better than his wife can.

## E. Their Homes, 12

**12 Let the deacons be the husbands of one wife, ruling their children and their own houses well.**

As in the same qualification Paul stated for elders, "husbands of one wife" is one possible way to translate the Greek, "one-woman man." Some Christians quite strictly interpret this qualification as a barrier to those who are divorced and remarried. Others see it as a description of a good man who is absolutely true to his wife and to her only.

The word "ruling" here has the positive meaning of overseeing or directing, and not the negative sense of being authoritative in an overbearing way.

## F. Their Reward, 13

**13 For they that have used the office of a deacon well purchase to themselves a good degree, and great boldness in the faith which is in Christ Jesus.**

Again, the word "used" means "served" in the office of a deacon. What do those who have done a good job in this servant role gain ("purchase") for themselves? What the KJV calls "a good degree" most of our newer versions call "a good standing." A fruitful deacon will be admired by the Christians he serves, and his ministry to them will bless him with greater confidence or assurance ("boldness") in his faith in the Lord.

സാൽ

## Evangelistic Emphasis

The quality of leadership in the church at Ephesus had apparently slipped considerably since earlier times. We can safely assume that at least some of the questionable teaching (chapter 1) done there was actually done by the local leadership, or at the least was done under their oversight and with their approval. Paul knows that to get the church back on the right track in its doctrine and worship, the shepherds need to be capable of leading the flock in the right direction.

With core Christian doctrine neglected in that church, and their worship services suffering as a result, the outlook for their spreading the gospel was not good. It may be that they had lost their initiative for evangelistic outreach. Paul felt it necessary to emphasize (chapter 2) that their prayers should include all mankind, and that God wants everyone to be saved and come to the knowledge of the truth. A church that has neglected major gospel truths itself is not likely to do much gospel evangelizing.

Paul and Timothy both had a passion for evangelism. They could never be content until the Ephesian disciples shared their zeal. This required good leadership. The standards listed in chapter three for church leaders indicate that God has a plan for his churches. He is guiding the Ephesian church toward good leadership, so they can be a functioning, evangelizing church.

SoCR

## Memory Selection

"Likewise must the deacons be . . . holding the mystery of the faith in a pure conscience." *1 Timothy 3:9* The responsibilities that go with the office of deacon are not as clearly defined in the Scripture, as are the duties of elders. In many churches today (though not all), deacons tend to be given practical duties such as assisting the elders/overseers. The sometimes delicate and always highly responsible job of caring for the church's benevolent/charitable work is often given to the deacons.

The first reference we have to deacons and their work is in Acts 6:1-8. There men were selected to distribute food to needy widows, so that the apostles need not spend their time doing this, but could devote themselves to teaching. It is from this situation that the concept of being assistants and serving the poor originates.

Regardless of how modern-day churches may adapt the office of deacon to fit their needs, our memory verse indicates the depth of Christian understanding and conviction the deacon must have if he is to do his work well.

The "mystery of the faith" he must hold doesn't mean mystery in the sense of a mystery novel or TV program. Especially as Paul uses it, it means understanding something that was once not known, but is now revealed to those who have spiritual discernment. It indicates a deep perception of Christian truth.

In Greek, the word deacon means servant. In the eyes of the Lord, that's a wonderful thing to be. (Read Matthew 25:31-46 about serving "the least" among the Lord's brothers.) The deacon who serves well, touches the very heart of Jesus Christ.

## Weekday Problems

I have had one friend, a gifted Christian woman, who was a deaconess in her church. It was a position that she valued, and she put her heart and soul into it. The two of us served together on committees in a horticultural society. As we would sit across the restaurant table from each other, presumably making plans for a flower show, the flowers usually got short shrift. She wanted to talk about her work for the church.

In the Scripture portion of our lesson, in the verses about deacon's qualifications, 3:11 says "Even so must their wives be . . ." and follows with several qualifications. As I look in the NIV, I see a footnote for wives that says "deaconesses." In the NAS the footnote says "either deacon's wives or deaconesses." (The same is true in Romans 16:1. Was Phoebe, a deaconess in the church at Cenchrea, or just a servant in the generic sense?)

To have deaconesses or not to have deaconesses, that is the question. Many churches, such as the one where my friend served, have answered the question in the affirmative. Others have hesitated to do so.

The church where I preach does not have an official position for deaconesses, but, thank God, we have dedicated women who serve without an official title. Our deacon's wives, for example, work as hard for our church as their husbands do.

We do not know for sure if the women mentioned in our lesson were deacon's wives, or officially deaconesses. Either way, let us thank God for the invaluable service of Christian women. Their good work solves many weekday problems.

# Chuckle

A friend was in front of me coming out of church one day, and the preacher was standing at the door as he always is to shake hands. He grabbed my friend by the hand and pulled him aside.

The pastor said to him, "You need to join the army of the Lord!"

My friend replied, "I'm already in the army of the Lord, Pastor."

Then the pastor asked, "How come I don't see you except at Christmas and Easter?

My friend whispered back, "I'm in the secret service."

# This Lesson in Your Life

Terms such as elder and deacon have a very churchy sound to them, don't they? If we add bishop, presbyter, pastor, overseer and shepherd to them, the list gets even churchier. None of the terms used in the Bible to describe church leaders are intended to be scary. Even though there are qualifications that go with these titles, those who wear them are not super-saints who have arrived at some elevated degree of holiness. We respect them, obey them, assist them, and appreciate their dedication, but realize that they are just as human as everyone else. Thus, we know they need all the support we can give them.

Now here comes a very important point. Please take the time to carefully read all the qualifications for leadership listed in our Scripture lesson. Include the part for wives. Virtually every point that is made for a qualified leader is also a goal for every Christian person.

You may have absolutely no aspirations to ever be a church leader. If the opportunity were offered you, you might decline it. The fact remains, though, that all Christians are working toward those basic qualification goals. (This assumes we make adjustments for points such as whether or not we are a husband, wife, parent, or head of a household.)

Let us look at some of an elder's qualifications and see how they fit. The first one sounds like a pretty tight fit. The bishop/elder must be blameless. Wow! It looks like we are starting out with a tough one. "Above reproach" is the way the modern translations word this. It has to do with reputation, both within and without the church. For example, we do not want to be a Saturday night sinner and a Sunday morning saint. We need consistent moral and ethical behavior. Our family members, neighbors, work-place associates, and the check-out clerk at the grocery store, need to speak well of our behavior.

When we think of being blameless or above reproach in this way, it becomes more doable. It's something of a Philippians 4:8-9 sort of thing. It includes being honest, just, and pure. It is following a "good report" lifestyle. We can see why church leaders need this quality. It is easy to see why all Christians should work toward it.

Let us look on down the list: The leader must be "the husband of one wife." Obviously, all Christians are not husbands (or wives). But if you are, or should ever become one, as a Christian you will want to be faithful to your spouse.

This lesson lets us know what the Lord expects our church leaders to be. We respect them for meeting His standard. Actually, it is just a common sense observation that these qualities should be the goal in all our lives as we mature spiritually. In this sense, "One size fits all." We get a clear picture of what God wants us all to be as we grow up in Christ.

278

**1. If a man desires the office of a bishop, how is this office described?**

He desires a good work. We might hope that deep thought and earnest prayer are involved, and that the Lord's will is a matter of concern with this person.

**2. How can we expect anyone to be "blameless"?**

The idea is to be above reproach, and there are no legitimate meaningful accusations that can be brought against him.

**3. What other terms might help explain what "vigilant" means? (It's one of the qualifications.)**

Modern translations tend toward "temperate." It is also associated with being sober minded and having self-control.

**4. What terms might help expand the meaning of "no striker?"**

The NIV uses "not violent but gentle." The NAS: not "pugnacious, but gentle."

**5. Why would one's relationship to his household and children be an important point for a church leader?**

The man who could not lead a properly functioning home and family cannot be depended on to lead a church.

**6. Why might being a novice (a newcomer to Christianity) be a problem?**

He would not have the depth and experience that might keep his office from "going to his head." He might forget that he is God's humble servant.

**7. Why would "the mystery of the faith" be associated with deacons?**

They must "keep hold of the deep truths of the faith" (NIV) in order to appreciate the importance of their work, and to do it properly.

**8. What does it mean that a deacon must "first be proved?"**

There must be some kind of time period when he has demonstrated the kind of person he is. He must not be selected without forethought.

**9. What happens when a deacon serves well (v.13)?**

He has a good standing in the church. He has demonstrated that he can be depended on to have a firm grasp of the faith.

**10. Our Devotional Reading (1 Peter 5:1-5) approaches elders from the point of shepherding. In v. 2, what should shepherds do for their flock?**

They should feed the flock of God, and take the oversight willingly. The shepherd's concern is for his flock.

Some anonymous wag, maybe with a touch of irreverence, asked a question that carries at least a slight sting of truthfulness. Why, he wanted to know, if Christians are supposed to be so happy, do so many of them look as if they had been baptized in vinegar. I will admit to having known a few vinegar-baptized and perpetually unhappy, complaining souls. Unfortunately, these people like to spread their misery. Fortunately, it does not have to be contagious. As a matter of fact, grouches usually have to add loneliness to their list of complaints. People tend to avoid them like the plague. We might call it quarantined for quarrelsomeness.

Some Bible commentator (whose name slips my memory) says "pessimistic Christian" is a contradiction of terms. Truth to be told, most Christians I have known are upbeat, optimistic people. Some are absolutely inspirational.

In this lesson, we are studying about church leaders. Maybe you have been blessed by having leaders who have lifted you up and made you a happier and better person. It may have been from the pulpit, the classroom, or perhaps on a more personal level. Maybe it was the choir director or a youth leader. Let us be optimistic enough to assume that you have received such a blessing.

During my own high school days, we had a young minister who could capture the attention even of my teenage brain. I was fortunate enough to spend many hours with him and his dear wife. They inspired and helped shape my lifelong thinking more than they ever knew.

During this same time frame, we had wise and gentle elders. I still tend to measure elders by my memory of them. I am not sure that, at the time, I actually appreciated them. It was in later years that I began to understand how valuable they had been for me and for the church of my growing-up years.

By no means, is it necessary to be a church leader in order to be a great influence for good. In our family, we had an aunt who saw to it that her nieces and nephews learned all the Bible stories that children need to know in order to reach adulthood not being pagans. In this department, Auntie got a head start on the preachers and everybody else.

You do not have to be anybody's aunt to touch their lives for the better. I can still recall the names of schoolteachers, who in addition to being good teachers of their subject matter, influenced me with their patience and kindness. I was not a dedicated geometry student, but had an excellent geometry teacher. She was a Christian and displayed the fruit of the Spirit in her classroom. She needed all the extra help she could get, and I believe the Lord helped her to help her students. During the several years I taught school, I remembered her example.

Thank the Lord for those who have inspired you. Thank Him for the opportunities you have to lift up others with your special touch. Oh yes, and avoid the vinegar.

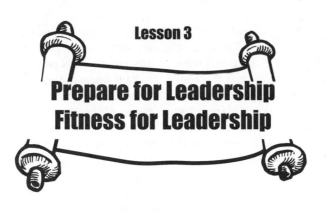

# Lesson 3

## Prepare for Leadership
## Fitness for Leadership

### 1 Timothy 4:6-16

If thou put the brethren in remembrance of these things, thou shalt be a good minister of Jesus Christ, nourished up in the words of faith and of good doctrine, whereunto thou hast attained.

7 But refuse profane and old wives' fables, and exercise thyself rather unto godliness.

8 For bodily exercise profiteth little: but godliness is profitable unto all things, having promise of the life that now is, and of that which is to come.

9 This is a faithful saying and worthy of all acceptation.

10 For therefore we both labour and suffer reproach, because we trust in the living God, who is the Saviour of all men, specially of those that believe.

11 These things command and teach.

12 Let no man despise thy youth; but be thou an example of the believers, in word, in conversation, in charity, in spirit, in faith, in purity.

13 Till I come, give attendance to reading, to exhortation, to doctrine.

14 Neglect not the gift that is in thee, which was given thee by prophecy, with the laying on of the hands of the presbytery.

15 Meditate upon these things; give thyself wholly to them; that thy profiting may appear to all.

16 Take heed unto thyself, and unto the doctrine; continue in them: for in doing this thou shalt both save thyself, and them that hear thee.

**Memory Verse**
1 Timothy 4:16

**Background Scripture**
1 Timothy 4:6-16

**Devotional Reading**
Philippians 3:17-4:1

Most of us feel a bit more secure if the pilot at the controls of the jet we are boarding has at least a tinge of gray around his temples. No cruise line will entrust a fine ship that cost them many millions to a young sailor who has just began to shave. Always they desire a mature, seasoned seaman to protect their investment and their passengers.

What does this tell us about pulpit

## For a Lively Start

No pastor's teaching to his church can rise above the life and character that the pastor models for them. If he preaches eloquent sermons about diligence and then lazes away his days, the church may follow his example instead of his preaching. In like manner, if a pastor thunders warnings about immorality, but all the while rationalizes personal dalliances with the opposite sex, his church

search committees who put a lid of 40 on the age of their candidates and really prefer a new pastor who is 28?

Paul warns the young pastor Timothy about the barrier he may face with his people because of his youthfulness. All of us learn by the mistakes we make in our early years. Young pastors are no exception. As their sheep, we must extend to young shepherds the same grace we expected at that age, and the young pastor must exercise special care not to let his lack of experience endanger his flock.

ℰ๑ଓ

may question his intentions to put into practice that which he preaches.

Therefore, Paul warned Timothy to be an example to his people in the way he lived, loved, and believed. For centuries Christians have told their teachers, "The way you live speaks more loudly than anything you say to us." Paul warned Timothy not to allow his youthfulness to detract from his ministry. Pastors with gray hair may find that temptation knows no age barrier.

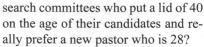

| Teaching Outline | Daily Bible Readings |
|---|---|
| I. Marks of a Good Minister—1 Timothy 4:6 | Mon. Stand Firm in the Lord *Philippians 3:17-4:1* |
| II. Warnings for a Young Minister—1 Timothy 4:7-11 | Tue. Trustworthy Service *Luke 19:12-23* |
| A. Avoiding Fables, 7 | Wed. Single-minded in Purpose *1 Chronicles 29:18-25* |
| B. Setting True Priorities, 8-9 | Thu God's Words in Your Heart *Deuteronomy 11:13-21* |
| C. Being Faithful and True, 10-11 | Fri. Taught and Led by God *Psalm 25:1-10* |
| III. Instructions for Timothy—1 Timothy 4:12-16 | Sat. Pursue Love *1 Corinthians 13:1-14:1* |
| A. Setting an Example, 12 | Sun. Guidance for Faithful Leaders *1 Timothy 4:6-16* |
| B. Establish Liturgy, 13 | |
| C. Using His Gift, 14 | |
| D. Honing His Life and Skills, 15-16 | |

# Verse by Verse

1 Timothy 4:6-16

## I. Marks of a Good Minister—1 Timothy 4:6

**6 If thou put the brethren in remembrance of these things, thou shalt be a good minister of Jesus Christ, nourished up in the words of faith and of good doctrine, whereunto thou hast attained.**

"These things" that Timothy is to remind his people, probably includes the latter verses of what we call Chap. 3 and the first five verses of Chap. 4—a section in which Paul shares the basic truths about Jesus. Paul then cautions Timothy about teachers who forbid marriage, insist on vegetarianism, and push for continuing Jewish diet rules. Timothy needs to instruct his people on such matters, nourishing them spiritually with solid truths and sound teaching.

"Whereunto thou hast attained" is ancient English that means Timothy's training has taught him not to stray into the offbeat teachings Paul lists.

## II. Warnings for a Young Minister—1 Timothy 4:7-11

### A. Avoiding Fables, 7

**7 But refuse profane and old wives' fables, and exercise thyself rather unto godliness.**

Dr. Eugene Peterson in *The Message* did a grand job of explaining what "profane and old wives' fables" might be. He calls them "silly stories . . . dressed up as religion." In the days of the Internet, we are being deluged with a flood of such tales that we do not repeat or forward to our friends. The last part of vs. 7 is well expressed in the RSV, "Train yourself in godliness."

### B. Setting True Priorities, 8-9

**8 For bodily exercise profiteth little: but godliness is profitable unto all things, having promise of the life that now is, and of that which is to come.**

**9 This is a faithful saying and worthy of all acceptation.**

Paul's remarks about physical exercise sound almost heretical to our present generation so obsessed with strict diets and physical fitness. It may well be that people today need to hear the apostle's balanced evaluation of physical versus spiritual fitness. The latter has eternal implications. Paul emphasized this teaching as credible truth worth accepting.

### C. Being Faithful and True, 10-11

**10 For therefore we both labour and suffer reproach, because we**

trust in the living God, who is the Saviour of all men, specially of those that believe.

**11 These things command and teach.**

Both Paul and Timothy, as well as all faithful spokesmen for the Lord since then, work hard and endure verbal mistreatment because they know their calling is from the one true God.

At least half a dozen times in the Pastoral Letters, Paul refers to God as our Savior (1 Tim. 1:1; 2:3; 4:10; Titus 1:3; 2:10; 3:4). Jude 25 also echoes this terminology.

Paul's instruction for Timothy to command and teach "these things" surely includes the matters covered in the early verses of Chap. 4. Since his original writing contained no chapter breaks, he may be referring to everything he has said so far in 1 Timothy.

### III. Instructions for Timothy—1 Timothy 4:12-16
#### A. Setting an Example, 12

**12 Let no man despise thy youth; but be thou an example of the believers, in word, in conversation, in charity, in spirit, in faith, in purity.**

Most of us probably have heard the little ditty that says, "I'd rather see a sermon than to hear one any day." This is what Paul is emphasizing in this verse. Older folks tend to discount the ideas of youth, especially if the young person has displayed what they consider poor judgment in dress, speech, or attitude. Paul warns Timothy to be aware of this and to be extra-careful not to give detractors reason to ignore him or even to belittle him.

Timothy's example for the Christians in Ephesus needed to be multi-faceted—in his speech ("in word"), in his general lifestyle (that's what "conversation" means in the KJV), in his loving ways of serving and getting along with others ("charity"), in his general attitude ("in spirit"), in his trust in the Lord and his loyalty to the truth ("in faith"), and in his morality ("in purity").

Any minister who slights even one of these areas gives people reason to doubt the content and character of his ministry. What we teach can never rise above who we are.

#### B. Establish Liturgy, 13

**13 Till I come, give attendance to reading, to exhortation, to doctrine.**

Unlike Leviticus, the New Testament nowhere offers us detailed instructions for how to structure a Christian worship service. Although we are given scattered warnings to avoid disorderly conduct or disruptive practices during worship times, particular liturgies are never specified. The apostles appear to have allowed individual congregations to praise the Lord in whatever format fit them and their needs. However, this verse does indicate that Paul thought a pastor ought to include at least these three elements. He ought to read Scripture, exhort his people, and teach them the truths of the faith. Worship that omits any one of these items probably is anemic.

#### C. Using His Gift, 14

**14 Neglect not the gift that is in thee, which was given thee by prophecy, with the laying on of the hands of the presbytery.**

Paul never does tell us precisely what spiritual gift had been imparted to Timothy. Some take "by prophecy" to mean that he was endowed with the gift of prophecy, but almost all newer Bible versions interpret this phrase as a description of how the gift came rather than what it was. The TEV says, for example, that the gift came to Timothy "when the prophets spoke and the elders laid their hands on you." "The presbytery" in this verse does not imply that Paul and Timothy were Presbyterians. The word means "the elders"—the lay leaders in some church (possibly Timothy's home congregation in Lystra, but Paul doesn't tell us which one), who imparted some gift to Timothy.

When the Lord has given any one of us a special gift, we are obliged to use that gift to bless all of our brothers and sisters in Christ. Each of us needs to hear Paul's admonition to young Timothy not to neglect the gift God gave him.

**D. Honing His Life and Skills, 15-16**

**15 Meditate upon these things; give thyself wholly to them; that thy profiting may appear to all.**

**16 Take heed unto thyself, and unto the doctrine; continue in them: for in doing this thou shalt both save thyself, and them that hear thee.**

We should not be led astray here by the word "profiting." Timothy was not in ministry to get rich. He was a prophet in a non-profit operation. For "thy profiting," almost all our modern Bible versions read "your progress."

People who could see that Timothy was maturing in his faith, growing in his ministry skills, and preaching content. Any pastor's spiritual growth bears the double fruit of improving him and blessing those he serves for Jesus.

## Evangelistic Emphasis

In the earlier chapters of this letter from Paul to Timothy, Paul has, so to speak, been clearing the deck for action. First, he dealt with the false teaching that had undercut God's work. Myths and controversies are no acceptable substitute for the gospel. Teachers who "do not know what they are talking about" (1: 7) should not be leading the Christian community. The church should not neglect the Lord's concern for all people in all nations. Public worship should reflect that this church represents the household of God, and has a solid foundation as the pillar and ground of the truth. Christ Jesus must remain their focus, because without question, the deep truths of the faith are centered in Him alone.

Paul has given Timothy guidelines for proper church leadership. The decks are clearing, things are more shipshape, and the church is beginning to move in the right direction.

This is going to involve Scripture, preaching, and teaching (v.13). This begins to sound like evangelism. Timothy had received a special gift for doing God's work. He was to be cautious about his life and his doctrine, and do things right. There had already been more than enough mistakes made in Ephesus. It was time to get to the business at hand. Timothy blessed both himself and his hearers. Then he preached the Word.

## Memory Selection

ഇ⊙ര

"Take heed unto thyself, and unto the doctrine; continue in them: for in doing this thou shalt both save thyself, and them that hear thee."

*1 Timothy 4:16*

Timothy was a man with talents too valuable to neglect. Some of his ability may have been given him by nature. Paul seems to have recognized this or he would not have selected him to be his traveling companion and trusted assistant. Paul would be careful about choosing the person who could help with his apostolic mission.

In addition to whatever his ancestral DNA had placed within him, Timothy had received a gift, a *charisma,* at his ordination. "Neglect not the gift that is in thee, which was given thee by prophecy, with the laying on of the hands of the presbytery" (v. 14). Paul had already mentioned this in 1:18. In 2 Timothy 1:6, we learn that, by Paul's hands, he had received a gift. (Perhaps at the same time as the event of 1:18?)

Multitalented Timothy had a lot to offer. Paul tells him to watch his own life and the doctrine closely. Much is at stake here. After what this church has already suffered, Timothy does not want to take a false step.

Perhaps this is a case of when much is given, much is required. With the backing of Paul and the Spirit's help, we expect that those who hear him will be listening to exactly what God wants them to know. We can feel confident that when Timothy watches the doctrine closely, the core values of Christianity, which have been so much a part of Paul's instruction to him, will be the heart of his teaching.

# Weekday Problems

I know a young man who was very good at what he did. He was well educated, highly motivated, had an exceptional work ethic, and knew the business he was in like the back of his hand.

There was a company over a thousand miles away that needed his expertise. He accepted their offer and arrived, ready to help them revamp a dysfunctional and inefficient way of doing business.

"But that's not the way we do it here," old timers on the job there would tell him, not realizing that doing it differently was what the business needed.

Do you suppose that Timothy found himself in a similar situation in Ephesus? He had to replace bad teachers. He had to revamp worship services. He had to establish valid doctrine in place of foolish fables. How long did it take before some recalcitrant church members finally realized that "That was then but this is now?"

Have you ever been in a position (maybe on the job, at church, school, a club, or even at home) where you helped bring about badly needed changes? Some people looked down on Timothy because of his youth. There will always be somebody who resists doing things the better way. Timothy called on his resources, watched his steps carefully, and worked hard. That is a good way to overcome a problem.

---

## New Courses for Guys

1. Introduction to Common Household Objects I: The Mop
2. Introduction to Common Household Objects II: The Sponge
3. Recycling Skills I: Boxes the Electronics Came In
4. Recycling Skills II: Styrofoam That Came in the Boxes the Electronics Came In
5. Retro? Or Just Hideous?: Re-examining Your 1970s Polyester Shirts
6. It's Yours, Mine, and Ours: Sharing the Remote
7. Directions: It's Okay to Ask for Them
8. Adventures in Housekeeping I: Let's Clean the Closet
9. Going Out to Dinner: Beyond the Pizza Hut
10. Romance: More Than a Cable Channel!

# This Lesson in Your Life

We have all kept track via TV newscasts of forest fires that just keep growing. California and other western states have some massive ones. One night's newscast will report ten square miles burned. Soon the burned-out area will have doubled and tripled. Finally the raging flames will be 40% contained, and cooler weather, shifting winds, or a good rainstorm will help the firefighters extinguish the flames.

Some problems have a traceable history much like a forest fire. Just as a careless camper lets his cooking fire spread into the forest, so a careless word or act grows into a red-hot problem. (James reminds us that just as a great forest is set on fire by a small spark, so the tongue is a fire that can become a life-ruining blaze.)

Have you ever noticed that some problems have a tendency to escalate? It is as though there is some unseen energy that keeps them going. The philosophy that says ignore it and it will go away just will not work. It is time to put more fire fighters on the line and call in more planes for dropping fire-retardant. (As we keep using the forest fire metaphor).

Have you ever had problems that seemed insolvable? Timothy's Ephesus situation might have looked that way to a lesser man than Paul and a smaller talent than Timothy's. Let us allow these two to teach us something about problem solving.

Timothy's youth was something of a problem. The old stuck-in-the-mud, let's-keep-things-the-way-they-are crowd would not like some young whipper-snapper upsetting their whole church scene. Paul wanted to save that church, not destroy it. He had the strategy to do it. Here is the plan.

Timothy will have to give some firm commands as far as his teaching is concerned. That is non-negotiable. He can overcome the youth issue by the example that he sets. As they see his life in action, his love, faith, and purity, this should do the job.

Do you think people such as you and I could work out at least some of our problems if we pick up a few pointers here? Can we find some principle that might work for us? Let's make a list.

Overcome evil with good.

Fight falsehood with truth.

Hate cannot stand up against love.

Holding a grudge does not work as well as forgiveness.

Getting even is not as nice as being kind to an opponent.

This list seems much too short.

Please see how much you can add to it.

**GETTING
THE FACTS STRAIGHT**

**1. What did Timothy need to do in order to be a good minister of Jesus Christ?**

He needed to remind the church what the Spirit had said about departures from the faith (vs. 1-4).

**2. As a good minister of Christ, what nourishment would Timothy find?**

Being a good minister would nourish him in words of faith and good doctrine.

**3. Timothy should refuse profane and old wives tales, but should train himself in what?**

He should avoid useless and unprofitable talk, which had been such a major part of the church's attention and teaching, and instead should train himself in godliness.

**4. Physical exercise has a limited benefit. What about godliness?**

Godliness is profitable for all things. If physical exercise is good (which it is), spiritual exercise is better.

**5. What kind of promises does godliness bring?**

It has the promise of this present life, as well as bringing benefits in the life to come.

**6. Why were Paul and Timothy willing to work and suffer reproach?**

They are willing to do this because they trust in the living God, who is the savior (preserver) of everyone, but especially is the (eternal) savior of believers.

**7. In what ways was Timothy to be an example to the believers?**

He should be an example by in his speech, his life, love, spirit, faith and purity. This church had experienced a severe lack of positive, upbuilding influences. Timothy is to demonstrate these excellent qualities.

**8. Paul hoped to come to Ephesus. In the meantime, what was Timothy to be doing?**

He was to give attention to the public reading of Scripture, to exhortation, and to teaching doctrine.

**9. In what way did Timothy receive the gift that helped him in his work?**

The gift was received with a prophetic utterance and the laying on of the hands of the presbytery.

**10. Who would benefit if Timothy took heed of himself and the doctrine?**

If Timothy continued in this both he and those who heard him would be saved.

We are going to be thinking here about something that will make us happier, brighter, more efficient, and all-around top-notch people. It is going to take us a while to get there, so please be patient. (Come to think of it, patience might be a major step toward our uplifting aspirations.)

Let us start with Solomon. He tells us that his proverbs will help us develop a disciplined life. Discipline is a risky topic for a man like Solomon. He was so rich that he had to work hard finding ways to spend his money. He had so many possessions that owning stuff got boring. He had more women than some small towns have as their total population. We give him credit though: he did compose some good proverbs, and the discipline he recommends is a good thing to have.

Have you guessed already? Discipline is what will make us happier. It is probably not one of our favorite words, which might help explain why there is so much unhappiness in the world.

Discipline does not have to be associated with punishment, like making a naughty child go stand in the corner. Maybe its being used in that way that gives it a negative connotation. It is actually a very positive word.

A disciplined life is going to be an orderly life. Sometimes it takes me five minutes to find a pen that will write. It can take longer than that to find a book that is not on the shelf where it should be. An excursion into my office closet presents a clear and present danger. Other areas of my life are kept more neat and tidy, but you can easily see how lack of discipline creates havoc. (And I am guessing that somewhere in your house there may be a junk drawer filled with things you do not need or want, and even if you did, you could not find them.)

A disciplined life is one of self-control. We all know how bad it can be when someone flies off the handle and says or does something that later causes regret, not to mention serious unhappiness. Discipline helps us get rid of bad habits and replace them with good ones. It keeps us from doing lots of misery-causing things and frees us up for happier times.

In our lesson, Paul told Timothy to be diligent and give himself wholly to certain things. That is discipline. It helped an entire church to be glad.

Take a close look. You can see how the word "discipline" bears a resemblance to "disciple." These words share a common language ancestor. Christians are disciples of the Lord Jesus. It is He who shapes our lives and gives direction to them. He sets boundaries for us within which we are safe, and beyond which danger lurks. We would have spiritual anarchy without His discipline.

Jesus told a group of believers that if they kept His teaching, then they were really His disciples, they would know the truth, and the truth would set them free (John 8:32). Being disciplined by Him brings freedom – freedom for all the good things that bring happiness and wellbeing.

## Lesson 4

# Worship Inspires Service All in the Family

## 1 Timothy 5:1-8, 17-22

Rebuke not an elder, but intreat him as a father; and the younger men as brethren;

2 The elder women as mothers; the younger as sisters, with all purity.

3 Honour widows that are widows indeed.

4 But if any widow have children or nephews, let them learn first to shew piety at home, and to requite their parents: for that is good and acceptable before God.

5 Now she that is a widow indeed, and desolate, trusteth in God, and continueth in supplications and prayers night and day.

6 But she that liveth in pleasure is dead while she liveth.

7 And these things give in charge, that they may be blameless.

8 But if any provide not for his own, and specially for those of his own house, he hath denied the faith, and is worse than an infidel.

17 Let the elders that rule well be counted worthy of double honour, especially they who labour in the word and doctrine.

18 For the scripture saith, Thou shalt not muzzle the ox that treadeth out the corn. And, The labourer is worthy of his reward.

19 Against an elder receive not an accusation, but before two or three witnesses.

20 Them that sin rebuke before all, that others also may fear.

21 I charge thee before God, and the Lord Jesus Christ, and the elect angels, that thou observe these things without preferring one before another, doing nothing by partiality.

22 Lay hands suddenly on no man, neither be partaker of other men's sins: keep thyself pure.

**Memory Verse**
1 Timothy 5:8

**Background Scripture**
1 Timothy 5:1-22

**Devotional Reading**
John 12:20-26

# *fo(us*

In the days before we had government programs to care for the elderly and disabled, the church served as the main source of aid for those who could not support themselves. The first major hospitals in America were founded by churches. Feeding programs like the Salvation Army predate government aid for the homeless. The Red Cross began as a Christian disaster relief effort. Through the ages, the Church has been the primary source of help for the helpless.

Churches still provide much-needed care for the working poor who fall through the cracks in health-care and feeding programs. Those who receive help such as food stamps and Social Security often do not receive enough to survive in our expensive times, so the church's assistance can be a crucial part of their sustenance. Paul outlines to Timothy wise rules for the church's widow-care program in the first century of our faith.

## *For a Lively Start*

ട്ര

Few churches turn away hungry people who seek food, even if those people are hell-raising pagans. If their kids are hungry, we feed them without requiring a morality test to qualify for aid.

Nevertheless, Paul reveals in 1 Timothy 5 a higher standard for the assistance to the poor and hungry within the church. Those who have thumbed their noses at the moral standards of the Christian faith should know that they are also closing the door to aid they might receive in their later years.

"Some widows have turned away to follow Satan," Paul notes (1 Tim. 5:15, TEV). Just because they are widows does not qualify them for routine church aid. They must be living in a way that upholds what the Church believes.

| Teaching Outline | Daily Bible Readings |
|---|---|
| I. Ministry to the Old and the Young—1 Timothy 5:1-2 | Mon. Chosen to Serve<br>*Acts 6:1-6* |
| II. Identifying a Widow Indeed—1 Timothy 5:3-8<br>A. Her Family, 3-4<br>B. Her Life and Faith, 5-6<br>C. The Clear Rules, 7-8 | Tue. Served by the Master<br>*Luke 12:35-40*<br>Wed. Support for Parents<br>*Mark 7:9-13*<br>Thu Honoring Elders<br>*Leviticus 19:31-37* |
| III. Remuneration for Church Leaders—1 Timothy 5:17-18 | Fri. A Widow's Gift<br>*Mark 12:41-44* |
| IV. Elders Who Sin—1 Timothy 5:19-21 | Sat. Assisting Widows<br>*1 Timothy 5:9-16* |
| V. Choosing Leaders Wisely—1 Timothy 5:22 | Sun. Duties Toward Believers<br>*1 Timothy 5:1-8, 17-22* |

# *Verse by Verse*

## 1 Timothy 5:1-8, 17-22

### I. Ministry to the Old and the Young—1 Timothy 5:1-2

**1 Rebuke not an elder, but intreat him as a father; and the younger men as brethren;**

**2 The elder women as mothers; the younger as sisters, with all purity.**

The same Greek word *prebuteros* can mean either an official elder in the leadership of a congregation or just a man who is elderly. Translators have to consider the meaning of the surrounding text to decide which significance the writer intends. From the admonitions that follow in these two verses, it seems clear that Paul is addressing first one age group in the church and then another, so almost all the newer Bible versions choose to translate "older man" in this instance. Paul is advising young Timothy to relate to older members as if they were his parents, and to younger members as if they were his siblings. Obviously, this means that he will treat none of the church women as sexual attractions, no more so than he would his own mother or sister.

### II. Identifying a Widow Indeed—1 Timothy 5:3-8

### A. Her Family, 3-4

**3 Honour widows that are widows indeed.**

**4 But if any widow have children or nephews, let them learn first to shew piety at home, and to requite their parents: for that is good and acceptable before God.**

Jewish communities, and the church after them, took good care of the widows and orphans among them, obeying God's instructions such as those in Deuteronomy 14:29; 24:17-21; and 26:12.

All women whose husbands were dead were widows, but not all of them had the same abject needs. Paul points out here that a woman who had relatives able to feed and care for her should expect them to bear that burden instead of holding out her hand to the church. The word for "nephews" in the KJV may mean "grandchildren" instead. Whomever the relatives may be, they show their true faith and piety—they "put their religion into practice" (NIV)—when they provide needed support for their elderly family members.

Paul believes that the younger relatives owe such care to their elders, since the older family members fed and clothed them when they were young.

Hence, they "requite" or "repay" their elderly kin when they feed them.

**B. Her Life and Faith, 5-6**

**5 Now she that is a widow indeed, and desolate, trusteth in God, and continueth in supplications and prayers night and day.**

**6 But she that liveth in pleasure is dead while she liveth.**

Not all widows who were truly alone ("desolate") in the world were eligible for the church's aid, Paul says. A true widow, in the sense that Paul is describing, would obviously trust in God, and show it by spending much time in prayer. In contrast, a widow whose only concern is herself and her own pleasures shows by her self-indulgence (RSV) that she is not devoted to the Lord. Such a person should not expect to be fed, clothed, or housed by the Lord, according to the apostle's instructions.

Is there a lesson here for the rest of us whose chief aim in life is how to amuse ourselves? Are we also "dead" while we are still alive?

**C. The Clear Rules, 7-8**

**7 And these things give in charge, that they may be blameless.**

**8 But if any provide not for his own, and specially for those of his own house, he hath denied the faith, and is worse than an infidel.**

Giving these things "in charge" is an out-dated way of telling Timothy to give the church clear instructions so that all may know what is expected of them (so that "they may be blameless").

Then Paul states the general rule for all Christians everywhere that all of us are responsible for caring for our own families ("his own house"). A person who allows a grandmother to be homeless or an elderly parent to go without necessary food obviously does not have Christ's love in their heart. They may sing loud hymns and endure long sermons, but they have denied the faith if they let their relatives starve. Even unbelievers do better than this. How can we expect the respect of our secular neighbors if we behave worse than they do?

**III. Remuneration for Church Leaders—1 Timothy 5:17-18**

**17 Let the elders that rule well be counted worthy of double honour, especially they who labour in the word and doctrine.**

**18 For the scripture saith, Thou shalt not muzzle the ox that treadeth out the corn. And, The labourer is worthy of his reward.**

Unlike vs. 1, the word "elder" most likely refers here to an official church leader. Such a person deserves "double honor"—both respect and remuneration—if he also serves as a preacher or a teacher in his church. Paul earlier warned that no person should desire to be a church leader in order to get rich (1 Tim. 3:3, 8), a warning which implies the possibility of remuneration for elders or deacons. Now the apostle expressly orders that those leaders who labor to teach the church should be paid.

To make this point, Paul quotes two scriptures. The first one is Deuteronomy 25:4, where the Lord commanded the Israelites not to muzzle their oxen that were forced to walk around all day long atop beds of grain to break the seeds loose from the chaff. "Corn" in the KJV is a mistake. Corn was an American crop, unavailable in Europe or the Holy Land in Bible times. The Greek word here means grain.

The second scripture Paul quotes contains Jesus' words in Luke 10:7, "The worker deserves to be paid."

## IV. Elders Who Sin—1 Timothy 5:19-21

**19 Against an elder receive not an accusation, but before two or three witnesses.**

**20 Them that sin rebuke before all, that others also may fear.**

**21 I charge thee before God, and the Lord Jesus Christ, and the elect angels, that thou observe these things without preferring one before another, doing nothing by partiality.**

Unfortunately, church leaders do sometimes go astray. Paul warns Timothy to proceed carefully if anyone comes to accuse an elder of wrongdoing. Such a charge should be heard only with two or three dependable witnesses. This policy will deter anyone with malicious accusations and prevent others who want to air petty complaints.

This entire matter of receiving charges against elders and rebuking them publicly for their sins is so serious that Paul calls God, Christ, and "the elect angels" to witness that he is giving this instruction to Timothy. No one seems to know exactly what Paul means by this description of angels. Some think he is referring to those who did not fall when Satan was cast out of Heaven. Others suggest that certain angels may have been assigned duties related to the church, such as serving as guardian angels to believers. "Elect" means "chosen," but it can also imply greater rank, just as the term "archangel" seems to acknowledge that Michael precedes other angels. All we know for sure here is that angels were witnesses to Paul's command. Beyond that, we are in the dark and guessing.

Paul's command is that Timothy should neither select new leaders nor should he discipline existing ones out of bias (NASB) or partiality. For the good of the church, Timothy's actions must be totally objective and fair just as our preferences must be when we deal with matters such as these.

## V. Choosing Leaders Wisely—1 Timothy 5:22

**22 Lay hands suddenly on no man, neither be partaker of other men's sins: keep thyself pure.**

This is a command about neither choosing leaders in haste nor colluding with those who have devious intentions, and is a continuation of the instructions in the preceding two verses. Timothy must stand above such underhanded, unworthy dealings in his administration of the church.

ℰℭ

## Evangelistic Emphasis

Christianity is a caring, giving, generous, benevolent, loving religion. It is what we are and who we are. We like to give.

Many members of the early church were very poor. Our lesson from Timothy gives specific guidelines for assisting those in the Ephesian church who needed help. Some truly needed the church's help. Others might be willing to accept it, but for various reason it was better not to include them. Plans were laid out so things would be done fairly. (You might also want to read Acts 6:1-7 about food distribution.)

Though it was not done to attract attention, when the church assisted its needy members, unbelieving neighbors and friends could not keep from knowing what was happening. They would see demonstrated the care that these disciples of Jesus had for each other. They would know about food on the table and a warm coat to wear. They had to be favorably impressed.

Jesus told the disciples that as He loved them, so they should love one another. By this all men would know that they were His disciples (John 13:34). Christian evangelism has a message that can be heard. Christianity in practice has a message that can be seen. The old adage, "Seeing is believing," suggests that Christian sharing enhances the believability of the evangelist's message.

## Memory Selection

ഇൻൽ

"But if any provide not for his own, and especially for those of his own house, he hath denied the faith, and is worse than an infidel."    *1 Timothy 5:8*

The recent widespread economic collapse put stress on American families in a way that we have not known since days of the Great Depression. The unemployed, under-employed, those who took cuts in pay, and those who lost retirement income, found themselves in a survival mode.

Hard times such as that bring to life our realization of how much we need each other. Families moved in with families, resources were shared, and in a very real way our Memory Verse lesson became a personal experience for many Christian people.

The church in Ephesus seems to have had quite a number of poor people in it. This probably had nothing to do with an economic collapse. It is just the way things were, and there was no government safety net. The church took care of those who truly needed its help.

However, it was expected that family would take care of family. That is the Christian way. Presumably, even pagans would do that much, and for a Christian not to do so would rank him as worse than an infidel.

We hear that "Everything old is new again." That ancient Christian core value, love and devotion to family, still holds true. It leads us to care for each other through adversity, and still works now just as it did in old Ephesus.

## Weekday Problems

Our congregation generously supports benevolent works in various parts of the world. This includes local causes, some connected with our church and some not. We try to see that none of our own membership suffers because of lack of funds. I will have to say that I am blessed to part of a caring, sharing church.

A couple of years ago, as our nation's recession moved into depression and our local unemployment and business failures increased, non-profit service organizations began to feel the pinch. Institutions that had traditionally fed and furnished emergency housing for the poorest of the poor were out of funds themselves. Their would-be donors were struggling.

Evening TV newscasts showed empty shelves in food banks and kitchens. Shelters for abused women and children had to limit service. Tax revenue was down resulting in lessened government programs. Our state was among the hardest hit by the housing crisis, and foreclosures were rampant.

We wanted to help stem the crisis, but our budget was maxed out. We found a solution to this problem. A young man in our church contacted a local food bank, which brought a huge food collection box to be placed in the church vestibule. Our people always had it filled to overflowing long before time for scheduled pick-up. Excess bags and boxes of groceries were stacked around the doorway on many Sunday mornings.

We solved the problem about how to help. We thought having an excess of food for the hungry was a good problem to have. We could use more like it.

---

# Bumper Stickers for Women

1. So many men, so few who can afford me.
2. God made us sisters, prozac made us friends.
3. If they don't have chocolate in heaven, I ain't going.
4. My mother is a travel agent for guilt trips.
5. If we are what we eat, I'm fast, cheap, and easy.
6. Coffee, chocolate, men . . . some things are just better rich.
7. I'm one of those bad things that happen to good people.
8. If you want breakfast in bed, sleep in the kitchen.
9. Dinner is ready when the smoke alarm goes off.
10. All stressed out and no one to choke.

# This Lesson in Your Life

It is said about missionaries that the one who gives away the most shirts, makes the most converts. There is no doubt a sadly true edge to that. It is possible to attract people by giving them material possessions, especially if they are living on a poverty level. However, a person who is simply bribed by Christian shirts is not a true Christian convert. Wearing a "Christian shirt" does not answer the question as to whether there is a Christian heart inside the wearer.

On the other hand, Christianity is a caring, giving, generous, benevolent, loving religion. It is what and who we are. We like to give. Continuing with the shirt metaphor, we will want to be reminded not to harm the person to whom we give the shirt. Whether we are talking about the mission field in some underdeveloped country, or helping our relatives, friends, neighbors, or fellow church members who are having a hard time, we should hand out the shirts wisely.

An example of the principle involved in this is seen in our government's efforts to help the poor. Various agencies have helped feed and house many who truly need and deserve assistance. To the contrary, the same good intention has been misused to create a welfare culture that can extend through generations. This is not making a political statement. It is simply an example of how generosity can help some and harm others.

Paul's instructions to Timothy about how to assist widows indicates that guidelines were needed. The church was not to say, "All widows please line up here to get your food and money." Paul seems to have sensed the probability that Christian benevolence would be misused by some. Apparently, some of the widows were living genuine Christian lives. Others (5:6) seemed to have been interested in a self-indulgent lifestyle. Age limitations and other factors were involved in eligibility for church assistance. This program called for wisdom and discretion. You and I as individuals, as well as our churches, will do well to take note.

Let us think for a moment about how we as individual Christians can use our money wisely to help the poor. Giving through our churches is the most obvious answer. You know (or can find out) how your church is helping.

Typically there are other organizations that also do a wonderful job helping the poor, the elderly, those with special needs, abused women and children, and others. Common sense tells us we need to know the reputation of any group we are interested in helping. There are those who are willing to scam us.

We Christians have lots of shirts to distribute. We just need to be careful about which shirt we give to what person, and why.

298

## GETTING THE FACTS STRAIGHT

**1. In what respectful way should Timothy give correction to an elder (older) man who needed admonition?**

He should rebuke him as a father. Verse 1 uses the term "elder" simply as an older person. In this verse and the next one it mentions younger men, and older and younger women.

**2. How are younger men, older women, and younger women to be treated?**

Younger men should be treated as brothers, older women as mothers, and younger women as sisters. All these groups are to be dealt with as Timothy would treat his immediate family members: respectfully, not harshly.

**3. To what group of widows should honor be given?**

Those who are widows indeed should be given proper recognition. Those who have family fall into a different category.

**4. If the widow has children or other close kin, what is their responsibility?**

Close kin should put their religion to practice at home by helping their own family members, and repay the care that has been given to them by the church.

**5. If anyone will not care for his own close relatives, how does Paul describe that person?**

He is worse than an infidel, who presumably would be caring for his kin. The idea points out that more should be expected from a Christian than an unbeliever.

**6. What does "counted worthy of double honor" mean? It refers to elders.**

All elders should be respected for what they do. Those who spend more time with the church's work, and especially if they preach and teach, should be paid for their labor.

**7. What Old Testament verse is used with reference to being worthy of being rewarded?**

Deuteronomy 25:4. "Thou shalt not muzzle the ox when he treadeth out the corn."

**8. There is a New Testament source for the wording about the laborer being worthy of his reward. Can you find it, and what was its context?**

Luke 10:7. Jesus sent out the seventy workers. Homes that received these workers should properly furnish them food and lodging.

**9. If anyone wanted to make an accusation against an elder, under what circumstances should it be done?**

The accusation should be heard only if there are two or three witnesses who bring the charges.

**10. What is the meaning of "Lay hands suddenly on no man, neither be partakers of other men's sins . . . ?"**

Care should be taken before anyone is appointed elder or deacon. To do so carelessly would make Timothy share the responsibility for the misdeeds they might commit.

A few years ago there was a real snafu in our local postal system (at least I hope it did not spread further than our area). Sometimes it took two to three weeks for our weekly church newsletter to be delivered. A three week old newsletter is not very newsy. The postal official to whom I spoke said he knew there was a really bad problem, and that it would definitely get fixed. Before that happened though, he said the problem was going to get much worse. It was fixed, but not before it got worse.

That was something of a good news/bad news situation, sort of like light at the end of the tunnel, but seen through a very long and dark tunnel. This business about the post office and the dark tunnel is to inform you that this page is going to be uplifting, but there will be some down spots first. Let us get right to it with one of those downers. While you are reading, keep Timothy's old folks in mind.

I have heard many people say that they just cannot bring themselves to visit in a nursing home. It is just too depressing. All those old folks confined to bed or wheelchair bound, with no real hope for getting better, is just too heartbreaking.

There is a sadness to becoming infirm or incapacitated, that is a fact. But after well over fifty years of ministry and visiting hundreds of people in countless care centers, I have come to see the beauty of well-run ones.

As I walk down the hallway and glance into the rooms while passing, I see residents who are clean, properly medicated, well fed, and resting in clean beds in clean rooms. It is wonderful to live in a land where this kind of thing is common.

One person whom I visit regularly in the care center has to be lifted out of bed into a wheelchair, then when it is time, lifted back into bed. I think it is great, not that he is incapacitated, but that there is someone there to lift him. He is also incontinent, and they keep him clean. He is diabetic, so they watch his diet and medication. He needs physical therapy and he gets it. Social Security is his only income, so except for that, we tax-payers cover his expenses. He grumbles some, but so what? When I leave his facility I feel good all over because I know he, and scores of others living there, have a staff on duty caring for them. The people of America have heart! Rejoice, and be glad that you are one of them.

My parishioner Ed was in an Alzheimer's unit. The last time I visited him, shortly before his death, he could not understand why I did not remember performing his wedding ceremony the week before. In his mind he was a newly-wed. Any form of dementia is heart-wrenching. We need to cherish and protect loved ones who suffer from it, and we must always remember those whose own memory is lost.

How do you suppose Paul and Timothy would feel about the care we are giving to those who need it? I think they would find it uplifting. We are part of a great and caring society. Aren't you glad to be a part of it?

300

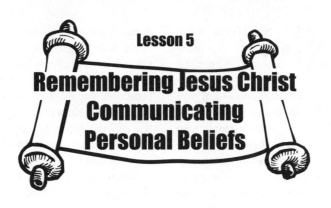

# Lesson 5

# Remembering Jesus Christ Communicating Personal Beliefs

## 2 Timothy 2:8-15

Remember that Jesus Christ of the seed of David was raised from the dead according to my gospel:

9 Wherein I suffer trouble, as an evil doer, even unto bonds; but the word of God is not bound.

10 Therefore I endure all things for the elect's sakes, that they may also obtain the salvation which is in Christ Jesus with eternal glory.

11 It is a faithful saying: For if we be dead with him, we shall also live with him:

12 If we suffer, we shall also reign with him: if we deny him, he also will deny us:

13 If we believe not, yet he abideth faithful: he cannot deny himself.

14 Of these things put them in remembrance, charging them before the Lord that they strive not about words to no profit, but to the subverting of the hearers.

15 Study to shew thyself approved unto God, a workman that needeth not to be ashamed, rightly dividing the word of truth.

---

**Memory Verse**
2 Timothy 2:15

**Background Scripture**
2 Timothy 2:8-15

**Devotional Reading:**
Titus 3:1-7

---

**focus** If you have gone to a nursing home to help lead worship for the residents, no doubt you have marveled to see some of the oldest folks in the circle—people who cannot tell you who they are or where they are—still able to join heartily in the singing, recalling every word of hymns they learned decades ago. The Church's hymns enshrine gospel truths in the depths of our souls at a level deeper than our rational thoughts.

No one recalls what melody the Church used with the hymn recorded in vss. 11-13, but the words have been preserved for us. Centuries after the names of the singers have been forgotten and the meter of the music lost, still the Church treasures the truths embodied in these ancient lyrics.

What music in today's worship do you expect to be blessing Christians 2,000 years from now?

ಜೊಡ

## For a Lively Start

When the apostle Paul delivers these words to his most trusted helper, Paul was back in prison. Not only is he in chains, but it is apparent from his later words in this letter that he expects soon to die for his faith. In the anticipation of death, would it not bless your soul to remember (as Paul commands in vs. 8) that the Jesus we worship and serve

was raised from the dead?

From the earliest moments of his ministry after his conversion in Damascus, Paul had faithfully proclaimed the resurrection of Jesus. Having seen the risen Lord, he had never had the slightest doubt that Jesus rose from the grave. Now with his own death drawing near, this truth surely takes on fresh meaning. How does Christ's victory over death abate our own fears of the grave?

| Teaching Outline | Daily Bible Readings |
|---|---|
| I. Remembering Jesus' Resurrection—2 Timothy 2:8-10 | Mon. Raised from the Dead *Acts 3:11-16* |
| A. Jesus Risen from the Dead, 8 | Tue. Descended from David *Romans 1:1-7* |
| B. Paul Imprisoned for This Truth, 9 | Wed. Our Savior *Titus 3:1-7* |
| C. Paul Suffering for the Elect, 10 | Thu Remembering Jesus' Sacrifice *Matthew 26:17-30* |
| II. An Ancient Hymn about Suffering—2 Timothy 2:11-13 | Fri. Proclaiming the Lord's Death *1 Corinthians 11:23-33* |
| III. Core Truths Versus Petty Squabbles—2 Timothy 2:14 | Sat. Now Is the Day of Salvation *2 Corinthians 6:1-10* |
| IV. A Workman Approved by God—2 Timothy 2:15 | Sun. Salvation in Christ Jesus *2 Timothy 2:8-15* |

# *Verse by Verse*

2 Timothy 2:8-15

## I. Remembering Jesus' Resurrection—2 Timothy 2:8-10

### A. Jesus Risen from the Dead, 8

**8 Remember that Jesus Christ of the seed of David was raised from the dead according to my gospel:**

Bible translators appear to be evenly split on whether Paul was telling Timothy to remember that Jesus was raised (as in the KJV, NKJV, and NLT among others) or simply to remember Jesus Christ who was resurrected (see the RSV, NIV, or TEV). Either reading fits the following comments of Paul, and although the emphasis of the two readings is different, the basic truth conveyed remains the same. In both readings, the resurrected Christ is recommended as the focus of Christians going through persecutions.

It is not hard to see why concentrating on the One who conquered death would be beneficial to believers who, like the apostle Paul, are facing the penalty of death for their faith. Knowing that a similar execution glorified the Lord instead of defeating Him could help these embattled Christians to face their fate with courage and hope.

Not quite so clear to us, however, is why Paul includes in his call for remembrance the fact that Jesus was a descendant of David. Most Bible scholars seem to agree that Paul alludes to Jesus' human ancestry to emphasize the Incarnation. Paul appears to be saying that Jesus, who defeated death, was a human being like us. Paul wants the suffering Christians to fix their eyes on the Man who died and rose again.

When he speaks of "my gospel," Paul is reminding Timothy that he has always preached this comforting truth about God who became a man to conquer death.

### B. Paul Imprisoned for This Truth, 9

**9 Wherein I suffer trouble, as an evil doer, even unto bonds; but the word of God is not bound.**

As Paul inspired these words, he has been imprisoned as a criminal ("an evil doer"). He is again chained to a Roman guard and now he faces execution, all because his preaching of the gospel of Jesus brought him to the attention of the governing officials. He may be in chains, but Paul exults that the gospel he has preached still spreads freely across the region. It is not restrained or chained. Nor can it be even today. In atheistic Iron Curtain lands where Christianity was outlawed for many decades, the gospel continued to be preached and men and women continued to be won to the Lord. Stalin and his officials could not squelch the Good News.

## C. Paul Suffering for the Elect, 10

**10 Therefore I endure all things for the elect's sakes, that they may also obtain the salvation which is in Christ Jesus with eternal glory.**

"The elect" means those who have been chosen by God. Christians across the Roman Empire are distressed by what is happening to their key leaders—men like Peter and Paul. Paul tells Timothy that he is willing to face any danger, suffer any pain, and pay any price—even his life—if "enduring all things" will result in the salvation of those whom God has chosen. If what the apostle suffers here on Earth results in their enjoyment of an eternity in Glory with the Lord, Paul thinks the result is worth whatever it costs him. The NLT simplifies this verse, telling us, "So I am willing to endure anything if it will bring salvation and eternal glory in Christ Jesus to those God has chosen."

Does the salvation of humans everywhere matter this much to us? Would we endure this kind of persecution in order to spread the gospel and save God's chosen children worldwide?

## II. An Ancient Hymn about Suffering—2 Timothy 2:11-13

**11 It is a faithful saying: For if we be dead with him, we shall also live with him:**

**12 If we suffer, we shall also reign with him: if we deny him, he also will deny us:**

**13 If we believe not, yet he abideth faithful: he cannot deny himself.**

What the KJV describes as a "faithful" saying, other Bible versions depict as a saying that is "sure" (RSV), "true" (TEV), or "trustworthy" (NLT, NIV). In other words, we can believe and trust the thoughts that follow.

Most Bible scholars believe the symmetrical words in these verses likely were an ancient hymn in which the beleaguered Christians in this era expressed their undaunted hope. No one could take away their hope because they knew whom their Savior was. No matter what happened to them, He would not let them down.

Almost all of the newer Bible versions alert us to the nature of this material by setting it in poetic or hymn format:

If we die with him,
we will also live with him.
If we endure hardship,
we will reign with him.
If we deny him,
he will deny us.
If we are unfaithful,
he remains faithful,
for he cannot deny who he is (NLT).

When our eyes see this, instantly we know we are not reading straight copy.

This hymn about dying and enduring hard times surely spoke to those who were facing such ends. How many would deny the Lord Jesus to escape torture? Some of them might weaken, the hymn admits, but Jesus would remain true to His people. He would never change.

## III. Core Truths Versus Petty Squabbles—2 Timothy 2:14

**14 Of these things put them in remembrance, charging them before the Lord that they strive not about words to no profit, but to the subverting of the hearers.**

Paul counsels Timothy again to have his people remember the instructions they have been given. One of Paul's most repeated exhortations was that the people in the Church avoid quarrels and arguments that would tear them down and impart no blessing to any of them. Striving "about words to no profit" seems to be a favorite activity of some believers. It undermines ("subverts"—KJV) their faith instead of building them up in the Lord.

## IV. A Workman Approved by God—2 Timothy 2:15

**15 Study to shew thyself approved unto God, a workman that needeth not to be ashamed, rightly dividing the word of truth.**

Based on the KJV's use of the word "study," many have used this verse to enjoin their people to be diligent in their study of God's word. Obviously, "dividing the word of truth" does involve time and effort spent to understand the Scriptures, but the word "study" actually has nothing at all to do with what we call studying. It is an older English term that means to do our best. Paul is counseling Timothy to use all his energy, time, and skills to be that kind of Kingdom worker that God would be highly pleased. One aspect of this labor would be his careful and responsible handling of the Scriptures.

"Rightly dividing" does not mean to discern its various sections, as some have concluded from a surface reading. Paul is telling Timothy to "teach correctly," "rightly handle," or to "explain accurately" the holy texts. Unfortunately, the archaic English terms used here have caused many to violate its instructions when they were explaining this very passage.

ಬಂದ

305

## Evangelistic Emphasis

In this lesson we find Paul in bonds, a prisoner awaiting his inevitable execution. Though in chains, he never took his eyes off the goal of spreading the gospel. There are no chains on the word of God, he said. He knew God's word would live and thrive even after his own death.

The Old Testament prophet Isaiah had said as much: "The grass withers and the flowers fall, but the word of our God stands forever" (40:8 NIV). This prophet also said that just as rain and snow water the earth and bring forth bread, so God's word will not return to him empty. It will accomplish His purpose (55:10-11).

Lines from Martin Luther's majestic hymn, "A Mighty Fortress," say it well.

> And though this world, with evil filled,
> Should threaten to undo us,
> We will not fear, for God hath willed
> His truth to triumph thru us.
> Let goods and kindred go,
> This mortal life also;
> The body they may kill:
> God's truth abideth still,
> His kingdom is forever.

Two thousand years after Paul wrote his last sentence and spoke his final word, we know that what he said about God's word not being chained holds true. God's church, His workers, and the Word are active in His service.

⊰⊱

## Memory Selection

"**Study to shew thyself approved unto God, a workman that needeth not to be ashamed, rightly dividing the word of truth.**" *2 Timothy 2:15*

It was Timothy's responsibility to instruct his fellow-teachers and fellow church members. He also needed to be aware of what was required of himself as their instructor. Paul reminds him that he should diligently work toward meeting God's approval. That is the acid test for any teacher of the Word. He should have no reason for shame when he is examined by God.

Anyone who teaches God's word must handle it accurately. It should not be tinkered with, treated lightly, or used for wrong purposes. It should be respected for what it is: God's word. It should never be dealt with in any way less than properly. Its presentation should meet God's approval.

Much of the teaching that was being done by certain workmen not only had no value, but ruined those who heard it. Two men were named who actually preached that the resurrection had already taken place, and this had destroyed the faith of some people. Timothy needed to keep warning them before God about their quarreling about words. They were quibblers, not teachers.

Timothy's job was not an easy one. He had to guard against being involved in the chatter that so many were using as a substitute for solid teaching. As Paul gave instruction to Timothy, at the same time he reminds us not to be led off into non-productive issues. God has a great message He wants delivered. Let us do it His way and do it well.

## Weekday Problems

My friends, Richard and Louise, had retired. The once-quiet neighborhood where they had lived for years was deteriorating. They were delighted to leave it and move into a lovely mountain retirement community.

They selected a nearby church and began attending there, looking for a new church home. The location was convenient, the people were friendly, but the preaching was shallow and without content.

They both insisted that there was nothing of any substance in the sermons. They did not give up easily, and continued attending there, thinking things would get better. Nothing improved. The big mystery (to them at least) was wondering why others were content with what was (or was not) coming from the pulpit.

Finally they went to a different church, not quite so conveniently located, but where they found biblical messages that were meaningful.

Their search for a good church (good pulpit may be more to the point), bears a resemblance to the problem Timothy faced in Ephesus. There was too much mindless chatter and too little constructive teaching in both these situations. This seems to have been an ongoing problem for Timothy, as Paul addresses it in both letters to him. My friends were able to find a happy solution to their problem. Here is hoping that you worship in a good church with great preaching.

# A Colorful Tale

I didn't know if my granddaughter had learned her colors yet, so I decided to test her. I would point out something and ask her what color it was. She would tell me, and always she was correct. But it was fun for me, so I continued. At last she headed for the door, admonishing me sagely, "Grandma, I think you should try to figure out some of these yourself!"

# This Lesson in Your Life

He was actually a well-meaning man. He was sincere in what he believed. He truly thought that it was his Christian duty to share with everybody else what he considered to be biblical insights that he had discovered and the rest of us had not. He was really big in the prophecy department and (in his own opinion) had Ezekiel and Daniel all sewed up, as well as Revelation. He knew all about God's plans for the unfolding history of Earth, which he had detected in their biblical hiding places. He knew which nations were going to invade which other ones, and who would win the battle. He did not know exactly when some of this would happen, except that it would be near the End. Working out the dates may have been the only area where unanswered questions lingered in his mind.

Having him for a friend was not easy. He pushed patience and tolerance to their outer limits as he insisted on sharing what he thought he knew.

I have all the respect in the world for men and women who make a serious study of those more difficult-to-understand parts of the Bible. My friend did not have a clue. He did not have the background or the ability to ever get a clue. This did not slow him down. I think his being clueless is what kept him going. A wiser man would not have forged ahead with his reckless abandon.

In 1 Timothy 1:4-7, Paul had written about those whose teaching promoted controversies rather than God's work. These people did not know what they were talking about, though they felt very confident. In our current lesson he warns about those who quarrel about points with no value and whose teaching is godless chatter. Timothy is reminded that in his own teaching he must correctly handle the word of truth.

Apparently, the false teachers about whom Paul warned Timothy were even more persistent than my friend was. The fact that, in both his letters to Timothy, they continued to be an issue lets us know they did not give up easily. At least my friend did not have access to a pulpit, as these fellows did. No church would have invited him to teach a Bible class, so he could not cause as much damage as they could.

As we read through portions of Scripture such as the verses that make up this lesson, we see that ancient problems can be modern ones. In Weekday Problems we saw a searching couple, desperate for well-grounded church teaching as they settled into a new community. My friend who considered himself an expert on prophecy meant well, but did not do anybody any favors as he tried to share his confused notions about things of which he did not know.

The issues Timothy dealt with still work their way into our lives today. That makes this lesson very useful to us. In our personal Bible study, in our interchange with friends, and in the Church's teaching program, we will always be challenged to handle the word of truth correctly.

**1. What two points about Jesus, used in Paul's preaching the gospel, did he tell Timothy to remember?**

He preached Jesus Christ, who was raised from the dead and descended from David.

**2. What did Paul say about preaching Jesus Christ (including that He was raised from the dead and descended from David)?**

He said this comprised the gospel he preached. Both these points are central to the story of Jesus.

**3. What offence had Paul committed that got him arrested and chained in prison?**

He was in trouble and in chains because of preaching the gospel. By doing this he was considered an evil-doer.

**4. Even though Paul was bound in chains, what did he say about the word of God?**

The word of God was not bound. (Gospel workers were preaching. In this letter he gives instruction for some of them.)

**5. Paul quoted what is believed to be an ancient Christian hymn (Vs. 11-13). What did it say about death and suffering?**

If we die with Christ we shall live with Him. If we suffer, we shall reign with Him. (Suffering and death would come to Paul soon.)

**6. In the hymn, if we believe not (if we are faithless), what does God do?**

God remains faithful regardless of our failure.

**7. How do we know that God will remain faithful?**

God cannot deny Himself. This is the nature of God. He will not go back on His word.

**8, Even during Paul's personal problems, he was concerned about how some were teaching improperly. In verse 14 what does he say about this?**

Timothy was to instruct them not to be quarreling about words. This was of no value and would subvert the hearers.

**9. Why was Paul willing to suffer for God's elect?**

He was willing to sacrifice in order to promote salvation in others.

**10. What instruction did Paul give for Timothy's own teaching?**

He was to study to show himself approved, a workman who did not need to be ashamed, and he was to rightly divide (correctly handle) the word of truth.

309

Singing is ready-made for joyful expression. True, some songs are very somber, but this is as it should be. Life runs the gamut from happy to sad, and our songs reflect that. I remember one Christmas season when I was away from home and visited a church's mid-week service. Most of the songs were on the order of "Joy to the World" and the spirit of the season. For reasons unknown to me, "We are going down the valley one by one, going toward the setting of the sun" worked its way into the service. Nobody asked me, but I thought it might have been better to have omitted that one, and to have sung "Joy to the World" a second time.

The early church used Psalms as its basic hymn book. We might assume that as David composed his psalms, he softly strummed his harp. This does not mean he did not know how to increase the volume and the tempo. Check out Psalm 150 for some cymbal clashing, trumpet blowing, tambourine shaking music. (David's family was musically talented. 1 Kings 4:32 says that his son Solomon composed 1005 songs.)

Our present lesson contains the words to what must have been one of the very earliest songs composed for Christian worship. Let's read it from the NIV:

If we died with him, we shall also live with him.
If we endure, we will also reign with him.
If we disown him, he will also disown us;
If we are faithless, he will remain faithful,
for he cannot disown himself.

The line about disowning Christ is a somber one. We know, though, that Jesus gave warning about those who would deny him before men (Matt. 10:32-33; Luke 12:9).

The first line in the song is an interesting one. I researched maybe a half-dozen sources to see what the commentators said about it. About half of them said the death spoken of is what we read in Romans 6, we die and are buried with Christ in baptism. The others insist just as assuredly that it is talking about dying as a martyr. Maybe you will join me in enjoying the best of all possible worlds. I can accept both interpretations, and not one to the exclusion of the other. (William Barclay's commentary comes down strongly in favor of martyrdom. He quotes Luther: "The Church is the heir of the Cross.") Any time we can exchange death for life, in whatever sense we are using the terms, is a happy time

This is a joyful song about being alive with Christ and reigning with him. It is about the faithfulness of our God. As we read this ancient hymn it inspires us, even as it did Timothy's generation. Christian music, both old and new, is a real pick-me-up for us all. ೞ೧ಬ

**Lesson 6**

# Praise Builds Us Up Assurances for Daily Living

## Jude 17-25

B ut, beloved, remember ye the words which were spoken before of the apostles of our Lord Jesus Christ;

18 How that they told you there should be mockers in the last time, who should walk after their own ungodly lusts.

19 These be they who separate themselves, sensual, having not the Spirit.

20 But ye, beloved, building up yourselves on your most holy faith, praying in the Holy Ghost,

21 Keep yourselves in the love of God, looking for the mercy of our Lord Jesus Christ unto eternal life.

22 And of some have compassion, making a difference:

23 And others save with fear, pulling them out of the fire; hat-

ing even the garment spotted by the flesh.

24 Now unto him that is able to keep you from falling, and to present you faultless before the presence of his glory with exceeding joy,

25 To the only wise God our Saviour, be glory and majesty, dominion and power, both now and ever. Amen.

April 10

**Memory Verses**
Jude 24-25

**Background Scripture**
Jude 17-25

**Devotional Reading**
2 Corinthians 4:1-12

Three times in the New Testament, praise is offered to the God "who is able."

In Romans 16:25, the apostle Paul begins his doxology at the end of the book of Romans by addressing our God who has the power to establish and strengthen us in Jesus.

Paul in Ephesians 3:20 concludes the first portion of that great book with a doxology that opens with praise to "Him who is able" to do far more for us than any may ask or think.

Now near the end of our New Testament, Jude finishes his letter with a grand doxology that begins with the same salutation to God who is able to keep His children from falling.

Our confidence rests upon the unequaled power of the One who saves us.

## For a Lively Start

Jude begins his short letter urging his readers to be true to "the faith once for all delivered to the saints" (vs. 3).

In those early days of the Church, all issues could be settled by an appeal to the common truths that had been shared with the first Christians by the apostles and by the first teachers that were taught and commissioned by the apostles.

Later in Jude's letter, he will remind us of predictions the apostles had made about scoffers who would belittle the believers and behave in scandalous ways. The apostles had in mind the decades right after their own ministry, but today we see a latter-day emergence of the same things—cynics who scoff at those who have faith and who want the rest of us to bless their blatant immorality.

| Teaching Outline | Daily Bible Readings |
|---|---|
| I. The Apostles' Predictions—Jude 17-19 | Mon. Treasure in Clay Jars<br>*2 Corinthians 4:1-12* |
| A. Immoral Scoffers, 17-18 | Tue. Praise from the Restored<br>*Jeremiah 31:2-9* |
| B. Unspiritual, Divisive Men, 19 | Wed. Live for the Glory of God<br>*1 Corinthians 10:23-31* |
| II. The Most Holy Faith—Jude 20-23 | Thu A Message That Builds Up<br>*Acts 20:28-35* |
| A. Built Up in the Lord, 20-21 | Fri. Protection From Evil<br>*John 17:6-19* |
| B. Showing Compassion to Doubters, 22 | Sat. The Good and the Right Way<br>*1 Samuel 12:19-25* |
| C. Reaching Out to Sinners, 23 | Sun. Build Yourselves Up in Faith<br>*Jude 17-25* |
| III. Jude's Doxology—Jude 24-25 | |

# *Verse by Verse*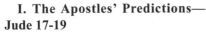

Jude 17-25

## I. The Apostles' Predictions—Jude 17-19

### A. Immoral Scoffers, 17-18

**17 But, beloved, remember ye the words which were spoken before of the apostles of our Lord Jesus Christ;**

**18 How that they told you there should be mockers in the last time, who should walk after their own ungodly lusts.**

Although Jude has written graphically in condemning words about the false teachers who were infiltrating the church in those late apostolic days, his language here indicates his genuine affection for those to whom he is writing. He calls them "beloved" and indicates that he fully expects them to treasure and respond to the warnings given to them earlier by the apostles.

In their last days, the surviving apostles were consistent in foretelling the coming of false teachers to ravage the churches. Paul told the Ephesian elders that imposters would arise from their own ranks—like wolves in sheep's clothing (Acts 20). Peter's second letter is filled with similar warnings about scoffers who would dismiss the church's belief in the End of time and the Judgment of the Lord.

These "mockers" are in focus here in Jude's letter. Likely, these charlatans are the same ones Jude has described so negatively in the body of his brief letter. His concern is more than just their wrong attitude and information about the End. He is more concerned that they are unworthy poseurs whose immoral lives and greed discredit anything they do or preach. In the preceding verses, Jude has already described their "ungodly lusts."

"The last time" Jude refers to in vs. 18 is common language used by the prophets to describe the Christian age. Peter began his famous Pentecost sermon in Acts 2 by quoting Joel's predictions for "the last days" or "the final times."

### B. Unspiritual, Divisive Men, 19

**19 These be they who separate themselves, sensual, having not the Spirit.**

The King James terminology here seems strange to our modern minds. "They who separate themselves" means that they divide churches, setting God's children at odds with one another. The sin of causing division is one of the few reasons the apostles gave for withdrawing fellowship from a wrongdoer (Titus 3:10-11).

"Sensual" in the RSV is translated "worldly." Other versions see in this term a contrast with the following phrase "having not the Spirit," so the NIV says these scoffers "follow mere natural instincts." Likewise, the TEV tells us they are "controlled by their natural desires." Thus, "natural" contrasts with attributes from "the Spirit." Jude's readers are led by the Spirit; the scoffers are not.

## II. The Most Holy Faith—Jude 20-23

### A. Built Up in the Lord, 20-21

**20 But ye, beloved, building up yourselves on your most holy faith, praying in the Holy Ghost,**

**21 Keep yourselves in the love of God, looking for the mercy of our Lord Jesus Christ unto eternal life.**

In these verses, Jude's metaphor is that of erecting a building on a solid foundation. We build our character, our attitudes, our habits, and our desires on our "most holy faith." Throughout the New Testament, the writers recognize that a core of truth had been imparted to the believers by the apostles. They refer to it as "the good deposit" (1 Tim. 1:14), "the tradition we passed on to you" (2 Thess. 3:6), or "the faith you were taught" (Col. 2:7). In more than two dozen passages, the New Testament writers speak simply of "the faith" (Heb. 4:14; 1 Tim. 4:7), meaning the basic doctrines and concepts included in the gospel preached by the apostles. Jude wants the Christians he addresses to base their lives and thinking on this sure footing of foundational truths.

They can build on these truths by doing several things, Jude says. They can earnestly pray in the Spirit. They can make sure they stay in the love

of God. They can eagerly hope for the mercy Jesus promises to us when He returns. Their present piety, their absolute devotion to the God of grace, and their unwavering anticipation of Christ's blessed return will be key ways for them to build up their lives and character in the most holy faith.

### B. Showing Compassion to Doubters, 22

**22 And of some have compassion, making a difference:**

In this verse, Jude tells his readers to show compassion to a certain group of people, but just who these people are is far from clear in the KJV. All our newer Bible versions explain in some way that the people who need our compassion are those who doubt—those who may waver in their faith. Unlike the ones in vss. 20-21 who build strongly upon a base of faith, these believers struggle with moments of uncertainty. Instead of condemning those who struggle, Jude calls for them to be treated with compassion.

### C. Reaching Out to Sinners, 23

**23 And others save with fear, pulling them out of the fire; hating even the garment spotted by the flesh.**

Two other groups of Christians need our loving attention, Jude tells us. In the first group are those who have slipped into various sins—sins so serious that they are in danger of hellfire. The exhortation and concern of believers who love them may "snatch" these people from that fire (TEV).

The latter group are those engaged in illicit sexual activity. Jude identifies the form of their immorality by mentioning the clothing they defile during their sinful activities. Notice that the target Jude identifies for the faithful Christians to "hate" is not the people who are sinning. Instead, he wants them to detest such immoral behavior, even to shun the items of clothing stained by such wrongdoing.

How many of us in the modern Church find sexual sins this offensive? On the other hand, how many of us have let our moral judgment be numbed by the bombardment of wicked behavior on prime-time televison? How many of us succumb to the current dogma of "tolerance" that would shame any Christian who speaks out against homosexuality or extra-marital sex? In a culture that idolizes serial adulterers in Hollywood, that passes more laws legalizing same sex marriages, and that brands preaching against immorality as a form of hate speech, we Christians need to be reminded by Jude that certain sins should be "hated." However, we do need to hear Jude's distinction that we should hate not the sinners, but the sins.

## III. Jude's Doxology—Jude 24-25

**24 Now unto him that is able to keep you from falling, and to present you faultless before the presence of his glory with exceeding joy,**

**25 To the only wise God our Saviour, be glory and majesty, dominion and power, both now and ever. Amen.**

Like the other great doxologies in the New Testament letters, this one lifts up our souls as it lifts up our God. Our security in His unfailing love is worth celebrating. He alone can keep us upright and blameless until the Day when we stand jubilant before Him in Glory.

Our saving God alone embodies true wisdom. We, like the countless angels on high, ascribe to Him glory and honor. In Him alone we recognize true authority and power both in this present age and for eternity.

Jude's letter may be brief, but it could not possibly end on a higher, more hopeful note.

ଈଓଔ

## Evangelistic Emphasis

We almost did not get the little book of Jude, at least not in its present form. He tells us that he had originally intended to write a treatise on salvation. Instead, circumstances demanded that he write concerning earnestly contending "for the faith which was once delivered unto the saints."

Salvation, Jude's first intended topic, is what Jesus is all about. The word Jesus means savior. We remember that the angel told Joseph to "call his name Jesus: for he shall save his people from their sins" (Matt. 1:21). Jesus described His mission as coming "to seek and save that which is lost" (Luke 19:10). The Great Commission is about preaching the gospel and saving people (Mark 16:15-16).

On the other hand, the topic Jude actually wrote about, contending for the faith, also emphasizes evangelism. Modern translations word this as the faith "once for all" delivered, which emphasizes the finality of its deliverance. In Scripture, the word faith frequently has reference to an individual's belief. For instance, you and I have faith. Jude uses it here in the sense of the entire body of Christian teaching. Jude is concerned because some unscrupulous people are perverting the Christian faith.

We preach Jesus as Savior. We proclaim the Christian faith. It was "once for all delivered." Jude would tell us not to change it. God got it right the first time.

## Memory Selection

ഇറയ

"Now unto him that is able to keep you from falling, and to present you faultless before the presence of his glory with exceeding joy, To the only wise God our Savior, be glory and majesty, dominion and power, both now and ever. Amen."                              *Jude 24-25*

These lovely words are called a doxology, which means they are praise to God. They are also a benediction, which literally means a good word. We usually think of a benediction as a closing prayer. As Jude writes these words perhaps we can say that he praises God as he closes his message with these good words. In this doxology, Jude says some things about what God does for us. He is able to make us stand. We constantly need His strength and guidance. He indwells us through His Holy Spirit. He instructs us in Scripture. He hears and answers our prayers. We are encouraged through the Church and our association with other Christians.

God is able to present us faultless in His presence. We are His workmanship. It is by the gift of His grace that we are saved through His Son (Eph. 2).

Jude recognizes Him as being the only wise God. He is the only real God. I have spent a very limited time in India. There are some dedicated Christians there, but most of the population is polytheistic. Such experiences make Jude's doxology/benediction all the more meaningful. Glory, majesty, dominion, and power to our only wise God now and forever more!

## Weekday Problems

James tells us not to count too heavily about what we will be doing next year. We do not even know what is going to happen tomorrow (James 4:13-17). That was the case with Jude. He had to change the topic of his treatise.

Many years ago, an elderly man told me a story about his grandfather. He left Germany and came to the States in order to escape European wars. He arrived in America just in time for our Civil War, and was killed while serving in the Union army. He did not find the peaceful life he thought he would have.

Here is another Civil War story. The first battle of the war was near a stream called Bull Run, near Manassas, Virginia. Wilmer McClain's farm house got damaged in the battle, so he moved his family to the quiet little hamlet of Appomattox Court House, far away from marching armies and whizzing cannon balls.

Little could Wilmer have guessed that five years later, General Ulysses S. Grant and General Robert E. Lee would meet in his Appomattox parlor, where Lee surrendered to Grant.

Has your life ever taken turns that you had not expected? How did you handle them? Jude, the German immigrant, and Wilmer would all tell us to do as James instructs us, and plan for the future by saying "If it's the Lord's will."

---

# Psychiatric Folksong

At three I had a feeling of

Ambivalence toward my brothers,

And so it follows naturally

I poison all my lovers.

But I am happy now I've learned

The lesson this has taught:

That everything I do that's wrong

Is someone else's fault.

—*Anna Russell*

---

# This Lesson in Your Life

Have you learned to appreciate the ancient prayers and songs that are included in Scripture? If not, you are missing something good. The Book of Psalms would be included among them, and many of them were used in Jewish worship gathering. We Christians have used many of them throughout the Church's history. In the church where I preach we have established the tradition of opening Sunday worship service with a reading from them. As in all churches, our hymn book contains several of them set to music.

Many people might consider the tiny book of Jude to be insignificant. If so, that would be blatantly ignoring the moving benediction with which he closes it. Those words from Jude's pen rank right up there with be best of doxologies.

One of the loveliest of biblical prayers is the priestly blessing God gave to Aaron and his sons (also called the Lord's benediction.) They were to bless the Israelites with it. As Christians, we still use it.

> The Lord bless you and keep you;
> The Lord make His face shine on you,
> And be gracious to you;
> The Lord life up His countenance on you,
> And give you peace.
> (Numbers 6:22-26 NAS)

It is not necessary for a Scripture passage to have originally been either a song or a prayer in order for it to be memorable, quotable, and beautiful. Perhaps we can call Ruth's words to Naomi a statement of commitment. (That is a poor way to describe something so lovely.) It has been set to music and we hear it sung at weddings. We are all familiar with it: "Intreat me not to leave thee, or to return from following after thee, for whither thou goest, I will go; and where thou lodgest, I will lodge; thy people shall be my people, and thy God my God."

A number of Scripture portions have been worked into our hymns. Habakkuk 2:20, for instance, we sing as "The Lord is in His holy temple; Let all the earth keep silence before Him; Keep silence, Keep silence, Keep silence before Him."

We sing the 23rd Psalm with variations on the wording, and set to several tunes. It goes without saying (but let us say it anyhow), that the Lord's Prayer makes a moving prayer-song.

Anybody who is familiar with Isaiah knows that Handel knew it well also. When we hear Handel's Messiah at Easter or Christmas, we are hearing words straight from that great Old Testament prophet Isaiah.

In this lesson we were blessed by Jude's benediction. Our lives will be greatly enriched if it triggers an appreciation in our hearts for the prayers and songs of the Bible. They are not only songs and prayers. They are Scripture.

## GETTING
## THE FACTS STRAIGHT

**1. To help stop false teaching, what solution did Jude offer?**
He told them to remember the words spoken earlier by the apostles of Jesus.

**2. What had the apostles said would happen in the last days?**
They had said that there would be mockers who would walk after their own ungodly lusts.

**3. What is the meaning in verse 19 that they "separate themselves?"**
The meaning is that they are divisive. Their teaching and practices create division within churches and between individuals.

**4. What are some other problems associated with these false teachers?**
They are sensual and do not have the Spirit. (A look at their behavior as reported by Jude makes this obvious.)

**5. In order to build themselves up, what foundation should they use?**
They are to build themselves up on their most holy faith. The implication is that their authentic faith will keep them on the right path.

**6. What does Jude tell them about their prayers?**
They should pray in the Holy Spirit. Read Romans 8:26-27. The Spirit helps us in our prayers when we do not know what to say. He also intercedes for us.

**7. What other points does Jude make that will help them?**
They should keep themselves in the love of God as they look for His mercy that will bring eternal life.

**8. There were differences in the degree to which some Christians were involved in false teaching and wrong behavior. What does "of some having compassion, making a difference" mean?**
A clearer translation would be "Be merciful to those who doubt" (NIV). An effort should be made to help them.

**9. What is one other category where the doubters may have ventured further into false ways?**
There are some that are so near the edge that saving them could be called snatching them from the fire.

**10. What caution should be observed in dealing with the doubters?**
Care should be taken not to become contaminated by their ungodly ways. Mercy should be mixed with fear.

Have you noticed that even when Bible writers are dealing with seriously corrupting issues that threaten the Church, they always seem to counterbalance the negative with something uplifting?

Jude certainly does that. He gives us some tips that will inspire us even when we are knee-deep in trouble. They might even help us avoid getting bogged down. His benediction alone makes an inspiring statement, but we will look elsewhere at some other things he tells us.

The people to whom Jude was writing were experiencing something of an invasion of their church by unbelievably godless influences. How could such things be done in the name of Christianity? Jude tells the people how to lift themselves above all the filth. His solution should work for us, too. It fits just about any situation where you or I might need an upward boost.

Boost yourselves up in the most holy faith, he says. The bedrock truths of Christianity give us a platform from which to operate. They furnish us a foundation from which to live day by day.

Here is an illustration. In the recent recession two of my Christian acquaintances lost their jobs. One of them approached the issue with the attitude of "Why is it always me who has trouble? Life has not been good to me. I have prayed, but nothing good has happened."

The other person said "I don't understand why this has happened. The Lord didn't cause it, but He can use it for good. Some good purpose will work its way into this."

The difference between these two men is too obvious to need further discussion.

Jude further states that when surround by difficulty we should pray in the Holy Spirit. Remember Romans 8:26-27. The Spirit helps us when we are weak. It even intercedes for us when we do not know how to pray. As a matter of fact, take the time to read the whole chapter and you will feel much better for having done so.

Keep yourselves in God's love, is another thing Jude says we need to do. We love Him because He first loved us. There is no fear in love. (Read 1st John 4.) Let us look at John 3:16, with the verse that comes before it. "Just as Moses lifted up the snake in the desert, so the Son of Man must be lifted up, that everyone who believes in him may have eternal life. For God so loved the world that he gave his one and only Son . . . ." That is how much God loves us.

What can make today a happier day? What can keep the day from being a grind? If we ever feel we are drowning in troubled waters, what will rescue us?

Jude says depend on your holy faith. Pray with the Spirit's help. Keep yourself in the love of God.

## Lesson 7

# Hosanna!
# Lavishing Praise

## Mark 11:1-11

And when they came nigh to Jerusalem, unto Bethphage and Bethany, at the mount of Olives, he sendeth forth two of his disciples,

2 And saith unto them, Go your way into the village over against you: and as soon as ye be entered into it, ye shall find a colt tied, whereon never man sat; loose him, and bring him.

3 And if any man say unto you, Why do ye this? say ye that the Lord hath need of him; and straightway he will send him hither.

4 And they went their way, and found the colt tied by the door without in a place where two ways met; and they loose him.

5 And certain of them that stood there said unto them, What do ye, loosing the colt?

6 And they said unto them even as Jesus had commanded: and they let them go.

7 And they brought the colt to Jesus, and cast their garments on him; and he sat upon him.

8 And many spread their garments in the way: and others cut down branches off the trees, and strawed them in the way.

9 And they that went before, and they that followed, cried, saying, Hosanna; Blessed is he that cometh in the name of the Lord:

10 Blessed be the kingdom of our father David, that cometh in the name of the Lord: Hosanna in the highest.

11 And Jesus entered into Jerusalem, and into the temple: and when he had looked round about upon all things, and now the eventide was come, he went out unto Bethany with the twelve.

**Memory Verse**
Mark 11:9

**Background Scripture**
Mark 11:1-11

**Devotional Reading**
1 Chronicles 16:8-15

"Palm Sunday" we call it in many of our churches. For many it is the beginning of Holy Week. It is the season when we focus both on the crowning of our King and on His atoning death and His victory over death.

On this jubilant morning in Jerusalem when Jesus comes riding into the Holy City on a donkey, His men have no idea what fateful events that week holds for them. But we know. We have read the rest of Mark's Gospel. Therefore, our own jubilation on Palm Sunday exceeds that of the cheering crowds along Jerusalem's main thoroughfare. They welcome a king to lead them in a historical victory. We welcome a King Who will lead us to eternal triumph in Glory.

They cry out, "Hosanna!" as an appeal to a Messiah who can lead them to victory over their Roman enemies. We shout, "Hosanna!"—"save us"—to the One who will help us win our struggle with the Enemy of all mankind.

## For a Lively Start

ଽଔ

People who were not raised on the farm may miss one of the significant miracles that happens on that first Palm Sunday. Those who have never tried to stay on the back of an unbroken, non-saddle-trained animal may not realize just how remarkable it is that the unridden donkey Jesus straddled bore Him docilely down the road without bucking Him off.

Years before this, the prophet Zechariah foretold that the Messiah would make His appearance astride a young donkey. "Behold, your King is coming!" the prophet heralded, and then described His humble mount. Jesus' men later recalled this prophecy as they reflected on the grand events of that day in Jerusalem.

| Teaching Outline | Daily Bible Readings |
|---|---|
| I. Jesus' Instructions—Mark 11:1-3<br>  A. Find the Colt in the Village, 1-2<br>  B. Dealing with the Owners, 3<br>II. The Apostles' Errand—Mark 11:4-7<br>  A. Identifying the Colt, 4<br>  B. The Owners' Challenge, 5-6<br>  C. Delivering the Colt, 7<br>III. The People's Praise—Mark 11:8-10<br>IV. Sundown at the Temple—Mark 11:11 | Mon. Call on God to Save<br>    *Psalm 55:16-22*<br>Tue. O Lord, Save Us<br>    *2 Kings 19:14-19*<br>Wed. At the Right Hand of the Needy<br>    *Psalm 109:21-31*<br>Thu The Lord Rescues<br>    *Psalm 22:1-8*<br>Fri. Sing Praises to the Lord<br>    *1 Chronicles 16:8-18*<br>Sat. Children Shout, "Hosanna!"<br>    *Matthew 21:12-17*<br>Sun. Welcome the King<br>    *Mark 11:1-11* |

# Verse by Verse

## Mark 11:1-11

### I. Jesus' Instructions—Mark 11:1-3

#### A. Find the Colt in the Village, 1-2

**1 And when they came nigh to Jerusalem, unto Bethphage and Bethany, at the mount of Olives, he sendeth forth two of his disciples,**

**2 And saith unto them, Go your way into the village over against you: and as soon as ye be entered into it, ye shall find a colt tied, whereon never man sat; loose him, and bring him.**

We do not know for sure where the village of Bethpage was located, but scholars agree that Bethany was about two miles southeast of Jerusalem. Made famous as the hometown of Mary, Martha, and Lazarus, Bethany turns out to be Jesus' place to lodge each night during Holy Week.

Slightly nearer to town was the Mount of Olives, often associated in Jewish tradition with the Messiah's coming. From this place just outside the city, Jesus dispatches two of His men to find and bring the donkey He will ride into town. No one knows for sure if Jesus was already familiar with this particular beast and its owners (hence His ability to describe it in detail and to predict the owners' reaction to His use of the animal). Some think Jesus is demonstrating miracle-working abilities in His knowledge of the donkey's location and the owners' immediate willingness for their colt to be used by the Savior.

Borrowing a donkey without previous permission from its owner would be tantamount to hot-wiring a Chevrolet on a mall parking lot without first asking its owner if that will be permissible.

#### B. Dealing with the Owners, 3

**3 And if any man say unto you, Why do ye this? say ye that the Lord hath need of him; and straightway he will send him hither.**

Whether He knows them or not, Jesus can correctly predict the owners' reaction when they see the two apostles taking their donkey. What would you do if you saw someone about to drive away in your pickup or your SUV? "Tell them the Lord needs the animal, but He will send him right back," Jesus instructs His men. If the owners have never met Jesus, this may well be a miracle—that they would surrender the colt so willingly. On the other hand, if the owners turned out to be someone Jesus had befriended in years past, He may be able, because of that friendship, to predict their willingness to lend Him the donkey.

What do you and I own that we would not make available to the Lord if He asked us to borrow it? What are we holding on to with tight fists, unwilling to surrender it to the use of the Lord?

## II. The Apostles' Errand—Mark 11:4-7

### A. Identifying the Colt, 4

**4 And they went their way, and found the colt tied by the door without in a place where two ways met; and they loose him.**

Jesus's men immediately go to the village and find the colt right where He told them they would. How available are we to do the Lord's bidding? Can we find lots of reasons to postpone or sidestep the tasks He lies before us?

### B. The Owners' Challenge, 5-6

**5 And certain of them that stood there said unto them, What do ye, loosing the colt?**

**6 And they said unto them even as Jesus had commanded: and they let them go.**

Do you sometimes look after your neighbors' property when they are out of town or away for some reason? It sounds like those who confront the borrowing apostles may not be the owners. They may just happen to be nearby and realize that two strangers do not really have any business walking away with their friend's donkey. Whether they are the owners or not, they are close enough to them to be able to grant permission for Jesus to use the colt. Good friends trust each other like this. The greater the trust,

the greater the freedom one feels to act on behalf of the other.

### C. Delivering the Colt, 7

**7 And they brought the colt to Jesus, and cast their garments on him; and he sat upon him.**

What do you do if you need to mount a donkey or a horse and you do not have a saddle blanket? No problem, these fellows say, and they throw their coats, sweaters, or robes on the back of the colt before they help Jesus take the reins.

Again we have to wonder what personal possessions we have that our natural sense of protectiveness or self-ishness would make us withhold from the use of the Church or some believer in need? These friends contribute their clothing without a moment's hesitation. Would we?

## III. The People's Praise—Mark 11:8-10

**8 And many spread their garments in the way: and others cut down branches off the trees, and strawed them in the way.**

**9 And they that went before, and they that followed, cried, saying, Hosanna; Blessed is he that cometh in the name of the Lord:**

**10 Blessed be the kingdom of our father David, that cometh in the name of the Lord: Hosanna in the highest.**

As Jesus and His entourage reach the city, hosts of strangers also offer their clothing to carpet the way for the Lord and His colt. Others cut tree branches for the same purpose. "Strawed" in the KJV is an archaic form and tense of the verb "strew." We likely would say that they "spread" the tree branches to further carpet the donkey's path. John tells us the branches were taken from palm trees (12:13); hence the familiar name for "Palm Sunday."

All along the way—both in front of the donkey and behind him—the people are shouting, "Hosanna!" which means, "Save us!" In their minds, Jesus is the Messiah coming to free His people from the oppression of Rome's occupying army. The "saving" they plead for is political, not spiritual. The King they herald is earthly, not heavenly.

"Blessed is he who comes in the name of the Lord," is a direct quotation of Psalm 118.26. During the religious festivals of the Jews in Jesus' day the people sang Psalms 115-118, using them to express their fervent hope that the Messiah would come to bring their nation back to the glory of King David's day. We are told that in response to the singing of these psalms, the people often shouted either "Hallelujah!" or "Hosanna!" in praise to the Lord.

From the second line of praise in Mark 11:10 it is clear that the people mean to express their messianic hopes as they greet Jesus on this occasion. They are welcoming the kingdom of great David. Coming "in the name of the Lord" means by His authority or with His power. These shouting crowds are acknowledging their belief that God sent Jesus to accomplish His purposes as the Messiah.

When we praise Jesus, are we also recognizing Who and what He is?

### IV. Sundown at the Temple—Mark 11:11

**11 And Jesus entered into Jerusalem, and into the temple: and when he had looked round about upon all things, and now the eventide was come, he went out unto Bethany with the twelve.**

Just what Jesus does in the Temple on this first Sunday in Holy Week is not clear from the Scriptures. Mark tells us Jesus goes inside and looks around, but in the evening He cuts short His visit. A surface reading of Matthew or Luke makes it sound as if the famous cleansing of the Temple took place late on Palm Sunday, but Mark clearly tells us this event happened the next day.

On this evening and on the next nights during Holy Week our Lord goes to the home of Mary and Martha and their famous brother Lazarus. Jesus and His friends enjoy the hospitality on Christ's last nights before the crucifixion. Surely, their friendship is a special blessing to Him at that hard time.

ഇരു

## Evangelistic Emphasis

Jesus and his disciples had climbed the steep and winding road that comes up to Jerusalem from Jericho. Prior to Jericho they had crossed the Jordan, not far from where John had baptized Him.

Now Jesus approaches Jerusalem, where the most significant events of all will take place for Him. First, though, He has a busy week ahead. It begins as He sends two disciples to bring a colt. They are to explain to anyone who asks that the Lord needs it.

One word in the explanation is significant. Jesus calls Himself "Lord."

"Son of Man" is what He usually called Himself. His Lordship will be fully declared three days following the event that will soon take place at Calvary.

On this day, that later generations will call Palm Sunday, He rides the cloak-covered colt down the palm and branch covered slopes of the Mount of Olives, toward Jerusalem and its magnificent temple. The exuberant crowd shouts "Hosanna!" "Crucify Him" will be shouted within a few days.

Jesus entered Jerusalem and went to the temple. He looked around at everything. What went through His mind? It was late in the day, so He went to Bethany. This was the calm before the storm.

We will tell the world about Jesus, including Palm Sunday, the events of Passion Week, and of Easter morning.

ഇൗരു

## Memory Selection

"And they that went before, and they that followed, cried, saying, Hosanna; Blessed is he that cometh in the name of the Lord."  *Mark 11:9*

To Jewish people, Psalms 113-118 were the Hallel, the praise psalms that were used in ascent to Jerusalem, and were used in connection with Passover and Tabernacles. (We can see a connection between Hallel and Hallelujah, which means praise God.) It was from these psalms that the crowd found expression for greeting Jesus. Psalm 118:25-26 says, "Save now, I beseech thee, O LORD: . . . Blessed be he that cometh in the name of the LORD . . . ." The word Hosanna means save now.

In addition to this, their prophet Zechariah had written (9:9), "Rejoice greatly, O daughter of Zion; shout, O daughter of Jerusalem: behold, thy King cometh unto thee: he is just, and having salvation; lowly, and riding upon an ass, and upon the foal of an ass."

The very fact that Jesus rode down the mountainside as He did, with crowds surging in front of Him and following close behind, that He allowed their shouts of blessing, and the fact that the beast He sat on had been foretold by the prophet, was His unmistakable announcement that He came as Christ the King.

He had known what this week would bring. On this day, He hears blessings shouted from the crowds. They call upon their ancient liturgy as they shout "Praise God" and "Save now." They lay down their cloaks and line His way with branches in His honor as He rides the little donkey into the City of David.

326

## Weekday Problems

A short attention span may be the problem at hand. Or again, it is more likely that they just did not fully comprehend what was happening. They may have been looking for a king who would put his crown in the closet, put on a general's uniform, and drive the Romans back to Rome.

In the cold light of the next day, what did those people think? The day before they had said "Blessed be the kingdom of our father David, that cometh in the name of the Lord." When they said "Hosanna in the highest," they were saying "God save us." What many of them meant was, "God save us from the Romans." When Jesus entered the city, walked through the temple, then quietly went to Bethany for the night, many of those who had cheered Him in the day, knew something had gone wrong.

If they had expected a nighttime bonfire rally with political speeches, or maybe to outright anoint Jesus as King David the Second of Israel, their day had ended badly. Nobody even organized a political action committee.

What present-day wrong reasons can you think of why anyone might follow Jesus? Can anybody join a church from wrong motives? What problems might possibly (or probably) develop when and if these things occurred? There is no reason why these unfortunate things should happen. There are more than enough good reasons to follow Him. Hosanna and Hallelujah!

## Dead Horse Theory

Dakota tribal wisdom says that when you discover you are riding a dead horse, the best strategy is to dismount. However, in managing any business we often try other dead-horse strategies, such as:

1. Buying a stronger whip.
2. Changing riders.
3. Saying things like, "This is the way we always have ridden this horse."
4. Appointing a committee to study the horse.
5. Arranging to visit other sites to see how they ride dead horses.
6. Doing a Cost Analysis to see if contractors can ride it more cheaply.
7. Appointing a tiger team to revive the dead horse.
8. Creating a training session to increase our riding ability.
9. Harnessing several dead horses together for increased speed.
10. Promoting the dead horse to a supervisory position.

# This Lesson in Your Life

Jesus teaches us so many things that we would have a hard time cataloging them all. In His own person He shows us what God is. Philip requested of Him, "Lord, show us the Father." Jesus' reply was "Anyone who has seen me has seen the Father" (John 14:8-9 NIV). Paul said of Jesus that "He is the image of the invisible God," and "In Christ all the fullness of the Deity lives in bodily form" (Col. 1:15; 2:9 NIV).

Though he was Deity, He washed the disciple's feet (John 13:1-17). He lifted humility and servanthood to an elevated status. The kneeling Servant, with towel and basin, speaks volumes.

Jesus had compassion on lepers, the blind, the infirm, and those who felt the pressures of life bearing down on them. (You might want to read Matthew 11:28-30.) He identified with the poor. Birds and foxes owned more than He did.

He taught absolute fidelity to the Father. "Thy will be done in earth, as it is in heaven," is how he taught us to pray (Matt. 6:10). As He prayed in Gethsemane on the night of His betrayal, and knowing the kind of death that awaited Him, He prayed "O my Father, if it be possible, let this cup pass from me: nevertheless not as I will, but as thou wilt (Matt. 26:39). "I do not seek to please myself but him who sent me," he said (John 5:30 NIV).

By His own sinless life He illustrated virtue and morality. It was never a matter of do as I say, not as I do. We have His own perfect life as a model. We should never set our sights lower. Even though we know we are far from perfect, still we do our best to live up to the example and the standards He set.

Jesus valued home and family. He honored marriage. He loved the little children. He loved His mother, and even as He suffered on the cross, made provision for her welfare.

Christ "is the head of the church: and he is the savior of the body." He "Loved the church, and gave himself for it" (Ephesians 5:23-25). These things being true, we should love and value it highly. It is not a take-it-or-leave-it option for us.

In our present lesson, and as we think further toward Good Friday and Easter morning, we see that Jesus was true to the Father (and to us) all the way. He was true to Himself. He did not waver from his purpose. He loved us to the end.

Luke 9:51 tells us that when it was time for Him to return to the Father, "He steadfastly set his face to go to Jerusalem." Much of what Matthew, Mark, Luke, and John tell us about Jesus happened as he made His way to that city and rode a borrowed donkey into town.

How does our lesson impact our lives? It introduces us to the most important week in human history. It brings us to the point that fully validates Jesus of Nazareth. It assures us that everything that He said or did should permeate every aspect of our lives.

**GETTING THE FACTS STRAIGHT**

1. As Jesus came from Jericho to Jerusalem He passed Bethphage and Bethany. After passing them, where did the road lead (before Jerusalem)?

It led them to the Mount of Olives, which slopes downward to Jerusalem. It provided the perfect setting for Jesus' entrance into the city.

2. On what task did Jesus send two of His disciples?

He sent them to a nearby village (unidentified), where they would find a colt that they should bring to Him.

3. What, as far as the use to which it had been put, was significant about the animal?

It had never been ridden. No one had sat upon it. This adds distinction to its important use by Jesus. It was part of prophetic Scripture (Zechariah 9:9).

4. If anyone asked why they were taking the colt, what were the disciples to say?

They were to say that the Lord had need of it. They added that He would return it to them promptly.

5. What is unusual about the use of the term "Lord." What did it signify?

Jesus usually did not emphasize that He was Lord, because His time had not come to be crucified. Using it here indicated that this is the time.

6. Why do we call this day Palm Sunday?

The crowd spread their garments and leafy branches on Jesus' pathway. John 12:13 says they took branches of palm trees. (And doesn't Palm Sunday sound better than Branch Sunday?)

7. The people shouted "Hosanna" to Jesus. What does this word mean?

It means "save now" and can be used as a prayer. Some Bible historians tell us that it eventually came to be used as a greeting.

8. If the people were shouting "Save us," from what did they want to be saved?

Probably most of them were wanting to be saved from the Romans, who occupied their land.

9. What is the significance of "Blessed be the kingdom of our father David, that cometh in the name of the Lord?"

The Jews were expecting a Messiah who would be an earthly king and gain freedom for them.

10. When Jesus entered the city what did he do?

He went in the temple and took a good look at everything there. He had been there before, so this was not His first time to see it. What do you suppose He was thinking about while he walked about and looked?

The death, burial, and resurrection of Jesus Christ are foundation events for Christianity. In 1st Corinthians 15, Paul identifies them as being what he preached. They constituted the saving gospel. Death and burial are sad events, but Jesus' death had an exceptional value attached to it. He died for our sins. He died so we could live. His death itself was a horrible event, but paying the cost for human sin gave purpose to it. That, plus the Resurrection, is good news. This good news is what we call the gospel.

It sounds like a contradiction in terms that we call Christ's crucifixion day Good Friday. The crucifixion itself was brutal, but Jesus endured it because He loves us. What happened on the cross that day was a history-changing event. It was bloody, but bloody for a purpose. His death successfully accomplished so much that can with good cause call it Good Friday. He died as our Passover Lamb, offering Himself as the atonement for our sins.

The Resurrection, of course, came after the sad part of the week, which we refer to as Passion Week or Holy Week.

Jesus' prayer life was invaluable to Him during that passion-filled week. It must have uplifted Him even during His suffering (The word "passion" applied to this week is used in the basic meaning of the word: suffering.) He prayed what is called His Intercessory Prayer (John 17) before going to Gethsemane. In it He prayed for Himself, His disciples, and for all believers. In Gethsemane's olive grove, He prayed while the disciples who had gone aside with Him slept. If they had been praying they would have been better prepared for what lay ahead.

Every one of us has dark nights of despair. Nothing approaching Jesus' passion, but we do have our troubles. James wrote (5:13) that when we are happy we should sing, but anyone who has troubles should pray. Praying will help us deal with troubles so we can start singing again.

We remember specific prayers that Jesus prayed, and have even given names to some of them. In your own experience are there times when you have prayed so fervently that the prayer stands out in your memory? Maybe you have gone through a week of prayer during some crisis, or one of thanksgiving for a blessing received. Possibly it was a prayer associated with some special place or occasion.

The garden where Jesus prayed was in an olive grove located on the lower slopes of the Mount of Olives, just above the Kedron Valley and across from Jerusalem. The location is still known. One moonlight night I went there with Christian friends and we prayed among the ancient trees. One in our group sang The Lord's Prayer for us. It was the kind of prayer time one does not tend to forget.

Jesus was God's Son, and often went to His Father in prayer. He prayed while nailed to His cross, right to the very end. The Bible says we should pray continually. When we do this, we are seeking the same Source of help that Jesus did.

## Lesson 8

# Christ Is Risen! Eternal Remembrance

### Matthew 28:1-17

In the end of the sabbath, as it began to dawn toward the first day of the week, came Mary Magdalene and the other Mary to see the sepulchre.

2 And, behold, there was a great earthquake: for the angel of the Lord descended from heaven, and came and rolled back the stone from the door, and sat upon it.

3 His countenance was like lightning, and his raiment white as snow:

4 And for fear of him the keepers did shake, and became as dead men.

5 And the angel answered and said unto the women, Fear not ye: for I know that ye seek Jesus, which was crucified.

6 He is not here: for he is risen, as he said. Come, see the place where the Lord lay.

7 And go quickly, and tell his disciples that he is risen from the dead; . . . .

8 And they departed quickly from the sepulchre with fear and great joy; and did run to bring his disciples word.

9 And as they went to tell his disciples, behold, Jesus met them, saying, All hail. And they came and held him by the feet, and worshipped him.

10 Then said Jesus unto them, Be not afraid: go tell my brethren that they go into Galilee, and there shall they see me.

11 Now when they were going, behold, some of the watch came into the city, and shewed unto the chief priests all the things that were done.

12 And when they were assembled with the elders, and had taken counsel, they gave large money unto the soldiers,

13 Saying, Say ye, His disciples came by night, and stole him away while we slept.

14 And if this come to the governor's ears, we will persuade him, and secure you.

15 So they took the money, and did as they were taught: and this saying is commonly reported among the Jews until this day.

16 Then the eleven disciples went away into Galilee, into a mountain where Jesus had appointed them.

17 And when they saw him, they worshipped him: but some doubted.

April 24

---

**Memory Verse**
Matthew 28:9

**Background Scripture**
Matthew 28:1-17

**Devotional Reading**
1 Corinthians 15:1-8

---

331

## focus

For Christians, belief in the bodily resurrection of Jesus is not optional. "If Christ has not risen from the dead," Paul insists, "then my preaching is useless and so is your faith" (1 Cor. 15:14).

Everything we Christians teach and believe rests upon the reality of the resurrection. The book of Romans begins with the assertion that Christ's identity as the Son of God was confirmed by His resurrection from the dead (1:4). Later in the same book Paul writes that our hope to live righteous lives and to overcome sin is based on the same power that raised Jesus from the grave (8:8-11).

If the events chronicled in Matthew 28 did not actually happen, then the whole Christian message must be discarded as a lie. It is a farce. Yet, if the account of Jesus' resurrection is genuine history, then Jesus stands as the unequaled, unchallenged Savior of man. He alone is the Living One.

ဆာၡ

## For a Lively Start

Most of us have stood brokenhearted beside a grave and said goodbye to someone we dearly loved. Parting with a dear friend or a precious loved one is never easy, but those of us who believe in the resurrection of Jesus see the entire experience from a different perspective than we might without that faith. We fully expect the One who conquered death to raise all of us back to life on the final Day.

How could we deal with death if we thought our loved ones were lost from us forever? How could we cope with our own death if we saw it as a dead end to a futile, purposeless life—one that had no dimension, no import, beyond our time on this planet? Because Jesus rose and His tomb indeed was empty, we face death today with hope instead of despair.

| Teaching Outline | Daily Bible Readings |
|---|---|
| I. The First Day Dawns—Matthew 28:1-7<br>  A. The Ladies Reach the Tomb, 1<br>  B. The Angel Opens the Grave, 2-4<br>  C. The Angel's Message, 5-7<br>II. The Ladies See the Risen Lord—Matthew 28:8-10<br>III. The Priests Bribe the Guards—Matthew 28:11-15<br>  A. The Guards' Report, 11<br>  B. The Priests' Cover-Up, 12-15<br>IV. Jesus Appears in Galilee—Matthew 28:16-17 | Mon. Good News of First Importance<br>     *1 Corinthians 15:1-8*<br>Tue. The Plot to Kill Jesus<br>     *Matthew 26:1-5*<br>Wed. The Judgment Against Jesus<br>     *Matthew 27:15-26*<br>Thu The Crucifixion of Jesus<br>     *Matthew 27:32-44*<br>Fri. Witnesses to Jesus' Death<br>     *Matthew 27:45-56*<br>Sat. Witnesses to Jesus' Burial<br>     *Matthew 27:57-61*<br>Sun. Witnesses to Jesus' Resurrection<br>     *Matthew 28:1-17* |

# *Verse by Verse*

## Matthew 28:1-17

**I. The First Day Dawns—Matthew 28:1-7**

**A. The Ladies Reach the Tomb, 1**

**1 In the end of the sabbath, as it began to dawn toward the first day of the week, came Mary Magdalene and the other Mary to see the sepulchre.**

The Jewish Sabbath was over at sunrise on Sunday, about 6 a.m. At the first possible moment the women who had served Jesus so faithfully—ladies like Mary Magdalene and another Mary not identified otherwise by Matthew (Luke calls her "the mother of James," which also would have been the mother of our Lord)—hurried to the sealed tomb to complete the embalming that had been delayed because the Sabbath hour had come.

**B. The Angel Opens the Grave, 2-4**

**2 And, behold, there was a great earthquake: for the angel of the Lord descended from heaven, and came and rolled back the stone from the door, and sat upon it.**

**3 His countenance was like lightning, and his raiment white as snow:**

**4 And for fear of him the keepers did shake, and became as dead men.**

The Gospels do not tell us where the women were when the earthquake shook the ground. They were somewhere en route to the burial site, but God's angel beat them to the tomb. By the time "the women" (Luke 23:55) got there, the angel had already removed the stone that had sealed the sepulchre. The angel sat on the stone, as if to indicate that moving it had been no big deal for him. The radiance of his face and the lustrous white of his clothing dazzled the guards ("the keepers"—KJV) and terrified them so that they first trembled and then were paralyzed by their fear. For a time—perhaps during the angel's conversation with the women—the guards were petrified from their encounter with the heavenly messenger.

**C. The Angel's Message, 5-7**

**5 And the angel answered and said unto the women, Fear not ye: for I know that ye seek Jesus, which was crucified.**

**6 He is not here: for he is risen, as he said. Come, see the place where the Lord lay.**

**7 And go quickly, and tell his disciples that he is risen from the dead; and, behold, he goeth before you into**

Galilee; there shall ye see him: lo, I have told you.

Just what the angel "answered" (KJV) Matthew doesn't tell us. In fact, most of the modern current Bible versions just say the angel "spoke" or "said" without implying that he was responding to comments or questions of the women.

The angel's message began as angelic messages always did: "Don't be afraid." The appearance of God's messenger had frightened the guards. Wicked guards opposing God's plan to save humanity deserved to be terrorized, but these women, intent on lovingly ministering to the body of God's dead Son, still reacted to the appearance of the angel as humans almost always did.

The angel set them at ease by telling them he understood their purpose for coming to the grave. He invited them to come inside the empty tomb and see for themselves the place where our Lord's body had lain. Then he commanded them to hurry to find the apostles to tell them the wonderful news.

What an honor God bestowed on all females when He decided to let these good women be the first humans to proclaim the Good News of the Resurrection!

## II. The Ladies See the Risen Lord—Matthew 28:8-10

**8 And they departed quickly from the sepulchre with fear and great joy; and did run to bring his disciples word.**

**9 And as they went to tell his disciples, behold, Jesus met them,** saying, All hail. And they came and held him by the feet, and worshipped him.

**10 Then said Jesus unto them, Be not afraid: go tell my brethren that they go into Galilee, and there shall they see me.**

The two Marys and Salome (Mark adds her name) did exactly what the angel bade them to do. Bubbling with joy at what they had just learned, they ran to share the Good News with the Eleven. What a marvelous surprise for them, however, when Jesus Himself interrupted their errand. He met them on the way and greeted them with a customary Hello. Do you suppose He would have shown Himself to them if they had disobeyed the angel? One has to wonder.

The statement that they "worshipped" Him means they bowed down to Him. The text makes this clear by telling us they took hold of His feet. Would you be frightened if you met a dead loved one who had already been buried? Would your gladness at recovering the departed be eclipsed by the eeriness of the whole experience? Jesus' first words to these devoted women admonished them not to be afraid.

Then Jesus repeated the angel's earlier instruction for the women to go tell the apostles to hurry to a place He had previously indicated to them in Galilee. There they also would see Him.

## III. The Priests Bribe the Guards—Matthew 28:11-15

### A. The Guards' Report, 11

**11 Now when they were going, behold, some of the watch came into the**

**city, and shewed unto the chief priests all the things that were done.**

While all of this was going on, the guards recovered from their stupor and went to tell the chief priest of the news that the dead man they had been guarding had disappeared. The King James word "shewed" means "disclosed" or "reported."

**B. The Priests' Cover-Up, 12-15**

**12 And when they were assembled with the elders, and had taken counsel, they gave large money unto the soldiers,**

**13 Saying, Say ye, His disciples came by night, and stole him away while we slept.**

**14 And if this come to the governor's ears, we will persuade him, and secure you.**

**15 So they took the money, and did as they were taught: and this saying is commonly reported among the Jews until this day.**

The chief priests and elders heard the guards' disturbing news and quickly schemed to explain the empty tomb. Losing a prisoner was a fatal offense under Roman law, but these corrupt leaders were not above spreading around whatever amount of money it took to placate everyone including the procurator ("the governor"—KJV). The public version of the cover-up would blame Jesus' apostles for stealing the body while the guards slept. The hefty bribe ("large money"—KJV) convinced the guards to live with this blight on their military records.

For many years our Jewish friends objected to the statement in vs. 15b that this cooked-up tale had been told among the Jews. They felt that Mat-

thew's words here were anti-Semitic. Such objections were silenced, however, when best-selling Jewish author, Rabbi Schonfield, a few years ago wrote a book called *The Passover Plot.* In this volume the rabbi summarized dozens of ways to explain the resurrection of Jesus. He proved the truth of Matthew's claim by leading off his list with the explanation the guards were bribed to tell, as described here in the final verses of Matthew.

**IV. Jesus Appears in Galilee— Matthew 28:16-17**

**16 Then the eleven disciples went away into Galilee, into a mountain where Jesus had appointed them.**

**17 And when they saw him, they worshipped him: but some doubted.**

The word "appointed" in vs. 16 means Jesus had pointed it out to them; on some earlier occasion He had given them directions to come to this particular place. Like the ladies, they fell at His feet when they saw the risen Savior. That is the meaning of the word "worshipped."

Matthew's admission that some of the apostles doubted what they were seeing and hearing should bolster our opinion of the veracity of the Gospel accounts. What other religion admits such weakness in their main leaders? Mark 16:14, tells us Jesus took to task a couple of the disciples who at first refused to believe He was alive. John affirms Matthew's admission by telling in more detail the story of Thomas, whose first reaction to the resurrection report was, "I will not believe." Converts like C. S. Lewis show us that convinced doubters often become the strongest believers of all.

## Evangelistic Emphasis

Just at dawn on the first day of the week two women, both named Mary, went to look at the tomb. They had seen it Friday just before evening when Joseph of Arimathea (assisted by Nicodemus, John 19:38-42) placed the body inside it and rolled a big stone in front of the entrance (Mk. 15:46). Now that Sabbath was passed, the women returned. (The other gospel writers let us know that there were other women along. Matthew focuses on these two.)

There was a violent earthquake. An angel from heaven came down, went to the tomb, rolled the stone back and sat on it. Mark tells us (16:2) that the women were worried about the heavy stone, wondering who would roll it away for them. That was no problem for the angel. It was just a convenient place for him to sit, once he had moved it. The guards were so frightened of him that they shook and became like dead men.

The angel knew why the women had come. They were looking for the crucified Jesus. As the angel spoke to the women, he gave them the first news of the Resurrection ever made on earth. "He is not here. He has risen, just as he said. Come and see the place where he lay."

As soon as they had looked, they were to go and quickly tell His disciples: "He has risen from the dead . . . ." These women were the first Christian evangelists. Their message, "He has risen from the dead" is our evangelistic emphasis.

### Memory Selection

ഇറ

"And as they went to tell his disciples, behold, Jesus met them, saying, All hail. And they came and held him by the feet, and worshipped him." *Matthew 28:9*

Two great surprises, and followed by a third. First, these women had no reason to think that in their lifetime they would actually see an angel, much less be spoken to by one. An even greater shock came when they were told that Jesus was not dead, but had risen. They were told He would meet His disciples in Galilee, and had no reason to think they would actually see Him within moments, if ever.

There he was! While they were obeying the angel, running to tell the disciples the wonderful news, they saw Him. He greeted them, and they came to Him, fell at His feet and held them, and worshipped Him.

They sensed immediately that He was divine and worthy of worship. This One who only three days earlier had been brutally beaten, scourged, knocked about, spit upon, crowned with thorns and mocked, then nailed to a cross and pierced with a spear, was standing before them. Without hesitation they humbled themselves before Him.

They had come this morning to see the tomb and further prepare the corpse for a respectable burial. They were continuing their ministry even after His death. That has all suddenly changed. He is no longer dead, and He repeats the angel's instruction that they should go tell the disciples.

# Weekday Problems

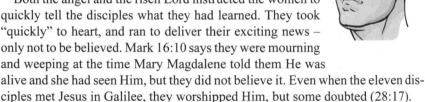

If we follow through from this lesson and observe the fallout from parts of it, we will discover problems aplenty, and be forewarned so we can avoid them.

Both the angel and the risen Lord instructed the women to quickly tell the disciples what they had learned. They took "quickly" to heart, and ran to deliver their exciting news – only not to be believed. Mark 16:10 says they were mourning and weeping at the time Mary Magdalene told them He was alive and she had seen Him, but they did not believe it. Even when the eleven disciples met Jesus in Galilee, they worshipped Him, but some doubted (28:17).

It is not as though these men had not been advised ahead of time about this. Jesus had told them, but they had never grasped it. It might be easier for us to understand their failure to understand it ahead of time, than to comprehend their reluctance to believe it when the evidence was before their eyes. Thomas did not see Jesus at the same time as the other disciples, and said he needed the evidence of his own sense of sight and touch. We have to give him credit for going the extra mile to authenticate the miracle. At the same time we remember the blessing the Lord pronounced on those who would believe without even seeing (John 20:24-29).

You and I will be well advised not to be judgmental toward these fellows. The New Testament contains many commands. It is overflowing with generous promises. It offers blessings beyond our right to expect. We have got our hands full in living in such a way that we show the Lord we actually believe it all.

## Resurrection Reflections

"There is no Easter apart from Good Friday. There is no resurrection without the cross, no rising with Christ except in dying to self that we might live again, or rather that the risen Christ might live through us."—*Leonard Wolcott*

"Let every man and woman count himself immortal, Let him catch the revelation of Jesus in his resurrection. Let him say not merely, "Christ is risen," but "I shall rise."
—*Philllips Brooks* (who also wrote "O Little Town of Bethlehem").

"On Easter Day the veil between time and eternity thins to gossamer." —*Douglas Horton*

# This Lesson in Your Life

Why do you suppose the angel appeared to the women rather than to the apostles to announce Jesus' resurrection? Why were not the leading apostles given the honor of telling the others? How did it happen that Jesus' first resurrection appearance was not to the assembled apostles, but to the women? We cannot answer these questions, but we can make some interesting observations.

Could it be so simple as that the women were in the right place at the right time? After all, they were the only ones who showed up at the tomb early on Resurrection morning. Could it be that this set off a series of coincidental events? The angel happened to be there when they arrived. Jesus happened to be there as they ran in His direction. No, we probably think. Announcing such a momentous event as the resurrection of the Son of God from the dead is not left to circumstantial happenings.

Why then, the women? Again, we cannot say. We can, however, learn some things about them that are significant, and may even give us some valuable pointers about our own relationship with the Lord.

Three hours of unnatural darkness, an earthquake, and unexplainable happenings along with the horrors of a crucifixion, was more than casual witnesses could handle. They went home remorsefully. Those who knew Jesus, including the women, remained (Luke 23:48-49). These women had followed Jesus from Galilee, and included among them were Mary Magdalene and Mary the mother of James and Joses (Matt. 27:55-56). Verse 61 says that while Joseph of Arimathea placed the body of Jesus in the tomb, Mary Magdalene and the other Mary were sitting opposite the tomb.

These two women had followed Jesus all the way down from Galilee, caring for His needs. They were there all the time, never deserting Him. In their own way they suffered as they witnessed His crucifixion. They followed Him to the tomb and saw Him placed inside it. They knew it was securely closed.

They prepared spices with which to prepare the body. As soon as Sabbath was over and the sun began to rise, they appeared at the tomb.

With Jesus all the way from Galilee, remained at the cross throughout the ordeal, witnessed His placement in the tomb, so what could we expect but that they would be there as early as possible following Sabbath. Their intention was to perform the only remaining service they could: see that His burial was proper.

Why did God select these women to be the first to learn and the first to tell about Jesus' resurrection? We are not given that answer, but we will all surely agree that they were an excellent choice.

These women set us a great example. We need to be completely dedicated to the Lord. We want to be faithful always. We will not be His fair-weather friends. Where He leads us we will follow. Each of us might want to think carefully about our Christian commitment. Is there anything more that we can do for Him?

**1. What three pieces of information are given to indicate when the women went to the tomb?**

They went to the tomb when the Sabbath was over, as dawn began, and on the first day of the week.

**2. What is the significance of the Sabbath in their going to the tomb? Why would it be mentioned?**

The Crucifixion and burial were on Friday. The Sabbath was from sundown Friday to sundown Saturday. Jews could not labor on the Sabbath (7th day). Early Sunday morning (1st day of the week) was the first time they could go there.

**3. When the angel came down there was an earthquake. At what other time very recently had there been an earthquake?**

At the time of Jesus' death "the earth did quake, and the rocks rent: (27:50-51).

**4. What did the angel do at the tomb?**

He rolled back the stone from the door and sat on it. (He opened up the tomb so the women and other witnesses could see that it was empty.)

**5. Who were the "keepers" who were afraid of the angel?**

They were the guards Pilate placed there to make sure none of Jesus' disciples removed the body (27:62-66). In verse 65, Pilate said "Ye have a watch" (You have a guard).

**6. What was there about the angel that was so frightening to the keepers?**

His appearance was like lightening and his clothing was as white as snow. This would be startling under any conditions, but especially when unexpected.

**7. Do we have any reason to think the women were also frightened when they saw the angel appearing in such a way?**

Yes. The first thing the angel said to the women was "Fear not." The whole scene took them by surprise. They had not expected the tomb to be open, and had certainly not expected to see an angel, regardless of how he looked.

**8. Did the angel know in advance why the women had come?**

Yes, he did know. He said "I know that ye seek Jesus." (We can feel assured that God would not send an angel to do a job and not give the angel full information about the situation.)

**9. What proof did the angel offer to the women that the tomb was empty?**

When he told them that Jesus was risen, he invited them to come see the place where he lay.

**10. What did the angel tell the women to quickly do?**

They were to inform the apostles that He was risen, and that they would see Him in Galilee.

The last week in the life of Jesus took place in and around Jerusalem. He had been there before on other occasions, and must have had many memories of the city. Luke tells us (2:41-52) of the time when as a child He went there with His parents to celebrate the Passover feast. He was twelve years old, and after his parents discovered He was not in the group of pilgrims as they returned to Nazareth, after three days of searching they found Him in the Temple. He was sitting with the teachers, both asking and answering questions. They were astonished at His understanding and answers. When Mary quizzed Him, He explained that He had to be about the things of His Father.

We might wonder if while He was in the Temple during the Passover week of His betrayal and crucifixion, He thought of the childhood visit when He spent time with the teachers there. For Him, these two Passovers were as different as night is from day.

Jerusalem is often called the Holy City, and Israel the Holy Land. It is inspirational just to remember some of the spiritually outstanding events that occurred there. Such things are why we add "Holy" to the names of these places.

Bethlehem, where Jesus was born, is only about seven miles south of Jerusalem. After His circumcision on the 8th day, and the time of purification (ritually required under the Law following birth of a child) was finished, Joseph and Mary took the infant Jesus to Jerusalem and presented Him at the Temple. There the righteous Simeon and the prophetess Anna rejoiced and prophesied (Luke 2:21-38). (This apparently happened before the visit of the Magi. When the family heard their warning, they fled into Egypt.)

Some day when you are bored, or cannot go to sleep at night, or you are depressed, try mulling over such things as these in your mind. We are not talking about serious study here. No research required. Just piece together some of the wonderful things you know about the Lord.

The present-day city of Jerusalem is not the city Jesus knew. The Romans completely destroyed it just a very few decades after His death. It has been fought over and rebuilt, and every new culture puts its stamp on it. The Muslims, the Crusaders, and the centuries have changed it. Yet, it is still Jerusalem, and we know our Lord was there, and at least in our minds we can follow His footsteps.

Jesus kept busy teaching during his final week. If we begin with His triumphal entry into Jerusalem, from that point on there is an amazing volume of teaching crowded into those days. If we are going to spend some time just reminiscing about Jesus in Jerusalem, we will want to remember His teaching.

Jesus was crucified within ten miles of the spot where He was born. You will be inspired and uplifted if you spend some time recalling the things you know that took place in His life in these hallowed spots.

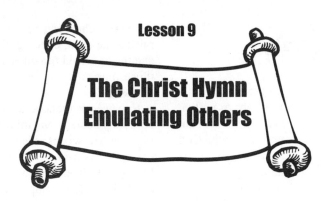

## The Christ Hymn Emulating Others

## Philippians 2:1-11

If there be therefore any consolation in Christ, if any comfort of love, if any fellowship of the Spirit, if any bowels and mercies,

2 Fulfil ye my joy, that ye be like-minded, having the same love, being of one accord, of one mind.

3 Let nothing be done through strife or vainglory; but in lowliness of mind let each esteem other better than themselves.

4 Look not every man on his own things, but every man also on the things of others.

5 Let this mind be in you, which was also in Christ Jesus:

6 Who, being in the form of God, thought it not robbery to be equal with God:

7 But made himself of no reputation, and took upon him the form of a servant, and was made in the likeness of men:

8 And being found in fashion as a man, he humbled himself, and became obedient unto death, even the death of the cross.

9 Wherefore God also hath highly exalted him, and given him a name which is above every name:

10 That at the name of Jesus every knee should bow, of things in heaven, and things in earth, and things under the earth;

11 And that every tongue should confess that Jesus Christ is Lord, to the glory of God the Father.

May 1

**Memory Verse**
Philippians 2:5

**Background Scripture**
Philippians 2:1-11

**Devotional Reading**
1 Peter 2:18-25

Bible scholars trying to explain what Paul means in vss. 6-7, have written many shelves of weighty books. Paul tells us that Jesus was equal with God but He "emptied" Himself ("But made himself of no reputation"—KJV).

Just what did Jesus give up, and in what circumstances? Often during His ministry we see Christ doing things only God could do—walking on water, changing water to wine, raising the dead, opening blind eyes, and the list could run on endlessly. In those moments He seems anything but "empty."

However, on other occasions we see Him fully human—anything but God-like—as He weeps, bleeds, sweats, dies. In those scenes He is completely like us with all our limitations and vulnerabilities. He is "empty" indeed.

In this lesson, we will touch only the surface of one of the deepest issues pondered by all who love Jesus.

## For a Lively Start

ೞೞ

For a generation now, the Rubicon of educational strategies has been to enhance the self-esteem of students. Kids who spell *cat* with a *k* must be praised for at least getting the phonetics right. Students who will never excel in serious academics must be touted as college-bound geniuses. God help the teacher who dares to hint that the class dunce is not an Einstein-to-be.

In our present culture, we find it hard to obey Paul's call in Philippians 2 for us to be willing to humble ourselves and count others more capable or more deserving than we are. When we spend our first 18 years being told how brilliant and talented we are, it is hard to reverse course and accept a realistic appraisal of who we really are. When you are so great, it is hard to be humble.

| Teaching Outline | Daily Bible Readings |
|---|---|
| I. Paul's Call for Unity—Philippians 2:1-2<br>II. Paul's Call for Humility—Philippians 2:3-4<br>III. An Ancient Hymn of Praise—Philippians 2:5-11<br>  A. Imitating the Mind of Christ, 5<br>  B. Jesus Equal with God, 6<br>  C. He Emptied Himself, 7<br>  D. He Became a Man, 8<br>  E. God Exalted Him, 9<br>  F. All Will Praise Him, 10-11 | Mon. Follow in Christ's Steps<br>  *1 Peter 2:18-25*<br>Tue. Good Lives Shown in Works<br>  *James 3:13-18*<br>Wed. Being Worthy of Jesus<br>  *Matthew 10:34-39*<br>Thu Lives Worthy of Your Calling<br>  *Ephesians 4:1-6*<br>Fri. Lives Worthy of the Lord<br>  *Colossians 1:9-18*<br>Sat. Lives Worthy of the Gospel<br>  *Philippians 1:27-30*<br>Sun. Living the Mind of Christ<br>  *Philippians 2:1-11* |

# *Verse by Verse*

Philippians 2:1-11

**I. Paul's Call for Unity—Philippians 2:1-2**

**1 If there be therefore any consolation in Christ, if any comfort of love, if any fellowship of the Spirit, if any bowels and mercies,**

**2 Fulfil ye my joy, that ye be likeminded, having the same love, being of one accord, of one mind.**

Paul's "if" at the beginning of this section really means "since." In his mind the qualities he lists in vs. 1 are in abundant supply in the Christian community. Since these things clearly characterize the relationships of believers, Paul reasons, then all of us ought to get along with each other.

In place of the KJV's "consolation," most of the newer Bible versions translate it as "encouragement." The TEV sees Christ as a source of strength for us. Obviously Christ does encourage and strengthen us. Paul expresses not the slightest doubt of this. In an interesting transfer, many of the newer versions, having abandoned the word *consolation* in the first phrase of vs. 1, now choose to use it in the second phrase: "If there is any *consolation* in love." However, several versions retain the KJV word choice and speak here of the "comfort" we receive from being loved.

Translators cannot seem to agree if the "fellowship" of the Spirit means that we share in and with Him or if we participate with one another in Him. It makes good sense either way, as Paul's original Greek allows either possibility.

No one today uses the word *bowels* the way they did back in King James' era. All of us use that word to describe the viscera in our lower anatomy. In the KJV, it often refers instead to emotions such as tenderness or compassion. Any friend who reads this verse in the KJV will likely misunderstand it unless we explain it to them.

Since all of Paul's positive things bind Christians together, he urges all of us to get along and display unity in Christ.

**II. Paul's Call for Humility—Philippians 2:3-4**

**3 Let nothing be done through strife or vainglory; but in lowliness of mind let each esteem other better than themselves.**

**4 Look not every man on his own things, but every man also on the things of others.**

"Vainglory" is an old English word that means conceit, false pride, or boastfulness. Much of the trouble in churches comes because somebody overestimates his or her abilities to lead, or they see a leadership role as a way to distinguish themselves above others. The NLT does a good job of presenting Paul's meaning here. "Don't be selfish; don't try to impress others." Instead, Paul urges us, let each one in the church count others better than ourselves. That is hard for most of us to do, isn't it?

Do you understand v. 4? The KJV phrasing seems a bit odd to our modern mind. We have little difficulty understanding it in the NKJV, "Let each of you look out not only for his own interests, but also for the interests of others." Unfortunately, the command is easier to understand than it is to obey.

### III. An Ancient Hymn of Praise— Philippians 2:5-11

### A. Imitating the Mind of Christ, 5

**5 Let this mind be in you, which was also in Christ Jesus:**

With this line Paul may be introducing one of the oldest Christian hymns. Many think the poetic format of the verses below indicate that it was a song. "Let this mind be in you" means "have this attitude." What attitude? Christ's attitude. Specifically, the attitude described in this grand hymn that follows.

Look at the way the NRSV formats vss. 6-11. This may help us see why so many Bible scholars refer to these verses as a hymn of praise:

6 who, though he was in the form of God, did not regard equality with God as something to be exploited,

7 but emptied himself, taking the form of a slave,
being born in human likeness.
And being found in human form,
8 he humbled himself
and became obedient to the point of death— even death on a cross.
9 Therefore God also highly exalted him and gave him the name that is above every name,
10 so that at the name of Jesus every knee should bend, in heaven and on earth and under the earth,
11 and every tongue should confess that Jesus Christ is Lord,
to the glory of God the Father.

### B. Jesus Equal with God, 6

**6 Who, being in the form of God, thought it not robbery to be equal with God:**

The word for "form" in Paul's language was different from the one that means outward shape or design. The word he uses here means the inner form—the true substance—of something or someone. Paul is telling us that Jesus was everything God was, and therefore, we must treat Jesus as an equal of God. Because Jesus knew this was His true nature, He did not have to try to cling to, to grasp that equality (some of these verbs are used in our later Bible versions to express the KJV term "robbery"). Instead, our Lord willingly surrendered this equality with the Almighty. In addition, Paul cites this as our example—the clear reason why none of us should try to hang onto claims of superiority or privilege in the Church.

### C. He Emptied Himself, 7

**7 But made himself of no reputation, and took upon him the form**

of a servant, and was made in the likeness of men:

When Jesus willingly became a human, He divested Himself of any pretense of being equal with God. For centuries, theologians have dwelled on this text, discussing when, how, and how much Jesus gave up when He "emptied" Himself of His deity. Others then discussed whether the emptying was eternal or only for the time He was on Earth. Most agree that He did become a man—a human in every way like us, the writer of Hebrews keeps stressing. This qualifies Jesus to serve as our High Priest. Paul's point here, however, is a different one. He calls us to have the same attitude that Jesus had when He willingly gave up His honored position.

### D. He Became a Man, 8

**8 And being found in fashion as a man, he humbled himself, and became obedient unto death, even the death of the cross.**

Not only did Jesus surrender Heaven and deity to become human, but also He accepted the humbling process resulting in His execution as a common criminal. Because He loved us, He accepted total humiliation.

### E. God Exalted Him, 9

**9 Wherefore God also hath highly exalted him, and given him a name which is above every name:**

"Whoever is humbled will be ex-alted," Jesus teaches us. This certainly came true in His case. The One who gave up all glory now has been promoted to a place above all. Like the one in Jesus' teaching who took the lowest seat, God has now said to Him, "Come up here to this place of greatest honor."

### F. All Will Praise Him, 10-11

**10 That at the name of Jesus every knee should bow, of things in heaven, and things in earth, and things under the earth;**

**11 And that every tongue should confess that Jesus Christ is Lord, to the glory of God the Father.**

The hymn Paul shares ends here with the lyrics of an even more ancient hymn from Isaiah 45:23.

The day will come when all creatures everywhere—in Heaven and on EarthBwill bow before our Lord and praise His name, even if they did not honor Him before that moment. His true greatness will be evident even to those who denied Him, much to their regret.

"Things under the earth" may refer to the nether regions with its satanic hordes. It may mean the dead, who will have been raised by Christ at His return. It could be simply a poetic hyperbole used to stress the whole sources of the praise that Jesus will receive from every imaginable creature.

&)C&

345

## Evangelistic Emphasis

The world is often not a nice place. We people have a tendency for causing this. When the world is really ugly, we have some graphic expressions to describe it. We might say it is a dog eat dog world out there, or it is red in tooth and claw. This suggests that we are behaving on a sub-human level.

Our lesson this week suggests behavior that is just the opposite of sub-human. It tells us to think and act like Christ. That is quite a contrast to the world's norm, and if we can do that, it cannot keep from having a positive impact.

We have the old expression, "I'd rather see a sermon than to hear one." Our lesson is ready-made to fulfill that wish. We can talk about love, tenderness, and compassion, but the point is made more strongly if we practice it.

There is definitely a human tendency toward selfishness. This makes it all the more impressive when anyone can behave in a generous, unselfish way and genuinely look out for the welfare of someone else. We Christians know that the grace of God and the mercy of Christ exemplify this fully. It is one thing to preach a sermon on grace or teach a lesson on love. A real-life demonstration will be more memorable.

When possible, we tell the gospel story. Christian evangelism works. We have 2,000 years of evidence for that. We can add lifestyle evangelism to the spoken variety. Even when we cannot tell about the Lord verbally we can demonstrate Him by how we think and act.

## Memory Selection

ॐ

**"Let this mind be in you, which was also in Christ Jesus."** *Philippians 2:5*

In his commentary on Philippians, British clergyman J. A. Motyer reminds us that each of the four Gospels tells the story of the Cross, and that its meaning is the main theme of the epistles. He points out, however, that the verses covered in our lesson "uniquely unfold the cross as seen through the eyes of the Crucified." He further notes that this enables us "to enter into the mind of Christ. We tread, therefore, on very holy ground indeed."

"Why did He do it?" we might ask. He was in the form of God. (This alone is a profoundly deep concept for limited human minds.) From this exalted position He humbled Himself to human life, and humbled Himself even further to the point of a sacrificial death. This is the mindset we are asked to adopt for our own.

Our Christian hymn writers have tried to capture the meaning. Here are the words of Henry Barraclough: "Out of the ivory palaces, Into the world of woe, Only His great eternal love Made my Savior go." Charles Wesley writes " 'Tis mystery all! The Immortal dies!" He closes this verse with "'Tis mercy all! let earth adore, Let angel-minds inquire no more."

In his commentary, Motyer closes his comments about the mind of Christ with "He looked at Himself, at His Father and at us, and for obedience' sake and for sinners' sake He held nothing back."

## Weekday Problems

The financial world was shaken when major American financial institutions needed to be bailed out with tax-payer money. Greed was the problem in at least some of these cases.

A New York investment mogul confessed to operating a 65 billion dollar Ponzi scheme, possibly the largest fraud ever on Wall Street. He had been trusted by individual investors and charitable foundations, and at one time had even been chairman of the Nasdaq stock exchange. Trust and credentials meant nothing when it was discovered that the money was not there.

It takes a lot of zeroes to make a billion dollars, and most of us do not need nearly that many when we total up our assets. We would like to think, though, that our local banker, home mortgage lender, credit card company, or the people at the corner hardware store, will treat us fairly and honestly. The ability to conduct business, whether large or small, is based on trust.

The interesting thing about our memory verse is that it requires more from us than basic honesty and trustworthiness. It calls for sacrifice. There will always be selfishness and greed in the world. You and I, though, as Christian men and women, are to follow Jesus and go the second mile. We learn sacrificial service from Him. We are to be givers, not self-seekers. That is the Christian way and it is not easy. It might even present a problem.

# Say That Again Please

*More Actual Headlines*

Include Your Children When Baking Cookies

Drunks Get Nine Months in Violin Case

Miners Refuse to Work after Death

Stolen Painting Found by Tree

Man Struck By Lightning Faces Battery Charge

Local High School Dropouts Cut in Half

New Vaccine May Contain Rabies

Hospitals Are Sued by 7 Foot Doctors

# Ths Lesson in Your Life

Warren W. Wiersbe tells an interesting story in his book, *Be Joyful, it Beats Being Happy* (A small book that is large on useful comments on Philippians). In the story, a reporter was interviewing a job counselor who had placed hundreds of workers in their vocations. The counselor was very successful and his placements fit well in the jobs he found for them.

When asked the secret of his success, the man replied: "If you want to find out what a worker is really like, don't give him responsibilities – give him *privileges*. Most people can handle responsibilities if you pay them enough, but it takes a real leader to handle privileges. A leader will use his privileges to help others and build the organization; a lesser man will use privileges to promote himself."

The point of this story leads us to Jesus. He was privileged to be in the very form of God. Rather than grasping that exalted position and holding on to it firmly, He gave it up with you and me in mind. He used his privilege for our sake, not his own. He did not think of Himself, He thought of others.

Our lesson encourages us to "Look not every man on his own things, but every man also on the things of others. Let this mind be in you, which was also in Christ Jesus." This lesson immediately works itself into our lives.

Wiersbe points out Scripture where God instructs us how to live with "one another":

We are to prefer one another, (Rom. 12:10).

Edify one another, (1 Thes. 5:11).

Bear each other's burdens, (Gal. 6:2).

Not judge one another, (Rom. 14:13).

Not judge but admonish one another, (Rom 15:14).

"Other" is the key word in putting sacrifice to work in our lives. We learn to make room for more than "Me and mine." Our English word "Ego" is actually nothing more than the word "I" in Greek. (See, you've been speaking Greek.) We brought it straight over from that language into English, and too much of it can get us into big trouble. Too much ego leaves too little room for others.

It is John's Gospel that tells us about Jesus washing the disciples' feet (Chapter 13). Many churches and various Christian organizations use the depiction of Him, bending on His knees and with wash basin in hand and draped towel, as a way of indicating that they take sacrificial service to heart.

By His very nature, He was in the form of God, but gave up this privileged position to become a servant. As He taught us to pray He said, "Thy will be done." There is no ego in this, and it ultimately led Him to the Cross. Our lesson verses give us a look into His mind, and tell us to let that be our mind also. If we do this, the lesson will be seen in our lives.

**1. What four "ifs" are included in verse 1?**

If any consolation (encouragement) in Christ, if any comfort from His love, if any fellowship of the Spirit, if any bowels and mercies (affection and compassion).

**2. When these things are in place, what are they to do to make Paul's joy complete?**

They are to be likeminded, have the same love, be of one accord and one mind.

**3. After having given these positive goals, what are they forbidden to do?**

They are to do nothing through strife or vainglory (vain conceit).

**4. Paul tells them what frame of mind to have as they consider others. What is to be their frame of mind and what are they to consider about others?**

They should have lowliness of mind (humility) as they consider others better than themselves.

**5. How are they to regard their own interests and the interest of others?**

They are not to look only to their own things (interests), but also to the things of others.

**6. How are they told to condition their minds?**

They are to let the mind of Christ be in them.

**7. Verse 6 describes Christ before He came to earth as a human. What does it say about Him?**

It says that He was in the form of God.

**8. How did Christ feel about being equal with God?**

He did not consider it robbery (something to be grasped, NIV and others).

**9. Christ made Himself of no reputation (made Himself nothing), and did what?**

He took the form of a servant and was made in the likeness of men.

**10. When Christ became a man, He humbled Himself and did what?**

He became obedient to death, even the death of the cross.

It was an unlikely setting for discussing church music. I was shopping for insurance and the salesman was sitting at my dining table with brochures and charts of numbers scattered all about. In very un-salesman-like fashion he kept changing the topic to church. He would give sales pitch for a few minutes, and then make some negative comment about the church in which he had grown up. He was very unhappy with it, so he and his wife and children had attended service in a different denomination. He did not like this church either, so I asked what the problem was with it. He did not like it because they sang too much. If he could find a church that did not sing he might like it better.

This was a very unusual complaint to hear about a church. He knew I was a minister and apparently thought I could help him. Needless to say, I could not – and neither did I buy any insurance, but not because of the singing.

Can you imagine going to church on Sunday morning and there not being any singing? It is unthinkable! Music is a powerful influence either for good or bad. Satan knows how to use it. Madison Avenue's commercials sing to us about everything from Chevrolets to mouthwash. With the right song a pop star can become a millionaire. Singing is part of living.

The earliest Christians were Jewish, and the Psalms were their hymn book. Very soon, it seems, specifically Christian songs were composed. Our present lesson contains an excellent example of one. The theology in it is good, as we would expect considering that it is preserved for us in the Bible. It is comprehensive in its praise for Christ. It speaks of Him in heaven before coming to earth, it tells what He did while here, and it tells of His exaltation after His ascension.

As an example of how it could have been sung in the early church, Ralph P. Martin's *Worship in the Early Church* presents it in an antiphonal form.

He, although He was in the divine Form,
Did not think equality with God a thing to be grasped;
But surrendered His rank
And took the role of a servant;
Becoming like the rest of mankind,
And appearing in a human role;
He humbled himself,
In an obedience that went so far as to die.
For this, God raised Him to the highest honor,
And conferred upon Him the highest rank of all;
That, at Jesus' name every knee should bow,
And every tongue should own that "Jesus Christ is Lord."

Can you visualize (or better still, can you hear) this being sung in your church, with you helping sing one of the antiphonal parts? It is a marvelous hymn to Christ. It is an uplifting blessing just to read it.

350

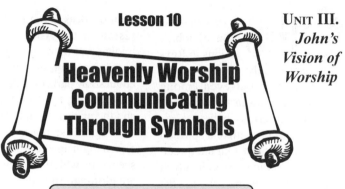

# Heavenly Worship Communicating Through Symbols

## Revelation 4:1-2, 6b-11

After this I looked, and, behold, a door was opened in heaven: and the first voice which I heard was as it were of a trumpet talking with me; which said, Come up hither, and I will shew thee things which must be hereafter.

2 And immediately I was in the spirit: and, behold, a throne was set in heaven, and one sat on the throne.

6b . . . and in the midst of the throne, and round about the throne, were four beasts full of eyes before and behind.

7 And the first beast was like a lion, and the second beast like a calf, and the third beast had a face as a man, and the fourth beast was like a flying eagle.

8 And the four beasts had each of them six wings about him; and they were full of eyes within: and they rest not day and night, saying, Holy, holy, holy, Lord God Almighty, which was, and is, and is to come.

9 And when those beasts give glory and honour and thanks to him that sat on the throne, who liveth for ever and ever,

10 The four and twenty elders fall down before him that sat on the throne, and worship him that liveth for ever and ever, and cast their crowns before the throne, saying,

11 Thou art worthy, O Lord, to receive glory and honour and power: for thou hast created all things, and for thy pleasure they are and were created.

---

**Memory Verse**
Revelation 4:2

**Background Scripture**
Revelation 4

**Devotional Reading**
Psalm 11

May 8

**focus** Interpretations of John's visions in Revelation vary widely not only from church to church but even among pastors and scholars in the same fellowship. What various believers see in the visions is not unlike a spiritual Rorschach inkblot test. Our interpretations say more about what is already in our heads and hearts than about what was in John's.

While we recognize the wide spectrum of ideas about each symbol and vision in the Apocalypse, we can rejoice that many who read the book come away with substantial agreement about some parts of it. All are lifted up, for example, by the pictures of Jesus and the names given to Him in John's writing. Most readers of the book also delight in the immense worship scenes in which God and the Lamb are glorified. In addition, virtually all come away from the book rejoicing that in the End the Christians—those on Jesus' side—win.

## For a Lively Start

Taking apart the apocalyptic visions of Revelation and analyzing them bit by bit is like dissecting a frog in biology class. You may learn a lot about the frog, but when you are done, that frog will never jump again.

Visions are made to be seen, not explained. They evoke intrinsic responses that can affect our hearts and emotions more than our way of thinking. They are designed to be seen as a whole, not in meaningless fragments.

If the curtain opens in a theater to reveal a lamp, a stuffed chair, a divan, and a picture on the wall, everyone in the theater concludes that they are looking at someone's living room. The total vision communicates. What if someone asks, "What does that chair *mean*?" Standing alone, it means nothing. Such are the apocalyptic symbols of John's Revelation.

| Teaching Outline | Daily Bible Readings |
|---|---|
| I. John's Invitation into Heaven—Revelation 4:1 | Mon. In the Holy Temple<br>*Psalm 11* |
| II. God on His Throne—Revelation 4:2 | Tue. Holy, Holy, Holy<br>*Isaiah 6:1-5* |
| III. The Four Creatures—Revelation 4:6b-8 | Wed. The Lord God Almighty<br>*Exodus 6:2-8* |
| A. Their Appearance, 6b-8a | Thu The King of Glory<br>*Psalm 24* |
| B. Their Praise to God, 8b | Fri. King Forever and Ever<br>*Psalm 10:12-16* |
| IV. The 24 Elders—Revelation 4:9-11 | Sat. Worship the Lord<br>*Psalm 96* |
| A. What They Do, 9-10 | Sun. You Are Worthy, O Lord<br>*Revelation 4:1-2, 6b-11* |
| B. What They Say, 11 | |

# *Verse by Verse*

Revelation 4:1-2, 6b-11

**I. John's Invitation into Heaven—Revelation 4:1**

**1 After this I looked, and, behold, a door was opened in heaven: and the first voice which I heard was as it were of a trumpet talking with me; which said, Come up hither, and I will shew thee things which must be hereafter.**

In last half of the first chapter of Revelation, John sees a vision in which the glorified Christ speaks to him in a voice like a trumpet blast and gives him instructions about writing down for the churches what he is about to see. The identity of this speaker seems to be clear to all Revelation readers because He identifies Himself as "the First and the Last" and "the Living One." Now John hears this same voice again. This time the Lord is inviting the aged apostle to come up into Heaven to see what the Lord will show him about "things which must be hereafter." Neither John nor Jesus tells us when the period "hereafter" begins. Those who study Revelation try to figure out this for themselves. In addition, as you might expect, there are about as many opinions on this as there are commentators on the book.

Was John invited bodily into Heaven, or was all of this a vision John saw while standing firmly on the ground on the Island of Patmos? Perhaps the next verse offers a clue.

**II. God on His Throne—Revelation 4:2**

**2 And immediately I was in the spirit: and, behold, a throne was set in heaven, and one sat on the throne.**

One decision all Bible translators must make repeatedly is whether the word "spirit" should be capitalized. The question is whether it refers to a person's own spirit or to God's Spirit. The KJV always translates the word with a lower-case *s* and lets the reader make his own call. Newer Bible versions often use the capital *S* to designate God's Spirit, but in this instance, they are about evenly split on whether John was over involved spiritually or whether he was "in the Holy Spirit." Both readings make good sense; yet, we have no way to tell which meaning John intended.

When John looked into Heaven—whether he was bodily there or in the spirit—John saw a throne with One sitting on it. If you try to *see* this vision, how big is this throne in your graphic image? No doubt, none of us will have the same image.

## III. The Four Creatures—Revelation 4:6b-8

### A. Their Appearance, 6b-8a

**6b . . . and in the midst of the throne, and round about the throne, were four beasts full of eyes before and behind.**

**7 And the first beast was like a lion, and the second beast like a calf, and the third beast had a face as a man, and the fourth beast was like a flying eagle.**

**8 And the four beasts had each of them six wings about him; and they were full of eyes within:**

The KJV's use of the word *beast* casts a rather scary, sinister pall over this scene when this may not be intended at all by John. Almost all the current Bible versions refer here instead to "four living creatures"—a much more positive image that seems to fit the rest of the vision. These creatures spend their time praising the God of Heaven. They are not evil, menacing beings.

The KJV confuses the image a bit by placing these creatures both in the middle of the throne and around it. The NIV conveys John's meaning when it tells us, "In the center, around the throne, were four living creatures."

We have never seen beings like this. It becomes clear as we read all of vs. 7 that John is describing their faces. A quick reading of Ezekiel's vision of the four creatures in Heaven shows where John borrowed some of this imagery. See Ezekiel 1:10 especially

for the four kinds of faces and the surrounding verses for similar images of multiple wings and an abundance of eyeballs.

We learn early on in Revelation that most of John's imagery has Old Testament roots. Very little of it is original with the apostle. His writing shows that he was a very good student of the Scriptures of his ancestors. We will be pressed to catch the meaning of the visions in Revelation if we have not paid careful attention to the Old Testament passages where John found them.

### B. Their Praise to God, 8b

**8b . . . and they rest not day and night, saying, Holy, holy, holy, Lord God Almighty, which was, and is, and is to come.**

The four living creatures give continual praise to God. Their words are not original. In Isaiah's vision of God's throne room, you will find Heaven ringing with the same words of praise (Isa. 6).

The description of God not only recognizes His immense power (He is the Lord God "Almighty"), but it also emphasizes His timelessness. Saying that He "was, is, and is to come" is like the name that God told Moses to use, "I AM." In every age—past, present, or future—He is.

## IV. The 24 Elders—Revelation 4:9-11

### A. What They Do, 9-10

**9 And when those beasts give glory and honour and thanks to him that sat on the throne, who liveth for ever and ever,**

**10 The four and twenty elders fall down before him that sat on the**

354

throne, and worship him that liveth for ever and ever, and cast their crowns before the throne, saying,

Again it is important here for us to try to *see* the vision. While the four living creatures are giving praise to the Eternal God, other remarkable activity is taking place before the throne. Can you *see* the "elders"—all 24 of them? What does an "elder" look like? The Greek word John uses implies advanced age, so something about their appearance must betray this. Can you see all two dozen of them prostrate before the Lord on His throne (Whose eternal nature is emphasized again in this verse)? Saying that they "worship" Him means they "bow down" before Him. The word describes their posture in His presence.

These elders wore crowns. John's original word for "crowns" here is *stephanos*, which means a crown awarded to a victor, as opposed to *diadem,* a crown worn by a ruler. In other words, the elders are not kings; they are winners. Their circle of thrones is a ring of honor, not a legislative gathering, nor an imperial council. The elders throw their crowns—the marks of their victory—before God's throne, acknowledging Him as the One Who enabled them to win.

Is the number of elders significant? Some think so. All of us can do the math, of course, and see that 24 is 12 two times. This causes some believers to suggest that this symbolic number encompasses the 12 tribes of Israel and the 12 apostles, thus including both the Old and the New Testament epochs. The math works but the interpretation is a guess unsupported by anything John tells us.

**B. What They Say, 11**

**11 Thou art worthy, O Lord, to receive glory and honour and power: for thou hast created all things, and for thy pleasure they are and were created.**

The elders around the throne echo the praises of the four living creatures, also ascribing "glory, honor, and power" to the One Who created everything, causing all things to be made as He pleased or for His delight. According to the elders, God is still producing things as He wishes. They say that creation is ongoing. While we are trying to *see* the vision, can we *hear* the elders' praise?

ಖಿಂಖ

## Evangelistic Emphasis

What a bright and colorful heaven John saw! It is an exciting and active place. From God's throne came lightning flashes and loud thunder. (The Old Testament depicts God's presence in this way:) On the throne sat one with the appearance of jasper and carnelian. Something like a shining, emerald rainbow surrounded the throne, with an expanse of crystal-like brilliance in front. There was nothing dull to be seen in all of heaven.

Four living creatures sang of God's holiness. They seem to represent all living things that dwell on earth. Twenty-four elders cast their golden crowns before the throne and they also praise God. We can see in them the twelve tribes of Israel plus the twelve apostles of Christ. It is as though the redeemed from both the Old and New Testaments are there. Heaven and earth praise God.

John received Revelation because the churches were suffering greatly, being persecuted by Rome and surrounded by a pagan world. The message John receives will be sent to them to give them hope and comfort. Hearing about John's look into heaven will help revive their faith.

We also get the vivid picture, and it is encouraging to us as well. It is a symbolic reminder to us that God is real and so is heaven. It is an incentive to stay busy evangelizing. Heaven should be shared with as many people as possible.

### ಸಃಝ

## Memory Selection

"And immediately I was in the spirit: and, behold, a throne was set in heaven, and one sat on the throne." *Revelation 4:2*

John had been sent to the rocky island of Patmos, used by Rome as a place of banishment. It must have been a grim and colorless place. Surrounded by this drabness he saw a door opened in heaven, and a trumpet-like voice said come up here and I will show you things that must take place after this.

Immediately he was in some state that he described as "in the spirit." "Look," he said, as he saw a throne with someone sitting on it. He was seeing God's throne and its surroundings. It was awesome, with lightening and peals of rumbling thunder coming from the throne. There was color and brilliance and movement.

It was reverent and worshipful. Around the throne were four living creatures, one human, one a domestic animal, another a wild beast, and one a flying bird. They praised God night and day. Just as impressive were twenty-four elders with golden crowns, and they worship in response to that of the living creatures.

John saw all this and more. If he had become discouraged during his exile and had wondered if God had forgotten him, this personal tour would assure him that all was well in heaven.

The struggling churches back in Asia (not Asia as we know it now, but the Roman province by that name) to whom John would send this book, would work their way through the symbolism and be thrilled with what they learned.

# Weekday Problems

Bill was a dedicated Christian with a firm faith and strong ties to his church. He loved the Lord and displayed Christian virtues in his life. He had many talents, and used them to help friends and neighbors. It was easy to like him.

In spite of seeming to be a person who had everything going his way, his life seemed to be headed down a wrong-way street. His marriage ended in divorce, much to the surprise of his friends. The small auto mechanic shop he owned went out of business. He could not keep up with his large competitors. His health took a nosedive with multiple complications.

He kept his faith, though. He said he prayed and trusted the Lord to be merciful, but one tragedy seemed to follow another. "Why?" he wondered.

In our lesson, John sees the wonders of heaven. He sees representatives of both heaven and earth praising God. He sees the mysterious splendor of His throne. Meanwhile, back in the Roman province of Asia, Christians are suffering.

The power of Rome is bearing down heavily on struggling churches. In temples dedicated to the divinity of the emperor, Christians are expected to say "Caesar is Lord." They are living in a hostile environment.

These persecuted believers trust the Lord, and must question why He does not deliver them from the cruelties that surround them. They believe that God is on His throne, but why does He not reach down to help them.

Have you ever wondered why God has not responded quickly to your prayers for help? Can you keep your faith when you have lost so much else? That is a challenge we Christians have to meet.

# Tender Mother's Day Sentiments

Joe Barnett tells of hearing a fellow on the radio interviewing mothers during the week before Mother's Day. "If you had it to do over again," the man asked one mother, "would you have children again?"

"Of course," was her immediate reply. "But not the same ones."

# This Lesson in Your Life

Heaven is the place where we all expect to spend eternity. Considering how heavily it figures in our hopes, we might wish we knew more details about it. What we do know exceeds our wildest expectations, and certainly exceeds what we deserve. (We remember that we are saved by grace, and not because we are such nice people that God has to let us in when we arrive at the pearly gates.)

Our strong convictions about heaven, being there for us when the time arrives, falls into the category of faith as Hebrews 11:1 defines it. That Scripture says faith is being sure of what we hope for and certain of what we do not see. We feel sure and certain about heaven, though it is a matter of hope not confirmed by sight.

First John 3:1-3 tells us that, "what we will be has not yet been made known. But we know that when He appears, we shall be like Him . . . ." Hebrews speaks of being sure and certain. John says, "we know." That is more than positive thinking; it is positive faith.

Much of what we know about heaven comes from Revelation, some of it in our present lesson. We do not spend much time reading in this book until we realize that most (but not all) of it speaks to us through powerful symbols. We do not take them literally, but know that the truth they convey comes in picture-language. We see the symbol and get the picture of what God wants us to know.

The Book of Revelation was to be read in the churches where John had preached. These Christians were struggling to survive. They needed help. What is God going to tell them (and us) about Himself and heaven? What can you and I find that is useful to our lives?

Let us take a look, to borrow John's frequent expression. (Over and over he says "I looked." There is a lot to see.) As some Bible students look at the appearance (red-colored jasper and carnelian) of Him who sat on the throne, they contrast this with the cool emerald-green of the rainbow. From the throne lightning flashes and thunder-claps rumble, and there were voices. In front of the throne is a sea of glass, clear as crystal. What have we seen when we see this?

One of the unique things about Revelation is that it encourages us to use our imagination. One concept of God is as our loving Father. That is an excellent image for us to have, but it is not the one portrayed in this lesson. My imagination tells me that we are seeing The Lord God Almighty in this heavenly scene. Those Christians who would first read this description were being opposed by the Roman Empire, the greatest power on earth. Maybe this is God's way of telling them (and us) that he is the supreme power of the universe.

We need to be careful as we read Revelation and not try to give some meaning to every little thing. We want to get the big picture. I have told you the big picture I see in this throne scene. I might add to it that I see a Holy Mystery. God is bigger than our minds. Heaven is so impressive. What do you see there?

## GETTING
## THE FACTS STRAIGHT

**1. What did John see and hear when he looked into heaven?**

He saw an opened door in heaven, and a voice like a trumpet speaking to him.

**2. What did the voice tell him to do?**

He was told to come up here and I will show you things that will happen afterward.

**3. How did John describe the condition in which he immediately found himself?**

He said that he was in the Spirit. He uses this expression in other places (1:10; 17:3; 21:10).

**4. What was the first thing John saw in heaven?**

He saw a throne with someone sitting on it.

**5. Describe the One who sat upon the throne, and its immediate surrounding?**

The One who sat upon the throne looked like a jasper and carnelian stone. It was surrounded by a rainbow that looked like an emerald.

**6. What was seated around the throne?**

There were 24 seats holding 24 elders clothed in white and wearing gold crowns.

**7. What does John say about the lamps?**

There were seven of them burning before the throne. They were the seven Spirits of God.

**8. The KJV says there were four beasts. They are more accurately described as living creatures. What four living creatures did they resemble?**

The first was like a lion, the second like a calf, the third had the face of a man, and the fourth was like a flying eagle.

**9. As the creatures worshipped God, what are they usually considered to represent? (This question is not answered in the text.)**

They are usually seen as categories of earth's living things. Both wild and domestic animals, birds, and humans, all join to worship God.

**10. When the 24 elders worshipped God, in what way did they subject themselves to Him?**

They fell down before Him and placed their crowns before Him.

The Book of Revelation does not get nearly the credit that it deserves. It is often shunned as being too mysterious to be meaningful.

It is intended to be an Uplift Book, not a downer. Let us see if we can take a look at our present lesson and find something encouraging and inspirational. This is not to suggest that it will ever be easy reading, but it should be a worthy undertaking. A blessing is pronounced on those who read or hear it (1:3).

It was originally to be sent to seven representative churches in the Roman province of Asia. We can visualize its being read aloud in their assembly, and listened to eagerly. These churches were in a survival mode and needing a pick-me-up. Their world was falling apart. This book was to give them an uplift.

John gets to look inside heaven. What he sees are symbols, but they stand for spiritual reality. He sees the throne of God and the activity that surrounds it.

There are 24 thrones (the Greek says thrones v, 4) surrounding the throne of God. They are occupied by 24 elders, each with a crown of gold. If we give ourselves a couple of minutes to read further in the chapter and get the picture of what is taking place here, we can easily conclude that these 24 represent the 12 patriarchs of Israel (their 12 tribes), plus the 12 apostles, representing Christians. It is a beautiful picture as God's faithful from the Old and New Testament worship Him.

There are also four living creatures surrounding the throne. As we read their descriptions (a man, a lion, etc.) they can easily represent all living things on earth, or we could say they represent nature. (We need to allow ourselves – and others – leeway in interpreting these symbols. We are looking for the big picture, and trying to see where Revelation is heading.)

These two groups, the elders and the living creatures, work in concert as they worship God. Day and night the living creatures never stop saying

> Holy, holy, holy
> is the Lord God Almighty,
> who was, and is, and is to come.

Whenever the creatures do this, the elders fall down, casting their crowns before God's throne, and say

> You are worthy, our Lord and God,
>
> to receive glory and honor and power,
> for you created all things,
> and by your power they were created
> and have their being.

This is a comforting scene. It is inspirational if we look at the symbols and find the reality. Admittedly, Revelation gets more complex as we read further and the plot begins to thicken. Good battles against evil and good wins. Let us approach this book with the eyes and ears of those to whom it was originally sent. It will bless us as it did them.

# Lesson 11

## Thankful Worship Where We Look in Times of Trouble

### Revelation 7:9-17

After this I beheld, and, lo, a great multitude, which no man could number, of all nations, and kindreds, and people, and tongues, stood before the throne, and before the Lamb, clothed with white robes, and palms in their hands;

10 And cried with a loud voice, saying, Salvation to our God which sitteth upon the throne, and unto the Lamb.

11 And all the angels stood round about the throne, and about the elders and the four beasts, and fell before the throne on their faces, and worshipped God,

12 Saying, Amen: Blessing, and glory, and wisdom, and thanksgiving, and honour, and power, and might, be unto our God for ever and ever. Amen.

13 And one of the elders answered, saying unto me, What are these which are arrayed in white robes? and whence came they?

14 And I said unto him, Sir, thou knowest. And he said to me, These are they which came out of great tribulation, and have washed their robes, and made them white in the blood of the Lamb.

15 Therefore are they before the throne of God, and serve him day and night in his temple: and he that sitteth on the throne shall dwell among them.

16 They shall hunger no more, neither thirst any more; neither shall the sun light on them, nor any heat.

17 For the Lamb which is in the midst of the throne shall feed them, and shall lead them unto living fountains of waters: and God shall wipe away all tears from their eyes.

**Memory Verse**
Revelation 7:10

**Background Scripture**
Revelation 7:9-17

**Devotional Reading**
Psalm 23

May 15

Those of us who serve the Lord in small, isolated congregations sometimes get discouraged and wonder if our limited efforts can make any real difference in the condition of the world or in the cause of Christ. This can happen to small-churchgoers in an age that tends to worship large communities and thinks that mega is always better.

Meditating on the heavenly scene in the last half of Revelation 7 should be an effective antidote to problems we have with spiritual sense of worth. Our own local church may be little, but all of us who serve Jesus are members of something so big that it spans centuries, cultures, and continents.

In Heaven, just the number of the martyrs from that one time of persecution overwhelmed the heavenly census takers. In Christ, we are related to those believers from every nation and language known on Earth. No other enterprise comes close to the scope of Christ's Church in which we serve.

## For a Lively Start

🔊🔉

When our hearts are broken by losses that seem too painful for us to bear, one common response is to turn inward and to tell ourselves that nobody else has ever hurt like we are hurting—that no one else has ever cried tears as bitter as our tears. Later, as we heal, we can see that we were wrong, but in the depth of our grief we may be blind to the suffering of others around us.

Grief recovery groups can help us to discover others sharing trauma just like ours. The countless multitudes of martyrs in Revelation 7 may be the largest grief support group ever assembled. All of them were killed for their faith. Now they knew that they had not been singled out unfairly for an unusual fate. Everybody in these scene around God's throne got there the same way.

| Teaching Outline | Daily Bible Readings |
|---|---|
| I. The Multitude of Martyrs—Revelation 7:9-10<br>  A. Who They Were, 9<br>  B. What They Said, 10<br>II. The Angels' Song—Revelation 7:11-12<br>III. The Elder's Question—Revelation 7:13<br>IV. His Answer—Revelation 7:14-17<br>  A. Martyrs for Jesus, 14<br>  B. Full-time Servants, 15<br>  C. All Troubles Ended, 16-17 | Mon. The Lord Is My Shepherd<br>    *Psalm 23*<br>Tue. God, the True Shepherd<br>    *Ezekiel 34:11-16*<br>Wed. The Good Shepherd<br>    *John 10:11-16*<br>Thu The Shepherd's Compassion<br>    *Matthew 9:35-38*<br>Fri. The Shepherd's Judgment<br>    *Matthew 25:31-40*<br>Sat. The Shepherd's Steadfast Love<br>    *Psalm 107:1-9*<br>Sun. The Lamb as the Shepherd<br>    *Revelation 7:9-17* |

# *Verse by Verse*

## Revelation 7:9-17

### I. The Multitude of Martyrs— Revelation 7:9-10

#### A. Who They Were, 9

**9 After this I beheld, and, lo, a great multitude, which no man could number, of all nations, and kindreds, and people, and tongues, stood before the throne, and before the Lamb, clothed with white robes, and palms in their hands;**

In this part of John's vision he returns to the throne room of Heaven. Now in addition to the four living creatures, the 24 elders around the throne, and the angels, John sees an uncountable multitude of people. The crowd is remarkable because of their diversity. In this vast throng, John sees people of every sort from nations, tribes, and language groups that span the planet. Scenes such as this should convince us that Heaven would not be a fun place for anyone who is consumed with racial prejudice. To a bigot, Heaven with its diverse population will seem like Hell.

The white robes appear repeatedly in Revelation as the attire of Christians who surround the heavenly throne. In other places (such as 7:14), we will be told that these robes have been washed and made white by the blood of the Lamb. The martyrs have been cleansed from their sins.

Some suggest that the palm branches in their hands may be symbols of victory and thanksgiving. Others point out possible connections between these palm-branch bearers and those on the original Palm Sunday when Jesus entered Jerusalem, but the link between the two scenes may be superficial at best.

#### B. What They Said, 10

**10 And cried with a loud voice, saying, Salvation to our God which sitteth upon the throne, and unto the Lamb.**

Instead of loud singing, the words of the innumerable throng are well described in the NLT as "a mighty shout." Nothing about this worship scene is restrained or solemn. The robust praise of the multitude rings through Heaven. We should note that those who have died for their faith are not complaining. They have not approached the throne to protest their fate. Instead, they draw near to praise the Almighty and the Lamb for providing salvation.

Our newer versions fill in some words to make the martyrs' praise make sense. God obviously does not need saving, as the KJV wording suggests here. Clearly, the martyrs are saying something other than this, such as the NLT and TEV translations that say, "Salvation *comes from* our God," or the NIV and NKJV which tell us that "salvation *belongs to* our God." The martyrs' message must be close to that of the apostle Peter when he told the Jewish court, "Nor is there salvation in any other, for there is no other name under heaven given among men by which we must be saved" (Acts 4:12, NKJV).

It is worth noting that the ones who honor God for providing salvation are the very people He did not rescue from physical torture or death. In their moment of greatest distress, no deliverance came to them from the One who alone could have saved them. Now that they are in Heaven, they can see that He loved them and provided them something far more valuable than physical safety.

## II. The Angels' Song—Revelation 7:11-12

**11 And all the angels stood round about the throne, and about the elders and the four beasts, and fell before the throne on their faces, and worshipped God,**

**12 Saying, Amen: Blessing, and glory, and wisdom, and thanksgiving, and honour, and power, and might, be unto our God for ever and ever. Amen.**

While the martyrs cry out their gratitude to God and the Lamb, the usual inhabitants of Heaven—the angels, the 24 elders, and the four living creatures

("beasts" in the KJV)—add their praise in a seven-fold doxology: blessing, glory, wisdom, thanksgiving, honor, power, might, all of these tributes ascribed to God eternally, with "Amen" both opening and closing the string.

Note the posture of the heavenly creatures. They fall prostrate before the throne. The word "worshipped" denotes posture instead of vocal content. It means they bowed down.

We moderns who are so accustomed to worship dominated by music come away from the Bible's heavenly worship scenes a bit surprised or disappointed when the great outpourings of praise usually are spoken rather than sung. So our minds brighten when vs. 12 in the NRSV and the NLT tells us the angelic beings were singing. That is exactly what we expected all along.

## III. The Elder's Question—Revelation 7:13

**13 And one of the elders answered, saying unto me, What are these which are arrayed in white robes? and whence came they?**

One of the 24 elders poses a question to John, not to obtain information but to make sure that John knows the answer. Indicating the vast multitude of white-robed martyrs, the elders asks John who (not "what") they are and where they came from?

## IV. His Answer—Revelation 7:14-17

### A. Martyrs for Jesus, 14

**14 And I said unto him, Sir, thou knowest. And he said to me, These are they which came out of great**

tribulation, and have washed their robes, and made them white in the blood of the Lamb.

John's reply is polite and tactful, like the way we speak to a traffic cop who is writing us a speeding ticket. John tells the elder, "I don't know, but you do." Indeed the elder does know. From his answer to John, we find out that the multitude are Christians who gave their lives for Jesus—believers who now stand sinless before God because of the blood of the Lamb that washed away their guilt.

Notice that the KJV tells us here that these martyrs "came out of great tribulation." They came to Heaven through a time of intense persecution and suffering. All of our later translations insert the word "the" before "great," so we read here about "the great tribulation." It is a subtle change, but it may reflect the doctrinal shift between the days of the KJV and this latest generation of Bible translators. During the past century, the influence of the Scofield Study Bible and of authors such as Hal Lindsay caused pre-millennial and dispensational viewpoints to replace the post-millennial theories that dominated the 18th and 19th centuries of Bible study. Most pre-millennial systems include a period called "the great tribulation" (although the teachers of this view do not agree among themselves as to when this period is to take place). We may be seeing the influence of this now common pre-millennial term when the translators change John's "great tribulation" to make it "*the* great tribulation," and this change does alter what we hear the elder telling us.

**B. Full-time Servants, 15**

**15 Therefore are they before the throne of God, and serve him day and night in his temple: and he that sitteth on the throne shall dwell among them.**

If there are clocks in the eternal realm, the redeemed martyrs stand on duty before God's throne available to serve Him continually.

Several newer versions indicate that vs. 15 begins a poetic section that continues through vs. 17. It may be one of the clearest passages in the Bible about what goes on between the time a person dies and the End of time.

**C. All Troubles Ended, 16-17**

**16 They shall hunger no more, neither thirst any more; neither shall the sun light on them, nor any heat.**

**17 For the Lamb which is in the midst of the throne shall feed them, and shall lead them unto living fountains of waters: and God shall wipe away all tears from their eyes.**

Those who came to Heaven through devastating persecution now enjoy an eternal rest from all their earthly troubles. Nothing will menace them as they stand in the Presence of God. The description here will later be echoed in Revelation 21.

## Evangelistic Emphasis

That gathering in heaven as described in our lesson is just too good to miss. Everybody who knows what is going on there will want to be included. There is an impressive roll-call (actually, all the saved).

The 12 tribes of Israel are there (even they are a symbol), each one with a symbolic 12,000 members each, 144.000 strong. This represents all of Israel. (Rom. 2:28-29; Gal. 3:29, 6:16 indicate that Christians are considered as being Israel.)

The next scene sees the heavenly gathering from another viewpoint.

Here there is a multitude too large to count. There are people from every nation, tribe, people and language, standing in the presence of the throne and the Lamb. They have white robes (they are saved), they hold palm branches (symbols of victory and thanksgiving), as they praise God.

We have found our evangelistic emphasis already. Nobody should be without the opportunity to hear the good news of God's salvation. This is what the Great Commission is about, and is to be a focus point for us.

These verses emphasize our responsibility to reach the broadest possible population with the gospel. If we picture ourselves in this heavenly gathering, maybe the person standing next to us will be there because we took our evangelistic responsibility to heart.

## Memory Selection

৪০০৪

"**Salvation to our God which sitteth upon the throne, and unto the Lamb.**" *Revelation 7:10*

The great multitude wearing white robes and gathered before the throne and in front of the Lamb have got it right. They understand salvation. (We would expect that of them; they are saved and in heaven.) Salvation does belong to God and to the Lamb. It is theirs'. They offer it. We accept it. It comes to us through their love, mercy, and grace.

Ephesians 1:4-10 makes this plain. It is because of God's great love for us and because He is rich in mercy, that He has made us alive in Christ Jesus. Chapter 2:8-10 (NIV) says "For it is by grace you have been saved, through faith – and this not from yourselves, it is the gift of God – not by works, so that no one can boast"

When Charles Wesley considered the Scripture contained in our lesson, he wrote this about our memory verse:

> The great congregation His triumph shall sing,
> Ascribing salvation to Jesus our King.
> "Salvation to God, who sits on the throne!"
> Let all cry out and honor the Son.
> Then let us adore and give Him his right,
> And honor and blessings with angels above,
> And thanks never ceasing and infinite love.

## Weekday Problems

Louise had been a member of her mid-sized church for over ten years. She loved everything about it. There had been a change of pastor during that time, but the replacement pastor was every bit as good as the previous one. She had developed a special friendship with a number of the church members, and had watched children grow into adults during her years there.

The one thing she loved most about this church was its music. The worship leader consistently worked the grandest of songs into the services. She marveled at the quality of his work. She appreciated fine music and was delighted to be in a church where it could be depended on.

She especially loved some of the ancient songs, those that had inspired Christians for centuries. There were verses in these songs that especially spoke to her. In the hymn "Jesus, the Very Thought of Thee," her favorite was "O Hope of every contrite heart! O Joy of all the meek! To those who fall, how kind Thou art! How good to those who seek!" It was meaningful to her to know that Christians had sung these words for over 800 years.

Much to her surprise and disappointment, the church changed much about its worship style. There was a new worship leader, and for all practical purposes the music she loved so much was a thing of the past. It was largely replaced by music that she considered light and without content.

What was Louise to do? From her point of view the heart of worship had been removed from this church, though everyone else seemed pleased. How can Louise reconcile this problem?

---

## Tombstones with a Twist

A stone in the Silver City, Nevada, cemetery:

> Here lies Butch,
>
> We planted him raw.
>
> He was quick on the trigger,
>
> But slow on the draw.

Boot Hill Cemetery in Tombstone, Arizona contains this marker for a Wells Fargo Co. station agent in the 1880's:

> Here lies Lester Moore
>
> Four slugs from a .44
>
> No Les No More.

# This Lesson in Your Life

We have to be impressed when we read in our lesson about the great multitude gathered before the throne of God. There were so many that no man could number them. Fortunately, God knows those who are His (2 Tim. 2:19). He can handle a big crowd. Every nation, tribe, people, and language was represented. It was truly an international gathering as far as their earthly background was concerned. As we see them in heaven, they are wearing white robes of the saved and carrying palm fronds of victory.

This reminds us of the worldwide scope of the Church. It reminds me of a situation that developed in the Baptist church that sits across the street from the church where I preach.

For some weeks as my wife and I arrived at our church on Sunday mornings, we would see families taking a short-cut across our parking lot, walking to the Baptist church. They were sometimes dressed colorfully, and we thought perhaps our neighboring church had begun a Spanish language service. (We have quite a few Hispanic friends and none of them dress particularly colorfully. Anyhow, that is what we thought.)

As it turned out, an article in our local newspaper explained what was happening. The church across the street had declined to 15 elderly members, who were considering disbanding and selling the property. Instead, through a series of circumstances (or was it the providence of God) this church began a ministry to Burmese immigrants.

In the 19th century a Baptist missionary worked among the Karen people of Burma (now known as Myanmar) and established churches. The Karen make up the largest minority in that country, and many have fled because of persecution.

Several years ago one Karen immigrant found her way to our neighboring church. A recent influx has brought 600 to our city, with several hundred more expected. Many of the arrivals are Baptists, or have Baptists Karen friends.

Here is the point of this story. From the work of a 19th century missionary, one descendant from his converts found her way to this church. Through her, many others from her persecuted tribe in Burma have found their way there also.

As for the elderly church members who were considering disbanding, they found themselves involved in a mission to these people who came from a rural mountainous region and needed help adapting to a new culture.

How does this fit into our lives? From the standpoint of the missionary who long ago went to Burma, his work is still alive in that land. For those of us who help send missionaries, we can hope for generations of results to follow. For those of us who stay at home, we can look for opportunities as we remember the 15 elderly members. When we all get to heaven, we can be glad God can recognize us even in such a big crowd.

**1. Describe the size of the crowd gathered before the throne and the Lamb.**

It was a multitude so large that no man could number it. (As the small, struggling churches in Asia read this, they might be encouraged to discover how many people there were who had followed God.)

**2. What were the origins of the crowd?**

They came from all nations and kindreds and people, and tongues. (The struggling churches might be encouraged to see how the church had spread worldwide,)

**3. What was there about this crowd that indicated their spiritual status?**

They wore white robes, which indicated they had been cleansed by Christ's blood. White signified purity. They carried palm fronds, a sign of victory and thanksgiving.

**4. What was the crowd saying in a loud voice?**

They were shouting "Salvation [belongs] to God, who sits on the throne and to the Lamb" NIV. (See Psalm 3:8.)

**5. What did the angels, the elders, and the four living creatures do?**

They all fell on their faces before the throne and worshipped God. They represent the entire creation.

**6. What did they say as they worshipped?**

They said Amen, and that Blessings, glory, wisdom, thanksgiving, honor, power, and might, be to God forever. They closed with another Amen (May it be so).

**7. One of the elders asked John who these people in white robes were, and from where did they come. How did John answer him?**

John said, "Sir, thou knowest." (John knew that the elder was better qualified to answer his own question.)

**8. Where did the elder say the people had come from?**

He said they had come from the great tribulation, and had made their robes white in the blood of the Lamb. (The seven churches were deep in tribulation. They will make the connection and see themselves in this picture.)

**9. "Therefore,"(because they have suffered and because they have washed their robes white) what is happening to them?**

Because of these things they are before the throne of God, serve Him day and night in His temple, and God dwells with them.

**10. What unpleasant things will never happen to these people in heaven?**

They will never hunger nor thirst, and the sun shall not beat on them, nor any scorching heat.

"Here be dragons." That's what we might have seen on the old maps, just before we got to the dropping off place at the end of the world. This, of course, would have been before Christopher Columbus with his three little ships helped convince the doubters that the earth was really shaped more like an orange than a pancake. Right beside that dragon-warning printed on the map, would have been the picture of a ferocious one (as though the artist had actually seen one and knew how it looked).

According to the legend (of which various versions tell differently), St. George managed to kill one. This sort of thing was the story-book goal of medieval knights. These days we no longer bother with dragons, but most of us wrestle an alligator now and then.

Well, actually, there is a horrible red dragon that we encounter in Revelation. There is also an ancient serpent and some really ugly beasts. Believe it or not, they all figure in a truly upbeat story. They are all symbols, so we do not have to worry about encountering one of them on a dark night. The fact that they are symbols, though, does not mean that we take them lightly. They represent some spiritual realities that are just as repulsive as the horrible creatures are themselves.

Just to keep anybody from worrying too much, we will do like the person who reads a mystery novel by looking at the last page first to see how the story ends. The Revelation story ends when the Lamb is victorious over all these wicked creatures.

The ancient serpent is the devil, Satan. He is called ancient because he is at least as old as the Garden of Eden. We remember the dirty work he did there, and know that he is still after you and me. The upbeat thing is that the One who is in us is greater than he. As we get toward the end of Revelation, he gets exactly what he deserves, and can never bother anybody again.

When the members of the seven churches first read about the fiendishly horrible and very powerful red dragon, they probably thought of the persecuting power of Rome. You and I do not have to worry about an emperor who thought he was divine, but we do have the pressures of a secular society, and a world in which governments are frequently ungodly. The dragon still keeps busy, but we have the Lamb on our side and know that the dragon is ultimately completely defeated.

What all this means is that Revelation is a book about victory. There is no instant gratification in it. It takes the long view. Ultimately all evil ceases to exist. At that time the Lamb of God and the One on the throne will welcome us to an eternity in the city of gold.

୫୬ଓ୧

## Lesson 12

# All Things New
# New Beginnings

## Revelation 21:1-8

And I saw a new heaven and a new earth: for the first heaven and the first earth were passed away; and there was no more sea.

2 And I John saw the holy city, new Jerusalem, coming down from God out of heaven, prepared as a bride adorned for her husband.

3 And I heard a great voice out of heaven saying, Behold, the tabernacle of God is with men, and he will dwell with them, and they shall be his people, and God himself shall be with them, and be their God.

4 And God shall wipe away all tears from their eyes; and there shall be no more death, neither sorrow, nor crying, neither shall there be any more pain: for the former things are passed away.

5 And he that sat upon the throne said, Behold, I make all things new. And he said unto me, Write: for these words are true and faithful.

6 And he said unto me, It is done. I am Alpha and Omega, the beginning and the end. I will give unto him that is athirst of the fountain of the water of life freely.

7 He that overcometh shall inherit all things; and I will be his God, and he shall be my son.

8 But the fearful, and unbelieving, and the abominable, and murderers, and whoremongers, and sorcerers, and idolaters, and all liars, shall have their part in the lake which burneth with fire and brimstone: which is the second death.

---

**Memory Verse**
Revelation 21:5

**Background Scripture**
Revelation 21

**Devotional Reading**
Isaiah 43:15-21

May 22

371

Although we are at times confused by the many competing interpretations of John's visions in Revelation, certain truths come through loud and clear to all who read the book. One of those truths is the promise here in Chapter 21 that God's children will one day be set free from all the sorrow and suffering in this life. Sickness, pain, grief, and tears will be over.

## For a Lively Start

ഇ‌ാ‌ര

Some softhearted Christians are nicer than God is. From the earliest verses of the Bible to its final lines, the Scriptures are quite clear in their warnings about the consequences of sin. God warned Adam and Eve that they would die if they disobeyed His instructions. Revelation draws to an end with clear predictions that those who persist in doing evil are headed

Just what God's precise timetable will be for restoring Paradise our Bible teachers do not agree. Whether this planet will be renovated or God intends to start anew elsewhere has long been debated. Some parts of John's vision seem to indicate one option while other parts lean toward the other. Nevertheless, almost all of us who read these final chapters of Revelation come away rejoicing that somehow God is going to give us a fresh start free from the blights in our fallen universe.

to the lake that burns. Sin destroys us. The Bible message is plain.

However, some God-fearing people find this hard to accept. Jesus spoke clearly about the fate in store for Satan and his angels. He spoke plainly words in warning that the wicked would share Satan's terrible end. The theology of some believers, however, has no place for Hell. John's words in vs. 8 indicate otherwise.

| Teaching Outline | Daily Bible Readings |
|---|---|
| I. A New Heaven and Earth—Revelation 21:1 | Mon. God Will Do a New Thing *Isaiah 43:15-21* |
| II. The Holy City—Revelation 21:2 | Tue. A New Commandment *John 13:31-35* |
| III. Everything New—Revelation 21:3-5 | Wed. A New Covenant *Luke 22:14-23* |
| A. God's Dwelling with Men, 3 | Thu A New Way of Life *Ephesians 4:17-24* |
| B. Earth's Agonies Ended, 4 | Fri. A New Jerusalem *Revelation 21:9-14* |
| C. A Message to Share, 5 | Sat. A New Light *Revelation 21:22-27* |
| IV. Life for God's Children—Revelation 21:6-7 | Sun. A New Heaven and New Earth *Revelation 21:1-8* |
| V. Death for the Wicked—Revelation 21:8 | |

# Verse by Verse

## Revelation 21:1-8
## I. A New Heaven and Earth— Revelation 21:1

**1 And I saw a new heaven and a new earth: for the first heaven and the first earth were passed away; and there was no more sea.**

John's language here has fueled much speculation about the blessings God plans for the faithful when the End comes. That God does plan to bless us beyond all imagination seems clear to all who read the final chapters of John's vision, but those who cherish the Scriptures have not been able to agree on what to expect.

Some Bible readers take their cue from Peter's predictions in 2 Peter 3 that the Earth and its universe will be completely destroyed. "On that Day the heavens will disappear with a shrill noise, the heavenly bodies will burn up and be destroyed, and the earth with everything in it will vanish," Peter tells us (3:10, TEV). On that final Day, he says, "The heavens will burn up and be destroyed, and the heavenly bodies will be melted by the heat" (3:12, TEV). Based on these graphic descriptions, many teach that everything connected with our present universe will cease to exist.

Of course, Peter goes on a verse later to use the same terminology John employs. Peter says God has promised us "new heavens and a new earth" (3:13, TEV). Keying on "new," some

link a dozen other texts to make the case that God will start afresh and He will create an entirely new universe for the redeemed—one that has not been spoiled by sin. Well studied Bible scholars have written thick books about what to expect in this very new cosmos.

Working with many of the same texts, though, a large number of Bible scholars through the centuries have theorized that the destruction Peter describes will simply be God's way to strip down our present planet so He can start over right here. Therefore, for these people, the "new heavens and new earth" will actually turn out to be this same planet made new.

Scholars make convincing cases for both schools of thought (and for a range of variations in between). What seems clear to all involved is that God is going to bless the faithful with a perfect place to live—a place free from today's turmoil and terrors. Just how He plans to do this, we cannot be sure.

What is the significance of the absence of the sea in God's new earth? The ancients saw the sea as a source of evil and chaos. Getting rid of it entirely might make the Earth seem a more benevolent place. A universe without a sea is a plus, John seems to be telling us, but nobody knows why for sure.

## II. The Holy City—Revelation 21:2

**2 And I John saw the holy city, new Jerusalem, coming down from God out of heaven, prepared as a bride adorned for her husband.**

It would be grand to know exactly what John saw in this vision. Can you imagine a whole city dropping down to the surface of a new earth—that city pristine, pure, and fancy like a bride decked out for her wedding day? Seeing this may take more imagination than some of us possess. We have seen expensively attired brides, but none of us has ever watched as a city descended from the skies. One thing John makes clear—this is not ancient Jerusalem he is seeing. It is "new" Jerusalem about to come alive on a new earth.

Ancient Jerusalem was God's point of contact with His people. They came here to worship Him. The priests ministered here continually. Perhaps the New Jerusalem contains some of those ideas, but this city would not have a Temple like the old one did. Since God lives in the new one, it will need no temple.

## III. Everything New—Revelation 21:3-5

### A. God's Dwelling with Men, 3

**3 And I heard a great voice out of heaven saying, Behold, the tabernacle of God is with men, and he will dwell with them, and they shall be his people, and God himself shall be with them, and be their God.**

The word "dwell" is the same as the word for "tabernacle." We are told in John 1:14 that the Word became flesh and He "lived"—literally, "tabernacled"— with men. Thus, John described Jesus' earthly ministry. Now John uses this word to describe God's presence among His people on the new earth.

These verses have a slightly different appeal when we read them in a newer version such as the NRSV and we see how vss. 3-4 are transformed as poetry.

### B. Earth's Agonies Ended, 4

**4 And God shall wipe away all tears from their eyes; and there shall be no more death, neither sorrow, nor crying, neither shall there be any more pain: for the former things are passed away.**

Vss. 3-4 are a grand announcement that thunders out to let everyone know just how uncomplicated the new universe will be. Most of our current Bible versions tell us the loud voice ("great voice"—KJV) booms out from the throne and not out of Heaven. This makes the vision more coherent, since John is in Heaven when he sees and hears all of this.

All the sources of pain in this world— "the former things"—all of these negative things are gone, the voice announces. What a glorious day!

### C. A Message to Share, 5

**5 And he that sat upon the throne said, Behold, I make all things new. And he said unto me, Write: for these words are true and faithful.**

God explains the announcement that just rang out in Heaven. All the pain and anguish of our earthly existence are now past, we were told by "the voice." God makes sure that John knows that this marvelous improvement has been His doing. "Behold, *I* make everything new," He points out to the apostle.

Earlier during the visions, John was cautioned by an angel not to write down something he heard or saw in Heaven, but God Himself instructs the apostle to write down the words he has just heard because these words are accurate and dependable. This description seems to refer to the two verses just before and not to the random statements that follow.

### IV. Life for God's Children—Revelation 21:6-7

**6 And he said unto me, It is done. I am Alpha and Omega, the beginning and the end. I will give unto him that is athirst of the fountain of the water of life freely.**

**7 He that overcometh shall inherit all things; and I will be his God, and he shall be my son.**

John reports that the Lord said to him, "It is done"—almost a verbatim repeat of the words John heard Jesus say on the cross, "It is finished" (John 19:30). The speaker here in vs. 6 likely is Jesus. See Revelation 1:8 where the glorified Christ identifies Himself with this same name. *Alpha* is the first letter in the Greek alphabet, *Omega*, the last. Therefore, Jesus is saying here, "I am the A and the Z, the first and the last." His claim here seems to be that He has accomplished the eternal heavenly plan for fixing the sin problem on Earth.

The offer of plentiful water was a powerful metaphor in a semi-arid land where water often was in short supply and quite difficult to obtain.

This water of life is available to God's people "freely."

Revelation is a book about winning. God and His people are the victors over Satan and over evil. The promises of eternal blessings in a close relationship to God are made to those who win. The "losers" are the wicked described in the next verse—people who have willfully disqualified themselves for living in Paradise with the Lord.

### V. Death for the Wicked—Revelation 21:8

**8 But the fearful, and unbelieving, and the abominable, and murderers, and whoremongers, and sorcerers, and idolaters, and all liars, shall have their part in the lake which burneth with fire and brimstone: which is the second death.**

All of these people headed to the lake of fire are bad to the core, not just normal humans subject to the flaws common to all humanity. Repeatedly, John identified those who had their sins washed white by Jesus' blood. Heaven will be full of these redeemed, penitent sinners. However, these wicked ones in vs. 8 are neither redeemed nor penitent.

"Fearful" denotes cowardliness and not normal, healthy fear. The TEV helps us by explaining that the "unbelieving" here are "traitors." Likewise, in the TEV we see that "the abominable" are "perverts." The word the KJV translates "whoremongers" refers to the entire range of sexual immoralities. "Sorcerers" includes those who practice all manner of black magic arts. All of these vile behaviors draw God's displeasure and will evoke dire consequences eternally, John tells us.

## Evangelistic Emphasis

By the time we read as far in Revelation as our present lesson, we have come to the time when the old order of things has passed away (v. 4). The world in which the ancient serpent Satan, the dragon, and other evil forces did their vile deeds is no more. For the first time in Revelation we hear the voice of God. The first thing He says is, "I am making everything new (v. 5).

This is God's ultimate renewal. In search of a way to date it we might say it comes at the end of time and the beginning of eternity. Actually, throughout the time of Jesus' ministry and the long history of gospel teaching, God had been providing spiritual renewal all along.

Jesus explained to Nicodemus that one must be born again (John 3), and had to clarify to him that this was a spiritual birth, and that without it no one can see the kingdom of God. (Everyone needs to get this new beginning taken care of in this life, long before we reach the new creation God will have waiting for us at the End.)

Paul wrote that, "if anyone is in Christ, he is a new creation; the old has gone and the new has come" (2 Cor. 5:17 NIV).

Such passages as these emphasize to us the need for evangelism. As we view the End Time and think in terms of preparation for entering the eternal kingdom, it makes obeying the Great Commission a high priority.

## Memory Selection

ಜಡಚ

"And he that sat upon the throne said, Behold, I make all things new." *Revelation 21:5*

How will our world end? Could it be by some nuclear conflagration that wipes out all living things? Will we pollute it to death? Will the environment collapse because of melting ice caps and other natural disasters?

This is not to suggest that nuclear devices are not dangerous or that we do not need to take care of our environment. However, Christians will remember that the One who made the world is still in control of it. When we sing, "This is my Father's world," we are making a statement of faith.

It is interesting that it is God Himself who says that He is making all things new. He does not have someone else say it for Him. It is He who tells John to write it down because the words are faithful and true. "It is done," God says. "I am Alpha and Omega, the beginning and the end." Alpha and Omega are the first and last letters in the Greek alphabet. God is A to Z in English.

"It is done." It is a done deal. No quibbling. These words from the Creator are spoken at the end of the earth as we know it, when the old order has passed away and He has made everything new. Much in chapters 21 and 22 describe God's new world.

How is the world going to end? It will end with a new beginning created by its original Creator.

# Weekday Problems

It did not take long for any of us as children to learn to deal with problems. If we fell down and hit our head on the sidewalk, it hurt. The fact that we survived to adulthood is an indication that we learned there are some things we try not to do, and that it is better to avoid a problem than to survive one.

Sin is a really big problem with big consequences. In our lesson there is a whole list of them that will keep us out of God's new creation and result in our being punished with the second death (v. 8).

If you were to be asked to make a list of sins that were this bad, how would you start your list? King Solomon made a list of sins, seven of them, that he says the Lord hates. You will find them in Proverbs 6:16-19. Paul made a list in Galatians 5:19-21. (Do not forget to read his list of virtues that follows.)

The sin that heads the list in our lesson is a surprising one. (Of course the list may, as he saying goes, "be in no particular order.") The KJV lists it as, "the fearful," though newer versions say "cowardice." Even as much as we value courage, would you have ever thought of cowardice as being a sin?

In the context of Revelation, this may have included those who yielded to the fear of persecution and even confessed that, "Caesar is Lord." In our own case, there may be times when we hesitate to "stand up and be counted," Perhaps some social pressure or other circumstance leads us deny the Lord by our action. This kind of cowardice is a sin. We can avoid the problem. Let us take the words of the Isaac Watts' hymn to heart: "I'm not ashamed to own my Lord, Nor to defend His cause; Maintain the honors of His Word, The glory of His cross."

## All Hymns Used to Be New Hymns

"Was it the organist's idea or yours that our peaceful worship service was shattered by that new hymn Sunday? The music was sacrilegious, something one would expect to hear in a den of iniquity, not a church! Don't expect me to even attempt the song next time!" (*Written in 1874 about "I Love to Tell The Story"*)

"Pastor, I am not a music scholar, but I feel I know appropriate church music when I hear it. Last Sunday's new hymn, if you call it that, sounded like a sentimental love ballad one might expect to hear crooned in a saloon. If you persist in exposing us to rubbish like this in God's house, don't be surprised if many of the faithful look for a new place to worship!" (A letter dated in 1864 concerning the hymn "*Just As I Am*")

# This Lesson in Your Life

It seems that someone has taken a poll on just about every topic that exists. How could TV newscasters fill their time slots without giving us the latest numbers on how many sunflowers there are in Kansas, or peach orchards in Georgia? That may mean that somebody, somewhere, probably knows the answer to the following question. Be that as it may, we will just tackle this question on our own.

In your observation, what are the two least used books in the New Testament? (Arrive at your answer by deciding which two you are less likely to use in your personal study and devotions. Which two are you the least likely to hear used as a sermon text or Scripture reading in church?)

My guess is that a great number of us might say Jude and Revelation. Jude is such a small book, and tucked in toward the end of the volume. Revelation is not the easiest reading in the world, especially when we get past chapter three. It is easy to pass over them. However, if Lesson Six from Jude, and these from Revelation, have helped us see their usefulness, then that itself is a valuable lesson.

Actually, some of the great Christian hymns are based on Revelation and have worked its message into our lives without our particularly having realized it. Take, for instance, Isaac Watts' "Lo! What a Glorious Sight." Christians have been singing these words for more than two and a half centuries. It begins: "Lo! What a glorious sight appears To our believing eyes! The earth and sea are passed away . . ." and the hymn continues, directly from our present lesson.

Here is one verse and the chorus from Clements' "In the Land of Fadeless Day," written in 1899.

In the land of fadeless day
Lies the city four-square;
It shall never fade away,
And there is no night there.
(chorus) God shall wipe away all tears.
There's no death, no pain, nor fears;
And they count not time by years,
For there is no night there.

Other hymns directly related to Revelation 21 include, "There is a Habitation" and, "Beyond This Land of Parting."

Our present lesson is an easy one to work into our lives. It is highly symbolic, of course, but so very comforting. The early Christians who first read it had lived under extreme pressures simply for having believed in Jesus. These last couple of chapters let them know what God had prepared for them in the hereafter. We share this comfort, because it is written to us, too.

## GETTING THE FACTS STRAIGHT

**1. John saw a new heaven and a new earth. What had happened to the old ones?**

The first heaven and earth had passed away, and there was no more sea. (Some Bible students understand the sea as representing a separation from God. In this case we can see why it would be gone.)

**2. He saw the holy city, the new Jerusalem coming down from heaven. For what was it prepared?**

The new Jerusalem was prepared as a bride adorned for her husband. Verse 9 says that the bride is the Lamb's wife.

**3. What did the great voice from heaven say about God being with men?**

His tabernacle will be with them (reference to living in a tent) and God Himself will be with them and be their God.

**4. What will happen with all unpleasantness?**

God will wipe away all tears, there will be no more death, neither sorrow, nor crying, nor pain.

**5. Previously we have read that a voice came from the throne, which might mean God was speaking indirectly through an angel. In verse 5, what indicates that this is actually God speaking directly (for the first time in Revelation)?**

The verse says "He that sat upon the throne said, 'Behold, I make all things new.'" God was the One who sat on the throne.

**6. In addition to the above, what did God say?**

He said "It is done. I am Alpha and Omega, the beginning and the end." Alpha and Omega are the first and last letters in the Greek alphabet. "The end" carries with it the idea of being the fulfillment, the culmination.

**7. What is promised to the person who overcomes?**

He will inherit all things. "I will be his God, and he shall be my son." (This would include the thought of children having the right to inherit from their Father.)

**8. The lake that burns with fire and brimstone is further identified as being what?**

The ungodly will have their part in the lake of fire and brimstone, which is the second death.

**9. Why will the heavenly city have not need of the sun or moon?**

The glory of God lights it, and also the Lamb is its light.

**10. Nothing defiled can enter the city. Who will be allowed in?**

The only ones allowed inside are "they which are written in the Lamb's book of life."

In his commentary on 1ˢᵗ Corinthians, Dr. F. W. Grosheide says some things about 13:10 that emphasize the uplifting nature of our lesson. It says, "when that which is perfect is come, then that which is in part shall be done away."

He notes that these words are not written only in reference to the special gifts that are mentioned in that chapter, but to the world. The world does not stand still, he says, and neither does time. Everything is moving quickly toward the end. He calls attention to 7:31: the world in its present form is passing away. Also Ephesians 1:9-10, about when the times will have reached their fulfillment.

As we mark off each day on our calendar, and each year replace it with a new one, we are approaching that time of fulfillment. This is exciting. And even though we do not know when it will arrive, we can read about it in our Revelation 21 lesson. We read about it there as if it were an accomplished fact.

"I saw a new heaven and a new earth: for the first heaven and the first earth were passed away, and there was no more sea." These words begin our lesson, and they describe, "when the perfect is come," and the world in its present form passing away.

A number of years ago, Doug Oldham made a very beautiful and moving recording of "The King is Coming." It sold so well that our local Christian book shops had trouble keeping it in stock. My wife especially loved it, and she would say it made her want to run outside and look to the sky to see if He was coming. Here is the first verse, with the chorus:

The market place is empty,
No more traffic in the streets.
All builders' tools are silent,
No more time to harvest wheat.
Busy housewives cease their labors,
In the courtroom no debate,
Work on earth is all suspended
As the King comes through the gate.

    Oh the King is coming,
    The King is coming,
    I just heard the trumpet sounding
    And now His face I see.
    Oh, the King is coming,
    The King is coming
    PRAISE GOD,
    He's coming for me.

In Matthew 16:27, Jesus says that He will come in the glory of His Father and with His angels. Let us keep our eyes heavenward!

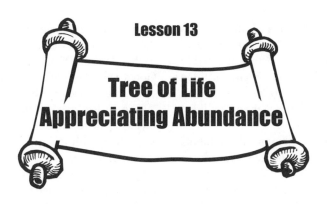

# Lesson 13

## Tree of Life
## Appreciating Abundance

Revelation 22:1-9

And he shewed me a pure river of water of life, clear as crystal, proceeding out of the throne of God and of the Lamb.

2 In the midst of the street of it, and on either side of the river, was there the tree of life, which bare twelve manner of fruits, and yielded her fruit every month: and the leaves of the tree were for the healing of the nations.

3 And there shall be no more curse: but the throne of God and of the Lamb shall be in it; and his servants shall serve him:

4 And they shall see his face; and his name shall be in their foreheads.

5 And there shall be no night there; and they need no candle, neither light of the sun; for the Lord God giveth them light: and they shall reign for ever and ever.

6 And he said unto me, These sayings are faithful and true: and the Lord God of the holy prophets sent his angel to shew unto his servants the things which must shortly be done.

7 Behold, I come quickly: blessed is he that keepeth the sayings of the prophecy of this book.

8 And I John saw these things, and heard them. And when I had heard and seen, I fell down to worship before the feet of the angel which shewed me these things.

9 Then saith he unto me, See thou do it not: for I am thy fellowservant, and of thy brethren the prophets, and of them which keep the sayings of this book: worship God.

**Memory Verse**
Revelation 22:2

**Background Scripture**
Revelation 22

**Devotional Reading**
Ephesians 3:14-21

May 29

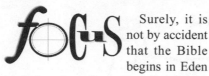 Surely, it is not by accident that the Bible begins in Eden and then it ends in Paradise where many of the features of the earlier Eden have been restored.

Most obvious among the symbols that take us back to Eden is the tree of life. When Adam and Eve sinned they were barred from Eden. One reason for their expulsion was to keep them from eating of the fruit of this tree and living forever. Now in John's vision of the Holy City, a tree of life grows on each side of the river, situated so that God's servants once more can have easy access to it.

The fruitfulness of the first Eden likewise is reproduced in the New Jerusalem, with fruit ripening in each month of the year. John surely is referring to the Genesis calamity when he tells us that nothing under the curse will be found in the city. Eden has returned in all its original blessedness and God's servants once again reside there.

## For a Lively Start

ഇന്റെ

One of the most amazing descriptions John gives us of the Holy City is his remark in 22:4 that God's servants living in the city will see His face. During the entire Bible before this moment in its final chapter, humans have been forbidden to see God. On countless occasions, He spoke to one or more of His people. They were allowed to hear Him. However, seeing Him would be fatal, they were warned.

In that famous story in Exodus 33 Moses was permitted to glimpse the back of God, but not His face. "You would not survive it," God told him. Several times in the Old Testament a person who thinks they have come too close to seeing God will exclaim, "Woe is me!" Now, in Heaven, at last God's people will be allowed to look His face and live.

| Teaching Outline | Daily Bible Readings |
|---|---|
| I. The Holy City—Revelation 22:1-5<br>A. The Water of Life, 1<br>B. The Trees of Life, 2<br>C. Free from the Curse, 3a<br>D. Servants of God, 3b-4<br>E. God Is the Light, 5<br>II. Faithful and True Sayings—Revelation 22:6<br>III. Christ's Blessing—Revelation 22:7<br>IV. Angel Worship Forbidden—Revelation 22:8-9 | Mon. Bowing Before the Father<br>*Ephesians 3:14-21*<br>Tue. A Glimpse of God's Glory<br>*Exodus 33:17-23*<br>Wed. The Throne of God<br>*Psalm 47:5-9*<br>Thu Living Water<br>*John 4:7-15*<br>Fri. The Tree of Life<br>*Revelation 2:1-7*<br>Sat. I Am Coming Soon<br>*Revelation 22:10-21*<br>Sun. Worship God!<br>*Revelation 22:1-9* |

# Verse by Verse

Revelation 22:1-9

## I. The Holy City—Revelation 22:1-5

### A. The Water of Life, 1

**22:1 And he shewed me a pure river of water of life, clear as crystal, proceeding out of the throne of God and of the Lamb.**

John had an ear for water metaphors. In the fourth chapter of his Gospel, he told of the time when Jesus offered the Samaritan woman "living water." Then in the seventh chapter of his Gospel, he included the time when Jesus addressed the festival crowds and offered them "rivers of living water" (which, according to John, referred to the Holy Spirit whom Jesus would give them). In vs. 17 of Revelation's final chapter, John invites anyone who is thirsty to come drink the water of life at no cost.

In John's earlier description of God's throne, he told us that before the throne was a sea of glass that looked like crystal (Rev. 4:6). Now the river that flows from the throne is described as "sparkling like crystal" (TEV) or "as bright as crystal" (RSV). Unlike so many polluted streams today, this river is pure.

### B. The Trees of Life, 2

**2 In the midst of the street of it, and on either side of the river, was there the tree of life, which bare twelve manner of fruits, and yielded her fruit every month: and the leaves of the tree were for the healing of the nations.**

The KJV in v. 2 seems to be positioning trees of life, one in the middle of the main street and one on either side of the river. Most of our newer versions think John's phrase about the middle of the street belongs to the verse above and therefore means to tell us that the river flows down the middle of the street. John seems to be suggesting a picture not unlike the section of Paris where the Seine River splits the picturesque boulevard, in effect flowing down the middle of it.

None of us has ever seen a tree that yields a dozen different kinds of fruit with a different type ready to harvest each month and with the additional benefit of leaves that have healing powers. This could mean the leaves have a medicinal value for people worldwide (sort of a universal health system), or it could imply that these leaves would heal rifts between the world's nations. John's reference to "healing" is vague.

### C. Free from the Curse, 3a

**3a And there shall be no more curse:**

The punishments Adam and Eve incurred for their sin got them evicted from Eden and ushered in suffering

383

and death as part of the human lot. God cursed the ground, making it less fruitful and thereby making man's labor strenuous. Childbirth now entailed travail for women. In Genesis 3 a gamut of punishments are described. This entire package is usually referred to as "the curse." Galatians 3:13 tells us that "God redeemed us from the curse." In the last half of Romans 5 the apostle Paul lists parts of the curse brought upon us by Adam and shows how Christ repaired each penalty. Vs. 3a tells us in effect that God has turned back the clock to the Beginning and has restored Eden to its pre-sin condition. John will go on to list evidences of the curse that will never be found in the New Jerusalem.

### D. Servants of God, 3b-4

**3b . . . but the throne of God and of the Lamb shall be in it; and his servants shall serve him:**

**4 And they shall see his face; and his name shall be in their foreheads.**

"His servants" could refer to the heavenly beings who perpetually praise the One on the throne, but more likely, it means all the redeemed who like the martyrs in Chapter 21 stand always night and day before the throne ready to serve their Maker and Savior.

We learned in John's vision in Revelation 4 and 5 that the Lamb is entitled to stand in the middle of God's throne. From that point on we see the two of them—God and the Lamb—together on the throne. One of the clearest and finest truths imparted to us through Revelation is the equality of God and Christ. The One who "emptied himself" (Phil. 2:7) to serve humanity on Earth returned to His former glory beside the Father in Heaven. Throughout John's vision the names reserved for God earlier in the Scriptures are now applied without hesitation to Jesus as well. Moreover, God and the Lamb share the throne.

### E. God Is the Light, 5

**5 And there shall be no night there; and they need no candle, neither light of the sun; for the Lord God giveth them light: and they shall reign for ever and ever.**

One of the Bible's most common images for evil is darkness. Satan rules over the kingdom of darkness (Eph. 6:12). Christians have been set free from the ignorance and evil of that dark realm (Col. 1:13). John favors this metaphor for evil. He uses it repeatedly in his letters, and he began his Gospel by telling us that Jesus is the one true light:

In him was life, and the life was the light of men. The light shines in the darkness, and the darkness has not overcome it. There was a man sent from God, whose name was John. He came for testimony, to bear witness to the light, that all might believe through him. He was not the light, but came to bear witness to the light. The true light that enlightens every man was coming into the world (1:4-10, RSV).

Now, as John writes the closing words in the Holy Scriptures, he returns to this figure to assure us that in Heaven no darkness or night will be known, for the true Light will always be there to illuminate that glorious realm. Vs. 5 repeats the descriptions in 21:23, 25.

## II. Faithful and True Sayings—Revelation 22:6

**6 And he said unto me, These sayings are faithful and true: and the Lord God of the holy prophets sent his angel to shew unto his servants the things which must shortly be done.**

The speaker here is the angel who chaperones John on this final grand tour of the Holy City. Likely, the "sayings" the angel commends here are the things John has heard since 21:9 when this angel became his escort, but some think this verse refers to the entire Apocalypse.

Several times during Revelation, some heavenly being has assured John that a particular vision or statement was "faithful and true." Usually the prompter added that it was worth writing down. In this instance, the angel confirms the dependability of what John has been seeing and hearing by attributing this latest revelation to the same source enjoyed by the holy prophets of old. If we trust them, then the angel tells us we have every reason to trust what John has written down for us.

Some interpreters of Revelation put heavy emphasis on the angel's description of John's vision as a revelation of "the things which must shortly be done." They may be right in limiting most of John's vision to events in the years soon after John wrote them down, but we do well to note that Heaven's time keeping seldom matches ours. Phrases such as "the last days" refer to an age that appears to have lasted almost 2,000 years. Therefore, God's "soon" may not match ours.

## III. Christ's Blessing—Revelation 22:7

**7 Behold, I come quickly: blessed is he that keepeth the sayings of the prophecy of this book.**

To "keep the sayings" may mean either to treasure them or to obey them.

One recurrent theme in the New Testament is the promise of Jesus' return. The early Church was motivated and shaped by this hope. In this verse and in the remainder of this final Bible chapter the Lord Jesus repeats this promise and stresses that He will not delay. However, as we just noticed, the Lord's use of the word "quickly" and our use of it is not always identical.

## IV. Angel Worship Forbidden—Revelation 22:8-9

**8 And I John saw these things, and heard them. And when I had heard and seen, I fell down to worship before the feet of the angel which shewed me these things.**

**9 Then saith he unto me, See thou do it not: for I am thy fellowservant, and of thy brethren the prophets, and of them which keep the sayings of this book: worship God.**

These two verses repeat a similar experience John describes in 19:10. They ring true with the consistent biblical message that we should never worship angels. Angels are created beings just as we are. The angel's message is clear: "Worship God."

ഇൗൽ

## Evangelistic Emphasis

In the midst of the glory that surrounds Revelation 22's description of eternal life with God, there is a sad, and at first look shocking, statement: "Let him who does wrong continue to do wrong; let him who is vile continue to be vile" (v. 11, NIV). Why is such a statement contained in this chapter? It is there because it is part of the reality of end time. On that day there will be no time for repentance. The time for conversion will be past. There will be no choices, no options, no easy outs, no sweetness and light for those who have rejected the Lord.

What we have seen in this Scripture sets the stage for evangelism. We need to be busy with it. There are some people who will never believe, but you and I do not know who they are. The responsibility is ours to spread the gospel, and the choice is theirs to accept or reject it.

Paul's charge to the evangelist is appropriate here: "Preach the Word, be prepared in season and out of season, correct, rebuke and encourage – with great patience and careful instruction. For the time will come when men will not put up with sound doctrine... They will turn their ears away from truth and turn aside to myths" (2 Tim. 4:2-4 NIV).

ॐ

## Memory Selection

"In the midst of the street of it, and on either side of the river, was there the tree of life, which bare twelve manner of fruits, and yielded her fruit every month: and the leaves of the tree were for the healing of the nations."

*Revelation 22:2*

Heaven is a beautiful city with a river running through it. The preceding verse describes the river as having the pure water of life, and being clear as a crystal. Most people in America are accustomed to pure water. That distinguishes us from millions in under-developed nations. Consequently, we are going to read this verse differently from them.

I've been in Pakistan a couple of times. Once, in a very small Christian village, I saw life as it might have been a thousand years ago. In the large irrigation canal, young boys were out in it bathing water buffaloes. A mother on the canal bank was bathing her infant child. Another woman was washing dishes and pots, while another did the family laundry. About this time, a beautiful girl walked down to the canal with a water pot balanced on her head. She had come to get household water.

I was in that remote village with a bishop in the Church of Pakistan, and we dedicated the space where those Christians would construct a mud-brick church building. When their pastor reads these verses to them about crystal clear water running through God's city, what will it mean to these people who have known only water that is just this side of murky?

Revelation's river is symbolic. These villagers know how to value that symbol. We all look forward to heaven's reality.

## Weekday Problems

The information John received concerning the End Time and the city of God was so very precious to him. He had suffered along with other Christians for so long, and now he had been given a look into the glories that await them all. He overflowed with appreciation to the angel who told and showed him these marvelous sights.

He fell down to worship at the feet of this angel. The angel told him not to do this, that he was a simply a fellow-servant along with John and the prophets. John should worship God. The direction and motivation for worship can be a real issue. Here is a little story about it.

Jerry was a very eligible bachelor. He was good husband material, and the women knew it. He was also a good Christian. It was unthinkable that he would marry and establish a family with anyone other than a Christian mate.

Beverly was not a Christian and had no particular interest in becoming one – at least until she met Jerry. To make a short story of it, she joined his church and eventually the two of them were married. She was attracted to Jerry, but not to the Lord. She was devoted to him but not to Him. What do you suppose the angel who spoke to John would say to her?

Is it possible that any of us might be motivated in our church relationship more out of family tradition, or because a loved one expects it of us, than out of love for the Lord? Worship God only, and out of right motivation, the angel might tell us.

## Church Signs

A smile is a curve that can set a lot of things straight.
Two rules of life: Rule 1, God is in control. Rule 2, See Rule 1.
God sends you flowers every spring: Thank Him.
Wal-Mart is not the only saving place. Come on in.
The mind grows by taking in. The heart grows by giving out.
The thing to spend on your children is time.
Pulling together can keep everyone from falling apart.
Patience is a virtue that carries a lot of wait.
There's a mighty GO in Gospel.
In the dark? Follow the Son.
Every home is a school. What are you teaching?
Love is a choice. Make a good one.
Without God we don't have a prayer.
Can't sleep? Try counting your blessings.

# This Lesson in Your Life

It is quickly noticeable as we read this lesson that there are two distinct groups of people involved. There are those who have washed their robes in the blood of the Lamb, a word picture that describes Jesus removing our sins and making us clean (v.14). They have His name written on their foreheads (v.4), which is to say His imprint is on their lives, and it indicates to Whom they belong. These are the people who came when they were invited, who were thirsty for the water of life, and wanted His gift (v.17).

On the other hand, there are those who are in an opposite situation. Right up until the very end they continued in their vile ways and wrongdoing (v.11). They are so corrupt that Scripture calls them dogs, and lists their horrible sins. They love and practice falsehood. These people are "outside," which is the saddest of places to be (v. 15).

What we are reading about here are consequences that result from choices, and this takes us directly into this lesson in our lives. These two very different groups of people did not get where they were by accident. It did not "just happen." It came about as the result of how they responded to the mercy, love, and grace of God.

Second Peter 3:9 tells us that the Lord is patient with us. He does not want anyone to be "outside" (as those mentioned above). Rather than perishing, He wants everyone to come to repentance. In this passage Peter describes the end of the world, and tells us that because we know the present world will end, we should live holy, godly lives and look forward to the day of God.

Being able to look forward to the day of God is a great blessing. Though He has given us the will to live out our lives here, and we value each day of life, we know that this world is not a forever thing. Knowing this, we hold more dearly to the expectation of a vastly greater life spent in the presence of the Father, the Son, the Spirit, and all the holy angels. We expect to be numbered with the heavenly multitude, including those whom we have loved on earth. This is our hope; it is our expectation. God has given us a choice to make, and we have accepted this as His gift.

As we read the last chapter in Revelation we are impressed that there are three witnesses who appear in it to assure us of its reality and truthfulness of its message: an angel, the apostle John, and Jesus Christ all speak to us.

We are impressed by verse 14: "Blessed are they that do his commandments, that they may have right to the tree of life, and may enter in through the gates into the city." We are thankful to God that in this life He has given us the opportunity to obey Him and to make this choice that has eternal consequences.

Because we look forward to the day of God, we thrill to hear Jesus say "Surely, I come quickly." In response, we all say, "Amen. Even so, come, Lord Jesus."

**GETTING
THE FACTS STRAIGHT**

**1. What was the source of the river? (It came from what location?)**

The river came from the throne of God, from Him. One commentary notes that the hymn, "Shall We Gather at the River?" mistakenly says the river "flows by the throne of God," not from it, and that it's important to know it is "from" God.

**2. Describe the river.**

It is a pure river of the water of life, and is clear as crystal.

**3. What kind of tree grew along either side of the river?**

It was the tree of life, with fruit year-round and healing leaves. Hendriksen's commentary says this represents the superabundant character of our salvation and the full communion we have with God. (Note also Gen. 2:9.)

**4. There will be no more curse in the city. Instead, what, thing very different from a curse will be there?**

The throne of God and of the Lamb will be there. Notice that by this wording God and the Lamb share the throne.

**5. Why will there be no night there?**

There will be no need of light from a lamp or from the sun, for the Lord God will give the light.

**6. What in verse 6 adds validity to Revelation?**

The angel says the words are faithful and true, and that the God of the prophets sent the angel with the message.

**7. What was John's reaction to the angel who had brought all this information?**

He fell down at the angel's feet to worship him.

**8. What was the angel's response to this?**

The angel told him not to do it, that he was a fellow servant with John's brothers, the prophets. (Notice that the answer places John on the level with the Old Testament prophets. This, along with the answer to question six. emphasizes that Revelation is Scripture.)

**9. What will happen to anyone who takes away or adds to the words of Revelation?**

Anyone who adds to it will have the plagues described in the book added to him. Anyone who takes away will have his share in the tree of life and in the holy city taken away.

**10. At the close of the chapter, what does the one who testified to these things say he will soon do? What follows this statement?**

He says "Surely I come quickly." This is followed by the response: "Amen. Even so, come, Lord Jesus."

Symbols are important to us. We need them because they point us to things we need to know or remember. They are a visual representative of some concept, idea, occurrence or thing. They "stand" for something.

On the battleground at Gettysburg there some very old "witness trees." They were growing there in 1863 when the battle was fought, and were (in a manner of speaking) witnesses to what took place. In recent years one of the locust trees on Cemetery Hill was struck by lightning. It made the news because it was growing there at the time and very near to the spot where Lincoln gave his Gettysburg Address. These trees stand for something, and add a special aura to that hallowed place. They represent "being there."

Russia has a bear for its symbol, and England uses the lion. In America we have the spread eagle, and these creatures signify a ferocious, protective image.

Revelation is replete with symbols. If we removed its symbols there would not be much left in the book. There are locusts that looked like horses with human faces with women's hair and lion's teeth, and tails with stingers. There is an enormous red dragon with seven heads and ten horns. There are hideous beasts that make England's lion look like a kitten.

With all these nightmarish creatures for comparison, do you remember the most striking symbol in the entire book? It is a little Lamb, with bloody stains and looking as if it had been slain. Can you imagine it? A dead-looking bloody Lamb gains the victory over all these ferocious satanic creations of horror.

In a fitting sense of the word, it is John the Baptist who introduces us to the Lamb. John was baptizing on the other side of the Jordan, near Bethany, when he saw Jesus coming toward him. He said, "Look, the Lamb of God, who takes away the sin of the world" (John 1:29 NIV).

The blood on the Lamb is easy to explain. Jesus said, "And I, if I be lifted up from the earth, will draw all men to Myself" (John 12:32 NIV). Nails and a spear- thrust brought the blood. The Cross and the Lamb are mighty symbols, and the two really cannot be separated from each other.

℘℘

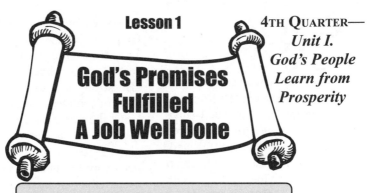

## Lesson 1

4TH QUARTER—
*Unit I.
God's People
Learn from
Prosperity*

June 5

# God's Promises Fulfilled A Job Well Done

## Joshua 1:1b-6; 11:16-19, 21-23

It came to pass, that the LORD spake unto Joshua the son of Nun, Moses' minister, saying,

2a Moses my servant is dead; now therefore arise, go over this Jordan, thou, and all this people, unto the land which I do give to them . . . .

3a Every place that the sole of your foot shall tread upon, that have I given unto you . . . .

4 From the wilderness and this Lebanon even unto the great river, the river Euphrates, all the land of the Hittites, and unto the great sea toward the going down of the sun, shall be your coast.

5 There shall not any man be able to stand before thee all the days of thy life: as I was with Moses, so I will be with thee: I will not fail thee, nor forsake thee.

6 Be strong and of a good courage: for unto this people shalt thou divide for an inheritance the land, which I sware . . . to give them.

**11:16-23**

16 So Joshua took all that land, the hills, and all the south country, and all the land of Goshen, and the valley, and the plain, and the mountain of Israel . . . .

17 Even from the mount Halak, that goeth up to Seir, even unto Baal-gad in the valley of Lebanon under mount Hermon: and all their kings he took . . . and slew them.

18 Joshua made war a long time with all those kings.

19 There was not a city that made peace with the children of Israel, save the Hivites the inhabitants of Gibeon: all other they took in battle.

21 And at that time came Joshua, and cut off the Anakims from the mountains, from Hebron, from Debir, from Anab, and from all the mountains of Judah, and from all the mountains of Israel: Joshua destroyed them utterly . . . .

22 There was none of the Anakims left . . . : only in Gaza, in Gath, and in Ashdod, there remained.

23 So Joshua took the whole land, according to all that the LORD said unto Moses; and Joshua gave it for an inheritance unto Israel . . . . And the land rested from war.

---

**Memory Verse**
Joshua 11:15

**Background Scripture**
Joshua 1:1-6; 11-12

**Devotional Reading**
Acts 26:1-7

# *fO**C**uS*

In Numbers 14 we read about the first time God brought His people to invade the Promised Land. Twelve spies—one from each tribe—explored the full extent of that fruitful land. They returned to the Israelite camp with samples of the fruit and with discouraging tales. "The warriors there are huge," they reported. "We could never defeat them." Therefore, Israel retreated and died in the desert.

## For a Lively Start

Many Bible readers are troubled by the carnage described in Joshua. Joshua and his troops commit genocide, slaughtering women, children, young and old.

This much killing will bother any sensitive soul, but it may help if we hear the Bible telling us that the blood

Now, under Joshua, God has brought His people back to Canaan to try again. This time God warns them—and Joshua often echoes that warning— "Be strong and of good courage." Lack of confidence and faith defeated Israel the first time. Joshua does not want this to happen again. Sure, the giants are enormous. Yes, the cities are massively fortified. However, Joshua keeps reminding his people, "The Lord our God will fight for us."

The only limit to God's power is what we think He cannot do.

ഇൗയ

did not flow because Joshua's men were savages. They killed because God told them to. Joshua 11:20 tells us, "It was the LORD himself who hardened their hearts to wage war against Israel, so that he might destroy them totally, exterminating them without mercy, as the LORD had commanded Moses" (NIV).

The prophets later explain that God was punishing Canaan's gross immorality, such as burning babies on their altars (Ezek. 20:27-38; Jer. 7; 19; 32).

| Teaching Outline | Daily Bible Readings |
|---|---|
| I. God's Charge to Joshua—Joshua 1:1b-6<br>   A. Cross the Jordan, 1b-2<br>   B. The Land Is Yours, 3-4<br>   C. I Will Back You Up, 5<br>   D. Divide the Land, 6<br>II. Successful Warfare—Joshua 11:16-19<br>   A. The Land Joshua Took, 16-17<br>   B. The Kings He Defeated, 18-19<br>III. Victory Over the Giants—Joshua 11:21-22<br>IV. Rest from War—Joshua 11:23 | Mon. Hope in God's Promises<br>   *Acts 26:1-7*<br>Tue. God's Promises to Israel<br>   *Romans 9:1-5*<br>Wed. Children of the Promise<br>   *Romans 9:6-12*<br>Thu. Children of the Living God<br>   *Romans 9:22-26*<br>Fri. Since We Have These Promises<br>   *2 Corinthians 6:14-7:1*<br>Sat. Abound in Hope<br>   *Romans 15:7-13*<br>Sun. God's Promises to Moses Fulfilled<br>   *Joshua 1:1b-6; 11:16-19, 21-23* |

# Verse by Verse

Joshua 1:1b-6; 11:16-19, 21-23

## I. God's Charge to Joshua—Joshua 1:1b-6

### A. Cross the Jordan, 1b-2

**1b . . .it came to pass, that the LORD spake unto Joshua the son of Nun, Moses' minister, saying,**

**2 Moses my servant is dead; now therefore arise, go over this Jordan, thou, and all this people, unto the land which I do give to them, even to the children of Israel.**

These verses link the history in the book of Joshua to the tales of Moses in the Pentateuch. Joshua had been Moses' right-hand man ever since the earliest days of the Exodus. In Exodus 18-20 we see Joshua as the first leader of Israel's army and then as Moses' attendant (this is the meaning of "minister" in 1b) at Mt. Sinai. Now Moses is dead and Joshua must take his place. Joshua will lead his people into the land God promised to them.

One of the most difficult times in the life of any nation, organization, or church is when a long-time trusted leader dies or retires. Often we find it hard to transfer our affections and trust to the successor. God's visible support of Joshua will help him bridge this gap as he assumes the mantle of his mentor.

### B. The Land Is Yours, 3-4

**3 Every place that the sole of your foot shall tread upon, that have I given unto you, as I said unto Moses.**

**4 From the wilderness and this Lebanon even unto the great river, the river Euphrates, all the land of the Hittites, and unto the great sea toward the going down of the sun, shall be your coast.**

God had been promising the land to Abraham's descendants ever since Genesis 11. Generation after generation He renewed the promise as part of His covenant with the Hebrews. Now the time has come for Israel to move into the land and make it their own.

Notice that the description of the real estate included everything from the desert south of the Negev up to and including the snow-capped peaks in Lebanon. East to west the land stretched from the Euphrates River (northern Iraq today) across what we call eastern Turkey (the powerful Hittite kingdom) all the way west to the shores of the Mediterranean Sea.

In the book of Joshua we see this promise fulfilled. God gives Israel all the land He promised to them and tells them it is theirs as long as they obey Him. Many believers—both Christians and Jews—think the land-grant promise still guarantees this territory to the Jews.

## C. I Will Back You Up, 5

**5 There shall not any man be able to stand before thee all the days of thy life: as I was with Moses, so I will be with thee: I will not fail thee, nor forsake thee.**

Anyone who has seen a large church make the adjustments to follow a new pastor after one whose ministry lasted several decades will appreciate what Joshua faces now that Moses is gone. God backs up His promises to Joshua. When Israel sees the flood-stage waters of Jordan back up to allow them to cross into Canaan, none of them will doubt after this that Joshua leads with the same authority and power God had vested in Moses.

God's promise never to leave or forsake Joshua becomes His promise to believers today (see Hebrews 13:5).

## D. Divide the Land, 6

**6 Be strong and of a good courage: for unto this people shalt thou divide for an inheritance the land, which I sware unto their fathers to give them.**

God's charge to Joshua to "be strong and of good courage" became Joshua's rallying cry to his people whenever they set out on a new stage of their conquest. As one of the two faithful spies, Joshua was acutely aware that a failure of courage would be fatal to Israel. The debacle at Kadesh-barnea (Num. 14) must not be repeated. God promises Joshua that he soon will get to divide the Promised Land to the various tribes if only he will trust in God's strength to win. After many centuries, God is ready to give His people the land He had promised to Abraham, Isaac, Jacob, and the many generations that had come after them.

## II. Successful Warfare—Joshua 11:16-19

## A. The Land Joshua Took, 16-17

**16 So Joshua took all that land, the hills, and all the south country, and all the land of Goshen, and the valley, and the plain, and the mountain of Israel, and the valley of the same;**

**17 Even from the mount Halak, that goeth up to Seir, even unto Baal-gad in the valley of Lebanon under mount Hermon: and all their kings he took, and smote them, and slew them.**

The first 11 chapters of Joshua tell in some detail how Joshua and his troops with God's aid wiped out the mighty Canaanite armies led by the fearsome kings who had intimidated the Israelites' ancestors. Vss. 16-17 summarize the preceding battle stories by telling us that Joshua's men now control all the territory from Egypt in the south to Mt. Hermon's snow-covered heights in the north. The Jews vanquished all the armies and killed their kings. Later in Joshua, the defeated kings will be listed by name and domain.

Although these early records in Joshua are easy and quick to read, the historian in vs. 18 will correct this impression by telling us that the conquest of Canaan took far more years than the hasty reading implies.

## B. The Kings He Defeated, 18-19

**18 Joshua made war a long time with all those kings.**

**19 There was not a city that**

made peace with the children of Israel, save the Hivites the inhabitants of Gibeon: all other they took in battle.

Later in the book of Joshua, as the various tribal divisions of land are described in detail, we will learn that in almost every tribe's area some nest of Canaanite defenders managed to hang on to their territory. Vs. 19 is right. These undefeated cities did not "make peace" with Israel. The Hebrew tribe who was given that land just failed to drive out the original owners and chose to leave them there, much to their later hurt.

### III. Victory Over the Giants— Joshua 11:21-22

**21 And at that time came Joshua, and cut off the Anakims from the mountains, from Hebron, from Debir, from Anab, and from all the mountains of Judah, and from all the mountains of Israel: Joshua destroyed them utterly with their cities.**

**22 There was none of the Anakims left in the land of the children of Israel: only in Gaza, in Gath, and in Ashdod, there remained.**

The KJV translation "Anakims" fails to recognize that *im* is a plural ending for Hebrew words (such as

*cherubim*, the plural of *cherub*). Adding an *s* to *Anakim* is the equivalent of doubling the *s*.

The first spies came back from Canaan terrified by the giants. These fellows were the Anakim, whose main lair was the mountainous regions of the land that later would be called Judah— the southern part of the Promised Land. The only giants who survived Joshua's attack were those in the Philistine strongholds along Canaan's southern Mediterranean shores. You may recall that Gath, mentioned here, was later the home of the famous giant Goliath who fought David.

### IV. Rest from War—Joshua 11:23

**23 So Joshua took the whole land, according to all that the LORD said unto Moses; and Joshua gave it for an inheritance unto Israel according to their divisions by their tribes. And the land rested from war.**

In the chapters that follow in Joshua, we are told the process used to divide the land among the tribes, and the actual dividing lines for the tribal portions are recorded quite precisely. A map of this era in a good study Bible or a Bible atlas will give us an instant view of detailed material that takes eight chapters to tell.

∞⌘

### Evangelistic Emphasis

Joshua has a tremendously difficult assignment given to him. He is to lead hundreds of thousands of people across a flooded river into a hostile land. When he gets there he is to defeat the local kings, take the territory and settle the tribes of Israel into their allotted areas.

As complicated and formidable as this seemed, there was a definite bright spot. God told him, "I will be with thee: will not fail thee, nor forsake thee." He was told that his way would be prosperous if he meditated on the book of the law and followed it closely (Vs. 5-8).

We see a principle here that is consistent throughout Scripture. God will not demand anything that is impossible. Further, when He gives a command, he will help with its fulfillment. Joshua had a big job ahead of him, but had the assurance that the Lord would be with him. That makes all the difference.

The Great Commission (Matt. 28:19-20) says we are to teach all nations. Mark 16:15-16 uses the words, "all the world" and "every creature." That is a lot of people waiting to be taught.

Just as God promised to be with Joshua, he makes the same promise to us. As Jesus gave the Commission to preach, He said, "I am with you always, even unto the end of the world." We have our work cut out for us. The Lord will help.

### Memory Selection

୫୦୯ଷ

"As the LORD commanded Moses his servant, so did Moses command Joshua, and so did Joshua; he left nothing undone of all that the LORD commanded Moses."                                    *Joshua 11:15*

By the time we arive at the point of our memory verse, Israel, under Joshua's command, has made great strides. They have crossed the Jordan, the walls of Jericho have tumbled down, and cities have fallen. The covenant has been renewed at Mt. Ebal (8:30-35). The sun has even stood still for them (10:12-13).

Joshua has been a busy man, and has done an amazing job. He has much to his credit. The spectacular results, though, ultimately lie with God. Whatever natural talents Joshua may have utilized, the main thing that he had going for him personally was his obedience to God. "He left nothing undone."

It takes a humble person to yield to God's will. It takes an exceptionally humble person to yield to God's will totally and always. God told Moses. Moses told Joshua. Joshua obeyed. It is that simple.

It is that simple except when you or I try to do it. At that point complications set in. Our best intentions fail. We slip up and fall down. As Paul said, we do what we do not want to do, and do not do what we want to do (Rom. 7:15-20). Is it not wonderful that we have a forgiving God?

We have to admire Joshua's record. He is a great role model. What do you suppose he said when he prayed? Maybe, "Thy will be done on earth as it is in heaven – and let it begin with me."

# Weekday Problems

Have you ever felt that your world was tumbling in around you? Maybe like the day the baby's fever kept rising, the dog chewed the new rug, the washing machine made its last gasp and shut down, and the postman delivered the checking account overdrawn notice from the bank. What is next? the young mother had to wonder. Some days (or weeks, months, or years) are difficult to survive, because life brings problems much greater than a chewed up rug.

Joshua's life was going about as smoothly as he might have wished, considering the weight he carried on his shoulders. He was successfully cleansing paganism from the land. However, some crafty Gibeonites got the better of him (chapter 9). Their city would have been on Joshua's list to be destroyed. They sent a delegation that pretended to be from a distant country, asking to make a treaty. Without consulting the Lord, the treaty was made and ratified by an oath. Later, when Joshua discovered the deception, he would not break the oath and did not destroy their city.

Joshua did not destroy Gibeon, but he did make its citizens become servants: wood cutters and water carriers. Would you say he made the best of a bad situation? After this episode he continued his good work.

Even those of us who trust the Lord and do our best to obey are going to have some bad times. Let us make the best of them, as Joshua did, and get on with our lives.

---

## Clear Profit

Two city boys paid a farmer cash for a mule. Two days later the mule got sick and died. When the city guys came to pick up their mule, the farmer told them the sad news, but he refused to return their money.

After some fussing, they said okay, but could they at least have the dead mule? The farmer was more than glad to be rid of it.

In town several weeks later, he bumped into the mule buyers. "I'm curious, guys," he asked. "What did you do with that dead mule?"

"Oh," they smiled, "we sold him."

"Sold him?" The farmer was incredulous. "Who would buy a dead mule?"

"It was simple," they explained. "We raffled him off for two bucks a chance. Finally got $884 for the critter."

"Wasn't the winner upset when he found out the mule was dead?"

"Yeah. He yelped some, so we returned his two dollars."

# This Lesson in Your Life

The challenge that Joshua faced was massive. His job was to claim the promise that God had made hundreds of years earlier to Abraham, who left Haran to go to the land that God would show him. That land was Canaan, and God promised it to him and his descendants. The only land that Abraham ever actually owned there was the burial site he purchased for his wife (Gen. 23).

There were cities In Canaan that had fine houses made of stone, but Abraham never lived in one. He, Isaac, and Jacob, three generations, lived in tents and moved from place to place with their herds. Abraham's grandson Jacob took the family to Egypt, where they eventually became slaves. After 400 years of bondage they spent 40 years wandering in the wilderness with Moses on their way to the Promised Land.

With the death of Moses, the responsibility of leading the children of Israel across the Jordan, and of conquering the land of Canaan that had been promised to them, fell on Joshua. Hundreds of years of history – centuries of waiting for the fulfilled promise – depended on Joshua's leadership. Obviously, he was going to need to listen closely to God's instructions for getting the job done.

What can you and I learn from this man that will impact our own lives? Is there some useable information here? Can we reach back (well over 3,000 years) and bring Joshua's values into today's world? Let us see what we can find.

Our memory verse can begin a list of values learned from Joshua. He obeyed God and left nothing undone. His was a total commitment. When God spoke to him (1:7) He instructed Joshua to turn neither to the right nor to the left in carrying out his instructions. It was straight ahead for this man. If all Christians had this kind of focus and determination, we might wonder what changes it would bring into the world. We can work on it in our individual lives and see how it works for us. This verse also commanded him to be strong and courageous. Service to God is not only quiet prayer and meditation. It calls for grit and backbone.

Joshua teaches us about accepting difficult and highly important responsibilities. He did not go around volunteering for the easy jobs and leaving the heavy work to others.

He was consistent throughout his lifetime. Numbers 11:28 tells us that since his youth he had assisted Moses. We do not know how young he was when he first began helping Moses, but we know he died at age 110 (Josh. 24:29). He did not rush into an early retirement in God's service.

Can you think of other ways we can apply this lesson in our lives?

**GETTING THE FACTS STRAIGHT**

**1. At what point in time did God speak to Joshua?**
It was after Moses died. Apparently it was following the 30 days of mourning following his death (Deut. 34:8).

**2. Joshua was commanded to arise and do what?**
He was to go over the Jordan with all the people in to the land that God was giving them.

**3. God was going to give them every place where a certain thing happened (something about their walking). What was it?**
God would give them every place that the sole of their feet tread upon, as He had said to Moses.

**4. What specific boundaries did God name for their territory?**
They would receive from the desert wilderness to Lebanon and the Euphrates River, to the Great Sea (Mediterranean).

**5. What kind of protection did God offer to Joshua?**
No one would be able to stand up against him. God would be with him all his life, and would not fail or forsake him.

**6. What personal characteristics did God demand from Joshua?**
He was commanded to be strong and of good courage.

**7. In 11:16-17, we're told that Joshua "took all that land." What, specifically, does it say he took? (It is OK to read your answer straight from the verses.)**
He took the hills, the south country, the land of Goshen, the valley, the plain, and the mountain of Israel with its valley.

**8. What did Joshua do with the kings he defeated?**
He struck them down and killed them.

**9. Was the war with these kings over with quickly?**
No, "Joshua made war a long time with these kings."

**10. Who were the only people (and their city) with whom Joshua made peace?**
He made peace with the Hivites in Gibeon. (Chapter 9 gives the details about how they deceived Joshua into making a treaty.)

King Ferdinand and Queen Isabella of Spain sent Christopher Columbus on his way with three little ships. Let us suppose the king and queen made a promise to Columbus. They promised that he and his descendants would regularly receive payment from the treasury of Spain.

In our imaginary story, let us fast-forward to the present time. In all the years since that promise was made, neither he nor any descendant ever received as much as a single coin. Let us further suppose that you are a descendant of Columbus. Would you be watching the mailbox hoping for a check from the Spanish government? Not likely. That promise is as dead as a doornail.

The time span in our little Columbus story covers more-or-less the time span that elapsed between when God made His promise to Abraham, and the time it was fulfilled. (At least the times are close enough to give us a general idea.)

This point is this: after many years, about 400 of them spent in Egyptian bondage, plus 40 wandering in the desert wilderness, Abraham's descendants were still expecting God's promise to come true. More importantly, God was still planning to keep His promise. Never for a moment had it been in question. You and I can feel assured that any promise God has made to us will be kept. We should not grow impatient. James says (1:12) that the person who perseveres will receive the crown of life God has promised to those who love Him.

Second Peter 1:4 says that God has given us His very great and precious promises. The preceding verse says that it is by His divine power that He gives us everything we need for life and godliness. This comes through our knowledge of Him who called us by His own glory and goodness.

This is God's promise to us that He will help us get through this world and ready for the next one. This is encouraging news, because it is not always easy to live a Christian life. In the verses that follow He gives us some excellent pointers to help us successfully get through life. Truth to be told, we all need all the help we can get. Let us take Him up on his promise.

First John 2:24-25 says that the person in whom the gospel message remains, and who remains in the Son and in the Father, has, "what He promised us – even eternal life" (NIV).

"Jesus Christ is the same yesterday and today and forever," Hebrews 13:8 (NIV) assures us. He will continue loving us and having our best interest at heart. God's dealing with us is not "iffy." It is not "Yes" and then "No." It is always positive and dependable. 2 Corinthians 1:20 says that God's promises to us are always "Yes" in Christ. We do not have to live too long before we discover life has some disappointments and failures. Some promises get broken. God does not disappoint. He never fails. He keeps His promises. He is a "Yes."

**Lesson 2**

# God Has Expectations Living by the Rules

### Joshua 1:7-16

Only be thou strong and very courageous, that thou mayest observe . . . all the law, which Moses my servant commanded thee: turn not from it to the right hand or to the left, that thou mayest prosper . . . .

8 This book of the law shall not depart out of thy mouth; but thou shalt meditate therein day and night, that thou mayest observe to do according to all that is written therein: for then thou shalt make thy way prosperous, and then thou shalt have good success.

9 Have not I commanded thee? Be strong and of a good courage; be not afraid, neither be thou dismayed: for the LORD thy God is with thee whithersoever thou goest.

10 Then Joshua commanded the officers of the people, saying,

11 Pass through the host, and command the people, saying, Prepare you victuals; for within three days ye shall pass over this Jordan, to go in to possess the land, which the LORD your God giveth you to possess it.

12 And to the Reubenites, and to the Gadites, and to half the tribe of Manasseh, spake Joshua, saying,

13 Remember the word which Moses the servant of the LORD commanded you, saying, The LORD your God hath given you rest, and hath given you this land.

14 Your wives, your little ones, and your cattle, shall remain in the land which Moses gave you on this side Jordan; but ye shall pass before your brethren armed, all the mighty men of valour, and help them;

15 Until the LORD have given your brethren rest, as he hath given you, and they also have possessed the land which the LORD your God giveth them: then ye shall return unto the land of your possession, and enjoy it, which Moses the Lord's servant gave you on this side Jordan toward the sunrising.

16 And they answered Joshua, saying, All that thou commandest us we will do, and whithersoever thou sendest us, we will go.

---

**Memory Verse**
Joshua 1:7

**Background Scripture**
Joshua 1:7-16

**Devotional Reading**
Deuteronomy 5:22-33

---

One of the Bible's more treasured descriptions of a godly man are the opening words of Psalm 1: "His delight is in the law of the Lord and in his law doth he meditate day and night."

In the generations before Christians wasted night after night watching mindless sit-coms or a non-stop diet of athletic events, it was common to see a much-used Bible on a table be- side an easy chair in the living room. Countless hours had been spent by the owner of that Bible as he meditated on its truths. Often that Bible reader was a respected leader in a nearby church.

As Joshua began his official leadership of his nation, God's first command to him was that he continually fills his heart and mind with the words of the law Moses had written down. Carefully observing God's laws would result in success and prosperity for Israel in their new land.

## For a Lively Start

ഇൻരു

Anyone who has served our country on extended overseas wartime duty knows what it means to be isolated from home and family for months or years at a time. Likewise, our men and women who serve as overseas missionaries go into this work knowing it will take them away from home perhaps for a lifetime.

The fighting men of three tribes— Reuben, Gad, and the half-tribe of Manasseh—promised Moses they would cross the river and fight to the war's end if he would allow their families to settle on the land east of Jordan. In vss. 12-16 Joshua is reminding these warriors of their earlier promise, and they assure him of their intent to be true to their word.

| Teaching Outline | Daily Bible Readings |
|---|---|
| I. God's Commands to Joshua— Joshua 1:7-9<br>  A. Know and Obey the Law, 7-8<br>  B. Be Courageous, 9<br>II. Joshua's Command to His Officers—Joshua 1:10-11<br>III. Joshua's Command to the Eastern Tribes—Joshua 1:12-15<br>  A. Remember Your Promise, 12-13<br>  B. Come Fight Without Families, 14-15<br>IV. The Three Tribes' Response, 16 | Mon. God's Commandments Given<br>    *Deuteronomy 5:28-33*<br>Tue. Listen and Learn<br>    *Deuteronomy 31:7-13*<br>Wed. Treasure God's Word<br>    *Psalm 119:9-16*<br>Thu. Walk in God's Ways<br>    *1 Kings 2:1-4*<br>Fri. As Long As He Sought God<br>    *2 Chronicles 26:1-5*<br>Sat. Teach Me, O Lord<br>    *Psalm 119:33-40*<br>Sun. The Key to Success<br>    *Joshua 1:7-16* |

# *Verse by Verse*

**Joshua 1:7-16**

## I. God's Commands to Joshua—Joshua 1:7-9

### A. Know and Obey the Law, 7-8

**7 Only be thou strong and very courageous, that thou mayest observe to do according to all the law, which Moses my servant commanded thee: turn not from it to the right hand or to the left, that thou mayest prosper whithersoever thou goest.**

**8 This book of the law shall not depart out of thy mouth; but thou shalt meditate therein day and night, that thou mayest observe to do according to all that is written therein: for then thou shalt make thy way prosperous, and then thou shalt have good success.**

Ever since the Garden of Eden the Lord has made it clear that, the way to prosper in His world is to do what He tells us to. He really does not have to punish those who disobey. Often the punishment is built into the law. Break it, and it will break you.

In vs. 7 the Lord connects being strong and courageous with being obedient to His laws. Later in the same verse, He connects Joshua's adherence to His laws to the success Joshua will have as his nation's leader. Both truths are important ones for any person elected to high office.

"The book of the law" would be what we call the Pentateuch. Those of us who have paid careful attention to its voluminous instructions can understand why Joshua would need to spend much of his time studying it in order to know all of its requirements.

Obeying these laws would assure Joshua's success at the helm. Obeying them would guarantee Israel's prosperity and success as a nation. Doing what God tells us to is also crucial to our own well-being as a nation. We ignore His rules at our risk.

### B. Be Courageous, 9

**9 Have not I commanded thee? Be strong and of a good courage; be not afraid, neither be thou dismayed: for the LORD thy God is with thee whithersoever thou goest.**

For the third time in nine verses, God commands Joshua to be strong and courageous. The importance of this comes clear when we remember that being weak and afraid cost one entire generation of Israel the right to enter and possess the Promised Land. Israel's fear of the giants coupled with their lack of dependence on God consigned Israel to 40 deadly years in the desert.

The reason God gives Joshua for not being afraid is that He the Lord will be with His people wherever they go in this conquest to win the land. God's people are never in the fray alone. Always He is with us. Repeatedly, Joshua will remind His people of this during the hard fighting that lie ahead.

## II. Joshua's Command to His Officers—Joshua 1:10-11

**10 Then Joshua commanded the officers of the people, saying,**

**11 Pass through the host, and command the people, saying, Prepare you victuals; for within three days ye shall pass over this Jordan, to go in to possess the land, which the LORD your God giveth you to possess it.**

Action is about to begin. After camping on the Plains of Moab for a period that almost doomed Israel's campaign to take Canaan (Num. 22-31), at last God's people are ready to cross the river and begin their assault on the land God promised them.

Joshua's order is quite practical. Prepare the food necessary for such an excursion. "Victuals" is a dated KJV term that means food. Joshua dispatches his officers to spread the word through the camp that in three days they will be on the move.

Good leaders always look ahead and make sure their people are equipped and prepared for the challenges that lie ahead.

## III. Joshua's Command to the Eastern Tribes—Joshua 1:12-15

**A. Remember Your Promise, 12-13**

**12 And to the Reubenites, and to the Gadites, and to half the tribe of Manasseh, spake Joshua, saying,**

**13 Remember the word which Moses the servant of the LORD commanded you, saying, The LORD your God hath given you rest, and hath given you this land.**

Numbers 32 contains the account of the request the eastern tribes made to Moses (before they were the eastern tribes). After Israel defeated Og, Sihon, and Balak—the kings on the east side of the Jordan—the tribal leaders of Gad, Reuben, and the half-tribe of Manasseh came to Moses with a proposal that they be allowed to settle down their families on the recently captured land. At first, Moses refused. It would not be fair to the other tribes; he told the men who came to him. A tough fight faced Israel when they crossed Jordan and took on the giants in that land. Everybody had to be part of that fight.

The leaders who asked for the land agreed. They assured Moses that their warriors would fight until the last battle had been won if he let them settle down their families and animals. With that promise firmly in place, Moses agreed for these tribes to move into the cities and farms Israel had conquered.

Now Joshua is reminding them of their promise. The "rest" he refers to in vs. 13 was the chance to end their wilderness wandering as they moved into their new homes in Gilead. Years later in Hebrews 4 that New Testament writer will teach at length about this same "rest," now applying the term to the entire land of Canaan and the relief the Israelites felt when they had a place to call home.

**B. Come Fight Without Families, 14-15**

**14 Your wives, your little ones, and your cattle, shall remain in the land which Moses gave you on this side Jordan; but ye shall pass before your brethren armed, all the mighty men of valour, and help them;**

**15 Until the LORD have given your brethren rest, as he hath given you, and they also have possessed the land which the LORD your God giveth them: then ye shall return unto the land of your possession, and enjoy it, which Moses the LORD's servant gave you on this side Jordan toward the sunrising.**

Perhaps implying a slight mistrust of the eastern tribes, or perhaps wanting to reassure the other tribes that Reuben, Gad, and the half-tribe of Manasseh were not getting a free ride, Joshua instructed the troops from these three tribes to march across the Jordan River out in front of the soldiers from the remaining tribes. So on the morning when Israel packs up and starts across the riverbed, these fighting men will lead the march.

Toward the end of the book of Joshua, when all the fighting in Canaan is ended, Joshua will release these faithful fighters to return home to their wives and children.

**IV. The Three Tribes' Response, 16**

**16 And they answered Joshua, saying, All that thou commandest us we will do, and whithersoever thou sendest us, we will go.**

The sincerity of these tribes seems to be unquestioned. Joshua's orders are acceptable to them. What they promised Moses they intended to fulfill.

Can people depend on us to keep promises we have made about things that may take a long time to work out?

℘℃

## Evangelistic Emphasis

Preparation, preparation, preparation: it paves the way for a successful outcome. Let us think about preparation needed before crossing the Jordan. First, Joshua told the people to prepare supplies for the crossing. Then he had to move the tribes from the plains of Moab where they were encamped, up to a spot nearer the river. He had to remind the tribes that preferred to live on the east side of the river of their responsibilities toward the tribes that would live across the river. All these things were preliminaries. The actual crossing would not be successful otherwise.

Just as Joshua had to prepare to do the work God had outlined for him, so do we. Evangelism is the spreading of the good news about Jesus Christ. We might want to do it without preparation, but this will not accomplish much.

Every person who wants to help spread the gospel should carefully study 1st and 2nd Timothy and Titus. Even if you are not an evangelist in the official sense of the word, every gospel teacher will find principles, as well as specifics, about teaching. The following are a few examples.

Paul tells Christian teachers to hold to the faith and keep a good conscience. They should be good examples in speech, life, faith, love, and purity. They should handle the word of truth correctly. Take Paul's admonitions to heart. They will help you prepare for the flooded rivers you may need to cross.

## Memory Selection

&)(CR

"Only be thou strong and very courageous, that thou mayest observe to do according to all the law, which Moses my servant commanded thee: turn not from it to the right and or to the left, that thou mayest prosper whithersoever thou goest."  *Joshua 1:7*

There is a very interesting word in our memory verse. It is the first one: "only." Something has been said previously that depends on "only." What has just been said is that no one will be able to stand up against Joshua, and that God will be with him and will not fail or forsake him. It is a promise, but a conditional one, made on the condition that Joshua observe the law and not veer away from it.

Someone might say, "I promise to give you a phone call tomorrow." This would be quite different from saying, "I promise to give you a phone call tomorrow only if I have any news to report by then." The "only" makes it conditional. Joshua is going to have to cooperate with God in order for this invasion of Canaan to succeed. Fortunately, Joshua has a good reputation for doing this (see 11:15).

In the memory verse, the fact that Joshua is to be strong and courageous seems tied to obeying the law. In our own contemporary society, we like the idea of being strong and courageous, but having to be obedient might go against the grain with many people. The fact is, strength and courage are often required in order to keep God's law. It is a point to be noted that the two great men in the entire exodus and Promised Land story, Moses and Joshua, are both obedient to the Lord.

## Weekday Problems

Bill was fortunate enough to land a very responsible position in a nationally prominent company. It paid well and the working environment was excellent. It was the kind of employment that might be considered a dream job. By the time he had been there a couple of years though, he began to feel cramped by the tightly regulated company protocol.

This was a nation-wide organization that had its operation down to a science. They knew what worked and what did not. The problem Bill had was that he (at least in his own mind) could see better ways of doing things. More and more he did them his way. His supervisor spoke with him about his going against policy. His supervisor's supervisor discussed it with him. Bill felt that his was the better way, and continued as usual.

The company suffered some setbacks and had to lay off some employees. Bill was among the first to lose his job. He could not understand why, of all people, he should have to go. After all, he knew more than the top level people did about how to run the business.

Can you understand why Bill lost his job? Can we see why Joshua had to follow God's plan for Canaan? Can we understand why God wants us to obey His commands?

## Father's Day Tributes

Three boys in the schoolyard are bragging about their fathers.

The first boy says, "My Dad scribbles a few words on a piece of paper, he calls it a poem, they give him $50."

The second boy says, "That's nothing. My Dad scribbles a few words on a piece of paper, he calls it a song, they give him $100."

The third boy says, "I got you both beat. My Dad scribbles a few words on a piece of paper, he calls it a sermon. And it takes eight people to collect all the money!"

# This Lesson in Your Life

This lesson gives us some valuable information about the early use of Moses' writings. At the time of our lesson what he had written was considered as the authoritative word of God and was the required standard for Joshua's conduct. If he did not follow it closely, he would not be a successful leader for Israel.

As background information, we read about Moses writing in what was called the Book of the Covenant (Exod. 24:1-7). He wrote down everything that the Lord had said to him while he was up on the mountain. This included everything from chapters 20 through 23. When he read the Book of the Covenant to the people, they responded that they would obey everything the Lord had said. We assume the book was written so there would be an official copy of the covenant. The people accepted it as containing God's commands. (For more about Moses' writing see Exod. 17:14; 24:4-7; Deut. 31:9, 11, 24, 26.)

Now let us return to Joshua and read 1:8, which follows our memory verse. "The book of the law shall not depart out of thy mouth; but thou shalt meditate therein day and night, that thou mayest observe to do according to all that is written therein: for then thou shalt make thy way prosperous, and then thou shalt have good success."

This book was recognized as the law Moses gave (v.7). It was a written body of literature that carried divine approval. What we are learning here is that in the 14th century B.C. there was a book of the law being used. It was read to all Israel (8:32-35), and in 24:25-27 Joshua called it the book of the law of God. It represents the early formation of our Bible.

This written law was valuable enough that Joshua was admonished to meditate on it day and night. This indicated that it was to reflect on it seriously and make it a part of his life. It would contribute to his spiritual growth.

This concept was developed further as the Psalms were written.

> Psalm 1:1-3
> Blessed is the man that walketh not in the counsel
> of the ungodly, nor standeth in the way of sinners,
> nor sitteth in the seat of the scornful.
> But his delight is in the law of the Lord;
> and in his law doth he meditate day and night.
> (Also read Psalm 119:15-16, 97.)

In this lesson we have our appreciation renewed for the written word. We get a glimpse of how God worked to provide it for us. We see how important it was to Moses, and for his successor Joshua. We see how the ancient Israelites received it. Second Peter 1:21 tells us that prophecy came as men spoke from God as they were carried along by the Holy Spirit. This lesson gives us a picture of the early stages in the development of our Bible.

**1. When the Lord spoke to Joshua and told him to be strong and courageous, it was in order that he might do what?**
It was so that he might do everything commanded in the law that Moses had commanded.

**2. What very narrow restrictions were placed on Joshua's obeying the law?**
He was commanded not to turn either to the right hand or to the left.

**3. If Joshua obeyed the law very carefully, what was promised to him?**
He would prosper wherever he went if he kept the law.

**4. What does it mean when Joshua is told not to let the law depart out of his mouth?**
The law should always be a part of who Joshua is. Anything he says should be acceptable to the law. It is something he should speak about and teach.

**5. What part of the command indicates how intimate the law should be in Joshua's life?**
He should meditate on it day and night in order that he will follow it closely.

**6. Why was Joshua assured that he need not be afraid or dismayed?**
God will be with him wherever he goes. He can be strong and courageous.

**7. Joshua planned to cross the Jordan in three days. What were the officers to tell the people about getting prepared?**
They were to get their victuals (supplies) ready. They would be moving from the plain of Moab to nearer the river. There were tents to be taken down and things to pack.

**8. Did any of the Israelites plan to live on the east side of the river rather than across it?**
Yes, the tribes of Reuben and Gad and the half-tribe of Manasseh had arranged earlier with Moses. They had large herds and there was good pastureland in certain areas there (See Numbers 32).

**9. Were any of them (the above in question 8) allowed to remain on the east side at the time the others crossed over?**
Yes, the women, children, and cattle could remain on the east side.

**10. Who, among the tribes that would remain on the east side, was required to cross the Jordan?**
The fighting men had agreed (and Joshua is reminding them) that they were required to help conquer Canaan before they could return to the east side.

It must be just one of the devil's dirty tricks. He has a whole bunch of them up his sleeves and distributes them freely wherever he thinks we might fall for one of them. Otherwise, how do we explain the fact that so many people seem to think that using Scripture as our guide takes all the pleasure out of life? I know a few people (fortunately only a very few) who behave as if the only good life is a raunchy one.

Am I the only person who thinks that on many TV programs, the Bible-believer, or "church lady," or clergyman, is often either a hypocrite or a creaky old dinosaur? Maybe I am over-sensitive about this, so we will not pursue it any further. Even so, there seems to be the perception among many that Christianity sucks the joy out of life. Nothing could be further from the truth. (We did not expect the devil to be interested in truth.)

In our lesson, the very thing that makes Joshua a hero is that he obeys God. He could not lead and would not be successful if he did not. Because he does obey the law, he is prosperous in everything that he does. He stands head and shoulders above the crowd and is strong and courageous. All this is because he's the kind of man who knows the value of meditating on the written word of God, and does it day and night. From what we read about the man in the Bible, he is a success story all the way through.

These Israelites whom Joshua is leading are on their way to the Promised Land, which is described as a land of milk and honey. They have been in bondage for centuries and have just finished 40 years of living in the wilderness, and are looking forward to a better life. They are about to receive God's promise. Milk and honey sounds much better to them than making bricks for Pharaoh. They are an excited and happy bunch of people.

I have not counted them, but somebody who has reports that in the four chapters of Philippians there are at least 19 times that Paul mentions joy, rejoicing, or gladness. All this from a man who is in prison! What do you suppose he must have been like when he was free and everything was going well?

Stuart Briscoe wrote a little book on Philippians, "Bound for Joy." In it he suggests that when we are in prison, or confined to a hospital bed, or a sink full of dirty dishes, or a desk, we should not be moaning about it. Rather, we should think of all the good things God has brought into our lives.

The words to the song, "I'm Bound for the Promised Land" were written in 1787. For all the years since, Christians have been singing about getting "to Canaan's fair and happy land," where "Shines one eternal day." "There God the Son forever reigns And scatters night away."

Nehemiah 8:10 reminds us that the joy of the Lord is our strength. Strong and joyful sounds like a good way to be. Let us try it.

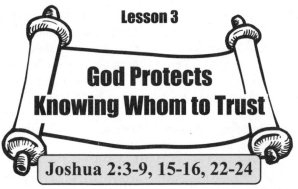

# Lesson 3

# God Protects
# Knowing Whom to Trust

## Joshua 2:3-9, 15-16, 22-24

And the king of Jericho sent unto Rahab, saying, Bring forth the men that are come to thee, which are entered into thine house: for they be come to search out all the country.

4 And the woman took the two men, and hid them, and said thus, There came men unto me, but I wist not whence they were:

5 And it came to pass about the time of shutting of the gate, when it was dark, that the men went out: whither the men went I wot not: pursue after them quickly; for ye shall overtake them.

6 But she had brought them up to the roof of the house, and hid them with the stalks of flax, which she had laid in order upon the roof.

7 And the men pursued after them the way to Jordan unto the fords: and as soon as they which pursued after them were gone out, they shut the gate.

8 And before they were laid down, she came up unto them upon the roof;

9 And she said unto the men, I know that the LORD hath given you the land, and that your terror is fallen upon us . . . .

15 Then she let them down by a cord through the window: for her house was upon the town wall, and she dwelt upon the wall.

16 And she said unto them, Get you to the mountain, lest the pursuers meet you; and hide yourselves there three days, until the pursuers be returned: and afterward may ye go your way.

22 And they went, and came unto the mountain, and abode there three days, until the pursuers were returned: and the pursuers sought them throughout all the way, but found them not.

23 So the two men returned, and descended from the mountain, and passed over, and came to Joshua the son of Nun, and told him all things that befell them:

24 And they said unto Joshua, Truly the LORD hath delivered into our hands all the land; for even all the inhabitants of the country do faint because of us.

---

**Memory Verse**
Joshua 2:24
**Background Scripture**
Joshua 2
**Devotional Reading**
James 2:18-25

---

How do we determine whom we can trust, especially in this age when so many con artists and scammers are prowling at all times?

The spies were meeting Rahab for the first time. Likewise, she had never laid eyes on them before. They did not have much choice but to trust her. Their lives depended on it right then. However, Rahab had to make a deci-sion on whether to risk her life to help these strangers. She suspected but had no way to know for sure just how much her own survival depended on them.

Trust is a fragile thing. How easily it can be forfeited. The spies warned Rahab that their promises to her were only as good as her treatment of them. If she betrayed them, the safety they had promised to her and her family would be lost. So they made a deal that depended in large part on their trust of each other. Even to this day, our life events are much like that.

## For a Lively Start  ℰↄ૦ૡ

What were these trusted men from the camp of God's people doing in the house of a prostitute? This question has troubled Bible readers for centuries—so much so that the NIV footnote suggests the alternative term "innkeeper" to describe her trade, as if she owned a Motel 6. Probably no translation has improved on the KJV's familiar "harlot" to identify her trade.

Someone has wisely asked where else in Jericho the spies could have expected to be welcomed with no questions asked. Others point out that this was a turning point in Rahab's life. The New Testament writers praise her as a woman of faith and courage, and Matthew lists her as an honored ancestor of King David and Jesus. If the gospel can be trusted, every church should have Rahab among them.

| Teaching Outline | Daily Bible Readings |
|---|---|
| I. The Official Inquiry—Joshua 2:3 | Mon. The Promises of God<br>*2 Corinthians 1:16-20* |
| II. Rahab's Brave Lie—Joshua 2:4-5 | Tue. God's Promises Kept<br>*Joshua 21:43-22:6* |
| III. The Spies Hiding Place—Joshua 2:6-7 | Wed. Rahab's Confession of God<br>*Joshua 2:10-14* |
| IV. Rahab's Testimony—Joshua 2:8-9 | Thu. Rahab's Pact with the Spies<br>*Joshua 2:17-21* |
| V. The Spies' Escape—Joshua 2:15-16, 22 | Fri. Rahab's Help Rewarded<br>*Joshua 6:22-25* |
|   A. The Open Window, 15 | Sat. Rahab and Her Works<br>*James 2:18-25* |
|   B. The Escape Route, 16, 22 | Sun. Rahab's Protection of the Spies<br>*Joshua 2:3-9, 15-16, 22-24* |
| VI. The Spies Report—Joshua 2:23-24 | |

# *Verse by Verse*

**Joshua 2:3-9, 15-16, 22-24**

## I. The Official Inquiry—Joshua 2:3

**3 And the king of Jericho sent unto Rahab, saying, Bring forth the men that are come to thee, which are entered into thine house: for they be come to search out all the country.**

In our culture, the officials knocking on our door would be the police or the FBI. If we really had foreign spies hiding on our property, lying about it and hiding them could very easily cost us our own freedom and even our lives. Rahab faces dire danger if the agents of the king find out she is concealing the spies. Someone must have given a tip to the city officials.

Was Rahab right to tell the lies she did? Later appraisals of her behavior in James 2 and Hebrews 11 would seem to mark this as one of those times when good sense and goodness dictated that the usual rules should be broken. Some believers are too brittle to recognize such moments, so the price others pay for the purity of their faith can be frightfully high.

## II. Rahab's Brave Lie—Joshua 2:4-5

**4 And the woman took the two men, and hid them, and said thus,**

**There came men unto me, but I wist not whence they were:**

**5 And it came to pass about the time of shutting of the gate, when it was dark, that the men went out: whither the men went I wot not: pursue after them quickly; for ye shall overtake them.**

"I wist not," is old English for "I didn't know." Rahab lies to the officers looking for the spies. Had she felt compelled to tell the truth regardless, the spies surely would have died. Similar situations have faced many good people in wartime—people such as Corrie ten Boom's family when they hid Jews from Nazi murderers.

"I wot not," is another tense of the same archaic English that means "I don't know." Rahab fashions a fancy fib, including the fiction that the spies have already slipped away and that she says she has no idea where they were headed.

Both Rahab's survival and that of the spies depends on her being an effective liar. If her nuances show the officers that she is misleading them, she and her new friends will be dead.

## III. The Spies Hiding Place—Joshua 2:6-7

**6 But she had brought them up to the roof of the house, and hid them**

with the stalks of flax, which she had laid in order upon the roof.

7 And the men pursued after them the way to Jordan unto the fords: and as soon as they which pursued after them were gone out, they shut the gate.

Rahab is not just a harlot by trade. She also must be a cloth producer. She has flax stalks laid out to dry on the flat roof of her multi-story shelter. The text tells us this home-in-the-wall has in the upper level an outer window that gives her a view of the terrain outside the walls of Jericho. Likely, the lower level opens out to the city street like a shopping mall where Rahab can sell her legitimate wares.

Hiding under drying vegetation would not be a pleasant experience, especially so if the sun is hot and if the flax still contains enough moisture to steam whatever it lies on. However, the stench of drying flax would be pleasant compared to anything the Jericho authorities will dish out if the spies fall into their hands.

The soldiers looking for the spies follow Rahab's false information, hurrying toward the Jordan in hope of catching the spies before they can return across the river.

## IV. Rahab's Testimony—Joshua 2:8-9

8 And before they were laid down, she came up unto them upon the roof;

9 And she said unto the men, I know that the LORD hath given you the land, and that your terror is fallen upon us, and that all the inhabitants of the land faint because of you.

Before they sleep that night, Rahab relates her understanding of the situation. She tells the spies how fearful Jericho's inhabitants are as Israel's army approaches their city. Everyone knows what Joshua's troops did to the formidable armies across the river. They do not expect to fare any better.

The tables have turned. Last time—40 years ago—the Israelites were terrified of the Canaanites. Now the people of Canaan "faint" with fear as Israel draws near. In each case, fear spells defeat.

## V. The Spies' Escape—Joshua 2:15-16, 22

### A. The Open Window, 15

15 Then she let them down by a cord through the window: for her house was upon the town wall, and she dwelt upon the wall.

Having an understanding with the spies—her life for their lives—Rahab again takes a huge risk, allowing the men to slip out her high window and slide down a rope. This part of the story lets us know that the "wall" of ancient towns was like a ring of condominiums and not just a stake fence like the wall of a western fort.

### B. The Escape Route, 16, 22

16 And she said unto them, Get you to the mountain, lest the pursuers meet you; and hide yourselves there three days, until the pursuers be returned: and afterward may ye go your way. . . .

22 And they went, and came unto the mountain, and abode there three days, until the pursuers were

returned: and the pursuers sought them throughout all the way, but found them not.

Having given the pursuers miss directions that headed them toward the escarpment of the river, Rahab now counsels the spies to go the other direction. The high country west of Jericho laid the opposite direction from Joshua's camp, so the searchers would not expect the spies to head out that way. "Go west," Rahab wisely instructs the spies. Not only is this a safe direction. It also will take the spies into some of the roughest terrain in the Promised Land. The spies can hide out there, and chances of their being spotted by locals will be slight.

Would you have followed the advice of a foreign harlot? Sometimes those who do not share our faith still have expertise that can bless us. We believers like it when our doctor is also a person with faith, but the superb skills of a vascular surgeon who has not met the Savior may be preferable to those of a believer with mediocre training or unsure hands. The wisdom and insights of unbelievers may be made to work for the good of the Kingdom. Rahab's wise strategies certainly blessed God's men as they planned the Jericho attack.

## VI. The Spies Report—Joshua 2:23-24

**23 So the two men returned, and descended from the mountain, and passed over, and came to Joshua the son of Nun, and told him all things that befell them:**

**24 And they said unto Joshua, Truly the Lord hath delivered into our hands all the land; for even all the inhabitants of the country do faint because of us.**

Through the ages, readers of this recital have wished that the historian had told us more about how the spies manage to cross Jordan when such a crossing seemed virtually impossible. They do cross over. The text tells us that. In addition, their report was just like the one that Joshua was aware of 40 years earlier when he returned from spying in Canaan. "The Lord will give us the land," they predicted as they told him how frightened the Canaanites were. It is precisely the report that Israel needed to prepare for the challenge before them.

જીભ

## Evangelistic Emphasis

Nerves are on edge on the west side of the swollen river. Stories have spread about the destruction Israelites bring. It is harvest season in Canaan, and farmers are wondering if they should risk going out into their open fields. Maybe they should go up to their hilltop shrine and make an offering of food to the gods. Perhaps it is serious enough that they should offer a child as a burnt offering. The gods are fickle. You never know!

On the east side of the river the Israelites are folding their tents and packing their gear, ready to move nearer the river, then across it. The Lord has instructed Joshua what is to be done, and they want to comply.

The Lord has promised Canaan to them and they are confident the time has come. God has given them the law. There are Ten Commandments plus many requirements involved in worship at the sacred tent. Moses had written the law down for them, and gave the copy to the Levites (Deut. 31:24-26). The first Commandment says they are to have only one God. The gods across the river are nothing but wood, stone, and metal.

The more things change the more they remain the same. Here you and I are, about three and a half thousand years after Moses and Joshua. Many people still follow the gods of this world; and God, the Father of our Lord Jesus Christ, still cares for His children – all pointing to the need for evangelism.

## Memory Selection

ഇറോ

"And they [the two spies just returned from Jericho] said unto Joshua, Truly the LORD hath delivered into our hands all the land; for even all the inhabitants of the country do faint because of us."

*Joshua 2:24*

The way Joshua sent his spies out and received their report when they returned is quite different from Israel's first spy episode. Moses sent twelve spies into Canaan, and when they returned, ten of them gave a fearful report in the presence of everyone. Their fear was contagious, and spread immediately. Joshua and Caleb gave the minority report: We can take the land (Num. 14:6-9).

Before entering Canaan Joshua needed information, so he secretly sent two spies. When they returned they reported to him, not to the people. As it turned out, they gave an optimistic report, but Joshua had taken the cautious approach. He apparently remembered the problems resulting from the earlier experience.

These two spies reported that the inhabitants of the land were melting in fear because of the Israelite threat. They had heard of the military success of Israel's army, and the reputation of Israel's God.

The favorable report the spies gave confirmed God's assurance given to Joshua that He would be with him and that Joshua would successfully lead the people to inherit the land. Their report was great news to Joshua's fighting men, and no doubt comforted everyone who depended on the success of the army. Begin the crossing.

## Weekday Problems

The spy business is pretty scary at best. There is always something going wrong. If you enjoy watching a spy thriller on TV, or love an exciting espionage novel, you know there are unexpected twists and turns that keep you on your toes. Will the spy get caught? If he is spying for the good guys, we hope not.

Joshua's two spies had a pretty close call in Jericho. Word got out to the king that they were at Rahab's place. She may have been a good seamstress in addition to her other line of business. She had flax drying on the flat roof of her house that she would later spin into linen thread. These two hideaways spent the night tucked away in flax bundles.

Rahab assured the king's searchers that the spies left town before the city gate was locked for the night. If they hurried, maybe they could catch them. Then she let Joshua's men out her window, and told them for safety's sake to hide in the mountains for three days. They knew Joshua was waiting for their report, but had no choice but to wait out the king's men who wanted to capture them.

It was these three days spent hiding in the mountains that interfered with Joshua's schedule. They doubled the time before he could get things underway, and he could not dare begin to cross Jordan before he heard from them.

We all know that unwritten law: If anything can go wrong, it will. What do you do when plans really get in a mess? We have to do what Joshua did, and his spies did. We make the best of the situation and get on with life.

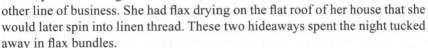

# Last Rights

When a gambler died, most of those attending his funeral were his professional friends. "Spike is not dead," the minister said in his eulogy. "He only sleeps." From the rear of the chapel a voice roared, "I've got a hundred that says he's door-nail dead."

At another funeral the preacher was inexperienced. Solemnly he pointed to the body in the coffin, and attempting to wax a bit eloquent, he launched an extemporaneous metaphor. "What we have here is only a shell," he opined. "The nut is already gone."

# This Lesson in Your Life

In nations where totalitarian regimes have been the norm for generations, the general population often has no concept of self-government. When freedom loving nations such as our own try to take democracy to such nations, one potential problem is that they're not prepared to make it work. They simply do not have the background for it.

Thinking along the lines of what kind of future a nation is prepared for, the Israelites did not have much going for them when they left Egypt. Four hundred years of servitude is not good preparation for nation building. That many centuries of taking orders from slave masters does not do anything toward organizing an army. If some think-tank had analyzed their future prospects, the outlook would have been bleak. From a human point of view they were in big trouble. At least back in Egypt they had food on the table. Their future was now uncertain at best, when judged by human standards.

"With God all things are possible," Jesus told His disciples (Matt. 19:26). That was true back when Joshua took over from Moses. Both of these men knew that and acted on it, and that is what got Israel as far as the Jordan River. Otherwise, they would have been wasting away out in the desert. Israel's future was in the hands of God. Where better could it have been?

God was the leader in charge of Israel's army. It was God who guided the nation. Joshua was the man through whom the Lord did His work. With God in control, all deficits were erased. All the dire predictions about Israel's success that humans might have made amount to nothing.

Who do you suppose holds your future and mine? We do not think that God is going to treat us like puppets on a string, but as people of faith, we depend on His being there for us. Joshua's experience teaches us to live our lives under God's control and guidance. Scripture leads us in this direction.

King Solomon's Proverbs are gems of practical wisdom, and 3:5-6 says:

> Trust in the LORD with all thine heart,
> and lean not unto thine own understanding.
> In all thy ways acknowledge him,
> and he shall direct thy paths.

Second Thessalonians 3:5 contains a one-sentence prayer that we should use for ourselves and all our friends (and enemies).

> May the Lord direct your hearts into
>
> God's love and Christ's perseverance (NIV).

God's leadership made possible for Israel what it could never have done on its own. Joshua and those whom he led remind us that we should trust God for guidance in our own lives.

**GETTING THE FACTS STRAIGHT**

**1. When Joshua's spies arrived in Jericho where did they go?**
They went to the house of a harlot named Rahab and stayed there.

**2. What was the report that the king of Jericho received?**
He was told that two Israelite spies had arrived and were in Rahab's house.

**3. What action did the king take in response to hearing about the spies?**
He commanded Rahab to bring the men forth because they had come to spy out the land.

**4. How did Rahab explain what had happened concerning the men?**
She said she did not know where they had come from, but just before the city gate was closed, they left the city. If the king's men hurried, they might be able to catch them.

**5. Where had Rahab hidden the spies?**
They were hidden among bundles of flax, up on the flat rooftop of Rahab's house.

**6. What kind of arrangement for her (and her family's) safety did Rahab work out with the spies?**
She asked that because of her kindness to the spies, they would see that she and her family were saved when the Israelites took the city.

**7. The spies agreed to Rahab's request. What kind of signal would the Israelites have to identify her house to keep it safe?**
Rahab was to tie a scarlet cord in the window. This would mark her house for safety.

**8. How did the spies manage to get out of Jericho safely?**
Rahab's house was built into the city wall. After dark she let them down through a window.

**9. What did she tell the spies they should do (after escaping Jericho) for their safety?**
The spies should hide for three days in the mountains, by which time the pursuers would have stopped searching.

**10. When the spies reported back to Joshua, what did they say?**
They told him that the Lord had delivered the land into Israel's hand, and the inhabitants were very frightened.

419

The Bible indicates that God has a tender spot in His heart for those who are disadvantaged in any way. Jesus defined His own ministry to John the Baptist in terms that emphasize this. When John was in prison, he sent his disciples to Jesus, asking if Jesus was the one to come, or if they should look for someone else. Jesus reassured John by telling him, "The blind receive their sight, and the lame walk, the lepers are cleansed, and the deaf hear, the dead are raised up, and the poor have the gospel preached to them" (Matt. 11:2-6).

The tender mercies of God are also seen in the Old Testament. We see them in our lesson about Joshua's invasion of Canaan. Though there is definitely a harshness in the warfare (which was to eliminate the abominable pagan religions), we also see God's grace that brings redemption.

Rahab, the harlot, makes for a fascinating and uplifting story. Her hiding the spies is only the beginning of it, but the beginning is a good place to start. She was a perceptive and intelligent person. She knew about Israel's crossing the Red Sea forty years earlier, and of what had happened with Israel since then. The evidence was compelling. She told the spies, "The Lord your God, He is God in heaven above, and in earth beneath" (2.11). We have no way of knowing if at this moment in her heart Rahab had forsaken the pagan gods of Canaan, but she had definitely made a major step in that direction.

We know that she and her extended family were saved from destruction when the walls of Jericho fell. We know that she continued to live among the Israelites (6:25). From that point, she is lost to us until we find her name in the most unexpected place. Who would have ever guessed that this woman would become an ancestress of Jesus of Nazareth? Matthew 1:5 (NIV), in giving Jesus' genealogy, says

Salmon the father of Boaz, whose mother was Rahab,

Boaz the father of Obed, whose mother was Ruth,

Obed the father of Jesse,

and Jesse the father of King David.

When we first became acquainted with Rahab, she was a prostitute in a pagan city in a pagan land. We would love to know the story of her life between what we read in Joshua and what we discover in Matthew. All we actually know is that our gracious and merciful God entered her life, though we don't know the specifics. We know that at some point she became the wife of Salmon and the mother of Boaz, who in turn married Ruth.

She is named along with other heroes of the faith in Hebrews 11:31. James 2:25 commends her for showing her faith by her works, and says she was justified by doing so. She was an amazing woman. She found an amazing God (more accurately, an amazing God found her), and she has an uplifting story to tell.

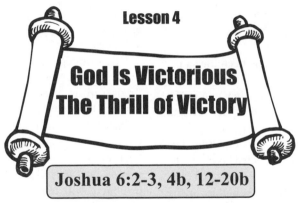

# Lesson 4

## God Is Victorious The Thrill of Victory

### Joshua 6:2-3, 4b, 12-20b

And the LORD said unto Joshua, See, I have given into thine hand Jericho, and the king thereof, and the mighty men of valour.

3 And ye shall compass the city, all ye men of war, and go round about the city once. Thus shalt thou do six days.

4 And . . . the seventh day ye shall compass the city seven times . . . .

12 And Joshua rose early in the morning, and the priests took up the ark of the LORD.

13 And seven priests bearing seven trumpets of rams' horns before the ark of the LORD went on continually, and blew with the trumpets: and the armed men went before them; but the rearward came after the ark of the LORD . . .

14 And the second day they compassed the city once, and returned into the camp: so they did six days.

15 And it came to pass on the seventh day, that they rose early about the dawning of the day, and compassed the city after the same manner seven times: only on that day they compassed the city seven times.

16 And it came to pass at the seventh time, when the priests blew with the trumpets, Joshua said unto the people, Shout; for the LORD hath given you the city.

17 And the city shall be accursed, even it, and all that are therein, to the LORD: only Rahab the harlot shall live, she and all that are with her in the house, because she hid the messengers that we sent.

18 And ye, in any wise keep yourselves from the accursed thing, lest ye make yourselves accursed, when ye take of the accursed thing, and make the camp of Israel a curse, and trouble it.

19 But all the silver, and gold, and vessels of brass and iron, are consecrated unto the LORD: they shall come into the treasury of the LORD.

20 So the people shouted when the priests blew with the trumpets: and it came to pass, when the people heard the sound of the trumpet, and the people shouted with a great shout, that the wall fell down flat.

---

**Memory Verse**
Joshua 6:16
**Background Scripture**
Joshua 5:13; 6:27
**Devotional Reading**
Psalm 98:1-6

---

In every age, it has been the same. God has always wanted His people to know that any victory they win in His service was the result of His strength and not theirs.

The apostle Paul was quoting Jeremiah when he instructed his converts, "Let him who boasts boast in the Lord" (1 Cor. 1:31, NIV). Whether in the days of the prophet or in those of the apostle, God deserved the credit for any success His people enjoyed. He still does.

God's strategy and power alone flattened Jericho. Not one of His warriors fired an arrow. Not one of the Israelites assaulted the city's walls. When this mighty fortress lay in rubble and dust, God's people knew the victory had been entirely His. As the Scriptures remind us, "It is God who works in us both to will and to do for his good pleasure" (Phil. 2:13).

෨෬

 **For a Lively Start**

Although not all have agreed, careful theologians through the centuries have made distinctions between the sin of murder and the killing involved in war. From the earliest days of the Church, the leaders of the faith have held that troops in "just wars" do not violate the Sixth Commandment when they must take life.

Scriptures such as the early chapters of Joshua support these distinctions. In the conquest of Canaan, the Lord repeatedly commands Joshua's army to kill everybody in town after town. Surely the One who so clearly tells His people, "You shall not murder" (Exod. 20:13) would not immediately tell them to violate that holy law. However, He does tell His people to kill. All through the Pentateuch, the Lord makes it clear that murder and killing are not necessarily the same thing.

| Teaching Outline | Daily Bible Readings |
|---|---|
| I. God's Battle Plan—Joshua 6:2-3, 4b | Mon. The Victory of Our God<br>*Psalm 98:1-6* |
| II. The First Six Days—Joshua 6:12-14 | Tue. A Victory to Anticipate<br>*Isaiah 25:6-10* |
| A. The Order of March, 12-13 | Wed. Victory Through Christ<br>*1 Corinthians 15:50-57* |
| B. Day Two Through Day Six, 14 | Thu. The Victory of Faith<br>*1 John 5:1-5* |
| III. The Seventh Day—Joshua 6:15-20 | Fri. A Petition for Victory<br>*Psalm 20* |
| A. Seven Times Around, 15-16 | Sat. Assurance Before the Battle<br>*Joshua 5:10-15* |
| B. Rahab Spared, 17 | Sun. God's Victory over Jericho<br>*Joshua 6:2-3, 4b, 12-20b* |
| C. God's Plunder, 18-19 | |
| D. Flat Walls, 20 | |

# Verse by Verse

## Joshua 6:2-3, 4b, 12-20b

### I. God's Battle Plan—Joshua 6:2-3, 4b

**2 And the LORD said unto Joshua, See, I have given into thine hand Jericho, and the king thereof, and the mighty men of valour.**

**3 And ye shall compass the city, all ye men of war, and go round about the city once. Thus shalt thou do six days.**

**4 And ... the seventh day ye shall compass the city seven times ....**

If we had been inside the city of Jericho, what would have been our response to this odd battle plan? From what Rahab told the spies we already know that everybody in the city is terrified. They have been for a long time. Watching Israel migrate across the Jordan must have changed fear to panic.

Now before His final blow God adds to the psychological stress for the people of Jericho. During the seven days leading up to their end, the citizens of Jericho must be petrified by the sudden God-ordered silence that falls on the camp of Israel. The normal chatter and bustle of two million people is suddenly replaced by absolute silence.

For six days, not a sound is heard out of the Israelites except during that brief period every morning while the priests sound rams' horns as they and the armed guard march around walls of the locked-down city. When the daily march is finished, the marchers sit silently in the camp of Israel and the eerie silence continues unbroken for the rest of that day.

The people inside Jericho's walls went into total panic and full alert on that first morning when the Israelites came marching toward the city walls with their holy ark. How puzzled they must have been when that first day's march ended without any ill effect on Jericho. By the time this happened three or four days, though, folks inside Jericho were getting used to the routine. "Here come those crazy Jews for their morning stroll," they must have told one another, assuming that it would end harmlessly just as it had on the previous days. Then on that seventh day the marchers did no quit after the first circuit but just kept circling the city. Can you imagine the fear that immobilized the people inside those walls?

### II. The First Six Days—Joshua 6:12-14

#### A. The Order of March, 12-13

**12 And Joshua rose early in the morning, and the priests took up the ark of the LORD.**

**13 And seven priests bearing seven trumpets of rams' horns before the ark of the LORD went on continually, and blew with the trumpets: and the armed men went before them; but the rearward came after the ark of the LORD, the priests going on, and blowing with the trumpets.**

The marches around the city begin early each day. The order of the march described in vs. 13 of the KJV is a bit confusing. Comparing any of the later Bible versions will help us see that the soldiers lead the march, followed by the trumpet-blowing priests, and then come the priests bearing the Holy Ark. Behind them come "the rearward" (KJV), or a rear guard of more armed men.

The line that says the priests "went on continually" does not refer to their preaching. It describes their constant trumpet blowing during the march, as does the later reference to "the priests going on." The NIV tells us here, "The trumpets kept sounding."

**B. Day Two Through Day Six, 14**

**14 And the second day they compassed the city once, and returned into the camp: so they did six days.**

To "compass the city" (as stated both here and earlier in vs. 3) is King James terminology that means to encircle the city. Day Two is a repeat of the first day march that surely puzzles the frightened citizens of Jericho. In addition, day by day nothing changes in the routine.

How long does it take us to get so used to something that we stop paying any real attention to it? God is lulling His victims before the big blow comes.

**III. The Seventh Day—Joshua 6:15-20**

**A. Seven Times Around, 15-16**

**15 And it came to pass on the seventh day, that they rose early about the dawning of the day, and compassed the city after the same manner seven times: only on that day they compassed the city seven times.**

**16 And it came to pass at the seventh time, when the priests blew with the trumpets, Joshua said unto the people, Shout; for the LORD hath given you the city.**

On the previous six days, the Israelite march started early, but this one kicks off just as soon as it gets light. They have a full day ahead of them. How long do you suppose it took them to circle the city once? That would depend on how large Jericho was, and we really do not know. Obviously, it was small enough for them to march around it seven times that last day and still have time enough to put to death any survivors and to gather the plunder for the Lord.

People inside the city surely must have panicked when the Israelites circle Jericho's walls a second time, and then a third, and just keep on going. All ears and eyes have to be trained on the Israeli actions by the time that fatal seventh march ends. The blasts of the trumpets and the shouts of the Israeli army are the last thing most of them will ever hear.

As the soldiers of Israel closed in to finish the destruction, Joshua reminded them that this victory was the Lord's. He handed the city to them. His strength and not theirs flattened this mighty fortress.

**B. Rahab Spared, 17**

**17 And the city shall be accursed, even it, and all that are therein, to the LORD: only Rahab the harlot shall live, she and all that are with her in the house, because she hid the messengers that we sent.**

Instead of "accursed," later versions of the Bible describe both the people and possessions of Jericho as being "devoted" (NIV) or "devoted to destruction" (NRSV). When describing the gold, silver, and other metal containers in Jericho, the same word is translated "sacred to the Lord." These things belong to Him and are not to be taken by the Israelites. Only Rahab and her family were exempted from this rule. Her faithful actions in Joshua 2 saved her family.

**C. God's Plunder, 18-19**

**18 And ye, in any wise keep yourselves from the accursed thing, lest ye make yourselves accursed, when ye take of the accursed thing, and make the camp of Israel a curse, and trouble it.**

**19 But all the silver, and gold, and vessels of brass and iron, are con-secrated unto the LORD: they shall come into the treasury of the LORD.**

The Lord warns the people that if they take into their camp any of the items marked for destruction, then the thief and the Israeli camp will also be marked for destruction. We see this warning come true in Joshua 7.

In the decades that would follow, the work of the Jewish priests would be well financed by the loot from this first Canaanite city. Just as Abraham paid tithes to Melchizedek after his victory over the northern kings, so the Israelites would be expected to tithe on the plunder taken in later Canaanite victories.

**D. Flat Walls, 20**

**20 So the people shouted when the priests blew with the trumpets: and it came to pass, when the people heard the sound of the trumpet, and the people shouted with a great shout, that the wall fell down flat . . . .**

Just as students shout at the top of their lungs when their sports teams meet fierce competition, so God's people erupt in mighty cries of victory when they hear the priests signal with the trumpets. In addition, as the old spiritual exults, "The walls of Jericho came tumbling down."

ഇരു

## Evangelistic Emphasis

Through the years many people have had a problem accepting the Israelite's complete annihilation of human life in the Canaanite cities. Some have thought that the God of the Old Testament is quite different from God in the New Testament.

It is probably not easy for us to grasp the whole story. This was not a racially inspired war, nor one simply to gain territory. It was not planned simply to kill humans. It was fought for the purpose of eradicating religion that was not simply false, but was horribly corrupt, ungodly, and depraved. (The pockets of paganism that were left remaining came back in later years to corrupt the Israelites.)

The first two of the Ten Commandments demand that there be no other gods besides God, and no idols shall be created (Exodus 20). (In our modern American society acceptance of all cultures, we may feel some pressures about these commands.)

In Romans 1:18-32 Paul describes the development and results of paganism. In Acts 17:16-34 he preaches to idol worshippers in Athens. Neither the apostles nor we go to combat for God with murderous weapons. We do, however, have the sword of the Spirit and the full armor of God (Eph. 6:10-18).

&)(&

## Memory Selection

"And it came to pass at the seventh time, when the priests blew with the trumpets, Joshua said unto the people, Shout; for the LORD hath given you the city."
*Joshua 6:16*

Have you ever noticed that sometimes God seems to make things easy for you? Maybe it was some situation that had troubled you greatly and you were afraid you could not handle? All of a sudden though, everything fell into place and worked out well.

At key times, God just opened the door up for the Israelites during the Exodus and conquering of the Promised Land. All they had to do was cooperate with God and then watch Him in action. As they left Egypt, He gave some instructions to Moses about holding his rod up and stretching his hand over the sea, and when he did this the waters divided. God makes it look so easy.

Much the same thing happened at the flooded Jordan, only this time the priests with the Ark of the Covenant stepped into the water. Again, God opened the door for them and told them to pass right through.

We find them now surrounding Jericho. They have marched, and the priests have blown trumpets, and this day they have done it seven times. Is God going to open the city gates as he opened the sea and river? That would sure be easier than using battering rams (of which they have none prepared).

They shout as instructed, the trumpets blare, and the wall tumbles down (except at Rahab's house). The Israelite soldiers climb through the rubble and take the city. There is no doubt as to who is leading this army. God is in charge.

## Weekday Problems

God's ways are not our ways, and sometimes we do not understand why He did what He did. He does have His own way of doing things, and no doubt that is for the better whether we understand or not. Still, His action often seems strange to us. Who, other than God, would have made a woman out of the man's rib? Who, other than God, would have solved the problem of rampant sin with an ark and a flood? Why did God promise Canaan to Abraham, yet wait hundreds of years to let His descendants have it?

Have you wondered why your own life has worked out as it has? You pray, you trust God for guidance, and sometimes things work out the way you think they should, but on occasions, they do not. You believe God answers prayer, but wonder why He answers them as He does. You believe in His providence, which is to say you believe He works in history, nature, and your own individual life. This is not the same as saying you have answers as to Why?

We all need to be on the cautious side in demanding answers from God. If we are not careful, we will be praying, "Not Thy will but mine be done." Hebrews 11 says that the walls of Jericho fell down because of faith. Marching round and round for seven days is a strange way to defeat a city, but it worked. Maybe we need more faith rather than more answers. You will be blessed if you read Psalm 139.

# What a Turkey!

"Lady, I couldn't sell you that parrot," the pet store owner apologized to a Christian customer. "He was owned by a sailor and he curses a blue streak."

But the woman persisted. She was convinced that with Christian love and firm discipline she could re-train the bird. When he started cursing, she warned the foul-mouthed parrot to hush or get put into the freezer for 10 minutes. He kept on spouting profanities, so into the freezer he went.

Ten minutes later she took out the shivering fowl who seemed totally penitent. "Pppplease, Illlady," he asked his new owner, "Wwwwould yyyyou ttttell mmme jjjjust oooone thththing? Wwwwhat ddddid thththat tttturkey ddddo?"

# This Lesson in Your Life

The archeology of ancient Jericho is not as decisive as we might wish it to be. At one time an archeology team thought they had found the wall ruins from Joshua's day. A few decades later another team pronounced the earlier conclusions mistaken. Maybe it does not make much difference. Considering that the walls fell down, we hardly expect them to be standing so they can be excavated by scientific teams.

Several decades ago I visited the excavations at Jericho. There are portions of several sets of walls built through the centuries after Joshua's time, and looking at them gives an idea of the formidable wall the Israelites might have seen. Off to the west stood the rugged desert mountains where the two spies hid. To the east just a few miles the Jordan River made its way to the Salt Sea, and beyond that, Mount Nebo and the top of Pisgah, from which Moses viewed the Promised Land.

In the Old Testament, Jericho was known as the City of Palms (plus, we might add, in the New Testament at least one sycamore tree for Zacchaeus to climb). Wealthy people built winter homes there for its 800-feet-below-sea-level climate. As we read about it in the Old Testament we do not visualize it as a winter vacation destination.

The city must have looked forbidding as the Israelites marched around it day by day. Walls high and strong, heavy gates tightly shut and locked, the ramparts bristling with spears, bows and arrows in the hands of angry men, and heavy rocks ready to be thrown down on Israelite attackers – all of which shows how deceiving appearances can be when God is involved.

Just a shout and some ram's horn blasts, and down the walls came. "Just" that, and by the power of God, what may have been the best fortified city in Canaan met its doom. Cities throughout Canaan were already frightened because of what they knew about the Israelites and their God. Most of them would have already heard about the crossing of the flooded river. Now, when word reached them of Jericho's destruction, the kings and their generals had to get busy conducting some desperate defensive planning.

We easily learn several things from this lesson. "Impossible" is not a word we use if God is involved. "Unexpected" is what we learn to expect. "Unusual" is normal. (Please feel free to add to this list.)

God surprises us with grace (which, by definition we do not earn or deserve). Divinity became a human. The Eternal One died. He loves us when we are unlovable. He paid an extravagantly outrageous price to purchase us (His Son's blood). He can reach people who are beyond reach (Rahab, the pagan prostitute). All these things we accept by faith, being sure and certain of things we hope for, but do not see.

**1. When Joshua was near Jericho, describe the man he saw.**

The man was standing in front of him with a drawn sword.

**2. Who did this man say he was (in what capacity had he come)?**

He had come as commander of the Lord's host (army).

**3. What was Joshua's reaction to the man's answer?**

He fell to the earth and worshipped.

**4. When Joshua asked the man what message the Lord had sent, how did the man respond?**

He told Joshua to pull off his sandals because the place where he stood was holy.

**5. What leads us to believe that this man was actually an appearance of God? (Answered is not to be found in this lesson.)**

This is apparently an appearance of God because he allows Joshua to fall down and worship. (See Rev. 19:10, where John tries to worship an angel.) Also, the man says the place where Joshua stands is holy. (See Exod. 3:1-6, Moses and the burning bush.)

**6. What was Joshua told to do for six days relative to Jericho?**

They were to march around the city one time for six days. The order of march was: An advanced guard first, followed by seven priests sounding ram's horn trumpets, followed by the ark, followed by a rear guard, and then the people, who were to remain silent. After this they went back to the camp.

**7. Describe what the Israelites were to do on the seventh day.**

They got up at daybreak and circled the city as before, except they did it seven times. The people were to keep silent until Joshua told them to shout.

**8. Describe what happened after they marched around the city for the seventh time.**

When the seventh circle had been completed Joshua gave the command to shout. The people shouted, the ram's horns sounded, the walls collapsed and the army went in and took the city.

**9. One section of the wall did not fall. Which one was it?**

Rahab's house was not destroyed. Also, she and her extended family were kept safe while the other inhabitants were killed.

**10. What happened to the articles in the city that were made of gold, silver, bronze and iron?**

These articles were consecrated to the Lord and went into His treasury.

429

One of my favorite poems by Robert Frost, that crusty old New Englander, is his "Mending Wall." In it he, along with his neighbor, each walks along his own side of the rock-wall fence, replacing the rocks that have fallen off during the winter.

He wonders why they even need a wall. The neighbor has pine trees and he has apple, and his apple trees are not going to bother the neighbor's pine cones. The neighbor insists that good fences make good neighbors.

He raises an excellent point when he muses that if he were going to build a wall, he would first ask who he was walling in or walling out, and who might take offence.

The people of Jericho built a wall around their city to protect themselves from all invaders – not that it did them any good in the final analysis. At least they could answer the poet's question about who they were walling out. (They had not counted on God.)

Let us fast-forward to the year AD 122. The Roman Emperor Hadrianus Augustus took a trip from Rome to the far edge of the then-known world, which was Britain. His empire extended that far. When he arrived at a certain point in Britain, he apparently came to the decision that this was far enough. He had a wall built all the way across Britain. It would mark the end of civilization and keep the barbarians out. The ruins of Hadrian's Wall can still be traced across the English countryside.

Much closer to our own time, the Communists built a wall dividing off their part of Berlin. It was built to fasten in their own people. It is not a good recommendation for any government when its citizens want to escape so badly that it has to fence them in.

How does God feel about walls? Actually, he tears them down, and this is where a powerful uplift comes for you and me. Before Christ there was a sharp dividing line between Jews and Gentiles. (Unless you are of Jewish descent, you are a Gentile.) Gentiles were cut off from the covenants of promise (such as we are studying in Joshua).

Christ's death destroyed the barrier, the dividing wall, between Jew and Gentile. He makes the two become one, and in this one body reconciles us all to God through the Cross (Eph. 2:14-16). Ephesians has much to say about unity. In 4:3-6 we are encouraged to keep the unity of the Spirit in the bond of peace. The gospel is about bonds, not barriers. These verses remind us that there is one body and one Spirit, "one Lord, one faith, one baptism; one God and father of all, who is over all and through all and in all" (NIV). We find our oneness in Christ.

Jericho's was not the last wall God destroyed, and we can rejoice in it. Edwin Markham's little verse reminds us of one way we can destroy dividing walls. "He drew a circle that shut me out, Heretic, rebel, a thing to flout. But love and I had the wit to win; We drew a circle that took him in."

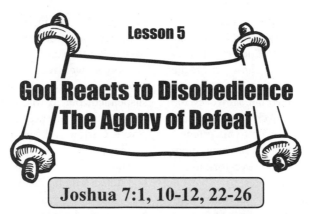

## Lesson 5

# God Reacts to Disobedience
# The Agony of Defeat

### Joshua 7:1, 10-12, 22-26

But the children of Israel committed a trespass in the accursed thing: for Achan, the son of Carmi, the son of Zabdi, the son of Zerah, of the tribe of Judah, took of the accursed thing: and the anger of the LORD was kindled against the children of Israel.

10 And the LORD said unto Joshua, Get thee up; wherefore liest thou thus upon thy face?

11 Israel hath sinned, and they have also transgressed my covenant which I commanded them: for they have even taken of the accursed thing, and have also stolen, and dissembled also, and they have put it even among their own stuff.

12 Therefore the children of Israel could not stand before their enemies, but turned their backs before their enemies, because they were accursed: neither will I be with you any more, except ye destroy the accursed from among you.

22 So Joshua sent messengers, and they ran unto the tent; and, behold, it was hid in his tent, and the silver under it.

23 And they took them out of the midst of the tent, and brought them unto Joshua, and unto all the children of Israel, and laid them out before the LORD.

24 And Joshua, and all Israel with him, took Achan the son of Zerah, and the silver, and the garment, and the wedge of gold, and his sons, and his daughters, and his oxen, and his asses, and his sheep, and his tent, and all that he had: and they brought them unto the valley of Achor.

25 And Joshua said, Why hast thou troubled us? the LORD shall trouble thee this day. And all Israel stoned him with stones, and burned them with fire, after they had stoned them with stones.

26 And they raised over him a great heap of stones unto this day. So the LORD turned from the fierceness of his anger. Wherefore the name of that place was called, The valley of Achor, unto this day.

---

**Memory Verse**
Joshua 7:1
**Background Scripture**
Joshua 7:1; 8:29
**Devotional Reading**
Romans 6:1-11

431

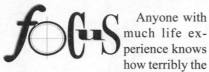

**focus**

Anyone with much life experience knows how terribly the misbehavior of one family member can hurt the rest of the clan. However, the consequences of Achan's sin appear to be disproportionate to his offense. The punishment for his sin seems more extreme than God's eye-for-an-eye fairness usually dictates.

One explanation is that Achan's offense took place in a time of war, so the equivalent of martial law would have been in effect. In America, we have had little experience with war on our soil, so we have known few times when normal civil rights and law were suspended, but in war zones, penalties for minor offenses may be quite severe. Curfew violators may be killed on the spot.

Another factor we cannot ignore is that Achan's theft violated God's holiness. Men like Uzzah (1 Chron. 13) or Nadab and Abihu (Lev. 10) found out how quickly that can cause death, even for good men.

## For a Lively Start

When some church project fails, or we hit one of those years when all our congregation's growth indicators go south, it is easy for us to become disappointed and to begin looking for a convenient scapegoat.

At such a moment, it is possible that, like Israel at Ai, we have sin in our camp. Times like that call for genuine penitence.

However, this may also be a time when we need to hear God reprimanding Joshua. "Stand up like a man!" the Lord orders Joshua in this dismal moment. He asks him, "Why are you prostrated there with your face in the dirt?" God might also be telling us to get our heads up and start trusting Him again to lead us to victory in His service.

| Teaching Outline | Daily Bible Readings |
|---|---|
| I. Achan's Sin—Joshua 7:1 | Mon. Victory Turned to Defeat<br>*Joshua 7:2-9* |
| II. Joshua's Dismay—Joshua 7:10 | Tue. The Reason for the Defeat<br>*Joshua 7:12-15* |
| III. God's Accusation—Joshua 7:11-12 | Wed. The Sin Revealed<br>*Joshua 7:16-21* |
| IV. Achan's Punishment—Joshua 7:22-26 | Thu. The Wages of Sin<br>*Romans 6:15-23* |
| A. The Evidence Revealed, 22-23 | Fri. The Work of the Advocate<br>*John 16:4b-11* |
| B. The Convicted, 24 | Sat. Dead to Sin, Alive to God<br>*Romans 6:1-11* |
| C. The Execution, 25 | Sun. The Outcome of Achan's Sin<br>*Joshua 7:1, 10-12, 22-26* |
| D. The Memorial, 26 | |

# Verse by Verse

**Joshua 7:1, 10-12, 22-26**

## I. Achan's Sin—Joshua 7:1

**1 But the children of Israel committed a trespass in the accursed thing: for Achan, the son of Carmi, the son of Zabdi, the son of Zerah, of the tribe of Judah, took of the accursed thing: and the anger of the Lord was kindled against the children of Israel.**

"Trespass" is the KJV word for "sin" (as in the Lord's Prayer, "Forgive us our trespasses"). God had clearly warned the Israelites not to be tempted to take for themselves any of the wealth in Jericho. Everything there belonged to Him. The word translated "accursed" carried a double meaning; first, the idea that any of the "accursed" items would convey a heavenly curse upon anyone who took them, and second, was the idea that these items were sacred and belonged to the Lord. Part of the first meaning may have been an implication that the possessions of the Canaanites might be contaminated and would expose a new owner to the diseases that plagued the original pagan owners.

Achan, the man who stole the dedicated items, is identified here as a great-great grandson of Judah, born through the line of Zerah, one of the twins Tamar bore in the Genesis 38 story.

Because of what one man did, God withdrew His support from the entire nation, and they learned of God's anger the hard way. God allowed them to be soundly defeated by the pagan defenders of the nearby fortress called Ai. If we allow serious sins to go undetected and unchallenged in our communities, do we fall under the same sort of divine displeasure?

## II. Joshua's Dismay—Joshua 7:10

**10 And the Lord said unto Joshua, Get thee up; wherefore liest thou thus upon thy face?**

Utterly devastated by the unexpected defeat his army suffered at Ai, Joshua lay face down on the ground and in bewilderment cried out to the Lord. Before God scolded him for the sin in the camp, He reprimanded Joshua for his reaction to his army's loss. "Stand up!" the Lord corrected him. Instead of acting like a loser, Joshua needed to be actively taking steps to deal with the root of the problem. Similarly, we please God more when we confront our weakness and our mistakes instead of complaining when things do not work out well.

### III. God's Accusation—Joshua 7:11-12

**11 Israel hath sinned, and they have also transgressed my covenant which I commanded them: for they have even taken of the accursed thing, and have also stolen, and dissembled also, and they have put it even among their own stuff.**

**12 Therefore the children of Israel could not stand before their enemies, but turned their backs before their enemies, because they were accursed: neither will I be with you any more, except ye destroy the accursed from among you.**

Achan's sin had numerous components: 1) He touched the tainted pagan property, 2) He stole what belonged to God, 3) He sneaked around ("dissembled"), 4) He hid the loot, 5) He lied about it, and 6) He mixed the polluted pagan stuff with his family's belongings. Our own sins seldom are simple, single-faceted offenses. Usually a sin involves several layers of guilt and affects people we never intended to hurt.

God explains to Joshua that this sin of Achan caused the disaster at Ai. Because one Israelite tampered with the accursed Jericho property, all of Israel became accursed. Are the ripples of our private sins this far-reaching and damaging?

The Lord made it clear to Joshua that Israel could no longer expect God to fight for them in the conquest of Canaan unless they dealt decisively with the thoughtless thief. Centuries later, the Lord required the Church to implement the same sort of quick and unflinching action to remove flagrant sin from the ranks of believers. "Those who sin are to be rebuked publicly, so that the others may take warning," Paul told Timothy (1 Tim. 5:20, NIV). The Corinthian church was told to dismiss one member who was boasting of scandalous behavior (1 Cor. 5). Those who look the other way and tolerate wickedness in their number may forfeit the Lord's favor and pay the kind of price Israel paid at Ai.

### IV. Achan's Punishment—Joshua 7:22-26

**A. The Evidence Revealed, 22-23**

**22 So Joshua sent messengers, and they ran unto the tent; and, behold, it was hid in his tent, and the silver under it.**

**23 And they took them out of the midst of the tent, and brought them unto Joshua, and unto all the children of Israel, and laid them out before the LORD.**

Achan's loot is publicly displayed. All the Israeli leaders can see the evidence of what he has done. Once the revered property reveals Achan as the offender who caused Israel's troubles, Joshua sends men to recover the loot from the tent floor where Achan tells them he buried it. The Scriptures warn us that we can be sure that our sins cannot be hidden and will be brought to light (1 Tim. 5:25; Mark 4:22; 1 Cor. 4:5). What is hidden in the darkness will be exposed in the light (Eph. 5:13). This account of Achan well illustrates the basic Bible truth that "nothing in all creation is hidden from

God's sight. Everything is uncovered and laid bare before the eyes of him to whom we must give account" (Heb. 4:13, NIV).

## B. The Convicted, 24

**24 And Joshua, and all Israel with him, took Achan the son of Zerah, and the silver, and the garment, and the wedge of gold, and his sons, and his daughters, and his oxen, and his asses, and his sheep, and his tent, and all that he had: and they brought them unto the valley of Achor.**

The valley of Achor is literally the Valley of Trouble. Achan's sin brings trouble upon his neighbors, just as our sins today may impair the love of those who depend upon us.

A verse like this one imposes a theological choice on us—one we cannot avoid. When we read this Biblical account, either we affirm that God always does what is right and holy—and we accept this event as one more demonstration of His justice and wisdom, or else we are troubled by the severity of Achan's punishment and start looking for ways to distance our God from what took place here.

## C. The Execution, 25

**25 And Joshua said, Why hast thou troubled us? the LORD shall trouble thee this day. And all Israel stoned him with stones, and burned them with fire, after they had stoned them with stones.**

Here is a fascinating analogy using the word trouble in a deadly serious conversation. Joshua uses the word *trouble* to describe both what Achan brought upon Israel and what Israel is about to do to him.

Does it help us to understand Achan's execution if we look back at the story and realize that this man's seemingly private sin cost 36 soldiers their lives and exposed the entire Hebrew army to possible annihilation by their revived enemies? If you were the parent or wife of one of those fatalities, would you think Achan got what was coming to him?

## D. The Memorial, 26

**26 And they raised over him a great heap of stones unto this day. So the LORD turned from the fierceness of his anger. Wherefore the name of that place was called, The valley of Achor, unto this day.**

Because of their lasting quality, people have been stacking stones for centuries. Their monuments symbolize either reminders of grand achievements or memoirs to make sure we do not forget atrocities. The pile of stones in the valley of Achor represents a fitting way to memorialize one of history's most ancient stoning that occurred in that valley of trouble.

For now, we leave this tragic valley of the Wadi Qilt. In due course, Isaiah 65:10 will come to rename this valley as a peaceably blessed place, and the writer in Hosea 2:15 will similarly transform its despair into hope.

෨෬

## Evangelistic Emphasis

What Achan did at Ai, and its tragic results, points out an essential truth we should include in our evangelism. Specifically, we need to remember that Christian life is not completed at conversion, but only begins there. We should not desert a convert the moment he or she comes to the Lord.

In Achan's situation, he had an excellent background. Like all his fellow-countrymen he was descended from father Abraham. We assume his voice was among those who pledged to obey Joshua just as they had obeyed Moses. Further, they all said anyone who did not do this should be put to death (1:16-18).. Achan was better at promising than at performing. He did not follow through on his commitment to Joshua and the Lord.

Let us look closely at the Great Commission: Jesus said we should "teach all nations, baptizing them in the name of the Father, and of the Son, and of the Holy Ghost." That is the first part, but there is more to follow. "Teaching them to observe all things whatsoever I have commanded you," is included.

True, salvation comes by grace through faith, but we do not want to preach a cheap grace. God's wonderful gift deserves heart-felt obedience. Good evangelism includes good follow-up. Achan leaves us a good example not to follow.

## Memory Selection

ഇറ

"But the children of Israel committed a trespass in the accursed thing: for Achan ... of the tribe of Judah, took of the accursed thing: and the anger of the Lord was kindled against the children of Israel." *Joshua 7:1*

"A chain is no stronger than its weakest link." We have all heard that saying, and Achan demonstrated how it works. Israel was the chain and he was the weak link. He broke and the whole chain suffered.

In one way or another, the results of sin and guilt end up being shared. There is no such thing as a sin that hurts only the person(s) who commit it. "We're not hurting anybody," is something we often hear said about sexual sins. Not so. Any one of us can name bad situations that can result that go well beyond the perpetrators of the sin.

You and I are not going to be stoned to death by our friends and neighbors when we sin, as Achan was. (Unless they resort to the lynch mob scene we used to see in the old western movies. We hope it does not come to that!) Our families may suffer because of our sin, but they are not going to be stoned along with us, and everything we own, including our dead bodies, burned to a crisp.

We are living in a different time and under much different circumstances than Achan did. That does not mean we should ignore his sad story. All sin is bad. It hurts the sinner (even now it sometimes kills), it damages families and other relationships, and weakens churches. Sin makes Satan happy. Let us try not to let that happen.

## Weekday Problems

This was Laura's senior year in high school, and she was enjoying every minute of it. She had recently learned that she was being accepted into a national honors group for the very top tier of students. This made her parents happy and added to their pride that she was receiving a four-year college scholarship.

A couple of Laura's friends could afford to shop in the most exclusive department stores in town. Whether it was jeans or jewelry, sweaters or shoes, they always had the top of the line. She had to do her own shopping in popular priced and discount stores. She did love her friend's beautiful purchases.

One of the guys who lived near her had graduated high school the previous year. She saw him often, and he always seemed to have money to spend, though he did not have a job. One day he asked her if she would like to earn money by delivering small packages for him. She turned down his offer immediately when she learned he wanted her to deliver drugs on campus. He would not let the matter rest, and eventually convinced her that he was going to keep selling drugs, the students were going to continue buying them, and she would not hurt anybody by making money delivering tidy little envelopes to kids on campus.

After a couple of weeks making easy money she was nabbed by the officers who had been doing surveillance on her drug-dealing "friend." Problems abound: court appearances, honors group and scholarship disappear, parents crushed, teachers disappointed, friends vanish, future uncertain. Achan found his problem in a conquered Canaanite city. Laura found hers' on a high school campus.

## Going to the Dogs

Called to a rural church for his first preaching assignment, the fledgling pastor showed up for his first sermon. One parishioner had brought his dog to church. "Kindly remove the animal from God's house," the preacher insisted.

After the service the deacons informed the preacher that the pup had been accompanying his master to worship for years and had never caused any trouble. So, that afternoon, the chastened clergyman stopped by the home of the dog's owner to apologize.

"Oh, don't worry about it, Reverend," the man replied. "It all worked out O.K. I wouldn't have had my dog hear that sermon for anything in the world."

# This Lesson in Your Life

In Achan we see a soldier who dutifully marched in Joshua's army and helped with the slaughter inside Jericho's fallen walls. In him we also see a man who foolishly marched along a classical path to sin,. He was neither the first nor the last to march his way right into sin.

We are all sinners, so we need to take note of Achan. There is probably a little bit of that man in all of us. First John 1:8 says that if we claim to be without sin we deceive ourselves and the truth is not in us. Achan is nobody's hero, but sometimes even a non-hero has a lot to teach us.

Achan knew the rules. He knew not to take anything, but he took something anyhow. How did he fall into this trap? He seems to have done it with his eyes wide open. My guess is he did a lot of rationalizing. He just talked himself into it by thinking things through and using what he thought was common sense.

Anybody, especially a soldier, knew that ever since there had been wars the tradition was that to the winners went the spoils. That is just the way things were. A soldier risked his life in a battle, and if he came through it alive and on the winning side, it was a small thing if he helped himself to whatever was available.

The lovely gleam of silver and gold caught his eye. He was not going to take that for himself, he might have said. He would take it for the security of his family. He had a wife and children to think about. With all of Canaan against Israel, the future could not be more uncertain. Who knew what might happen? If he died in battle, at least he would have provided for his family. As for the beautiful robe from Babylon, that was just a little bonus.

The Bible does not give us any information about how he managed to dig a hole under his tent floor and bury his contraband. It is hard for us to imagine that his family was not involved in some way. There cannot be too much privacy in a tent. It is just the nature of sin that it spreads itself like a contagious germ.

We have all seen the signs as we drive down the street: "We Buy Gold." Achan had about five pounds of silver and a pound and a fourth of gold. Any of us could sell that much precious metal for a big handful of dollars. That was no minor temptation that Achan found in Jericho.

It is not likely that any of us are going to sin on purpose. We are not going to say, "I think I'll go out and do some sinning today." As with Achan though, the possibility for sin is there and we might fall victim to it.

James 1:13-15 tells us that when we are tempted, it is our own evil desire that causes us to be dragged away and enticed. He does not leave us any wiggle-room for excuse making. Rationalization will not work. He sees this as a conception to death process. When desire has conceived, it gives birth to sin. When sin is full-grown, it gives birth to death. If Achan could have been calm enough to think clearly before they started throwing stones at him, he might have said "Amen" to what James wrote.

**1. What did Achan do that was forbidden?**

He took some of the possessions that had belonged to the citizens of Jericho. All silver, gold, brass and iron, was to go into the Lord's treasury (6:18-19), and Achan helped himself to some silver and gold.

**2. What was the Lord's reaction to Achan's sin?**

The Lord's anger "was kindled against the children of Israel."

**3. While still at Jericho and planning his next attack, Joshua sent men to spy out what city and its countryside?**

He sent them to take a look at Ai, a relatively small city, but next in Joshua's logical line of attack.

**4. What report did the men bring back concerning Ai?**

They reported that only two or three thousand soldiers should be needed because they were few at Ai.

**5. Joshua sent about three thousand men to conquer Ai. Were they victorious? How did the battle go?**

This was a huge defeat for Israel. Joshua's men fled, and thirty-six were killed as they were chased by Ai's defenders.

**6. How did the Israelites respond to this unexpected defeat?**

"The hearts of the people melted, and became as water."

**7. What did Joshua do that demonstrated his feelings about what happened?**

He tore his clothing and fell face down before the ark and stayed there until evening. He (and Israel's elders) put dust on their heads.

**8. What was the Lord's reaction to Joshua's mournful position face down on the ground?**

The Lord told him to get up, and asked why he was down on his face.

**9. When it was revealed that Achan had hidden the forbidden items under the floor of his tent, why did he say he had taken them?**

He simply said that he saw the spoils; he coveted them and took them.

**10. What happened to Achan, his entire family and all his possessions?**

They were stoned to death and then burned. They piled a great heap of stones over Achan.

439

We have been studying some exceptionally heavy material. The sturdy, protective walls of a well fortified city have collapsed. An army of Israelites clamored through the rubble and killed every living thing inside, with the exception of Rahab's people. Men, women, children, animals, were all put to the sword. What rating would a movie get if it showed all this in graphic detail?

All this, of course, meant victory for Joshua. Following wiping out Jericho so completely, he confidently sent three thousand men to take the much smaller town of Ai. His men fled in disarray as they were fiercely chased by Ai's defenders. Thirty-six Israelis were killed in this melee. Joshua was shocked, devastated, embarrassed that his troops turned their backs to the enemy. He prostrated himself on the ground before the ark and put dust on his head.

This picture has gone from bad to worse. We need something uplifting from it. As we might expect, it is God who provides the uplift, both literally and figuratively. While Joshua was face to the floor with dirt on his head, God appeared and said "Stand up! What are you doing down on your face" (7:10 NIV)? God told this groveling man to lift himself up and do something positive.

There is a time for humility and mourning. There are times when constructive action is needed. God knew that a serious transgression had been committed and he wanted Joshua to get to the bottom of it. Nothing good was going to happen until Joshua began taking care of business.

Just as soon as the affair with Achan was finished, we find a renewed spirit. The whole attitude changes for the better, as we read in 8:1, "The Lord said unto Joshua, Fear not, neither be thou dismayed: take all the people of war with thee, and arise, go up to Ai: see, I have given into thy hand the king of Ai . . . ."

Joshua had been dealing with a serious problem, and he let it paralyze him into inaction. That is the very kind of thing the Lord will help us to avoid... Scripture offers an alternative for us when we, like Joshua, tend to accept an overload of care.

This song will be sung in the land of Judah . . .
Thou wilt keep him in perfect peace, whose mind
is stayed on thee: because he trusteth in thee.

Isaiah 26:1-3

Rejoice in the Lord always ... The Lord is near . . .
Do not be anxious about anything, but in
everything, by prayer and petition, with thanksgiving,
present your requests to God. And the peace of God,
which transcends all understanding, will guard your
hearts and your minds in Christ Jesus.

Philippians 4:4-7 (NIV)

ഇൻ

440

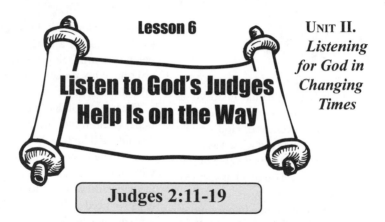

**Lesson 6**

## Listen to God's Judges Help Is on the Way

### Judges 2:11-19

And the children of Israel did evil in the sight of the LORD, and served Baalim:

12 And they forsook the LORD God of their fathers, which brought them out of the land of Egypt, and followed other gods, of the gods of the people that were round about them, and bowed themselves unto them, and provoked the LORD to anger.

13 And they forsook the LORD, and served Baal and Ashtaroth.

14 And the anger of the LORD was hot against Israel, and he delivered them into the hands of spoilers that spoiled them, and he sold them into the hands of their enemies round about, so that they could not any longer stand before their enemies.

15 Whithersoever they went out, the hand of the LORD was against them for evil, as the LORD had said, and as the LORD had sworn unto them: and they were greatly distressed.

16 Nevertheless the LORD raised up judges, which delivered them out of the hand of those that spoiled them.

17 And yet they would not hearken unto their judges, but they went a whoring after other gods, and bowed themselves unto them: they turned quickly out of the way which their fathers walked in, obeying the commandments of the LORD; but they did not so.

18 And when the LORD raised them up judges, then the LORD was with the judge, and delivered them out of the hand of their enemies all the days of the judge: for it repented the LORD because of their groanings by reason of them that oppressed them and vexed them.

19 And it came to pass, when the judge was dead, that they returned, and corrupted themselves more than their fathers, in following other gods to serve them, and to bow down unto them; they ceased not from their own doings, nor from their stubborn way.

July 10

**Memory Verse**
Judges 2:17

**Background Scripture**
Judges 2; 21:25

**Devotional Reading**
Psalm 78:1-8

The era of the Judges was a low point in Israel's spiritual history—a time when even the best people seemed to have little awareness of God's rules for life. "Every man did what was right in his own eyes," the final verse of the book explains, and often what seemed right was terribly wrong.

We seem to be coming into a similar time in America—a time when biblical morality no longer is the measure used by the majority, a time when deviant behaviors are being normalized and anyone who dares to speak out is branded as a bigot.

The book of Judges offers one ray of hope. Even in that benighted time, the morality and faith of the people seemed to rally whenever God allowed a leader with faith. Under that person's influence, the nation drew nearer to the Lord. Perhaps we need to be praying for God to raise up such leaders today.

ഇരുട്ട

### For a Lively Start

Although the book of Judges describes a moral Dark Age in Israel, the writing style in the book shows surprising sophistication. At the end of Deborah's saga we will find a classic ballad as good as any in more literate times. Moreover, the basic format, like the home-base melody in a great piece of classical music, echoes repeat-edly. Each judge's tale begins with the same leading line, "The people of Israel again did what was evil in the Lord's eyes," so God "gave them up into the hands" of some enemy, who afflicted Israel until the Lord "raised up a judge."

Before long the reader of Judges will begin to hear the familiar tune that says, "A new judge is coming." The writer's technique works well to help us follow a rather puzzling tale of moral confusion.

| Teaching Outline | Daily Bible Readings |
|---|---|
| I. Israel Forsakes the Lord—Judges 2:11-13<br>  A. The God Who Freed Them from Egypt, 11-12<br>  B. The Gods of Canaan, 13<br>II. God Punishes This Unfaithfulness—Judges 2:14-15<br>  A. Enemies Allowed to Dominate, 14<br>  B. No Divine Help in Battle, 15<br>III. God Raises up Judges—Judges 2:16-18<br>  A. Deliverance from Enemies, 16-17<br>  B. God Hears Israel's Groaning, 18<br>IV. Israel Slides Back into Idolatry—Judges 2:19 | Mon. The Snare of Other Gods<br>  *Exodus 23:20-33*<br>Tue. A Covenant to Obey God<br>  *Joshua 24:19-27*<br>Wed. Better to Obey and Heed<br>  *1 Samuel 15:17-23*<br>Thu. God's Wrath for the Disobedient<br>  *Ephesians 5:6-20*<br>Fri. An Ignorant Generation<br>  *Judges 2:1-10*<br>Sat. Teaching the Next Generation<br>  *Psalm 78:1-8*<br>Sun. A Cycle of Stubborn Sin<br>  *Judges 2:11-19* |

# *Verse by Verse*

**Judges 2:11-19**

**I. Israel Forsakes the Lord— Judges 2:11-13**

**A. The God Who Freed Them from Egypt, 11-12**

**11 And the children of Israel did evil in the sight of the LORD, and served Baalim:**

**12 And they forsook the LORD God of their fathers, which brought them out of the land of Egypt, and followed other gods, of the gods of the people that were round about them, and bowed themselves unto them, and provoked the LORD to anger.**

The sin identified in vs. 11 is idolatry. The rather odd spelling of "Baalim" has no reference to the soundalike prophet's name, Baalam. Instead, *im* in Hebrew pluralizes a word just like *s* in English. Therefore, in modern syntax, our newer Bible versions tell us here that Israel served "the Baals." Baal, in its various manifestations, was a fertility god the Canaanite people worshiped with orgies of drunkenness and sex and with human sacrifices involving their children.

God had led His people out of Egypt. As long as they remembered His mighty acts of deliverance, they humbled themselves before Him and obeyed His instructions. However, later generations would entertain debauchery that characterized the pagan worship in Canaan. The Lord's anger was aroused not just by petty jealousy but more so because His people would lower themselves to such decadence.

**B. The Gods of Canaan, 13**

**13 And they forsook the LORD, and served Baal and Ashtaroth.**

God was distressed when He saw them defiling themselves with the sordid immorality common to those who worshiped the fertility gods and goddesses.

**II. God Punishes This Unfaithfulness—Judges 2:14-15**

**A. Enemies Allowed to Dominate, 14**

**14 And the anger of the LORD was hot against Israel, and he delivered them into the hands of spoilers that spoiled them, and he sold them into the hands of their enemies round about, so that they could not any longer stand before their enemies.**

The Lord's displeasure with His people in this instance was not just mild irritation. He became "furious" with them (TEV). He "burned with anger" (NLT). He got so upset with them that He allowed various enemies—first one nation and then another—to dominate them.

What a contrast this is to the days of Joshua. When Israel was true to the Lord under Joshua's strong leadership, no enemy army could withstand their attack. No king could successfully oppose them because the Lord fought for His people. However, in story after Judges story the Lord repays Israel's evil by allowing neighboring enemies to conquer His people.

### B. No Divine Help in Battle, 15

**15 Whithersoever they went out, the hand of the LORD was against them for evil, as the LORD had said, and as the LORD had sworn unto them: and they were greatly distressed.**

"Whithersoever" is old English for "wherever." In those periods when Israel was disobedient to the Lord, He allowed them to fail in war no matter where they turned. It was just as He had warned them through Moses and then later through Joshua. If they chose to serve the Lord, He would fight for them and protect them. If they chose to turn away to do evil and follow other gods, they could not expect the Lord to defend them. Without His aid, times got tough. The enemy nations oppressed them with great cruelty. God let it happen in order to punish them for their evil.

### III. God Raises up Judges— Judges 2:16-18

### A. Deliverance from Enemies, 16-17

**16 Nevertheless the LORD raised up judges, which delivered them out of the hand of those that spoiled them.**

**17 And yet they would not hearken unto their judges, but they went a whoring after other gods, and bowed themselves unto them: they turned quickly out of the way which their fathers walked in, obeying the commandments of the LORD; but they did not so.**

Vs. 16 explains why the series of judges showed up during the days recorded in this Bible book. The Lord "raised" them up as leaders who could rescue their people from the mistreatment of whatever enemy held them at that time. Does God raise up godly leaders to give our land comfort after times of unfaithfulness?

Vs. 17's classic KJV phrase "they went awhoring after other gods" embodies a favorite metaphor of the prophets. It is an appropriate metaphor, since the pagan worship involved so much illicit sexual activity. God throughout Scripture calls Himself Israel's husband. The name of the pagan god Baal also means husband. So God portrays the situation here as a struggle between two suitors for the same woman, the nation of Israel. When His people chose Baal, God says they are being unfaithful to Him like a wayward wife.

Israel's ancestors in Joshua's time had been faithful. They had obeyed God, but in contrast, the rather confusing phrases in the end of vs. 17 say that the people in the days of the judges did not obey Him.

### B. God Hears Israel's Groaning, 18

**18** And when the LORD raised them up judges, then the LORD was with the judge, and delivered them out of the hand of their enemies all the days of the judge: for it repented the LORD because of their groanings by reason of them that oppressed them and vexed them.

The Lord will call judge after judge to lead Israel in repeated victory over intermittent enemies. This verse describes the period that would follow each judge's success. Leaders like Deborah, Gideon, and Samson answered the call to free their people from oppression.

Just as God heard the cries of the Hebrew people during their slavery in Egypt, now He again hears their mournful cry for relief from the cruelty of their conquering enemies. In the same way, the Lord hears us when we cry out to Him in our moments of greatest distress. When times are worst for us, we need to pray and watch for His deliverance.

### IV. Israel Slides Back into Idolatry—Judges 2:19

**19** And it came to pass, when the judge was dead, that they returned, and corrupted themselves more than their fathers, in following other gods to serve them, and to bow down unto them; they ceased not from their own doings, nor from their stubborn way.

Unfortunately, the people of Israel always seem to regress. When their liberating judge dies, they revert to their doomed pagan idolatry. Moreover, that choice opened the door for another period of enslavement by another aggressive enemy.

"Their own doings" means the people's way of living instead of the way God had commanded. They stubbornly wanted to do things their way, even when that choice obviously is causing them untold suffering.

℘〰℀

## Evangelistic Emphasis

Just a glimpse into Judges lets us know all too quickly that Israel was in a spiritual decline. Not only had they not eliminated the Canaanite pagans from the land, but many Israelites had begun to worship their gods.

While there are millions of faith-filled Christians in our own country, still we seem to be steadily moving toward a more secular society. We cannot assume that Christian values are the norm in America.

Historically, wars have prompted population migrations. Recent wars have brought millions of people to us who have carried their foreign (to us) religions with them. The religious landscape of America is changing.

We can observe the spiritual and moral decline of Israel during the time of the judges. We are aware of the ever-changing social and religious conditions in America. It should be an easy step for us to take warning from what happened in ancient Israel and be aware of our own nation's present need to put emphasis on preaching the gospel.

The Cross carries a powerful message. Jesus said, "But I, when I am lifted up from the earth, will draw all men to myself" (John 12:32 NIV). You and I have the privilege of telling others about this.

## ಇ⊃ಛ

## Memory Selection

"...They would not hearken unto their judges, but they went a whoring after other gods, and bowed themselves unto them: they turned quickly out of the way which their fathers walked in, obeying the commandments of the LORD, but they did not so." *Judges 2:17*

The Israelites made a terrible mistake in possessing the Promised Land by allowing Canaanite paganism to remain there. During Joshua's time, as well as the period of the judges, they did not fulfill God's requirement that they displace the Canaanites and break down their shrines.

Not only did they allow paganism to remain, but they also committed spiritual adultery ("went a whoring after") by participating in it. We can take "spiritual adultery/whoring after" in the figurative sense of being unfaithful to God. We can also make a literal use of the terms, for much pagan worship consisted of sexual orgies. Commandments one, two, and seven out of the Ten were ignored. We might wonder what happened with the remaining ones.

You and I will do well to remember that we are warned to keep away from idolatry. Paul reminds us that among other evils which we are to "mortify" (put to death), we should include "covetousness, which is idolatry" (Col. 3:5). Paul also reminds us that there is a force at work that he calls the god of this age. It blinds the minds of unbelievers so that they cannot see the light of the gospel (2 Cor. 4:4). During the period of Israel's judges, Satan worked through paganism. For you and me, he uses a more subtle approach. We want to be on the watch for any of his dirty tricks.

446

## Weekday Problems

"What's this younger generation coming to," we old-timers sometime say. It does appear (to many people in my age bracket) that Judeo-Christian morality (which is to say biblical morality), is no longer the standard of measurement that it should be.

I try to be cautious in passing such judgments. I have recently done research on one of my great-great-grandfathers, who was a Methodist circuit-riding preacher in Arkansas in the 1840s and 1850s. The clergyman who wrote the book I was using, a history of Arkansas Methodism during that period, stressed the need for more preachers, because the younger generation was forsaking religion. Maybe so. Maybe not. I can count six different Christian denominations where my ancestor's descendants regularly fill church pews each Sunday.

There is no doubt, though, about the younger generation that followed that of Joshua. When Joshua's generation "were gathered unto their fathers," there arose a generation "which knew not the LORD" and did not remember the works He had done for Israel. They forsook the God of their fathers and worshipped the Canaanite pagan gods.

Every new generation faces the same problem. They have to demonstrate to the old one – more importantly to their loving God, that He is alive in their hearts, and that they will share His gospel with the next new generation.

---

# Daffynitions

*An optimist:* A fellow who puts his shoes back on when the preacher says, "Finally."

*Ecumenism:* Getting to know the opposite sects.

*An egotist:* Someone who is always me-deep in conversation.

*A cult:* The church down the street from yours.

*A will:* A dead give-away.

---

# This Lesson in Your Life

The central problem with the Israelites who were born following Joshua's leadership is that they forsook God. They had no memory (Did they chose not to remember?) of the mighty works of God in delivering their ancestors from bondage and into Canaan. They did not remember *who* they were, or how they got to *where* they were. They forgot that the land of Canaan was the Land of Promise, and that their lives were part of that promise. They were neglecting God's gift to them.

They chose to live in the 'here and now" of paganism. If temple prostitutes and sexual "worship" encouraged good crops and large herds of farm animals, that made "Do not commit adultery" seem like an out-of-date concept. They had no time for God. They forsook Him. There is a lesson here for our lives.

How could we possibly forget God, we might ask. The answer is, we can do it all too easily. The number of diversions available to us is astounding. Considering the hours spent on the work week, there is not time enough remaining in a simple 24 hour day to do all the things that are available. This is not counting time to eat breakfast each morning and take the garbage out at night. Some of my friends who are retired keep busier than others who have full time jobs.

It amazes me how so many people find time for social networking via computer. (Wondering about that, is one of the self-righteous foibles that I enjoy.) Those very people who enjoy this diversion may wonder why I enjoy genealogy. Why, they might well ask, would I want to spend time researching dead people when I could be enjoying real-time living ones. They would have a good point.

There is a purpose for discussing how we spend time. It leads to how we might forget God. The old Israelites got involved in paganism. There are plenty of evil ways that you and I might be led away from God, but for the moment, let us just think about the innocent ones. Hebrews 2:1 says we should pay careful attention to what we have heard about the Lord, lest we slip away. Newer translations say "drift away." Let us think about this.

It is very unlikely that we are going to decide deliberately to turn our backs on God. We are not going to say, "I'm forgetting God." What we might do, though, is inadvertently slip away, like a drifting boat that accidentally eases out into the lake. We are not going to rev up the boat's motor and go high-speed away from God. We would never do that. We would be more likely to get so busy living that bit by bit we would forget the One who gave life to us. It is not necessary to be an evil, sin-loving person in order to forsake God. It does not require worshipping in a Canaanite pagan shrine. It can be done innocently and unintentionally when we get too involved with self and the busy work of enjoying the blessing God has made available to us. We appreciate the gifts. Let us remember the Giver of all good things.

## GETTING
## THE FACTS STRAIGHT

**1. After God freed the Israelites from Egypt what did the children of Israel do?**
The children of Israel did evil in the sight of the Lord, and served other gods. v. 11

**2. After the generation of Joshua and the elders who served with him died, what happened to the Israelites?**
They forsook the Lord and worshipped other gods. They did not remember the works the Lord performed as he brought their ancestors out of Egypt. v.12

**3. In what way had the Israelites deserted the Lord?**
They deserted the Lord to serve fertility gods and goddesses. v. 13

**4. How did the anger of the Lord manifest itself?**
Enemies of Israel were allowed to conquer them as repayment for their evil ways.

**5. For Israel's disobedience to the Lord, what was a major cause of their distress?**
The Lord was against the Israelites for their evil ways and withheld divine help in their battles. v. 15

**6. What did the Lord do to help the Israelites to rescue them from their enemies?**
The Lord raised up Judges to deliver them. v.16

**7. Did the Israelites follow reformation efforts of the Judges?**
No. The degenerate Israelites were not effectually and thoroughly reformed. They reverted to idolatry by serving unworthy gods and goddesses. v. 17

**8. Hearing the cries for help from the Israelites, What did the Lord do?**
The Lord called for leadership and He was answered by Judges to guide Israel to freedom from oppression. v.18

**9. When liberating Judges pass away, were their reformations maintained?**
No. When their Judge was dead, the Israelites reverted to their pagan idolatry as a contradiction to their reformers. v.19

**10. As Israel slides back towards idolatry, what happens to the godforsaken?**
Those that have forsaken the good ways of God, which they have once known and profess, commonly grow most daring and desperate in sin, and have their hearts most hardened...until God is angered by or takes pity on them. God does not desert.

**449**

Here is a little story. Once upon a time there were two oaken buckets. Each day they were taken from the cottage to the village well and filled with fresh water. By nightfall they were always empty. The next morning they would be taken back to the village well, and the cycle would begin all over again. Day in, day out, it continued.

One night as they sat empty and dry on the table in the cottage, one bucket said to the other: "I'm so discouraged. No matter how full we are filled in the morning, by night we're always dry. It never fails." The other bucket replied: "I'm so encouraged. No matter how dry we are at night, we're always filled the next morning. It never fails."

We have the choice as to which of these buckets we want to be. The Lord never fails, but we may have some dry times. The people of Israel certainly went through some difficult days during the time of the judges. As a matter of fact, there were repeated patterns (with variations) through which they went. As outlined in the "Old Testament Survey" (LaSor, Hubbard and Bush), here is their cycle:

The people "do evil" by serving other gods.
God sends a nation to oppose them.
The people cry out to God.
He raises up a judge deliverer.
The oppressor is defeated.
The people have rest.

There is goodness and a severity with God (Rom. 11:22). He is both kind and stern. The Israelite's unfaithfulness brought His sternness, but His gentle mercy rescued them over and again. My guess is that some of them thought God came down hard on them and treated them roughly. We all hope there were some insightful people among them who saw the gentle Shepherd trying to keep his straying sheep in the safety of the fold.

We have a good God. He is kind and merciful. He is generous, even sacrificial. His Son embodies His very Being. He sent His Holy Spirit. We are Christ's spiritual Body, His Church. He has provided us with Scripture, such as the Book of Judges which shows us how much He loves even a rebellious people. No matter how dry the Israelites (or we) are in the evening, He will refresh us in the morning.

It is of the LORD'S mercies that we are not consumed,
because his compassions fail not.
They are new every morning: great is thy faithfulness.
The LORD is my portion, saith my soul;
therefore I will hope in him.
Lamentations 3:22-24

# Lesson 7

## Use God's Strength Help from Unexpected Sources

### Judges 3:15-25, 29-30

But when the children of Israel cried unto the LORD, the LORD raised them up a deliverer, Ehud the son of Gera, a Benjamite, a man lefthanded: and by him the children of Israel sent a present unto Eglon the king of Moab.

16 But Ehud made him a dagger which had two edges, of a cubit length; and he did gird it under his raiment upon his right thigh.

17 And he brought the present unto Eglon king of Moab: and Eglon was a very fat man.

18 And when he had made an end to offer the present, he sent away the people that bare the present.

19 But he himself turned again from the quarries that were by Gilgal, and said, I have a secret errand unto thee, O king: who said, Keep silence. And all that stood by him went out from him.

20 And Ehud came unto him; and he was sitting in a summer parlour, which he had for himself alone. And Ehud said, I have a message from God unto thee. And he arose out of his seat.

21 And Ehud put forth his left hand, and took the dagger from his right thigh, and thrust it into his belly:

22 And the haft also went in after the blade; and the fat closed upon the blade, so that he could not draw the dagger out of his belly; and the dirt came out.

23 Then Ehud went forth through the porch, and shut the doors of the parlour upon him, and locked them.

24 When he was gone out, his servants came; and when they saw that, behold, the doors of the parlour were locked, they said, Surely he covereth his feet in his summer chamber.

25 And they tarried till they were ashamed: and, behold, he opened not the doors of the parlour; therefore they took a key, and opened them: and, behold, their lord was fallen down dead on the earth. . . .

29 And they slew of Moab at that time about ten thousand men, all lusty, and all men of valour; and there escaped not a man.

30 So Moab was subdued that day under the hand of Israel. And the land had rest fourscore years.

**Memory Verse**
Judges 3:15
**Background Scripture**
Judges 3:7-31; 21:25
**Devotional Reading**
Psalm 27:7-14

# fOCuS

Have you noticed that the Bible seldom describes even its main characters? How tall was Abraham, for example? What color were his eyes or his hair? We do not have a clue. The only time the Bible's characters are described is when that part of their appearance matters in the story.

Therefore, we know from the start that the outcome of this account

## For a Lively Start

We know nothing about Ehud except this one account about his courage. He put his life on the line to free his people. As we observe both his bravery and his braininess in plotting the overthrow of King Eglon, we can see why the Lord singled out Ehud as the right one to become a judge of Israel.

In the judge stories that follow, Bible

requires us to know that Ehud is left-handed and that Eglon...well, obese may be an understatement.

Sure enough, Ehud's clever strategy for getting his weapon through security depends on his left-handedness. Those that are right-handed wear their swords on their left hip. Ehud could expect a less-than-alert security man to pat down that hip, thus allowing the left-handed assassin to slip through with his sawed off sword strapped on the unchecked side. Moreover, his victim's obesity helped the short sword to vanish in the dead king's abdomen.

୫୬୦୪

readers sometimes are puzzled when they see righteousness often was not one of the qualifications God looked for when He was choosing a new champion. Instead, God usually picked the new judge because he or she was the toughest person in the territory. At times, they were also the meanest and the most immoral. Therefore, we may not go to this part of the Bible to find heroes to emulate.

| Teaching Outline | Daily Bible Readings |
|---|---|
| I. Ehud Raised up as Judge—Judges 3:15a<br>II. Ehud Assassinates Eglon—Judges 3:15b-22<br>  A. Delivering the Annual Tribute, 15b<br>  B. Ehud's Special Sword, 16<br>  C. A Private Audience with the King, 17-20a<br>  D. A Message for the King, 20b-22<br>III. Ehud's Escape—Judges 3:23-25<br>  A. His Unseen Departure, 23<br>  B. Delay in Finding the Body, 24-25<br>IV. Victory over Moab—Judges 3:29-30 | Mon. The Lord Is My Stronghold<br>*Psalm 27:1-6*<br>Tue. Wait for the Lord<br>*Psalm 27:7-14*<br>Wed. A Cry for Help<br>*Habakkuk 1:1-5*<br>Thu. In God I Trust<br>*Psalm 56:1-11*<br>Fri. May the Lord Give Strength<br>*Psalm 29*<br>Sat. God Will Protect and Deliver<br>*Isaiah 31:1-5*<br>Sun. God Raises Up a Deliverer<br>*Judges 3:15-25, 29-30* |

# *Verse by Verse*

**Judges 3:15-25, 29-30**

## I. Ehud Raised up as Judge—Judges 3:15a

**15a But when the children of Israel cried unto the LORD, the LORD raised them up a deliverer, Ehud the son of Gera, a Benjamite, a man lefthanded:**

This judge story, like most of the others, begins in vs. 12 with the familiar line, "The children of Israel did evil again in the sight of the LORD," so He allowed the Moabites to defeat them and subject them to cruel oppression. However, just as in Egypt when God's people cried out in their misery, again the Lord hears His people and has mercy upon them.

The text says He raised up for them a "deliverer" or, as the TEV tells us, "a man to set them free." We call these deliverers "judges"—a word that means nothing like it does today when we use it to refer to legal magistrates presiding in courtrooms. "Hero" or "military champion" would be closer to the biblical term.

Strangely enough, the name of this left-handed deliverer, Ehud, in Hebrew literally means "son of my right hand." His left-handedness made Ehud able to slip through security with a sword when the king's guards searched for weapons on the side where right-handed men would wear them.

## II. Ehud Assassinates Eglon—Judges 3:15b-22

### A. Delivering the Annual Tribute, 15b

**15b . . . and by him the children of Israel sent a present unto Eglon the king of Moab.**

This "present" that Ehud takes to the king is identified in almost all our newer Bible versions as "tribute" or, even more precisely, as "tribute money" (NLT). It was part of the price Eglon exacted from his Hebrew subjects. Evidently, the gift was so sizeable that, as the next verses indicate, it took several men to deliver it to the king.

### B. Ehud's Special Sword, 16

**16 But Ehud made him a dagger which had two edges, of a cubit length; and he did gird it under his raiment upon his right thigh.**

In order to slip a weapon past Eglon's bodyguards, Ehud fashioned for himself a special two-edged sword. Like a sawed-off shotgun, this 18-inch weapon could be hidden under his robes, strapped to his right thigh. Most men wore their sword on their left thigh, so Ehud was gambling that

Eglon's bodyguards would do a careless search and miss his concealed weapon. His ruse worked.

## C. A Private Audience with the King, 17-20a

**17 And he brought the present unto Eglon king of Moab: and Eglon was a very fat man.**

**18 And when he had made an end to offer the present, he sent away the people that bare the present.**

**19 But he himself turned again from the quarries that were by Gilgal, and said, I have a secret errand unto thee, O king: who said, Keep silence. And all that stood by him went out from him.**

**20a And Ehud came unto him; and he was sitting in a summer parlour, which he had for himself alone.**

Ehud further fooled the king and his guards by going about the delivery of the tribute money in a routine way. Only after the tribute had been presented did he send away his helpers and return to Eglon's palace. He got as far away from the palace as a landmark near Gilgal—called "quarries" in the KJV but identified by most Hebrew scholars as stone statues or idols.

When Ehud got face to face with Eglon again, he kept the king from being apprehensive by flattering his ego. "I have a secret message for you from my God," he confided to the rotund one. Taking the bait, Eglon told Ehud to hush until all the servants and royal attendants were out of hearing.

All of this was happening in what the KJV calls "a summer parlour." The NRSV calls it his "cool roof chamber"—in other words, not a secure area inside a substantial stone palace. It was the king's personal retreat area, so it was somewhat secluded from the usual traffic of the palace.

## D. A Message for the King, 20b-22

**20b And Ehud said, I have a message from God unto thee. And he arose out of his seat.**

**21 And Ehud put forth his left hand, and took the dagger from his right thigh, and thrust it into his belly:**

**22 And the haft also went in after the blade; and the fat closed upon the blade, so that he could not draw the dagger out of his belly; and the dirt came out.**

Eglon was ready and eager to hear some privileged message from the God of the Israelites. Imagine his horror when that "message" turned out to be Ehud's sawed-off sword, which Ehud thrust into the mid section of the corpulent king. The sword must have been razor sharp and Ehud's stroke must have been forceful, for the sword was completely buried, handle and all. The "haft" in the KJV we would call the "hilt." The sword went in so deep that Ehud could not retrieve it. Ehud's guards likely would not have known what killed their obese master if his intestines had not drained out of the sword's entryway. God's message to Eglon was final and fatal.

## III. Ehud's Escape—Judges 3:23-25

### A. His Unseen Departure, 23

**23 Then Ehud went forth through the porch, and shut the doors of the parlour upon him, and locked them.**

Ehud made good his escape from the king's summer porch by wisely locking the doors and slipping out the back way so that the king's servants did not know he was gone. Ehud was long gone before the palace attendants realized anything was amiss.

**B. Delay in Finding the Body, 24-25**

**24 When he was gone out, his servants came; and when they saw that, behold, the doors of the parlour were locked, they said, Surely he covereth his feet in his summer chamber.**

**25 And they tarried till they were ashamed: and, behold, he opened not the doors of the parlour; therefore they took a key, and opened them: and, behold, their lord was fallen down dead on the earth . . . .**

Some time after Ehud had fled, the king's servants began to wonder if they needed to check on their sovereign. When they found the doors to the private chamber locked, however, they delayed their entry, fearing that they might embarrass the king. "Covering his feet" (KJV) leaves us scratching our heads. If we check several of the newer Bible versions, we will see that the royal servants surmised that the king was on the palace commode "relieving himself" or "using the latrine." Therefore, they were slow to barge in.

As the minutes of quietness ticked by, the servants became more anxious ("ashamed"). Finally they unlocked the door to the king's chamber and found him dead on the floor.

**IV. Victory over Moab—Judges 3:29-30**

**29 And they slew of Moab at that time about ten thousand men, all lusty, and all men of valour; and there escaped not a man.**

**30 So Moab was subdued that day under the hand of Israel. And the land had rest fourscore years.**

Vs. 28 tells us that when Eglon was dead, Ehud rallied the Israelite troops and killed a host of Moab's best soldiers who were trying to flee across the Jordan River to get back to their homes. "Lusty" means strong or able-bodied.

Thus, through the daring and cleverness of Ehud, the Lord set His people free from bitter bondage to the Moabites and they enjoyed 80 good years.

ഓരോ

## Evangelistic Emphasis

The period of the judges was a stressful time for Israel. They would forsake the Lord and enter into paganism, then find themselves overwhelmed by enemy forces. They would repent, call on the Lord, and He would rescue them by giving them a judge who could lead them to victory and peace. It was when they "hit bottom" that they realized they needed help to get back up.

This same principle applies to today's unbelievers, and sends a message to those of us who want to lead others to the Lord. Tragedies of whatever kind cause people to re-evaluate life. Any calamity, can trigger a deeper look into life's values – what is truly important and what is not.

This kind of situation has been described as being a window of opportunity. People who previously had closed themselves off from the good news of the gospel might become more receptive as they perceive the turmoil and vacancy in their lives. This is a time when they need answers.

Jesus had compassion on the multitudes who were "distressed and downcast like sheep without a shepherd" (Matt. 9:36 NAS). He told his disciples that the harvest was plentiful, but workers few. They should pray the Lord of the harvest to send out workers into His harvest. This is where you and I can enter the picture.

ॐ

## Memory Selection

"When the children of Israel cried unto the Lord, the Lord raised them up a deliverer, Ehud . . . a man lefthanded . . . ." *Judges 3:15*

There are times when we wish the Bible would give us more information about some situation it is relating to us. Other times, such as the events surrounding Ehud the judge, we are given interesting tidbits of details that fit neatly into the story. We know Ehud is left-handed, which helps him slip the dagger from his right thigh. We know the king who is to get the dagger plunged through his stomach is fat. This caused him to rise out of his chair slowly and present a large and easy target for Ehud's surprise left-handed thrust. This has all the makings of a thriller novel – but it is true.

The Lord raised up some interesting characters to serve as judges. They were more qualified for the military than what we think of as judicial, so we do not want to be thrown off by the word "judge."

On the battlefield Ehud probably kept his opponents guessing. They never knew what he might do next. It was while Ehud was delivering the tribute that Israel paid him that he managed to get the king's guards out of the room. When Ehud said he had a message to him from God, the king hefted his heavy body out of the chair. Ehud's dagger delivered a surprise message.

Ehud was a smooth operator, but he got the job done. In battle his men killed 10,000 opponents and gained eighty years rest for Israel.

## Weekday Problems

Tom came from a family that did well to show up at church on Easter and Christmas. Tammy, on the other hand, grew up attending Sunday school and church regularly. By young adulthood though, this did not mean much to her.

They started dating in their mid-twenties, and like so many other young couples, were soon living together (without marriage, we need to insert.)

They both had jobs, and enjoyed buying expensive adult toys. Their apartment was filled with about every electronic entertainment gadget on the market. Two nice cars, plus a boat, water skies and snow skies, and an off-road vehicle begins the inventory of what filled their lives.

At some point they began to notice that their married friends were planning for children and a future. These friends enjoyed living, but had a life larger than fun and games. There was a deeper side to them. Bit by bit Tom and Tammy began to realize that there was a huge vacancy in their lives.

The Christian values that her parents had instilled in her began to call out to Tammy. She and Tom realized that they had made consuming gods out of what should have been incidental entertainment and recreation. They saw that their relationship with each other was shallow and not up to Christian standards.

This story has a storybook ending. They are now married, dedicated Christians, and thank the Lord for the new life He has given them. (We can see that He still rescues and gives peace, even as to Israel under the judges.)

## Just One of the Guys

Rev. Robert Runcie, retired Archbishop of Canterbury, tells of the time when he boarded a train in England and discovered to his surprise that all the passengers in that particular car were patients at a mental institution. They were enjoying a day in the countryside.

The hospital attendant soon began counting the patients to be sure all of them were there. "One, two three, four, five . . ." She came to Runcie and asked, "Who are you?"

"I'm the Archbishop of Canterbury," Runcie told her.

He said the attendant smiled indulgently and pointed at him as she continued counting, ". . . six, seven, eight . . . ."

# This Lesson in Your Life

Those old Israelites left themselves open to all sorts of trouble. They should have seen it coming down the road. How could they have been so blind? They knew that God's promises to Joshua and their ancestors had been conditional. Israel must obey God. That was the necessity. If they did this, God would give them success. Without their obedience, God sent invaders to subjugate them.

These people abandoned God in a big way. They worshipped at pagan shrines where "sacred" prostitutes were common. They intermarried with Canaanites and accepted their moral and spiritual standards. As we look back at them (from our safe distance), it is puzzling to us why they could not see what was happening. As we read further in Judges, we see that they repeatedly fell away every time God rescued them

It is easy for us to pick them to pieces for their foolish disobedience. It may be hard for us not to follow in their footsteps. We are not likely to feel threatened by Canaanites. Worshipping at a hilltop pagan shrine does not sound tempting us at all. The fact is, though, that we are faced by the moral equivalent of Canaanite paganism.

First John 2:15-16 speaks to us about loving the world. John is using the word "world" in a special way. He is not talking about the material universe or the population of earth itself (as in "God so loved the world). He is referring to the world without godliness – the world that has chosen to forsake God. (Does this sound like the Israelites in out study?) John is warning us about becoming involved with evil things in the world. Here is what he says:

> Love not the world, neither the things that
> are in the world. If any man love the world, the
> love of the Father is not in him.
> For all that is in the world, the lust of the
> flesh, and the lust of the eyes, and the pride
> of life, is not of the Father, but is of the world.

These words from the New Testament sound very much like a message that God might have sent the Israelites in the generation following Joshua. Paul wrote (1 Cor. 15:33 NIV), "Do not be misled: 'Bad company corrupts good character.'" a warning needed by the Israelites who were intermarrying with pagans. Jesus taught (Matt. 624) that we could not serve two masters. This is true whether one of the masters is pagan Baal, or the gods of materialism that tempt us.

Reading such Scriptures as these is a sharp reminder that you and I face, in principle at least, the same temptations as the Israelites. Let us not make the same mistakes they did. The events in our Joshua studies occurred a long time ago, but the lessons they teach dovetail right into our contemporary world.

GETTING
THE FACTS STRAIGHT

**1. Israel has sinned on numerous occasions. When Israel sins, what does God do?**

When Israel sins, God presents a new oppressor.

**2. Why do you think God calls out the oppressor's guard?**

God punishes the sins of his own people, that the flesh being destroyed, the spirit may be saved.

**3. When Israel prays again, whom did God send, and from which tribe did he belong?**

God presented Ehud as the new deliverer from the tribe of Benjamin.

**4. What is significant about Ehud's tribe?**

The name Benjamin signifies the son of the right hand. Yet many of them were left-handed, giving the positive advantage and benefit of surprise.

**5. What did Ehud do for Israel's rescue from the hands of the Moabites ?**

He saved the oppressed by destroying the oppressors. As a minister of divine justice, he put to death the Moab king Eglon.

**6. How did Ehud arrange circumstances that led to his mission of freedom?**

Ehud went on his errand to Eglon, offered his present with the usual ceremony and expressions of dutiful respect, the better to shade what he intended and to prevent suspicion.

**7. How did Ehud approach the king of Moab?**

Ehud asked for a private audience, and obtained it in a summer parlor. He told the king he had a secret message for him. The king ordered his attendants to leave.

**8. What was the message of Ehud's errand?**

Ehud demands and receives Eglon's attention to a message from God. Ehud tells Eglon that a message from God can best be felt, not to the ear, but to the heart— into which the fatal blade was thrust—the sword of God.

**9. What was the consequence of Ehud's victorious actions?**

The consequence of this victory was that the power of the Moabites over Israel was broken. The country was cleared of these oppressors, and the land had a rest for 80years.

**10. Can you cite other biblical stories that this lesson brings to mind?**

Among your other recollections, the lesson contains motifs of oppressor carnal security and deprivations of discretion; God's contempt for such royalty; a knife-felled fatted calf as an acceptable sacrifice to divine justice; and with less macabre, the Son of God requiring Peter to sheath his sword.

Here is a challenge for you. Read carefully through Judges 3 and see how much of an uplift you get. At first it looks like pretty depressing reading. There is one failure by Israel followed by another. They just never seemed to get it right, and kept falling into the same trap. There is an account of palace intrigue, where a fat enemy king gets killed by his left-handed Israelite foe. That is a victory for Israel, but some Bible students think Ehud the judge did not do this piece of work in an honorable fashion. (Getting ahead of our story, Sampson was not always an outstanding gentleman, so if we compare Ehud to Sampson, Ehud comes out looking good.)

There is some outstandingly encouraging information in this chapter. We just have to look for it. With all the gloom and doom in this chapter, the grace of God shines through. (Gloom and doom is when we most appreciate the grace of God). God is unchangeable. He is always the same. We Christians have the same God as we are reading about in Judges. He a God of grace now, and was a God of grace then.

Let us look for God's grace in this chapter. Here is an example.

Israel did evil, forgot God, served pagan gods (v.7).

God was angry with them, made them serve a pagan king (v.8).

Children of Israel cried out to the Lord (v.9).

God raised up Othniel to deliver them (v.9).

The Israelites were under the pagan king's domination for eight years, and had clearly brought this punishment on themselves by serving pagan gods. However, when they cried out to God, He rescued them, even though they had deliberately sinned against Him. This is a testimony to the power of prayer. It is a testimony of the grace of God. They did not deserve what God did for them. That is God's grace in action.

By the time we get to verse 12, Othniel the judge dies and, "the Israelites did evil again in the sight of God." The same pattern plays out again, and this time it is left-handed Ehud whom God raises as their judge-deliverer. It repeats still again, and Shamar, who killed 600 men with an ox goad, becomes judge.

As we read further in Judges, God continues to rescue these undeserving people. Should this remind us of Ephesians 2:4-5; 8-9? "But God, who is rich in mercy, for his great love wherewith he loved us, Even when we were dead in sins, hath quickened us together with Christ, (by grace ye are saved)" "For by grace are ye saved through faith, and that not of yourselves: it is the gift of God."

It may come as something of shock to our systems, but the fact is that you and I are in the same boat with these ancient Israelites. We are sinners saved by grace. "To the only wise God our Savior, be glory and majesty, dominion and power, both now an ever. Amen" (Jude 25).

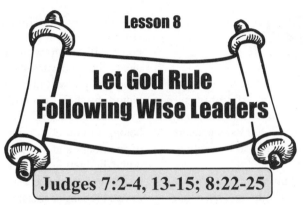

## Lesson 8

# Let God Rule
# Following Wise Leaders

## Judges 7:2-4, 13-15; 8:22-25

And the LORD said unto Gideon, The people that are with thee are too many for me to give the Midianites into their hands, lest Israel vaunt themselves against me, saying, Mine own hand hath saved me.

3 Now therefore go to, proclaim in the ears of the people, saying, Whosoever is fearful and afraid, let him return . . . and there remained ten thousand.

4 And the LORD said unto Gideon, The people are yet too many; bring them down unto the water, and I will try them for thee there: and it shall be, that of whom I say unto thee, This shall go with thee, the same shall go with thee; and of whomsoever I say unto thee . . . .

13 And when Gideon was come, behold, there was a man that told a dream unto his fellow, and said, Behold, I dreamed a dream, and, lo, a cake of barley bread tumbled into the host of Midian, and came unto a tent, and smote it that it fell, . . . that the tent lay along.

14 And his fellow answered and said, This is nothing else save the sword of Gideon the son of Joash, a man of Israel: for into his hand hath God delivered Midian . . . .

15 And it was so, when Gideon

heard the telling of the dream, and the interpretation thereof, that he worshipped, and returned into the host of Israel, and said, Arise; for the LORD hath delivered into your hand the host of Midian.

8:22 Then the men of Israel said unto Gideon, Rule thou over us, both thou, and thy son, and thy son's son also: for thou hast delivered us from the hand of Midian.

23 And Gideon said unto them, I will not rule over you, neither shall my son rule over you: the LORD shall rule over you.

24 And Gideon said unto them, I would desire a request of you, that ye would give me every man the earrings of his prey. (For they had golden earrings, because they were Ishmaelites.)

25 And they answered, We will willingly give them. And they spread a garment, and did cast therein every man the earrings of his prey.

**Memory Verse**
Judges 7:15
**Background Scripture**
Judges 6; 8; 21:25
**Devotional Reading**
1 Samuel 2:1-10

461

Those of us who serve the Lord today as members of impressive mega-churches can be blessed by paying close attention to God's concerns about sending Gideon to war with too large an army.

The Lord thinned out the ranks of the Israelite army to less than one-hundredth of its original size—from 32,000 to 300—before He Okayed Gideon's attack on the Midianite horde. "If you go with too many soldiers," the Lord warned His new judge, "your people will think they won the victory by their own military might."

Is there a danger that we who belong to churches with a multitude of members and with multi-million-dollar budgets might credit our own resources for any success we may have in evangelism or missions? How can we guard against this?

ഇൻൽ

## For a Lively Start

God never seems to be troubled by Gideon's repeated need to be reassured that the power of the Lord really is backing him. Soon after God called Gideon to lead Israel against Midian's huge army, Gideon put out the fleece and asked the Lord to distribute the nighttime's heavy dew in a way to prove the call really was divine. Instead of scolding Gideon, the Lord did what Gideon asked.

Now when the Lord sees that Gideon is hesitant to risk an attack when he is so very out-manned. He's proactive in giving His new leader assurance that God will guarantee him victory. When Gideon hears the sentry's dream, he hurries home and rouses his handful of troops to begin the battle.

What kind of assurances does the Lord give His leaders today?

| Teaching Outline | Daily Bible Readings |
|---|---|
| I. Reducing the Army's Size—Judges 7:2-4 | Mon. No Holy One Like the Lord *1 Samuel 2:1-10* |
| A. God's Concern, 2 | Tue. Follow the Lord Only *Deuteronomy 13:1-5* |
| B. The First Riff, 3 | Wed. Suffering Oppression *Judges 6:1-10* |
| C. The Second Culling, 4 | Thu. I Will Be with You *Judges 6:11-16* |
| II. The Reassuring Dream—Judges 7:13-15 | Fri. A First Act of Obedience *Judges 6:25-32* |
| A. The Sentry's Dream, 13 | Sat. Seeking a Sign from God *Judges 6:36-40* |
| B. Its Interpretation, 14 | Sun. The Lord Will Rule *Judges 7:2-4, 13-15; 8:22-25* |
| C. Gideon's Reaction, 15 | |
| III. Reward for Gideon—Judges 8:22-25 | |

# Verse by Verse

Judges 7:2-4, 13-15; 8:22-25

## I. Reducing the Army's Size— Judges 7:2-4

### A. God's Concern, 2

**2 And the LORD said unto Gideon, The people that are with thee are too many for me to give the Midianites into their hands, lest Israel vaunt themselves against me, saying, Mine own hand hath saved me.**

God and Gideon have two opposing concerns. Gideon thinks his army is pitifully small compared to that army in the Midianite camp. Attacking the enemy with such a tiny force seems almost like suicide. However, the Lord's situation appraisal is somewhat different. God fears that a victory won by Gideon's 32,000-man army will tempt the Israelites to "vaunt themselves"— to boast of their own might. Such boasting, God warns Gideon, would be "against me." Does God feel this way whenever we dare to take credit for our own successes?

Paul had something like this in mind when he warned his converts, "Let him who boasts boast in the Lord" (2 Cor. 10:17).

### B. The First Riff, 3

**3 Now therefore go to, proclaim in the ears of the people, saying, Whosoever is fearful and afraid, let him return and depart early from mount Gilead. And there returned of the people twenty and two thousand; and there remained ten thousand.**

Can you imagine the exodus that would take place if the army commander in Iraq or Afghanistan assembled his troops and told any of them who had any misgivings or fears to climb on the airplane and fly home? Gideon reduced his army to less than one-third of its original size by this ploy.

No doubt, Gideon was shaken by this drastic reduction in troop deployment, but God still thought the Israeli army was too big.

### C. The Second Culling, 4

**4 And the LORD said unto Gideon, The people are yet too many; bring them down unto the water, and I will try them for thee there: and it shall be, that of whom I say unto thee, This shall go with thee, the same shall go with thee; and of whomsoever I say unto thee, This shall not go with thee, the same shall not go.**

God's second method of culling the army was ingenious. When the troops were allowed to go to the river to drink, nobody warned them in advance that if they laid down their weapons and knelt down to drink, they would be sent home. Those who held onto their weapons and reached down with one hand to scoop up water from the river—these men were the real soldiers in the crowd. They had a true sense of the enemies' presence and the seriousness of the mission.

The last half of vs. 4 is confusing in the KJV. The NIV clarifies it. God tells Gideon, "Take them down to the water, and I will sift them for you there. If I say, 'This one shall go with you,' he shall go; but if I say, 'This one shall not go with you,' he shall not go." Then in vs. 5 we hear God's explanation of who He will select to stay versus who will be sent home. Gideon winds up with a only 300 men. No wonder he was uncertain about the wisdom of attacking.

## II. The Reassuring Dream— Judges 7:13-15

### A. The Sentry's Dream, 13

**13 And when Gideon was come, behold, there was a man that told a dream unto his fellow, and said, Behold, I dreamed a dream, and, lo, a cake of barley bread tumbled into the host of Midian, and came unto a tent, and smote it that it fell, and overturned it, that the tent lay along.**

The verses right before this one tell us that sending Gideon down to the Midianite camp during the night is God's idea. The Lord wants His new judge to be confident as he leads his troops on this dangerous mission. So God arranges for Gideon to reach the perimeter of the huge Midianite camp just as one of the sentries is telling his

friend about a curious dream he had the night before.

The dream is like a comedy cartoon scene. Loaves of barley bread do not usually come out of the oven large enough to flatten a tent in the middle of an army camp, but this one did. Of course, all sorts of weird things happen in dreams. The KJV phrase "that the tent lay along" is an archaic way of saying "so that the tent lay flat on the ground."

### B. Its Interpretation, 14

**14 And his fellow answered and said, This is nothing else save the sword of Gideon the son of Joash, a man of Israel: for into his hand hath God delivered Midian, and all the host.**

What really catches Gideon's attention is the second sentry's interpretation of his friend's dream. With absolutely nothing in the details of the dream that would point either to Israel or to Gideon, this man predicts that the God of the Jews will let Gideon's army defeat the hordes of Midian.

When Gideon hears this explanation of the dream, he knows then why God has sent him down to reconnoiter the enemy camp. Now Gideon has a feeling that he and his army will prevail.

### C. Gideon's Reaction, 15

**15 And it was so, when Gideon heard the telling of the dream, and the interpretation thereof, that he worshipped, and returned into the host of Israel, and said, Arise; for the LORD hath delivered into your hand the host of Midian.**

The interpretation of the dream is so incredible and its impact on Gideon so profound that he bows down to the

Lord (that is the literal meaning of the word translated "worshipped"). Now Gideon knows not only that his army will win. He also knows that God has singled him out for special encouragement. Now there can be no remaining doubt that God is on his side.

Fired by this realization, Gideon hurries back to his own camp and awakens his troops. He rousts them from their beds as he assures them "we are going to win!"

### III. Reward for Gideon—Judges 8:22-25

**22 Then the men of Israel said unto Gideon, Rule thou over us, both thou, and thy son, and thy son's son also: for thou hast delivered us from the hand of Midian.**

**23 And Gideon said unto them, I will not rule over you, neither shall my son rule over you: the LORD shall rule over you.**

**24 And Gideon said unto them, I would desire a request of you, that ye would give me every man the earrings of his prey. (For they had golden earrings, because they were Ishmaelites.)**

**25 And they answered, We will willingly give them. And they spread a garment, and did cast therein every man the earrings of his prey.**

After Gideon and his men vanquished the Midianite army, some of the Israelites on the west side of the Jordan threaten him because he had not invited them to share in the war and, therefore, in the plunder. Gideon finally reminded them that they had the honor of catching and killing two of the most powerful Midianite chiefs. This means they got significant treasures from the former possessions of those chiefs.

For the most part, however, the people of Israel expressed gratitude and honor to Gideon, thanking him for his role in freeing them from Midian's cruel reign. After the battle, they invite him to become their ruler, but Gideon assures them that neither he nor his sons have any desire to hold such an office.

Yet, there is one thing that he does request as payment for his services; he requests part of the jewelry taken from the dead or routed Midianites, which included the many earrings worn by the enemy soldiers. (Have you noticed how many Midianite soldiers we have among us nowadays?) The KJV makes it sound like Gideon asked for all of the earrings. Newer versions such as the NIV, NLT, and NRSV phrase Gideon's request to include just a single earring from the booty for each Israeli soldier. The people gladly agree to do what Gideon asked. Even if the last reading is correct, he winds up wealthy. The donated golden earrings weigh about 43 pounds.

80CB

465

## Evangelistic Emphasis

Satan is the great deceiver, and does his dishonorable business under many guises. We would hardly expect him to show up at our door and say "I'm the evil one, and have come to cause you heartache and misery." He appeared to Eve as a friend who had come to set her straight about God. He told her that the reason God did not want her to eat of the forbidden fruit was that she would become as wise as the Creator. Eve fell for his story, and as her descendents, we have done a good job of making this a family tradition.

Paul wrote (2 Cor. 11:14-15) that Satan masquerades as an angel of light, and his servants are going to appear as being righteous. That is about as dishonest as dishonesty gets to be, and lets us know what kind of opponent Satan is. He does a good job of making evil look innocent, and sometimes even good.

He tricked the Israelites regularly. Joshua had given them God's warning about keeping away from false gods. The warning was repeated during the time of the judges. Yet the lure of pagan gods promised good crops and increasing herds of animals, associated with sexually oriented worship in their shrines.

Throughout all ages and in every nation, Satan does his work. Take time to read Romans 1:14-17. Paul says the gospel is the power of God for salvation to everyone who believes. It is the remedy for Satan's trickery.

## Memory Selection

ଈୠଈ

"And it was so, when Gideon heard the telling of the dream, and the interpretation thereof, that he worshipped, and returned into the host of Israel, and said, Arise; for the Lord hath delivered into your hand the host of Midian."
*Judges 7:15*

Gideon needed to be reassured again and again that God would give him victory over the Midianites. As one way of helping shore up Gideon's weak faith, God told him to go into the enemy's camp and listen to what he could hear. As Gideon and his servant walked among the Midianites, he overheard one of them telling his friend about a dream. In it a loaf of barley bread rolled into the camp, hit a tent and knocked it flat. His friend interpreted this as being the sword of Gideon of Israel, into whose hand God had delivered Midian.

There is much about Gideon that we do not know, including why he was so unsure that God was actually leading him. Was he unsure about God? Was he unsure that he was interpreting God's signs and instructions properly? Maybe somewhere deep inside him were self-doubts, a lack of self-assurance that he was man enough to do God's work. Once he got his faith issues settled he served God and Israel well.

What about your faith and mine? Hebrews 11:1 says it should work even when we hope but do not see. Thomas, the apostle, had to see the evidence before he could believe in the Resurrection. Read John 20:24-29 to see what Jesus says about those who believe without seeing.

# Weekday Problems

Even though most Israelites had gone off after other gods, Gideon apparently had kept his faith in the God of Israel. However, Gideon's father, Joash, maintained a pagan shrine. It contained an altar to Baal and a wooden symbol of Asherah, the female deity (called a grove in the KJV, and an Asherah pole in newer translations). Gideon was possibly the only member of the family who did not worship at this shrine. We can instantly see a potential conflict here.

God instructed Gideon to tear down his father's pagan shrine and build an altar to the Lord instead. Gideon took ten servants and did this during the night, because he was afraid of his father's family and the townspeople. The next day the townspeople demanded that Joash bring Gideon out, for he must die. Joash realized that Baal had no power or he could have killed Gideon for having destroyed his shrine. If Baal is really a god, he told the hostile crowd, let him defend himself. We can hope that this represents a permanent turn-around for Joash. We wonder what Gideon's relationship had been with his family through the years. Matters of faith can cause conflict.

Take time to read Matthew 10:32-39. Jesus tells us that family relationships must not keep us from following Him. Many people have to make the decision as to where their loyalty lies. Family and friends must not keep us from the Lord. A decision to follow Jesus may result in unbelieving family members doing so. Gideon's father seems to have had a complete change in his thinking.

# Groaners

1. A bicycle can't stand alone because it is two tired.

2. Time flies like an arrow. Fruit flies like a banana.

3. She had a boyfriend with a wooden leg, but she broke it off.

4. A chicken crossing the road is poultry in motion.

5. If you don't pay your exorcist, you get repossessed.

6. With her marriage she got a new name and a dress.

7. Show me a piano falling down a mine shaft and I'll show you A-flat minor.

# This Lesson in Your Life

When a large homebuilding developer begins a new project, perhaps construction of hundreds of homes in a new subdivision, there are no hammers and nails to be seen at this stage. There are no plumbers or cement trucks. There are no deliveries of building supplies. These things come later.

Bulldozers and graders come first. They clear and shape the landscape. They dig out and push away unwanted foundations from previous buildings. They remove brush and unwanted growth. They level ridges and fill in gullies.

This is much the way God intended for the Israelites to build their nation in Canaan. The pagan gods and lifestyle had to be cleared away before godly construction could begin. We have seen in Joshua and Judges how they failed at this. In almost monotonous repetition they fall away from God, begin following paganism, then return to God. They never cleared the land before building.

Our lesson in Judges has a very literal example of clearing off before building. Gideon's father, Joash, had a family shrine devoted to both the male and female god and goddess of the Canaanites. God commanded Gideon to tear down and destroy this shrine, and he did so. After the heathen shrine was out of the way, God asked Gideon to build an altar at that place, and to offer sacrifice on it. Put first things first – clear away the evil, then build for God.

We can easily see a lesson for our own lives here. When we become Christians we should clean up our lives to prepare room for the Lord and the Holy Spirit to work. It is not enough just to get rid of the bad things that used to be there, but we are to build a life of good things.

Jesus taught a parable about this. Cleaning the evil out of our lives can backfire if not followed through by building something good. In Matthew 12:43-45, He tells about an evil spirit that came out of a man, wandered around for awhile, then returned to that man. It found its old dwelling place swept, cleaned, put in order, but unoccupied. It then went out and found seven other spirits even more evil than itself, and they all moved into the empty space. It is one thing to get rid of evil. It is another to replace it with godliness.

Let me tell you a very short story about a drug addict. You will get the point even before you finish reading it. This young man had just finished a compulsory drug counseling program. He said he wanted to stay clean. He needed a place to live, and accepted the hospitality of one of his drug-dealing "friends." Can you see how this person needed to bulldoze some trash out of his life, before trying to rebuild it? He needed to tear down shrines to his addiction, but did not. You do not even need me to tell you what happened to him.

Gideon teaches us all a lesson. Listen to God. Clear away evil influences and practices. Replace them with God-oriented thoughts and deeds.

**GETTING THE FACTS STRAIGHT**

**1. Who were the oppressors named in chapter 6?**

They were oppressed by the Midianites, the Amalekites, and other tribes from the east (v.3).

**2. What was the name of the judge that God raised up to be their deliverer?**

The Lord provided Gideon, the son of Joash from Ophrah.

**3. When the angel of the Lord appeared to Gideon, what happened to the sacrifice (a young goat and some cakes) when Gideon placed it on a rock?**

The angel touched the sacrificial offering with the tip of his staff. Then fire came out of the rock and consumed the sacrifice.

**4. Gideon was ordered by God to destroy Joash's pagan shrine. He did so with the help of ten servants. Why did they do it during the night?**

Gideon was afraid of his family and the townspeople. They would not have approved of this.

**5. When the townspeople wanted to kill Gideon after discovering what he had done, what did Gideon's father say to them?**

Joash said if he (Baal) be a god, let him plead for himself. Joash seems by this time to realize that Baal is powerless.

**6. Gideon asked God for a sign, using fleece. What was the first test with the fleece?**

Gideon would put a fleece on the ground overnight. In the morning, if the fleece was wet and the ground around it dry, that would be the sign. (The next night the test was the opposite: dry fleece and wet ground.)

**7. The Lord said that Gideon had too many soldiers. Any who were afraid should return home. After all these left, how many men were left? How many returned to their homes?**

Gideon had 10,000 men remaining. 22,000 returned to their homes.

**8. Why did God want to reduce the number of fighting men?**

God wanted Israel to know that it was He who would defeat the enemies. If Israel had a large army, they might think they had done it by themselves.

**9. God reduced the number of soldiers again, this time by the method in which they drank water. What was the final number of men left to fight?**

The number was reduced to 300, which would remove all doubt as to whether Israel took credit for the victory.

**10. What would the Israelite soldiers do to make their enemies think they were surrounded by a huge army?**

The 300 were divided into three groups, and surrounded their enemies. On a signal, each of them would sound a trumpet, break a pitcher, and display a torch.

Sometimes less is more.

In preparing food, a few choice spices are more satisfying than dumping in some of everything that is in the spice cabinet. Without just a touch of salt, food is bland – too much and it is inedible, not to mention unhealthy. The right amount of sunshine helps the body produce Vitamin D. Too much can cause skin cancer. Not often, but occasionally, before my wife leaves for work she will say "Look closely. Am I wearing too much jewelry?"

She says the rule of thumb is that when you are finished dressing, take off at least one piece of jewelry. That way you are not as likely to overdo it.

However, with armies preparing for battle more is normally what is wanted. More "boots on the ground" gives the commanding general the overwhelming force needed to overcome the enemy.

Except not always.

God was in charge of Gideon's battle against the Midianites and their supporting tribes. He deliberately reduced His army from 32,000 fighting men to only 300. His enemies were countless desert camel-riding warriors, but less is what He wanted. (My eighth grade English teacher said we should use "few" for things that can be counted, and "less" for things that cannot such as salt or water. My apologies to Mrs. Whitten for not saying, He wanted "fewer." Anybody who can count to 300 should know better.)

God has a wonderful way of using small numbers. The human inhabitants of Eden came to a grand total of two. After He destroyed the sinful world, He started things all over by saving one family in an ark. Of all the millions to choose from, He selected one man, Abraham, to be the father of the faithful. Of the numerous nations, all of which belonged to Him, He selected insignificant Israel as His chosen one, His treasured possession.

He bypassed the families of Jerusalem's theological elite and went to Nazareth, where He selected a young maiden through whom His Son would come to earth in the flesh. From one congregation of orthodox Jews in Jerusalem, His Church spread around the world. He turned the world upside down, starting with only 12 men, one of whom was a disastrous failure.

His Scripture tells us that "There is one body, and one Spirit," and we have "one hope." There is "One Lord, one faith, one baptism, One God and Father of all, who is above all, and through all, and in you all." To this very significant list of ones He adds, "unto *every __one of us__* is given grace according to the measure of Christ (Eph. 4:4-7).

Sometimes less is more.

ഓൻ

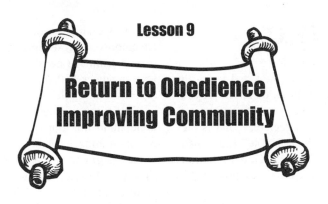

## Lesson 9

# Return to Obedience Improving Community

## Judges 10:10-18

And the children of Israel cried unto the LORD, saying, We have sinned against thee, both because we have forsaken our God, and also served Baalim.

11 And the LORD said unto the children of Israel, Did not I deliver you from the Egyptians, and from the Amorites, from the children of Ammon, and from the Philistines?

12 The Zidonians also, and the Amalekites, and the Maonites, did oppress you; and ye cried to me, and I delivered you out of their hand.

13 Yet ye have forsaken me, and served other gods: wherefore I will deliver you no more.

14 Go and cry unto the gods which ye have chosen; let them deliver you in the time of your tribulation.

15 And the children of Israel said unto the LORD, We have sinned: do thou unto us whatsoever seemeth good unto thee; deliver us only, we pray thee, this day.

16 And they put away the strange gods from among them, and served the LORD: and his soul was grieved for the misery of Israel.

17 Then the children of Ammon were gathered together, and encamped in Gilead. And the children of Israel assembled themselves together, and encamped in Mizpeh.

18 And the people and princes of Gilead said one to another, What man is he that will begin to fight against the children of Ammon? he shall be head over all the inhabitants of Gilead.

July 31

**Memory Verse**
Judges 10:16

**Background Scripture**
Judges 10:6; 11:33; 21:25

**Devotional Reading**
2 Corinthians 7:5-11

# focus

Are you sometimes fed up with the responsibilities of an employee or child, so much so that you run out of patience and declare, "That is the last straw! I have had it." If so, then you can understand God's reaction to the repeated unfaithfulness of the Israelites.

Repeatedly, the Lord had bailed them out of the troubles they brought upon themselves when they abandoned Him to worship various pagan gods. He empowered rescuers to deliver His people from the oppression of some foreign power. In thanks, they just kept repeating the cycle.

Identifying this cycle may help us understand the motif chosen by the writer of Judges. Most stories of the judges begin with the same refrain: "The people again did what was evil in the sight of the Lord. They ignored Him and worshiped the Baals. Then God gave them to the hands of their enemies." An endless cycle.

## For a Lively Start

ॐ ॐ

Judges 10, the writer introduces the story of the judge named Jephthah, which follows in the next chapter. It is a memorable account, but one that perplexes many of us. God uses Jephthah to free His people from oppression, but Jephthah is an evil man. Probably he was chosen by Israel precisely because he was the worst rogue in the neighborhood. Someone said he must have been the original Hell's Angel. It took somebody that rough to defeat the Ammonites.

Jephthah's tragic vow forced him to offer his only daughter as a sacrifice. It takes us back to God's instructions about vows in Leviticus 27 and in Numbers 30, possibly preparing us to understand other Old Testament stories that involve vows.

| Teaching Outline | Daily Bible Readings |
|---|---|
| I. Israel's Appeal for Help—Judges 10:10 | Mon. Grief Leading to Penitence<br>*2 Corinthians 7:5-11* |
| II. God's Refusal to Help—Judges 10:11-14 | Tue. The Path to Forgiveness<br>*1 Kings 8:46-50* |
| A. His Reminder of Past Aid, 11-12 | Wed. New Hearts and New Spirits<br>*Ezekiel 18:25-32* |
| B. No Help This Time, 13-14 | |
| III. Israel's Confession—Judges 10:15 | Thu. Unless You Repent<br>*Luke 13:1-9* |
| IV. God Changes His Mind—Judges 10:16 | Fri. God's Loving Reproof<br>*Revelation 3:14-22* |
| V. The Search for a Rescuer—Judges 10:17-18 | Sat. Proclaiming Repentance and Forgiveness<br>*Luke 24:44-49* |
| A. Their New Oppressor, 17 | Sun. Repentance and Submission<br>*Judges 10:10-18* |
| B. Finding a Deliverer, 18 | |

# *Verse by Verse*

## Judges 10:10-18

### I. Israel's Appeal for Help—Judges 10:10

**10 And the children of Israel cried unto the LORD, saying, We have sinned against thee, both because we have forsaken our God, and also served Baalim.**

Israel was in deep trouble, suffering at the hands of an invading nation. They recognize that they have brought this mistreatment upon themselves because they forsook their God and turned instead to serve the Baals—the pagan gods of the Canaanites around them.

"Baalim" is an archaic KJV form of the plural form of the word "Baal." In its plural form, it usually includes all the pagan gods of Canaan.

Like most sinners reeling in the misery caused by their sins, the children of Israel are able to see why they are in trouble. By the time a sinner realizes what mistakes he has made, it is often too late to repair the damage.

### II. God's Refusal to Help—Judges 10:11-14

#### A. His Reminder of Past Aid, 11-12

**11 And the LORD said unto the children of Israel, Did not I deliver you from the Egyptians, and from the Amorites, from the children of Ammon, and from the Philistines?**

**12 The Zidonians also, and the Amalekites, and the Maonites, did oppress you; and ye cried to me, and I delivered you out of their hand.**

God has a long memory. He can recall all the times before the Exodus when he heard the moans of His people in Egyptian slavery in Moses' time. His reference to helping His people against the Amorites probably refers to the history recorded in the book of Joshua. Thus, this divine recitation of past deliverances reaches back many generations.

Since Ammonites were inhabitants of the area of Moab, the Lord likely is citing Ehud's work here. Shamgar was covered in one verse in Judges, but he did set his people free from Philistine oppression. Zidonians (or the people of Sidon, to use the more modern spelling) likely points to the brave campaign of Deborah and her forces against enemies from northern Canaan. Israel was afflicted by Amalekites since Exodus 17, but it seems likely that the Lord is referring here to a later event such as the one in Judges 3:13, when Ehud finally broke their power over Israel. The reference to "Maonites" puzzle Bible scholars, for the village of Maon is dismissible as trouble to the Israelites. The Septuagint version amends the Hebrew text here to refer to "Midianites." This change seems to fit this list of times when God delivered His people from their enemies, for this would include the heroic leadership of Gideon.

### B. No Help This Time, 13-14

**13 Yet ye have forsaken me, and served other gods: wherefore I will deliver you no more.**

**14 Go and cry unto the gods which ye have chosen; let them deliver you in the time of your tribulation.**

God asks His people when they cry out for His help that when He has come to their aid many times in the centuries before this, but what did it accomplish? Every time they regressed into idolatry. Instead of being grateful to Him for setting them free from cruel masters, they have foolishly chosen to worship the gods of the people who had mistreated them.

Therefore, God says, "Enough is enough." If they want help, He says, let them cry out to the gods they have chosen in place of Him. Let these gods help this time.

If we keep looking somewhere besides God for solutions to our life problems—if we trust our wealth, our education, our scientific advances to fix the problems we make in our lives—should we be surprised if God tells us to depend on those institutions instead of bothering Him? If we turn repeatedly to alcohol, to drugs, to pornography, or to sexual immoralities to find relief from life's pains, this text implies that God just might leave us to find our comfort in these ruinous options.

### III. Israel's Confession—Judges 10:15

**15 And the children of Israel said unto the LORD, We have sinned: do thou unto us whatsoever seemeth good unto thee; deliver us only, we pray thee, this day.**

When God refused to aid them this time, the children of Israel saw how foolish they had been and they confessed their sin. So strong was their need for the Lord's help that they submitted themselves to whatever retribution He might see fit to impose upon them. Do whatever You need to, they told Him, but we desperately need Your deliverance. In effect, they were praying for God to grant them another judge who could end the suffering the Ammonites were inflicting.

Those who have struggled with alcohol, drugs, or other addictions know that they usually fail to recognize how desperate the situation is until they hit rock bottom. Then, after a long period spent in denial, finally they reach out to God for whatever grace it takes to be free from sin.

### IV. God Changes His Mind—Judges 10:16

**16 And they put away the strange gods from among them, and served the LORD: and his soul was grieved for the misery of Israel.**

True penitence caused Israel to rid themselves of the pagan gods and turn back to the Lord. When God saw their change of heart, the NRSV tells us that He "could no longer bear to see them suffer."

How blessed we are to serve a God who loves us. Unlike the mythical gods and goddesses of other religions, He takes no pleasure in seeing His children suffer.

In this case, God retreated from His refusal to help and allowed Jephthah to become a liberating judge to relieve His people.

## V. The Search for a Rescuer— Judges 10:17-18

### A. Their New Oppressor, 17

**17 Then the children of Ammon were gathered together, and encamped in Gilead. And the children of Israel assembled themselves together, and encamped in Mizpeh.**

The Ammonites now threatened to increase their oppression of the Israelites. This conflict was located in Giliead, on the eastern side of the Jordan. Some mistake the "Mizpeh" mentioned here for "Mizpah" on the other side of the river—a town made famous by the prophet Samuel. This present Mizpeh appears to be a reference to Ramoth-mizpeh, a place in Gilead identified in Joshua 13:26; 20:8. Israel's first-rate force is camped here, but their hope of resisting the Ammonite attack seems futile unless the Lord intervenes. Hence their prayers.

### B. Finding a Deliverer, 18

**18 And the people and princes of Gilead said one to another, What man is he that will begin to fight against the children of Ammon? he shall be head over all the inhabitants of Gilead.**

Israel began an intensive search for a rescuer who could lead them in the battle with the Ammonites. They were so afraid that they agreed to let he who saves them, become their ruler in Gilead. Thus begins the story of Jephthah.

ЅꙨ

## Evangelistic Emphasis

Evil, in whatever form it appears, has a tendency to spread. It only becomes increasingly evil as it continues to spread into any areas it can enter. Paul's description of ungodly peoples teaching fits evil exceptionally well. He said it "will eat as doth a canker" (2 Tim. 2:17). ("Spread like gangrene," NIV. NAS footnotes this as "cancer.")

Satan's evil influence spreads like a disease in the human body, destroying and consuming as it goes. It has the unwholesome characteristic of being contagious. It spreads from one person to another and from one place or society to another. Left alone, it grows like a health pandemic.

The Israelites in our lessons regularly strayed away from God and followed the pagan gods. There were a number of these gods, each with its own attraction. Our present lesson gives the discouraging news that the Israelites had added some new ones to those they worshipped (10:6). This was evil spreading itself.

This comes as a warning to us. The "germ" of evil will infect us unless we take precautions. It is not likely to be a pagan shrine, but evil will search for a way.

We are also reminded of the need for evangelizing. Truth is what overcomes error. Light dispels darkness. Jesus said the sick need a physician, and that is why He reaches out to sinners (Matt. 9:12). He is the remedy to evil's infectious spread.

## Memory Selection

### ෨෬

**"And they put away the strange gods from among them, and served the LORD: and his soul was grieved for the misery of Israel."** *Judges 10:16*

It comes as no surprise to us that Israel was worshipping strange gods. They had made a habit of it. This is the third lesson we have studied from Judges, and we have one more remaining. In all four we find the Israelites doing this, and it points out something we all need to remember: Sin is very alluring. It looks good. (Eve found the forbidden fruit "pleasant to the eyes." A green persimmon or a rotten apple would not have tempted her.) Satan is evil, but he is not dumb. He does not go around peddling shriveled fruit. Whatever he offers is more likely to be polished and attractive. It will be attractive at least until he gets us hooked. Once we are in his control he may lead us down dark alleys filled with filth and slime. How else can we explain depraved perversions and addictions? Paul wrote about the fruitless deeds of darkness where shameful things are done in secret (Eph. 5:11-12).

By the time the Israelites got themselves very deeply into paganism they would find themselves face to face with grisly horrors. Even human sacrifice was practiced in the service of some gods.

It does not seem to be sin that the Israelites found repulsive or undesirable. It was the fact that they were in servitude to foreign powers that made life hard for them. This seems to be what brought them to repentance. (The memory verse speaks of God's concern for their suffering. Check out the Uplift Page.)

# Weekday Problems

When it was time for fun and games, the Israelites easily worshiped at the pagan shrines. When they got into deep trouble from their oppressors, and it lasted long enough that they could not stand it any longer, they repented and returned to the living God who never failed to restore them.

The pagan religions did not spend much time being concerned about morality. To the contrary, much of pagan worship was immoral by the light of God's law. It is an easy-going religious life when immorality gives you credit with the gods. There were both male and female prostitutes commonly associated with Canaan's major shrines. It is obvious that holiness was not a priority, and their lax standards made the God of Moses and Joshua seem stern and restrictive.

We Christians believe that there is one God, who is the Father of our Lord Jesus Christ. On the other hand, we know we are surrounded by other gods, and each in its own way can ensnare us. Anything that stands between us and God – anything we allow to substitute for God – becomes an idol to us. Having spent time recently studying Judges, I was taken aback recently by something on the TV news. By the stadium entrance a young man was being interviewed about his support of our professional basketball team, even when it had lost a long string of games. He said, "Man, this is my shrine. It's my temple." He may not have meant it, but he came close to sending a shiver down my spine.

## Wizened Wisdom

1. Eventually you will reach a point when you stop lying about your age and start bragging about it.

2. Don't let anyone tell you you're getting old. Squash their toes with your rocker.

3. The older we get, the fewer things seem worth waiting in line for.

4. Some people try to turn back their odometers. Not me. I want people to know why I look this way. I've traveled a long way and some of the roads weren't paved.

5. The golden years are really just metallic years, gold in the tooth, silver in your hair, and lead in the rear.

# Ths Lesson in Your Life

We are given the names of 12 judges. They were a mixed bunch. Three of them appear in this lesson: Tola, Jair, and Jephthah. We are not told much about Tola, but he led Israel for 23 years, which sounds good. Jair adds some local color to the story. He was from the east side of the Jordan and had 30 sons. We are left not knowing how many wives were involved. Each of his 30 sons had a donkey that he rode. When they all gathered at Jair's house they must have had a noisy parking lot. There were 30 towns in Gilead that they controlled, so everything worked out evenly. We can see why the area was given a name that meant "the settlement of Jair."

Jephthah is more interesting. He, too, was from east of the Jordan, and was a mighty warrior. His mother was a prostitute, but his father had other sons by his wife. When they were grown, the wife's sons drove Jephthah away because they did not want to share the inheritance with him. He went to the land of Tob, which was probably to the northeast.

The Ammonites made war against Israel, and Jephthah's old home territory needed him to come back and be their commander. He drove a hard bargain, and said they were the people who hated him. Why did they want him now? He ended up being head of all the people, as well as commander.

He turned out to be a diplomat as well as a warrior. He engaged in a series of discussions with the king of the Ammonites, asking why he wanted war. They discussed events in their history and who had rights to what land. The Ammonites could not be appeased, and attached Israel. The Lord was with Jephthah's forces and they devastated 20 towns and subdued Ammon.

There is actually more in our lesson about this judge, but let us just stop at this point and get a lesson for our life from what we already know. It takes someone who has been through the thick of battle to know how horrible war can be. It was the Union's Civil War General Sherman who said, "War is hell." Jephthah knew this also, as no doubt the both of them created a lot of it during their military careers. Given a choice, though, Jephthah would rather talk than fight.

This mighty warrior sets the example for us to avoid fighting if we can. That is what Paul said in Romans 12:18: "If it be possible, as much as lieth in you, live peaceably with all men." There is a sad story in Philippians 4. Two women are named who had been Paul's fellow-laborers in the gospel. They were probably delightful people, and we would have enjoyed knowing them and being around them. They had some sort of falling-out though, and what we remember about them is their disagreement. It is a pity that they entered and exited Bible history with this reputation. Jesus said, "Blessed are the peacemakers: for they shall be called the children of God" (Matt. 5:9).

I think Jephthah would suggest that a good lesson for our lives is this: It is better to talk than fight.

1. **Jair and Jephthah were both from Gilead. In what way did being from Gilead make their location distinct from the other judges?**

Gilead was on the east side of the Jordan River. The other judges were from the west side, where most of the tribes were located and most Israelite activity took place.

2. **What three things do we know about Jair's sons?**

He had 30 sons. They rode 30 ass colts. They had 30 cities.

3. **After Jair's death the Israelites resumed worshipping false gods. Into whose hands did the Lord give them?**

God gave them over to the Philistines and the children of Ammon.

4. **What was distinctive about these locations? (Philistines and Ammon.)**

The Philistines were on the extreme west, along the coast. Ammon was on the extreme east, on the edge of the desert. Israel was surrounded by enemies.

5. **When the Israelites asked God for help, He reminded them that he had saved them from various enemies previously. They had always forsaken Him, and He was not going to deliver them. What did he tell them to do?**

"Go and cry unto the gods which ye have chosen; let them deliver you in the time of your tribulation."

6. **Israel told the Lord, "We have sinned." They put away the strange gods. How did the Lord respond to this?**

After Israel's repentance, the Lord's "soul was grieved for the misery of Israel."

7. **Jephthah was Israel's next judge. Gilead was his father. What do we know about his mother?**

His mother was a harlot.

8. **Gilead had other sons by his wife. What did these sons do to Jephthah?**

They forced him to go away because they did not want to share the inheritance with him. He settled in the land of Tob.

9. **When the Israelites were threatened with war, they sent for Jephthah to come be their commander. What position did he receive besides that commander?**

He insisted on the position and got it: he was head of all the people.

10. **Rather than go right to war, what tactic did Jephthah try first with the king of Ammon?**

He sent messengers to the king asking why he wanted to go to war. He reasoned with him about ownership of the land. (This accomplished nothing and war followed.)

In first year Greek class, we normally did vocabulary work in a routine fashion. However, on the day we had *agape* introduced, the professor spent the entire period lecturing on that single word. It was one of the more memorable hours in my educational life. This is the Greek word normally used for "love" in the New Testament. We usually think of *agape* as Christian love.

He discussed the various aspects of love, and ways the word is used. In the professor's mind, he had distilled what seems to me to be the most workable definition of Christian love. Love is when you want only the very best for someone. This makes it possible for us to love our enemies. Thinking of love in this way lifts it above emotion and whims of the moment. It gives love a solid footing.

If we love God in this way, we will genuinely want His will to be done on earth even as it is in heaven. God is love and He loves us. He wants only what is best for us.

As we study in Judges we see God's love in action. The section in 10:6-16 is an excellent example. Israel had behaved in typical fashion and was deep into idol worship, having forsaken God again. They had reached out and included gods from neighboring nations in their paganism. God used the Philistines (to the west along the coast), and the Ammonites (on their far eastern side), to shatter and crush them. They were caught in the middle of two powerful enemies. Even here we see the love of God. He was not being vindictive. He was providing the only incentive to which Israel responded that would lead them back to Him. This is what was best for them under the circumstances.

Israel cried out to God that they had sinned against Him. It is interesting that God does not immediately give them what they want. He drives a lesson home to them. He reminds them of the past times He has come to their rescue, and tells them to go pray to the pagan gods and let them deliver them from their trouble. (We would describe this as tough love.)

The lesson seems to have been taken to heart. They came back to God and again said, "We have sinned." They added to it that God could do to them whatever seemed good to Him. They put away their pagan gods and served the Lord. (This reminds us of John the Baptist demanding fruits that went along with repentance.)

After this, we find these tender words: The Lord's "soul was grieved for the misery of Israel." The NAS words this, "He could bear the misery of Israel no longer." His heart went out to them. God wanted only the best for them. He loved them.

God loves you. He wants only the best for you.

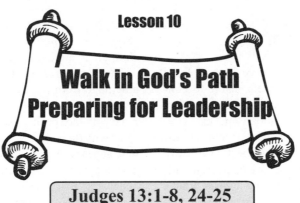

## Lesson 10

# Walk in God's Path Preparing for Leadership

## Judges 13:1-8, 24-25

And the children of Israel did evil again in the sight of the LORD; and the LORD delivered them into the hand of the Philistines forty years.

2 And there was a certain man of Zorah, of the family of the Danites, whose name was Manoah; and his wife was barren, and bare not.

3 And the angel of the LORD appeared unto the woman, and said unto her, Behold now, thou art barren, and bearest not: but thou shalt conceive, and bear a son.

4 Now therefore beware, I pray thee, and drink not wine nor strong drink, and eat not any unclean thing:

5 For, lo, thou shalt conceive, and bear a son; and no razor shall come on his head: for the child shall be a Nazarite unto God from the womb: and he shall begin to deliver Israel out of the hand of the Philistines.

6 Then the woman came and told her husband, saying, A man of God came unto me, and his countenance was like the countenance of an angel of God, very terrible: but I asked him not whence he was, neither told he me his name:

7 But he said unto me, Behold, thou shalt conceive, and bear a son; and now drink no wine nor strong drink, neither eat any unclean thing: for the child shall be a Nazarite to God from the womb to the day of his death.

8 Then Manoah intreated the LORD, and said, O my Lord, let the man of God which thou didst send come again unto us, and teach us what we shall do unto the child that shall be born.

24 And the woman bare a son, and called his name Samson: and the child grew, and the LORD blessed him.

25 And the Spirit of the LORD began to move him at times in the camp of Dan between Zorah and Eshtaol.

Aug. 7

**Memory Verse**
Joshua 13:24-25

**Background Scripture**
Joshua 13; 21:25

**Devotional Reading**
Romans 2:1-8

Couples who have longed for a child and have been unable to conceive one find a special joy when they learn, as did Manoah and his wife, that they are going to become parents. Such parents tend to bestow an extra level of love and care upon their children when they finally appear. What a contrast we see between these eager parents who waited and prayed for their offspring and those who either abort their babies or consider their children an annoying burden.

The Scriptures tell us, "Sons are a heritage from the LORD, children a reward from him" (Ps. 127:3, NIV). Even with the special instructions that came with their child, Manoah and his wife appear to have been delighted to have a son. The Bible commands all believers, "Bring up your children in the discipline and instruction of the Lord" (Eph. 6:4, NRSV).

## For a Lively Start

ಬಂಐ

Most of us who grow up with any Bible instruction will learn the stories of Samson while we are still children. If we fail to study Judges 13-16 again when we are mature, however, we may never really know these stories. One reason is that no thoughtful person teaching Bible lessons to children will delve into the "adult" aspects of the Samson stories. Another reason is that the recurring references to the work of the Holy Spirit in Samson's life take us to depths few children can fathom.

When we read concerning Samson in vs. 25 that "the Spirit of the LORD began to move him at times," this requires us to see the events in this judge's later life through a lens that most juveniles cannot access.

| Teaching Outline | Daily Bible Readings |
|---|---|
| I. The Theme of Judges—Judges 13:1 | Mon. God's Righteous Judgment *Romans 2:1-8* |
| II. The Angel's Announcement—Judges 13:2-5 | Tue. Separated to the Lord *Numbers 6:1-8* |
| A. The Barren Couple, 2 | Wed. The Holy and the Common *Leviticus 10:8-11* |
| B. The Good News, 3 | |
| C. The Nazirite Restrictions, 4-5a | Thu. Keep the Commandments *Deuteronomy 5:6-10* |
| D. The Baby's Destiny, 5b | |
| III. Manoah Finds Out—Judges 13:6-8 | Fri. Hold Fast to God *Deuteronomy 10:12-21* |
| A. His Wife Fills Him In, 6-7 | |
| B. Manoah's Prayer, 8 | Sat. Wonders for God's Followers *Judges 13:15-23* |
| IV. Samson Is Born and Matures—Judges 13:24-25 | Sun. God Prepares a Deliverer *Judges 13:1-8, 24-25* |

# *Verse by Verse*

**Judges 13:1-8, 24-25**

## I. The Theme of Judges—Judges 13:1

**1 And the children of Israel did evil again in the sight of the LORD; and the LORD delivered them into the hand of the Philistines forty years.**

This familiar line alerts us to the fact that we are about to meet another judge. Once again, the cycle of deliverance followed by disobedience shifts back to deliverance. This time the Philistines dominate Israel for 40 hard years before the Lord hears Israel's cries and sets about to give them relief. That relief will take more than two decades to develop, for Samson has to grow up before he is man enough to deal with the Philistines, and even his total victory will not come until Samson is well into his adult years.

## II. The Angel's Announcement—Judges 13:2-5

### A. The Barren Couple, 2

**2 And there was a certain man of Zorah, of the family of the Danites, whose name was Manoah; and his wife was barren, and bare not.**

How many barren couples in the Bible received through the Lord the news of a coming child? An angel announced the conception of John the Baptist to his father Zacharias. The Holy Spirit confirmed the news to Elizabeth after John moved in her womb when Mary greeted her. Mary was not barren, of course, although being virgin also would result in her being childless at that point. To her the angel Gabriel brought the news of her coming pregnancy, and then he repeated the announcement to Joseph. Years before Jesus' birth, barren Hannah learned from an aged prophet that she would bear the much greater prophet Samuel. Now we have this record of the time when Manoah and his wife find out from an angel about their unexpected pregnancy.

"Bare not" at the end of vs. 2 is an Elizabethan English spelling of our word "bear." It refers to childbearing and implies nothing about nudity or the lack thereof.

### B. The Good News, 3

**3 And the angel of the LORD appeared unto the woman, and said unto her, Behold now, thou art barren, and bearest not: but thou shalt conceive, and bear a son.**

Why did the angel appear first to the mother-to-be and not to her husband to begin with? Likewise, Gabriel approached Mary with the news of Jesus'

483

birth before he surprised Joseph.

**C. The Nazirite Restrictions, 4-5a**

**4 Now therefore beware, I pray thee, and drink not wine nor strong drink, and eat not any unclean thing:**

**5 For, lo, thou shalt conceive, and bear a son; and no razor shall come on his head: for the child shall be a Nazarite unto God from the womb:**

"Beware, I pray thee" in our newer Bible versions means "be careful" or "be cautious." Samson's mother must obey the angel's strange instructions with great care, for from the moment of his conception he will be devoted to God with what was called a Nazirite vow.

As we debate abortion issues and try to determine exactly when life begins, we cannot afford to ignore the implications of this passage.

In his instructions to Samson's mother-to-be, the angel summarizes the requirements of a Nazirite vow as they are delineated in Numbers 6. Most men who took this particular vow did so for a specific length of time, as in the case of the apostle Paul, who resolved to be a Nazirite until he got to Jerusalem on the next festival day (Acts 18:18-21). A man who took this vow promised the Lord that no razor would touch his head during the vow (so in Paul's time men often started off with their heads shaved). They agreed not to drink wine or alcoholic beverages for the duration of the vow. They also pledged to use special care in abiding by the Jews' dietary and sanitation laws. The combination of prohibitions could be quite restricting. The prohibitions were voluntarily accepted as an act of spiritual discipline as in Lenten fasts in some Christian fellowships.

In all newer versions and Bible dictionaries, the spelling of the name of the vow is *Nazirite* instead of *Nazarite*, as in the KJV. The modern spelling helps us avoid the possible confusion of this vow's name with Jesus' hometown, Nazareth, or with the modern Nazarene denomination. The vow has no connection to either, as the spelling with two *i*'s indicates.

**D. The Baby's Destiny, 5b**

**5b . . . and he shall begin to deliver Israel out of the hand of the Philistines.**

Now we discover God's special interest in this baby. He will be God's answer to the pleading of the Israelites for relief from their enemies.

How many babies being carried in their mother's womb today does God have destined as solutions to problems faced by His people in many places?

**III. Manoah Finds Out—Judges 13:6-8**

**A. His Wife Fills Him In, 6-7**

**6 Then the woman came and told her husband, saying, A man of God came unto me, and his countenance was like the countenance of an angel of God, very terrible: but I asked him not whence he was, neither told he me his name:**

**7 But he said unto me, Behold, thou shalt conceive, and bear a son; and now drink no wine nor strong drink, neither eat any unclean thing: for the child shall be a Nazarite to**

484

God from the womb to the day of his death.

Manoah's wife (whose name we never know) tells him about her exciting visit with God's angel. Her description of an angel is quite interesting. It is obvious from her account that the angel frightened her—so much so that she did not dare ask him who he was and where he came from. Still, she seemed to be convinced that she had talked to a heavenly messenger.

She told Manoah both the news of the baby to be born and of the lifelong Nazirite vow imposed on their child. Any family with a child that requires careful and continuous medical attention can appreciate how much the Nazirite vow restrictions affected the home of Samson's parents.

**B. Manoah's Prayer, 8**

**8 Then Manoah intreated the LORD, and said, O my Lord, let the man of God which thou didst send come again unto us, and teach us what we shall do unto the child that shall be born.**

Manoah's reaction to his wife's startling news is to pray for God to send the angel back so they can find out more about the child He is sending and the care they need to give him to prepare him for the Lord's purposes.

**IV. Samson Is Born and Matures—Judges 13:24-25**

**24 And the woman bare a son, and called his name Samson: and the child grew, and the LORD blessed him.**

**25 And the Spirit of the LORD began to move him at times in the camp of Dan between Zorah and Eshtaol.**

Nine months later, Samson is born and named. Again the old English spelling of "bear" as "bare" could be confusing, but less so here than earlier.

Half a verse later Samson is maturing into a man. With maturity comes also the moving of God's Spirit in this man God has brought to set his people free from the Philistines' cruel bondage. In the chapters that follow, we will have to ponder each event and ask how Samson's actions are the Spirit's way of using him to provoke the Philistines into a confrontation he can win.

The location of Samson's boyhood home is important to his life mission. Several newer versions call his home village Manaheh Dan. In their footnotes, some of them explain that the words here literally mean the "Camp of Dan," as in the KJV translation. Its location was strategically located between the Philistine settlements of Zorah and Eshtaol—a location almost guaranteeing Samson's conflict with the enemies of his people.

ഹൗൽ

485

**Evangelistic Emphasis**

God has used a fascinating group of men and women to do His work. Some stand out as being exceptionally admirable and others do not. Names such as Seth, Enoch, Noah, Abraham, Moses, Elijah and Isaiah, shine brightly along with others we could include in this list.

Then there is Samson.

None of us would want our sons to grow up and become a Samson. We would not want our daughters to marry a Samson. We would not even want to have a cousin or an uncle like him. Who knows what he might do when he came to the family reunion?

Nevertheless, Samson's name is recorded in Hebrews 11 as a hero of the faith.

Even with all his impulsiveness and reckless behavior, his chasing after Philistine women, and his all-around irresponsible lifestyle, God managed to use him. (Some Bible students see Israel's rebellious behavior reflected in him. Do you suppose any of his contemporaries saw this?)

God chose him even before his conception, apparently to do one particular work: oppose the Philistines. He did it well enough that even with all his flaws, he fulfilled this faith responsibility.

There is work that God wants you and me to do (and it is not to behave like Samson). He wants us to be godly and Christ-like to let others know about the Father and His Son.

ഇറ

**Memory Selection**

"And the woman bare a son, and called his name Samson; and the child grew, and the Lord blessed him. And the Spirit of the Lord began to move him . . . ." *Judges 13:24-25*

We see God planning as he brought Samson on the scene. In Canaan's earlier history, the Philistines had not been major players. However, they have become the dominate political and military power and God will deal with them. His working through the God-fearing couple, Manoah and his wife, and the birth of their son Samson, sets the stage for some impressive events. The Philistines will be dealing with God at work as Samson comes their way.

We notice in our memory verse that little is said about Samson's childhood. He was born, he grew, and the Lord blessed him. Actually, those few words, plus the fact that he was born to loving parents, suggests a favorable childhood for him. His parents reverenced God, which is a definite plus for any child.

Our memory verse says that the Spirit of the Lord began to move him. The Keil and Delitzsch commentary on this verse says, "The Spirit of Jehovah began to thrust him . . . denoting the operation of the Spirit of God within him, which took possession of him suddenly, and impelled him to put forth supernatural powers." It further says, "The meaning of this verse, which forms the introduction to the following account of the acts of Samson, is simply that Samson was there seized by the Spirit of Jehovah, and impelled to commence the conflict with the Philistines.'

## Weekday Problems

John Milton, who lived in the 1600s, wrote a dramatic poem entitled "Samson Agonistes." (Agonistes is a word that means Samson was engaged in a struggle.) In the poem, we hear Samson musing about his life. He is blind, a slave of the Philistines, and is about to be taken in to their banquet hall where he pulls the temple down on everyone. Here are a few lines from the poem.

> Why was my breeding ordered and prescribed
>> As of a person separate to God,
>> Designed for great exploits . . .
> Ask for this great Deliverer now, and find him
>> Eyeless in Gaza, at the mill with slaves,
>> Himself in bonds under Philistian yoke . . .
> But what is strength without a double share
>> Of wisdom?

It sounds like a bad pun to say that Samson's strong point was his strength. In the poem, he sees a great need for wisdom to go along with muscle. We will avoid many problems if we ask God for wisdom to accompany our God-given talents and strong points. Maybe we could even ask for a double share of wisdom.

---

# How to Install
# Your Own Home Security System

1. At the Goodwill Store buy a pair of men's work boots, size 14-16 (well used).

2. Place them on the front porch along with a copy of *Gun and Ammo* magazine.

3. Put a couple of BIG dog dishes next to the boots and magazine

4. Leave this note on your door:

Hey Bubba,Big Jim, Duke, Slim, and Me have gone for more ammo. We'll get back in about 1 hour. Don't mess with the pit bulls—they got after the mailman this morning and messed him up real bad. I don't think Killer took part in it, but it was hard to tell from all the blood. Anyway, I locked all the dogs in the house. Better just wait outside till we get back. Cooter

# This Lesson in Your Life

God can take a less than perfect situation and make it work for good. More to the point, He can do this with very unfavorable circumstances. Take, for instance, Joseph being sold to a passing caravan of Ishmaelite traders. They were coming from Gilead with their camels loaded with spices, balm, and myrrh, on their way to Egypt. Joseph's jealous brothers saw in them a way to get rid of him without having to commit murder. The Ishmaelites bought him for twenty shekels of silver and took him to Egypt where they sold him. This piece of treachery on the part of the brothers influenced the subsequent history of Israel. They meant it for evil but God used it for good. (Genesis 37, 45, 46.)

A New Testament example is Onesimus the run-away-slave. His escapade worked to his own conversion, was helpful to Paul in prison, and resulted in the touchingly beautiful letter of Paul to Philemon.

Our immediate case in point, of course, is Samson. By most standards, his personal life might be described as a colossal train wreck. He was crude, boorish, and immoral – you can name his failings without reading them here. Yet God used him to do an important work and the Bible recognizes his faith in action (Heb. 11:32).

There are two points we want to notice that will help us adapt this lesson to our lives. One is that we need to be aware that things are not always what they seem. This is especially true when God is involved (as we have noticed in the previous paragraphs). God assesses things differently than we do from our human point of view. Daniel 4:17 says that He is sovereign over the kingdoms of men, and sets over them anyone He wishes. This includes the lowliest of men. Some of them may well have been the pagan kings who troubled Israel during the time of the judges.

To us, Samson was not a nice person. We can be sure his misbehavior did not escape God's notice, but he did what God intended him to do in opposing the Philistines. The pagan Canaanite kings were cruel and oppressive toward Israel, but they served God's purpose when they forced the Israelites back to Him.

The second point we can use is brought to our attention by our Devotional Reading, Romans 2:1-8. We need to be careful about being judgmental. This, of course, includes our sitting in judgment on Samson. It approaches this from several directions, one being that we might be condemning ourselves when we condemn someone else. God judges truly; yet, our judgment may be one-sided. In addition, we do not want to oppose God's goodness, forbearance, and patience, all of which helps lead people to repentance.

God worked through Samson, a less than perfect person. We want God to work through us, less than perfect also. Isn't there a lesson in there somewhere?

## GETTING
## THE FACTS STRAIGHT

**1. Who were the oppressors of Israel during Samson's time?**
The Philistines oppressed Israel during Samson's time. There were five cities, located along the coastline.

**2. For how many years did the Philistines oppress Israel?**
They oppressed Israel for forty years.

**3. What was Samson's father named, and to which tribe did he belong?**
Samson's father was Manoah, from the tribe of Dan.

**4. Manoah's wife was barren. When the angel appeared to her, what did he say concerning this?**
He told her that she was barren, but would now conceive and bear a son.

**5. Why did the angel place restrictions on her diet?**
Her son was to be a Levite from the womb, and she should observe the dietary restrictions given in Numbers 6.

**6. Manoah asked the Lord to send the angel again. Did the angel make another appearance?**
Yes, the angel came and appeared to the wife while she was sitting in the field. She ran and brought Manoah.

**7. Manoah prepared a burnt offering on a rock. A flame came up from the rock. How did the angel make his exit?**
The angel ascended in the flame of the altar.

**7. It was when the angel ascended in the flame that Manoah realized he was an angel and not just a man. Of what was he afraid would happen?**
He thought they had seen God and would die.

**8. How did his wife assure him that they would not be killed?**
She explained that if they were to be killed, God would not have accepted their burnt offering, and would not have shown or told them the things that He did.

**9. The Bible gives a very short account of Samson's youth. What does it tell us?**
It simply tells us that Samson was born, that he grew, and that the Lord blessed him.

**10. What are we told about when the Lord began to move in Samson?**
The Spirit of the Lord began to move in him at times while he was in his home territory of Dan.

**489**

In many ways, studying Judges has a depressing edge to it. The pagan kings were oppressive, the pagan gods were despicable, and the Israelites repeatedly abandoned God in spite of His goodness to them. This pattern pretty well continues through the whole book. There is one redeeming factor that gives uplift to the otherwise sad story: God is in it. When God is at work, there is something good to be found.

In their book, *Old Testament Survey*, La Sor, Hubbard, and Bush, summrize the central truth of Judges. It points us in an uplifting direction.

Here are a few of their lines:

> The lesson from each of the judges is, above all,
> that those who are dedicated to Yahweh can be
> used by Yahweh. Elements in their lives may not
> be in keeping with the Lord's will. Their methods
> may not stand up as exemplary . . . Again and again
> God's servants fall short in their private and public
> thoughts and acts. Something to censure can be
> found in almost everyone mentioned in Hebrews 11 . . . ."

God can and does use those who are dedicated to Him. This is wonderful news to everyone who wants to serve Him. There is an important statement made in 2 Timothy 2:19, where the topic is how to be a good worker for God. It says, "The Lord knows those who are his" (NIV). The Lord knows our hearts. He knows our motivation. He knows our level of dedication.

Even with the shortcomings that are obvious in some of the judges, God had raised each one up. His Spirit was in them. He used them to help Israel, His children. He will use us also. Be encouraged by this.

Another faith-building lesson that comes through Judges is that God is the ultimate savior. There is a sense in which each judge saved Israel from its oppressors, and each one probably did have certain talents that helped him be effective. The deciding factor, though, in every judgeship, was the action of God.

Jephthah, for instance, was a mighty warrior, but he said it was the Lord who gave him the victory over the Ammonites (12:3).

We can come through our study in Judges feeling good because we know God's judgment is superior to our judgment. He uses imperfect people, which means he can and does use you and me. Whether it is with the judges or with us, it is He who empowers and saves. Paul said, "I can do all things through him who gives me strength" (Phil. 4:13 NIV). We can depend on that same Source. We know the One in whom we have believed. We know we can trust Him with everything until that very last day (Read 2 Tim. 1:12). Our strength is in Him.

℘℩℘

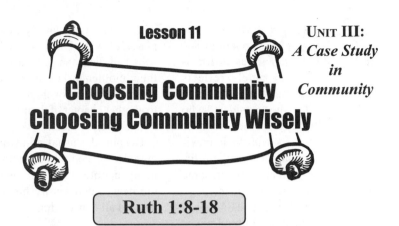

# Lesson 11

## Choosing Community
## Choosing Community Wisely

### Ruth 1:8-18

And Naomi said unto her two daughters in law, Go, return each to her mother's house: the LORD deal kindly with you, as ye have dealt with the dead, and with me.

9 The LORD grant you that ye may find rest, each of you in the house of her husband. Then she kissed them; and they lifted up their voice, and wept.

10 And they said unto her, Surely we will return with thee unto thy people.

11 And Naomi said, Turn again, my daughters: why will ye go with me? are there yet any more sons in my womb, that they may be your husbands?

12 Turn again, my daughters, go your way; for I am too old to have an husband. If I should say, I have hope, if I should have an husband also to night, and should also bear sons;

13 Would ye tarry for them till they were grown? would ye stay for them from having husbands? nay, my daughters; for it grieveth me much for your sakes that the hand of the LORD is gone out against me.

14 And they lifted up their voice, and wept again: and Orpah kissed her mother in law; but Ruth clave unto her.

15 And she said, Behold, thy sister in law is gone back unto her people, and unto her gods: return thou after thy sister in law.

16 And Ruth said, Intreat me not to leave thee, or to return from following after thee: for whither thou goest, I will go; and where thou lodgest, I will lodge: thy people shall be my people, and thy God my God:

17 Where thou diest, will I die, and there will I be buried: the LORD do so to me, and more also, if ought but death part thee and me.

18 When she saw that she was stedfastly minded to go with her, then she left speaking unto her.

**Memory Verse**
Ruth 1:16

**Background Scripture**
Ruth 1:8-18

**Devotional Reading**
Romans 10:5-13

Aug. 14

491

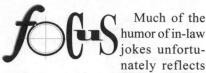

Much of the humor of in-law jokes unfortunately reflects the sad truth that many families find it hard to assimilate the "outsiders" who marry into their circle. When we try to merge two families with their inevitable cultural variations and their different ways of problem solving, some conflict seems to be unavoidable.

How fortunate Naomi and Elimelech had been that their sons found wives who fit into their family in a loving, peaceful way. Even when Naomi's sons had died, the girls' affection for their mother-in-law is evident. Her unselfish desire for them to move on to another chapter of their lives speaks of her love for them.

Despite the usual adjustments required to get comfortable with in-laws, many people will later testify that the new united family blessed them beyond all expectation.

ഇ൬ൽ

## For a Lively Start

After enduring a famine and three family funerals, Naomi was bitter about her lot in life. Before her troubles, she evidently had embodied her name, which means Pleasant. When she finds her way back to her original village, she tells her longtime friends to call her Mara, which means bitter. As Naomi urges her widowed daughters-in-law to return to their homes and find new husbands, she apologizes to them for getting them tangled in her troubles. To describe her sad lot in life, she says in vs. 13, "The Lord himself has raised his fist against me" (NLT).

Why are people so quick to blame God for their heartaches and troubles? Job made that mistake, crediting God for all the disasters Satan heaped upon him. This serious theological error can cause a faith crisis like Naomi's in this story.

| Teaching Outline | Daily Bible Readings |
|---|---|
| I. Naomi Tells the Girls to Go Home—Ruth 1:8-9 | Mon. The Lord of All<br>*Romans 10:5-13* |
| II. The Girls Refuse—Ruth 1:10 | Tue. Bound Together in Christ<br>*Romans 12:3-8* |
| III. Naomi Cites More Reasons—Ruth 1:11-13 | Wed. Seeking Unity in Community<br>*Romans 14:1-9* |
| IV. Orpah Goes; Ruth Stays—Ruth 1:14 | Thu. Restoring Community<br>*Genesis 50:15-21* |
| V. Naomi Urges Ruth to Go—Ruth 1:15 | Fri. Protecting Community<br>*Exodus 1:8-21* |
| VI. Ruth Pledges Faithfulness—Ruth 1:16-17 | Sat. Seeking Comfort in Community<br>*Ruth 1:1-7* |
| VII. Naomi Ends Her Pleading—Ruth 1:18 | Sun. Choosing Community<br>*Ruth 1:8-18* |

# *Verse by Verse*

**Ruth 1:8-18**

## I. Naomi Tells the Girls to Go Home—Ruth 1:8-9

**8 And Naomi said unto her two daughters in law, Go, return each to her mother's house: the LORD deal kindly with you, as ye have dealt with the dead, and with me.**

**9 The LORD grant you that ye may find rest, each of you in the house of her husband. Then she kissed them; and they lifted up their voice, and wept.**

Naomi's proposal to her daughters-in-law expresses her unselfish love for them. A lesser person might have trapped the young women, dooming them to live as childless unmarried women, in order to retain their companionship and their youthful ability to attend to the older woman's needs. Not Naomi. Urging them to go find husbands and begin a new chapter in their young lives, she assures them of her continued love even if they leave her as she is urging.

It is clear from vs. 9 that these three women truly love one another. The Scriptures give us no details about their life together before this moment, nor are we given a clue as to whether their spouses perished in a single disaster, epidemic, or whether they were taken in separate incidents. The women have clearly been through three funerals together, but their loving relationship seems to have grown strong even before misfortune descended upon them.

## II. The Girls Refuse—Ruth 1:10

**10 And they said unto her, Surely we will return with thee unto thy people.**

At first, Ruth and Orpah reject Naomi's suggestion. Naomi has confided in them that she is planning to return to her remaining family in the Bethlehem area. The famine that drove her and her family to Moab has broken. Now that all the men in Naomi's family have died in this foreign land, she has no reason to remain here. In fact, her only realistic hope for a decent future is to go back to live among the people who know and love her.

## III. Naomi Cites More Reasons—Ruth 1:11-13

**11 And Naomi said, Turn again, my daughters: why will ye go with me? are there yet any more sons in my womb, that they may be your husbands?**

493

**12** Turn again, my daughters, go your way; for I am too old to have an husband. If I should say, I have hope, if I should have an husband also to night, and should also bear sons;

**13** Would ye tarry for them till they were grown? would ye stay for them from having husbands? nay, my daughters; for it grieveth me much for your sakes that the hand of the LORD is gone out against me.

As the book of Ruth will illustrate fully in its later chapters, God's rules for His people required a young childless widow to maintain her connection to the family of her dead husband. The nearest kinsman in that family was required by God's law to father a child by this widow—a child who would then legally inherit his dead father's property (see Deuteronomy 25:5-10). This custom is the background of Naomi's reasoning as she urges Ruth and Orpah to go find Moabite husbands. She is too old to start a new family and provide them new husbands within her clan. Even if she had new sons starting that very day, it would not be reasonable to expect these young women to wait for those boys to grow up and marry them.

Naomi is being harshly, bitterly realistic. She sees no reasonable way for them to comply with the requirements of Moses' law, and she loves Ruth and Orpah too much to let them grow old and childless. It is simply their misfortune to have been drawn into the relationship with an insecure, elderly, and godforsaken woman.

**IV. Orpah Goes; Ruth Stays—Ruth 1:14**

**14** And they lifted up their voice, and wept again: and Orpah kissed her mother in law; but Ruth clave unto her.

Again, Naomi's suggestion that they leave her reduces all them to tears. After Naomi's fuller explanation and urging, Orpah agrees and departs after kissing her. However, Ruth refuses to abandon the older woman. "Clave" is an archaic English past tense of the verb "cleave." The TEV says Ruth "hung on" to Naomi. The NLT reads that she "clung tightly" to her mother-in-law.

**V. Naomi Urges Ruth to Go—Ruth 1:15**

**15** And she said, Behold, thy sister in law is gone back unto her people, and unto her gods: return thou after thy sister in law.

Having finally convinced Orpah to see things her way, Naomi redoubles her efforts to persuade Ruth to return to her Moabite culture. We do learn from vs. 15 that Naomi realizes that sending the girls back home involves sending them back to serve their pagan gods instead of the Lord. Once more Naomi urges Ruth to be sensible and go back to her former home and its ways, just as Orpah has done.

**VI. Ruth Pledges Faithfulness—Ruth 1:16-17**

**16** And Ruth said, Intreat me not to leave thee, or to return from following after thee: for whither thou goest, I will go; and where thou lodgest, I will lodge: thy people shall be my people, and thy God my God:

**17** Where thou diest, will I die, and there will I be buried: the LORD do so to me, and more also, if ought but death part thee and me.

Probably there are no words, more treasured, in the book of Ruth than this pledge of faithfulness by Ruth. It has inspired many poems, songs, and sermons. Updated from the KJV syntax and set in poetic form in the NRSV, it reads as follows:

Do not press me to leave you
or to turn back from following you!
Where you go, I will go;
where you lodge, I will lodge;
your people shall be my people,
and your God my God.
Where you die, I will die—
there will I be buried.
May the LORD do thus and so to me,
and more as well,
if even death parts me from you!

## VII. Naomi Ends Her Pleading— Ruth 1:18

**18 When she saw that she was stedfastly minded to go with her, then she left speaking unto her.**

Naomi lost this argument. During the centuries since then, we have honored Ruth for her unshakeable loyalty to her aging mother-in-law. The KJV vocabulary here is an outdated surprise. Saying Ruth was "minded" to go with Naomi means she was "determined" to go. Saying that Naomi "left" speaking is an antiquated way of saying she "quit" speaking to Ruth.

Sometimes when we can see, as Naomi does, that we are not going to convince another person to see things our way, we do well to imitate her wisdom—just be silent.

ৡয়ঝ

## Evangelistic Emphasis

Shortly before Joshua died, he gathered Israel at Shechem and renewed God's covenant with them (Josh. 24). He spoke of what God had done for Israel, and then he gave them a choice: "Choose you this day whom ye will serve ... But for me and my house we will serve the LORD (24:15).

As we studied through Judges, we saw Israel undecided between the pagan gods and the living God. Every generation or so, they would revert to paganism. They had trouble choosing God and remaining faithful.

In our study in Ruth, there are still choices to be made. The two sons of Elimelech and Naomi married women from Moab. The chief god there was Chemosh, a horrible deity. As events developed, these two women each made a choice about God.

Our studies in Joshua, Judges, and Ruth, combine to remind us of the responsibility and privilege God gives us to share the Word. In evangelism we offer a choice. We want everyone to know the work of the Father, Son, and Holy Spirit. They should know about God, and that He loved the world enough to send his Son. They need to know about Jesus, who is the Christ, and His sacrifice on the cross, and what that accomplished. They should know about the comfort and guidance of the Spirit. If they know this, they can make an informed choice.

## Memory Selection

"And Ruth said, Intreat me not to leave thee, or to return from following after thee: for whither thou goest, I will go; and where thou lodgest, I will lodge: thy people shall be my people, and thy God my God." *Ruth 1:16*

Ruth's touching words to her mother-in-law are among the most beautiful to be found in the Old Testament. They are among the highest expressions of faith in the entire Bible.

The Davis and Whitcomb commentary suggests that, "they are a good example of what Christ had in mind when He uttered the words recorded in Matthew 19:27-30." In this passage, Peter asked the Lord "We have left everything to follow you! What then will there be for us?" Jesus answered, "I tell you the truth, at the renewal of all things, when the Son of Man sits on his glorious throne . . . everyone who has left houses or brothers or sisters or father or mother or children or fields for my sake will receive a hundred times as much and will inherit eternal life."

As we read Ruth's words, they speak to us of total love, devotion, and trust. It is no wonder that they are repeated so often in wedding ceremonies. They speak to us of stable homes, enduring love, and complete faith in the God of Israel.

We need to remember that Ruth was a Moabite widow, impoverished and walking along the long road to Israel when she spoke these words. She did not know what lay ahead, but she loved Naomi deeply and had faith that would find refuge for her under the wings of a loving and faithful God.

# Weekday Problems

The book of Ruth is set in the time of the judges. There is famine in the land, and Elimelech, Naomi, and their two sons are suffering. This may the same famine as in Judges 6:1-6. If not, it must have been one just as devastating. Elimelech could not feed his family.

They lived in Bethlehem, which means "House of Bread." However, this family from the House of Bread had none. They emigrated to neighboring Moab, and for a time this probably seemed a good solution to the problem. One by one, though, the men of the family died. What once had been a solution now became a problem. Naomi was in a most difficult situation.

A few evenings ago, my wife and I watched the very old movie, "The Grapes of Wrath" on TV. During dust bowl days, an extended family left Oklahoma and traveled west on Route 66, confident that California was their Promised Land. They were not welcomed there with open arms.

During the height of the recent recession, a man who had lost his job traveled over a thousand miles and arrived in our city, confident he would find work here. He discovered that our city was one of the hardest hit by the recession.

At some time in life, every one of us is likely to hit a brick wall. It may be economic, or it could be something else. There is no guarantee the solution will come easily. Perhaps Naomi and Ruth can give us some survival tips.

---

## British Brass

*Actual excerpts from Royal Navy and Marines officer fitness reports:*

- His men would follow him anywhere, but only out of curiosity.
- I would not breed from this officer.
- He has carried out each and every one of his duties to his entire satisfaction.
- He would be out of his depth in a car park puddle.
- This young lady has delusions of adequacy.
- Since my last report he has reached rock bottom and has started to dig.
- She sets low personal standards and then consistently fails to achieve them.
- He has the wisdom of youth and the energy of old age.
- Works well when under constant supervision and cornered like a rat in a trap.
- This man is depriving a village somewhere of an idiot.

# This Lesson in Your Life

It is just the nature of things that we have to make choices. We have no choice but to make them. If we should be tempted to say, "I'm not going to make that decision," we have made the decision to do nothing, which may have been a very bad choice.

We see any number of choices being made in the first chapter of Ruth. Let's look at a few, evaluate some of them, and see if we can learn anything from them.

There was famine in Israel and Elimelech's family was having a hard time eking out a living. There was no sign of improvement to be detected, and he was a desperate man. Just the other side of the Salt Sea in Moab things were better, and he was tempted to make the move. They would be foreigners there, and Chemosh was their god. There was food there, and they could still be faithful to the God of Israel. These things and more went through Elimelech's mind. Finally he said, "Let's move to Moab."

Knowing what we do about what happened to this family, do you think Elimelech made a wise choice? We have the advantage of hindsight, and he could not read the future. He did the best he could.

While in Moab, his two sons married Moabite women. Israelites were forbidden to marry pagans. What can we say about their choice? Considering that one of these women, Ruth, became an ancestress to Jesus, we are forced to see the providence of God at work. These things we are reading about did not happen through circumstance, yet the men and women who are involved had no way of knowing this. They were simply making the choices that seemed best at the time.

After the death of the three men, and the famine around Bethlehem had ended, Naomi made the choice of returning home. We would say that was a wise one, wouldn't we? Her two daughters-in-law now have a decision to make. Do they stay in Moab, or go with Naomi? Their prospects probably look brighter in Moab and riskier in Israel. We know how the story works out, and again, we have to see the providence of God working His will through all these events.

We all make choices every day, and some of them will determine how our lives go. We decide to attend a particular school, accept a certain job, or move to some city. There we meet the person we will marry, or some other life-changing events take place. Assuming we are people of faith and ask God for direction in our lives, will this help us make right choices? If something goes wrong (we remember that three men died in Moab) how do we handle that? In our minds, can we work a tragedy into God's providential guidance?

James tells us (1:5-7) that if we lack wisdom, we should ask our generous God and He will give it to us. He says we must ask in faith. Here are a couple of wise choices: Ask God for wisdom to make choices. Keep faith in Him.

498

## GETTING
## THE FACTS STRAIGHT

**1. During what time period is the Book of Ruth set?**

Ruth takes place during the days when the judges ruled.

**2. What tragic occurrence in the land caused Elimelech to move to Moab?**

Elimelech went to Moab because there was a famine in the land.

**3. What was the name of Elimelech's wife and two sons?**

Naomi was Elimelech's wife. The sons were named Mahlon and Chilion.

**4. The two sons married women from Moab. What were their names?**

Mahlon was married to Ruth. Chilion was married to Orpah.

**5. When Naomi and Ruth returned to Bethlehem, Naomi told the people not to call her Naomi, but to call her Mara. What is the significance of these names?**

Naomi means pleasant. Mara means bitter. Naomi felt that God had dealt bitterly with her.

**6. At what time of the year did Naomi and Ruth arrive in Bethlehem?**

They arrived at the beginning of barley harvest. This was probably in April.

**7. How did Naomi describe how she left Bethlehem and how she returned?**

She said she went out full, and the Lord had brought her back empty.

**8. In what way had Ruth indicated that she accepted the God of Israel rather than the gods of Moab?**

As she let Naomi know she intended to stay with her and go to Bethlehem, she said that Naomi's God would be her God.

**9. When Orpah decided to remain in Moab, what does the Bible say she did, and Ruth did (The contrast between the two)?**

It says, "Orpah kissed her mother in law; but Ruth clave unto her."

**10. What indications do we have that Orpah found it difficult to remain in Moab and not go with Naomi?**

At first she went with Naomi and Ruth, and cried when Naomi encouraged them to return. It was only when Naomi insisted that she decided to return, and again they cried, and she kissed Naomi.

"Everybody loves a lover," so the old saying goes. Maybe that is why Ruth is such a popular Biblical heroine. We all love Ruth. We all love the Book of Ruth, which is a love story.

This peasant Israelite family, made up of Elimelech, Naomi, and their sons Mahlon, and Chilion, were a bright spot during a time when Israelites were often wandering in spiritual and moral darkness. We remember, from our study in Judges, how fickle the Israelites often were. Elimelech's family lets us know that there were always individual Israelites who kept their faith in God.

The Book of Ruth comes as a breath of fresh air and a sunbeam of light shining during the dreary period of the judges. While so much violence and intrigue was taking place in Israel, this book gives us a different perspective. Though Judges and Ruth are set in the same historical period, the two books are as different as night from day.

Ruth obviously loved her mother-in-law. This gives us a good feeling about their relationships in their little family clan, while the three men in the family were still alive. Orpah, the daughter-in-law who decided to remain in Moab, wept as she made her decision to part from Naomi. It was not an easy decision for to her to make. The three deaths plus the decision to return to Bethlehem marked the end of what must have been an admirable family group. That part is sad, but it figures into the story.

Love empowers us to undergo hardships. Naomi and Ruth set out on their walk to Bethlehem. It may have been something on the order of a 75 mile trip. (One commentary says 50; another, 75.) From the hills of Moab, they descended about 4,500 feet down the dusty road to cross the Jordan. From there, they climbed not quite that many feet up into the hills of Judah. They arrived in Bethlehem at barley harvest, probably April.

Here is where the poverty to prosperity part of the story unfolds. The much younger Ruth accepts the responsibility for gleaning in the grain fields so both she and Naomi can eat. She joins the other poverty-stricken people who collect what the harvesters have left behind. Along comes the well-to-do land owner in whose barley field Ruth is working. The rest of the story is history.

Boaz and Ruth marry. Soon, Naomi will be the grandmother to little Obed, who lies in her lap as she cares for him. As time passes, Obed becomes the grandfather of David, who becomes Israel's great king. About a thousand years later Jesus would be born in Bethlehem, descended in the flesh from this line.

The faith of Ruth the Moabites is used by God as he develops His plan of salvation. In this lovely story we see how God enters the ordinary events of ordinary people to work out His will in the world. We are inspired as we see the Creator's intimate concern for daily events, and how He works through humble people to fulfill His divine purpose.

# Lesson 12

## Empowering the Needy Depending on the Community

### Ruth 2:8-18

Then said Boaz unto Ruth, Hearest thou not, my daughter? Go not to glean in another field ... but abide here fast by my maidens:

9 Let thine eyes be on the field that they do reap, and go thou after them: have I not charged the young men that they shall not touch thee? and when thou art athirst, go unto the vessels, and drink of that which the young men have drawn.

10 Then she fell on her face, and bowed herself to the ground, and said unto him, Why have I found grace in thine eyes, that thou shouldest take knowledge of me, seeing I am a stranger?

11 And Boaz answered and said unto her, It hath fully been shewed me, all that thou hast done unto thy mother in law since the death of thine husband: and how thou hast left thy father and thy mother, and the land of thy nativity, and art come unto a people which thou knewest not heretofore.

12 ... A full reward be given thee of the LORD God of Israel ....

13 Then she said, Let me find favour in thy sight, my lord; for that thou hast comforted me, and for that thou hast spoken friendly unto thine handmaid, though I be not like unto one of thine handmaidens.

14 And Boaz said unto her, At mealtime come thou hither, and eat of the bread, and dip thy morsel in the vinegar. And she sat beside the reapers: and he reached her parched corn, and she did eat ....

15 And when she was risen up to glean, Boaz commanded his young men, saying, Let her glean ... and reproach her not:

16 And let fall also some of the handfuls of purpose for her, and leave them, that she may glean them, and rebuke her not.

17 So she gleaned in the field until even, and beat out that she had gleaned: and it was about an ephah of barley.

18 And she took it up, and went into the city: and her mother in law saw what she had gleaned: and she . . . gave to her that she had reserved after she was sufficed.

**Memory Verse**
Ruth 2:12
**Background Scripture**
Ruth 2; 3; Leviticus 19:9-10
**Devotional Reading**
Proverbs 22:1-9

Aug. 21

# fOCuS

God's compassion for the poor and the homeless lay behind His rules for harvesters. In Leviticus 19:9-10 and Deuteronomy 24:19-22 the Lord explains that a Hebrew reaping grain or grapes should not go back to retrieve any produce left behind, nor should the workers pick up any grain they happened to drop. Instead, the poor were to be allowed to come into the fields or vineyards to pick up what was left behind. Harvesting the leftovers was called gleaning. Farmers like Boaz who welcomed gleaners on their property obviously loved and obeyed the Lord.

Gleaning virtually vanished until recent times when American tax laws encouraged farm corporations to allow food bank volunteers to glean fruit or vegetables that were being left to rot. Today, we commonly see senior citizen volunteers or trustee convicts doing the difficult stoop labor to pick up left-behind crops to be distributed to feeding programs for the poor.

## For a Lively Start

ഇൗ

Our first look at Boaz in Ruth 2 lets us know that he is a high-principled man with a soft heart. Unlike some in every age, he is free of the bigotry that would have shut a Moabite stranger out of his fields. One reason he gives, for his kindnesses to Ruth, lets us know that he feels compassion for a widow like Naomi. His heart is loving and unselfish, so he does all he can to aid Naomi and Ruth.

"We just ask that you remember the poor," was the only requirement the apostles and James made when they blessed the ministry of Paul and Barnabas to the Gentiles. In every age God's people have helped the helpless. For centuries, the Church was the only source of significant aid for the sick and hungry. People like Boaz reached out to take care of their neighbors.

| Teaching Outline | Daily Bible Readings |
|---|---|
| I. Boaz's Kindness to Ruth—Ruth 2:8-16 | Mon. Sharing Bread with the Poor *Proverbs 22:1-9* |
| A. Boaz Invites Her to Glean, 8-9a | Tue. Provision for the Poor *Leviticus 19:1-10* |
| B. Boaz Gives Protection and Water, 9b | Wed. Generosity in the Kingdom *Matthew 20:1-15* |
| C. Ruth Asks Why, 10 | Thu. Sharing Equally *1 Samuel 30:21-25* |
| D. Boaz Explains His Kindness, 11-12 | Fri. Ready to Share *1 Timothy 6:11-19* |
| E. Ruth Thanks Boaz, 13 | Sat. Taking Initiative *Ruth 2:1-7* |
| F. Boaz Does More for Ruth, 14-16 | Sun. A Kind Benefactor *Ruth 2:8-18* |
| II. Rewards for a Hard Day of Work—Ruth 2:17-18 | |

# *Verse by Verse*

## Ruth 2:8-18

**I. Boaz's Kindness to Ruth—Ruth 2:8-16**

**A. Boaz Invites Her to Glean, 8-9a**

**8 Then said Boaz unto Ruth, Hearest thou not, my daughter? Go not to glean in another field, neither go from hence, but abide here fast by my maidens:**

**9a Let thine eyes be on the field that they do reap, and go thou after them:**

When Boaz's workers identify the stranger who is gleaning in his grain field, the farmer immediately goes out of his way to make sure Ruth feels welcome. His workers report that Ruth came early to the field and worked non-stop in the hot morning sun. Gleaning is stoop labor. Picking up the dropped heads of grain hour after hour turns out to be hard work that yields far less than a regular harvester can expect to reap.

Boaz speaks kindly to Ruth and tells her not to go off to somebody else's property to glean. Evidently, he has some female servants working in the field. For safety's sake he advises Ruth to hang close to the other women—to work in whatever field they choose to work on a particular day.

**B. Boaz Gives Protection and Water, 9b**

**9b . . . have I not charged the young men that they shall not touch thee? and when thou art athirst, go unto the vessels, and drink of that which the young men have drawn.**

Working alone in a field with a crew of men could be a dangerous situation for a lone woman. Boaz tells Ruth he has warned his men to keep their hands off the Moabitess. Even the boss' warnings would not guarantee her total safety, but it would certainly increase her security. They knew they would have to deal with Boaz if they abused Ruth.

An equally valuable favor extended by Boaz is the right to drink from the water provided in the field for Boaz's workers. Carrying a full day's supply of drinking water from town to the field every day would add greatly to Ruth's labors. Boaz knows this, so he lightens her load by offering access to his water.

**C. Ruth Asks Why, 10**

**10 Then she fell on her face, and bowed herself to the ground, and said unto him, Why have I found grace in thine eyes, that thou shouldest take knowledge of me, seeing I am a stranger?**

Ruth's response to Boaz's generosity is one of grateful courtesy. Bowing low to acknowledge his rank above her and her sense of dependence on his largess, Ruth expresses surprise that this stranger would be so kind to an alien. She wants to know why he is taking such good care of her.

To "take knowledge of" her is King James phrasing that means "to pay attention to."

### D. Boaz Explains His Kindness, 11-12

**11 And Boaz answered and said unto her, It hath fully been shewed me, all that thou hast done unto thy mother in law since the death of thine husband: and how thou hast left thy father and thy mother, and the land of thy nativity, and art come unto a people which thou knewest not heretofore.**

**12 The LORD recompense thy work, and a full reward be given thee of the LORD God of Israel, under whose wings thou art come to trust.**

Boaz told Ruth he already knew more about her than she realized. As a member of Elimelech's family, he was aware of the Naomi losses. Someone had told him about Ruth and what a sacrifice she had made willingly to help take care of her aging mother-in-law. It surely would not be a light thing for a person voluntarily to leave their parents and the land where they had grown up to establish a new life among strangers in an unfamiliar culture. Boaz knew Ruth was doing all of this for Naomi, and he appreciated that. His kindness was a way he could thank Ruth for all she was doing to help his relative.

Boaz's words in vs. 12 give us another clue that he is a man of genuine faith. He invokes a blessing from the God of Israel upon this Moabite woman he has just met—a woman who has demonstrated her newly placed trust in the God he knows and serves.

In this last line, there is a veiled suggestion that Boaz realized Ruth has not come to his field just by accident or luck. He knew that she and Naomi have identified him as a close relative of Ruth's dead husband, and therefore a possible candidate to fulfill God's law in Deuteronomy 25. The woman he has just met saw him as a potential mate, not because of romance but because of faith.

### E. Ruth Thanks Boaz, 13

**13 Then she said, Let me find favour in thy sight, my lord; for that thou hast comforted me, and for that thou hast spoken friendly unto thine handmaid, though I be not like unto one of thine handmaidens.**

The connecting words for the phrases in this verse in the KJV make it confusing. The NRSV clarifies by telling us that Ruth says to Boaz: "May I continue to find favor in your sight, my lord, for you have comforted me and spoken kindly to your servant, even though I am not one of your servants."

### F. Boaz Does More for Ruth, 14-16

**14 And Boaz said unto her, At mealtime come thou hither, and eat of the bread, and dip thy morsel in the vinegar. And she sat beside the reapers: and he reached her parched corn, and she did eat, and was sufficed, and left.**

**15 And when she was risen up to glean, Boaz commanded his young**

men, saying, Let her glean even among the sheaves, and reproach her not:

16 And let fall also some of the handfuls of purpose for her, and leave them, that she may glean them, and rebuke her not.

After his first visit with Ruth, Boaz is convinced that his earlier opinion of her was accurate, so he extends to her even more kindnesses. He invites her to eat with his field workers, sharing the food he provides for their lunch.

"Sufficed" in vs. 14 is the King James way of saying she "ate until she was full." After she finishes eating and goes back to work in the field, Boaz instructs his men both to allow her to glean near them without giving her any trouble, and to purposely drop extra grain on the ground when they see her working close behind them. That night when she gets home and Naomi sees how much grain Ruth has gleaned that day, she is delighted because she knows Boaz is showing them special favor for this amount to be possible.

## II. Rewards for a Hard Day of Work—Ruth 2:17-18

17 So she gleaned in the field until even, and beat out that she had gleaned: and it was about an ephah of barley.

18 And she took it up, and went into the city: and her mother in law saw what she had gleaned: and she brought forth, and gave to her that she had reserved after she was sufficed.

"Even" in vs. 17 is archaic English for "evening." As the day is ending, Ruth threshes the grain she has retrieved from the ground. To explain to modern readers how much grain is in an "ephah," the NIV footnote says it was about three-fifths of a bushel. Taking a different tack, the TEV says Ruth wound up with about 25 pounds of clean grain.

Ruth arrived home late; and Naomi has already eaten her fill ("was sufficed"), but the older woman thoughtfully set aside what was left over for Ruth's supper.

80CR

## Evangelistic Emphasis

In any context, God's way is the best way. In all situations, family, business, social, or whatever, godly attitudes and conduct win out every time. People can behave in an ungodly way, and some spend their entire life doing that, but they do so at their own loss.

As we enter the second chapter of Ruth, we have three main characters in the story: Naomi, Ruth, and now Boaz comes on the scene. In some ways they are very different from each other. Naomi is the elderly, poverty-stricken widow. Ruth is the foreigner among them, also in poverty. Boaz is the prosperous land owner. There is one underlying principle that unites the three: they all want to do things God's way. That is why the Book of Ruth has a happy ending.

Whether we are reading in the Old or the New Testament, it is clear that God's way is the superior way. This brings us to the topic of evangelism. At its heart, evangelism is telling about Jesus and the Cross. The results of accepting this wonderful gift of God's grace and Christ's love, is to develop a godly, Christ-like life. In other words, we want God's will to be done on earth as it is in heaven, and we want it to happen to each of us. We want to share this with others. That is what evangelism is all about.

## Memory Selection

ಐಇೞ

**"The LORD recompense thy work, and a full reward be given thee of the LORD God of Israel, under whose wings thou art come to trust."** *Ruth 2:12*

The Keil and Delitzsch commentary notes that, "In these words of Boaz we see the genuine piety of a true Israelite." (This reminds of what Jesus said about Nathanael: "Here is a true Israelite, in whom there is nothing false" John 1:47 NIV). The setting of Ruth is in the days of the judges, a period when many in Israel did not share Boaz's godly wisdom and devotion.

As we read about Boaz and Ruth, it is interesting if we realize that they were possibly contemporaries with Gideon, whom we first met in Judges 6. (If not him, then some similar setting.) We remember that Gideon's father was a pagan, and the Israelite townspeople were upset because Gideon destroyed his father's shrine to the gods. The contrast of Boaz to the many Israelites who had forsaken God, makes him stand out all the more as a man of faith and character. It also reminds us that even in the dark days of Judges, there were some who kept their faith.

In David Atkinson's "The Wings of Refuge," he points out that in Boaz' prayer we see his awareness of being a member of the covenant family of the God of Israel. We see his understanding that God is the Lord. Boaz saw the grace of God in terms of wings of refuge. The more we learn of Boaz the more we come to respect him. He blesses us with his words and his deeds.

## Weekday Problems

In the state where I live, workers in two nationwide grocery chains are threatening to go on strike this week. As you can imagine, both newspaper and television reporters are interviewing people on both sides of this conflict. The union representing the workers is sponsoring TV ads. Some workers (union members) who disagree with the union's demand for a strike are picketing their own union. Shoppers are being interviewed as they leave the stores, and have strong views both pro and con. Temporary workers are being hired in case the strike occurs. It is a real labor/management struggle.

Our dear friend Boaz avoided such conflict. So did his workers. As Boaz entered his field, he blessed his reapers: "The LORD be with you," he said. They replied, "The LORD bless thee." (We have not heard any of this kind of talk in this week's TV strike-threat interviews.) Boaz furnished water, bread, and parched grain for his workers – enough to share with Ruth. There was enough parched grain that Ruth saved some for Naomi.

The well-to-do farmer, Boaz stands out in stark contrast to the rich farmer in Jesus' parable (Luke 12:15-21). Boaz was no fool. He knew how to be rich toward God and kind to his laborers. I seriously doubt that the grocer CEOs will sit down with union leaders for a discussion conducted in the spirit of Boaz and his workers. Could such a thing make some problems go away?

---

# Just for fun

Give me a sense of humor, Lord,
Give me the grace to see a joke,
To get some humor out of life,
And pass it on to other folk!

✳ ✳ ✳

Auto mechanic to customer:
"I couldn't repair your brakes, so I made the horn blow louder."

✳ ✳ ✳

Patience is the ability to idle your motor
when you feel like stripping the gears.

✳ ✳ ✳

Q. What's the difference between a choir director and a terrorist?
A. You can negotiate with a terrorist.

# This Lesson in Your Life

Ruth is a book about relationships. Not relationships only, but they stand out especially strongly in it. None of us is an island to himself; no one really stands alone. To some degree we all interrelate with others. Relationships can be either good or bad. Ruth has some exceptionally wholesome ones, as we shall see here.

Naomi's relationship with her daughters-in-law was considerate, and showed genuine concern for their welfare. If they accompanied her to Bethlehem, she knew they would be abandoning family and culture. With her, she felt they would remain widows in a strange land, but if they remained in Moab they could find husbands and have children.

The years Ruth and Orpah, with their husbands, had spent with Elimelech and Naomi must have been pleasant. Otherwise, they would have been happy to part company with Naomi. We cannot fault Orpah for returning home. It was a sensible thing to do, and Naomi had encouraged it. The decision making time was emotionally wrenching for the three of them, and tears flowed. Ruth was motivated by an exceptionally strong bond of love.

After Naomi and Ruth arrive in Bethlehem we observe their relationship develop further. Ruth goes out each day and works hard gleaning in the barley fields. She makes sure she provides enough grain for Naomi, who in turn is solicitous for the younger woman's welfare and working conditions. It may be that Naomi is too elderly or otherwise incapable of gleaning, so Ruth accepts the responsibility of providing for her.

Boaz works his way into this picture very smoothly. We first see him as he enters the harvest scene, where he and his laborers give God's blessings to each other. He inquires about the new woman is who is gleaning. Neither he nor his reapers seem concerned that she is foreigner. It is very possible that her Moabite clothing is different from that of the Israelite workers; she may speak with a foreign accent, or even have some racial distinctions apparent in her face. If so, it does not seem to be important to Boaz or his laborers.

Boaz treats Ruth respectfully and generously, and demands that his workers do also. As the relationship progresses, Boaz is careful to observe every legal step regarding next of kin. This process concerns Law of Moses legalities, and he does it by the book. There is land that is Naomi's through her deceased husband, and marriage to Ruth the widow of a kinsman, and Boaz works his way through them one by one. Behind the scenes is Naomi, busy and happy, seeing that Ruth says and does all the right things. Boaz, though, gives us the most thorough example of the kind of godly relationship we should have with one another.

Do you suppose you and I can keep all our relationships working smoothly? Romans 8:28 says all things work for the good for those who love the Lord.

## GETTING THE FACTS STRAIGHT

**1. What was Boaz' family connection with Naomi?**
Boaz was a kinsman to Naomi's late husband Elimelech.

**2. What request did Ruth make of Naomi concerning obtaining food?**
She asked to be allowed to go into the fields of anyone with whom she could find favor to pick up leftover grain.

**3. By happenstance she went into whose field to glean?**
She went into the field that belonged to Boaz, Elimelech's kinsman.

**4. When Boaz asked his workmen who the young woman was, how did they respond?**
They explained that this was the woman who had come back to Bethlehem from Moab with Naomi.

**5. After learning who she was, what did Boaz tell Ruth to do?**
He told her to not to work in any other fields, just his only, to stay near his servant girls, and the men were instructed not to harm her. Also, she should get drinking water from what his men supplied.

**6. What strange (to us) custom did Naomi have Ruth do regarding Boaz at the threshing floor?**
Naomi instructed Ruth to go to the threshing floor after Boaz was asleep, and lie down at his feet. It was connected with the fact that he was the kinsman-redeemer.

**7. How did Boaz respond when he discovered Ruth at his feet?**
Boaz said that she was very kind to him, that he was not the nearest of kin, but he would see if that person wanted to claim the right. If not, he would marry her.

**8. At what time did Ruth leave the threshing floor?**
Boaz told her to lie down until morning. She arose very early and left before anyone would know she was there.

**9. What did Boaz send to Naomi with Ruth as she left the threshing floor?**
He sent six measures of barley with her, probably about as much as she could carry, so she would not return empty to Naomi.

**10. When Ruth told Naomi what Boaz had said about being kinsman, what did Naomi say he would do?**
Naomi said Boaz would not rest until he had finished taking care of the matter.

We Christians believe that a benevolent Creator brought into being everything that exists in the universe. As His acts of creation progressed, He saw that everything was good. That is exactly the kind of world we would expect to come from His hands.

We have every confidence that at the creation God did not treat His universe as if it were a giant clock, to be wound up, set on a shelf to be ignored, and eventually allowed to run down due to His neglect. We believe that He keeps watch over the world. Hebrews 1:2-3 tells us that the created universe is sustained by His powerful word. He upholds what He created. We believe that He takes a personal interest in His people. When Paul preached in Athens, he used the words of Greek poets who said that it is in God that we live, move and have our being. We are His offspring (Acts 17:24-28). We are not orphans left alone. We have a loving Father.

God gives us what we need to meet life's uncertainties. In the book of Ruth we see this exemplified beautifully, as when Boaz spoke of the God of Israel, under whose wings Ruth had come to trust. We picture perhaps a powerful mother eagle in her nest of hatchlings, guarding them with strength and gentleness. Under such a protective and caring Lord this otherwise vulnerable woman found her refuge. It is possible that Deuteronomy 32:11 inspired Boaz to use this imagery. (In Matthew 23:37, Jesus told Jerusalem that He would be to them like a mother hen gathering her chicks under her wings, but they refused.) Here are more passages picturing God's protective wings: Exodus 19:4; Psalm 17:8; 91:4.

We believe in God's providence, that He works in ways we do not see to help get us through life. When Ruth went out to glean, "her hap was to light on a part of the field belonging unto Boaz" (2:3). "Her hap" is a quaint way of saying she happened to go into Boaz' field. She apparently went there by happenstance, not knowing to whom the field belonged. We see that God's hand was in her selection, yet from her point of view this was not obvious at all. Without her awareness, God placed her where she needed to be. God acts within the framework of our normal daily lives, perhaps most often without our ever knowing it. We might want to be careful about saying something "just happened."

You and I are blessed with God's faithful love. Our lives fall within His providence, believing that ultimately He will bring about what is best for us. A line in David Atkinson's "The Wings of Refuge" goes like this: "'Providence' says that God is there, God cares, God rules, and God provides." We see this in the Book of Ruth. Let us expect it in our lives.

ℬℭ

# Respecting Community Standards
# Caring for One Another

## Ruth 4:1-10

Then went Boaz up to the gate, and sat him down there: and, behold, the kinsman of whom Boaz spake came by; unto whom he said, Ho, such a one! turn aside, sit down here. And he turned aside, and sat down.

2 And he took ten men of the elders of the city, and said, Sit ye down here. And they sat down.

3 And he said unto the kinsman, Naomi, that is come again out of the country of Moab, selleth a parcel of land, which was our brother Elimelech's:

4 And I thought to advertise thee, saying, Buy it before the inhabitants, and before the elders of my people. If thou wilt redeem it, redeem it: but if thou wilt not redeem it, then tell me, that I may know: for there is none to redeem it beside thee; and I am after thee. And he said, I will redeem it.

5 Then said Boaz, What day thou buyest the field of the hand of Naomi, thou must buy it also of Ruth the Moabitess, the wife of the dead, to raise up the name of the dead upon his inheritance.

6 And the kinsman said, I cannot redeem it for myself, lest I mar mine own inheritance: redeem thou my right to thyself; for I cannot redeem it.

7 Now this was the manner in former time in Israel concerning redeeming and concerning changing, for to confirm all things; a man plucked off his shoe, and gave it to his neighbour: and this was a testimony in Israel.

8 Therefore the kinsman said unto Boaz, Buy it for thee. So he drew off his shoe.

9 And Boaz said unto the elders, and unto all the people, Ye are witnesses this day, that I have bought all that was Elimelech's, and all that was Chilion's and Mahlon's, of the hand of Naomi.

10 Moreover Ruth the Moabitess, the wife of Mahlon, have I purchased to be my wife, to raise up the name of the dead upon his inheritance, that the name of the dead be not cut off from among his brethren, and from the gate of his place: ye are witnesses this day.

**Memory Verse**
Ruth 4:5
**Background Scripture**
Ruth 4
**Devotional Reading**
Philippians 1:3-11

Aug. 28

511

 "What God the Father considers to be pure and genuine religion is this," the Scriptures tell us, "to take care of orphans and widows in their suffering" (Jas. 1:27, TEV). This was one of the main purposes behind the rules God laid down for Israel in Deuteronomy 25:5-10. In effect, the requirement that the closest male relative marry the widow of a man who died childless was God's Social Security plan for Israel's widows.

Men who honored and obeyed this law, as Boaz did, showed that they honored the Lord and shared His concern for those who might otherwise be left in dire circumstances. On the other hand, men like the relative who cared more about his own inheritance line than about Naomi demonstrated both a lack of compassion for others and an unwillingness to obey the clear commands of the Almighty. If we turn our backs on the poor even today, we turn our backs on God.

## For a Lively Start

Boaz may have been a bit slyer than some realize. He clearly wants to marry Ruth and thereby to help Naomi, but the other relative—nearer in kinship to Mahlon than Boaz is—has first dibs on redeeming the dead man's property. Is there a hint in the text that Boaz knows his competitor is so racially prejudiced that he will never agree to marry a woman from Moab? Is Boaz playing this bargaining chip when he reminds the other man that he will acquire the foreign woman along with Mahlon's land?

If this is a correct reading of the story, what a delightful turn of justice takes place here when the man's prejudice costs him any rights to a profitable land deal. He pays a high but just price for his bigotry.

| Teaching Outline | Daily Bible Readings |
|---|---|
| I. Witnesses at the City Gate— Ruth 4:1-2 | Mon. Pray for the Faith Community *Philippians 1:3-11* |
| II. Boaz and the Closer Kinsman— Ruth 4:3-4 | Tue. The Blameless Walk *Psalm 15* |
| A. Boaz Offers the Land Deal, 3 B. The Other Man Accepts, 4 | Wed. Integrity of the Heart *1 Kings 9:1-5* |
| III. The Deal Falls Through—Ruth 4:5-8 | Thu. Walking in Integrity *Psalm 26:1-11* |
| A. Boaz Mentions Ruth, 5 B. The Kinsman Backs Out, 6 C. The Sandal Exchange, 7-8 | Fri. Integrity Provides Security *Proverbs 10:6-11* |
| | Sat. Persisting in Integrity *Job 2:1-9* |
| IV. Witnesses Verify the Deal—Ruth 4:9-10 | Sun. Following Community Standards *Ruth 4:1-10* |

# Verse by Verse

## Ruth 4:1-10

**I. Witnesses at the City Gate— Ruth 4:1-2**

**1 Then went Boaz up to the gate, and sat him down there: and, behold, the kinsman of whom Boaz spake came by; unto whom he said, Ho, such a one! turn aside, sit down here. And he turned aside, and sat down.**

**2 And he took ten men of the elders of the city, and said, Sit ye down here. And they sat down.**

The syntax of the Elizabethan English in these verses seems strange to us, but most of us can manage to comprehend what Boaz says and does. The city gate was the place where the elders of a Hebrew town took care of business such as the transfer of property ownership. As Boaz promised Ruth the night before at the threshing floor, he asked of the intentions of the one relative who had a closer relationship than Boaz did to Ruth's late husband.

Some of the modern Bible versions complicate the story right here by using unfamiliar terms to describe this relative. The NIV calls him in vs. 1 the "kinsman-redeemer." Most KJV readers are likely to ask, "What is that?" A footnote in the NRSV clarifies this term by calling this next-of-kin "the one with the right to redeem"—

meaning his kinship entitles him to purchase Mahlon's land. As Boaz will point out in this encounter, that right to redeem property also entailed the requirement to father a child by the widow-owner of the land.

Since this particular land/wife deal has the potential to become complicated, Boaz makes sure that ten reliable witnesses observe the transaction. This is the equivalent of legal witnesses and a notary public verifying a will today.

**II. Boaz and the Closer Kinsman—Ruth 4:3-4**

**A. Boaz Offers the Land Deal, 3**

**3 And he said unto the kinsman, Naomi, that is come again out of the country of Moab, selleth a parcel of land, which was our brother Elimelech's:**

To the next-of-kin, Boaz offers the first option on the land that belonged to Elimelech (Naomi's husband) and his sons. Legally, the man's position on the family tree entitles him to purchase this obviously desirable piece of property. Boaz knows this, so he makes sure to handle this transaction legally.

**B. The Other Man Accepts, 4**

**4 And I thought to advertise thee, saying, Buy it before the inhabitants,**

and before the elders of my people. If thou wilt redeem it, redeem it: but if thou wilt not redeem it, then tell me, that I may know: for there is none to redeem it beside thee; and I am after thee. And he said, I will redeem it.

The meaning of the word *advertise* has changed since the KJV translators used it here. Back then, it meant to "tell" or to "inform" or to bring something to someone's attention. In essence, Boaz tells his relative that he thinks he should share with him the news that Elimelech's land is about to be sold.

"The inhabitants" mentioned here are those who occupy the seats beside the city gate—the witnesses to this entire transaction. Among them surely are some of the elders of the city.

With the man informed of the land sale and with respected witnesses present to confirm the man's response, Boaz presses him for an immediate decision. "If you do not want to buy the land," Boaz tells him, "I am going to buy it." As Boaz surely expected, his competitor quickly agrees to buy it. He wants Elimelech's land. It must have been a good farm.

### III. The Deal Falls Through— Ruth 4:5-8
#### A. Boaz Mentions Ruth, 5
**5 Then said Boaz, What day thou buyest the field of the hand of Naomi, thou must buy it also of Ruth the Moabitess, the wife of the dead, to raise up the name of the dead upon his inheritance.**

Having baited the trap by offering the relative his legal right, Boaz calls his attention to the fine print on this contract. Whoever gets Naomi's land also gets Mahlon's widow, the Moabite girl who came home with Naomi. The land-buyer's duty is to father a child by Ruth to inherit the dead man's name and property.

#### B. The Kinsman Backs Out, 6
**6 And the kinsman said, I cannot redeem it for myself, lest I mar mine own inheritance: redeem thou my right to thyself; for I cannot redeem it.**

Immediately the relative reverses course. He will take a pass on the land purchase, attractive though it may be, and allow Boaz to buy the farm. The reason he gives for this change of heart is his fear that any child he fathered by Ruth to become Mahlon's heir might somehow disturb his own estate. As much as he would like to have Naomi's land, he is not willing to take the chance of tangling up the inheritance line for his present children. At least, this is the reason he publicly states. For centuries, Bible readers have speculated that this relative may be married to a shrew that would boil him in oil if he showed up with a brand new young foreign wife, but of course, he cannot very well state such fears as his reason for avoiding the deal. Nor would he likely admit it to the witnesses if his real reason for passing up the property was racial prejudice. Whatever his real reason may be, the next-of-kin stands down and allows Boaz to buy the land—and marry Ruth as well.

#### C. The Sandal Exchange, 7-8
**7 Now this was the manner in former time in Israel concerning redeeming and concerning chang-**

ing, for to confirm all things; a man plucked off his shoe, and gave it to his neighbour: and this was a testimony in Israel.

8 Therefore the kinsman said unto Boaz, Buy it for thee. So he drew off his shoe.

The shoe (more likely sandal) exchange here conforms perfectly to the rules laid down in Deuteronomy 25:5-10. If brothers are living together and one of them dies without a son, his widow must not marry outside the family. Her husband's brother shall take her and marry her and fulfill the duty of a brother-in-law to her. The first son she bears shall carry on the name of the dead brother so that his name will not be blotted out from Israel. However, if a man does not want to marry his brother's wife, she shall go to the elders at the town gate and say, "My husband's brother refuses to carry on his brother's name in Israel. He will not fulfill the duty of a brother-in-law to me." Then the elders of his town shall summon him and talk to him. If he persists in saying, "I do not want to marry her," his brother's widow shall go up to him in the presence of the elders, take off one of his sandals, spit in his face and say, "This is what is done to the man who will not build up his brother's family line." That man's line shall be known in Israel as The Family of the Unsandaled (NIV).

If the "unsandaled" next-of-kin in this case ever contests the transaction because Boaz got the land he wanted, all Boaz needs to do is to produce the man's sandal and the witnesses who saw how he acquired it.

## IV. Witnesses Verify the Deal— Ruth 4:9-10

9 And Boaz said unto the elders, and unto all the people, Ye are witnesses this day, that I have bought all that was Elimelech's, and all that was Chilion's and Mahlon's, of the hand of Naomi.

10 Moreover Ruth the Moabitess, the wife of Mahlon, have I purchased to be my wife, to raise up the name of the dead upon his inheritance, that the name of the dead be not cut off from among his brethren, and from the gate of his place: ye are witnesses this day.

Just as Boaz promised Ruth at the threshing floor the night before, he swiftly resolves the possible legal conflict between him and the next-of-kin. In strict adherence to the legal standards of that day, he claims both the land and the wife of his dead relative, Mahlon.

In the final verses of this chapter, we will learn the real importance of the whole story of Ruth. Boaz and Ruth are destined to become the great-grandparents of King David. This means they also are ancestors of our Lord Jesus. This strange land deal in Bethlehem sets the stage for a far more important Bethlehem event several centuries later.

෧ඞ

## Evangelistic Emphasis

Boaz may well be one of the more fascinating people in the Old Testament. He is certainly an admirable one in a number of ways. Everything he does seem to have been done right. If he had any outstanding character flaws, or even any minor ones, the historian who wrote Ruth neglected to tell us about them.

Whatever business needed attending to he did promptly and well. Just look at how efficiently he handled the legal business at the city gate. He could teach us a thing or two about evangelism. It is not something to be put on the back burner and neglected.

Paul gave Timothy the following charge: "Preach the Word. Be prepared in season and out of season; correct, rebuke and encourage – with great patience and careful instruction. For the time will come when men will not put up with sound doctrine" (2 Tim. 4:2-3 NIV).

Jesus told the disciples that as long as it was day, "we" must do the works of the One who sent Him. "Night is coming, when no one can work," He told them (John 9:4). Jesus included Himself and the disciples when He said this. (The original language uses the plural.)

We have the examples of Boaz, Paul's charge, and the words of Jesus. We have evangelistic emphasis.

ഇറ

## Memory Selection

"Then said Boaz, What day thou buyest the field of the hand of Naomi, thou must buy it also of Ruth the Moabitess, the wife of the dead, to raise up the name of the dead upon his inheritance." *Ruth 4:5*

In Jewish law and custom there were two family protections available that show up here. One protects family property (Lev. 25:23-28). If the property is sold, a kinsman can redeem it so it will not pass out of family hands. (Actually, land was not sold in the sense we think of selling. It all reverted to the seller in the year of Jubilee. All land was considered owned by God.)

The other family protection was to preserve the name of a husband who died childless (Deut. 25:5-10). The widow was not to marry outside the family. The brother of the deceased was to take her as his wife and the first son would carry on the name of the deceased.

The details of how these practices were carried out are not clear to us, and some of them seem to have been modified as time passed. They are actually two separate sets of regulations. Boaz, though, skillfully blended them together as he presented the case before the town elders and the man who was closer kin than he. The unnamed man who was closer kin to Elimelech had the legal right to redeem the land and to marry Ruth if he chose to do so.

When Boaz told him about the land, he agreed to redeem it. However, Boaz told him that, to do this, he would also need to marry Ruth. When he heard this, he backed out of the entire process. This, of course, is what Boaz wanted to happen.

## Weekday Problems

"All, or nothing at all." There may be times when that is a good policy. Other times, though, it might not work so well. Actually, there might be times when it is both good and bad at the same time, depending on who you are and what you want. Take, for instance, the two men standing inside Bethlehem's city gate in the presence of ten town elders, transacting legal business.

The gentleman, who is described to us only as the next of kin to Elimelech, wanted only half of what was available. He wanted land but not a wife. When he discovered the only way he could get the land was to take all that was offered, he declined. He had preferred nothing at all, and used as his reason that marriage might endanger his own inheritance.

Boaz, on the other hand, wanted it all, got it all, and we are glad he did. (It would have really messed up this story if the other man had gotten the girl.) Boaz had a big heart. By this time in the story, Ruth seems to have stolen the romantic part of it, but he had a good heart toward Naomi and wanted to do what was right by her. Also, he was willing that his first son would preserve the name of Mahlon. That takes a generous heart. He was an "All" man. Are you and I "All" in our commitment to doing God's will?

---

# Out of the Clear Blue Sky

Two men survived a plane crash on an isolated South Pacific Island. One of them panicked when he found out the island was uninhabited and had no source of food or water. "We're dead!" he moaned to his friend.

"Oh, don't worry. We're going to be O.K. I make $250,000 a week."

"And how could that possibly help us here?" the worry-wart screamed. "We don't have any food. We have no water. Man, I tell you, we're dead!"

"Calm down," his friend reassured him. "I told you I make $250,000 a week. What I didn't tell you is that I'm a Baptist, and I tithe. I promise you, my pastor will find us."

---

517

# This Lesson in Your Life

The Book of Ruth immediately gets us involved in families. It begins the family of Elimelech and Naomi, along with their two sons Mahlon and Chilion. This family soon expands to include Ruth and Orpah. As time passes we reach a point in the story when only Naomi and Ruth survive as the family unit. It is as we find these two women alone in Bethlehem that the story takes a sharp turn, and the family begins to expand in a fascinating way.

God has placed emphasis on human families since the very creation. It was in the Garden that He said, "Therefore shall a man leave his father and his mother, and shall cleave unto his wife: and they shall be one flesh" (Gen. 2:24). The Old Testament is filled with "begats" as it traces family lines through the generations.

Within the past few years, I have gotten interested in genealogy. (It sounds more personal if you call it family history.) In genealogy, one of the first things to become obvious is that we cannot choose our ancestors. If great-grandpa was a horse thief, we cannot make him into a saint. We are stuck with him. At one time I thought I had found an ancestor who was a Mississippi riverboat gambler, but that was a false lead. My wife's niece said she would trade me two of her Presbyterian preacher ancestors for him, but unfortunately, I had nothing to swap.

Our lesson in Ruth has some significant genealogy, as it traces the tribe of Judah down to King David. Boaz and Ruth are included in his ancestry. This is especially interesting because Matthew's genealogy of Jesus includes the same names as we find in Ruth. The name of every individual who is included in Ruth is part of God's preparing for the birth of Jesus of Nazareth. Who they were, who they married, what child was born – affects all our lives because it leads to Jesus. Boaz and Ruth's child, Obed, was born in Bethlehem. This was a cause for rejoicing throughout the town. Centuries later another Child would be born there and even heaven's angels rejoiced. Our study in Ruth is a prelude to His birth. Here is what Luke wrote about the family connection (2:1-7):

"And Joseph also went up from Galilee, out of the city of Nazareth, into Judea, unto the city of David, which is called Bethlehem; (because he was of the house and lineage of David:) to be taxed with Mary his espoused wife, being great with child. And so it was, that while they were there, the days were accomplished that she should be delivered. And she brought forth her firstborn son, and wrapped him in swaddling clothes, and laid him in a manger; because there was no room for them in the inn."

The Son of God came to earth as a human; we call this the "incarnation."

Our lessons in Ruth affect our lives because of the part they play in this great plan of God.

518

## GETTING
## THE FACTS STRAIGHT

**1. Why did Boaz go to the city gate in order to transact legal business?**

There were no court systems or organized structures to handle legal cases. The area in front of the city gate was a public place where city elders could witness events such as the one Boaz brought to their attention.

**2. How many city elders were selected to hear the case Boaz presented?**

There were ten of them. This is probably the number that custom called for during this time period. In addition to the elders, however, there were a number of townspeople present who also said they would be witnesses.

**3. What was the first point of business Boaz introduced to the man who was next of kin to Elimelech?**

The first thing Boaz brought to their attention was the piece of land that had belonged to Elimelech. Naomi wanted to sell it.

**4. At first the next of kin wanted to buy the land. What made him change his mind?**

When Boaz told him he would also be required to take Ruth as his wife, he did not want to do this, so he declined the land.

**5. Why did the next of kin take off his shoe?**

This was a customary indication of a denial in such cases. It may have in some way symbolized that the person doing so had no right to tread on the property. This, however is unclear. but has been suggested as a possibility.

**6. In what words did Boaz clarify to the witnessing elders precisely what had been transacted?**

In verses 9 and 10, he said that he had bought from Naomi, all that belonged to Elimelech, Chilion, and Mahlon, and had purchased Ruth to be his wife, to raise up an inheritance for the dead (Mahlon).

**7. All the people who were at the gate and the elders said that they witnessed the transaction. What was their attitude toward Boaz?**

They wished for him abundant children, and that he would have a good reputation, and be famous in Bethlehem.

**8. When a son is born to Boaz and Ruth, for whom are the women of the city excited?**

It is Naomi who gets their attention. They even say, "There is a son born to Naomi."

**9. What was the name given to Ruth's son?**

He was called Obed.

**10. Trace the genealogy from Obed to King David.**

Obed was the father of Jesse. Jesse was the father of David.

Redemption is a great theme in the New Testament, and it centers on the work of Jesus Christ. It is an uplifting concept. We get an introduction about how redemption works in the action of Boaz toward Naomi and Ruth. As a matter of fact, one of the purposes of the book of Ruth may be to explain redemption's meaning. In his commentary, David Atkinson quotes another author, D. A. Leggett, who writes the following passage about Boaz' part in this great drama:

> In the actions of Boaz as goel [redeemer] we see foreshadowed the saving work of Jesus Christ, his later descendant. As Boaz had the right of redemption and yet clearly was under no obligation to intervene on Ruth's behalf, so it was with Christ. As Boaz, seeing the the poor widows, came to their rescue because his life was governed by Yahweh and His laws, so also of the Messiah it is prophesied that his life would be governed by the law of God and that he would deal justly and equitably with the poor and with those who were oppressed.

Boaz offered security, protection, hope, and help to Naomi and Ruth, and gave it to them freely. This came at some cost to him since he accepted responsibility for them and paid the price of the land. This he voluntarily and gladly did. (We contrast his action toward the two widows with that of the next of kin, who did not want to be involved.) Further, we contrast what Boaz did with Christ's redeeming work, and immediately see the similarity.

Scripture speaks to us movingly about Jesus as our redeemer. In Revelation 5, John was "in the Spirit" and saw the throne of God, and in the center of it was a Lamb, looking as if it had been slain. Those who were around the throne fell down before the Lamb and sang a new song, saying that He was slain, and had redeemed us to God by His blood, and had made us a nation of kings and priests for God.

Even Job, speaking from the distant past of history, expected to see the Redeemer. "I know that my Redeemer lives, and in the end he will stand upon the earth. And after my skin has been destroyed, yet in my flesh will see God: I myself will see him with my own eyes – I and not another. How my heart yearns within me!" (19:25-27 NIV)

We are inspired by the redeemer Boaz, great-grandfather to the great King David. We are even more inspired by David's greater Son, Jesus of Nazareth, who redeems us from sin and unto God.

(There are numerous biblical references to redeemer/redemption. Here are some of them: Psalm 130:7; Isaiah 59:20; Romans 3:24; Galatians 4:4-5; Ephesians 4:30; Colossians 1:14; Titus 2:11-14; Hebrews 9:12; 1 Peter 1:18-29,)